AQA Law

A2

Exclusively endorsed by AQA

Emma Bateman
Guy Blundell
Peter Smith
John Wilman

Series editor
Richard Wortley

Nelson Thornes

Published in 2009 by:
Nelson Thornes Ltd
Delta Place
27 Bath Road
CHELTENHAM
GL53 7TH
United Kingdom

09 10 11 12 13 / 10 9 8 7 6 5 4 3 2

A catalogue record for this book is available from the British Library

ISBN 978 0 7487 9866 7

Cover photograph: Alamy/Image 100
Illustrations by Paul McCaffrey; additional illustrations by eMC Design Ltd

Page make-up by eMC Design Ltd

Printed and bound in Spain by GraphyCems

Acknowledgements

The authors and publisher are grateful to the following for permission to
reproduce photographs and other copyright material in this book:

p5 Science Photo Library/Ian Hootom; p11 Topham/FNP-STAR; p116 Rex
Features/Richard Young; p129 Fotolia; p170 © Crown Copyright/MOD 2009;
p192 iStockphoto; p199 courtesy of The Advertising Archives; p208 courtesy of
the Skegness Standard; p254 Getty Images/Bob Thomas; p289 Getty Images/
Time & Life Pictures; p326 Alamy/Alex Segre; p335 Rex Features/Sipa Press;
p338 Moviestore; p340 Corbis/Hulton-Deutsch Collection; p346 Corbis/Derek
Hudson/Sygma; p346 Getty Images; p361 Getty Images/Time & Life Pictures;
p365 Alamy/David Willis; p393 Topfoto/UPP.

Every effort has been made to contact the copyright holders and we apologise if
any have been overlooked. Should copyright have been unwittingly infringed in
this book, the owners should contact the publishers, who will make corrections
at reprint.

Contents

Unit 4C
Concepts of law   319

AQA introduction

Nelson Thornes has worked in partnership with AQA to ensure this book and the accompanying online resources offer you the best support for your A Level course.

All resources have been approved by senior AQA examiners so you can feel assured that they closely match the specification for this subject and provide you with everything you need to prepare successfully for your exams.

These print and online resources together **unlock blended learning**; this means that the links between the activities in the book and the activities online blend together to maximise your understanding of a topic and help you achieve your potential.

These online resources are available on  which can be accessed via the internet at **www.kerboodle.com/live**, anytime, anywhere. If your school or college subscribes to this service you will be provided with your own personal login details. Once logged in, access your course and locate the required activity.

For more information and help visit **www.kerboodle.com**

Icons in this book indicate where there is material online related to that topic. The following icons are used:

🔆 Learning activity

These resources include a variety of interactive and non-interactive activities to support your learning.

✅ Progress tracking

These resources include a variety of tests that you can use to check your knowledge on particular topics (*Test yourself*) and a range of resources that enable you to analyse and understand examination questions (*On your marks …*).

ⓘ Research support

These resources include *WebQuests*, in which you are assigned a task and provided with a range of web links to use as source material for research.

▮ How to use this book

This book covers the specification for your course and is arranged in a sequence approved by AQA.

The book content is divided into chapters matched to the sections of the AQA Law specification for Units 3 and 4. Units 3A Criminal law (fatal and non-fatal offences against the person) and 3B Contract law cover Unit 3, and Units 4A Criminal law (offences against property), 4B Tort and 4C Concepts of law cover Unit 4. The chapters within each section provide full coverage of the AQA specification.

The features in this book include:

In this topic you will learn how to:

Each chapter is made up of two or more topics. At the beginning of each of these topics you will find a list of learning objectives that contain targets linked to the requirements of the specification.

 Key terms

Terms that you will need to be able to define and understand.

 Key cases

Cases that demonstrate a key legal concept.

 Links

These refer you back to other points in the book that consider similar points, or to the AS book to refresh your memory on key points and cases.

 Activities

Things for you to do that will reinforce the information you have just learned.

 Examiner's tip

Hints from AQA examiners to help you with your study and to prepare you for your exam.

You should now be able to:

A bulleted list of learning outcomes at the end of each topic summarising core points of knowledge.

 ## Web links in the book

As Nelson Thornes is not responsible for third party content online, there may be some changes to this material that are beyond our control. In order for us to ensure that the links referred to in the book are as up-to-date and stable as possible, the websites are usually homepages with supporting instructions on how to reach the relevant pages if necessary.

Please let us know at **kerboodle@nelsonthornes.com** if you find a link that doesn't work and we will do our best to redirect the link, or to find an alternative site.

Table of cases

Table of statutes

UNIT 3A Criminal law
(fatal and non-fatal offences against the person)

Introduction

Chapters in this unit:

1 Murder and voluntary manslaughter

2 Involuntary manslaughter

3 Non-fatal offences against the person

4 Defences

Unit 3 gives candidates a choice between the study of criminal law and contract law. The unit constitutes 50 per cent of the overall marks for the A2 section of the qualification, and 25 per cent of the overall marks for the A Level qualification. The Unit 3 examination is of 1.5 hours' duration. Candidates must answer one question. The examination paper will include both criminal law and contract law questions: Questions 1 and 2 being criminal law and Questions 3 and 4 being contract law. Candidates who choose criminal law will have to select one question to answer as will candidates who have chosen contract law. Each question is divided into three parts, all of which must be answered.

Each question is worth 75 marks. Each part is worth 25 marks. Parts (a) and (b) will be a test of your ability to select and apply the law to the given scenario, and part (c) will require an evaluative discussion of a stated area of the specification. All areas of the specification, including the defences, are possible questions for a critical evaluation including proposals for reform. The one exception is that no critical evaluation question will be asked on involuntary manslaughter.

All questions require essay style answers. In Parts (a) and (b), attainment of high grades is dependent on correct identification of the issues raised by the question, sound explanation of each of the points and clear application of the law to the facts disclosed. This may involve some consideration of alternatives where the law lacks clarity in its application to the scenario. In Part (c), illustration may be in many forms for example, legislation, cases, research, statistics, material from the media, and these need to be put into a coherent argument to answer the question set. Further exam tips are provided throughout each topic and at the end of the chapter.

Unit 3A comprises four chapters:

1 **Murder and voluntary manslaughter:** concerned with the law with respect to murder and manslaughter.

2 **Involuntary manslaughter:** explains the law on involuntary manslaughter.

3 **Non-fatal offences against the person:** considers the law on non-fatal offences against the person.

4 **Defences:** concerned with the defences to the offences dealt with in Chapters 1–3.

1 Murder and voluntary manslaughter

1 Murder

Murder is an example of unlawful homicide. Homicide is the killing of one human being by another. It can be lawful or unlawful. One example of lawful homicide would be where a person kills another in self-defence, using no more than reasonable force in the circumstances. Another would be the killing of the enemy by a soldier on active duty in wartime. Unlawful homicides include manslaughter, both voluntary and involuntary, (see the next chapter), and murder. Murder is the most serious form of unlawful homicide.

In this chapter we shall examine the definition of murder. We shall also find what must be proved in order to prove guilt in a case of murder.

Definition of murder

Murder is a common law offence, and has never been defined by statute. The most commonly accepted definition is the one given by the early 17th-century judge, Sir Edward Coke. He defined murder as:

> ... the unlawful killing of a reasonable person in being and under the King's (or Queen's) peace with malice aforethought, express or implied.

The first part of this definition, the unlawful killing of a reasonable person in being and under the Queen's peace, describes the *actus reus* of murder. The second part, with malice aforethought, express or implied, describes the *mens rea* of murder. Both elements will be discussed in detail in the course of this chapter.

The *actus reus* of murder

'Unlawful killing'

As was stated at the beginning of this chapter, some killings might be lawful. Such killings are recognised by the law as being justified. For example, a person who kills while acting in self-defence, or in the prevention of a crime, provided that the force used was reasonable in the circumstances, will not be guilty of an unlawful killing. Similarly, some killings might be authorised, such as those which take place during a war, or judicial executions in countries where the death penalty is carried out.

Omissions

In the majority of unlawful killings, the action which brings about the death presents few problems. It may be the result of shooting, stabbing, strangulation and so on. However the death may be the result not of a positive act, but of an omission, or failure to act. If the accused has a duty towards a person and fails to carry out that duty and death results, then the *actus reus* of murder may exist. As has been seen in your AS law module, there are certain situations where this may happen. These include:

■ a duty arising from a relationship such as that between parent and child such as *Stone v Dobinson* (1977)

■ some other such duty undertaken voluntarily, such as looking after a child or an elderly relative

a duty arising from the accidental creation by the defendant of a dangerous chain of events such as *Miller* (1983). It should be noted that no one died in *Miller*, but there remains potential liability for an omission.

A 'reasonable person in being'

The only problems usually posed by this part of the definition are those concerning the opposite ends of human existence. Can the foetus in the womb be a 'reasonable person in being'? And what of a person who is being kept technically alive by means of a life support machine, but is 'brain dead'?

A foetus in the womb, having no existence independent of its mother, is not defined in law as 'in being'. It is only considered to be such when it has been fully expelled from its mother's body. It is not clear whether this is the case if the umbilical cord remains uncut, or if it is yet to take its first breath. However, if the foetus in the womb is deliberately injured and the child dies from these injuries after having been born, then the attacker would be criminally liable. This was decided in the *Attorney-General's Reference (No. 3 of 1994)* (1997); the verdict, however, would be likely to be manslaughter (see Chapter 2, Involuntary manslaughter), rather than murder.

Doctors are permitted to switch off life support machines of people who are 'brain dead', without being liable for unlawful homicide. It would seem therefore that one who is 'brain dead' is not generally considered to be a 'reasonable person in being'. Although there are no cases directly on this point, the related cases of *Malcherek and Steel* (1981) (dealt with later under Causation) would tend to confirm this.

'Under the Queen's peace'

The killing of an enemy in war is not murder, as such a person is not 'under the Queen's peace'. It would, however, be considered the *actus reus* of murder to kill a prisoner of war.

Prosecution for murder

A feature of the crime of murder is that a British citizen can be tried in the domestic courts for a murder alleged to have been committed in the United Kingdom or in any other country.

A prosecution for murder can be brought at any time after the death of the victim. However, if death occurs more than three years after the injury which caused it, the consent of the Attorney-General is required to prosecute for murder. The same is true where a person has already been found guilty of an offence which was connected to the circumstances of the death.

Causation

The principles of causation have been studied in AS Law. It has to be proved that there is a direct and unbroken link between the defendant's act and its criminal consequence. The death of his victim has to be the direct result of the defendant's conduct. There must be no intervening act breaking the chain of causation. There must be both factual and legal causation. Factual causation is that the death would not have happened but for the conduct of the defendant. Legal causation requires the act to be the operating and substantial cause of the death. If the chain of causation is broken, then there is no liability for unlawful homicide. This does not necessarily mean, however, that there is no liability for the initial act – for example, for assault occasioning actual bodily harm.

Activities

Using only the material you have read so far in this chapter, do you think that the *actus reus* of murder is present in the following cases? Give reasons for your opinions.

1. Arnold and Bert are steeplejacks. High up on a factory chimney, Bert pulls out a gun, points it at Arnold, and says that he is going to kill him for having an affair with his wife. Arnold lunges at Bert to knock the gun from his hand, and in doing so causes Bert to fall backwards off the scaffolding to his death.

2. Cheryl has agreed to look after her aged uncle Dennis. He is dependent on various prescription drugs, but Cheryl, tired of the responsibility towards him, deliberately fails to get them for him. As a result of this, he dies.

3. Eric, during the course of an argument, stabs his pregnant girlfriend. She recovers, but gives birth to their child prematurely. As a result of the premature birth, the child dies shortly afterwards.

Link

A case which illustrates this point is *White* (1910), which you will have seen on p169 of *AQA Law AS*.

Key cases

White (1910): mother died of a heart attack before poison administered by her son could take effect; chain of causation was broken.

Pagett (1983): police bullet killed girl being held as a human shield by defendant; defendant responsible for her death.

Cato (1976): mutual injection of drugs was more than a minimal cause of death.

Blaue (1975): refusal of blood transfusion following stabbing not the main cause of death.

Factual causation

In **White (1910)**, the defendant put poison in his mother's drink with the intention of killing her. She took a little of the drink, but died of a heart attack before the poison could take effect. There was no evidence that the heart attack was in any way the result of the poison. There was therefore no direct link between White's act and his mother's death, and he was acquitted of murder. He was, however, found guilty of attempted murder.

A more controversial case illustrating actual causation is **Pagett (1983)**.

The defendant, armed with a shotgun, was attempting to resist arrest. He forcibly held a 16-year-old girl in front of him as a human shield, and fired at the police officers. Instinctively, the police fired back at him, killing the girl. Pagett was tried for murder. He argued that it was not he who fired the shot which killed the girl. This was true, but it was held that, but for his action, the girl would not have been killed. His conduct was the direct actual cause of her death. He was convicted of manslaughter.

Legal causation

The cause of death in unlawful homicide can vary between the substantial and the minimal. Stabbing a victim in the chest is clearly a substantial cause of death. The problem lies with the other end of the spectrum. The law does not require conduct to be substantial, but it must be more than a minimal cause of the death. A defendant can be guilty of unlawful homicide even if his conduct only contributed to the death, or if he was only one among others who contributed to it.

There must be a more than 'slight or trifling' link. An extreme example of a minimal cause would be if a person pricks the finger of another who is in the course of bleeding to death following an accident. The further loss of blood from the pin-prick may accelerate the death, but it could only be said to be a minimal cause.

In **Cato (1976)**, two drug addicts had spent the night injecting each other with a mixture of heroin and water. In the morning, both were extremely ill, and one of them died. The other was charged with his friend's manslaughter. The Court of Appeal held that the heroin need not necessarily have been the only cause of death, but it was more than a minimal cause, and one which accelerated the moment of the victim's death.

'Taking the victim as he finds him'

When considering the chain of causation, it is necessary to bear in mind that the consequences of a person's conduct might be affected by unknown circumstances. For example, an attacker might hit someone on the head with a baseball bat in the course of a robbery. Normally, this might produce no more than a sore head and bruising. Unknown to the assailant however, the victim has an unusually thin skull, and dies of his injuries. It is no good the defendant protesting that he didn't know about the thin skull; he must take the victim as he finds him. If a person's injuries are made more serious by some unusual physical or mental condition, then a defendant is liable for such injuries. This is usually known as the 'thin skull rule'.

The case which illustrates this rule is **Blaue (1975)**.

The victim, a young woman, was stabbed by the defendant. It was necessary for her to have a blood transfusion, but her religion, (she was a Jehovah's Witness), did not allow this. She died, and the defendant was found guilty of murdering her. It was no good his maintaining that a blood transfusion would have saved her; he had to take his victim as he found her.

New intervening acts

It is possible for the chain of causation to be broken by some new and independent event. In this case, the defendant will no longer be responsible for the consequence, providing that the intervening event is sufficiently different and serious. The intervening event could be the result of an act by a third party, some unforeseeable happening, or by the victim himself.

A case illustrating the first of these situations is **Jordan (1956)**.

The victim had been stabbed in the stomach, and following treatment in hospital, his wounds were healing well. An antibiotic was given to him, and a large intake of liquid. It had previously been found that he had an allergy to the drug, and that he shouldn't be given large amounts of liquid. He suffered a severe allergic reaction and died. It was held that the actions of the medical staff were the main means of death, not the initial stab wound. There was a sufficiently independent intervening act, and the defendant was not guilty of murder.

However, it is unusual for medical treatment to be held to break the chain of causation. The two cases of **Smith (1959)** and **Cheshire (1991)** are illustrations of this.

A soldier had been stabbed in the lung during a barrack-room brawl. He was taken to the medical centre, but was dropped on the way. When he eventually got there, the medical staff attempted to give him artificial respiration by pumping on his chest. This worsened his condition and he died. Although the treatment he had received drastically reduced his chances of survival, his original attacker was found guilty of his murder.

A victim had been shot in the stomach and thigh. In hospital, a tube was inserted in his throat to help him breathe more easily. As a result of rare complications following this tracheotomy, the victim died. The complications had not been noticed by the doctors. Although his wounds at the time were no longer life-threatening, his original assailant was held responsible for his death.

At the beginning of this chapter, when considering 'reasonable persons in being', the cases of *Malcherek and Steel* (1981) were mentioned. Both cases involved switching off the life-support machines of victims who were considered to be 'brain dead'. *Malcherek and Steel* (1981) established that such switching off does not break the chain of causation, and therefore death is the result of the assailant's action.

Action taken by the victim

It is not difficult to imagine situations where a victim who feels threatened takes drastic action to escape, and in doing so is injured or is killed. Consider the case of a person who dies as a result of jumping from a first storey window to escape an attacker. Does this action break the chain of causation? Is the death the direct result of the attacker's action, or the independent act of the victim? It depends, of course on the nature and seriousness of the threat. If the threat to the victim is serious, then it would be more reasonable for him to take the evasive action which resulted in his injury. In such a case, the chain of causation would not be held to be broken. If, on the other hand, the threat was of a relatively trivial or minor nature, then drastic evasive action would be held to break the chain of causation. Two cases which illustrate this point both involve jumping out of moving cars.

Key cases

Jordan (1956): wrong administration of drug in hospital was a new intervening act.

Smith (1959): clumsy and inappropriate treatment of a soldier following a stabbing did not break the chain of causation.

Cheshire (1991): the victim, whose wounds were no longer life-threatening, died as a result of unusual complications; there was no break in the chain of causation.

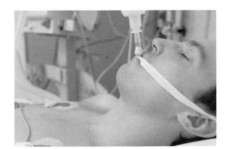

Fig. 1 Malcherek *established that switching off life support does not break the chain of causation, and therefore death is the result of the assailant's action*

Roberts (1971): victim jumped from moving car to avoid sexual advances; chain of causation was not broken.

Williams (1991): victim broke the chain of causation because his reaction was unreasonable.

Activities

What do you think the criminal liability might be in the following cases?

1 Gert is unable to tolerate her unhappy marriage to Harry any longer. After Harry has gone to bed, she takes a knife and stabs him. Unknown to her, the equally desperate Harry was already dead, having taken a large overdose of drugs half an hour earlier.

2 Mahmoud is attacked by Naseem and suffers serious, though not fatal, injuries. On its way to take Mahmoud to the hospital, the ambulance is involved in a high-speed car crash in which the driver of the ambulance and Mahmoud are killed.

3 Oona is on a fairground ride, during the course of which the person next to her attempts to indecently assault her. Desperate to get away, she jumps out and, being hit by the following car, is fatally injured.

Key cases

Vickers (1957): vicious attack on an old lady was enough for the intention to murder.

In **Roberts (1971)**, the driver of the car turned off down a side road and subjected his passenger to unwanted sexual advances. She jumped out of the moving car in order to escape, and was injured. It was held that the defendant was liable for her injuries. There was a direct line of causation between his conduct and her injuries which had not been broken by her act.

In **Williams (1991)**, on the other hand, the victim jumped out of a moving car because he alleged that there had been an attempt to steal his wallet. Because this was held to be an unreasonable reaction under the circumstances, and disproportionate to the threat, it was held that the chain of causation had been broken by the victim's intervening act. The defendant was not liable for the victim's injuries.

You should now be able to:

- state the definition of murder
- explain the *actus reus* and *mens rea* of murder, giving cases as examples
- evaluate causation in relation to murder.

2 The *mens rea* of murder

'Malice aforethought, express or implied'

This is the *mens rea* of murder as defined by Coke. Case law has identified some extensions of this definition. There is no requirement for 'malice' to be present. It is possible to imagine a situation where a killing takes place from motives of love or compassion. An example might be of a parent who gives a fatal overdose of drugs to a child suffering from an intolerably painful terminal illness, *Gray* (1965). 'Aforethought' does not need any previous planning or thinking about it beforehand, merely that the intention to kill does not occur after the act. The *mens rea* of an unlawful killing is an intention to kill or cause grievous bodily harm.

If a defendant who kills has either of these intentions, then he is guilty of murder. Notice that this is the case even when the defendant does not expressly intend to kill his victim. The intention to cause grievous, (meaning serious), bodily harm is enough for a conviction for murder.

This was established in **Vickers (1957)**, a decision confirmed by the House of Lords in *Cunningham* (1982).

In *Vickers* (1957), the defendant had broken into the cellar of an old lady's shop. When she discovered him there, he attacked her savagely by punching her and kicking her in the head. She died from her injuries. The court held that an intention to inflict grievous bodily harm, resulting in the death of the victim, was enough to imply the necessary intention for murder.

Foresight of consequences

The express intention to kill usually poses no problems. For example, a terrorist who puts a bomb on a passenger airliner, resulting in its blowing up at 35,000 feet can safely be assumed to intend the death of his victims. Similarly, implied intention can often be safely inferred where the defendant clearly intended to cause serious injury, as in *Vickers* (1957), (above).

The main difficulty arises when the defendant's main aim is not to kill or cause serious injury, but to achieve some quite different end. Several cases over the years have attempted to clarify this matter by examining the question of foresight. How far can intention to kill or cause serious injury be inferred from the defendant's foreseeing the consequences of his actions? This was considered in the cases of **Maloney (1985)**, **Hancock and Shankland (1986)** and **Nedrick (1989)**.

In *Maloney* (1985), the defendant had been drinking with his stepfather, a man with whom he was apparently on good terms. In the early hours, the two men had challenged each other as to who could be first to load his gun and be ready to fire. Maloney won, pointed his gun at his stepfather, pulled the trigger and killed him instantly. He maintained that he had no intention whatever of killing or causing injury; it was 'just a lark'. Following the direction of the judge at his trial, he was found guilty of murder. The House of Lords, however, allowed his appeal, and changed the verdict to manslaughter. They held that nothing less than the actual intention to kill or cause serious harm should constitute the necessary *mens rea* for murder. The mere foresight of probable death or serious injury was not in itself intent, though it could be evidence from which a jury might infer intention.

In *Hancock and Shankland* (1986), the House of Lords further developed the decision in *Maloney* (1985). Two striking miners had dropped large blocks of concrete from a bridge over a road into the path of a taxi with a police escort taking a non-striking miner to work. One piece of concrete hit the taxi's windscreen, killing the driver. The defendants claimed that their only intention was to block the road, not to kill or injure anyone. In allowing their appeal and substituting a verdict of manslaughter, the House of Lords ruled that in such a case the degree of probability of death or injury was of paramount importance. It was suggested that juries should be directed that:

- the greater the probability of a consequence, the more likely it is that the consequence was foreseen
- if the consequence was foreseen, the greater the probability is that it was also intended
- juries must be reminded that the decision is theirs to be reached upon a consideration of all the evidence.

In *Nedrick* (1989), the defendant had poured paraffin through the letterbox of a house with the intention of frightening the woman who lived there. A child died in the resulting fire. The defendant's appeal against his conviction for murder was allowed. The Court of Appeal suggested that the jury should consider the following:

- Do they feel that death or serious injury was the virtually certain result of the accused's voluntary act?
- Did the accused foresee that death or serious injury was the virtually certain result of his act?

If the answer to both was 'yes', then the jury could reasonably infer that the accused intended the consequences of his act.

A further development took place in the case of **Woollin (1998)**, in which the defendant lost his temper while feeding his baby son. He threw the baby against a wall, and it died of its injuries. In allowing Woollin's appeal against a conviction for murder, the House of Lords approved the direction given in *Nedrick* (1989), provided that the word 'find' was substituted for 'infer'. The jury therefore should not 'find' the necessary intention, unless the answers to the questions above are 'yes'. This would

Key cases

Maloney (1985): defendant killed his stepfather in drunken game; nothing less than the actual intention to kill or cause serious harm should be the *mens rea* in murder.

Hancock and Shankland (1986): striking miners dropped concrete blocks into the path of a taxi, killing its driver; foresight of consequences may amount to intention, but it is up to the jury.

Nedrick (1989): a child died in a fire caused by the defendant; the jury should ask itself two questions; if the answer to both is 'yes', it may infer the probable intention.

Woollin (1998): the defendant killed his baby son in a fit of temper; if the answers to the questions in *Nedrick* (1989) are 'yes', the jury must find, rather than infer, intention.

Key cases

Matthews and Alleyne (2003): victim died as a result of being thrown into a river: foresight of consequences as being the same as intention is more like a rule of evidence.

seem to suggest that the House of Lords again found in *Woollin* (1998) that foresight of consequence amounts to intention, when in *Moloney* (1985) it had ruled that it was not necessarily so.

Foresight of consequences was again considered in **Matthew and Alleyne (2003)**, in which the defendants had thrown their victim from a bridge into a river. They knew that he could not swim, and they left the scene before he could reach safety. The victim drowned. The defendants argued on appeal that the direction given at their trial suggested that foresight of consequences was the same as intention. However, the Court of Appeal regarded foresight of consequences being the same as intention to be more as a rule of evidence. A jury in such a case is entitled to find the existence of intention, but does not necessarily have to. Despite what the Court of Appeal may have considered to be a technical misdirection, it decided that it would not have made any difference to the jury's decision. The conviction of Matthews and Alleyne was therefore upheld.

Conclusion

The best way of expressing the present position is as follows:

A person commits murder when he kills another with the necessary intent.

Intention for murder is nothing less than the intention to kill or cause serious bodily harm. The defendant's foresight of the consequences of his actions is no more than evidence from which the jury may infer intent.

Activities

What do you think might be the liability for murder in the following cases? Give your reasons.

1   Peter is in severe financial trouble. He places some bogus cargo in a freight plane, primed with a bomb and timed to explode in mid-air. In this way he hopes to claim insurance on the phoney goods. The plane is destroyed at 30 000 feet, and all the crew are killed as a result.

2   Quin interferes with the power steering of his girlfriend Rosie's, car with the intention of preventing her from meeting a secret lover. On leaving her drive, Rosie tries to turn into the road, but cannot avoid an approaching vehicle. The oncoming car crashes into her, and she is killed immediately.

3   Tracey, a member of an extreme terrorist group, enters a pub carrying a holdall containing a bomb. She shouts a warning, and immediately runs out. Very shortly afterwards, the bomb explodes, killing three people who were unable to get out in time.

You should now be able to:

■ explain the law relating to murder

■ apply the law to given scenarios.

3 Voluntary manslaughter: provocation

The difference between voluntary and involuntary manslaughter

When considering the law relating to murder, we saw that it was necessary to establish that the defendant had the intention to kill or cause serious bodily harm. This is, of course, in addition to committing the act causing death.

The distinguishing factor between voluntary and involuntary manslaughter is that, whereas voluntary manslaughter requires the same degree of intention as murder, involuntary manslaughter does not.

Involuntary manslaughter occurs when a person is killed as the result of a wide variety of situations. These can vary between the extremes of death during the commission of a serious crime, to death following an act of carelessness. The spectrum is wide, but in all cases of involuntary manslaughter there is no intention by the defendant to cause death or serious harm. Involuntary manslaughter will be considered in detail in Chapter 2.

Voluntary manslaughter is the outcome of a situation where a defendant who would otherwise be guilty of murder, is able successfully to plead one of two specific defences. These defences are defined in the Homicide Act 1957. They are:

 provocation
 diminished responsibility.

The result of successfully pleading one of these defences is that the defendant is found guilty of manslaughter, and not murder.

The Homicide Act 1957, s3

Provocation had been a common law defence before the passing of the Homicide Act 1957. If a person could show that he was provoked by another to such an extent as to lose self-control, then he could plead a defence to murder. The Homicide Act 1957, s3, set out this defence as follows:

> Where, on a charge of murder there is evidence on which the jury can find that the person charged was provoked (whether by things done or by things said or by both together) to lose his self-control, the question whether the provocation was enough to make a reasonable man do as he did shall be left to be determined by the jury.

It goes on to say:

> … in determining that question the jury shall take into account everything both done and said according to the effect which, in their opinion, it would have on a reasonable man.

It can be seen from this that the Act lays down a two-fold test to be applied by the jury:

1 Was the defendant provoked to lose his self-control? (The 'subjective test'.)

2 Would a reasonable man have lost his self-control in the circumstances? (The 'objective test'.)

In this topic you will learn how to:

 distinguish between voluntary and involuntary manslaughter

 state the definition of provocation

 explain provocation as a partial defence to murder

 explain cases that illustrate circumstances that can amount to provocation

 explain cases that illustrate circumstances that can amount to loss of self-control

 explain cases that illustrate circumstances that can fulfil the objective test

 apply the rules to a given situation.

Provocation – the subjective test: was the defendant provoked enough to lose self-control?

In determining whether the defendant was provoked into losing self-control, it is necessary to examine the precise meaning of 'provocation'. Section 3 of the Homicide Act says it is things 'done or said or both'. Usually provocation will be aimed specifically and deliberately at the defendant by the victim. It may be, however, that the provocation is not deliberate, or may not necessarily be aimed at the defendant himself. It is enough that there were 'things done' which caused the loss of self-control.

Many different kinds of behaviour have been held to constitute provocation. These include:

- a physical attack on the defendant
- an assault not on the defendant but on those close to him (*Pearson* (1992))
- the crying of a small baby (*Doughty* (1986))
- mockery following sexual abuse (*Camplin* (1978))
- the supplying of drugs to the defendant's son (*Baillie* (1995))
- the denial of theft of another's property (*Smith* (2000)).

These cases will be described in the following section.

Loss of self-control

As mentioned above, many different kinds of behaviour have been held to be enough to amount to provocation.

- In *Pearson* (1992), it was held that the ill-treatment of the defendant's younger brother by his father was enough to cause the defendant to lose self-control. In this case the acts which provoked the defendant were not aimed at him but at his brother.
- In *Doughty* (1986) the continual crying of his three-week-old son caused the defendant to lose control and kill him. Clearly, the provocation in this case could not be said to have been deliberate.

Under the common law, the loss of self-control had to be 'sudden and temporary' such as to render the accused 'so subject to passion as to make him for the moment not master of his mind'. This was stated in the case of *Duffy* (1949) and has been applied in cases following the passing of the 1957 Act.

Problems can arise from this. If the loss of self-control must be 'sudden and temporary', what if there is a lapse of time between the provocation and the reaction to it? This has happened in a number of cases. It would seem that the longer the lapse of time, the less likely it would be that the defence of provocation would succeed.

In *Baillie* (1995) a father killed the dealer supplying drugs to his son. Although there was a lapse of time during which the defendant armed himself, it did not necessarily preclude a sudden and temporary loss of self-control. In *Ibrams and Gregory* (1981) on the other hand, it had been found that as there had been no provocation for a period of three days before the killing, there could not have been a sudden loss of self-control.

The issue is highlighted by cases involving women who have been abused by their partners over a long period of time. In these cases the woman concerned suddenly 'snapped' and killed her abusive partner, despite a lapse of time since the last instance of abuse. It has been said that the requirement that provocation must be sudden and temporary disadvantages women, who tend to be less likely than men to react suddenly. Two cases of **Ahluwalia (1992)** and **Thornton (1996)** serve to illustrate this 'slow burn' situation.

In *Ahluwalia* (1992) the defendant had been abused by her husband over many years. One night before he went to sleep, her husband threatened her with violence the next day. When he was asleep, she poured petrol over him and set him alight. She was convicted of murder. The Court of Appeal disallowed her appeal on the ground of provocation, holding that there was too long a delay. The court did, however, uphold her appeal on the grounds of diminished responsibility. (See Topic 4.)

In *Thornton* (1996), Sara Thornton faced a retrial for the murder of her husband. He had been a heavy drinker, and had consistently physically abused her. After one incident, she went to the kitchen to calm down. She looked for a weapon, took a carving knife and sharpened it. She then returned to the living room where she stabbed her husband to death. She was convicted of murder and her first appeal failed, the Court of Appeal holding that there had not been a sudden and temporary loss of self-control. At her second appeal the court held that it was possible that a minor incident could act as the last straw and trigger a sudden final loss of control, following a long build-up of provocation. A retrial was ordered at which, in 1996, the jury acquitted her of murder.

Lack of restraint following loss of control

In **Richens (1993),** the defendant's girlfriend was allegedly raped. He confronted the culprit, who contended that the woman had been a willing partner and had consented to sex. The defendant became enraged and stabbed him to death. The Court of Appeal accepted the plea of provocation, stating that it did not require the accused to have such a loss of control that he did not know what he was doing. It was enough that the loss of control made him unable to restrain himself from doing what he did.

Provocation – the objective test: would a reasonable man have lost his self-control in the circumstances?

This test asks the question, 'Would a reasonable man have lost his self-control in the circumstances?' In turn, it raises another question as to what constitutes a 'reasonable man'. Traditionally, before the passing of the Homicide Act 1957, the courts had ruled that the reasonable man was an adult, normal both physically and mentally. This test comes from the case of *Bedder* (1954), where the defendant, who suffered from impotence, was taunted by a prostitute for his failure to have sex with her. It was held in this case that the jury should have been asked to consider the effect of the mockery on a reasonable, normal (that is, non-impotent) man.

This was developed in the case of **Camplin (1978)**.

The defendant was a 15-year-old boy. He had been at the house of an older man, who forcibly abused him sexually, and then laughed at him. The defendant lost his self-control, seized a heavy pan and hit his abuser over the head, killing him. The House of Lords ruled that the term 'reasonable man' was not confined to the adult male, but 'a person having the power of self-control to be expected of an ordinary person of the sex and age of the accused'. Furthermore, would the reasonable man, sharing the characteristics of the accused, be similarly provoked, and react to the provocation as the accused did?

Key cases

Ahluwalia (1992): defendant waited for her husband to fall asleep before killing him; because of this delay, provocation was not available as a defence.

Thornton (1996): the defendant killed her husband after a delay following an abusive incident. 'Last straw' could trigger final loss of self-control.

Richens (1993): provoked defendant may know what he is doing, but be unable to restrain himself.

Camplin (1978): 15-year-old boy killed his tormentor with a chapati pan: 'reasonable man' test not confined to the adult male.

Fig. 2 *At Sara Thornton's second appeal against the conviction for the murder of her husband the court held that it was possible that a minor incident could act as the last straw and trigger a sudden final loss of control, following a long build-up of provocation. A retrial was ordered at which, in 1996, the jury acquitted her of murder*

This rule may be summarised as a two-part test as follows:

■ Would a reasonable man have lost his self-control in the circumstances?
■ Would the reasonable man, sharing the characteristics of the accused, be similarly provoked and react to the provocation as the accused did?

Characteristics

In *Camplin* (1978) the defendant was a 15-year-old boy. Other characteristics were identified by the House of Lords as being possible objects of provocation. They include, apart from age and sex: race, colour, ethnic origin, physical deformity, impotence (as in *Bedder* (1954)) and a painful medical condition where the provocation is a blow to that part of the body. Pregnancy and menstruation might also be relevant where women are concerned, if that was the object of the provocation.

Power of self-control

In *Thornton* (1996), referred to earlier, the Court of Appeal stated that the 'battered wife syndrome' might be taken into account when assessing the likelihood of a person being easily provoked. It was not certain, however, how far other conditions, such as injuries causing shortness of temper, or other mental abnormalities, could be taken into account. These conditions in any case would be more relevant in the defence of diminished responsibility, (see below). Two cases illustrate somewhat different approaches.

Luc Thiet Thuan (1996) was a case from Hong Kong. The defendant, as the result of a head injury following a fall, had several times lost his self-control in response to only minor provocation. The Privy Council held that any mental infirmity which reduced the power of self-control below those of an ordinary person could not be ascribed to the ordinary person for the purposes of the objective test. His appeal against a conviction for murder was dismissed.

In **Smith (Morgan) (2000)**, the defendant killed a man in the course of an argument about some stolen tools. He was convicted of murder, but the Court of Appeal substituted the conviction for manslaughter. The court held that the trial judge had been wrong to tell the jury to ignore the defendant's severe clinical depression, (which might have reduced his power of self-control), in considering whether a normal reasonable man would have acted in such a way. The House of Lords agreed with the Court of Appeal, and thus the reasoning in *Luc Thiet Thuan* (1996) (above) was rejected.

This confusion in the law was to some extent resolved in another Privy Council case **Holley (2005)**, this time from Jersey.

The defendant, Holley, was a chronic alcoholic. On one occasion while drunk he killed his girlfriend with an axe. He admitted the killing, claimed provocation, but was found guilty of murder. The Privy Council, comprising nine judges, all of whom were Law Lords, disapproved of the decision in *Smith (Morgan)* (2000), and reaffirmed the decision in *Luc Thiet Thuan* (1996). Lord Nicholls, delivering the majority verdict (6:3), considered the objective test 'whether the provocation was enough to make a reasonable man do as he did'. He said that the jury must consider the effect of that provocation of a person of the same age and sex as the defendant, but with ordinary powers of self-control. The jury should not take into account any individual peculiarities such as mental abnormality or intoxication. These would be matters better left to a consideration of the defence of diminished responsibility.

> ### Key cases
>
> **Luc Thiet Thuan (1996)**: head injury resulting in reduced power of self-control could not be taken into consideration in the objective test.
>
> **Smith (Morgan) (2000)**: victim was killed in an argument over stolen tools; clinical depression may reduce the power of self-control.
>
> **Holley (2005)**: drunken defendant killed his girlfriend with an axe; *Smith (Morgan)* (2000) disapproved and *Luc Thiet Thuan* (1996) reaffirmed.

In the cases of *James and Karimi* (2006), the Court of Appeal dismissed the joint appeals of two defendants convicted of murder. The court held that it is the decision of the Privy Council in *Holley* (2005), rather than that of the House of Lords in *Smith (Morgan)* (2000) which should be followed as a correct statement of law on this point. Importantly, it was agreed, even by the minority three judges who dissented in that case, that the majority decision in *Holley* (2005) has now settled the matter.

Conclusion

The objective test can now be summarised as follows:

■ Was the provocation enough to make a reasonable man behave in the same way as the defendant?

■ Would a person of the same age and sex as the defendant, but with ordinary powers of self-control, have reacted in the same way to the provocation?

■ Individual peculiarities such as mental abnormality or intoxication should not be taken into account.

Activities

Consider whether the defence of provocation could be successful in the following situations:

1 Usha and Vikram work in the same office together. Usha is constantly taunting Vikram about the well-known infidelities of his wife. On one occasion, unable to stand it any longer, Vikram grabs a paperknife and stabs Usha in the heart, killing her instantly.

2 Wayne is a drunkard and a bully, and has been physically abusing his wife Yvette for years. One night he comes home drunk from the pub, threatens Yvette with violence and then falls asleep on the sofa. Yvette puts on her coat and goes outside to calm down. She sees a building site further down the road. After searching for a while, she finds a pickaxe which she carries home. She attacks the sleeping Wayne with it and kills him.

3 Zak suffered an injury to his head a year ago which has left him with a very short temper. One day a workmate criticises him for being slow. In a rage, Zak grabs him by the throat and strangles him.

You should now be able to:

■ explain the law relating to provocation

■ apply the law to given scenarios.

AQA Examiner's tip

When assessing the defence of provocation, ask yourself the following questions.

■ Was the defendant provoked? Does the behaviour of the victim fall within 'things done and said' which would constitute provocation? Would a reasonable man sharing the same characteristics as the defendant have been similarly provoked?

■ Was there a 'sudden and temporary' loss of self-control?

■ If the defendant was provoked, would a reasonable man of the same age and sex as the defendant, with ordinary powers of self-control have reacted in the same way as the defendant?

In this topic you will learn how to:

■ state the definition of diminished responsibility

■ explain the relationship of diminished responsibility as a partial defence to murder

■ explain cases that illustrate circumstances that can amount to abnormality of mind and causes of abnormality of mind

■ explain cases that can illustrate circumstances that can amount to substantial impairment

■ apply the rules to a given situation.

4 Voluntary manslaughter: diminished responsibility

The Homicide Act 1957, s2(1)

The defence of diminished responsibility was also introduced by the Homicide Act 1957. The defence of insanity, (see Chapter 4, Defences), had existed before then, and still does. However, the test for insanity is too narrow to include many of the mental problems which people can suffer from. The verdict when a person successfully pleads insanity is 'not guilty by reason of insanity'. The result of successfully pleading the defence of diminished responsibility, as with provocation (above), is to change the verdict to one of manslaughter.

Section 2(1) of the Homicide Act states that:

> *Where a person kills ... another, he shall not be convicted of murder if he was suffering from such abnormality of mind (whether arising from a condition of arrested or retarded development of mind or any inherent causes or induced by disease or injury) as substantially impaired his mental responsibility for his acts and omissions in doing or being a party to the killing.*

A person who pleads diminished responsibility must therefore prove that:

■ he was suffering from an abnormality of mind

■ this was caused by arrested or retarded development of mind or an inherent cause or disease or injury

■ this abnormality of mind substantially impaired his mental responsibility for the killing.

A defendant who puts forward this defence must prove it on the balance of probabilities.

Abnormality of mind

Abnormality of mind covers many different kinds of medical condition, such as psychotic disorders, clinical depression, and epilepsy. It can also be the result of post-natal depression, (**Reynolds (1988)**), pre-menstrual tension (**English (1981)**) and battered wife syndrome (*Ahluwalia* (1992), described in Topic 3).

Byrne (1960) was an early case following the Homicide Act 1957 which examined the issue of abnormality of mind. The defendant was a sexual psychopath, who strangled a young woman and then mutilated her body. At his trial he was found guilty of murder. On appeal, however, the Court of Appeal substituted a conviction for murder for one of manslaughter.

The court said that:

> Abnormality of mind ... means a state of mind so different from that of ordinary human beings that the reasonable man would term it abnormal. It seems to us to be wide enough to cover the mind's activities in all its aspects, not only the perception of physical acts and matters, and the ability to form a rational judgement as to whether an act is right or wrong, but also the ability to exercise willpower to control physical acts in accordance with that rational judgement.

Byrne was not able to resist the impulse to gratify his perverted desires, therefore the defence of diminished responsibility was available to him. Though the verdict was changed to manslaughter, the court saw no reason to alter his sentence of life imprisonment.

Key cases

Reynolds (1988): a young mother killed her mother with a hammer: post-natal depression could cause diminished responsibility.

English (1981): a woman who killed could bring evidence to show that her responsibility had been impaired enough by pre-menstrual tension to admit the defence of diminished responsibility.

Byrne (1960): sexual psychopath's inability to control his perverted desires could plead diminished responsibility.

Causes of abnormality of mind

Section 2(1) of the Homicide Act 1957 lists the causes of abnormality of mind as follows:

- A condition of arrested or abnormal development of mind. Examples of this would be that of a grown person with the mental age of a child, or someone with an abnormality such as that displayed by Byrne, (above).
- Any inherent cause. This must come from within the defendant, not be something caused by an external factor such as drugs or alcohol. (*Di Duca* (1959), and *Tandy* (1989), described below).
- Induced by disease. This could include post-traumatic stress disorder or reactive depression as the result of some event affecting the defendant. (See *Skelton* (1994), *Hampson* (1999) and *Lawson* (2001)).
- Induced by injury. A head injury, for example, might cause a person to behave in an irrational way. (See *Luc Thiet Thuan* (1996), above).

Whatever cause of diminished responsibility is put forward by the defendant at his trial, it is necessary for medical evidence to be produced to support it.

Substantial impairment

Section 2(1) of the Homicide Act states that the defendant's abnormality of mind must be such that it 'substantially impaired his mental responsibility for his acts or omissions'.

The extent to which the defendant's abnormality of mind 'substantially impairs' his responsibility for his acts is a question for the jury to decide. It was held in *Gittens* (1984) (see below) that the impairment must be 'more than minimal'; it has to be substantial. It need not, however, be total. It is of course a matter of degree, upon which the jury must come to a decision based on the facts of the case (*Byrne* (1960)). If there is no evidence from which the jury could reasonably conclude that there was substantial impairment, the judge can withdraw the point from them.

The effect of intoxication

As was stated in the section above, the abnormality must be from an inherent cause. It does not include the abnormality of mind which might come from being drunk or under the influence of drugs. To that extent, the effect of taking alcohol or drugs cannot in itself be pleaded in defence under s2(1). The general defence of intoxication is further considered in Chapter 4.

In **Tandy (1989)** the issue of intoxication was raised in the defence of diminished responsibility. After drinking the best part of a whole bottle of vodka, the defendant had strangled her 11-year-old daughter. The defence maintained that the defendant's alcoholism amounted to a disease, and also that her drinking was, as a result, involuntary. The Court of Appeal dismissed Tandy's appeal against a conviction for murder. It held that drunkenness was not an abnormality of mind, and only if the brain had been injured by alcoholism, or the drinking had become wholly involuntary, might a defence of diminished responsibility succeed. If the defendant merely failed to resist the impulse to drink, and only the first drink was voluntary, she could not claim diminished responsibility. Unfortunately this case still did not settle the question as to whether alcoholism could be a 'disease' in the meaning of s2(1).

A problem arises when the defendant, as well as suffering from an abnormality of mind, is also under the influence of alcohol or drugs at the time of the killing. Should a jury separate out the intoxication and consider only the abnormality of mind in isolation from it?

Key cases

Tandy (1989): the defendant, when intoxicated, killed her young daughter; she tried to plead alcoholism as a cause of diminished responsibility.

Gittens (1984): defendant killed while suffering from depression combined with drink and drugs: was the depression on its own enough to impair his responsibility for his act?

Dietschmann (2003): the defendant had killed while suffering from a mental abnormality combined with intoxication; did the abnormality on its own substantially impair his responsibility?

This point is illustrated by the case of **Gittens (1984)**. The defendant killed his wife and step-daughter while suffering from depression, combined with the effect of drink and drugs. At his trial, the jury had been invited to decide whether it was the depression or the intoxication that was the main cause of the defendant's mental state. He was convicted of murder. The Court of Appeal held that the jury should have been directed to disregard the effect of the drink and drugs, and then consider whether the other cause (depression) was sufficient to impair the defendant's responsibility for his acts. Because of this misdirection, a verdict of manslaughter was substituted for murder.

This decision was approved in **Dietschmann (2003)** by the House of Lords. The Court of Appeal had upheld the conviction for murder. The defendant, who was suffering from an 'adjustment disorder', had killed another man whom he felt had been disrespectful to the memory of the defendant's lately deceased aunt. At the time of the killing, the defendant had consumed a large amount of alcohol. On his further appeal, the House of Lords approved the decision in *Gittens* (1984). Lord Hutton said that whether the defendant would still have killed had he not been intoxicated is irrelevant. The important question for the jury is whether his mental abnormality, disregarding his intoxication, substantially impaired his responsibility for his actions.

Activities

Consider whether the defence of diminished responsibility might be successful in the following situations:

1. Andy is a 38-year-old man who has the mental age of a six-year-old. When his neighbour, Beth, calls him 'stupid', he flies into a rage and stabs her to death.

2. Callum suffers from a painful ulcer on his leg, which causes him to be very irritable. After taking some painkillers, he goes out to the local pub, where he drinks seven pints of strong lager, followed by several whiskies. At the end of the evening, he gets into an argument with another customer, Dwayne, whom he imagines is making fun of him. He grabs a heavy ashtray and smashes it over Dwayne's head, killing him.

3. Ellie, 16, has recently given birth in circumstances of secrecy. Suffering from stress and post-natal depression, she goes to visit her aunt Flo. Far from being sympathetic, Flo launches into a criticism of Ellie's lifestyle. Ellie seizes a pair of kitchen scissors and stabs Flo to death.

You should now be able to:

- explain the law relating to diminished responsibility
- apply the law to given scenarios.

2 Involuntary manslaughter

Introduction

In the last chapter we saw that the crimes of murder and voluntary manslaughter both required a particular degree of intent. The intention in both crimes was the intention to kill or cause grievous (serious) bodily harm. In voluntary manslaughter, the charge is reduced from murder if the defendant can successfully prove one of the specific defences to murder. The important difference between voluntary and involuntary manslaughter is that in involuntary manslaughter the defendant does not intend to kill or cause serious harm.

This will inevitably mean that the range of involuntary manslaughter is very wide. Death may result from an extremely dangerous act at the one extreme, to some relatively minor degree of carelessness at the other. The maximum sentence for involuntary manslaughter is life imprisonment. It is, however, discretionary, (see Unit 3A, Evaluation of fatal and non-fatal offences against the person). A judge may therefore pass a sentence which reflects the seriousness of the offence, from life imprisonment to, if such a sentence is justifiable in the circumstances, even a non-custodial one.

In this chapter we will consider three forms of involuntary manslaughter. They are:

- gross negligence manslaughter
- unlawful act manslaughter, (sometimes called constructive manslaughter)
- subjective reckless manslaughter.

In this topic you will learn how to:

- state the meaning of involuntary manslaughter
- explain the meaning of gross negligence manslaughter
- explain cases that illustrate gross negligence manslaughter
- apply rules to a given situation.

Key cases

Bateman (1925): doctor's negligent treatment of his patient resulted in death: 'gross negligence' was the basis for criminal liability.

Donoghue v Stevenson (1932): snail in ginger beer: key case in negligence which established the principles of duty of care and the neighbour test.

1 Gross negligence manslaughter

Gross negligence manslaughter is when a person dies as a result of the negligence of another, and the degree of negligence by the defendant is sufficiently serious as to make him criminally liable for the death. It was in the case of **Bateman (1925)** that 'gross negligence' by the defendant was referred to as the basis for criminal liability.

The test stated in that case was:

> does the conduct of the accused show such disregard for the life and safety of others as to amount to a crime against the state and conduct deserving of punishment?

In *Andrews* (1937), it was stated that where there is a charge of gross negligence manslaughter, simple lack of care which would constitute civil liability is not enough. For the purposes of the criminal law, a very high degree of negligence is required to be proved before the crime is established.

The statement in *Andrews* (1937) was made by Lord Atkin, who five years earlier, in the case of **Donoghue v Stevenson (1932)**, had formulated the test for negligence in civil cases.

In *Donoghue* v *Stevenson* (1932) it was stated that a duty of care was owed to:

> … persons who are so closely and directly affected by my act that I ought reasonably to have them in contemplation as being so affected when I am directing my mind to the acts or omissions which are called into question.

Adomako (1994): anaesthetist failed to notice disconnected tube during an operation; he was convicted of gross negligence manslaughter.

Stone and Dobinson (1977): defendants breached duty towards old lady in their care; she died and they were convicted of manslaughter.

Litchfield (1998): contractual duty of care owed towards crew by ship owner and master; three crew died when ship driven onto rocks.

Wacker (2002): 58 illegal immigrants suffocated on Channel crossing; duty owed for the purposes of manslaughter, even though victims were complicit in a crime.

The leading modern case on gross negligence manslaughter is **Adomako (1994)**, in which the defendant was an anaesthetist during an eye operation. During the operation, the tube supplying oxygen to the patient became disconnected. After suffering a heart attack, the patient later died as a result of brain damage. It was testified at the trial that a competent anaesthetist should have noticed the disconnected tube within seconds. The defendant's failure to do so was described as 'abysmal'. His conviction for gross negligence manslaughter was subsequently upheld by the House of Lords.

Adomako (1994) established that the elements required to prove gross negligence manslaughter are:

■ a duty of care exists on the part of the defendant towards the victim
■ there is a breach of that duty of care, which causes death
■ the gross negligence is such as to be considered criminal by the jury.

Duty of care

Lord Mackay said in *Adomako* (1994) that the ordinary principles of negligence in civil law, (as outlined in *Donoghue* v *Stevenson* (1932), above), should apply when ascertaining whether a duty of care existed, and if so, whether it was breached.

A case illustrating this is **Stone and Dobinson (1977)**. The defendants had undertaken the care of Stone's elderly sister. She became bedridden and unable to care for herself. As the result of the defendants' failure to feed her or get medical help, the old lady died. They had owed her a duty of care, because they had voluntarily agreed to look after her. The breach of this duty of care resulted in their being convicted of manslaughter.

A breach of duty can also occur where there is a contractual situation, as in the case of **Litchfield (1998)**, where it was held that the owner and master of a sailing ship owed a duty to the crew. The defendant sailed knowing that engine failure was likely owing to the fuel being contaminated. Three crew members died when the boat was driven onto rocks. The case of *Singh* (1999) established that a duty towards tenants was owed by the defendant, who had a duty to manage and maintain property. A faulty gas fire had resulted in the deaths of some of his tenants.

The case of **Wacker (2002)** established that a duty of care is owed to one with whom the defendant is complicit in a crime. The defendant had agreed to carry illegal immigrants in his lorry on a cross-channel ferry. The air vent enabling them to breathe had been closed for the duration of the crossing. The crossing took an hour longer than usual, and the result was that 58 of the immigrants died of suffocation. The Court of Appeal held that although a civil action could not arise from this situation, (because the victims and defendant had been complicit in the commission of a crime) a duty of care existed for the purposes of a criminal case of manslaughter. This decision was based partly on a matter of public policy, and it may have opened the door to other duties of care being recognised in future.

Gross negligence

The cases of *Bateman* (1925) and *Andrews* (1937), mentioned at the beginning of this topic, established that the degree of negligence amounting to manslaughter must be far greater than that in a civil case. For criminal liability, the negligence has to be 'gross' and go 'beyond a mere matter of compensation between subjects', (*Bateman* (1925)).

In *Adomako* (1994), the House of Lords approved the test in *Bateman* (1925). The then Lord Chancellor, Lord Mackay said:

> The jury will have to consider whether the extent to which the defendant's conduct departed from the proper standard of care incumbent upon him, involving as it must have done a risk of death to the patient, was such that it should be judged as criminal.

It is the jury then, taking into account all the evidence, which must decide whether the breach of duty of care was serious enough to amount to gross negligence. Having regard to the risk of death, did it amount to a criminal act or omission? If the jury thinks it did, then the verdict is guilty of gross negligence manslaughter. The following further cases of **Finlay (2001)** and **Edwards (2001)** illustrate this.

In *Finlay* (2001), a scout leader was in charge of a party of scouts when one of them, a 10-year-old, fell to his death on Snowdon. There was evidence that several of the proper safety procedures had not been followed, but the jury felt that the defendant's conduct did not show such disregard for life and safety as to amount to gross negligence. He was acquitted of manslaughter.

In *Edwards* (2001), a couple had allowed their seven-year-old daughter and her friend to play on a railway bridge. They had promised to warn them if a train approached, but the children were killed by a train which the defendants had not seen. They had ignored an obvious and serious danger, or had decided to take the risk, and this amounted to gross negligence. The jury found them guilty of manslaughter.

The case of **Misra and Srivastava (2004)** raises another interesting aspect of gross negligence manslaughter. A patient had died as the result of the negligence of two doctors, who were convicted of gross negligence manslaughter. On appeal, the defendants argued that the jury had been asked to define a hitherto unknown crime. This was incompatible with their human rights, especially the right not to be punished for an act not defined as an offence at the time it was performed. The House of Lords held that the offence was compatible with the defendants' human rights. The jury had been asked to decide, as a matter of fact, whether the defendants' negligence was so reprehensible as to amount to 'gross' negligence, thereby agreeing with the pre-existing definition of the crime.

Risk of death

In *Adomako* (1994), Lord Mackay referred in his judgement to the 'risk of death'. The law does not seem to be clear on this point, but in a charge as serious as manslaughter, it is logical that this test is applied. In *Bateman* (1925) the test for determining whether there was a risk of death was a 'disregard for the life and safety of others', and in *Stone and Dobinson* (1977), a risk to the 'health and welfare' of the victim. Both were approved in *Adomako* (1994).

Mens rea

Since the very essence of involuntary manslaughter is that the defendant does not have the intention to kill or cause serious harm, that aspect of *mens rea* is not present. It will be necessary though, in a case where the defendant creates a dangerous situation, to show that he had the intention of doing so. In many cases, the intention takes the form of recklessness.

Consider the liability for gross negligence manslaughter in the following cases.

1 Geoff is the driver of a train on a rural branch line. Because he is looking at the list of runners in the 3.30 race at Beverley that day, he fails to notice a signal at red. Rounding a bend, the train hits a closed crossing gate and ploughs into a car. The driver of the car is killed.

2 Hank, together with his mate Ian, has stolen a car. As a result of his driving too fast, the car crashes. Ian is seriously injured but Hank suffers only slight bruising and whiplash. Hank runs away from the scene without summoning any medical help for Ian. Medical help would have saved him, but none being forthcoming, Ian dies of his injuries.

3 Jim is an electrician. He is called to Kylie's house to do some rewiring. Having double-booked himself, Jim is in a great hurry to get to another job. In his haste, he inadvertently wires up the mains electricity to the plumbing. Kylie is electrocuted when she tries to turn on the tap in her kitchen.

You should now be able to:

- explain the law relating to gross negligence manslaughter
- apply that law to given scenarios.

In this topic you will learn how to:

- explain the meaning of unlawful act manslaughter
- explain cases that illustrate unlawful acts, the dangerous nature of an act and substantial cause of death
- explain the *mens rea* requirements of unlawful act manslaughter
- apply the rules to a given situation.

2 Unlawful act manslaughter

In the common law, a person who killed while committing what was then called a felony, (a serious criminal act), was guilty of murder through the doctrine of 'constructive intent'. This meant that the intention of the defendant was 'constructed', or built up, from the facts of his unlawful and dangerous act. Felony murder was abolished by the Homicide Act 1957. However, it survives in part in 'constructive manslaughter', better known now as unlawful act manslaughter.

To prove that a defendant has committed unlawful act manslaughter, it is necessary to prove that he has committed an act which is:

- unlawful
- dangerous
- the one which causes death
- an unlawful act for which the defendant had the *mens rea*.

The unlawful act

This must be a criminal offence. A civil wrong could not amount to an unlawful act for this purpose. An act which is the result of ignorance or foolishness would not be enough, if no criminal offence is involved.

In the case of **Lamb (1967)**, the defendant and his friend had been playing with a loaded revolver. There were two bullets in the chamber of the gun, but both men thought that neither bullet would fire unless it was opposite the barrel. Lamb pointed the gun at his friend and pulled the trigger. Because the cylinder revolved, a bullet from the next chamber was fired. His friend was killed. Although dangerous and fatal, the act of pointing the gun was held not to have been unlawful. His friend was not in fear of harm at the time, so there was no assault in the technical sense, (see Chapter 3, Non-fatal offences against the person). Therefore there was no criminal offence, and Lamb's appeal against his conviction for manslaughter was allowed.

In most cases, the unlawful act resulting in death would be some kind of physical assault. It could be some other crime, however, such as burglary, arson or criminal damage, provided that it may be likely to cause injury.

There must be an unlawful act. An omission, (failure to act; see 'Causation' in Chapter 1, Murder and voluntary manslaughter), could not give rise to liability for unlawful act manslaughter. In this respect, unlawful act manslaughter differs from murder, voluntary manslaughter and gross negligence manslaughter.

Dangerous act

What constitutes a dangerous act? The test for this is an objective one, and can best be expressed in the words of Edmund Davis LJ in *Church* (1966). He said that:

> The unlawful act must be such as all sober and reasonable people would inevitably recognise must subject the other person to, at least, the risk of some harm resulting therefrom, albeit not serious harm.

The important points to note about this are that:

- it need not be the accused who necessarily foresaw the harm, but any 'sober and reasonable' person
- the risk may be only 'some harm', not necessarily serious harm.

The harm need not be aimed at the victim. If the defendant commits an unlawful act upon one person, and another dies as a result, he still may be guilty of unlawful act homicide. An illustration of this is the case of **Mitchell (1983)**, in which the accused punched someone during an argument in a post office queue. The man who was attacked fell back and knocked over an old lady causing her injuries from which, shortly afterwards, she died. It was enough that the initial assault was unlawful and dangerous. It was foreseeable by a reasonable person that some injury might be caused to someone.

It is important to note that the harm intended must be actual physical harm. It is not enough merely to frighten someone. The case of **Dawson (1985)** illustrates this point. In *Dawson* (1985) there was an attempted robbery of a filling station by three masked men armed with pickaxe handles. The victim, the petrol station attendant, had a heart attack and died. It was held that the fear caused to the attendant was not an act dangerous enough in itself to warrant a conviction for manslaughter.

But what if it is obvious from the outset that someone is frail and vulnerable? In that case the 'reasonable person' would realise that harm could follow from the victim's condition. To commit an act causing fear and apprehension in such a situation might well mean a conviction for manslaughter, if death is the consequence.

The dangerous act may not be intended to cause harm to a person. It is enough for harm to be aimed at property, if an individual dies as a result. So long as it accords with Lord Davis's description, (above), then it could mean liability for dangerous act manslaughter. An example of such a case is that of *Goodfellow* (1986), (which will be dealt with later at the end of this topic). His conviction for manslaughter was upheld on the grounds that he had intentionally committed an unlawful act (arson), which any reasonable person might foresee would cause harm, and death had resulted.

Substantial cause of death

The unlawful act must be the substantial cause of death. In this respect the same general principles, such as the chain of causation and the thin skull rule, apply to manslaughter as to murder.

Key cases

Mitchell (1983): scuffle in post office queue resulted in old lady dying after being knocked down; defendant guilty of manslaughter, despite harm not being directed at the victim.

Dawson (1985): petrol station attendant died from heart attack caused by fear; not a dangerous enough act to warrant manslaughter conviction.

Key cases

Corion-Auguiste (2004): firework thrown into bus station; old lady died in panic rush; defendant's act direct cause of death.

Kennedy (2007): victim injected himself after being given drug by defendant; chain of causation broken, and no noxious substance administered by the defendant; no manslaughter.

Shohid (2003): the original attack on the victim on a railway station was serious enough to be the cause of the resulting death, even though it was not the main cause.

Carey (2006): a girl, while running away home after a fight, died as a result of a heart disease; the original punch was held not to be the cause of her death.

Attorney-General's Reference (No. 4 of 1980) (1982): girl died after a series of unlawful acts, any one of which could have caused death; it was not necessary to prove which particular act was responsible.

In **Corion-Auguiste (2004)**, the defendant threw an 'air bomb' firework in a crowded enclosed bus station. In the general panic, passengers rushed for the exits and an elderly lady was knocked over in the rush. She struck her head and died later in hospital. The defendant was convicted of unlawful act manslaughter. His act was the direct and substantial cause of the victim's death.

In **Kennedy (2007)**, the defendant, at the request of the victim, filled a syringe with heroin. He gave it to the victim in order for the victim to inject himself. The victim died as a result of the drug, and the defendant was found guilty of unlawful act manslaughter. The House of Lords, on quashing the conviction, held that the victim's voluntary act in injecting himself had broken the chain of causation. The unlawful act relied on by the prosecution, (Offences against the Person Act (1861) s23, causing a noxious substance to be administered to the victim), could not be said to have taken place. The victim, an adult, made a voluntary and informed decision to act in the way he did. Contrast this case with *Cato* (1976), (described in Chapter 1, Murder and voluntary manslaughter, Topic 2), where the defendant and the victim injected each other.

The unlawful and dangerous act need not be the sole cause of death, so long as it was not trivial.

This principle is illustrated by the case of **Shohid (2003)**, in which the defendant was one of a group of men who attacked the victim and his friend on the platform of a railway station. The victim and his friend were forced onto the railway track, and the friend was able to climb back onto the platform. The victim, however, was prevented from doing so by some of the attackers, not including the defendant, and was killed by a train. Upholding the defendant's conviction for manslaughter, the Court of Appeal held that the original attack was sufficiently serious as to be a cause of the subsequent death, and it was not necessary that it should be the only cause.

In **Carey (2006)**, however, the original attack was not held to be serious enough to be the cause of death. Three girls started a fight in which a fourth suffered only minor bruises. This girl later ran away but collapsed after running about 100 m. Her death was from an inherent heart disease which had been aggravated by her running. The girls who started the fight were convicted of manslaughter based on the unlawful act of affray. The convictions were quashed on appeal on the grounds that the victim had not been running away from a serious threat, but merely to get home. The only dangerous act directed at her was a single punch, which was not the cause of her death. Furthermore the acts of violence and threats in the affray were not dangerous enough for a reasonable person to have foreseen any serious harm to the victim.

What if the death of a victim is the result of a series of unlawful acts by the defendant? If it cannot be proved which particular act caused the death, it is sufficient to show that any one of them could have been. This is illustrated by **Attorney-General's Reference (No. 4 of 1980) (1982)**. The defendant pushed the victim head-first over the rail on a landing so that she fell on her head to the floor below. He then dragged her upstairs by a rope tied round her neck. Finally, he cut her neck with a knife before cutting up and disposing of the body. The Court of Appeal held that the defendant could properly be convicted of manslaughter even though it could not be shown which unlawful, dangerous or grossly negligent act was the actual cause of death.

Mens rea

In order to prove unlawful act manslaughter, there must be a positive act. An omission will not do. The act itself must have been intentional; it must have been accompanied by the *mens rea* to commit that act. There need not, of course, have been any intention to cause harm, as in the case of **Newbury and Jones (1976)**. The defendants were two teenage boys. As a train approached, they pushed a piece of paving stone over the parapet of a bridge. It hit the train, went through a window and killed the guard. Upholding their conviction for manslaughter, the House of Lords held that a defendant could be convicted of unlawful act manslaughter even if he did not foresee that his act might cause harm to another. He need not be aware that his act was unlawful, nor need he intend, or consider the risk of, injury. It was enough that he realised what he was doing and had the intention of doing it. Moreover, the risk of injury must have been obvious to a reasonable adult of normal intelligence.

In **Le Brun (1991)**, the defendant had, without intending any serious harm, hit his wife on the chin during an argument outside their house. She fell unconscious and he dragged her away in order to avoid detection. In doing so, he caused her head to hit the pavement hard enough to fracture her skull. She died as a result and the defendant was convicted of manslaughter. Upholding the verdict, the Court of Appeal held that although the original act was not the direct cause of death, that act and the cause of her death were both part of 'the same sequence of events'. The original punch was intentional, and that was enough.

Overlap between gross negligence and unlawful act manslaughter

The case of **Goodfellow (1986)** is an example of a case where the defendant could have been found guilty of both unlawful act and gross negligence manslaughter. His intention was to set fire to his council house, a plan described by a friend whom he told about it as 'a stupid idea'. He determined to carry out the scheme, nonetheless. He intended that the adults should rescue the children and all should escape unharmed. The fire would be blamed on a neighbour allegedly throwing a fire bomb through the window, and he and his family would be moved by the council to other accommodation. The fire spread so rapidly that three people were unable to escape, and died as a result. In addition to the unlawful act aspect, the defendant had acted in such a manner as to create an obvious and serious risk of causing physical injury or death to some person. He had recognised that risk and had nonetheless gone on to take it recklessly. In other words, he could be said to have been grossly negligent.

> ### Key cases
>
> **Newbury and Jones (1976)** Boys killed a train guard by pushing stone off a bridge; enough for manslaughter that the defendants realised what they were doing and intended to do it.
>
> **Le Brun (1991):** man punched his wife, who fractured her skull and died as he dragged her away unconscious; it was enough that the original punch was intentional.
>
> **Goodfellow (1986):** defendant deliberately set fire to his accommodation in order to get an alternative; three people died in the fire; he was convicted of unlawful act manslaughter.

> ### Activities
> Assess the liability for unlawful act manslaughter in the following scenarios.
>
> **1** In a fight outside a night club, Liam punched Matt. Matt fell to the ground where Liam gave him a half-hearted kick to the head and walked away. Matt had a very thin skull, and died as a result of the kick.
>
> **2** Nick was trespassing on the land of Ollie, a farmer. When Ollie confronted him, Nick became aggressive. Fearful for his safety, Ollie turned to run but had a heart attack and died.
>
> **3** Paddy thought it would be amusing to drop breeze blocks from a bridge over a canal to see if he could cause a boat to sink. He dropped one block onto a narrow boat passing below, hit Qasim, who was at the tiller, and killed him.

You should now be able to:

- explain the law relating to unlawful act manslaughter
- apply the law to given scenarios.

In this topic you will learn how to:

- explain the meaning of subjective reckless manslaughter
- explain the arguments relating to the need for and existence of subjective reckless manslaughter
- analyse the scope for reform in this area.

Key cases

Gemmel and Richards (2004): two boys caused great damage by starting a fire; conviction quashed, as their youth should have been taken into account when considering their foresight of risk.

Lidar (1999): man drove car away with another leaning in through a window; guilty of reckless manslaughter.

3 Subjective reckless manslaughter

In unlawful act manslaughter, the unlawful act must be objectively dangerous. The risk of some serious injury to someone must be obvious to a reasonable adult of normal intelligence. This was seen in the case of *Newbury and Jones* (1976). This takes no account of the defendant's age and mental capacity. In non-fatal assaults, the test is a subjective one. It is usually referred to as having the same meaning as in *Cunningham* (1957); the defendant either intended injury or realised that there was a risk of injury and took that risk.

The subjective test for recklessness is further illustrated by the case of *Stephenson* (1979). The defendant was a tramp who sheltered in a hollow of a haystack. Feeling cold, he lit a fire. The haystack was destroyed. The Court of Appeal quashed his conviction because although a normal person would have expected the haystack to be destroyed, the defendant was a schizophrenic and did not realise this. This point should have been left to the jury.

The subjective rule was later restated by the House of Lords in the case of **Gemmel and Richards (2004)**. Two boys, 11 and 12 years old respectively, had lit some newspapers and put them in a wheelie bin. They had thought that the papers would burn themselves out, but the fire spread and caused damage to the extent of £1m to a shop and nearby buildings. The Lords quashed their convictions, overruling the trial judge's direction that no allowance should be made for the youth of the defendants. The rule now is that a defendant can now only be guilty if *he* realises the risk of damage – a purely subjective test.

Where the defendant is aware of a significant and highly probable risk of serious injury and causes death, he is guilty of reckless manslaughter. This is illustrated by the case of **Lidar (1999).** The defendant drove away from a pub with two passengers in the car and a third leaning in through the car window. After driving about 200 m, and the car travelling at about 30 mph, the man leaning in through the window caught his foot in a wheel and fell out of the car. He died as the result of being hit by another vehicle. The defendant was found guilty of manslaughter, and this was affirmed on appeal. At the appeal, Lord Evans said that there is nothing in *Adomako* (1994) to exclude reckless manslaughter.

It would seem that both exist in parallel; indeed gross negligence and recklessness may well mean the same thing. What distinguishes these kinds of manslaughter from unlawful act manslaughter is that they do not require the performance of an unlawful activity.

Stephenson (1979) and *Gemmel and Richards* (2004) related to the Criminal Damage Act 1971. The subjective test when applied to manslaughter would mean that a defendant would only be guilty of manslaughter if, at the time of his act, he:

- intended injury
- realised that there was a risk of death or injury, and took that risk regardless.

Summary of involuntary manslaughter

The forms of involuntary manslaughter may be summed up as follows:

Table 1

Gross negligence manslaughter	Unlawful act manslaughter
■ There is the breach of a duty of care owed by the defendant to the victim, causing death.	■ The defendant commits an act which is unlawful.
■ The negligence is so serious as to give rise to criminal liability.	■ The unlawful act must be a criminal offence.
■ The risk of death, to be considered criminal, should mean a 'disregard for the life and safety', or a risk to the 'health and welfare' of the victim.	■ The act must be dangerous. ■ The act must be the one which causes death.
■ It is for the jury to decide whether the gross negligence should be considered to be criminal.	■ The defendant must have had the *mens rea* for the unlawful act.
■ The activity of the defendant at the time is not in itself unlawful or dangerous, for example, hospital treatment (*Adomako* (1994)) or sailing a ship (*Litchfield* (1998)).	

Subjective reckless manslaughter

This occurs where the defendant at the time of his act:

■ intended injury, or

■ realising there was a risk of injury, took that risk regardless, and

■ the death of the victim followed as a result.

Differences between the kinds of manslaughter

The important distinction to bear in mind is that:

■ unlawful act manslaughter requires the performance of an unlawful (criminal) activity

■ gross negligence and subjective reckless manslaughter do not.

In addition:

■ unlawful act manslaughter requires there to have been an act, not an omission

■ gross negligence and subjective reckless manslaughter can result from an omission.

You should now be able to:

■ explain subjective reckless manslaughter

■ analyse the need for development and clarification of this.

■ **Activity**

Roxanne is a 15-year-old who has severe learning problems. One day she decides to make some chips. She puts a pan of cooking oil on the gas ring, leaving it to heat up. While this is happening, she goes across the road to see a friend. She forgets about the oil, which boils over causing a severe blaze which destroys the house. Her bedridden grandmother upstairs is killed in the fire.

Key terms

Law Commission: a full-time body made up of five Commissioners and a consultant, together with a staff of civil servants. Its brief is to 'keep under review all the law with which (it is) concerned with a view to its systematic development and reform ...'

4 Reform of the law of involuntary manslaughter

Whilst the AQA specification does not involve evaluation of involuntary manslaughter, it is useful to look at the criticisms and proposals for reform in the context of homicide generally and the Concepts of law essays in Unit 4C.

Over the years there have been various suggestions as to why and how the law relating to involuntary manslaughter should be reformed. Indeed this is true of all homicide offences. It its preamble to its 2006 report, the **Law Commission** stated that:

> The law relating to homicide in England and Wales is a rickety structure set upon shaky foundations. Some of the rules have remained unaltered since the 17th century, even though it has long been acknowledged that they are in dire need of reform. Other rules are of uncertain content, often because they have been constantly changed to the point that they can no longer be stated with any certainty or clarity.

Fig. 1 *The Law Commission is concerned with development and review of the law*

Gross negligence manslaughter

The main criticisms of the law relating to gross negligence manslaughter are:

■ Gross negligence manslaughter is based on the civil law concept of negligence. The burden of proof in a criminal case is different from that required in a civil case. In a criminal case the burden of proof is 'beyond reasonable doubt'. In civil cases the burden of proof is less stringent, being 'on the balance of probabilities'. This could cause confusion to a jury.

■ In gross negligence manslaughter the jury is asked to determine whether or not negligence is 'gross', and thus amounting to criminal liability. In effect, the jury is asked to decide whether a crime has been committed by deciding if the behaviour of the defendant is criminal.

■ In practice, the above means that the jury is being asked to determine the boundaries of manslaughter. This means that verdicts may be inconsistent, depending on the opinions of individual juries.

■ Even if the defendant did not realise that there was a risk of injury, he is still liable. Unlike the case in non-fatal offences against the person, (see Chapter 3, Non-fatal offences against the person), he does not need to have foreseen the risk of injury. In this, the law is inconsistent.

Unlawful act manslaughter

With reference to unlawful act manslaughter, the main criticisms are as follows:

■ It is a very wide-ranging offence. For example, at the one extreme is the case of *Shohid* (2003). This was where the victim was prevented from climbing onto the platform of a railway station and was killed by a train. In this case it could be said that the act was on the very borderline between murder and manslaughter. At the other extreme is the case of *Mitchell* (1983). The death of the old lady knocked over in a post office queue by a man recoiling from the defendant's punch could be said to be on the borderline between manslaughter and unfortunate accident. Even taking into account a judge's discretion to vary sentences, is it right that such a wide variation of offences should go by the same title? The Law Commission said in 2006:

> the law is too generous to some who kill by 'reckless' conduct, that is those who … do realise that their conduct involves an unjustified risk in causing death … but press on regardless as guilty only of manslaughter.

■ The *mens rea* for unlawful act manslaughter can exist at a very low level. In *Mitchell* (1983), for example, there was no more than the intention to punch the man with whom the defendant was arguing. There was certainly no foresight of death.

■ The defendant may not have realised that there was the risk of harm, but because of the objective nature of the test as to whether an act is dangerous or not, he is still liable.

Manslaughter generally

Is there any practical point in classing involuntary manslaughter under three different categories? They all share the same basic characteristics. This is certainly true of gross negligence manslaughter and reckless manslaughter.

Suggested reforms

Not all commentators agree either as to the nature of the problems, or the solutions to them. It is generally agreed though, that clarification and simplification of the law of involuntary manslaughter might be desirable. The need to narrow the crime of involuntary manslaughter has apparently already been accepted by the Government (Home Office, *Reforming the Law on Involuntary Manslaughter: The Government's Proposals* (2000)).

The draft criminal code published in 1989 proposed that a person will be guilty of manslaughter if he causes another's death by:

■ intending to cause serious personal harm.

■ being reckless whether death or serious personal harm will be caused.

In its recommendations for the reform of the law of homicide, published in 2006, the Law Commission recommended that all involuntary manslaughter should be reclassified under the simple heading of 'manslaughter'. It would be:

■ by gross negligence as to the risk of death; or

■ by a criminal act that the defendant intends to cause some injury or is aware involves a serious risk of causing some injury; or

■ by participating in a criminal joint venture in which there was an obvious risk that someone might be killed.

This last point is aimed at tackling gang violence. Those who help or encourage in attacks in which the victim is murdered would be made guilty of manslaughter if it was obvious that murder might be committed by the perpetrators.

Manslaughter would still be punishable by discretionary life imprisonment.

Notice that this proposal would result in the following changes:

■ It would eliminate the largely artificial distinction between gross negligence and reckless manslaughter.

■ It includes a subjective element in the test for awareness of serious risk of injury.

The Law Commission said in the introduction to the report:

> We will recommend that, for the first time, the general law of homicide be rationalised through legislation. This structure must be set out with clarity, in a way that will promote certainty and in a way that non-lawyers can understand and accept.

Whether Parliament has the time or the inclination to undertake such a major piece of legislation remains to be seen.

How to write an essay on law reform

Table 2 might be helpful in conjunction with the proposed reforms outlined above and in Chapter 1, Murder and voluntary manslaughter.

Table 2 *Criticism and possible reforms of the laws on manslaughter*

Criticism	Possible reforms
Gross negligence manslaughter	
■ Civil test for negligence used in a criminal case.	■ All involuntary manslaughter should be reclassified simply as 'manslaughter'. (See 'Reclassification of homicide' on page 66.)
■ Jury's role in determining criminal liability.	
■ No foresight of injury required by defendant.	■ Defendant showed gross negligence as to the risk of death.
Unlawful act manslaughter	
■ Very wide-ranging offence.	■ Degree of blame should be considered. The worst kind would be 'second degree murder'. (See Chapter 1, Murder and voluntary manslaughter.)
■ Low level of *mens rea* required.	
■ Objective test for dangerous act.	■ The defendant intends to cause some injury, or should be aware of the consequences of his act; a subjective test.
Subjective reckless manslaughter	
■ Differs little from gross negligence manslaughter.	■ Reclassification would do away with distinction.

Activities

1 Identify areas in the law of involuntary manslaughter which you consider to be less than satisfactory.

2 Discuss any proposals for reforming the law of involuntary manslaughter.

You should now be able to:

- evaluate the law relating to gross negligence manslaughter, unlawful act manslaughter and subjective reckless manslaughter
- describe proposals for reform in those areas
- construct an appropriate essay on these topics.

5 Problem solving

How to approach a problem on homicide

Study the flow chart on the next page. From it you will see that many different possibilities are listed. It is probable that not all of them will be relevant to a scenario you are faced with. Many of them, however, will be, and the technique is to work through the possibilities methodically, eliminating those which clearly do not apply, and dwelling on those which are of direct relevance to the case. Here are some hints as to how to go about it.

- Read the facts carefully. Do they remind you of a case that you have studied? Very often examination questions are formulated with decided cases in mind.
- Identify the crime you are being asked about. Is it essentially about murder, or manslaughter? If it is the latter, what kind of manslaughter?
- Identify the particular part of the law which is at issue in the problem. Is it about causation, or intention, or whether negligence is 'gross', and so on?
- Note any potential clues. If, for example, the age of a person is mentioned, or his or her mental state, that will often be an indicator of a possible route to follow.
- Work logically through the possibilities of the scenario. Remember to illustrate your arguments as liberally as you can by reference to decided cases. Ensure that the cases you mention are relevant. The ideal is to quote the case correctly, complete with date. However, don't worry if you can't remember the date. Also, it is better to describe a case, if the name slips your memory, than not to mention it at all. Say, for example, 'As in the case where the defendant threw a firework into a bus station', if you can't remember *Corion-Auguiste* (2004). Always quote key legislation, (such as The Homicide Act 1957, for example), where relevant.
- It is possible that you may not be able to arrive at a definite decision about the guilt of the defendant. It is enough that you show that you know the issues involved and the law relating to them. It is quite acceptable to say, for example, 'On the evidence of the facts given, it would appear that the defendant is probably guilty of gross negligence manslaughter. On the other hand, if the jury considers ...' and so on.
- Leave time to read your answer through carefully. If you have forgotten to quote a key case, put it in as a footnote.

In this topic you will learn how to:

- apply the law to problem scenarios involving a death
- construct an essay evaluating the law of homicide and its various forms.

Below is a flow chart showing liability for homicide following the killing of one person by another.

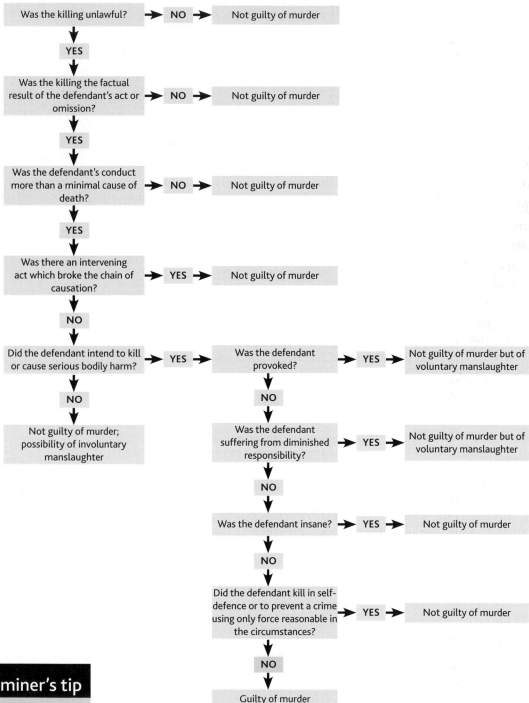

Fig. 2 *Flow chart for liability for homicide*

You should now be able to:

■ answer problem questions involving death

■ construct an appropriately reasoned answer, quoting authority where necessary.

3   Non-fatal offences against the person

1 Assault and battery

Assault and battery are together referred to as 'common assault' but it needs to be recognised that they are two separate and distinct offences. The essential difference between the two is that the offence of assault is causing the victim to fear harm (but with no requirement that harm is actually suffered) whereas the offence of battery is the actual infliction of harm. The terms assault and battery can be confusing since the word assault is more normally understood to describe an act of physical harm as opposed to a mere fear of such harm.

Assault and battery were traditionally common law offences and all the principles still derive entirely from decided cases in accordance with common law principles. The offences are, however, recognised by statute law and s39 of the Criminal Justice Act 1988 (CJA 1988) provides that they be tried summarily with a maximum sentence of six months' imprisonment or a fine. *Little* (1992) ruled that the offences should be considered statutory offences despite the fact that s39 does not provide any definitions but only fixes the penalty and tariff.

It follows from the fact that assault and battery are two distinct offences that, in theory, one can be committed without the other. Both offences are committed when, in full view of the victim, the accused pulls back his fist and then punches since harm is feared when seeing the fist pull back (the *assault*) and then inflicted with the punch (the *battery*). However, only a battery is committed if the punch is made from behind since then the victim has not feared the harm. Conversely, only an assault is committed if the fist is pulled back but the accused misses the victim.

Assault

Actus reus

In **Ireland; Burstow (1997)** the House of Lords confirmed that an **assault** is committed when the accused intentionally or recklessly causes the victim to apprehend immediate and unlawful violence.

The *actus reus* of assault is:

- an act
- causing the victim to apprehend immediate and unlawful violence.

An act

An act or words from the defendant must cause the victim's fear. An assault cannot be committed by omission. An act might be waving a knife or might be a gesture such as the accused running his finger across his throat to indicate slitting.

In **Constanza (1997)** the court ruled that *words alone* were sufficient for an assault. Here the accused stalked the victim and his harassment campaign included sending her 812 letters. It was held that the contents of those letters were assaults since the victim read them clearly as threats, even though there was no reinforcing physical gesture. It follows that e-mails and texts and all other forms of written communication can also constitute assaults.

The decision in *R v Burstow* (1997) went even further than *Constanza* (1997) and ruled that silence could amount to an assault in the form of silent telephone calls made by the accused to the victim.

In this topic you will learn how to:

- state the meaning of assault and battery
- distinguish between assault and battery
- explain cases that illustrate assault and battery
- apply the rules to a given situation.

Key terms

Assault: intentionally or recklessly causing the victim to apprehend immediate and unlawful violence.

Key cases

Ireland; Burstow (1997): silent telephone calls can be an assault. The case for immediacy is made if the victim fears the 'possibility' of an immediate attack and this fear does not have to be rational.

Constanza (1997): words alone can be an assault.

Words spoken by the defendant will prevent an act from being an assault if the words make it clear that the accused is not intending to cause the harm that is otherwise suggested by his conduct. This principle comes from the old case **Tuberville v Savage (1669)** where the defendant placed his hand on his sword angered by comments made to him. This might have constituted an assault since it could cause another to fear an immediate attack but it was accompanied by the words: 'If it were not for assize time I would not take such language.' These words clearly meant that he was not going to use his sword because the criminal judges were in town.

Causing the victim to apprehend immediate and unlawful violence

We need to break this phrase down to examine how the courts apply this principle. There are a number of aspects to the definition that need to be considered:

Causing

This merely is the application of the principles of causation that you have studied at AS level.

Apprehend

If the victim does not *apprehend* immediate force then an assault has not been committed. In *Lamb* (1967) two friends were playing with a revolver. One of the men was shot dead by the other but there was no assault because the shot man had not appreciated that the gun would fire and so could not apprehend immediate force.

The victim does not have to actually *fear* violence and the word 'apprehend' equally means *anticipating* violence. A heavy-weight boxer may not be frightened at the idea of a slap from a frail elderly woman but if he stands in front of her expecting that slap, then theoretically it qualifies as an assault.

Immediate

Traditionally it has been held that the victim must fear *immediate* violence and not violence at some time in the near or distant future. However, the law has now taken a more liberal view of the meaning of 'immediacy' in part to allow courts to achieve justice for victims of harassment and stalking campaigns.

In **Smith v Chief Superintendant of Woking Police Station (1983)** the victim was at home in her ground floor flat wearing only her night dress when, terrified, she suddenly saw the accused staring in at her through the window from her garden. The accused was unable to enter the flat since the doors and windows were locked but the court ruled that the requirement of immediacy was satisfied if the victim 'did not know what the defendant was going to do next, but whatever he might be going to do … was something of a violent nature.' This suggests that 'immediate' does not mean the same as 'instantaneous'.

In *R v Burstow* (1997) the House of Lords ruled that the case for immediacy was proved if the conduct of the accused caused the victim to apprehend the 'possibility' of an immediate attack. Such fear does not even have to be rational in the panic of the moment provided that it is genuinely held.

Unlawful violence

The use of the word 'violence' can be misleading. The phrase 'apprehend immediate and unlawful force' is often used as an alternative way of stating the principle of assault because the victim is not required to apprehend any injury, pain or harm for the purposes of proving the offence. In fact, assault can be committed even where the 'force' apprehended is a mere touch provided that touch is unwanted. This leads onto the final requirement of unlawfulness. Generally, a lack of consent to the feared violence or force will make it unlawful but this principle and its exceptions will be discussed below under battery.

Mens rea

The *mens rea* of assault was stated in *Savage* (1992) as an intention to cause the victim to apprehend immediate and unlawful violence or recklessness as to whether such an apprehension is caused. The intention can be direct or oblique intention. The recklessness is *Cunningham* (1957) recklessness so the defendant must realise that his acts or words could cause the victim to apprehend violence.

Battery

Actus reus

The *actus reus* of **battery** was stated in *Ireland; Burstow* (1997) as the application of unlawful physical force on another. The victim does not have to suffer any pain or injury.

In **Collins v Willcock (1984)** it was decided that 'any touching of another person, however slight, may amount to a battery'. In this case a police officer had committed a battery by taking hold of the arm of a woman suspected of soliciting for the purposes of prostitution. This had been done to detain her but with no intention to make an arrest.

A slap, a kiss, throwing a drink over someone and even touching the victim's clothes has been suggested as meeting the requirements of a battery. In *Thomas* (1985) a school caretaker rubbed the hem of a pupil's skirt and the court held that touching a person's clothes is equivalent to touching the person and could therefore be a battery.

Of course, most common assault batteries do involve some degree of albeit minor harm so that grazes, scratches, minor bruising, reddening of the skin, superficial cuts and black eyes are all appropriate for a charge of 'assault by beating' contrary to s39 CJA 1988.

Unlawful physical force

The fact that the victim has not consented to the battery will usually make the act unlawful. However, genuine consent will not always make the act lawful and this is discussed in detail together with the other criminal defences which you will study in Chapter 4, Defences.

Certain force is lawful even without consent such as the reasonable force applied in self-defence. Police officers may use reasonable force in the prevention of crime but only is so far as the law deems necessary for them to carry out their duties. The officer in *Collins v Willcock* (1984) was held to have committed a battery because he was not arresting her and therefore had no need to take her arm.

It would be absurd to make all touching without consent an offence since unwanted physical contact is almost unavoidable in everyday situations. Lord Goff recognised this in *Collins v Willcock* (1984):

 Examiner's tip

Remember that the rules for oblique intention apply to all the non-fatal assaults you study in this chapter and the cases and principles relevant to oblique intention you studied for the fatal offences will be appropriate to use for the non-fatal assaults as well.

Key terms

Battery: intentionally or recklessly applying unlawful physical force on another.

Key cases

Collins v Willcock (1984): followed earlier cases to rule that the slightest touch (holding an arm in this case) can amount to a battery.

 Examiner's tip

Whilst it is fine to refer to the Charging Standard in an examination essay, you must appreciate that it has no legal status and its purpose is only to assist prosecutors in choosing the correct offence to charge. It is useful to know because you can check that you are considering the right non-fatal offence but do not use its examples of injuries to support your arguments in an exam because it has no relevance to deciding the guilt of the defendant.

> Most of the physical contacts of ordinary life are not actionable because they are impliedly consented to by all who move in society and so expose themselves to the risk of bodily contact. So nobody can complain of the jostling which is inevitable from his presence in, for example, a supermarket, an underground station or a busy street; nor can a person who attends a party complain if his hand is seized in friendship, or even if his back is (within reason) slapped.

However, if the contact exceeds what is generally held to be acceptable (such as a hand squeezed tightly and at length until it hurts or a person is repeatedly slapped on the back) then the *actus reus* of battery might still be established.

Indirect batteries

Most batteries are force applied directly by one person to another. However, it has been long established that batteries can be inflicted *indirectly*. In *Martin* (1881) the accused placed an iron bar across the exit in a theatre, turned off the lights and shouted 'fire'. Several people were hurt in the ensuing crush and the conduct was held to constitute a battery.

More recently was the case of **DPP v K (1990)**, where a 15-year-old schoolboy hid sulphuric acid in a hand drier in a school toilet block. He had no intention of causing harm and planned to remove it later. However, in the meantime, a fellow pupil used the drier and was sprayed by the acid which caused severe scars on his face. The court confirmed that common assault could be committed by an indirect act. This principle was developed further in **Haystead v Chief Constable of Derbyshire (2000)**, where the accused punched a woman, causing her to drop her baby. The court held that the defendant had effectively used the woman as a weapon to injure the baby and he was held liable. The defendant would also have been liable under the principle of transferred malice which is discussed below in relation to *mens rea*.

Omissions

Unlike assault, a battery can be committed by an omission but only where there is a duty to act. This limits the scenarios where omission might be relevant but there is one interesting reported case where the defendant had created a dangerous situation and then failed to act. In *Santana-Bermudez* (2004) the accused was asked, but failed, to inform a police officer searching him that he had a hypodermic needle in his pocket. The officer was injured when she put her hand in his pocket and the court ruled that his failure to tell her of the needle satisfied the requirements of the *actus reus*.

Mens rea

The *mens rea* of battery was confirmed in *Venna* (1976) as the intention to apply force to another or recklessness as to whether such force is so applied. It is important to note that the intention or recklessness is only required for the act of physical contact itself and not in respect of harm that might arise from such contact.

Remember that the defendant might be liable under the doctrine of transferred malice as illustrated in *Latimer* (1886). In this case the defendant intentionally hit A with his belt, but the belt rebounded and accidentally hit B. The defendant had the *mens rea* for the attack on A and this was transferred to the act upon B which satisfied the *actus reus* of battery. The doctrine only operates where the *mens rea* and *actus reus* coincide for the same crime as they did here.

■ **Key cases**

DPP v K (1990): confirmed that a battery can be committed by an indirect act.

Haystead v Chief Constable of Derbyshire (2000): developed the rule that an indirect act can be a battery by finding that a woman who had dropped her baby after being punched had been used as an 'instrument' to commit the battery.

Activities

Identify which offences might have been committed in the following scenarios and use case authorities to back your argument:

1 Alice has been sponsored for charity to hug as many people as she can in 60 minutes. She sees Ben in the street and shouts 'I am going to give you a great big hug!' Ben does not want to be hugged by a stranger and replies 'No thanks, not today.' Alice ignores this and hugs him anyway.

2 Ellie has recently split up from her violent boyfriend Carl. She is sitting in a bus in a traffic jam when she receives a text from him saying 'You are going to die.' Terrified, she looks out of the window and sees him sitting in a café on the other side of the road.

You should now be able to:

■ explain and distinguish the offences of assault and battery

■ explain the law to given scenarios.

2 Sections 47, 20 and 18 of the Offences Against the Person Act 1861

Common assault deals with the least serious cases of harm and more serious injuries will be charged under ss47, 20 or 18 of the Offences Against the Person Act 1861 (OAPA 1861). These are statutory offences but the sections only provide the basic definitions of each offence and case law is heavily relied upon to explain the meaning of the terms used in setting out the offences.

Section 47 of OAPA 1861

Section 47 deals with the least serious cases of harm. Section 47 states:

> Whosoever shall be convicted on indictment of any assault occasioning actual bodily harm shall be liable to imprisonment for not more than five years.

The offence is triable either way depending on the gravity of the assault.

Actus reus

As you have seen at AS, the key elements in the *actus reus* are the words:

■ assault

■ occasioning

■ actual bodily harm.

Assault

The term 'assault' under s47 means either an assault or a battery according to the cases and principles set out for common assault above.

Occasioning

An assault or battery will only be charged under s47 if it *occasions* actual bodily harm. If there is no such harm then the charge will be brought under s39 CJA 1988. 'Occasion' appears to mean the same as 'cause' and the normal rules of causation apply as confirmed in *Roberts* (1971). The facts of this case were that the victim jumped from a moving car fearing a sexual assault when the accused told her to undress and tried to remove her coat. The court needed to consider whether her actions

In this topic you will learn how to:

■ state the meaning of the offence of assault occasioning actual bodily harm

■ state the meaning of the offence of assault inflicting grievous bodily harm

■ state the meaning of the offence of wounding

■ state the meaning of the offence of wounding or causing grievous bodily harm with intent

■ explain the *actus reus* and *mens rea* of each offence

■ distinguish between each of the offences

■ explain cases that illustrate each of the offences

■ apply the rules to a given situation.

in jumping out of the car had broken the causal chain. The court ruled that the chain was still intact since her actions could 'reasonably have been foreseen as the consequence of what he was saying or doing.' The judgement recognised that a victim will not necessarily act in a sensible manner in a moment of fright but added that a defendant might not be held responsible if the victim does something 'daft' or unexpected that no reasonable man could be expected to foresee.

Where the accused directly physically attacks their victim then causation is immediately established and no further discussion is required.

Actual bodily harm

The word 'actual' refers to the fact that, unlike common assault, there must be some form of physical or psychological injury caused to the victim. **Assault occasioning actual bodily harm** can be very minor harm and indeed was described in **Miller (1954)** as 'any hurt or injury calculated to interfere with the health or comfort of the victim' provided it is more than 'transient and trifling'.

The definition of actual bodily harm was extended to hair being cut without the consent of the victim in *DPP* v *Smith* (2006). Here, the defendant forced down the head of his former girlfriend and chopped off her pony-tail. The defence tried to argue that hair could not be treated as 'bodily' harm since it was dead tissue above the scalp. The court disagreed, however, and determined that hair was to be treated as part of the body and noted that cutting a woman's hair without her consent is a 'serious matter amounting to actual (not trivial or insignificant) bodily harm'. It was also stated, *obiter*, that if paint or a similar material was put on the hair, that could also be actual bodily harm.

Injuries such as a loss of or a broken tooth, loss of consciousness, minor cuts requiring medical treatment (such as stitches), minor fractures and extensive bruising as injuries would normally be charged under s47.

Psychiatric as well as physical harm can be regarded as actual bodily harm and this was confirmed in **Chan Fook (1994)**. In this case a victim had been subjected to aggressive interrogation and locked in a room when having been suspected of stealing an engagement ring. The Court of Appeal ruled that the term actual bodily harm could cover psychiatric harm but only if medical experts could prove that the state of mind caused in the victim was evidence of an identifiable clinical condition and 'mere emotions such as fear, panic and distress' when unrelated to such a condition would not be considered actual bodily harm.

In needs to be noted that the definition of actual bodily harm from *Miller* (1954) is therefore not adequate as a principle to be applied to psychiatric harm cases since these cases require a more serious degree of harm amounting to a clinical condition.

Mens rea

The combined House of Lords appeal of *Savage; Parmenter* (1992) confirmed that the *mens rea* for common assault is sufficient to establish the *mens rea* for a s47 offence. Accordingly, the *mens rea* is either intention or recklessness as to causing the victim to apprehend immediate and unlawful violence, or intention or recklessness as to the application of unlawful force. The crucial point to note here is that no extra *mens rea* need be proved as regards the harm caused by the assault or battery. The accused does not have to have intended or even had foresight of the slightest bodily harm provided that he intended or had foresight of the actual assault or battery itself and that this assault or battery caused the harm.

Key terms

Assault occasioning actual bodily harm: an assault or battery causing an injury that is more than trivial but less than serious harm.

Key cases

Miller (1954): actual bodily harm is 'any hurt or injury calculated to interfere with the health or comfort of the victim' that is not 'transient or trifling'.

Chan Fook (1994): psychiatric harm can be deemed actual bodily harm provided that expert evidence proves that the harm is a symptom of an identifiable clinical condition and not just 'mere emotions'.

The facts of **R v Savage (1992)** explain this principle. Mrs Savage was in a pub when she spotted her husband's ex-girlfriend. Mrs Savage went over to the other women and said 'Nice to meet you darling' and threw the contents of her glass of beer at her. But as well as being soaked by the beer, the victim's wrist was also cut by a piece of broken glass as Mrs Savage dropped the glass after throwing the beer. Mrs Savage said that she had not meant to drop the glass and insisted that she had only intended to throw the beer without any intention to injure the victim. Nor had she realised that there was any risk of injury. Her argument was that she could, at most, be liable under s39 for common assault battery for covering her victim with beer but she could not be liable under s47 because she did not have the necessary *mens rea* for the more serious actual bodily harm that followed when the glass broke. However, the Court of Appeal decisively ruled that provided there was proof of an assault (using the common assault definitions for the *actus reus* and *mens rea*) then the case for a s47 offence was made by simply proving that this assault caused (occasioned) the actual bodily harm.

This confirmed the position in **R v Roberts (1971)** where the defendant had the *mens rea* for the battery as he had intended to touch the girl's coat but had not intended nor had foresight even of the fact she might suffer minor injuries. He was convicted under s47 because he had the necessary *mens rea* for common assault battery and this battery had *caused* the actual bodily harm.

Mrs Savage appealed her case to the House of Lords, which heard it together with an appeal in the case of **DPP v Parmenter (1992)**, where a defendant had played with his son so roughly that he had caused injuries to him. The defendant in this case also argued that he did not have the required *mens rea* for the actual bodily harm caused by the assault. By awkward coincidence, the Court of Appeal hearings of both cases had taken place on the same day but the judges in *Parmenter* (1992) came to a different conclusion and ruled that it was necessary to find that the defendant had been subjectively reckless not only in respect of the battery but *also* in respect of the actual bodily harm caused! Fortunately, the House of Lords established some certainty on the matter by confirming the Court of Appeal ruling in *Savage* (1992) and overruling *Parmenter* (1992) on the grounds that the law on the necessary *mens rea* for s47 was correctly stated in *Roberts* (1971).

Section 20 of OAPA 1861

Section 20 of OAPA 1861 states:

> Whosoever shall unlawfully and maliciously wound or inflict any grievous bodily harm upon any person, either with or without any weapon or instrument, shall be guilty of an offence and shall be liable... to imprisonment for not more than 5 years.

Section 20 is a more grave offence than s47, despite the fact that the maximum sentence for both is five years. The offence is triable either way.

Actus reus

As has been seen at AS, the offence can be committed in either of two ways:

1 unlawful **wounding**, or

2 unlawful infliction of **grievous bodily harm**.

The defendant is charged with wounding *or* grievous bodily harm. If the wound has also inflicted grievous bodily harm, then the prosecution must choose from the two offences depending on which reflects the true nature of the assault.

JCC v Eisenhower (1994): a wound must break the continuity of the skin and internal bleeding is not sufficient.

DPP v Smith (1961): grievous bodily harm means no more and no less than 'really serious harm'.

R v Burstow; R v Ireland (1997): a s20 offence can be committed without an assault or battery involving either direct or indirect force and 'inflict' should have the same meaning as 'cause'.

R v Bollom (2004): injuries caused to a child or elderly person will be more serious than the same injuries caused to a strong, healthy adult.

R v Dica (2004): recklessly transmitting a disease to an unknowing victim was ruled to be inflicting grievous bodily harm.

AQA Examiner's tip

Students commonly make the mistake of stating that a wound must be serious enough to satisfy the definition for grievous bodily harm or conversely that grievous bodily harm has not been committed unless there is a wound. This is not the case: grievous bodily harm can be committed without a wound and a non serious wound can amount to unlawful wounding.

Wounding

A wound takes place when both layers of the skin are broken and there is usually blood loss. In **JCC v Eisenhower (1994)** the victim was hit in the eye with a pellet fired from an air pistol. He suffered ruptured blood vessels in his eye but the court held that there must be 'a break in the continuity of the skin' to constitute a wound for the purposes of s20 and internal bleeding was not sufficient. Scratches, abrasions and burns will not be considered wounds (unless the second layer of skin is broken) and nor will broken bones and internal ruptures. The definition of 'skin' includes the inner lining of cheeks and lips. This definition leads to the strange conclusion that a pin prick to the skin that draws blood can be classed as a wound.

Grievous bodily harm

A minor wound might be charged as a s20 offence but any other bodily harm under s20 must be 'grievous'. In **DPP v Smith (1961)** the House of Lords ruled that 'grievous' means no more and no less than 'really serious'. In *Saunders* (1985) it was held that 'serious harm' would suffice and the word 'really' was not necessary. Psychiatric harm can be grievous bodily harm provided that it is sufficiently serious (**R v Burstow (1997)**). The Charging Standard list includes broken bones, injuries requiring lengthy medical treatment and injuries causing a substantial loss of blood or permanent disability or disfigurement.

R v Bollom (2004) ruled that the victim being elderly or a child is relevant to the grievousness of the harm since their injuries will tend to more serious than the same injuries to a 'six foot adult in the fullness of health'. In this case a 17-month-old baby suffered extensive bruising and abrasions and this was treated as grievous bodily harm.

If the victim suffers minor injuries which, taken as a whole, amount to serious harm then this has been held to constitute grievous bodily harm despite the fact that the injuries viewed separately would not satisfy the seriousness required for s20. This was decided in *Brown and Stratton* (1998), where the victim was beaten and suffered multiple injuries including concussion, bruising, lost teeth and a broken nose and these minor injuries were considered together be chargeable under s20 as grievous bodily harm.

The grievous bodily harm must be 'inflicted' upon the victim. It had been argued in the past that 'inflict' has a narrower meaning than 'cause' used in s18 in respect of wounding and grievous bodily harm with intent. At its narrowest interpretation in *Clarence* (1888) 'inflict' was understood to need an assault or battery requiring the application of direct force. In this case the court held that the defendant had not inflicted grievous bodily harm on his wife when he infected her with gonorrhoea on the basis that her consent to sexual intercourse meant that there had not been a battery.

However, in *Wilson* (1996) it was held that an offence under s20 could be committed without any need for an assault or battery. This was confirmed in **R v Ireland (1997)**, where the House of Lords ruled that there was no necessity to apply direct or indirect force. The prosecution only needed to prove that the defendant caused the victim to suffer grievous bodily harm. Lord Hope added that for practical purposes 'the words 'cause' and 'inflict' may be taken to be interchangeable.

Removing the requirement for an assault or battery under s20 led to the development of 'biological' grievous bodily harm in **R v Dica (2004)**, where the defendant was knowingly suffering from HIV and infected two women through consensual sex. Dica was convicted and the court ruled that *Clarence* (1888) 'should have no further relevance' in cases where the defendant knows that they are suffering from HIV or some other serious sexual disease and recklessly transmits it to the unknowing victim through consensual intercourse.

Unlawfulness

The last issue to discuss is the fact that a wounding or grievous harm needs to be unlawful in order to be an offence and in most cases a simple lack of consent by the victim will render the act unlawful. However, there are instances where, even if the victim has consented, the defendant will still be liable and this is discussed in Chapter 4, Defences.

Mens rea

The wounding or grievous bodily harm must be done '**maliciously**' but it was confirmed in *Cunningham* (1957) that this merely means that the defendant must intend to inflict the harm or be subjectively reckless as to whether such harm might occur.

The leading case of **R v Mowatt (1976)** established the crucial principle that the prosecution does not have to prove that the defendant intended or foresaw the wound or the grievous bodily harm. The case is proved provided the defendant intended or foresaw that *some* harm *might* occur. Lord Diplock stated in his judgement:

> It is quite unnecessary that the accused should have foreseen that his unlawful act might cause physical harm of the gravity described in the section, i.e. a wound or serious physical injury. It is enough that he should have foreseen that some physical harm to some person, albeit of a minor character, might result.

Lord Diplock's words were the subject of scrutiny in *DPP* v *A* (2000), where a 13-year-old boy had mistakenly shot his friend in the eye whilst meaning to fire below knee level. The magistrates' court dismissed the s20 charge but prosecution appealed on the basis that the word 'maliciously' had been wrongly applied and the Divisional Court allowed the appeal. The magistrates had taken their definition from *Stone's Justices' Manual* but this reputable publication had mistakenly stated that the defendant needs to foresee that the harm *would* occur as opposed to the correct interpretation that the harm *might* occur.

Section 18 of OAPA 1861

Section 18 provides:

> Whosoever shall unlawfully and maliciously by any means whatsoever wound or cause any grievous bodily harm to any person, with intent to do some grievous bodily harm to any person, or with intent to resist or prevent the lawful apprehension or detainer of any person, shall be guilty of an offence, and being convicted thereof shall be liable…to imprisonment for life.

This is a much more serious offence than s20, despite the similarities in language used to describe the assault. It is triable on indictment only and the maximum sentence is life imprisonment.

Actus reus

The *actus reus* is unlawfully wounding or causing grievous bodily harm to the victim. The meanings of the words 'wound' and 'grievous bodily harm' are exactly the same as for s20 and the defendant needs only to 'cause' these injuries with the normal rules of causation applying.

Section 18 also covers wounding and causing grievous bodily harm when resisting arrest and this charge will be preferred where it might be easier to prove that the defendant intended to resist arrest than prove that he intended to cause grievous bodily harm.

Key terms

Maliciously: for the purposes of s20 this means intending the harm or being reckless as to whether such harm might occur (*Cunningham* (1957)).

Key cases

R v Mowatt (1976): established that the defendant will be liable under s20 provided that he intended or foresaw 'some physical harm to some person, albeit of a minor character …'

Again, the wound or grievous bodily harm must be unlawful and the comments above in relation to s20 apply equally to s18.

Mens rea

The vital difference between s20 and s18 is the level of *mens rea*. Recklessness is sufficient to establish *mens rea* for s20 but only intention will suffice for s18. Furthermore, it is not enough to intend *some* harm, but instead prosecution must prove that the defendant intended to cause *grievous* bodily harm. Note that any wounding must be intended to cause grievous harm. If the defendant intended serious harm then he will be convicted under s18 even if the wound turns out to be a minor injury.

The word 'maliciously' is interpreted to mean that the defendant must intend serious harm. In respect of resisting arrest and detention it has been suggested that 'maliciously' means that the defendant will be liable if they foresee (as opposed to intend) that serious harm might result from their conduct.

Oblique intention as well as direct intention applies to s18. Therefore, according to the test in *Nedrick* (1986), if the defendant foresaw that grievous bodily harm was virtually certain to result from his conduct then he will be liable under s18. Oblique intention will satisfy the *mens rea* for common assault, s47 and s20 but prosecutors will prefer to prove a *mens rea* of recklessness for these lesser offences since this is easier to establish than indirect intention.

Activities

1. Raz and Kieran are enjoying an afternoon at an outdoor swimming pool when a heated argument breaks out between them. Raz tells Kieran to calm down but Kieran, now even more angry, pushes Raz into the water. As he falls, Raz cracks his head on the side of the pool and the cut requires stitches. Raz climbs out of the pool and, furious, starts to chase Kieran who runs straight out of the swimming pool complex and onto the road where he is knocked down by a speeding car. He suffers a broken leg and ruptured spleen. Consider what offences that Raz and Kieran might have committed.

2. Make up a fight scenario which will require the application of the law from both *R v Mowatt* (1976) and *JCC v Eisenhower* (1994) when considering whether any offence has been committed. Then provide the answer setting out the relevant potential offences and the principles from both these cases together with any other cases you use.

3. Find an article in a newspaper or online giving details of a court hearing where the defendant has been convicted of an offence under ss47, 20 or 18 of the OAPA 1861. Explain how the facts of the case satisfy requirement of the *actus reus* and *mens rea* for each relevant offence.

You should now be able to:

- explain and distinguish the offence of actual bodily harm, wounding, grievous bodily harm and grievous bodily harm with intent

- explain and apply the law to given scenarios.

4 Defences

💡✔

1 Introduction to defences in criminal law

The AQA law specification for Unit 4 sets out the defences that will be included. These are insanity, automatism, intoxication, consent, self-defence/prevention of crime. Defences become relevant when the *actus reus* of an offence has been committed with the applicable *mens rea*. Therefore, in your answers to the scenario-based questions you are well-advised to discuss the offences and then consider the application of any relevant defence.

The defence of insanity is too narrow to include many of the mental problems which people can suffer from. This is why the Homicide Act 1957 introduced the partial defence of diminished responsibility. The verdict given when a person successfully pleads insanity is 'not guilty by reason of insanity'.

The defence of automatism requires an external factor which distinguishes it from insanity. However, the defence will not be available if the defendant was responsible for creating the automatism.

The defence of intoxication through drink or drugs is sometimes said not to be a defence at all but incapacity to form the *mens rea* of the crime. If this is considered as an idea, then it is obvious that the defence will not be of universal application, only applying when the defendant is incapacitated by drink or drugs. In any event, since some offences involve intoxication (being drunk in a public place or driving whilst unfit through drink or drugs), it is logical that the defence of intoxication will be of application in the *mens rea* aspect of an offence.

Self-defence/prevention of crime are a mixture of defences that largely apply to crimes involving violence so have important application to some of the offences within this unit.

The defences are to some extent interlinked. The challenge is to select the appropriate defence or defences for the individual problems.

You should now be able to:

- outline the range of defences available in the AQA specification
- understand the effect of a defence to a crime
- understand how to approach problem questions involving a defence.

In this topic you will learn how to:

- outline the range of defences in the syllabus
- explain the effect of a successful defence to a crime
- state an appropriate method of applying a defence to problem questions.

2 The defence of insanity

Insanity as a defence is relevant only at the time the offence was committed. Insanity after that is only of relevance if the defendant stands trial or not. The defendant must prove that, on the balance of probabilities, he was insane at the time of the offence. If the prosecution wish to raise the issue of the defendant's insanity, they must prove that beyond reasonable doubt. This is because everyone is presumed to be sane.

If the defence is found to exist, the defendant is not found 'not guilty', but a special verdict of 'not guilty by reason of insanity' is given. Under the Criminal Procedure (Insanity and Unfitness to Plead) Act 1991 the

In this topic you will learn how to:

- explain the meaning of the defence of insanity
- distinguish between insanity and diminished responsibility
- explain cases that illustrate the defence of insanity
- apply the rules to a given situation.

court has a range of options available. For the offence of murder, the court must make a hospital order restricting the defendant's discharge indefinitely. For any other offence, the court may make one of the following orders:

- A hospital order and an order restricting discharge either for a limited or unlimited period of time.
- A guardianship order.
- A supervision and treatment order.
- An order for absolute discharge.

The law relating to the defence of insanity comes from the case of **M'Naghten (1843)**. This case involved the attempted assassination of the then Prime Minister, Sir Robert Peel. The defendant missed, but killed Peel's secretary, Edward Drummond. Medical opinion suggested he was mentally ill and this resulted in the House of Lords setting out rules for use in such cases.

The rules were set out in the case as follows:

> That if the accused was conscious that the act was one which he ought not to do; and if the act was at the same time contrary to law, he is punishable. In all cases of this kind the jurors ought to be told that every man is presumed to be sane, and to possess a sufficient degree of reason to be responsible for his crimes, until the contrary be proved to their satisfaction: and that to establish a defence on the ground of insanity, it must be clearly proved that at the time of committing the act the party accused was labouring under such a defect of reason, from disease of the mind, as not to know the nature and quality of the act he was doing, or as not to know that what he was doing was wrong.

This sets out three key issues that must be established for the defence to succeed:

1 Defect of reason.

2 Caused by disease of the mind.

3 So that the defendant does not know the nature and quality of his act or as not to know that what he was doing was wrong.

Defect of reason

The concept of defect of reason is based on an inability by the defendant to use powers of reason, rather than his failing to use his powers of reason. Thus a person who is confused or absent minded is not insane and, indeed, may have a defence to a crime as lacking the *mens rea*. This can be seen in the case of **Clarke (1972)**, where the defendant was charged with stealing from a supermarket. What had happened was that she transferred some items from the supermarket's basket to her own bag and left the shop without paying for these items. She claimed that she must have put the items in her bag in a moment of absent-mindedness and had no intent to steal. She suffered from diabetes, a number of domestic problems and clinical depression which could cause her to be absent-minded. At her trial the judge said this was a defence of insanity, so she quickly withdrew the defence (in 1972 there were not the current options on a finding of insanity). On appeal, the court decided that she was not deprived of reason, merely temporarily absent-minded. She was not, therefore, insane, but could be found not guilty as she lacked the *mens rea* for the offence of theft.

Key cases

M'Naghten (1843): this case set out the test for the defence of insanity; there are three key areas of the test: defect of reason, disease of the mind and the defendant does not know the nature and quality of his act.

Clarke (1972): a person who is confused or absent-minded is not insane; thus an absent-minded person putting things in her own bag rather than a supermarket basket may be not guilty of theft if the jury recognise she did not have the *mens rea* for theft.

Caused by disease of the mind

The term 'disease of the mind' is a legal term and not a medical term. This is because the law is concerned with whether the defendant should be liable for his acts. The disease of the mind must be a physical disease, rather than one brought about by external factors such as drugs. It can be a permanent state or a temporary state – hence the fact that where the defence is successful, the defendant remains in the control of the court (for example, at a secure hospital) for an indeterminate period.

The court has attempted to decide what constitutes a disease of the mind over many years. It is perhaps best to look at the cases as examples of a disease of the mind and they should not be seen as an exclusive list. The key is to distinguish the diseased mind from the unaffected mind.

In the case of **Kemp (1957)**, the defendant suffered from arteriosclerosis which affected the flow of blood to his brain. This sometimes caused a temporary lack of consciousness. During one such episode he attacked his wife with a hammer and killed her. The court decided that this was a case of insanity rather than automatism (see Topic 3) and, more importantly, established the fact that a disease of the mind could be temporary and the actual medical condition of the brain was not, in itself, relevant. Devlin J stated: *'In my judgment the condition of the brain is irrelevant and so is the question whether the condition of the mind is curable or incurable, transitory or permanent.'*

In **Bratty (1963)**, Lord Denning approved the statement set out above from Devlin J. He added that any mental disorder which was demonstrated by violence that was prone to occur was a disease of the mind. This should be seen as an additional pointer rather than a limiting factor on what amounts to a disease of the mind. Lord Denning was anxious to protect the public from people who suffered in this way. *Bratty* (1963) involved a plea of insanity and automatism by the defendant. The defendant suffered from a psychomotor epileptic seizure during which the strangulation of a girl took place. The effect of this type of seizure is that the victim of it may carry out purposeful acts whilst in an unconscious state. In this case he was driving his van with the girl in the passenger seat. He took off her tights and strangled her with them. The court said that this type of seizure could amount to insanity and gave the court the opportunity to distinguish insanity from automatism.

In **Sullivan (1984)**, the defendant kicked and injured his friendly elderly neighbour during a minor epileptic fit. The fact that this was only temporary did not preclude it from being a defence of insanity. It would not be a defence of automatism as that required an external factor. This, and other decisions regarding epileptic fits, demonstrates very clearly that the legal definition of insanity is very different from the medical definition.

So that the defendant does not know the nature and quality of his act or as not to know that what he was doing was wrong

The expression 'nature and quality' merely refers to the physical quality of the act. This means that the defendant proves any of the following:

- That he did not know what he was doing.
- That he did not appreciate the consequences of his act.
- That he did not appreciate the circumstances in which he was acting.

In these situations he lacks *mens rea* but because this is a result of his insanity, the special verdict is given rather than being acquitted.

- The idea that he did not know that what he was doing was wrong means that he had the *mens rea* for the offence but because of his insanity he did not know it was wrong. This does not distinguish

Key cases

Kemp (1957): arteriosclerosis caused occasional lapse of consciousness in the defendant; whilst he was suffering from this disease, he killed his wife by hitting her with a hammer; this was treated as insanity.

Bratty (1963): a psychomotor epileptic seizure could amount to insanity.

Sullivan (1984): a minor epileptic fit can amount to insanity in law rather than automatism as automatism requires an external factor.

Key cases

Windle (1952): the defendant did know the nature and quality of his act and that what he was doing was wrong so he could not rely on the defence of insanity.

between legal and moral 'wrongness'. It seems that a common sense approach to this will prevail – the issue is rarely raised, although it became central in the case of **Windle (1952)**. In that case the defendant killed his insane wife. He pleaded his own insanity, but had originally given himself up to the police saying, 'I suppose I'll hang for this!' As this showed he knew the nature and quality of his act and that what he was doing was wrong, he was convicted of murder, a hanging offence at the time.

Conclusion

The defence of insanity is a rarely used defence today as it has a special verdict rather than an acquittal. It was a more popular defence when there was the death penalty for murder and before the introduction of diminished responsibility in the Homicide Act 1957. Defendants are not keen on the indeterminate nature of the orders made under a special verdict and often withdraw or do not propose the defence. This is one reason why the issue of insanity can be raised by the prosecution. The vital elements of the defence revolve around the distinction between internal and external factors and the idea of a disease of the mind.

Application of the defences of insanity to problems in the examination

In the examination there are often questions involving the defence of insanity. Discussion of this defence is suggested whenever a character in the scenario appears to be mentally unstable, for example hearing voices.

Activity

Consider the criminal liability of in the situation below, taken from the 2007 case of Johnson, and consider the defence of insanity to the offences that you find he has committed:

The appellant in June 2006 was leading an independent life at a block of flats in Barnes. It is plain that he was subject at the time to delusions and to clear auditory hallucinations, which the psychiatrists, who have seen him as a result of the events which we shall describe, had no difficulty in diagnosing as amounting to paranoid schizophrenia.

In another flat in the block in which he lived was a man called Alan Taylor. It is plain that he was somewhat uneasy about the behaviour of the appellant and rightly so as it transpired, for, on 20 June 2006 at about three o'clock in the afternoon the appellant forced his way into Alan Taylor's sitting room while Alan Taylor was watching television. The appellant shouted very aggressively, although it was difficult to make sense of what he was saying. He was holding a large kitchen knife, with which he stabbed Alan Taylor first in the left shoulder. When Alan Taylor tried to protect himself he suffered four deep stab wounds and many small lacerations to his fingers. The applicant then, fortunately having not caused fatal injuries, left the flat and Alan Taylor was able to call the emergency

services. He was found in a serious condition, having lost a great deal of blood. After two weeks in hospital, he was happily released and it would appear, again fortunately, that he has made a good recovery.

The story of that afternoon did not end at Alan Taylor's flat, because the appellant turned up at the home of a person who considered himself to be a friend, called Russell Pidworth, at Mortlake Cemetery. Russell Pidworth was not there but his father was. There was a serious incident in the doorway of that house, when it would appear as though the appellant was seeking to obtain entry, asking for Russell. He was carrying a knife, which was clearly the knife with which he had injured Alan Taylor. He was shouting and swearing and accused Russell of 'noncing my sister'. He threatened Russell Pidworth's father, who was there at the time, but bravely, it would appear, was able to at least calm him to the extent that eventually the appellant left. It subsequently transpired that Russell had two days earlier seen the appellant in the cemetery holding a knife and thrashing out at shrubs; and when he, Russell, asked what he was doing the appellant complained at that stage about an Indian man in a shop 'who has been noncing my sister'.

www.bailii.org/ew/cases/EWCA/Crim/2007/1978.html

You should now be able to:

- state and apply the law of the defence of insanity.

3 The defence of automatism

Automatism requires the defendant to show that his act was:

- involuntary
- due to an external factor.

An involuntary act

The defendant's act must be involuntary in that that his mind is not controlling his limbs in a purposeful manner. This is similar to **Bratty (1963)**, considered in insanity, where the defendant claimed that 'a blackness came over him'. In that case Lord Denning said.

> No act is punishable if it is done involuntarily and an involuntary act means an act which is done by the muscles without any control by the mind such as a spasm, a reflex action or a convulsion; or an act done by a person who is not conscious of what he is doing, such as an act done whilst suffering from concussion or done whilst sleepwalking.

However, it should be noted that this has to be a total lack of awareness, just not partly automatic as in the case of **Attorney-General's Reference (No. 2 of 1992)**, where the defendant killed two people whose car was on the hard shoulder of the motorway. He claimed he was driving his lorry 'without awareness', caused by driving for a long time on the motorway and was in a trance-like state. The court decided that he was still partly in control so automatism did not apply.

The external factor

This requirement is that the automatism has been caused by an external factor such as a blow on the head rather than an internal factor such as a disease. This has already been seen in the topic of insanity. It follows from this that the automatism must not be self-induced – this is the case with self-administered drink or drugs. Automatism is self-induced when it results from the defendant's actions or failing to take action. This can be seen in the case of **Quick (1973)**, set out below.

The difference between insanity and automatism

This distinction is key to the understanding of these defences. The basic rule is that insanity results from factors internal to the defendant and automatism arises as a result of external factors. This is sometimes known as insane automatism and non-insane automatism.

In *Quick* (1973), the defendant was a nurse alone on duty in a ward at a hospital where a paraplegic spastic patient, unable to walk, was sitting watching television. Half an hour later, the patient had sustained two black eyes, a fractured nose, a split lip which required three stitches, and bruising of his arm and shoulders. There was undisputed medical evidence that these injuries could not have been self-inflicted.

The defendant admitted that he had been drinking and that his drinks had included whisky and a quarter of a bottle of rum, but his was not a defence of intoxication. He also said that he was, and had been since the age of seven, a diabetic and that that morning he had taken insulin as prescribed by his doctor. After taking the insulin he had had a very small breakfast and no lunch. On many occasions he had been admitted to hospital either unconscious or semi-conscious due to hypoglycaemia, which is a condition brought about when there is more insulin in the bloodstream than the amount of sugar there can cope with. At the start of the imbalance the higher functions of the mind are affected. As the effects of the imbalance become more marked, more and more mental functions are upset, and unless the hypoglycaemia is reversed (for

In this topic you will learn how to:

- explain the meaning of the defence of automatism
- distinguish between insane and non-insane automatism
- explain cases that illustrate the defence of automatism
- apply the rules to a given situation.

 Key cases

Bratty (1963): sets out the key definition for disease of the mind.

Attorney-General's Reference (No. 2 of 1992): automatism requires a total lack of awareness, not just partial control.

Quick (1973): highlights the distinction between automatism from external factors and insanity from internal factors when related to a diabetic condition; taking insulin is an external factor.

example by giving the sufferer a sugar lump) he can go into coma. In the later stages of mental impairment a sufferer may become aggressive and violent without being able to control himself or without knowing at the time what he was doing or having any recollection afterwards of what he had done.

As the defendant's condition arose as a consequence of an external factor (the insulin) the defendant could rely on a defence of automatism rather than insanity.

In **Hennessey (1989)**, the defendant was charged with taking a motor car without authority and driving while disqualified. He claimed that he was suffering from hyperglycaemia (high blood sugar level caused by diabetes) at the time because he had not taken any insulin to stabilise himself, nor eaten properly for days, and as a result was acting unconsciously. The court decided that the defence of automatism was not available to him as the diabetes was an internal factor. The only possible defence for a jury to consider was insanity.

Conclusion

The defence of automatism revolves around the distinction between internal and external factors and the idea of a disease of the mind.

Application of the defences of insanity and automatism to problems in the examination

In the examination, there are often questions involving the defence of insanity or automatism. Discussion of these defences is suggested whenever a character in the scenario appears to be mentally unstable, for example hearing voices. Automatism is the factor to consider when the character is said to be sleep walking or not conscious of what he is doing.

> **Key cases**
>
> **Hennessey (1989):** highlights the distinction between automatism from external factors and insanity from internal factors when related to a diabetic condition; lacking insulin is an internal factor.

> **Activity**
>
> Consider the scenario set out below. You should discuss both offences and possible defences.
>
> For many years, Janine believed that fairies and pixies lived at the bottom of her garden. She now also believes that, as a result of population growth, they have expanded to inhabit parts of the garden of her neighbour, Kenneth.
>
> Janine was looking out of her bedroom window when she saw Kenneth digging in his garden. Believing that Kenneth was destroying the fairies' and pixies' homes, she rushed into the garden. As she went out, she picked up an old shotgun that had been left behind by her first husband. She believed the gun was unloaded and she was about to take it to hand in at a weapons amnesty. She then started to shout and wave the shotgun at Kenneth. Unfortunately, the shotgun was loaded and went off, injuring Kenneth who fell to the ground.
>
> Janine was shocked by what had happened and thought she had killed Kenneth. She began to move in a trance-like manner to where Kenneth lay. She thought Kenneth was dead so dragged him to her compost heap where she covered him in leaves. Some days later he died of exposure.

You should now be able to:

■ state and apply the law of the defence of automatism

■ distinguish between insanity and automatism.

4 The defence of intoxication

Intoxication can be either voluntary or involuntary. In general, where the intoxication is voluntary, a person should not be excused from the consequences of their actions. This is because that person is responsible for being in the state of intoxication that impairs their judgment. Intoxication, however, can be used to show that the defendant could not form the necessary *mens rea* for the offence with which he has been charged. In that sense, it can provide a defence.

The law distinguishes between voluntary and involuntary intoxication and the effect that has on different offences, the offences being divided into those of basic intent and those of specific intent. The result that will be discussed below can be seen in Fig. 1 below.

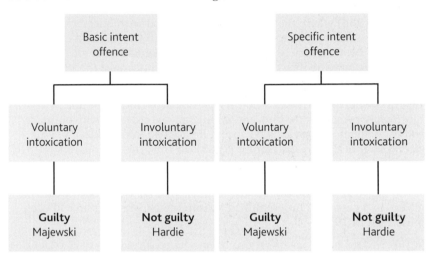

Fig. 1 *The effect of intoxication*

Voluntary and involuntary intoxication

Voluntary intoxication is where the defendant takes the drink or drugs of his own free will. Involuntary intoxication is where a person does not know he was taking alcohol or an intoxicating drug. In such cases, there will only be a defence if the *mens rea* for a crime was not formed. Involuntary intoxication can arise where:

- the defendant's drinks were spiked with alcohol or drugs such as where a drug is slipped into a soft drink or alcohol is added without the defendant's knowledge
- the defendant takes drugs prescribed by his doctor in accordance with the instructions
- the defendant takes a non-dangerous drug, although not prescribed to him, in a non-reckless way.

If involuntary intoxication is to be a defence, it must be shown that the effect of the intoxication is that the defendant was, as a result of the intoxication, unable to form the *mens rea* of the offence. This is not always possible as can be seen in the case of **Kingston (1994)**. In that case, at a trial in the Lewes Crown Court in March 1992, the defendant, Barry Kingston and a man named Penn were jointly indicted on a count of indecent assault on a youth aged 15. The defendant, who had paedophiliac homosexual tendencies (which he normally controlled fully), was blackmailed by two former business associates who arranged for Penn to photograph and audio-tape him in a compromising situation with the boy. Sedative drugs were found in Penn's flat when it was searched and the prosecution claimed that Penn had laced the

In this topic you will learn how to:

- state the definition of the defence of intoxication
- distinguish between crimes of basic and specific offence
- distinguish between the effect of voluntary and involuntary intoxication
- explain the effect of mistake when intoxicated
- explain the law relating to Dutch courage
- apply the rules to a given situation.

Key cases

Kingston (1994): a defendant can only use the defence of involuntary intoxication if the court is convinced that because of being intoxicated the defendant lacked the required *mens rea* for the offence; in the case, the court said that an intoxicated intent was still an intent.

boy's drink. Kingston's defence was that Penn had also laced his drink. Kingston said that he had seen the boy lying on the bed but had no recollection of any other events that night and had woken in his own home the next morning. He said that he would never have committed the offence had he not been affected by the drug. The House of Lords stated that involuntary intoxication was not a defence to a charge if it was proved that the defendant had the necessary intent when the offence was committed, even though he was not to blame for the intoxication. Lord Mustill saw this case as one of disinhibition – the taking of the drug (whatever it was) lowered his ability to resist temptation, so that his desires overrode his ability to control them.

Where the defendant does not realise the strength of the alcohol or drug he has taken, it does not make the intoxication involuntary. The fact that the intoxication remains voluntary can be seen from the case of **Allen (1988)** where the defendant was charged with buggery and indecent assault following an evening drinking in the pub and some wine given later by a friend. His claim that he did not realise the alcoholic strength of the wine that he had been given did not make the intoxication involuntary.

Where the defendant takes a non-dangerous drug, although not specifically prescribed to him, the taking may be treated as involuntary and may therefore provide a defence if he does so non-recklessly. This can be seen in the case of **Hardie (1985)**. In this, the defendant's relationship with Mrs Hardie had broken down and she had insisted that he must leave. He did not wish to do so, but on the morning of 2 January 1982, he packed a suitcase. At about lunchtime he found two bottles of tablets in a cabinet. One contained Valium which Mrs Hardie had been prescribed in 1974.

Whilst he had never taken Valium before, he took one about 12 o'clock to calm him down but it did not have much effect. He and Mrs Hardie had then gone shopping and he had taken two more in front of her and she had said, 'take as many as you like, they are old stock and will do you no harm'. He took two more shortly afterwards and shortly thereafter on return to the house he had fallen into a deep sleep and could thereafter remember only odd periods for the rest of the day.

It was not disputed that he must have started the fire for he was alone in the bedroom when it started. Having started it, he emerged, returned to the sitting room to be with Mrs Hardie and her daughter, Tonia, and stayed there. Shortly afterwards Mrs Hardie heard sounds from the bedroom, went there and found smoke and flames coming from the wardrobe. There was evidence that before, at the time of and after the fire the defendant was showing signs of intoxication and that such signs might have resulted from the taking of Valium some hours earlier.

The court decided that this did not necessarily amount to voluntary intoxication. The jury should be directed that if they came to the conclusion that, as a result of the Valium, the defendant was, at the time, unable to appreciate the risks to property and persons from his actions they should then consider whether the taking of the Valium was itself reckless. The courts later decided that there was a distinction between 'dangerous' drugs including those where it is 'common knowledge' that the taker 'may become aggressive or do dangerous or unpredictable things' or make the defendant incapable of appreciating risks (amphetamines and LSD being well-known examples), and non-dangerous drugs such as Valium. Where the drug can be said to be dangerous, there may be recklessness in self-administering it which would be the case when the drug was well known for causing the effects.

■ **Key cases**

Allen (1988): intoxication remains voluntary even where the defendant claims he did not know the strength of the drink or drugs.

Hardie (1985): the voluntary consumption of dangerous drugs might be conclusive proof of recklessness; this is not the case with non-dangerous drugs, and a jury should have been directed to consider whether the defendant had been reckless in consuming the Valium.

The distinction between crimes of basic intent and specific intent

The principle is that intoxication is a defence to crimes of specific intent and not those of basic intent. The key case with respect to this is **Majewski (1977)**. In that case during the evening of 19 February 1973 the defendant and his friend, Leonard Stace, who had also taken drugs and drink, went to The Bull public house in Basildon. Stace became involved in a disturbance. Glasses were broken. The landlord asked Stace to leave and escorted him to the door. As he did so, Stace called to Majewski: 'He's putting me out.' Majewski got up and prevented the landlord from getting Stace out and abused him. The landlord told them both to go. They refused and a brawl followed. Majewski was violent and abusive and spat in the landlord's face. When the police came, a fierce struggle took place to get him out. He shouted at the police: 'You pigs, I'll kill you all, you f—— pigs, you bastards.'

The House of Lords considered the whole aspect of intoxication and came to the conclusion that self-induced intoxication can only be raised as a defence to crimes of specific intent, but not to crimes of basic intent.

The difficulty arises in that whilst the term 'specific intent' had been used in previous cases, 'basic intent' had not. Indeed it was not wholly clear what was meant by specific intent. It seems that a crime of basic intent is one where there is a general criminal intent rather than a sort of ulterior intent that the defendant wishes to achieve from his *actus reus*. Self-induced (voluntary) intoxication is no defence to a crime of basic intent as the defendant's actions in becoming intoxicated voluntarily is in itself reckless behaviour – he knows there is a risk he will behave badly or criminally, but goes ahead anyway. This distinction is sometimes summarised as specific intent crimes require the *mens rea* of intention and basic intent crimes only recklessness.

For many crimes, there are variations that have the specific intent crime as the more serious offence, with a lesser offence of basic intent. An example is basic criminal damage under s1(1) of the Criminal Damage Act 1971 and aggravated criminal damage which is destroying or damaging property with intent to endanger life under s1(2) of the Act. The 'with intent to endanger life' is the specific intent crime. Thus, a defendant who had the *actus reus* and *mens rea* for both offences but was voluntarily intoxicated at that time, might be able to show that he was so intoxicated that he could not form the specific intent of the aggravated crime and thus only be convicted of the lesser, basic offence. However, not all 'specific' intent offences have a corresponding 'basic' intent offence. A typical example of this is theft.

The offences that we have considered in this unit can be categorised as follows:

Table 1 *Specific and basic intent offences*

Basic Intent Crimes	Specific Intent Crimes
Offences Against the Person Act 1861 s47	Offences Against the Person Act 1861 s18
Offences Against the Person Act 1861 s20	Murder
Assault	
Battery	
Involuntary manslaughter	

Key cases

Majewski (1977): this case made the distinction between crimes of basic intent and crimes of specific intent.

Key cases

Attorney-General for Northern Ireland v Gallagher (1963): if the *mens rea* is formed before the intoxication, as in Dutch courage, there will be no defence of intoxication; in this case the intention to kill his wife was formed before he got drunk.

It should also be noted that if the *mens rea* is formed before the intoxication, as in 'Dutch Courage', there will be no defence of intoxication. This can be seen in the case of **Attorney-General for Northern Ireland v Gallagher (1963)**. In this case, the defendant decided to kill his wife. He went out and bought a bottle of whisky and a knife. He drank the whisky and became so drunk that he could not form the *mens rea* for murder (an intention to kill or cause really serious harm); then he killed his wife. As he had formed the intention to kill her before he became intoxicated, he had no defence of intoxication.

Conclusion

The first distinction is between voluntary and involuntary intoxication. Involuntary intoxication is a defence, but only where the intoxication is completely involuntary. The defence of intoxication applies differently to offences of specific intent and those of basic intent. It is essential, therefore, to understand the distinction between the two.

In the examination, there are often questions involving the defence of intoxication. Discussion of this defence is suggested whenever a character in the scenario takes an alcoholic drink or drugs, whether illegal or legal. It may well be the case that you decided, after due consideration, that the defence will be unsuccessful. Nevertheless, you must make that discussion.

Activity

Consider the scenario set out below. You should discuss both offences and possible defences.

Rob drank a few glasses of wine and then took a rowing boat out onto the river with Salma. Unknown to him, someone had slipped a drug into the wine and, by the time that he began rowing, he was already feeling rather confused. Tom, who was walking along the riverbank, jeered at Rob and then threw a stone at him, striking him in the chest. Rob stood up and persistently shouted and shook his fist, even though the boat was rocking dangerously. Shortly afterwards, the boat overturned and Salma, who could not swim, drowned in the river.

You should now be able to:

■ state the law of the defence of intoxication.

In this topic you will learn how to:

■ state the definition of the defence of consent

■ apply the rules to a given situation.

 Key cases

Airedale NHS Trust v Bland (1993): the court is the only body that can give lawful permission for discontinuing life support for those in a persistent vegetative state.

5 The defence of consent

The defence of consent is, in many ways, not a defence at all as it could be argued that there has been no unlawful act. The issues are deciding what a person can consent to and the genuineness of the consent. We will consider them in this order:

■ What offences can a person consent (and not consent) to?
■ Is the consent genuine?

What offences cannot be subject to a defence of consent?

A person cannot consent to being killed (murder), hence the difficulties with euthanasia and turning off life support machines. In **Airedale NHS Trust v Bland (1993)**, Anthony Bland was badly crushed at the Hillsborough football disaster. He was left permanently unconscious, in a persistent vegetative state. The unanimous opinion of all the doctors who had examined him was that there was no hope whatsoever of recovery or improvement of any kind in his condition. Whilst he continued to breathe unaided and his digestion continued to function, he could not see, hear, taste, smell, speak or otherwise communicate, was incapable of voluntary movement, could not feel pain and had no cognitive function. Three years later the hospital applied to the court for a ruling whether it would be lawful to discontinue artificial hydration and nutrition, resulting inevitably in his death.

The House of Lords decided:

■ Artificial nutrition and hydration is regarded as a form of medical treatment.

■ There is no distinction between an omission to treat a patient (withholding) and discontinuance of treatment once commenced (withdrawing).

■ In making the decision whether or not to provide medical treatment the question to be asked is whether it is in the best interests of the patient that his life should be prolonged.

■ Previously stated wishes of the patient and the views of close relatives should be taken into account in the assessment of best interests.

Euthanasia or assisted suicides remain an area where, despite the apparent consent of the victim, the law does not permit this activity. This is confirmed in the case of **Pretty (2002)**. Dianne Pretty suffered from motor neurone disease which left her paralysed. She wanted her husband to be able to assist her suicide without fear of prosecution so that she could choose the time of her death and die with dignity. She argued that Article 2 (right to life) of the European Convention on Human Rights protects the right to life and the right to choose the manner of death.

However, the House of Lords and the European Court did not find that Article 2 created a right to die and indeed that the need to protect vulnerable citizens justified the prohibition of assisted suicide.

What activities that might be an offence can a person consent to?

There are a number of areas where the law allows consent, although the extent of the consent may be limited. This was discussed in detail in **Brown (1993)**. This case involved consenting homosexuals who performed sado-masochistic acts in private. Whilst at the time many perceived the acts as distasteful, and immoral, the question before the court was whether the individuals could consent to these activities. The court confirmed that consent is allowed as a defence to battery, but not to more serious injuries as the law insists that there are limits to the defence of consent when injuries are more serious than common assault (ss47, 20 and 18): it is not in the public interest for people to harm each other for no good reason. The court stated that the defence is not available for injuries more serious than common assault unless they fell into one of the 'recognised exceptions'. A list was given including 'properly conducted games and sports, reasonable surgical interference and dangerous exhibitions'.

Normal sports activities

Many sports involve some physical contact and the risk of injury inflicted by another. The problem comes in the extent of the consent. Clearly, a person consents to being hit and possibly to very serious injuries in a boxing match, perhaps the most famous case being that of Michael Watson in 1991. Whilst the event is being properly conducted and

Pretty (2002): assisted suicide is a criminal offence and is not a breach of the victim's human right (right to life).

Brown (1993): the leading case on consent which set out the parameters for the defence.

supervised within the rules, there is consent. When the incident goes beyond the rules and regulations of the sport, then there is the potential for criminal liability. This can be seen from the case of *Barnes* (2004). In this case, the victim suffered a serious leg injury following a tackle during an amateur football match. The Court of Appeal decided that criminal proceedings should only take place in those situations where the conduct was sufficiently serious. Most sports had their own disciplinary procedures that covered most situations and physical injury was an inevitable risk of sport, and those taking part consented to such injury.

Before a prosecution was considered the following would need to be considered:

- The type of sport.
- The level at which it was played.
- The nature of the act.
- The degree of force used.
- The extent of risk of injury.
- The state of mind of the person causing the injury.

The court also noted that in the heat of the moment excessive force might be used but that was unlikely to be criminal.

Normal social intercourse

This covers things such as shaking hands, tapping someone on the shoulder to draw their attention to something, hugging, etc. It should be noted that a person can withdraw their consent, thus making the action potentially criminal.

Medical procedures, dentistry, piercing, tattooing and blood tests

Most surgical treatment can be readily consented to either expressly by signing consent forms, having the forms signed by a parent or guardian for a child and by implied consent in emergencies. This consent can be refused or withdrawn at any time

With respect to blood tests, under the Police Reform Act 2002, the situation where it appears to the constable that the person is, for a medical reason (not, for example, because he cannot understand English) incapable of giving a valid consent. This will normally be because the person is unconscious. In that situation, the constable may now request that a blood specimen be taken, thus giving a statutory consent to the test.

With respect to piercing and tattooing, this can be consented to but is regulated by statute such as the Tattooing of Minors Act 1969.

Horseplay and sexual activities

Lord Mustill in his dissenting speech in **Brown (1993)**, said, whilst discussing the law on horseplay:

> As a matter of policy the courts have decided that the criminal law does not concern itself with these activities, provided that they do not go too far. It also seems plain that as the general social appreciation of the proper role of the state in regulating the lives of individuals changes with the passage of time, so we shall expect to find that the assumptions of the criminal justice system about what types of conduct are properly excluded from its scope, and what is meant by 'going too far' will not remain constant.

This is relevant to unregulated sports and games and is a rather more physical form of social intercourse. It includes the usual pushing and shoving between friends, arm wrestling, etc. The problem comes when it gets out of hand or is clearly not consented to as it is bullying. A typical

Key cases

Brown (1993): even though the activities were fully consensual, the defendants were convicted because the acts were intentional, and, also because of the moral view taken; the conviction was not interfered with by the European Court of Human Rights, under the name of *Laskey v UK* (1997)

case is the case of **Jones (1986)**, where a group of boys gave another 'the bumps' by tossing him in the air. The defendants were entitled to be acquitted if the jury decided that they were indulging in 'rough' and undisciplined sport or play, not intending to cause harm, and genuinely believing that the injuries which occurred in the course of the horseplay occurred with the victim's consent.

With respect to sexual activities, the law is concerned on moral grounds with respect to extreme sexual activities, however consensual, and the transmission of diseases such as Aids. In *Brown* (1993), the victims and the defendants were involved in consensual sado-masochistic homosexual activities that did not result in permanent injury or hospitalisation. Despite the consensual nature of the activities the defendants were found guilty – the European Court of Human Rights confirming that there was no breach of human rights in imposing criminal sanctions for such activities. This follows the established principle that it is not in the public interest that people should cause each other actual bodily harm for no good reason.

The case of *Dica* (2004) established that the transmission of disease (at least sexual ones) can be criminal and the question is then one for the jury on the issue of consent. Clearly someone who is not told that their partner is HIV positive cannot consent to the risk of infection as a result of unprotected sex, but this does not deal with the issue of the victim's ability to understand the implications of the activity, or where drug users share needles or inject each other.

It is important to reiterate that the defence is only relevant where the *actus reus* and *mens rea* of the crime have been established. Thus, if the defendant has no *mens rea*, the defence of consent is irrelevant. This can be seen in the case of **Simon Slingsby (1995)**, where the defendant caused internal injuries to a woman partner from the signet ring he was wearing. At the time of the incident, neither the defendant nor the victim was aware of the injury or the cause of it until the subsequent seriousness as a result of the wound becoming septic became apparent. Her death was not the result of a criminal act as the defendant lacked the *mens rea* for unlawful act manslaughter, so the issue of consent was irrelevant.

Is the consent genuine?

The fact that the victim appears to consent does not mean that the consent is genuine. If the victim is a child or is mentally retarded, then the consent may not be valid. The question is whether the victim has sufficient understanding and intelligence to give consent. This can be seen in the case of **Burrell v Harmer (1967)**, where the defendant tattooed two boys who were aged 12 and 13 with their consent. The defence of consent was not allowed, as the court felt that the boys were unable to understand the pain involved whilst recognising what a tattoo was. Age in itself does not mean there is no consent, but the failure to appreciate the nature of the act does form the basis of the lack of consent.

Where the victim consents only through fear, it is a question of whether the threats are sufficient to warrant the consent. This would be in line with the defence of duress. However, where the consent is obtained by fraud, it will not be a valid consent. The fraud must be as to the nature of the act. This can be seen in the case of **Tabassum (2000)**, where women consented to a breast examination carried out by the defendant in the erroneous belief that he was medically qualified. The offence had taken place because the women, who had consented to being touched purely for medical purposes, had not consented for any other purpose. This seems inconsistent with **Richardson (1998)**, where consent to dental treatment was accepted as a defence even though the patients did not know that the defendant had been disqualified from practice. This latter case seems inconsistent with the case of *Dica* (2004) and so perhaps should be disregarded.

Application of the defence of consent to problems in the examination

In the examination, there are often questions involving the defence of consent. Discussion of this defence is suggested whenever a character appears to submit to the offence. It may well be the case that you decided, after due consideration, that the defence will be unsuccessful. Nevertheless, you must make that discussion.

Activity

Consider the scenario set out below. You should discuss both offences and possible defences.

Emma, who was 12 years of age but looked older, paid for her tongue to be pierced and a stud inserted by Farah. Emma's tongue rapidly developed a serious infection which required hospital treatment. The treatment was administered by George, a newly qualified doctor. George misinterpreted Emma's medical record and gave her an antibiotic drug which her body could not tolerate. This resulted in her death.

You should now be able to:

■ state the law of the defence of consent.

In this topic you will learn how to:

■ state the definition of the defence of self-defence/ prevention of crime

■ distinguish between self-defence and prevention of crime

■ apply the rules to a given situation.

6 The defence of self-defence/prevention of crime

This topic is sometimes called public and private defence. This is because the common law defence of self-defence is extended and, to some extent superseded, by the statutory defence of public defence (prevention of crime) under the Criminal Law Act 1967, s3. As the two do overlap, the idea of self-defence is still relevant as it may be that a person is defending themselves from someone who is not, in fact, committing a crime, for example because that person is insane.

Self-defence is just defending yourself or another, whereas the statutory defence deals with prevention of crime. These are two separate defences. The two overlap and are essentially the same but should be treated separately.

Criminal Law Act 1967, s3

This section provides:

> A person may use such force as is reasonable in the circumstances in the prevention of crime, or in effecting or assisting in the lawful arrest of offenders or suspected offenders or of persons unlawfully at large.

The following points need to be considered:

■ The necessity of force.

■ The reasonableness of force.

The necessity of force

The basic principle is that the use of force is not justified if it is not necessary. It will be necessary if it is seen to be so in the circumstances which exist or which the defendant genuinely believed existed. This can be seen from the case of **Gladstone Williams (1987)**, where a man saw a woman become the victim of a robbery by a youth. This man struggled with the robber with a view to stopping him and handing him to the police. At this point the defendant appeared and took the view that the man was attacking the youth and stepped in to protect the youth. The defendant was successful in pleading prevention of crime, even though he was mistaken as to the actual facts. His defence is based on what he genuinely believed was happening.

The defence comes into operation even if the attack has not yet taken place providing it is imminent. In other words, the defendant does not have to wait for an attack to start but can get in the first blow. The difficulty with this is establishing that the force he uses is reasonable. However, it is clear that the defendant does not have a duty to retreat as far as possible before using force which was the case under the old law. This can be seen from the case of **Bird (1985)**. The facts of the case were that on 10 March 1984 the defendant, Debbie Bird, was celebrating her 17th birthday. There was a party at a house in Harlow. There was a guest at the party called Darren Marder, who became the victim. He and the defendant had been friendly and had been going out together between about January and the middle of 1983. That close friendship had come to an end, but Marder arrived at the party with his new girlfriend and an argument broke out. The defendant told Marder to leave, and he did.

A little later he came back and a second argument took place. The defendant poured a glass of Pernod over Marder, and he retaliated by slapping her around the face. When she was later held up against a wall she lunged at Marder with her hand, which was the hand which held the Pernod glass. The glass hit him in the face, broke, and took out his eye. The court decided that it was unnecessary to show an unwillingness to fight and there were circumstances where a defendant might reasonably react immediately and without first retreating, as in this case. The force was not reasonable in terms of what had happened, but was reasonable with respect to what she thought might happen when pinned against the wall.

The reasonableness of force

The jury have the task of deciding whether, in all the circumstances, the defendant used reasonable force. The jury, of course, can take as long as they need to balance the facts, the facts as the defendant believed them, the circumstances of the attack, the time available to the defendant to decide on his course of action, and balance the risk to himself against the risk of harm to the victim. The defendant usually does that in a split second so he may use excessive force. If that is the case, that excessive force is unlawful.

Lord Morris of Borth-y-Gest said in the case of **Palmer (1971)**:

> It is both good law and good sense that a man who is attacked may defend himself. It is both good law and good sense that he may do, but may only do, what is reasonably necessary. But everything will depend upon the particular facts and circumstances. … It may in some cases be only sensible and clearly possible to take some simple avoiding action. Some attacks may be serious and dangerous. Others may not be. If there is some relatively minor attack it would not be common sense to permit some action of retaliation which was wholly out of proportion to the necessities of the situation. If an attack is serious so that it puts someone in immediate peril then immediate defensive action may be necessary. If the moment is one of crisis for someone in imminent danger he may have to avert the danger by some instant reaction.
>
> If the attack is all over and no sort of peril remains then the employment of force may be by way of revenge or punishment or

by way of paying off an old score or may be pure aggression. There may no longer be any link with a necessity of defence. Of all these matters the good sense of a jury will be the arbiter. If there has been no attack then clearly there will have been no need for defence. If there has been attack so that defence is reasonably necessary it will be recognised that a person defending himself cannot weigh to a nicety the exact measure of his necessary defensive action.

The famous cases of Corporal Clegg, a soldier on a checkpoint in Northern Ireland in the 1990s faced with what might be a terrorist attack, and Tony Martin in 2001 who shot and killed a 16-year-old intruder with a pump action shotgun demonstrate the extremes to which a jury must go when considering what amounts to reasonable force.

Conclusion

A person may use such force as is reasonable in the circumstances in the prevention of crime, or in effecting or assisting in the lawful arrest of offenders or suspected offenders or of persons unlawfully at large. The key aspects of the defence are the necessity of force and the reasonableness of force.

Application of the defence of self-defence/prevention of crime to problems in the examination

In the examination there are questions involving the defence of self-defence. Discussion of this defence is suggested whenever a character in the scenario is reacting to a threat of violence made against him.

Activity

Consider the scenario set out below. You should discuss both offences and possible defences.

Ali, who was aged 55, had been on bad terms with Bill, aged 32, over an alleged attack by Ali on Bill's young daughter. By chance, they found themselves together in the house of a mutual friend. Bill was heard to say, 'I am going to do that pervert.' Shortly afterwards, encouraged by his friend, Colin, Bill began punching and kicking Ali. As he was falling to the floor, Ali took a knife from his pocket and slashed Bill's arm. Bill reeled backwards, bleeding heavily. Ali suffered from a broken nose and broken ribs.

You should now be able to:

■ state the law of self-defence/prevention of crime.

3A   Review and examination techniques

Answering questions on criminal law in Unit 3A

To complete an examination paper in criminal law successfully, you must both prepare carefully beforehand and deploy a range of skills when actually answering questions.

In preparing for an examination, you may find the following guidelines helpful:

- Make sure you have a thorough understanding of the key principles relating to each crime and defence. Be aware that each crime consists of rules relating to the existence of an *actus reus* and *mens rea*. There may also be issues of causation and there may be a defence available.

- Be prepared to illustrate key principles with the use of authority. Authority means a case or an Act of Parliament demonstrating the principle in question or a case explaining a point about the Act of Parliament.

- With respect to cases, you should be able to explain the principle that the case illustrates. It is helpful to have an outline knowledge of the facts of the case, as that gives a useful example, but it is not necessary to know the facts in great detail or to memorise the date of the case.

- With respect to Acts of Parliaments, you need to be able to cite the relevant section number, as well as the name and date of the statute, and to be able to explain in your own words what the section says. It is preferable to quote the key extract from the section of an Act of Parliament so that you use the correct legal term.

- Make sure you frequently practise writing answers to past papers and similar examples, and ensure that you pay attention to the feedback that you receive. You do not want to be in the position of trying out your problem-solving skills for the first time in the examination. No one gets everything right the first time and everyone benefits from experience.

- Pay attention to your written English. There are five marks awarded for using good English, organising information clearly and using legal vocabulary accurately and at appropriate places. Five marks may not sound very much but it could be the difference between two grades, especially as the other A Level law examinations also carry marks for the quality of your written communication. When you practise exam answers, be aware of the need to produce organised answers (not random points churned out in the hope that something will be correct) and take the time to check spellings.

- When looking at a problem scenario, begin by identifying the characters involved. You need to know who the victims and possible defendants are. Be sure to read the question carefully and answer only what you are asked. If the question asks you about the criminal liability of Character A, you will waste time if you discuss what Character B's criminal liability might be.

- Then consider which crimes are relevant. There are actually only a limited number of crimes on the specification, and you should be able to run through them in your mind. You might consider whether there are several possible offences arising out of the same incident. If the question relates to homicide, start with murder and then consider whether in fact the question relates to manslaughter. The examiner often helps you by requiring you to consider, for example, involuntary manslaughter.

■ Restrict yourself to discussing the law covered by the specification. You may well think that a character in a problem has committed a property offence or has been negligent, but these things are not being examined on this paper, and a discussion of them is unlikely to gain you marks (except for negligence in the context of gross negligence manslaughter).

■ When writing about a particular crime, make sure you deal with all aspects of the *actus reus* and *mens rea*, but say very little about those parts that are not in question. Concentrate on those where the application of the law to the problem is not clear and then conclude (taking into account any defences that might be apparent).

■ Give a concise explanation of the relevant legal principles. Do not waste time talking about related, but irrelevant, matters that you happen to know about. If, for instance, a question is clearly about s18 of the Offences Against the Person Act 1861, assault may well be irrelevant.

■ Where you can, give the names of relevant cases to illustrate the legal principles you are discussing. You do not have to explain the fact of the case unless you think it helps your discussion.

■ Be aware that it is not enough just to explain the law. You need to go on to apply the law to the scenario. This means that you need to discuss what the position of the characters is, and make sure you do it at each stage of your answer.

■ When answering an evaluative question, make sure you focus on the area of law asked in the question.

■ Don't be worried if there doesn't seem to be a definite answer. Sometimes scenarios are written deliberately to pose awkward questions. Discuss both sides of an issue and consider the application of the law for both views.

You should now be able to:

■ complete an answer to a scenario question in criminal law in an organised fashion with the purpose of gaining as high a mark as possible.

Read this scenario, together with its questions, and then complete the activities that follow it.

Scenario 1

Farrah, who was 14 years old, began to receive notes through the post which contained drawings of dead bodies and statements such as 'This will be you'. In consequence, she became very reluctant to leave the house and had to have specialist counselling for depression and panic attacks. Eventually, Farrah's mother, Gill, discovered that the notes were being sent by Isi, a girl in Farrah's class at school, and she went round to confront Isi at her house. When she did so, a furious argument broke out on the doorstep, during which Isi grabbed Gill's hair and slapped her very hard three or four times. Gill then managed to push Isi, who tripped over the doorstep and fell backwards through a glass door panel, suffering deep cuts to her arm and face. Isi's father, Jack, was very angry about these events. Whilst driving through town, he saw Farrah's 13-year-old brother, Karl, walking along the street. He rapidly braked, forced Karl into the car, and drove off into the countryside. When the car stopped at a junction, Karl managed to jump out and run away. Jack panicked and drove off, and so did not see that, almost immediately, Karl was struck by a car driven by Leon as it came round a bend. Karl was thrown into a ditch and Leon drove away without stopping. Karl was not discovered until the next day, by which time he had died from his injuries.

1   **(a)**   Discuss the criminal liability of Isi and of Gill.   *(25 marks)*

       (b)   Discuss the criminal liability of Jack and of Leon for the involuntary manslaughter of Karl.   *(25 marks)*

Question (a):

1. Isi's possible liability in relation to Farrah is for the offences of assault and assault occasioning actual bodily harm. This requires you to discuss the issues of fear of 'immediate' violence, psychiatric injury, and *mens rea*. You might also discuss unlawful and malicious infliction of grievous bodily harm.

2. Isi's possible liability in relation to Gill is the offence of battery or possible assault (battery) occasioning ABH).

3. Gill's possible liability in relation to Isi is for unlawful and malicious wounding/infliction of GBH. You need to discuss issues of the definition of the relevant injury and of *mens rea* (discussion of assault occasioning actual bodily harm may also be needed).

4. Discuss the plea of self-defence by Gill concentrating on the need for force, and proportion in force used.

5. Prepare a paragraph by paragraph plan for each character and each offence, marking on where you will use cases to support your explanations.

6. Write full answers based on your plans. Use continuous prose, make sure your information is organised and that your spelling is accurate.

Question (b):

1. In relation to Jack you need to discuss the offence of unlawful act manslaughter based on the unlawful abduction (seen in general terms, as kidnap/false imprisonment (no technical detail required as it is not part of the specification) or, perhaps, as battery with continuing threat amounting to an assault).

2. A discussion of causation issues involving the attempted escape and the role of Leon.

3. In relation to Leon – the offence of gross negligence manslaughter. Your argument may be based on either or both of Leon's acts in driving into Karl, or his omission in failing to assist or get help for him.

4. As with question (a), a paragraph by paragraph plan for each character and each offence, marking on where you will use cases to support your explanations.

5. Finally, write a full answer based on your plans.

Now read this second scenario and attempt the questions that follow it.

Scenario 2

Early one morning, Alan was standing on a stepladder, washing the windows of his house with a powerful detergent solution. Bob and Chris came walking noisily up the street, having spent all night out, drinking alcohol. Bob shouted something and suddenly veered across the street in Alan's direction, followed by Chris, who was trying to take hold of his arm. Alan was convinced that Bob was coming to knock him off the stepladder, and quickly got down and threw the bucket of detergent solution over Bob. Some of the solution also went over Chris, causing him to suffer an extreme allergic reaction which required hospital treatment for damage to the skin on his face. In fact, though very drunk, Bob had merely wanted to have a friendly talk to Alan.

Dave, who lived in the same street as Alan, had become obsessive about cleaning his car and ensuring that he could park it outside his house. He suffered great stress and became angry when he was prevented from doing either. He had begun to believe that his neighbours, Edward in particular, were splashing his car with mud and deliberately parking immediately outside his house to stop him parking there. When Dave saw Edward park there, he rushed out and told him to move his car. Edward swore at him before walking off. Dave went into his kitchen, seized a knife, and ran after Edward. As he heard footsteps behind him, Edward turned and a brief struggle took place, during which Dave stabbed Edward in the leg. The stab wound severed a main artery and Edward rapidly bled to death.

1 **(a)** Discuss the criminal liability of Alan and of Bob arising out of the incident in the street. *(25 marks)*

   (b) Discuss the criminal liability of Dave for the murder of Edward. *(25 marks)*

3A Evaluation of fatal and non-fatal offences against the person

Introduction

This chapter aims to consider the areas of the law of contract that you have studied (apart from involuntary manslaughter that does not need to be evaluated in this AQA specification). For each part that you do need to evaluate, there are a number of points made that you can use to develop your arguments. You should remember that every aspect of the law has its good and bad points. Indeed, in criminal law, these may well vary with the point of view of the person considering the law; a victim may view the law differently to the accused and the general public may view the law differently again.

As you will appreciate, a great deal of time and care is taken by experts when drafting an Act of Parliament. Nevertheless, statutes have to be interpreted in the light of the infinite range of human behaviour, and according to the ever-changing nature of society and the way in which business operates. The common law, too, has developed to accommodate these changes. Over the years, judges refine and clarify the law to reflect the needs of the time. In many cases this is entirely successful, and adds to our understanding of what the law is on a particular point.

It also often happens, however, that a particular area of law is capable of ambiguity, and we find that conflicting decisions occur. There is a real risk that injustices might happen as a result. In these cases, there comes a point where it may be necessary to introduce reforms. These would take the form of new legislation, and their aim would be to:

- clarify existing areas of difficulty or ambiguity
- change the law where necessary
- introduce new laws to reflect present needs.

Each of the topics are evaluated in turn. You should be able to write an essay on each topic so as to be prepared fully for the exam.

1 Murder

Murder

There are several aspects of the law relating to murder which are considered to be in need of change or clarification. The main ones are:

- The necessary intent.
- The use of force in self-defence.
- The mandatory life sentence.

Intent

In *Moloney* (1985), Lord Bridge said that in the great majority of cases it would be enough for a trial judge to ask the jury to consider whether the prosecution had satisfied them that the defendant had intended a particular consequence. In cases where there is a shooting or stabbing, there is usually no problem. However, establishing *mens rea* in cases where the prime intent was not to kill, will inevitably involve problems. What did the defendant intend? What did he foresee might happen as the result of his act? Only the defendant himself can possibly know what was in his mind at the time. In cases like *Moloney* (1985), even the defendant himself might not have known.

As things stand at the moment, a person who intends to cause serious bodily harm and actually causes his victim's death is guilty of murder. But should a defendant whose only intention is to cause serious bodily harm be as guilty of murder as one who deliberately sets out to kill? And what of the defendant whose main intention is not even to cause serious bodily harm? As was seen above, the defendants in *Hancock and Shankland* (1986) maintained that their only motive was to block the road. They did not intend to cause serious bodily harm, let alone death. They were both convicted of murder, although this verdict was changed on appeal to one of manslaughter. It is the foresight of consequences which causes the main area of concern. This is an area which subsequent cases, (as considered above), have done little to clarify.

Over the years it has often been suggested that the criminal law be **codified**. This would mean that murder would be included in new legislation. A draft criminal code was produced in 1989, in which the following definition of murder was proposed:

> A person is guilty of murder if he causes the death of another –
>
> **a** intending to cause death; or
>
> **b** intending to cause serious personal harm and being aware that he may cause death.

This would mean that a defendant who did not intend to kill, but had the intention as described in (b), above, could still be found guilty of murder. This would happen only if the jury was sure that the defendant was aware that his action could cause death. However, no such attempt at codifying the criminal law has yet been made, probably due to shortage of parliamentary time.

As to what the word 'intention' actually means, some help is provided by the Criminal Justice Act 1967. Section 8 of this Act states that:

> A court or jury in determining whether a person has committed an offence:
>
> **a** shall not be bound in law to infer that he intended or foresaw a result of his actions by reason of its being a natural and probable consequence of those actions, but
>
> **b** shall decide whether he did intend or foresee that result by reference to all the evidence, drawing such inferences from the evidence as appear proper in the circumstances.

Again, the Law Commission in its report *Offences Against the Person and General Principles* (1993) proposed that the word 'intentionally' should be defined thus:

> A person acts intentionally with respect to a result when:
>
> **a** it is his purpose to cause it; or
>
> **b** although it is not his purpose to cause it, he knows that it would occur in the ordinary course of events if he were to succeed in his purpose of causing some other result.

The introduction of this reform would go a long way towards clarifying the rather confusing situation caused by *Woollin* (1998) and *Matthews and Alleyne* (2003).

Self-defence

The Criminal Law Act 1967, s3 states that a person may use 'such force as is reasonable in the circumstances' in self-defence or to prevent a crime being committed. What is reasonable depends on what the defendant honestly and instinctively thought the needs of the moment to be. The situation as it stands at present therefore is that a person who kills in self-defence, or to prevent a crime, either:

▪ has a complete defence, in which case he is innocent of the charge of murder; or

▪ if his use of force is considered to be disproportionate, he is found guilty of murder.

It can be seen therefore that the dividing line between what is reasonable force in the circumstances and what is not determines either complete guilt or compete innocence. This harsh all-or-nothing situation results in the defendant either walking free from the court, or being sentenced to life imprisonment. It is clearly unjust that a person who oversteps the mark of what is reasonable force, usually in a situation of considerable stress, faces a term of life imprisonment. Two cases illustrate the problems arising from these situations.

In **Clegg (1994)** the defendant was a soldier on duty in Northern Ireland before the peace settlement. He was at a road checkpoint when a car came towards him at high speed. Seeing that it was not going to stop, he fired at it. His last shot hit a girl passenger in the back seat and killed her. Evidence showed that the car had already passed him when he fired that final shot. It was held that under the circumstances neither he nor anyone else was any longer in danger, therefore his plea of self-defence or defence of another should not succeed. He was found guilty of murder, a decision which was upheld on appeal.

In **Martin (Anthony Edward) (2001)**, the defendant lived alone in an isolated farmhouse in East Anglia which had been burgled in the past. On this particular occasion, Martin, woken by the sounds of someone entering his property, took his shotgun and fired without warning into the darkness. One of the intruders, 16-year-old Fred Barras, was shot in the back and killed. Martin was found guilty of murder. On appeal his plea of self-defence was rejected on the grounds that the force he had used was unreasonable. However, his conviction was reduced to manslaughter on the grounds of diminished responsibility. He was freed in 2003.

This case caused some disquiet. In February 2005, the Crown Prosecution Service and the Association of Chief Police Officers jointly issued a leaflet containing new guidelines. These aimed at reassuring householders that they would not necessarily face prison as a result of tackling intruders who were burgling their homes. If householders do what they 'honestly and instinctively believe is necessary in the heat of the moment', they will be unlikely to end up in court. This is the case even if a weapon is used and the intruder is seriously injured or killed. In addition, the law does not expect that a householder has to be attacked before he uses force to defend himself. Householders are reminded that they are not entitled to use force maliciously, or by way of retribution or revenge. The leaflet states that, 'As a general rule, the more extreme the circumstances and the fear felt, the more force you can lawfully use in self-defence'.

It has been suggested by the Law Commission that self-defence might be made a partial defence, resulting in a conviction for manslaughter rather than murder. An alternative suggestion was that if the mandatory life sentence for murder were to be abolished, judges would have the discretion to pass suitable sentences in such cases.

Mandatory life sentence

The **mandatory** life **sentence** for murder was laid down by the Murder (Abolition of the Death Penalty) Act 1965. The reason for this was that murder is generally held to be the most dreadful of crimes and deserves the maximum sentence permitted by the law. There was also an element of appeasement of those who opposed the abolition of the death penalty.

A judge must impose life imprisonment on any person aged 18 or over who is found guilty of murder. A person between the ages of 10 and 17 is 'detained at Her Majesty's pleasure'. This means indefinitely, until such a time as it is deemed safe to return him to society.

Objections to the mandatory life sentence are often put forward, however. It is suggested that although murder is a dreadful crime and deserves to be punished, there is no latitude for the judge to vary the sentence according to the seriousness of the killing. Murders cover varying degrees of seriousness. On the one hand, there are the cold-blooded serial killers like Sutcliffe or the Wests, and ruthless terrorist bombers belonging to extremist groups. On the other hand, there are those who kill from motives of compassion, ('mercy killers'), or those like Anthony Martin who overstep the limits of reasonable force in self-defence. All convictions for murder, of whatever degree of seriousness, attract the same sentence – life imprisonment. Another objection to the mandatory life sentence is that, in order to avoid it, inappropriate verdicts of manslaughter might be returned. This has happened in the case of so-called 'mercy killings', where the defence of diminished responsibility has been accepted on the flimsiest of evidence to avoid a conviction for murder.

Suggestions for reform of the law in this matter continue to be made. If life imprisonment usually does not mean 'for life', then why call it life imprisonment, and why insist on it being passed? One suggestion is to abolish the mandatory life sentence and make it **discretionary**. Other crimes, such as manslaughter, rape, wounding with intent, and indeed attempted murder, attract a maximum of life imprisonment. It is, however, discretionary; the judge may impose any sentence up to and including life imprisonment, according to the seriousness of the offence. If the punishment for murder were to be discretionary life imprisonment, a judge would have the power to impose life (meaning for life) for the most serious murders. For other killings, he could impose a term of years reflecting their relative seriousness.

Another suggestion is that different degrees of murder could be introduced. In this way, the most serious murders would attract a mandatory life sentence. Less serious ones would attract a discretionary life sentence. The Law Commission in its recent report on homicide, (2006) recommended that voluntary manslaughter should be reclassified as 'second degree murder'.

When imposing the mandatory life imprisonment for murder, a judge has the power to recommend that the defendant serve a minimum number of years before being eligible for release. He can also recommend that the defendant should never be released; life imprisonment meaning literally for life. By making such recommendations, a judge can reflect the seriousness of the offence. It may be for this reason that no moves have yet been made to abolish the mandatory life sentence.

Key terms

Discretionary sentence: the judge has the power to pass any sentence up to and including the maximum laid down by law; for example, theft carries a maximum sentence of seven years; a judge may sentence offenders to anything from an absolute discharge to the maximum seven years, depending on the seriousness of the offence.

2 Voluntary manslaughter

The potential areas of reform to the law of voluntary manslaughter necessarily centre on the two defences which give rise to it.

Provocation

One of the main difficulties with the defence of provocation is raised by the wording of the section in the Homicide Act which created it: '… the provocation was enough to make a reasonable man do as he did …'

The question has to be asked, can any man be described as 'reasonable' if he reacts to provocation to such an extent that he kills? Furthermore, there is no real consensus on what is meant by a 'reasonable man'. Certainly judges over the years have found it a difficult concept to explain, and have not so far produced a convincing definition.

The judiciary have had problems with the required power of self-control. The different approaches in *Luc Thiet Thuan* (1996) and in *Smith (Morgan)* (2000), lead to the Privy Council decision in *Holley* (2005). This would appear to be adopted, particularly given the cases of *James and Karimi* (2006). Whilst this whole episode in English law calls into question the doctrine of precedent and the role of the Privy Council, it reflects the problem that lawyers have in dealing with an uncertain and changing law on provocation.

Another objection to the law as it stands at the moment is that there seems to be an almost endless range of conduct capable of provoking. It could be vicious bullying at one end of the scale. At the other end there is the case of *Doughty* (1986). Here, the defendant was 'provoked' by the crying of a very small baby, the provocation coming from conduct which was entirely innocent. In all kinds of situations it follows that often where a defendant alleges he was provoked, that provocation allows a defence for anger. There is no such defence where a defendant kills from love, compassion, fear or despair.

These shortcomings were pointed out by the Law Commission in its 2003 consultation paper on the special defences to murder. As yet, no action has been taken by way of reform.

There is also a widespread feeling that it is a defence which favours men, who are more likely to experience sudden loss of self-control. As is illustrated by cases such as *Ahluwalia* (1992) and *Thornton* (1992), women are more prone to the 'slow burn' syndrome. This state of affairs has to some extent been alleviated by using the defence of diminished responsibility.

The question of reform in this area is a difficult one. The Law Commission suggested that if the mandatory life sentence for murder were to be abolished, the defence of provocation could also be done away with. This would allow the judge to pass a sentence which would reflect the circumstances of the case. The objection to this course of action is that it would be left to the judge to decide on the degree of self-control expected by society. Surely that would be better left to a jury.

Diminished responsibility

The main problems with this defence are:

- The words of s2 of the Homicide Act are not clear as to what constitute the causes of abnormality of mind.
- Unlike other defences, the burden of proof is on the defendant. In the case of provocation, the defence only has to raise the issue, and the prosecution has to disprove it. This is not the case with diminished responsibility, where the defendant has to show, on the balance of probabilities, that there were circumstances that would warrant that defence.

There have been various proposals for reform of the law in this area. The Law Commission's consultation paper, 2003, (referred to above in reform of the law of provocation), felt that the words in brackets in s2 of the Homicide Act have given rise to conflicting opinions of what they mean. Cases over the years have shown significant differences of opinion between doctors as to what conditions fall within this definition. They also raised the question as to whether 'substantial impairment of mental responsibility' should be a matter settled necessarily by the medical profession. Should psychiatrists be asked to give their opinions on what are felt by many people to be essentially moral issues?

The draft Criminal Code, published in 1989, (referred to in reform of the law of murder, above), proposed the following definition of diminished responsibility:

1 A person who, but for this section, would be guilty of murder is not guilty of murder if, at the time of his act, he is suffering from such mental abnormality as is a substantial enough reason to reduce his offence to manslaughter …

2 … 'mental abnormality' means mental illness, arrested or incomplete development of mind, psychopathic disorder, and any other disorder or disability of mind, except intoxication.

3 Where a person suffering from mental abnormality is also intoxicated, this section applies only where it would apply if he were not intoxicated.

If adopted, this wording would have widened the definition of the causes of mental abnormality, as in (2) above. It also would have dealt, in (3), with the problem of the intoxicated defendant.

In addition, this proposal would have shifted the burden of proof to the prosecution to disprove the defence once the defendant has raised evidence of it. This would have brought it into line with the defence of provocation. It would have had the benefit of causing less confusion to juries where a defendant pleads both defences to murder.

Reclassification of homicide

The 2006 report on homicide by the Law Commission suggested that voluntary manslaughter should be reclassified as a 'second degree murder'. It would still attract a discretionary life sentence, as it does now. Reclassifying it as a degree of murder would recognise the fact that the killing was intentional rather than accidental.

A summary of the Law Commission's proposals is as follows:

First degree murder (mandatory life sentence) would cover:

1 intentional killing; or
2 killing with an intention to cause serious injury, in the awareness that there is a serious risk of causing death.

Second degree murder (discretionary life sentence; guidelines on minimum terms) would cover:

1 killing with intent to do serious injury
2 killing with intent to cause some injury or fear or risk of injury, in the awareness that there is a serious risk of causing death; and
3 killing with the intent for first degree murder, but where a defence of provocation, diminished responsibility or suicide pact succeeds.

Manslaughter (discretionary life sentence) would cover the various kinds of involuntary manslaughter as exist at the moment, (see Chapter 2, Involuntary manslaughter).

By introducing a three-tier structure of homicide, the Law Commission suggested that it would 'give the jury in homicide trials greater power to reflect in their verdict the extent to which the offender was at fault in killing'.

As yet, no action has been taken on these proposals.

Activities

1 Look at the comments on the offences you have studied in this chapter and make a table with a list of criticisms of the present law on the offences on one side and a matching list of proposed reforms on the other.

2 Look at any murder or voluntary manslaughter case you have studied or one that is in the media currently and discuss the effect of the proposed reforms on that case.

You should now be able to:

■ evaluate the law relating to murder, provocation and diminished responsibility

■ describe proposals for reform in those areas

■ construct an appropriate essay on these topics.

3 Non-fatal offences

It is unanimously accepted that the law on non-fatal offences is in need of reform. A Law Commission Report published in 1993 described the OAPA 1861 and law of common assault as 'inefficient as a vehicle for controlling violence' where 'many aspects of the law are still obscure and its application erratic'. It is routinely criticised as being chaotic, unjust, irrational, outdated and unclear. The essential problem lies with the fact that the OAPA 1861 is Victorian legislation that was never intended to be a logical and consistent set of rules applying to non-fatal offences. Instead, it was a piece of legislation that simply brought all the then applicable laws into one Act. Hence the sections are randomly ss47, 20 and 18 because the Act also includes other sections setting out the law on matters as diverse as poisoning and kidnapping. As a consequence there is no uniformity of language used between the sections and nor is there a coherent hierarchy in respect of the seriousness of the offences. Matters are made worse by the fact that the legislation suffers from poor drafting allowing a woeful lack of explanation of *mens rea* and failure to define terms. We add to this the basic problem that the courts are having to apply a piece of legislation drafted in the reign of Queen Victoria to situations created in a very different modern society. We shall look at these criticisms in more detail before considering any proposed reforms. Much of material that you study in this topic is ideally suited for further discussion in Unit 4C when you study Concepts of law.

Language

Key words and phrases used in ss47, 20 and 18 are not defined in the statute so need to be explained through case interpretation. It is not appropriate that statutory offence terminology such as 'actual', 'grievous' and 'bodily harm' is continually evolving through cases and appeal processes and this can only lead to inconsistent decision making.

Another criticism is that much of the language is old fashioned, badly drafted and used inconsistently. An example is the use of the word 'maliciously' at ss20 and 18 which is not defined in the Act. It was interpreted in *R* v *Cunningham* (1957) to cover recklessness but its usual and modern meaning would usually imply bad motive and wickedness. Furthermore, whilst 'maliciously' provides the only clues as to *mens rea* under s20 it has no purpose whatsoever in s18, where the *mens rea* is made clear by the words 'with intent'.

We have previously touched upon the fact that even the word 'assault' is used inconsistently by those drafting the relevant legislation and there are no clear statutory explanations as to what is meant by an assault or a battery. The term 'common assault' is correctly understood to mean both of the distinct offences of assault and battery. This confusing use of terminology is compounded by vague drafting which results in s39 of the CJA 1988 referring to 'common assault and battery' but s40 of that Act only referring to 'a common assault'. Section 47 of the OAPA 1861 only uses the word 'assault' when this is also meant to cover battery.

The use of the word 'inflict' in respect of grievous bodily harm under s20 as opposed to 'cause' in s18 has also been subject to criticism. 'Inflict' was originally understood to have a narrower meaning than 'cause' and requiring an assault or battery, but it has now been established in *R* v *Ireland*; *R* v *Burstow* (1997) that neither is necessary and 'inflict' should be given the same meaning as 'cause'. This interpretation has been criticised for permitting liability under s20 where there is insufficient fault on the part of the defendant to justify such a serious conviction. If an assault or battery is not required then, in theory, I might be held liable for the serious psychiatric harm caused to my friend by telling her she looked a fright on her wedding day. I might not have intended to cause her harm but if I knew that she was a depressive and that this comment might severely aggravate her condition, then I could have the necessary *mens rea* of subjective recklessness. Strangely, I would not be liable if her psychiatric harm only amounted to actual bodily harm since an assault is required under s47. It does not seem right that it is easier to prove a s20 charge than the lesser charge of s47.

The meaning of 'wounding' is also not set out in the Act and case law has provided that it means a breaking of both layers of the skin. This does not match the normal understanding of the word and, as pointed out earlier, this means that a person can be charged under s20 for wounding by merely pricking their victim's finger with a pin. However, the Charging Standard recommends that such minor injuries including small cuts and lacerations would be more appropriately charged under s47. It must be remembered, however, that the Charging Standard is designed only as a set of guidelines to assist prosecutors to choose the appropriate charge. It is not legally binding upon the courts and liability, once the charge is determined, will be decided in accordance with statute and case authority.

Hierarchy of seriousness

Section 39 of the CJA 1988 and ss47, 20 and 18 were not designed to work as one coherent hierarchy of offences. Accordingly, there is not a logical sentencing structure that reflects the seriousness of each offence.

The legal philosopher HLA Hart wrote that this 'might bring the law into disrepute' as 'principles of justice or fairness between different offenders require morally distinguishable offences to be treated differently and morally similar offences to be treated alike.'

There is a potential for overlap between s39 of the CJA 1988 and s47 since the threshold of harm that qualifies as actual bodily harm is set very low and includes all harm (save for serious harm and some wounds) that is considered more than 'transient and trifling' (R v *Miller* (1954)). Hart would argue that injuries at the lower scale of s47 and those charged under s39 of the CJA 1988 are morally similar and the significant disparity between the respective sentences of five years and six months is therefore unjust. Even more surprising is the fact that although grievous bodily harm is a much more serious offence than actual bodily harm, the maximum sentence for both s20 and s47 is five years. The sentence then jumps to life imprisonment for s18, which might seem a disproportionate increase when the difference between the two offences is one of motive only, as the harm requirement is the same.

Mens rea

According to *R* v *Roberts* (1971) a person is liable for actual bodily harm under s47 where there was only recklessness or intention as to causing a battery. Similarly under *R* v *Mowatt* (1976) liability for grievous bodily harm will arise where the defendant intended only minor harm or was reckless as to the fact that some physical harm might be caused to some person. This has been criticised as failing to match the punishment to the culpability of the defendant and therefore unjust.

Outdated

The legislation was drafted in a different age and needs updating to modernise the language and to better reflect the concerns of modern society. Lord Steyn commented in *Ireland*; *Burstow* (1997) that 'the Victorian legislator … would not have in mind psychiatric illness' but illnesses affecting the mind are now an established area of medical health and legislation needs to reflect this. Remember also that the telephone was not invented in 1861, let alone e-mail and text! Judges found ways to establish liability for psychiatric harm in the stalking cases but the liberal interpretations they imposed upon the wording of the Act in order to achieve this have been the subject of much criticism. Stalkers can now be prosecuted under the Protection from Harassment Act 1997 as opposed to the OAPA 1861. This Act provides that a person will be sentenced to up to five years imprisonment if convicted of 'a course of conduct (which) causes another to fear, on at least two occasions, that violence will be used against them.'

Judges also had to strain interpretation to convict the defendant for grievous bodily harm in *Dica* (2004). The Act is not suitable to deal with the prevention of the spread of Aids or indeed any other sexually transmitted diseases.

Reforms

Widespread criticism of the legislation governing the non-fatal offences led to the Criminal Law Revision Committee publishing proposals for reform in 1981. These proposals formed the basis of the **Law Commission Report 1993** and an attached draft Bill which was never put before Parliament. The new Labour government produced a draft Bill in 1998 essentially in the same form as the Law Commission Bill. The **1998 draft Bill** includes the following proposals:

■ Statutory definitions are provided for assault and battery.

Key terms

Law Commission Report 1993: the Report 'Legislating the Criminal Code: Offences Against the Person and General Principles', which includes a draft Bill.

1998 draft Bill: the draft Offences Against the Person Bill issued by the government (and based upon the proposals of the Law Commission Report 1993) which is included in a Consultation Document entitled 'Violence: Reforming the Offences Against the Person Act 1861'.

■ Section 47 is replaced by the offence of intentionally or recklessly causing injury to another person with a maximum prison sentence of five years. Prosecution will no longer need to prove that the injury was caused by an assault or battery. 'Injury' is defined to mean 'physical injury' which includes pain, unconsciousness and any impairment of a person's physical condition and also 'mental injury' which includes any impairment of a person's mental health.

■ Sections 20 and 18 are replaced by the separate offences of recklessly causing a serious injury to another and intentionally causing a serious injury to another. The maximum prison sentences are seven years and life imprisonment respectively. There is no longer any reference to wounding so the problem that a minor wound can be charged under these sections is removed. The troublesome word 'inflict' is removed and all references are to 'caused'.

■ The harm intended or foreseen must correspond to the offence committed contrary to the *mens rea* principles in *Roberts* (1971) and *Mowatt* (1976). Accordingly, the reckless defendant will only be convicted under the new s47 if he has foresight of the *injury* as opposed to the battery that caused it and he must have foresight of serious injury to be convicted for grievous bodily harm.

■ Save for the offence of intentionally causing serious injury, 'physical injury' does not include disease and therefore a person will only be liable if he *intends* to infect another with a serious sexual disease and reckless infection will not be an offence.

■ Intention and recklessness are defined.

The draft Bill is clearly an improvement but has, nevertheless, attracted criticism. Such criticism includes the argument that the offence replacing s47 should also be divided into two separately punishable offences based on recklessness or intent as there is no logic as to why the different *mens rea* should only be relevant to serious injuries. Furthermore, the definition of 'injury' still fails to establish a clear dividing line between what might constitute an injury and what would be charged as the lesser charge of assault. 'Serious' is still not defined and the term 'assault' continues to be used to mean both an assault and a battery.

In his forward to the 1998 draft Bill, the Home secretary pledged his government's commitment to modernising and improving the law. Regrettably, the Bill has yet to be enacted and the courts are still relying upon the OAPA 1861.

Activities

1 Using case authorities from this section explain how the courts have interpreted the following words:

■ actual

■ grievous

■ bodily harm.

2 Write down some reasons as to why it might be a disadvantage that these words are not defined in the OAPA 1861.

3 Make a table with a list of criticisms of the present law on non-fatal offences on one side and a matching list of proposed reforms on the other.

4 The defences

Evaluation of the defence of insanity and automatism

Insanity and automatism have been combined because the substantive law on these defences is so intertwined.

A typical criticism of the defence can be found in a House of Commons debate in 1967, when Dr Winstanley said:

> These rules were formulated following the case of Daniel M'Naghten and they are still in force despite the fact that they have been almost constantly subjected to criticism and attack, not only by the medical profession but by lawyers and members of the general public.
>
> I do not need to repeat the various attacks that have been made over the years, but it is interesting to note that as long ago as 1874 the noble Lord, Lord Bramwell, giving evidence to the Select Committee on the Homicide Law Amendment Bill in June, 1874, said that the present law lays down such a definition of madness that nobody is hardly ever really mad enough to be within it. That is the kind of view which has been held by the many people who have frequently criticised this form of the law. We had much criticism at the time of the Royal Commission on Capital Punishment, since when we have had a general acceptance of the fact that the M'Naghten Rules, while they provide a basis, do not necessarily provide a satisfactory one.
>
> Briefly, the important rules – two of them; there are others which are less important today – provide that a person can only be found insane in relation to a criminal act if, first, he is unaware of the nature and quality of the act which he is doing, or, secondly, if he is so aware, that he is not aware that that particular act is wrong.
>
> Many people have held that we should alter the law to embody provisions to cover the type of mental abnormality which could result in a person, while he was aware of what he was doing, or while he might be aware that what he was doing was wrong, was none the less subject to an uncontrollable impulse or otherwise unable to control his behaviour.

Source: http://hansard.millbanksystems.com

There are a number of points to consider about the defence. They are:

- the shift of the burden of proof
- the definition of insanity
- the ineffectiveness of the verdict
- the scope of the defence.

The shift of the burden of proof

There is a different standard of proof depending on whether the defence or the prosecution raise the issue of insanity. This is likely to confuse a jury, or at least be deemed an irrelevant distinction by many. This also conflicts with the *Woolmington* v *DPP* (1935) principle that the burden is always on the prosecution to prove the offence, not to prove a defence.

The definition of insanity

The definition of insanity is said to be 'medically irrelevant'. The legal definition of insanity has not advanced significantly since 1843; in 1953 evidence was given to the Royal Commission on Capital Punishment that doctors even then regarded the legal definition to be obsolete and misleading. The distinction between internal and external factors relating to diabetes and hyperglycaemia and hypoglycaemia is particularly arcane.

In any event, no one would recognise that a diabetic person was insane purely as a result of their condition!

The rules currently do not distinguish between defendants who represent a public danger (the claimed main purpose of the special verdict) and those who do not. Illnesses such as diabetes and epilepsy can be controlled by medication.

The ineffectiveness of the verdict

A finding of insanity can be an indefinite place in a secure hospital, whereas a conviction for murder or grievous bodily harm with intent may well result in a life sentence that does not mean life and be given a tariff of between ten and fifteen years. In these circumstances, most defendants would prefer the conviction and sentence. Given the numbers of prisoners with severe mental problems (if not insanity), it appears that few consider raising the defence of insanity.

Article 5 of the European Convention on Human Rights provides that a person of unsound mind may only be detained where proper account of objective medical expertise has been taken. It is not always the case that a plea of insanity can be said to have done so. It is to be noted that there is likely to be a human rights challenge on all indeterminate sentences.

The scope of the defence

The Butler Committee recommended that proof of severe mental disorder should be sufficient to negate responsibility. This would create a presumption of no criminal responsibility where there is proof of a severe mental disorder. However, this assumes a lack of criminal responsibility simply because there is evidence of some sort of mental dysfunction, rather than establishing a standard of criminal responsibility. This may be seen to be an interesting view of fault based liability. This then questions the application of the defence to all crimes rather than those involving *mens rea* only.

Law reform

The Law Commission's 10th programme of Law Reform includes:

Project 7: unfitness to plead and the insanity defence

1.20 The current law is based on rules formulated in the first half of the 19th century when the science of psychiatry was in its infancy. Those rules are in need of reform. There are important unresolved issues which include the scope of a trial of the facts following a finding of unfitness to plead. In addition, there is a need to reconsider the relationship between automatism and insanity and that between diminished responsibility and insanity.'

www.lawcom.gov.uk

It is not known when the report will be completed, but it is clear that there will be proposals for reforming the law.

Evaluation of the defence of intoxication

The defence of intoxication is a relatively modern invention – the law originally took the view that if you were intoxicated, you should be criminally responsible as you got yourself into that state. The current law does not depart significantly from this, but does distinguish between voluntary and involuntary intoxication and does distinguish between a certain basic criminal responsibility and crimes where a specific intention must be formed by the defendant.

There are a number of criticisms to make of the law:

- The distinction between specific and basic intent.
- The relationship of intoxication to other defences.
- The level of intoxication and the relationship of alcohol and drugs.

The distinction between specific and basic intent

The general law takes a subjective approach to *mens rea*. If there is no subjective *mens rea* there should be no liability as can be seen in the case of *R v G and R* (2003). The case of *Majewski* (1977) ignores this subjective approach for basic intent crimes. For specific intent crimes the orthodox approach will be applicable. However, for basic intent crimes, which are normally high in volume, the moral questionability of getting drunk is appreciated and a pragmatic approach is adopted. Intoxication is ignored and *mens rea* is constructed. It is asked what the *mens rea* would be like if the person were sober.

The distinction also requires judges to decide whether each criminal offence is one of basic or specific intent. This seems not to be settled as can be appreciated from the appeal in the case of **Heard (2007)** the offence of sexual assault contrary to s3 of the Sexual Offences Act 2003 was one of specific or basic intent. It seems surprising that Parliament does not make it clear in drafting an Act.

There are also some bizarre anomalies – for example attempted rape is a crime that can be defended by a plea of intoxication, rape cannot.

The relationship of intoxication to other defences

In the case of **Richardson and Irwin (1999)** the defendant students were messing around after drinking and held their friend over the balcony of his room. Unfortunately he fell and was severely injured. The court decided that the jury should consider the effect of alcohol on the consent to this horseplay.

In the defence of insanity, if the defendant's drink or drug taking produces a disease of the mind he can be found insane under the M'Naghten rules. This was discussed in the early case of *Davis* (1881) and approved in both *Beard* (1920) and *Gallagher* (1963).

Evaluation of the defence of consent

There are a number of points to consider about the defence. They are:

- the problem of informed consent
- consent and euthanasia
- individual freedom and its restriction.

The problem of informed consent

As has been seen in the cases discussed above, the law does not seem to fully recognise the situation where the consent has been given without a full appreciation of all the facts. This seems to negate consent from young people (*Burrell* v *Harmer* (1967)) but not always to adults who might otherwise reconsider their position as in *Richardson* (1998) and *Tabassum* (2000). This confusion needs clarifying.

Consent and euthanasia

The case for euthanasia is often argued on the basis of freedom to make decisions about life or medical treatment. This is also seen as an issue of consent. However, the principle also entails a responsibility to act ethically. While a patient is capable of giving valid consent, a doctor has no authority to treat the patient unless that consent is given. However, the patient cannot ethically refuse treatment with the intention to bring about his own death. This ethical objection to suicide is reflected

> ### Key cases
>
> **Heard (2007)**: in this case the court had to decide whether the offence of sexual assault contrary to s 3 of the Sexual Offences Act 2003 was one of basic or specific intent.
>
> **Richardson and Irwin (1999)**: the court decided that the effect of alcohol should be taken into account when considering the defence of consent

in law. Assisting a suicide is an offence but committing suicide is not. This is because people who try to kill themselves need help rather than punishment. There is therefore no legal right to suicide, and therefore no right to involve others in killing oneself. intentionally deprive oneself of life.

If the law were to allow some individuals to volunteer for euthanasia, this would also threaten the right to life of others, especially the elderly, the gravely ill and the disabled. Legalisation of euthanasia would make a clear statement to society that it was permissible for private citizens (e.g. doctors) to kill because they accepted the view that a patient's life was no longer worthwhile. Thus, cases such as Anthony Bland's required the courts to authorise his death. This seems to be a transfer of power to a small group of people, but the rules set up are so stringent that the individual's rights are paramount and the system will not allow easy decisions to terminate the life of any person with or without their consent.

Individual freedom and its restriction

It is difficult to understand that individual activities done with consent should not be lawful. However, the state does interfere where those individual freedoms are perceived in being used in an immoral manner and where the consent may not be freely given despite the appearance of so being. This can be seen in the case of *Brown* (1993).

Evaluation of the defence of self-defence/prevention of crime

There are a number of points to consider about the these defence in addition to those that you have studied in evaluating the law on murder in Chapter 1, Murder and voluntary manslaughter. They are:

- What is appropriate force?
- The all or nothing approach.

What is appropriate force?

In assessing the reasonableness of the force used, these questions need to be asked:

- Was the use of force justified? Was there a need for any force at all?
- Was the force used excessive in the circumstances?

These questions are answered on the basis of the facts as the accused honestly believed them to be as we have seen in the case of *Gladstone Williams* (1987). This is a subjective test. There is, however, an objective element to the test as the jury must then go on to ask themselves whether, on the basis of the facts as the accused believed them to be, a reasonable person would regard the force used as reasonable or excessive.

An example of the complexity of the defence can be seen in the case of *Armstrong Braun* (1998). In that case, the assault took place on a building site near Wrexham. The victim, a Mr Orritt, was using a mechanical digger when the defendant came up to him. The reason for the defendant's presence was that there had been a long-standing concern (which the defendant shared) for the fact that there was a habitat of Great Crested Newts on the site. The defendant was a 58 year old local County Councillor who had a sincere wish to protect the Great Crested Newt and to preserve its habitat. When he came on to the site, he took a wooden stake from a nearby fence and tried to use it to jam the foot controls of the digger. He also struck the roll bar of the digger once with the stake. He told Mr Orritt he was committing a crime. Mr Orritt then became angry and chased the defendant, who struck him once with the stake on his arm. The defendant genuinely thought this was the minimum necessary to stop the machine or to protect himself.

In his judgment, Brooke LJ said:

> On a number of occasions in recent years the Law Commission has drawn to the attention of Parliament the desirability of codifying the law of self-defence which causes a good deal of difficulty in its application to the lower courts, and this is another example of a case which has become quite unnecessarily complicated because of the theoretical glosses that might be applied to the uncodified law.

This can be seen in the problem that arises in a person's viewpoint. In the present case, for example, a defendant who asked himself what degree of response would be considered reasonable by people concerned about the destruction of our natural environment, might come up with a very different answer than if he were to judge his acts by the standards of building workers or property developers!

The all or nothing approach

This approach cannot work fairly as the whole point of the defence is that a person is either guilty or not guilty. If the defendant is guilty despite attempting to persuade the court to accept the defence, then he has the opportunity to use the circumstances as a plea in mitigation. This is satisfactory except in the case of murder where the defendant would still receive a life sentence and any other tariff type sentence that might be pertinent at the time. It can also be said that the defendant might have just tipped the balance as to unreasonable force.

Conclusion

All the defences have criticisms that can be made. It should also be noted that there are positive aspects as well as negative aspects of that criticism. You should be aware of that in constructing your essay to the part (c) answers in the exam. You should also note that any question on evaluation of the defences may well not focus on just a single defence.

Activities

1. Construct a chart of all the defences in the specification for this unit listing positive and negative criticisms that you have learned.

2. Plan an essay based on evaluating each of the following:
   - Insanity and automatism.
   - Consent and self-defence.
   - Intoxication.

You should now be able to:

- evaluate the individual defences
- state proposals for reform of the defences.

Contract law

Introduction

Unit 3 gives candidates a choice between the study of criminal law and contract law. The unit constitutes 50 per cent of the overall marks for the A2 section of the qualification, and 25 per cent of the overall marks for the A Level qualification. The Unit 3 examination is of 1.5 hours' duration. Candidates must answer one question. The examination paper will include both criminal law and contract law questions: Questions 1 and 2 being criminal law and Questions 3 and 4 being contract law. Candidates who choose criminal law will have to select one question to answer as will candidates who have chosen contract law. Each question is divided into three parts, all of which must be answered.

Each question is worth 75 marks. Each part is worth 25 marks. Parts (a) and (b) will be a test of your ability to select and apply the law to the given scenario, and part (c) will require an evaluative discussion of a stated area of the specification. All areas of the specification, including the remedies, are possible questions for a critical evaluation including proposals for reform. The one exception is that no critical evaluation question will be asked on discharge of contract.

All questions require essay style answers. In Parts (a) and (b), attainment of high grades is dependent on correct identification of the issues raised by the question, sound explanation of each of the points and clear application of the law to the facts disclosed. This may involve some consideration of alternatives where the law lacks clarity in its application to the scenario. In Part (c), illustration may be in many forms for example, legislation, cases, research, statistics, material from the media, and these need to be put into a coherent argument to answer the question set. Further exam tips are provided throughout each topic and at the end of the chapter.

Unit 3B comprises five chapters:

5 **Formation of contract:** concerned with the formation of contract.

6 **Contract terms:** deal with the terms of a contract.

7 **Vitiating factors:** considers the law with respect to misrepresentation.

8 **Discharge of contract:** concerned with the discharge of contracts.

9 **Remedies:** examines the remedies available for a breach of contract.

5 Formation of contract

1 Offer

The study of the law on contract will always start with the offer. This will be followed by an acceptance (Topic 2) that creates an agreement which may become a legally binding contract if other factors are also present (Topics 3, 4, and 5). The public believe they understand the meaning of an offer but as will be seen it has a very specific definition in law. This topic will consider the definition of an offer, what may appear to be an offer but is not, when an offer is created/ended and, finally, how an offer is communicated.

The offer

The nature of an offer

An **offer** is the first step in the creation of a contract. For example, Rameez wishes to sell his car and tells Leanne that his car is for sale to her for £1,000. Rameez is the **offeror** and Leanne is the **offeree**. The next step is accepting the offer.

Rameez has made a statement to Leanne which is an offer. A valid acceptance by Leanne will legally bind him to the terms of the offer which will lead to the creation of a binding contract.

It is important to distinguish between a **bilateral contract** and a **unilateral contract**.

Most contracts tend to be a bilateral contract where one party has made a promise to the other (to transfer ownership of the car) in return for the other's promise (to make a payment of £1,000).

An example of a bilateral contract is the agreement made between Rameez and Leanne for the purchase of the car.

A unilateral contract is when one party (Party 1) has promised to pay the other party (Party 2) a sum of money if Party 2 performs a certain act but Party 2 makes no promise in return to perform the act.

An example would be if Person A promises to pay Person B £500 if he repaints her caravan on Thursday. Person A has made a promise to pay Person B but that person is under no obligation to perform the act. If he decides on Thursday to repaint the caravan then there is an acceptance of the offer (see Topic 2) but Person A can do nothing if Person B chooses not to perform the task.

Who makes the offer – different situations

Sometimes one party wishes to commence negotiations with the other party rather than make an offer. For example, Rameez may suggest to Claire that she should look at his car as he is thinking of selling it for about £1,000. This may seem like an offer but is not – Rameez has merely made the first step in the negotiation process. This step is called an 'invitation to treat'. An invitation to treat may appear to be an offer but is an attempt by a party (usually a seller) to encourage the other party (the buyer) to make an offer.

In this topic you will learn how to:

- define an offer
- explain the nature of an offer
- distinguish between an offer and an invitation to treat
- explain when an offer is made
- describe the rules that decide when an offer comes to an end
- describe the different methods of, and importance of, communication of an offer
- apply the rules to a given situation.

Key terms

Offer: a statement of intent to be legally bound by the terms of the offer if it is accepted.

Offeror: a person making an offer to another person.

Offeree: a person receiving an offer from the offeror.

Bilateral contract: both parties to the agreement have obligations to perform.

Unilateral contract: only one party has obligations to do something.

Key cases

Pharmaceutical Society of GB v Boots Cash Chemists (1953): goods in a self-service store are an invitation to treat, not an offer.

Fisher v Bell (1961): a knife with a price label on it in a shop window was only an invitation to treat.

Partridge v Crittenden (1968): an advertisement in a newspaper that offered wild birds for sale was an invitation to treat not an offer for sale.

Carlill v Carbolic Smoke Ball Co. (1893): an advertisement could contain an offer if it was clearly meant to be taken seriously and the advertisement indicated the offeree should take a particular 'course of action'.

There are many examples of invitations to treat. They include:

Self-service displays

Goods on a shelf in a supermarket are an invitation to treat and not an offer, as shown in **Pharmaceutical Society of GB v Boots Cash Chemists (1953)**. Boots was prosecuted for offering medicines for sale without a pharmacist being present. This was an offence under the Pharmacy and Poisons Act 1933. The court decided that Boots were not guilty as the offer was made by the customer at the checkout. The invitation to treat invites the customer to make an offer to buy the goods from the seller. This rule allows a shopkeeper to refuse a sale under contract law, e.g. if the wrong price has been attached to the goods.

Shop window displays

A shop window display is only an invitation to treat. The customer makes the offer once inside the shop, as in the case of **Fisher v Bell (1961)**, where a shopkeeper was prosecuted under the Restriction of Offensive Weapons Act 1959, because he displayed a knife in the shop window with a ticket. He was found not guilty as he was not offering the knife for sale, it was an invitation to treat.

Advertisements

Advertisments in a newspaper or magazine are purely invitations to treat such as in the case of **Partridge v Crittenden (1968)**.

Lots at an auction

At an auction the auctioneer makes invitations to treat and the bidders make offers. The auctioneer then accepts the highest bid by banging his gavel. The bidder may withdraw an offer at any time up to the auctioneer's acceptance.

Situations <u>not an invitation to treat</u>

Sometimes what may seem like an invitation to treat may actually be an offer such as in the case of **Carlill v Carbolic Smoke Ball Co. (1893)**.

The company advertised its smoke ball stating if the buyer purchased the product, used it correctly and then caught the 'flu, the company would pay £100 in compensation. The advertisement also stated the company had deposited £1,000 with its bank as security for the compensation. Mrs Carlill bought the product used it and caught the 'flu. The advertisement was an offer, which Mrs Carlill had accepted by purchasing and then using the item (the 'course of action'). The court was also influenced by the words relating to the specific compensation promised and the money on deposit, which the court decided would show to a potential buyer that the company was serious in its claims.

This case is authority for two important propositions:

■ An advertisement may constitute an offer to the whole world, i.e. to anyone who reads it.

■ Acceptance may not have to be communicated to the offeror (see Topic 2).

Termination of an offer

Once an offer exists it is open for acceptance by the offeree. It may then become very important whether the offer is still in existence as if not then no agreement can flow from it. An offer can end (be terminated) in a variety of ways, some of which are explained below:

If properly withdrawn

If the offer is properly withdrawn *before* acceptance then no offer exists.

For example, Rameez may offer the car to Leanne but then withdraw the offer before she has accepted which results in the offer terminating.

In **Routledge v Grant (1828)** a seller of a house said the house was available for purchase for six weeks. The offeror then informed the offeree the offer had been withdrawn. The offeror was entitled to withdraw the offer before the offeree had accepted it. An example of an improperly withdrawn offer can be found in **Byrne v Van Tienhoven (1880)**.

The specified time for acceptance has passed

If the offer is stated to be open for acceptance until a particular date then it no longer exists after that date. In *Routledge v Grant* (1828) the offer would have automatically terminated after the six-week period had expired.

The offer terminates if a reasonable time has passed

In many situations an offer has no time limit placed upon it. The court allows the offer to exist for a *reasonable* time. The court will consider all the circumstances when reaching its decision, demonstrated in **Ramsgate Victoria Hotel v Montefiore (1866)**, where the defendant offered to buy shares in the hotel on 8 June. The hotel tried to accept the offer on 23 November, but the defendant no longer wanted the shares. The court decided that the five-month gap was too long and the offer had lapsed.

It would not be reasonable to expect an offer to buy shares to exist for six months as the value of shares fluctuates dramatically.

The offer is rejected

The rejection of an offer will terminate that offer. The making of a counter-offer is treated as a rejection (see Topic 2 and the case of *Hyde* v *Wrench* (1840)). Leanne would reject the offer by replying to Rameez that she would not buy the car, *or* by agreeing to buy the car but suggesting a price of £900.

Death of one of the parties

The general rule is that if the offeree dies the offer terminates. However, if the offeror dies an offeree's acceptance may still be valid (provided the death was unknown to the offeree).

By acceptance

If the offeree properly accepts the offer then the offer no longer exists, as it is now part of the agreement. If Leanne responds to the offer of Rameez by replying 'yes' then the offer is ended and an agreement is created. Rameez may no longer alter the terms of the offer, as it no longer exists.

Communication of the offer

The offeror must communicate the offer to the offeree – the offeree cannot accept an offer of which he has no knowledge. There are different ways of communicating an offer:

- An offer can be to one person or the whole world: see *Carlill* v *Carbolic Smoke Ball Co.* (1893).
- The offer must be communicated to the offeree. **Taylor v Laird (1856)** shows that an offer cannot be accepted unless the person who is seeking to accept it knows of its existence.
- An offer may be withdrawn at any time before an acceptance. Suppose Rameez offers his car to Leanne for £1,000 and states the offer will remain open for acceptance until 12 noon on Monday 16 June. In reliance on this statement Leanne drives a 100 mile round trip to view the car and is so impressed with its quality that she asks her local garage to check it out for her at a cost of £50. The report is favourable

Key cases

Routledge v Grant (1828): an offer can be revoked at any time even if it is said to be open for a fixed period that has not yet ended.

Byrne v Van Tienhoven (1880): Van Tienhoven offered goods to Byrne and then sent a letter withdrawing the offer; this letter arrived after Byrne had accepted the offer, so the withdrawal letter was not effective.

Ramsgate Victoria Hotel v Montefiore (1866): an offer made to buy shares in a company had lapsed when the company responded five months later; the person making the offer was entitled to assume the company did not want him to invest.

Taylor v Laird (1856): a captain's claim for wages failed as on the return trip he worked as an ordinary crewmember but did not tell the owner of his change of status.

but before she can accept the offer Rameez telephones her on Sunday 15 June to withdraw the offer. Even though Rameez has withdrawn the offer before the stated date Leanne will be unable to recover any of her expenses from Rameez.

■ The withdrawal of an offer must be communicated to the offeree. This links in with 'termination' of an offer. If Rameez wishes to withdraw his offer to Leanne he must communicate that withdrawal to her. He may either do this or a third party on his behalf and in either event Rameez has only to take reasonable steps to bring the withdrawal to Leanne's attention.

■ The terms of the offer must not be vague. The parties cannot reach agreement if the words of the offer are too vague, as demonstrated in **Guthing v Lynn (1831)**. In the scenario, if Rameez offers his car to Leanne at a 'reasonable price' there can be no valid acceptance of such an offer.

Activities

1 Look at a local or national newspaper and consider whether the advertisements are offers or invitations to treat.

2 Create your own advertisements, one to be an offer and the other an invitation to treat. What are the main differences?

You should now be able to:

■ understand the nature of an offer

■ explain the rules in relation to an offer

■ apply the law to given situations.

In this topic you will learn how to:

■ define acceptance

■ explain the different methods of acceptance

■ describe the different methods of, and importance of, communication of acceptance

■ apply the rules to a given situation.

Key terms

Acceptance: the unconditional agreement to all the terms of the offer.

Key cases

Hyde v Wrench (1840): a counter-offer ends the original offer.

Stevenson v McLean (1880): an enquiry about whether credit was available did not reject the offer, which could still be accepted.

2 Acceptance

Acceptance is the second step in the formation of a contract. If Leanne wishes to purchase the car offered by Rameez then she must communicate that acceptance to him in a positive manner. The simplest example is that she says 'Yes, Rameez, I agree to buy your car for £1,000'.

There are various rules concerning acceptance, which are set out below:

The acceptance must be unconditional

A crucial element of acceptance is that it must be an agreement to all the terms of the offer. If the offeree tries to vary the terms of the offer then the offer is terminated *and* there cannot be a valid acceptance. For example in **Hyde v Wrench (1840)** Wrench offered his farm to Hyde for £1,000. Hyde agreed to buy the farm but for £900, which Wrench refused. Hyde then said he would pay the original £1,000. Wrench was entitled to refuse this suggestion as Hyde had terminated the original offer when he made his counter-offer of £900.

Request for information

An offeree may sometimes ask the offeror for information concerning the terms of the offer. This request for information does not terminate the offer. In **Stevenson v McLean (1880)** the purchaser asked if delivery of iron could be staggered. The purchaser sent a telegram to the seller accepting the offer but in the meantime the seller sold the iron to a third party claiming the purchaser had made a counter-offer. The court decided the purchaser had made an enquiry not a counter-offer so the original offer still existed.

Form of acceptance

Acceptance may be in any form, e.g. it may be verbal, written or a gesture. However, if the offer states the acceptance must be in a specified form, e.g. a letter, then any other type of acceptance is unlikely to be valid such as in the case of **Yates Building v Pulleyn (1975)**, where acceptance was only effective if the acceptance of that right was by 'recorded' delivery). The acceptance was sent by first class post and received but this was not classed as valid acceptance.

Communication of acceptance

Whether an acceptance must be communicated to the offeror depends on the contract being bilateral or unilateral.

In unilateral contracts, the acceptance need not be communicated to the offeror. For example, Mrs Carlill did not have to inform the Carbolic Smoke Ball Company that she had accepted their offer. Her conduct alone was sufficient for acceptance.

In bilateral contracts the general rule is that the acceptance must be communicated to the offeror. This can be seen in **Felthouse v Bindley (1863)**. An uncle wanted to buy his nephew's horse and wrote a letter saying 'If I hear no more about him I shall consider the horse mine for £30'. The nephew wanted to sell to the uncle so did nothing as suggested but told the auctioneer who held the horse not to sell it. In error, the auctioneer still sold the horse to a third party. The third party was entitled to the horse as the uncle and the nephew never had an agreement. The nephew's acceptance was never communicated to the uncle.

The rule for the communication of acceptance is sensible as it allows for there to be certainty between the parties as to whether an agreement is made or not. However, the court chose to ignore both parties' wishes in this case.

The 'postal rule'

The **postal rule** was created in the early 1800s and is an exception to the general rule concerning communication of acceptance for a bilateral contract. The rule, shown in the case of **Adams v Lindsell (1818)**, tries to balance the interests of two innocent parties. What happens if the offeree's letter of acceptance is delayed in delivery or is never delivered at all?

The rule *only* applies where use of the ordinary postal system is the specified *or* reasonable method of acceptance. It is unlikely this rule applies to private couriers, but there is no precedent.

Household Fire Insurance v Grant (1879) and *Holwell Securities* v *Hughes* (1974) decided that even if the letter never arrives there is still acceptance provided the letter was correctly stamped and addressed and if the offeror stated the acceptance 'must be received by notice in writing' the acceptance must be received and placing the letter in the post-box was not sufficient.

The probable reasons for the postal rule are based on business efficiency (i.e. what else could the offeree have done?) and acknowledgement of the practicalities of business (i.e. in balancing the rights, responsibilities and expectations of innocent parties, the postal rule is an acceptable compromise).

Problems with the postal rule in modern society

There is some uncertainty whether the postal rule applies to more modern methods of communication such as text messages, emails, faxes, pager messages, telexes, etc. There is case law that clarifies certain points but not all. The case of **Entores Ltd v Miles Far East Co. (1955)** would seem to suggest that the postal rule does *not* apply to some methods of instantaneous communication, e.g. by telephone or by telex.

 Key cases

Yates Building v Pulleyn (1975): any requirement as to manner of acceptance must be complied with for acceptance to be valid.

Felthouse v Bindley (1863): a statement that if nothing further was heard then a contract would be made was not sufficient to be the positive act required for acceptance.

Adams v Lindsell (1818): the postal rule states that a letter of acceptance takes effect at the moment of posting.

Household Fire Insurance v Grant (1879): if the postal rules apply, acceptance takes place when the letter is posted even if does not arrive.

Entores Ltd v Miles Far East Co. (1955): a telex was sent and the court decided the telex took effect when it was *received*, i.e. the postal rule did not apply.

Key terms

Postal rule: postal acceptance takes effect when the letter of acceptance is posted; 'posted' means that the letter is in the control of the Post Office or one of its employees authorised to receive letters.

In *Brinkibon Ltd* v *Stahag Stahl GmbH* (1982): the court confirmed the Entores decision and stated:

> … it would seem … that the communication should take effect at the time when the [offeree] could reasonably have expected it to be read.

The courts seem reluctant to extend the postal rule to methods of communication outside the postal system itself.

The case of **Mondial Shipping and Chartering BV v Astarte Shipping Ltd (1995)** clarified two particular and important points concerning communication of acceptance. First, if an acceptance is sent out of office hours the acceptance will only be effective once office hours restart. Second, the postal rule does not apply to faxes (and, by implication, does not apply to other modern forms of communication).

Electronic Commerce (EC Directive) Regulations 2002

Under the Regulations any organisation or service provider that sells goods or services on the internet from a website must follow certain requirements in order for there to be a valid contract between the purchaser (the Regulations are aimed at protecting consumers rather than businesses) and the seller.

These requirements are: the service provider must provide receipts for orders (offers by the purchaser) without delay, allow purchasers to amend orders (offers) easily before sending the order (offer) and to provide name and address (geographical and electronic) of the service provider.

These Regulations do not alter the rules on offer and acceptance outlined above but do allow the consumer some protection. It is the purchaser who makes the order (offer) based on the invitation to treat provided on the website. However, to protect the customer the contract is voidable if the basic information described is not given in the invitation to treat.

An incident in 1999 indicated the application of the common law rules of offer and acceptance to an advertisement on a website. A large electronic retailer mistakenly advertised televisions for sale at £30 when the correct price was £300. Many customers contacted the retailer 'accepting' the retailer's 'offer' but it was concluded that the advertisement was an invitation to treat, the purchasers were making the offer and the retailer was entitled to reject those offers.

Consumer Protection (Distance Selling) Regulations 2000

If a commercial supplier is supplying goods or services to a consumer and the contract is made, for example, by an exchange of letters, faxes, emails, by tele-shopping or by website trading then the consumer is entitled to a 'cooling-off' period in which the contract may be ended by the consumer.

The consumer has the right to cancel the contract within seven working days of the consumer's receipt of the goods.

The Regulations do not alter the common law rules of offer and acceptance but do allow the consumer some protection when having made a valid contract and then having second thoughts.

Offer and acceptance problems

The examiner frequently sets questions based either wholly or partly on offer and acceptance. These questions are usually easily identifiable as they involve what appears to be an offer but may be an invitation to treat. This will be linked with an acceptance that may be valid but will have a potential problem with communication.

Key cases

Mondial Shipping & Chartering BV v Astarte Shipping Ltd (1995): the postal rule does not apply to faxes; it should be noted that where items to which the postal rule do not apply arrive outside office hours, communication will not take place until office hours.

The answer should identify the topics under review, state the relevant law clearly and concisely and then apply that law to the question. Inevitably, there will be room for discussion of the application of the law and the examiner will not necessarily be expecting a definitive answer.

For example, one previous exam question was as follows:

> Brian was a member of the Alpha Wine Club. He received a letter from the Club which stated 'As one of our most valued customers, Brian, we offer you this opportunity to buy a case of French red wine at the specially low price £95. Stocks are limited, so reply within five days to be certain of getting your wine'. Brian sent an email that same day to order a case of the wine. However, though the email was received by the Club, it was accidentally deleted by a trainee customer service employee before it had been dealt with. Consequently, Brian did not receive the wine, which had sold out by the time that he queried the lack of delivery. Subsequently, Brian discovered that, had he obtained the wine, he could have re-sold it for £150 on the open market'.
>
> Taking into account the rules on formation of a contract, consider whether Brian has any rights and remedies against the Alpha Wine Club in connection with the case of red wine.

A good answer would first deal with the communication to Brian and discuss the status of the letter. The answer should define an offer and an invitation to treat, with examples, and discuss the different consequences if the letter is an offer or an invitation to treat, i.e. if an offer then Brian's email is an acceptance, if an invitation to treat is Brian's email an offer?

The good answer should then define an acceptance and, in particular, discuss whether the acceptance (*if* the letter is an offer of course) has been communicated, which involves a discussion of the 'postal rule' and whether it applies to the modern method of communication in this question.

 Link

The answer should also cover remedies and this is dealt with in Chapter 9, Remedies.

Activities

1. Explain the postal rule and justify its existence.
2. Describe the effect of an offeree's acceptance by email which is never received by the offeror.

You should now be able to:

- understand the nature of acceptance
- explain the rules in relation to acceptance
- apply the law to given scenarios.

In this topic you will learn how to:

■ define consideration

■ distinguish between sufficiency and adequacy of consideration

■ explain the meaning of past consideration

■ explain the situation where there is part performance and performance of an existing duty

■ describe the function of consideration

■ apply the rules to a given situation.

Key terms

Consideration: some right, interest or profit benefiting one party and is a loss or responsibility suffered by the other party.

Adequacy: whether something is of equivalent value or comparable in price.

Sufficiency: when the consideration is real, tangible and has some value.

Key cases

Thomas v Thomas (1842): Mrs Thomas remained in the family home after her husband's death provided she paid rent to Mr Thomas's estate of £1 per year; this was not a commercial rent, but the contract between Mr Thomas and his widow was valid as the adequacy of the consideration was irrelevant.

Chappell & Co. v Nestlé (1960): for tax reasons the court had to decide whether chocolate wrappers were consideration; the court decided they were as they were real, tangible and had some value, even though Nestlé threw them away once received.

3 Consideration

Consideration is what passes from one contractual party to another; each party in a contract must give something of value.

Consideration is traditionally thought of as money, goods or services. However, in modern cases the courts seem willing to define almost anything as consideration even if that element is not part of the contract.

The usual attitude of the courts to consideration (and to formation of contracts generally) is to attempt to reach a decision which allows the court to enforce what the parties have agreed. Our commercial and business world is based on contractual obligations and the court does not like allowing parties to escape these obligations.

Consideration need not be adequate but must be sufficient

The court's view is that the **adequacy** of consideration is a matter for the parties to decide and is best shown in the case of **Thomas v Thomas (1842)**. The court will not interfere if one party has made a bad bargain.

To be sufficient, consideration must:

■ be real (the consideration must exist)

■ be tangible (the consideration must be definite, e.g. a vague promise may not be definite enough for **sufficiency**)

■ have some value (even if of a nominal amount).

The case of **Chappell & Co. v Nestlé (1960)** demonstrates the criteria in action.

Past consideration

To be valid, consideration must be a mutual exchange of promises. If one party carries out an act voluntarily and a second party later promises to pay for or contribute to this act then this is called 'past' consideration. The promise to pay by the second party is not good consideration as it is a promise to pay for something that has already happened. The first party is not able to enforce the promise of the second party as there is no valid contract. In **Re McArdle (1951)** some family members redecorated the family home and other family members then promised in writing to contribute a fixed sum to the cost of redecoration but never did. No payment was due as the promise to pay was for something that had already occurred: it was past consideration so there was no contract.

There is an exception to this rule from the old case of **Lampleigh v Braithwaite (1615)**, when a party:

■ requests a service from another and

■ the promise of payment can be implied into the request.

This exception may apply in commercial situations where the payment is implied due to the context of the facts. In *Re Casey's Patents* (1892) a manager worked on patents for a company, which then promised him a one-third share in the patents. The company then refused to share the patents claiming past consideration. The manager was entitled to the share as it was implied that when he worked on the patents he would receive payment of some form.

Part payment of a debt in place of the whole debt gives no consideration

This rule from **Pinnel's case (1602)** is that a creditor is able to claim the remainder of a debt even if the creditor has agreed with the debtor that a part payment by the debtor will clear the debt.

In a scenario, Miriam owes Vicky £600 for costumes. Vicky may agree to accept £500 and confirm that the balance of £100 will be written off.

However, under Pinnel's rule Vicky is still entitled to claim the £100. The reasoning behind the rule is that Vicky is 'giving' something to Miriam (a reduction in the debt) but what is Miriam giving in return? As Miriam is not supplying any form of consideration for the reduction in the debt there is no valid agreement as to the part payment so the original debt is still outstanding.

In **Foakes v Beer (1884)** Foakes owed Beer £2,000 and they agreed he would repay by instalments and Beer would do nothing more. Beer then asked for interest and Foakes refused. Foakes was giving Beer no consideration to be allowed to pay by instalments, therefore Beer was entitled to sue for the whole amount and to claim interest.

The above case should be compared with **D & C Builders v Rees (1966)**, when builders were owed £482 by Rees but agreed to accept £300 in full settlement as the builders were near bankruptcy. The builders were able to claim the balance of £182.

There is a subtle difference between these two cases. In *Rees* the reduction in payment had been obtained by the use of economic pressure on the builders who had a cash-flow problem. In *Foakes* there was no such pressure and the original arrangement as to payment by instalments had been reached with mutual consent. It could be argued that the *Rees* decision is correct but in *Foakes* some flexibility could, and should, have been allowed to Foakes, who was trying to resolve the dispute on terms fair to both parties.

The law appreciates that Pinnel's rule may seem harsh, so exceptions have developed.

- *Accord and satisfaction*: If the debtor agrees to pay a smaller amount on a date earlier than originally agreed *or* in cash when a cheque was originally agreed then the debtor has provided consideration for the new agreement. Alternatively, if the creditor agrees to accept something other than money for the whole debt this is good consideration even if the item provided is not comparable in value to the debt. This is another example of the rule about adequacy of consideration.

- *Promissory estoppel*: If one party to an existing contract (the promisor) promises to vary the contract (for the other's benefit) and the other party relies on that promise to vary then the promisor cannot go back on the promise, i.e. the promisor is 'estopped' from breaking the promise.

Lord Denning's statement in **Central London Property Trust Ltd v High Trees House Ltd (1947)** appears to be in direct conflict with the decision in *Foakes*. If Beer could break her promise not to sue why cannot High Trees House Ltd sue in the *High Trees* case? Lord Denning's comments in *High Trees* seem to indicate consideration was not a crucial element of a contract. This was a radical view and the courts have been cautious in allowing this new principle to develop.

In *Re Selectmove* (1995) a company owed tax to the Inland Revenue. An agreement was reached that the tax owed would be paid by instalments and Selectmove commenced payment. The Inland Revenue then claimed the whole debt, which would put Selectmove into liquidation. Selectmove argued that it had relied on the Inland Revenue's promise not to sue and that Lord Denning's principle from *High Trees* was applicable. The Inland Revenue was not bound by the agreement and, applying the principle from *Foakes*, the whole debt was due.

This case is of interest in that Selectmove also argued the principle from *Williams* v *Roffey Bros & Nichols (Contractors) Ltd* (1990) would allow the agreement with the Inland Revenue to stand. The Williams case is

dealt with in the section below (existing duty) and is further evidence of
the reluctance of the courts to extend the *High Trees* principle.

An existing duty

If a contractual party performs an existing duty (and no more) then this
performance cannot be consideration for a new contract. This is shown
in the case of **Stilk v Myrick (1809)**.

In the scenario, Vicky has contracted to manufacture twelve costumes for
£600 (contract 1). Vicky then discovers the cost of material has suddenly
increased. As a result she asks if Miriam agrees to pay an additional £10
per costume making a new total of £720 (contract 2). Miriam agrees but
then pays only the original £600. Is the additional £120 due?

The court will ask what consideration both parties were giving for
contract 2. Obviously Miriam is paying the extra £120 but Vicky is
manufacturing the costumes that she was contracted to complete in
any event. Vicky is merely performing her 'existing duty' and that is not
sufficient to be valid consideration for contract 2. The additional £120 is
not payable.

This principle was followed in **Collins v Godefroy (1831)**, where the
promise of payment for the performance of a public duty (attending court
under a court order) was not enforceable as there was a public duty to
attend court anyway.

The situation may be complicated by the involvement of a third party.

In the scenario, Miriam may have agreed that Vicky would deliver the
costumes by Monday 23 June. Siobhan (the third party) supplies some of
the material to Vicky for the manufacture of the costumes and has agreed
with Vicky to supply the material by 20 May. Miriam wanted to ensure
the costumes were ready by the 23 June so agreed to pay Siobhan an extra
£100 (in addition to Vicky's fee to Siobhan) if the material is supplied to
Vicky by 20 May.

Miriam has agreed to pay Siobhan (a third party) to perform a duty
Siobhan is already contracted to perform for Vicky. If Siobhan delivers the
material on time is she entitled to the additional £100? The answer to
this question is, perhaps surprisingly, yes.

This principle was set out in *Scotson v Pegg* (1861), when Scotson agreed
with X to deliver coal to anyone nominated by X. X nominated Pegg (the
third party) and Scotson made his delivery. For reasons not relevant to
this topic Scotson sued Pegg and Pegg claimed there could be no contract
as Scotson was only performing a duty for Pegg which Scotson had to
perform anyway under Scotson's contract with X. In this situation it
is possible to offer the same consideration to two different parties so
Scotson was successful against Pegg.

In certain circumstances the courts have been willing to allow what
appears to be an existing duty to be classed as valid consideration for a
new contract. Two examples are:

1   If what is given is more than was originally expected, as in **Hartley v
    Ponsonby (1857)**

2   If performance of the existing duty gives the other party a 'benefit'. As
    will be seen from the Williams case below, the court may give a wide
    meaning to the definition of benefit.

An important case is **Williams v Roffey Bros & Nichols (Contractors)
Ltd (1990)**, when a developer contracted with a builder (Roffey) to
refurbish some flats. There was a condition that if Roffey did not
complete by a specified date then Roffey would have to pay daily

compensation to the developer until completion. Roffey subcontracted the roofing work to a roofer (Williams) for £20,000. Unfortunately, Williams encountered labour problems and it appeared to Roffey that the roofing work would overrun the completion date Roffey had agreed with the developer. Roffey suggested to Williams he would pay an extra £10,300 to allow Williams to employ more labour to ensure the roofing work was completed on time. Williams agreed and managed to complete the roofing work on time so Roffey did not have to pay the developer any compensation for late completion. Roffey refused to pay the extra £10,300, arguing that Williams was merely performing an existing duty and the principle from *Stilk* v *Myrick* (1809) applied. The Court of Appeal decided the extra payment was due to Williams as Roffey was receiving benefits from Williams, namely:

- the extra payment ensured Williams continued the roofing work and did not stop in breach of contract with Roffey; and
- the extra payment allowed Williams to complete on time so Roffey avoided his potential liability to the developer for late completion; and
- the extra payment avoided Roffey the trouble and expense of engaging other people to complete the roofing work.

This case is seen as very significant as it has widened the limits of what the courts may consider as valid consideration.

Activities

1. Explain, in your words, the difference between 'adequacy' and 'sufficiency' in respect of consideration.

2. Describe two examples of when Pinnel's rule would not apply to part payment of a debt.

3. A student wants to make holiday money so visits a property without warning, mows the lawn, weeds and cleans the paths. He then asks the owner for payment who promises him £20. Can the student insist on payment?

You should now be able to:

- understand the principle of consideration
- explain the rules in relation to consideration
- apply the law to given scenarios.

In this topic you will learn how to:

■ define privity of contract

■ distinguish between privity of contract and consideration

■ explain the exceptions to the doctrine of privity of contract

■ describe the function of the Contracts (Rights of Third Parties) Act 1999

■ apply the rules to a given situation.

Key cases

Dunlop Pneumatic Tyre Co. Ltd v Selfridge (1915): Dunlop manufactured tyres and sold some to Dew, who agreed not to resell them below a certain price; Dew resold to Selfridge on the basis of the same term not to resell below a certain price; Selfridge then resold below this price and Dew refused to sue, so Dunlop sued Selfridge; Dunlop was not a party to the contract between Dew and Selfridge, so the claim failed.

Tweddle v Atkinson (1861): a person cannot sue or be sued successfully under a contract unless that person has provided consideration under the contract.

Shanklin Pier v Detel Products (1951): the strict privity rule can be avoided by finding a collateral contract in a case such as this.

4 Privity of contract

The rule of privity in contract is that only those who are parties to the contract are bound by it and can benefit from it.

The justification for this rule, seen in **Dunlop Pneumatic Tyre Co. Ltd v Selfridge (1915)**, is that it would be unfair for two parties to make a contract that would bind a third person to do something and conversely it would be unfair for that third person to sue either or both of the contracting under that contract.

Relationship between privity and consideration

The rule of privity can be seen as based on a rule of consideration in that 'consideration must move from the promisee'.

In **Tweddle v Atkinson (1861)** two fathers agreed with each other to pay an agreed amount each to their son and daughter respectively when the couple married. The written contract stated it was made for the couple's benefit. The couple married, the bride's father paid his agreed share but the son's father had died. The trustees of this father's estate refused to make the payment so the son sued his late father's estate. The son lost his claim as he had provided no consideration under the contract and was not a party to the contract made between the two fathers.

This rule is seen as causing injustice and the courts have on occasions tried to ignore the rule.

In *Jackson v Horizon Holidays Ltd* (1975) Mr Jackson booked a holiday for himself and his family, which turned out to be very disappointing. Mr Jackson sued Horizon Holidays for damages for himself and his family. The Court of Appeal held that it would be unfair to limit the award of damages to Mr Jackson and so the claims of his family were allowed even though, strictly, they were not parties to the holiday contract, which was in Mr Jackson's sole name.

General exceptions – agency, collateral contracts, restrictive covenants

The courts and Parliament created certain, limited, exceptions when the rule of privity would not apply.

Agency

An agency situation arises when one person, the agent, is authorised to make a contract on behalf of another person, the principal.

In a valid agency situation the principal will be bound by the terms of the contract even though he did not make the contract himself. The principal and the agent are treated by the courts as being one person, and that person is a party to the contract.

Collateral contracts

The court may be able to avoid the strict rule of privity by finding a second contract alongside the main agreement.

In **Shanklin Pier Ltd v Detel Products Ltd (1951)**: Shanklin Pier contracted with a painter for their pier to be painted and insisted on a particular type of paint provided it would last for 7–10 years. The manufacturer of the paint (Detel) gave that assurance to the painter. The paint lasted only three months and Shanklin Pier sued Detel. On the face of it Shanklin Pier should lose the case under the privity rule as they had no contract with Detel, however, the court decided that a second (collateral) contract between Shanklin Pier and Detel existed alongside the original contract between Shanklin Pier and the painter.

Restrictive covenants

A restrictive covenant exists under land law when a purchaser of land promises the seller in the contract of purchase (the 'initial contract') that he will not do something on the land and that covenant then 'runs with the land'.

This means that all subsequent purchasers of that land are legally bound by that promise even though they are not parties to that initial contract.

In **Tulk v Moxhay (1848)**: Tulk sold a garden in Leicester Square, London, to Elms. The initial contract contained a restrictive covenant that Elms would not build on this land. Elms sold to Moxhay, who intended to build on the land. Tulk could enforce the covenant against Moxhay even though there was no direct contract between them: the covenant had run with the land and Moxhay was bound by it.

Contracts (Rights of Third Parties) Act 1999

Under this Act someone who is *not* a party to a contract (a 'third party') may enforce the contract against either or both of the actual parties to the contract if:

1 the third party is expressly identified by name, or as a member of a class or as answering a particular description, *and*

2 the contract *expressly* provides the third party may enforce the contract, *or*

3 the contract term is an *attempt* to confer the benefit of the term on the third party.

Point 1 means, for example, an unborn baby may use the Act if properly described.

Points 2 and 3 mean the third party may enforce the contract if the contract either states that to be the case or that is how the contract may be interpreted. In this respect the case of **Nisshin Shipping Co. Ltd v Cleaves & Co. Ltd (2003)** confirmed the court will use the objective test of what reasonable contracting parties would have thought the relevant term(s) of the contract meant.

However, if 'on a proper construction of the contract' it appears the parties did not intend the term to benefit a third party then the Act will not apply. The parties to the contract therefore have the right to exclude the Act from benefiting a third party. Most commercial contracts now include such a term so the impact of the Act is not as great as was anticipated.

It should be noted that if the contract contains an exclusion and/or limitation clause then the third party may use the rules concerning the unenforceability of such clauses (discussed in Chapter 6, Contract terms, Topic 5, Control of exclusion and limitation clauses: common law approaches).

> ### Key cases
>
> **Tulk v Moxhay (1848)**: restrictive covenants (part of land law) are an exception to the privity of contract rule.
>
> **Nisshin Shipping Co. Ltd v Cleaves & Co. Ltd (2003)**: the test for what reasonable contracting parties would have thought the terms of the contract meant is an objective test.

> ### Activities
>
> 1 Define what privity of contract means.
>
> 2 Create an example of how the 1999 Act may affect the rights of a third party.

You should now be able to:

■ understand the nature of privity of contract

■ explain the rules in relation to privity of contract and the exceptions

■ apply the law to given scenarios.

5 Intention to create legal relations

There may be a valid offer and acceptance, valid consideration from all parties and those interested in the contract are all parties (privity) to the contract – but there may still not be a legally binding contract.

When parties agree something with each other they do not always believe or intend that if either breaks the agreement the other will be able to sue. It would not be possible for the courts to decide every single dispute based on all these situations.

Intention to create legal relations ('legal intent') must exist between the parties for the agreement to become legally enforceable.

If the agreement is made in a *social* or *domestic* situation then the law presumes there is *no* legal intent. The court will consider the subject matter of the agreement as much as the status of the parties involved. For example, if a father (a farmer) agrees to sell his combine harvester to his farmer son for £10,000 then the court presumes there is no legal intent but there is likely to be a valid contract once the court takes the context of the contract into account.

If the agreement is in a *commercial* or *business* situation then the law presumes there *is* legal intent unless there is evidence to the contrary.

It must be noted that these are only presumptions (i.e. starting points) for the court and other evidence may allow the court to alter its view.

Social and domestic arrangements

Social arrangements

Agreements between friends are unlikely to have legal intent.

In **Simpkins v Pays (1955)** a lodger, her landlady and the landlady's daughter regularly entered 'fashion' competitions on the basis that any prize money would be shared equally. All three contributed to the entry fee and one form was sent off containing all three entries and was in the sole name of the lodger. The lodger received the prize money of £750 but did not share the winnings as agreed. Although the agreement was made in a social setting the court decided the involvement of money (both the equal contribution to the entry fee and the possibility of winning a substantial sum) had created legal intent between the parties so the winnings had to be shared.

In **Parker v Clarke (1960)**: Mr and Mrs Parker (a young couple) agreed to sell their home and move in with, and care for, an older couple (Mr and Mrs Clarke). In return Mr and Mrs Clarke agreed to leave them their home in their wills. Mr and Mrs Parker sold their home, gave some money to their daughter to buy a flat and moved in with Mr and Mrs Clarke. Mr Clarke altered his will to leave the property to Mr and Mrs Parker. An argument followed and Mr and Mrs Clarke evicted the younger couple. There was legal intent between the parties as Mr and Mrs Parker had given up their financial security by selling their home. Further, by altering his will, Mr Parker had shown he expected to be legally bound by the agreement.

Domestic arrangements

Agreements between family members are not usually legally binding, as demonstrated in **Balfour v Balfour (1919)**.

This case should be contrasted with **Merritt v Merritt (1970)**, where Mr Merritt deserted his wife and agreed to pay her a regular monthly amount from which she would pay the mortgage on their former home. Mr Merritt defaulted in his payments. There was legal intent as the parties

Key cases

Simpkins v Pays (1955): if money (usually more than a small amount) is exchanged or financial security is put at risk then there may be legal intent in an agreement made in a social setting.

Parker v Clarke (1960): evidence of legal intention can come from surrounding circumstances such as selling a home and changing a will.

Balfour v Balfour (1919): Balfour went abroad to work and agreed to pay his wife £30 a month but did not pay as agreed; there was no enforceable contract as this was a domestic agreement.

Merritt v Merritt (1970): a more formal written agreement between husband and wife as to some financial arrangements following a marital split can be legally binding.

were separated when the agreement was made and it was not therefore a domestic arrangement.

In **Jones v Padavatton (1969)** a mother bought a house for her daughter to live in while the daughter studied to be a barrister. They had an argument and the mother tried to evict the daughter from the property. The daughter claimed she had an enforceable contract with her mother. There was no legal intent as this was a domestic arrangement.

The *Jones* case was a split decision in the court. There was evidence both in support of and against the existence of legal intent. The case highlighted how important the presumptions are when deciding such cases and if the initial presumption had been the other way the court's final decision may have been different.

Commercial agreements

In the **Esso Petroleum Co. Ltd v Customs and Excise (1976)** case the company gave out world cup coins with little value with every four gallons of petrol. Customs and Excise wanted to charge tax on the coins so the court had to decide if there was legal intent in respect of the agreement to supply the coins. Normally, promotional advertising by a company is not seen as having legal intent but the House of Lords decided by a majority that there was legal intent. Esso did not profit directly from the supply of the coins but did profit from the increased sales of petrol as a result of the promotion.

In **Jones v Vernon's Pools (1938)** the pools company inserted a term in its competition form stating '… this agreement will not create a legal relationship and is binding in honour only'. Jones said his winning form had been lost and claimed his winnings but there was no enforceable agreement as the 'honour clause' removed all legal intent from the agreement.

Activities

1 What are the two presumptions used by the court to assist in deciding if there an intent to create legal relations?

2 Give an example of a domestic agreement to which you have agreed – is it legally binding?

3 Explain the reason for the different decisions in the *Esso* and *Jones* cases.

You should now be able to:

- understand the principle of intention to create legal relations
- apply the law to given situations.

Key cases

Jones v Padavatton (1969): allowing a child who is a student to live in a house bought specially by a parent is merely a domestic arrangement.

Esso Petroleum Co. Ltd v Customs and Excise (1976): an agreement made in a business setting is presumed to be legally binding unless there is evidence that shows a different intent.

Jones v Vernon's Pools (1938): it is possible to exclude legal liability by the use of an express term in the agreement to that effect.

6 Formation of contract – overview

How to attack a problem involving formation of contract

It will be usual for the exam question to state specifically that the question in respect of the scenario relates to the 'formation of a contract'. You are therefore made aware that the topics under review are those covered in this chapter. It is unlikely that one question will cover all five topics.

If the question involves, for example, an advert and/or negotiations and/or a delayed or failed acceptance then the question covers offers, invitations to treat and acceptance. If the scenario involves friends, relatives, work colleagues, neighbours, etc., then the question involves intention to create legal relations. If one of the parties makes a bad bargain and/or promises to pay for something after the event and/or asks for more money having already agreed to carry out the task for a lower amount then the question covers consideration. Finally, the scenario may involve a father making a contract with a builder for repair work to the house belonging to the father's son – this involves privity and whether the son may enforce the contract against the builder.

You must always identify the area(s) of law under review and then apply the relevant law to the question. This allows you to concentrate on explaining one area of law and then its application without the confusion of other rules of law, principles and cases. This also allows the examiner to evaluate the answer in a logical manner.

For example, an exam question from January 2006 was:

> Paul was a talented artist with little business knowledge. He asked his brother, Richard, to assist him to promote his work for one year. Richard agreed to do so in return for a commission of 15 per cent on all sales of Paul's work during that year. After eight very successful months, Richard told Paul that he wanted 20 per cent commission for the remaining four months. Though he agreed, Paul never paid any extra commission and, at the end of the year, refused to do so.
>
> Having regard to the relevant elements in the formation of contract, consider whether Richard has any rights and remedies against Paul in connection with the unpaid extra commission.

You must first identify the topics involved. The reference to an agreement between brothers should immediately indicate that *intent to create legal relations* is relevant. Richard has asked for more money (the *extra* commission) and this should indicate that *consideration* is relevant and in particular *existing duty*.

A good answer would first deal with the intent to create legal relations. The answer should explain the different presumptions that exist in commercial and family agreements (with reference to cases as examples), decide which type of agreement exists and then outline the consequences to the parties if there is, or is not, an intent to create legal relations.

The good answer should then define consideration and the rule about performing an existing duty and whether that is good consideration or not. There are various cases to which reference should be made and the answer should discuss whether Richard is supplying something extra which justifies the application of the *Williams* v *Roffey* principle.

You must read the question carefully and take time to consider what are the relevant topics contained within the question. It is very important that explanation and application of relevant elements of contract formation is used. No credit will be given for a discussion of offer, acceptance or privity. The answer should also cover remedies and this is dealt with in Chapter 9, Remedies.

How to write an essay evaluating the law on formation of contract

The (c) examination question is different to the (a) and (b) questions, which are based on the scenario described in the question. The typical (c) question will ask you to 'critically analyse the law of formation of a contract and to include any appropriate suggestions for reform'. There are 25 marks each for questions (a) and (b) and also 25 marks for question (c) so this question must be given the same consideration as the other two.

The examiner will be expecting an accurate explanation of areas of the law of contract formation. There must also be a discussion of the fairness, relevance and clarity of those areas. Inevitably, all areas of law are not perfect and a description of that law and a logical criticism of that law are required. The examiner will also be expecting to see sensible suggestions as to how the law could be improved or whether, in all the circumstances, reform is not appropriate or possible.

You should also explain areas of relevant law that work well, are clear and/or fair as 'critically analyse' does not mean all the analysis results in suggestions for reform of bad law.

Activities

1 Prepare a list of the main headings for offer, acceptance, consideration, privity and intent to create legal relations.

2 Use this list to create your own examination question covering at least two of these topics.

3 Create a further question using the remaining three topics.

You should now be able to:

- answer problem questions involving formation of contract
- evaluate the law relating to formation of contract
- describe proposals for reform of those areas
- construct an appropriate essay on these topics.

Contract terms

Key cases

The Moorcock (1889): if the business of the contract could not be carried on without the term and if, when the contract was made, an independent third party (the 'officious bystander') had asked the parties if a particular term should be in the contract and both parties would have replied 'Oh, of course', then that term will be implied into the contract by the court.

1 Terms of a contract

The terms of a contract are what the parties have agreed between themselves and define the extent and limit of their respective obligations.

Mike is a car dealer and has advertised a moped for sale in his local newspaper for £1,750 (an invitation to treat). James visits Mike to view the moped, considers its condition and makes an offer of £1,250 that Mike rejects. James asks for confirmation that the moped is a 2006 model, that it only has one previous owner (Mike) and that it will be supplied with a full tank of petrol. During the negotiations, Mike confirms the above three points and states the price of the moped is now at a reduced price of £1,500. James makes an offer to buy the moped for £1,500, which Mike accepts, pays in cash and drives it away.

There are terms of this contract that James will pay £1,500 for the moped and in return Mike will transfer ownership and possession of the moped to James.

Basic terminology

Express and implied terms

The terms of a contract are usually what the parties have expressly agreed between themselves and are stated in the contract (whether verbally or written). In the scenario, one express term is that the price for the moped is £1,500. However, sometimes the law will imply a term or terms *into* a contract or *cancel* a term or terms in a contract whether or not the parties agree.

A term can be implied *into* a contract in four different ways:

1 The 'business efficacy' and the 'officious bystander' tests

The court will imply a term into a contract if the term is *necessary* to make sure the contract works on a businesslike basis. Two tests were set out in **The Moorcock (1889)** as being required before a term is implied.

In *The Moorcock* (1889) the defendant owned a harbour and hired out moorings for boats to unload their cargo. A boat owner hired a mooring and paid the fee. It was accepted that both parties realised the boat would rest on the seabed when the tide was out and the boat landed on sharp rocks under the mooring and sank. There was no term in the contract about the safety of the mooring so the boat owner could not sue for breach of contract. The court implied a term into the contract to cover the mooring's safety so the boat owner succeeded in the claim for breach of contract. The court decided a term about the safety of the mooring was necessary for the contract to be effective and both parties, if asked, would have agreed such a term was required.

2 Terms implied by custom

A term may be implied into a contract if such a term would exist as a matter of custom. For example, it was the agreed farming practice that a tenant farmer, on being given notice to quit by the landlord, would be allowed compensation for the seeds and labour he had put into the land and from which the landlord would benefit (*Hutton* v *Warren* (1836)). That term would be implied in such a contract.

3 *Terms implied by the Sale of Goods Act 1979*

See Topics 2, 3 and 4.

4 *Terms implied by the Supply of Goods and Services Act 1982*

See Topics 2, 3 and 4.

A term may be *excluded* in one of three ways:

    a **If the term is not incorporated in the contract**
        See Topic 5.

    b **Terms prohibited by the Unfair Contracts Terms Act 1977**
        See Topic 6.

    c **Terms prohibited by the Unfair Terms in Consumer Contracts Regulations 1999**
        See Topic 6.

Conditions, warranties and innominate terms

Once it is decided there is a particular term in a contract (whether it is expressly agreed or implied) it is necessary to evaluate which of the three types of term it is.

Condition

A **condition** is a term that is fundamental to the contract, i.e. without that term the contract would be pointless. When a condition is breached, such as in **Poussard v Spiers (1876)** the victim may repudiate the contract (end the contract) if desired and/or sue for damages (compensation).

Warranty

A **warranty** is a minor term of the contract. When a warranty is broken the victim may sue *only* for compensation and the contract will continue, shown in the case of **Bettini v Gye (1876).**

Innominate (indeterminate) terms

Sometimes it is difficult to tell if a term is a condition or a warranty and these are know as **innominate terms.** Here the court will look at the consequences of the breach of the term and then decide. For example, if the breach has a serious result then it is likely to be classed a condition so the victim may repudiate the contract and/or sue for damages.

In **Hong Kong Fir v Kawasaki Kaisha Kasan (1962)** a company hired a cargo boat for two years and a term was that the boat was 'fitted for ordinary cargo service'. During the two years' hire the boat was out of action for repairs for 18 weeks (17 per cent of the hire period). The court could not tell from the wording of the contract if the term was a condition or warranty. By looking at the result of the breach the court concluded the time lost was not too serious so the term was a warranty and only compensation could be claimed.

Exclusion and limitation clauses

An *exclusion* clause is a term of the contract that tries to exclude the liability of one of the parties if that party breaches another contractual term.

A *limitation* clause is a term of the contract that tries to limit the extent of that liability rather than exclude liability entirely.

Courts believe that parties to a contract should be allowed to agree to whatever terms of a contract they wish – even if such a term excludes or limits one party's rights against another. However, the courts are also aware that when contracts are negotiated one party may be at a

---

Key terms

Condition: a term that is fundamental to the contract, i.e. without that term the contract would have been pointless.

Warranty: a minor term of the contract, i.e. the contract would have been made without the term.

Innominate terms: a term in a contract that can be treated as either a condition or a warranty depending on the nature of the breach of the term.

Key cases

Poussard v Spiers (1876): Poussard's inability to sing the lead role in an opera for the first six days of performance was a breach of condition; the opera promoter was able to end the contract and replace the singer.

Bettini v Gye (1876): a singer contracted to attend rehearsals and the actual performances of a show, missed some of the rehearsals but attended all the performances; this was a breach of warranty so the theatre could only claim compensation and the singer could continue the contract.

Hong Kong Fir v Kawasaki Kaisha Kasan (1962): this case is an example of the courts considering an innominate term.

disadvantage to the other, for example a consumer dealing with a large commercial company. The result of such terms may prove harsh on the victim so over the years courts have developed rules limiting the creation of these types of terms.

Further, Parliament has created Acts and Regulations to restrict the validity and/or extent of such terms in certain circumstances.

Distinction between terms and representations

Representations

Before a contract is agreed the parties will usually have negotiated the terms of the contract. One party may have made a statement (a 'representation') on which the other party is relying but the representation is never included in the final contract (whether oral or in writing). The victim will wish to claim the representation is a term of the contract while the party in breach will claim it is just a statement with no legal effect.

In the scenario, Mike stated during negotiation that the moped had only one previous owner (himself), which James later finds to be untrue. That statement was never included in the final contract (for whatever reason) so James is unable to sue for breach of a term of the contract. He may be able to sue under Misrepresentation (see Chapter 7, Vitiating factors) but this is more complicated and less easy to prove than a breach of contract. The court has developed guidelines to help it decide whether a statement made in negotiations has actually become a term of the contract or remains a mere representation.

Is the statement a representation or a term?

The guidelines are as follows:

1   The importance attached to the representation

In **Couchman v Hill (1947)** an auction catalogue stated that a heifer (a young female cow) was unserved (a maiden cow). Before bidding started a farmer asked the seller and auctioneer for confirmation of this, as it was important to him. They both confirmed so the farmer bought the heifer. However, it was pregnant and died while calving. The statement made to the farmer was so important it became a term of the contract so the farmer could claim for breach of contract.

2   Special knowledge or skill of the party making the representation (the Representor)

In **Oscar Chess Ltd v Williams (1957)** a private seller sold his car to a dealer, stating it was a 1948 model (which he believed) but it was actually a 1939 model. The contract did not refer to the age of the car but as the seller had no expertise in selling cars and the dealer relied on their own skill the statement was not a term of the contract.

The above should be contrasted with **Dick Bentley Ltd v Harold Smith Motors (1965)** when a car dealer stated a car had done 20,000 miles when it had actually done 100,000 miles. The contract made no mention of mileage. The statement had become a term of the contract as the dealer had special knowledge/skill so the buyer could sue for breach.

3   The time between making the representation and the contract

In **Routledge v McKay (1954)** a seller of a motorbike said it was a 1942 model when it was actually a 1930 model. The written contract was made seven days after this representation and did not refer to the year of the bike so the representation did not become a term of the contract.

Key cases

Couchman v Hill (1947): the more important the statement, the more likely it will become a term of the contract rather than just a representation.

Oscar Chess Ltd v Williams (1957): the court is more likely to decide the representation has become a term of the contract if the representor has special knowledge or skill.

Dick Bentley v Harold Smith Motors (1965): the dealer in this case had special knowledge making the representation a term of the contract.

Routledge v McKay (1954): sometimes the time gap between the representation and the making of the contract is so long that the court considers it would be unfair to make the representation part of the contract.

4 Is the agreement is in writing?

In *Routledge*, if the parties have taken the time and trouble to put the contract into a written form then the court presumes everything the parties wanted is in the written contract.

The relationship between common law and statutory aspects of the law

In relation to the terms of a contract the examiner will expect the student to understand and apply the common law rules and the statutory rules and how both aspects relate.

For example, in relation to express and implied terms, it should be noted that there are two ways in which the common law may imply a term into a contract (points 1 and 2 on p94); there are two ways that statute implies a term into a contract (points 3 and 4 on p95); there is one way common law may prohibit a contract term (point a on p95); and there are two ways statute may prohibit a contract term (points b and c on p95).

- The common law is *not limited* to the type of term to be implied. As can be seen from the *Moorcock* and *Hutton* v *Warren* cases, terms were implied into the respective contracts to cover the 'safety' of the mooring and the 'loss of profit' when leaving tenanted land.

- Statute is *limited* as the type of term to be implied. Topics 2, 3 and 4 cover the relevant statutes in detail but, in summary, the statutes imply terms as the quality of goods when sold or transferred and/or the standard of services supplied and the time for completion of the contract.

- The common law may exclude *any type* of term from a contract if the requirement of point a on p95 is not followed.

- Statute is *limited* to prohibiting exclusion and/or limitation terms (absolutely or allowing the term if reasonable) or, in consumer contract only, prohibiting *any type* of term if 'unfair'.

Activities

1 Mike and James did not expressly agree that the registration documents for the moped would be handed over on payment of the £1,500. Would this term be implied into the contract?

2 Mike stated the moped had only one previous owner (himself) but this was never made a term of the contract. If James discovers there is more than one previous owner would this statement be a representation or become a term of the contract?

3 The parties agreed that the moped would be supplied with two new tyres. James discovers the tyres are second-hand and worn. This is a breach of contract by Mike – but is it a breach of condition, warranty or an innominate term?

You should now be able to:

- understand the principles behind contract terms.

In this topic you will learn how to:

■ state the limits of the syllabus for implied terms

■ distinguish between Sale of Goods and Supply of Goods and Services.

2 Implied terms 1

Your study will be limited to ss13, 14(2) and 14(3) of the Sale of Goods Act 1979 ('the 1979 Act') and to the study of ss3, 4, 13 and 14 of the Supply of Goods and Services Act 1982 ('the 1982 Act').

Scope of Sale of Goods Act 1979

One of the most important principles of contract law is that parties are allowed to make whatever contract they like (unless, for example, the contract is for an illegal purpose). This principle is called 'freedom of contract'.

This principle means that a party may, if they wish, make a bad bargain and the court will not intervene. This may sometimes be unfair, especially if one party is financially weaker than the other. Parliament decided that statute should protect this weaker party and passed the 1979 Act. This Act implies certain terms into contracts for the *sale of goods* that will protect the consumer should the goods, for example, prove defective.

Scope of Supply of Goods and Services Act 1982

Parliament also wanted to protect parties in contracts for the *supply of work and materials* linked to the work and so passed the 1982 Act. Where such a contract involves the transfer of goods to a party, similar terms to the 1979 Act are implied as to description, quality and fitness for purpose of the goods. In relation to the work provided (services) there are terms implied that the services will be carried out with reasonable care and skill and, unless the contract specifies a certain period, the work will be completed within a reasonable time.

Activities

1 James drives the moped away and the engine immediately seizes due to an internal defect. Even though the contract did not specifically refer to the quality of the moped, a term is implied that the moped will be of 'satisfactory quality'. James may now sue Mike under that implied term. What else could prove wrong with the moped that would mean it was not of satisfactory quality?

2 James may return the moped to Mike for its annual service. If the contract makes no reference to the quality of Mike's work and no time limit is specified for the work, does James have any remedy if the service is inadequate and Mike takes three weeks to complete the job? If James has a claim, under which Act would it be made?

You should now be able to:

■ understand the distinction between Sale of Goods and Supply of Goods and Services.

3 Implied terms 2

Section 2(1) of the 1979 Act defines a contract for the sale of goods as 'a contract by which a seller transfers or agrees to transfer the property in goods to the buyer for a money consideration, 'called the price'.

The relevant terms implied in the sale of goods contract are set out in ss13–14 of the 1979 Act.

Sale of Goods Act 1979 s13 – meaning, application, remedies and examples

Section 13 of the 1979 Act states when goods are sold by description or by sample, there is an implied condition that they will correspond with the description or sample.

If the buyer examines and selects the goods then s13 will still apply.

This implied term about description is a condition so a breach of that term allows the buyer to repudiate (terminate the contract) and/or claim damages (compensation).

This term is implied into *all* contracts for the sale of goods whether the sale is private or commercial.

In **Beale v Taylor (1967)** the seller advertised a car as 'Herald, convertible, white 1961' but the car was actually two cars welded together and only the back half was a 1961 model. The advertisement was a description and as the car did not conform to this description there was a breach of s13. This was a breach of a condition the buyer could repudiate (reject the car) and/or claim damages (compensation).

Section 13 may sometimes result in what appears to be a harsh decision. In **Moore & Co. v Landauer & Co. (1921)** tinned fruit was described as being in cases of 30 tins per case. Some cases contained 24 tins but the buyer received the correct number of tins in total. The seller was in breach of s13 and so the buyer could reject the goods and/or claim damages.

Because of this unfairness, the Sale and Supply of Goods Act 1994 (the 1994 Act) created a new s15(A) of the 1979 Act so that a breach of the implied term will be treated as breach of warranty if:

- the buyer is a business (i.e. not a consumer); *and*
- the breach is so slight that it would be unreasonable to allow the buyer to reject the goods.

A breach of warranty will allow the buyer to claim damages only and the contract will continue so the goods may not be rejected.

Remedies

See s14(3) on p100.

Sale of Goods Act 1979 s14 (2) – meaning, application, remedies and examples

Section 14(2) of the 1979 Act states when goods are sold by a seller *in the course of a business* there is an implied condition that they will be of '**satisfactory quality**'.

The 1994 Act replaced the word 'merchantable' in the 1979 Act with the word 'satisfactory' but the cases pre-1994 are still helpful guidelines on the application of s14(2). It should be noted that s14(2) does *not* apply to a private sale.

In this topic you will learn how to:

- explain the meaning of ss13, 14(2) and 14(3) Sale of Goods Act 1979
- distinguish between ss13, 14(2) and 14(3) Sale of Goods Act 1979
- apply ss13, 14(2) and 14(3) Sale of Goods Act 1979 to given situations
- describe and apply the remedies available where ss13, 14(2) and 14(3) Sale of Goods Act 1979 have been breached.

Key cases

Beale v Taylor (1967): description is given a wide meaning and applies to colour, size, age, weight, etc.

Moore v Landauer (1921): s13 is applied strictly with apparently harsh results

Key terms

Satisfactory quality: goods that meet the standard that a reasonable person would regard as satisfactory, taking account of any description of the goods, the price (if relevant) and all other relevant circumstances.

The quality of goods includes their state and condition and the following (among others) are aspects of the quality of goods:

- Fitness for all the purposes for which the goods of the kind in question are commonly supplied.
- Appearance and finish.
- Freedom from minor defects.
- Safety and durability.

Key cases

Bartlett v Sidney Marcus (1965): s14(2) applies to both new and second-hand goods.

Crowther v Shannon Motor Co.: here the court took the view that satisfactory quality related to normal expectations relating to the goods sold

In **Bartlett v Sidney Marcus (1965)** a buyer purchased a second-hand Jaguar being told the clutch needed repair. The clutch needed more work than anticipated but the court held there was no breach of s14(2). The court held the car was still usable and defects were to be expected in such second-hand cars.

This decision can be contrasted with the case below when more could be expected of a second-hand car.

In **Crowther v Shannon Motor Co. (1975)** the car had covered over 82,000 miles at purchase and after another 2,300 miles the engine broke. The court held such a car should reach 100,000 miles so there was a breach of s14(2).

Under the Sale and Supply of Goods to Consumers Regulations 2002 (which came into force on 31 March 2003) relevant circumstances may now include:

> … any public statements on the specific characteristics of the goods made…by the seller, the producer or his representative, particularly in advertising or on labelling.

This means statements made in national advertising and/or by manufacturers may affect a seller's liability under s14(2).

An example of the application of 'relevant circumstances' is *Bramhall v Edwards* (2004), when a motor-home was a few inches wider than allowed by regulations. The buyer claimed the goods were of an unsatisfactory nature and therefore in breach of s14(2). Evidence was given that the authorities ignored such minor matters so the claim was unsuccessful. This decision shows the court is willing to take all relevant matters into account when deciding whether a breach has occurred or not.

Remedies

See s14(3) below.

Sale of Goods Act 1979, s14(3) – meaning, application, remedies and examples

Section 14(3) of the 1979 Act states that when goods are sold by a seller *in the course of a business* and the buyer expressly or impliedly makes known to the seller any particular purpose for which the goods are being bought, there is an implied condition that the goods are reasonably fit for that purpose.

Section 14(3) applies whether or not the purpose made known by the buyer is the purpose for which goods of that particular type are commonly supplied.

However, s14(3) will not apply if:

- the buyer does not rely on the skill or judgment of the seller, or
- it was unreasonable for the buyer to rely on the skill and judgment of the seller.

These exceptions may occur if, for example, the buyer told the seller specifically that he did not want the seller's advice on the suitability of the goods for the stated purpose or examined the goods and that examination would have made it clear the goods were unsuitable.

In **Griffiths v Peter Conway (1939)** a buyer of a Harris tweed coat had very sensitive skin but did not tell the seller this fact. The coat caused dermatitis. The buyer did not claim under s14(2) as the coat was of satisfactory quality (it could be worn) but claimed the coat was not fit for its purpose for the buyer. As the seller had no knowledge of the buyer's circumstances (the extra sensitive skin) then the coat was fit for its purpose.

The rule to be drawn from this decision is that for s14(3) to apply a buyer must ensure the purpose for the goods is clearly stated *and* the seller must be informed of any unusual circumstance surrounding the use of the goods by the buyer.

Section 14(2) would appear to have a wider application than s14(3) in this respect. The Court of Appeal has stated s14(2) is concerned with the basic quality of the goods supplied while s14(3) is limited to a case where the claimant has relied on the seller's skill and judgment.

In **Jewson Ltd v Boyhan (2003)** the seller supplied boilers for the buyer's flats. Unfortunately the boilers affected the energy efficiency rating of the flats and their value fell. The buyer claimed under ss14(2) and 14(3) but both claims were unsuccessful. The boilers were satisfactory as boilers for flats and the buyer had not relied on the seller's judgment of the suitability of the boilers for these particular flats.

This recent decision confirms the comment made above about *Griffiths* v *Peter Conway* (1939).

Remedies

Under ss13, 14(2) and 14(3) the victim may repudiate the contract and/or sue for damages.

Repudiation

The victim may choose to terminate the contract due to the breach of the implied condition. In effect, the victim is entitled to the return of the price paid but must return the goods that do not fit their description, are not of satisfactory quality or are not fit for their purpose. This remedy may prove attractive to the victim as they may then recommence their search for the appropriate goods with their financial position restored to its original position.

The right to reject the goods may be lost if, for example, the goods have been *accepted* by the victim. Under s11(4) of the 1979 Act where a buyer has accepted goods a breach of condition will *not* allow the buyer to repudiate the contract and reject the defective goods. This could cause unfairness as the buyer may purchase an item and not use it for some time. If, when used the item is found to be in breach of ss13 and/or 14, the buyer's only remedy would be damages as the buyer had the item for some time.

The 1994 Act amended the 1979 Act to redefine when the buyer is held to have 'accepted' goods. The 1994 Act defines acceptance as when:

- the buyer tells the seller the goods are accepted; or
- the buyer does something inconsistent with the seller's ownership of the goods; or
- the buyer keeps the goods without telling the seller they are rejected within a reasonable time.

Key cases

Griffiths v Peter Conway (1939): there is relationship between s14(2) and s14(3); claims and goods may be of satisfactory quality and yet not fit for their purpose.

Jewson v Boyhan (2003): here the court decided that the buyer had not relied on the seller's skill and judgment.

A case showing the unfairness of the original section is *Bernstein* v *Pamson Motors Ltd* (1987), when Bernstein purchased a new car but only managed to drive it 142 miles before he fell ill and the car was not then used for three weeks. When next used the car was found to have serious defects and Bernstein was stranded in an isolated part of the country. Bernstein claimed a breach of the implied conditions under the 1979 Act and attempted to claim repudiation and to reject the car. As Bernstein had retained the car for three weeks this was long enough for Bernstein to have accepted the car and the right to reject was lost.

The decision in this case raised controversy. It was felt that the innocent victim was left unable to claim a rejection of an expensive item that failed to meet any of the requirements of the implied conditions of the 1979 Act. The victim's only claim was for damages (see Damages below).

This point was reconsidered in **Clegg v Olle Anderson (2003)**, when Clegg purchased a new yacht in August 2000 and was told immediately that the keel was substantially heavier than specified in the contract. Clegg negotiated with the seller and then rejected the yacht by letter in March 2001. The court confirmed that the *Bernstein* (1987) case was no longer good law and that Clegg was entitled to reject the yacht under the 1979 Act as amended by the 1994 Act.

As a general rule therefore, a buyer with a claim under s13, ss14(2) or 14(3) should reject the goods as soon as possible so that repudiation has a practical and positive result for the buyer.

Damages

As an additional or sole remedy, the victim may choose to claim damages (i.e. compensation for the losses incurred due to the breach of one or more of the implied conditions).

Damages are explained in detail in Chapter 9, Remedies, but to summarise: the aim of contractual damages is to put the victim in the position they would have been had the contract been performed properly. In the scenario, if the moped is not delivered then James may elect to repudiate (reclaim the £1,500 paid to Mike) and then to claim the expense incurred in purchasing an equivalent moped. For example, James may now have to pay an extra £250 for an equivalent moped.

In the Bernstein (1987) case, Bernstein recovered the cost of making his way home, the loss of a full tank of petrol, £150 for a 'totally spoilt day comprising nothing but vexation' and compensation until Bernstein purchased a replacement car.

Key cases

Clegg v Olle Anderson (2003): explained that the Bernstein case is no longer good law and the rule as to reasonable time for rejection is looked at by the courts more sympathetically.

Activities

1. In the scenario in Topic 2, what if the moped is described as having a complete service history but Mike is unable to provide any documentation? Which, if any, of the 1979 Act's sections may assist James?

2. James has purchased the moped, uses it for ploughing his allotment and the moped's engine seizes. Which, if any, of the 1979 Act's sections may assist James?

3. The problems listed in the activities above have occurred but Mike was not a dealer and the moped sale was a private sale. What difference, if any, would this situation make to your answers?

You should now be able to:

■ understand the operation of ss13, 14(2) and 14(3) Sale of Goods Act 1979.

4 Implied terms 3

This topic covers a discussion of terms implied into a contract when a service is being supplied and/or goods are transferred by one party to another.

Dan is the owner of a garage that sells cars, car parts and carries out repairs. Aimee agrees for Dan to fit four new tyres to her old car. This is a contract for the supply of a service (the fitting of the tyres) *and* the transfer of goods (the new tyres). Dan finds four *used* tyres and fits them, but takes five weeks to complete the task and then forgets to tighten the wheel nuts with the result that Aimee crashes.

Aimee would have various claims under the 1982 Act, which are discussed below.

Supply of Goods and Services Act 1982 s3 – meaning, application, remedies and examples

Section 3 of the 1982 Act states:

> … where, under a contract for the transfer of goods, the transferor transfers … the goods by description … there is an implied condition that the goods will correspond with the description.

This means where one party contracts with another party for the supply of services which includes the transfer of ownership of goods, the 1982 Act implies a condition into the contract that the goods will fit their description.

The principles involved are very similar to those for s13 of the 1979 Act. It must be noted that s3 is effective for *all* contracts not just those made between a consumer and a business.

An example of a s3 situation would be if Aidan (a bricklayer) agreed with his customer Craig that he would build a new garden wall with reclaimed red brick. Craig accepts Aidan's quote for the job but Aidan builds the wall using new red bricks. Craig would have a claim for breach of a condition of the contract as the goods transferred to Craig (the bricks) do not correspond with their description.

Supply of Goods and Services Act 1982 s4 – meaning, application, remedies and examples

Section 4 of the 1982 Act states:

> … where, under … a contract [for the transfer of goods], the transferor transfers the property in goods in the course of a business, there is an implied condition that the goods supplied under the contract are of satisfactory quality and/or are fit for their purpose.

The principles involved are very similar to those for s14(2) and (3) of the 1979 Act above. Note that s3 is effective *only* for contracts made in the course of a business.

An example of a s4 situation would be as above but, instead of being new, the bricks were crumbling, lopsided and damaged. Craig would have a claim under s4 as the goods were supplied in the course of a business, with a service and are not of satisfactory quality nor fit for their purpose.

In this topic you will learn how to:

- explain the meaning of ss3, 4, 13 and 14 of the Supply of Goods and Services Act 1982

- distinguish between ss3, 4, 13 and 14 of the Supply of Goods and Services Act 1982

- apply ss3, 4, 13 and 14 of the Supply of Goods and Services Act 1982 to given situations

- describe and apply the remedies available where ss3, 4, 13 and 14 of the Supply of Goods and Services Act 1982 have been breached.

Supply of Goods and Services Act 1982 s13 – meaning, application, remedies and examples

Section 13 of the 1982 Act states:

> In the contract for the supply of a service where the supplier is acting in the course of a business, there is an implied term that the supplier will carry out the service with reasonable care and skill.

This term will only be implied where the service is supplied *in the course of a business.*

The implied term is equivalent to the standard of care expected in a claim in tort, i.e. has the supplier of the service achieved a *reasonable* level of care and skill in performing the work?

In **Thake v Maurice (1986)**, a surgeon who performed a vasectomy that proved unsuccessful was not liable under s13, as he had used reasonable care and skill. The court accepted that some vasectomies naturally heal.

It is important to note that the patient in the *Thake* case could have made a contract with the surgeon that contained an *express* term confirming a successful vasectomy. Here, the patient would succeed and would not require s13. The victim only requires the implied term of s13 if there is no express term in the contract that covers the situation.

Supply of Goods and Services Act 1982, s14 – meaning, application, remedies and examples

Section 14 of the 1982 Act states:

> In the contract for the supply of a service where the supplier is acting in the course of a business, there is an implied term that the supplier will carry out the service within a reasonable time.

Note again this term will only be implied where the service is supplied *in the course of a business.*

Section 14 assists a consumer when there is no specific term in the contract as to the time to be taken for the service to be completed and the service has not been completed or has taken longer than expected to complete.

Remedies

It is important to note that ss3 and 4 of the 1982 Act refer to the implied terms as *conditions*. This means a breach of such a term allows the victim to claim repudiation and/or damages. However, the same principles as stated above for the 1979 Act will apply and the right to repudiate (and therefore to reject the goods) may be lost if the goods are accepted.

However, ss13 and 14 do not refer to conditions but to implied *terms*. This implied term will be treated as an innominate term and the victim of a breach of such a term will only be able to repudiate the contract if the consequences of the breach are serious.

As a result under ss13 and 14 of the 1982 Act the victim can *always* claim damages but may only claim repudiation successfully if the consequences of the breach are serious. For a discussion of innominate terms see Topic 1, Terms of a contract and for repudiation and damages see Topic 3, Implied terms 2.

Activities

1 There was no agreed contractual term as to when Dan would complete the fitting of the tyres so s14 applies. The court would decide whether five weeks to fit four tyres was a reasonable period or not. It seems an excessive period but what test would the court use to decide on Dan's potential liability?

2 Dan has supplied four used tyres rather than new tyres. Would Aimee's claim in this respect be under the 1979 or 1982 Act? Justify your decision.

You should now be able to:

■ understand the operation of ss3, 4, 13 and 14 Supply of Goods and Services Act 1982.

5 Control of exclusion and limitation clauses: common law approaches

Exclusion and limitation clauses (terms) are briefly explained in Topic 1, Terms of a contract.

The general principle of control

A valid and enforceable exclusion or limitation clause will seriously affect a victim's right to bring any successful claim against the party in breach of contract.

In **L'Estrange v Graucob (1934)** a café owner bought a cigarette vending machine and signed a contract that she did not read. One term stated that if the machine did not work then no claim could be made under the Sale of Goods Act 1893 (the equivalent to the current 1979 Act). The machine did not work and even though the implied term of the contract as to fitness for purpose of the goods had been breached the exclusion clause meant the café owner's claim failed.

The courts wished to protect those who have agreed to a term, or terms, in a contract that are prejudicial to them because they had no choice. In consequence, for an exclusion or limitation clause to be valid it must comply with strict rules. These rules allow the courts to *control* the legality of such clauses.

Incorporation

To become part of the contract the exclusion or limitation clause must be effectively 'incorporated' into the contract like any other term, i.e. it must become a valid and enforceable contractual term. The courts have considered various ways in which such 'terms' may succeed or fail in becoming part of the contract:

1 Signature: if a party has signed a contract then that party is bound by all the terms within that contract whether or not that party has read the contract or not. That is the situation that applied in *L'Estrange* v *Graucob* (1934) (see above).

2 Notice: this form of incorporation of the clause in the contract may occur in two situations:

   a If an exclusion/limitation clause is set out, or referred to, in a document which is handed to the party *when* the contract is made *and* that party either knew or should have known that the document contained such a clause.

In this topic you will learn how to:

■ explain the general principles behind exclusion and limitation clauses

■ explain the concept of incorporation

■ describe the main purpose rule

■ explain the operation of overriding oral statements

■ apply the rules in a given situation.

Key cases

L'Estrange v Graucob (1934): courts are not keen on interfering with the terms of a contract voluntarily made between parties.

In **Chapelton v Barry Urban District Council (1940)** Chapelton sat on one of the Council's deckchairs, paid the fee when the attendant arrived and was given a 'receipt' on the reverse of which was an exclusion clause. The chair collapsed, Chapelton was injured and the Council denied liability claiming a valid exclusion clause. The clause was not part of the contract of hire as it was contained in a mere receipt, which Chapelton would not have expected to contain such a clause.

A different scenario occurred in **Olley v Marlborough Court Hotel (1949)** when Mr and Mrs Olley checked into a hotel, paid in advance and went to their bedroom. Mrs Olley then saw a notice on the back of the bedroom door that excluded the hotel's liability for any personal property stolen from the hotel. Mrs Olley's fur coat was taken from her room due to the hotel's negligence. The hotel was liable as notice of the exclusion clause was not drawn to Mrs Olley's attention when the contract was made at the reception desk.

b   The exclusion/limitation clause is displayed *where* the contract is made *and* reasonable notice of its existence is given to that party.

This manner of incorporation is difficult to identify when it is not clear when the contract is actually made. A good example is **Thornton v Shoe Lane Parking Ltd (1971)**, when Thornton decided to use the Shoe Lane car park for the first time. A notice outside the entrance stated 'All cars parked at owner's risk' ('notice 1'). Thornton drove his car to the car park barrier, paid his fee and was given a ticket from the machine that contained, in small print, a notice 'This ticket is issued subject to the conditions of issue displayed on the premises' ('notice 2'). Inside the building was another notice stating Shoe Lane Parking was not liable for any property damage or personal injury ('notice 3'). When collecting his car Thornton was injured due to the negligence of Shoe Lane Parking. Thornton's contract with Shoe Lane Parking incorporated notice 1 as Thornton had notice of it before making the contract. Notice 2 was not sufficient as it was too vague and notice 3 was not incorporated, as Shoe Lane Parking had not taken sufficient steps to draw Thornton's attention to it.

The *Thornton* case is an example of a case where the exemption clause is not displayed when or where the contract is made (notice 3 was displayed inside the car park when the contract had already been made) and nor had reasonable notice of the clause been given (the small print on the barrier ticket – notice 2 – was not sufficient for this purpose).

3   Previous course of dealing: in **Spurling v Bradshaw (1956)** the parties had previously contracted when the victim had received notice of the other party's exclusion clause but had never bothered to read it. On the final contract the victim did not receive notice of the clause until after the contract was made. The other party lost the goods, the subject matter of the contract, and relied on the exclusion clause. The parties had a previous course of dealing so the victim was aware of the other party's standard exclusion clause and was therefore bound by it.

However, this case should be contrasted with **Hollier v Rambler Motors (AMC) Ltd (1972)**, when a customer had previously dealt with a garage on three to four occasions in five years when an exclusion clause had been part of the garage's contract. There was no such clause in the contract in dispute and the Court of Appeal decided the clause was not incorporated under the 'previous course of dealings' principle.

Main purpose rule

Even if the clause is incorporated into the contract the courts may not allow the exclusion or limitation clause to be effective if that clause affects the main purpose of the contract.

A classic example would be in a contract for the carriage of goods. The term as to the route would be fundamental to the contract as the importance of the time for delivery of the goods is crucial. The goods may deteriorate and/or lose value and/or be required for a specified purpose and if a different route is used time is wasted. Because of this importance any exclusion or limitation clause would have no affect on a breach of the term as to the specified route.

In **London and North Western Railway v Neilson (1922)** some important theatrical properties were to be delivered by railway by a certain route. The address labels became detached and the stationmaster innocently sent the items to various wrong destinations. The railway company was unable to rely on its exclusion clause as the main purpose of the contract was the delivery of the items by a specified route and that obligation could not be excluded.

The courts accept it is not always possible to identify the 'main purpose' of a contract so the use of this rule by a victim of a breach of contract is not always successful.

Overriding oral statements

This rule is only effective if 'an express specific oral promise' is given which is inconsistent with the exclusion or limitation clause.

The **Couchman v Hill (1947)** case was dealt with in Topic 1 (Terms of a contract). The auction particulars gave notice of the exclusion clause so it was incorporated into the contract. The clause was not effective as the 'express specific oral' promises by the auctioneer and seller overrode the clause.

Key cases

LNWR v Neilson (1922): the main purpose rule can override an exclusion clause.

Couchman v Hill (1947): if an exemption or limitation clause is incorporated into a contract it may be overridden by an express promise given before, or at the time of, the making the contract.

Activities

Danielle is the owner of a rundown and badly maintained car park in the centre of town. Entry to the car park is by payment at a barrier and then through a dimly lit archway to the car park. The car park has many potholes and rubble, including broken glass, tin cans and fast food cartons. Danielle has placed a handwritten sign at the far end of the archway that states:

'Danielle hereby gives notice that she is not liable for any harm or injury suffered by any user of this car park.'

James is a regular visitor to town and always parks his moped in Danielle's car park. On this occasion he pays the fee at the barrier but cannot see the notice as a large branch from a tree covers it. As he parks his moped in the car park a broken bottle cuts one of the tyres, his moped swerves and he falls off, breaking his arm. His moped is badly damaged.

1. Consider the above and Danielle's notice. Discuss whether the notice contain an exclusion or limitation clause?

2. Presuming it is an exclusion clause, has it been incorporated into James' contract with Danielle – and, if so, how?

3. Presuming the clause is incorporated, do you think James can rely on either the 'main purpose rule' or the 'overriding statement rule' to successfully claim the clause is not effective? What are the reasons for your conclusion?

You should now be able to:

- understand and explain the common law approach to exclusion and limitation clauses
- apply the law to problem situations.

6 Control of exclusion and limitation clauses: statutory approach

If the exclusion or limitation clause passes the common law tests in Topic 5 then it is incorporated into the contract. Parliament has created rules that give further protection to the victim of a breach of contract who may have no claim, or a limited claim, due to the valid exclusion or limitation clause. The clause is a valid and enforceable term of the contract but *may* become invalid and unenforceable due the relevant Act of Parliament and/or Regulation.

Control within the Sale of Goods Act 1979

The relevant sections of the 1979 Act are:

■ Section 13: In *all* contracts when goods are sold by description or by sample, there is an implied condition that they will correspond with the description or sample. If the buyer examines and selects the goods then s13 will still apply.

■ Section 14(2): When goods are sold by a seller *in the course of a business* there is an implied condition that they will be of 'satisfactory quality'.

■ Section 14(3): When goods are sold by a seller *in the course of a business* and the buyer expressly or impliedly makes known to the seller any particular purpose for which the goods are being bought, there is an implied condition under s14(3) that the goods are reasonably fit for that purpose. This is the case whether or not the purpose made known by the buyer is the purpose for which goods of that particular type are commonly supplied.

Control within the Supply of Goods and Services Act 1982

The relevant sections of the 1982 Act are:

■ Sections 3 and 4: These sections are the equivalent to ss13, 14(2) and 14(3) respectively of the 1979 Act but cover goods transferred under a contract of service.

■ Section 13: In a contract for the supply of services, when the supplier is acting in the course of a business, there is an implied term that the supplier will carry out the service with reasonable care and skill.

■ Section 14: In a contract for the supply of a service, when the supplier is acting in the course of a business, there is an implied term that the supplier will carry out the service within a reasonable time.

General control within the Unfair Contract Terms Act 1977

Despite its title the Unfair Contracts Terms Act 1977 (UCTA) does not cover all contracts or unfair terms but concentrates on exclusion and limitation clauses in an attempt to protect **consumers** and others who may be unjustly prejudiced by such clauses. UCTA covers areas of law not within the AQA specification and this study is limited to the relevant sections of the 1979 and 1982 Acts outlined above.

Sale of Goods Act 1979 and Supply of Goods and Services Act 1982: UCTA invalidates *any* exclusion or limitation clause inserted in a consumer contract to cover breaches of:

■ the implied conditions of description (s13), satisfactory quality (s14(2)) and fitness for purpose (s14(3)) in the 1979 Act

■ the equivalent implied terms under ss3 and 4 of the 1982 Act.

It is therefore essential that the victim must satisfy the requirement of being a consumer.

What if the buyer of the goods does *not* deal as a consumer? UCTA allows the implied conditions above to be excluded or limited by the seller but only to the extent that the exclusion or limitation satisfies the 'reasonableness' requirement of UCTA.

Section 11 of UCTA states the requirement of reasonableness is satisfied if: '... the term shall have been a fair and reasonable one to be included having regard to the circumstances which were, or ought reasonably to have been, known to or in the contemplation of the parties when the contract was made'.

Factors the court will consider are:

▪ the relative strength of the parties' bargaining positions
▪ whether the customer was given any inducement to agree to the exclusion or limitation term
▪ whether the customer should have known of the term
▪ whether the goods were altered or adapted at the customer's request.

It should be noted that any contractual term excluding or limiting liability for death or personal injury due to negligence is automatically ineffective.

Supply of Goods and Services Act 1982 ss13 and 14: UCTA applies to these implied terms and the reasonableness test must be applied *and*:

▪ the victim of the exclusion or limitation clause must be a consumer

or

▪ the victim has agreed to the contract on the other party's written standard terms of business.

Obviously in the area of law where reasonableness is under scrutiny each case must be decided on its own facts and it is difficult to identify a common thread or trend in the decisions. However, the following do give some guidance in this respect.

In **George Mitchell Ltd v Finney Lock Seeds Ltd (1983)** the purchaser agreed to buy a particular white cabbage seed but the seller provided the wrong seed and the purchaser's crop failed causing a loss of £63,000. The contract contained a clause limiting the seller's liability to £200 being a refund of the price of the seed. The House of Lords decided the clause was unreasonable, as the sellers could have protected themselves by insurance without increasing the cost of the seed and it was the general practice in the trade not to rely on such clauses.

The above decision should be compared to **Watford Electronics Ltd v Sanderson CFL (2001)**, when computer software did not function properly and caused the purchaser losses. The sales contract included a clause excluding liability and a clause limiting liability to a refund of the purchase price. The Court of Appeal decided both clauses were reasonable. The contract had been the subject of much negotiation so the purchaser was fully aware of the clauses and their possible impact, there was no real difference in bargaining power between the parties and the purchaser had used similar clauses in his contracts when selling products to others.

The Court of Appeal confirmed in **Granville Oil & Chemicals Ltd v Davis Turner & Co. Ltd (2003)** that, in general, the Court of Appeal would not wish to interfere with the terms of a commercial agreement negotiated between parties of equal bargaining power, i.e. an exclusion and/or limitation clause in such a contract is likely to be classed as reasonable.

▪ **Key cases**

George Mitchell v Finney Lock Seeds (1983): the clause was an unreasonable clause as the company relying on the clause could easily have been insured against the excluded losses.

Watford Electronics Ltd v Sanderson CFL (2001): a much negotiated exclusion clause was reasonable.

Granville Oil & Chemicals Ltd v Davis Turner & Co. Ltd (2003): in general, the court would not wish to interfere with a freely negotiated commercial contract.

General control within the Unfair Terms in Consumer Contract Regulations 1999

These regulations replaced Regulations made in 1994. The 1999 Regulations (UTCCR) are applied alongside UCTA and cover *every* term in a contract made between a *consumer* and a *seller or supplier*, not just exclusion or limitation clauses. If the UTCCR consider a term to be *unfair* then that term will not be contractually binding. However, UTCCR only protect a consumer.

Regulation 3(1) states: A consumer is '...a natural person ... acting for purposes which are outside his trade or profession'.

This definition means that, unlike under UCTA, a business can *never* be a consumer under UTCCR.

Regulation 3(1) states: A seller or supplier is '... any natural or legal person who, in contracts covered by these Regulations, is acting for the purposes of his trade, business or profession ...'.

Contracts covered by these Regulations means contracts made between a consumer and a seller or supplier containing terms that have not been 'individually negotiated'.

A term will not have been *individually negotiated* if the contract was prepared in advance and the consumer had no opportunity to influence the wording and meaning of the term. It is for the seller or supplier to prove the term was individually negotiated.

Regulation 5(1) states:

> Unfairness is '...any term which [is] contrary to the requirement of good faith [and] causes a significant imbalance in the parties' rights and obligations arising under the contract, to the detriment of the consumer'.

Schedule 2 of UTCCR lists, as examples, certain factors to be considered by the court:

- The relative bargaining strength of the parties.
- A term requiring the consumer to pay a disproportionately high amount of compensation for a breach.
- A term requiring the consumer to complete obligations even if the seller or supplier does not perform his.
- Special requirements placed on the consumer.

N.B. Regulation 6(2) states the UTCCR will *not* apply if the term is in plain, intelligible language *and* relates to:

- a core contractual term *or*
- the adequacy of the price or remuneration for goods or services provided.

The reasoning here is that the purpose of UTCCR is to protect consumers from hidden injustice. This exception is likely to be interpreted restrictively by the courts to ensure consumers are still protected.

There are only a few cases that show how the senior courts have interpreted and applied UTCCR. As with UCTA, each case is decided on its own facts and will only give a limited indication of how the courts view the Regulations. The main area for discussion will be on what is, and what is not, regarded as an unfair term.

In **Director General of Fair Trading v First National Bank plc (2001)** the consumer signed the supplier's pre-typed standard contract that

Key cases

Director General of Fair Trading v First National Bank plc (2001): a clearly set out term with respect to interest payments to a bank were fair.

included a term that interest on outstanding amounts would be charged even after a court judgement. This meant even if the court reduced the contractual instalments the balance of the debt would still attract interest at the original rate. The Director General issued the claim on behalf of many complainants and The House of Lords decided the term was not unfair. The three main reasons for this decision were that payment of interest on a judgment debt was not unusual, a lender would be expected to want its loan repaid plus interest and the particular term was set out clearly within the contract.

This decision should be compared with **Bairstow Eves London Central Ltd v Smith (2004)**, when an estate agent's commission agreement stated that if payment was late the commission would increase from 1.5 per cent to 3 per cent. The High court decided this term was unfair even though the original commission was for 3 per cent and the reduced commission of 1.5 per cent only applied if payment was made early.

Key cases

Bairstow Eves London Central Ltd v Smith (2004): a term doubling estate agents commission in the event of late payment was unfair.

Activities

Zoë and Mitch are the owners of an electricians' business ('Z and M') and supply electrical goods and services. Elissa visits their shop to purchase an expensive light fitting which is described as 'silver'. Elissa arranges for Z and M to fit the fitting but unfortunately Mitch omits to earth the fitting and Elissa is badly electrocuted. Elissa then discovers the fitting is only made of cheap steel and the internal wiring is defective. Elissa complains but is referred to the reverse of her pre-printed contract with Z and M which states in small print that there is no liability for any goods or services provided by Z and M.

1   Elissa is unhappy about the fitting being steel not silver and she now realises Mitch did not wire the fitting satisfactorily. Outline under what statutory provisions Elissa could bring a claim against Z and M.

2   Discuss whether you think the term in the contract excluding liability is effective to protect Z and M from Elissa's claims.

3   List the major differences between UCTA and UTCCR.

You should now be able to:

■ understand and explain the statutory approach to exclusion and limitation clauses

■ understand the interaction of the common law and statutory approaches

■ apply the law to problem situations

■ construct an appropriate essay on these topics.

7 Overview of contract terms

How to attack a problem involving contract terms and exclusion clauses

It will be usual for the exam question to state specifically that it relates to the rules on 'terms in a contract'. You are therefore made aware that the topics under review are those covered in this chapter, i.e. express or implied terms, the three types of term, exclusion and limitation clauses and whether a statement is a term or a representation. It is unlikely that a question will cover all these topics.

If the question involves, for example, negotiations between the parties and/or an exclusion clause or an apparently unfair term then the question covers representations and terms, UCTA and UTCCR. If the scenario involves a party breaching what is clearly a term, the answer should explain and discuss the types of term and the different rights the victim may have. A question on terms will often be linked with a question on formation of a contract, so one, or some, of the topics in Chapter 5, Formation of contract, may be relevant.

You must always identify the area(s) of law under review and then apply the relevant law to the question. This allows you to concentrate on explaining one area of law and its application without the confusion of other rules of law, principles and cases. This also allows the examiner to evaluate the answer in a logical manner.

For example, one previous exam question in January 2008 was as follows:

> Sara was at a family party when she mentioned to her cousin, Tom, that she needed to rent a car for a fortnight's touring holiday. Tom ran a car repair business and he said he would provide her with a car. In return, she agreed that she would do some urgent secretarial work for him at his garage when her holiday was over. The car broke down on the second day of Sara's holiday. When she learned that it would take a further two days to repair, and that Tom could not supply a replacement car, Sara told Tom that the deal was off and she hired a car for the remainder of her holiday at a cost of £250. Tom had to pay £300 to employ a secretary from an agency to do the urgent secretarial work.
>
> Taking into account the rules on formation of a contract and on terms in a contract, consider what rights, duties and remedies, if any, are available to Sara and to Tom arising out of their agreement in connection with the car and the secretarial services.

You must first identify the topics involved. Sara wanted a car for touring so what type of term relates to the supply of the car – a condition perhaps? What is the effect of the breach of that term by Tom – repudiation and/or damages for Sara? Perhaps Sara is in breach and, if so, to what is Tom entitled?

The question could have referred to an exclusion clause and the answer should discuss whether the clause was incorporated and whether UCTA and UTCCR affected the validity of the clause.

The remainder of the question relates to intention to create legal relations as Sara and Tom are related, and consideration (is secretarial work good consideration for the hire of a car?), which are topics from Chapter 5, Formation of contract.

The answer should also cover remedies, and this is dealt with in Chapter 9, Remedies.

How to write an essay evaluating the law on contract terms and exclusion clauses

The (c) examination question is different to the questions (a) and (b) which are based on the scenario described in the question. The typical (c) question will ask you to 'critically analyse the law of contractual terms and exclusion clauses and to include any appropriate suggestions for reform'. There are 25 marks each for questions (a) and (b) and also 25 marks for question (c) so this question must be given the same consideration as the other two.

The examiner will be expecting an accurate explanation of relevant areas of the law. There must also be a discussion of the fairness, relevance and clarity of those areas. Inevitably, all areas of law are not perfect and a description of that law and a logical criticism of that law are required. The examiner will also expect sensible suggestions as to how the law could be improved or whether in all the circumstances reform is not appropriate or possible.

You should also explain areas of relevant law that work well, are clear and/or fair as 'critically analyse' does not mean all the analysis results in suggestions for reform of bad law.

Activities

1 Briefly outline in your own words, with headings, the rules on incorporation and the effect of UCTA and UTCCR.

2 How would you simplify UCTA and UTCCR?

You should now be able to:

■ answer problem questions involving terms in a contract

■ evaluate the law relating to terms in a contract

■ describe proposals for reform of those areas

■ construct an appropriate essay on these topics.

Vitiating factors

In this topic you will learn how to:

■ state a definition of misrepresentation

■ explain the definition of misrepresentation.

Key terms

Misrepresentation: an untrue statement of fact made by one party to a contract to the other, during negotiations, which induces the other party to enter the contract but which is not a term of the contract.

Representor: the party who makes the untrue statement to the other party.

Representee: the party who receives the untrue statement and becomes the victim in the case.

1 Misrepresentation

Misrepresentation is when a party to a contract has made a statement during negotiations, on which the other party has relied, but the content of the statement does not become a term of the contract. If the other party does not comply with the content of the statement the victim has no claim as the statement is not a contractual term.

This situation is clearly unfair on the victim so common law, and statute, have created the modern law of misrepresentation. The victim, in the situation described above, is now able to claim that the untrue statement forms the basis of a claim and may be awarded damages and/or a remedy called rescission, which is explained below.

The nature of misrepresentation

Adam is thinking about replacing his moped as he has obtained a new job, which pays a higher salary, but he must now commute twenty miles per day. Adam is concerned that his current moped will not prove reliable enough so looks in the local paper for suitable second-hand mopeds. He finds an advert describing what appears to be a suitable replacement.

Adam makes an appointment to view this moped and meets with the seller, Tristan. Adam asks for confirmation that the moped is reliable and that there is a full service history which Tristan confirms. Adam agrees to purchase the moped and both parties sign a short contract which states the names of the parties, the moped's registration and the agreed sale price. Adam hands over the cash and receives a bundle of papers from Tristan.

On his trip home the new moped breaks down and Adam discovers the bundle of papers contains an incomplete service history. The moped is checked by a local garage which states the moped was in for regular repairs when owned by Andy who sold it to Tristan. Adam is very unhappy and asks Tristan for his money back. Tristan refuses, saying there is nothing in the contract about 'reliability' or 'full service history'. Tristan is correct so Adam cannot sue for breach of contract and is left with a moped which is almost valueless. What can he do? If it had not been for Tristan's statements Adam would not have purchased the moped.

What are Adam's losses?

■ He has wasted the cost of buying the moped.

■ He has spent money with the garage on pointless repairs as the moped is not worth repairing.

■ He will either lose his job or have to pay for a taxi to and from his new job until he manages to purchase an adequate replacement.

Case law has developed which allows a party in Adam's position to succeed in a claim and Parliament has also become involved in this area and created the Misrepresentation Act 1967. A person (the **representor**) who makes untrue statements to another (the **representee**) may be liable for those statements even if the statement does not form part of the contract – this is called misrepresentation.

Statements made before, or at the time of, the contract are called 'representations'. It should be noted that representations may, in certain circumstances, become terms of the contract and lead to a claim for breach of contract (see Chapter 6, Contract terms, Topic 1, Terms of a contract). This topic is only concerned with representations that *do not* form part of the contract.

An untrue representation is called a misrepresentation. The result of a misrepresentation is that the contract is voidable, i.e. the victim has the choice of continuing with the contract or not.

Untrue statement

To be a misrepresentation the statement must be untrue. Two situations need to be considered here.

First, a representor may make a statement which is true but does not continue with the statement to reveal the whole truth. The maker of the statement has a duty to continue and reveal the whole truth of the situation.

In **Dimmock v Hallett (1866)** a seller of land told the purchaser there were tenants on the land (which the purchaser wanted) but failed to complete the statement by saying all the tenants had handed in notices to quit and were leaving. This part truth was a misrepresentation.

Second, if a statement by the representor is true when made but becomes untrue or inaccurate before the contract is made then the representor must clarify the change. If the representor remains silent this can be a misrepresentation as the original statement is misleading the victim.

In **With v O'Flanagan (1936)** a GP told the purchaser of his practice that it produced a certain annual income. However, between the statement and the contract the GP fell ill and many of the patients left the practice making the original statement inaccurate. The non-disclosure by the GP of the drop in annual income was a misrepresentation.

Material fact

The statement must be one of material fact and will not be a misrepresentation if it is an opinion or merely an advertising 'puff'. In **Bisset v Wilkinson (1927)** during negotiations a farmer told the purchaser of his land that he thought the land would graze 2,000 sheep, which proved to be inaccurate. As the farmer had never grazed sheep on the land and the purchaser knew this, the statement was one of opinion and so could not be a misrepresentation.

A statement of intention to act in a particular way in the future may be a statement of fact if the representor did not have that intention when making the statement. In **Edgington v Fitzmaurice (1885)** a company issued a prospectus, to encourage investment in the business, stating the money invested would be used in a particular way (which the company never intended to do). This statement of intent was an untrue statement of fact and therefore a misrepresentation.

Finally, a misrepresentation does not have to be in words but may also be made by actions or conduct as shown in **Spice Girls Ltd v Aprilia World Service BV (2000)**. All five members of the Spice Girls took part in the filming of a promotion for Aprilia which was to form part of an advert for Aprilia scooters, but one of the group left, making the promotion and the contract worthless. The group knew when making the promotion that one of the group would be leaving and this was a misrepresentation.

Key cases

Dimmock v Hallett (1866): the maker of a statement has a duty to continue and reveal the whole truth of the situation.

With v O'Flanagan (1936): the maker of a statement has a duty to clarify any change to the truth of the statement before the contract is made.

Bisset v Wilkinson (1927): a pure conjecture is a statement of opinion and therefore cannot be a misrepresentation

Edgington v Fitzmaurice (1885): a statement in a company prospectus about the way in which the company intended to use money raised from investors was a representation and not just a statement of future intention so could be relied on and therefore become a misrepresentation when the statement turned out to be false.

Spice Girls Ltd v Aprilia World Service BV (2000): a misrepresentation does not have to be in words but may also be made by actions or conduct.

Fig. 1 *All five members of the Spice Girls took part in the filming of a promotion but one of the group left, making the promotion and the contract worthless. The group knew when making the promotion that one of the group would be leaving and this was a misrepresentation*

Made by a party to the contract to the other

The statement must be made by one party to another. There is no misrepresentation when the untrue statement is made by a third party, i.e. someone not a party to the contract.

During negotiations

In **Roscorla v Thomas (1842)** after a contract had been made for the sale of a horse, the seller said to the purchaser that the horse was '… sound and free from vice' but the horse was uncontrollable. The purchaser had no claim as the statement was made after the contract had been made.

Induces the other party to enter the contract

It is not enough for the victim to prove the statement is untrue as the statement must be important to the making of the contract.

In **Attwood v Small (1838)** the seller of a mine made an untrue statement to the purchaser about the earning capacity of the mine. The buyer instructed a surveyor to confirm this statement, which the surveyor did (incorrectly). The purchaser bought the mine and then discovered the statement to be untrue. There was no misrepresentation as the purchaser relied on the survey report and not the seller's statement.

It is not a defence for the maker of the statement to claim:

■ the victim could have discovered the truth by taking reasonable steps
■ the victim was unreasonable in relying on the untrue statement.

In **Redgrave v Hurd (1881)** the seller of a business misled the purchaser as to the true earnings of the business. The purchaser had documents available to him before he signed the contract which showed the statement to be untrue but the purchaser chose not to read them and relied on the seller's statement. It was irrelevant the purchaser could have discovered the untruth by reading the documents supplied and this was still a misrepresentation.

An example of the second situation is **Museprime Properties Ltd v Adhill Properties Ltd (1990)** when the purchaser of property relied on inaccurate statements made in auction particulars. The defendant argued that no 'reasonable' purchaser would have relied on these statements, as the statements should have raised doubts about the sense of purchasing the property. The only relevant question was whether the purchaser had relied on the statements (which he had): what the reasonable person would, or would not, have done was irrelevant.

Is not a term of the contract

The statement must *not* be intended to form part of the contract. If the statement is intended to be legally binding then it becomes a term of the contract and cannot remain a representation. If the term is untrue then this forms a claim for breach of contract. It should be noted that claims for misrepresentation and breach of contract are mutually exclusive. However, s1 of the Misrepresentation Act 1967 does now allow a claimant to bring a claim for both misrepresentation and breach of contract.

See *Couchman* v *Hill* (1947) mentioned in Chapter 6, Contract terms, Topic 1, Terms of a contract, when the statement about the 'unserved' heifer was so important that it became a term of the contract.

Silence and misrepresentation

English law is, generally, based on the principle that a party to a contract should be allowed to profit from their superior knowledge and is under no positive obligation to reveal the truth unless asked for a particular piece of information.

In **Fletcher v Krell (1873)** a woman applied for a job of governess. She was not asked and did not volunteer that she was a divorcee (which, due to the morals of the period, would mean she would not be offered the position). There was no misrepresentation as the applicant was under no duty to disclose her status and she was not asked about it.

Exceptions (i.e. when silence may be a misrepresentation)

Relationship of trust

If a relationship is based on trust then silence by the representor may prove to be a misrepresentation. This trust will exist in relationships between lawyer and client, parent and child and in similar situations.

In **Tate v Williamson (1866)** a financial adviser advised his client to sell some land at an undervalue to clear debts. The adviser then purchased the land at half its value but did not tell his client. The silence by the adviser that he was to buy the land was a breach of trust and was a misrepresentation.

Contracts of 'utmost good faith'

An example of such a contract is an application for insurance when non-disclosure would result in the insurance company charging a lower premium than would otherwise be the case.

In **Lambert v Cooperative Insurance Society (1975)** a woman renewed her jewellery insurance without telling the insurance company her husband had recently been convicted of conspiracy to steal. This was an important fact which would have affected the insurer's decision whether to renew the insurance and, if so, at what premium. The silence of the woman was a misrepresentation and the company was entitled to declare the policy void.

> **Key cases**
>
> **Fletcher v Krell (1873)**: there is no common law obligation to disclose information that has not been requested, and silence will not be a misrepresentation.
>
> **Tate v Williamson (1866)**: the silence by the adviser was a breach of trust and was therefore a misrepresentation.
>
> **Lambert v Cooperative Insurance Society (1975)**: silence of the claimant with respect to material facts for a contract of insurance was a misrepresentation.

> **Activity**
>
> Study some advertisements in the media and consider if they are mere representations or terms of the contract.

You should now be able to:

■ understand the meaning of misrepresentation.

2 Types of misrepresentation

When the representor makes an untrue statement of fact before a contract is entered into, there are various alternatives as to what that person will have been thinking at the time of making the statement. The law of misrepresentation has developed in an attempt to cover these different situations and there are now three main types of misrepresentation:

■ Fraudulent misrepresentation: when the representor had intentionally lied about a fact or been reckless as to its truth.

■ Negligent misrepresentation: when the representor had been careless about the truth of a statement.

■ Innocent misrepresentation: when the representor honestly believed the statement was the truth.

Re-read the scenario at the start of Topic 1. First, Tristan may have known the moped was unreliable and did not have a full service history but lied to Adam in order to obtain the best sale price possible. Second, Tristan may have made the statements off the top of his head without checking if they were true or not. Finally, Tristan may have genuinely, but mistakenly, believed the statements he made to be true.

Fraudulent misrepresentation and remedies

This type of misrepresentation has its origins in the common law and is called the 'tort of deceit'. This is when the representor has made a statement that the representor knows to be untrue or is reckless as to whether it is true or not, i.e. the representor has been fraudulent in respect of the truth of the statement. Consider what was in Tristan's mind in the first part of the scenario described above.

In **Derry v Peek (1889)** a tram company used horses to pull its trams. The directors of the company believed that under a recent Act of Parliament the Board of Trade would consent to the company using motor-driven trams and that this consent was a formality, but did not check. The use of horse-drawn trams would make the company more profitable and the directors advertised for investors for the company on this basis. The company did not obtain the consent and the company shares dropped in value. The purchasers of the shares sued for their losses but this was not a fraudulent misrepresentation as the directors were only careless as to whether what they said was true.

Remedies for fraudulent misrepresentation

The victim of a fraudulent misrepresentation will be very unhappy with the position in which they find themselves. For example, Adam has lost out financially and will also incur future expenses. The law has developed two remedies available in a claim for misrepresentation:

Rescission

This is an equitable remedy which means the court will only award it if it is fair to do so in all the circumstances. Rescission means the parties are returned to the positions they were in before the contract was made. The justification for this rule is that the misrepresentation means the contract was entered into by the victim under a misapprehension of the true situation, i.e. if the victim had known the truth there would have been no contract.

> ### Key cases
>
> **Derry v Peek (1889)**: a fraudulent misrepresentation is when the person making the statement has made a statement which he knows to be untrue or is reckless as to whether it is true or not.

Damages

Damages is the title of the order made by the court that one party should pay the other money as a form of compensation for losses and harm suffered. There are two principles to consider:

First, because the claim is based on the 'tort of deceit' the court will award damages even if they are not foreseeable to the defendant, provided causation can be proved.

In **Smith New Court v Scrimgeour Vickers (1996)** the victim had been induced by an untruthful statement to buy shares in a company for 82p per share when their true market value was 78p. The victim discovered the lie and sold the shares, now worth only 30p–49p per share. The question was whether the award of damages was limited to those foreseeable at the time (i.e. the difference between the price paid and the true value of the shares) or based on the actual loss to the victim. The court awarded the victim damages based on the difference between the amount paid of 82p and the final sale price, which is more than the usual award of damages in a contractual situation.

Second, the calculation of contractual damages is usually based on putting the victim in the position they would have been in had the contract been completed properly. Damages based on misrepresentation aim to put the victim in the position they were in before the misrepresentation occurred. However, the court seems willing to take the view that contractual damages may be appropriate in certain circumstances.

In **East v Maurer (1991)** the representor sold his hairdressing business to the victim stating he would not open another salon in the same area which he then did. The victim suffered a loss of profit that was only recoverable under breach of contract not misrepresentation. The court decided the victim would have purchased a different business if the truth had been known. The calculation of damages awarded him the profit he would have earned from that business.

Negligent misrepresentation and remedies

This type of misrepresentation is when the representor has been careless and in breach of duty as to whether a statement is true or not. There are two types of negligent misrepresentation:

Common law

Until 1964 the common law gave the victim no remedy for a negligent misrepresentation as the only claim allowed was that for fraudulent misrepresentation.

In **Hedley Byrne & Co. Ltd v Heller & Partners Ltd (1964)** the victim asked the bankers for a company named Easipower for a financial reference in respect of Easipower. The bankers supplied the reference which had been negligently prepared and stated Easipower to be in a good financial position. The victim relied on this reference and entered into a contract with Easipower which then went into liquidation owing the victim money. The victim sued the bankers for these losses and, in principle, the bankers were liable to the victim for these losses.

Various conditions were set out by the House of Lords before such a claim would be successful. These conditions have been considered and refined by later decisions. The two main conditions and the ones that cause the most difficulty are that there must be a 'special relationship' and 'proximity' between the victim and the representor.

> ### Key cases
>
> **Smith New Court v Scrimgeour Vickers (1996)**: because the claim is based on the 'tort of deceit' the court will award damages even if they are not foreseeable to the defendant.
>
> **East v Maurer (1991)**: here the calculation of damages awarded him the profit he would have earned from that business.
>
> **Hedley Byrne & Co. Ltd v Heller & Partners Ltd (1964)**: a claim for a misrepresentation based on negligence would be allowed.

In **Goodwill v British Pregnancy Advisory Service (1996)** a married man (M) had a vasectomy and was told he need take no further contraceptive precautions. M had an affair with Miss Goodwill (G) who followed the advice and took no precautions herself. G fell pregnant and sued the BPAS for negligent misrepresentation. The court decided the claim would fail as, amongst other reasons, there was no special relationship between the BPAS and G. The BPAS was not employed to confer a benefit on M's future sexual partners.

However, in **Esso v Marden (1976)** Esso let a garage to Mr Marden and told him during negotiations that the garage would sell 200,000 gallons of petrol per year. Esso did not check with the local council and under planning law the layout of the garage had to be altered so the petrol sales were a lot lower than stated. Esso was liable as it had been careless and there was proximity between the parties as they were involved in negotiations for a contract.

Misrepresentation Act 1967

Section 2(1) of the Misrepresentation Act (the '1967 Act') created a statutory liability for negligent misrepresentation which does not require there to be a 'special relationship' or 'proximity' between the parties. All that is needed is for there to be a misrepresentation which results in a contract and the victim suffers loss.

An important aspect of the 1967 Act is that once the victim has proved there was a misrepresentation the onus is then on the representor to prove that there were reasonable grounds to believe the statement was true. This reverses the burden of proof in civil cases when it for the victim to prove the case. As a result, the 1967 Act is preferable for the victim to use than *Hedley Byrne* (1964).

In **Howard Marine v Ogden & Sons (1978)** a company wanted to hire barges to carry earth and asked for advice about capacity and was told by the representor the barges carried 1,600 tons when the correct capacity was 1,055. The company relied on the advice and it took longer than anticipated to complete the job. The company had proved a misrepresentation and the representor had not proved it had reasonable grounds to believe its statement was true.

Remedies for negligent misrepresentation

▪ Rescission (see fraudulent misrepresentation on p118)

and/or

▪ Damages

Under *Hedley Byrne* the damages are based on tort and are those that are reasonably foreseeable. However, there is some confusion about damages under the 1967 Act. The case below shows the principle applied by the Court of Appeal and, although criticised by academics and queried in other cases, the stated principle appears to be the current law for damages under s2(1). The principle is that damages under s2(1) are not subject to the reasonable foreseeability rule and are based on how damages are measured under fraudulent misrepresentation.

In **Royscot Trust Ltd v Rogerson (1991)** a car dealer negligently misrepresented to a finance company the amount of a deposit paid for a car by a purchaser. The finance company lost money when the purchaser defaulted on the hire-purchase agreement. The Court of Appeal confirmed the damages for negligent misrepresentation under the Act are based on tort and also confirmed that the reasonable foreseeability test does not apply to s2(1) damages.

Innocent misrepresentation and remedies

Innocent misrepresentation is when the representor genuinely believes the statement to be true and is not at fault.

Remedies for innocent misrepresentation

Rescission and damages are not both available for innocent misrepresentation (as for fraudulent and negligent misrepresentation) but only as alternative remedies.

- Rescission (see fraudulent and negligent misrepresentation)

or

- Damages: There is no *right* to damages for an innocent misrepresentation. The court has discretion to award damages instead of rescission. The type of damages is probably foreseeable and not as under the tort of deceit.

Rescission as a remedy

Rescission may no longer be available to the victim in certain situations. Rescission is an equitable remedy and the court will always use discretion when deciding if this remedy is appropriate or not.

Impossibility of restitution

In **Clarke v Dickson (1858)** the representor misled the victim about the shares in a partnership. By the time the victim discovered the true facts the partnership had been converted into a limited company. Rescission was not available as the victim could not return a partnership to the representor.

The contract is affirmed

The victim may choose to affirm the contract in some way even though they are aware of the misrepresentation. In these circumstances the victim is no longer able to claim the contract should be set aside due to their own affirmation of its existence.

In **Long v Lloyd (1958)** a seller misrepresented that a lorry had a certain fuel consumption. The purchaser discovered the misrepresentation and returned the lorry for repairs to which the seller had agreed to contribute. Rescission was not allowed as the purchaser had affirmed the contract by returning the lorry for repair.

Delay

A delay (for whatever reason) in bringing the claim for misrepresentation to court will mean rescission is not available as a remedy.

In **Leaf v International Galleries (1950)** a seller misrepresented a painting as a Constable but the purchaser only became aware of the misrepresentation when trying to sell it five years later. Rescission was not allowed due to delay.

Third party has gained rights

If a third party has gained an interest in the goods then rescission will not be granted as this would be unfair on the innocent third party.

In **Lewis v Averay (1972)** a seller of a car was misled by the purchaser as to the purchaser's true identity. As a result the seller allowed the purchaser to take the car before the cheque cleared. In the meantime, the purchaser sold the car to an innocent third party and the purchaser's cheque then bounced. The seller's only effective remedy was to claim rescission and to ask for the car to be returned to him by the third party. The seller's claim for rescission failed as in the circumstances it would be unfair to deprive the third party of the car purchased in good faith.

> **Key cases**
>
> **Clarke v Dickson (1858)**: rescission is not allowed if the parties cannot be restored to their pre-contractual position.
>
> **Long v Lloyd (1958)**: the claimant had affirmed the contract even though aware of the misrepresentation and so could not claim rescission.
>
> **Leaf v International Galleries (1950)**: delay in bringing the claim for misrepresentation to court will mean rescission is not available as a remedy.
>
> **Lewis v Averay (1972)**: where a third party has gained an interest in the goods then rescission will not be granted.

■ Activity

It will be usual for the exam question to state specifically that the law of misrepresentation is to be applied to a given scenario. This allows you to know exactly what area of the law is expected in the answer. The question may also require the application of another area of law as well, e.g. a question involving misrepresentation will often also contain a question about breach of contract relating to the same scenario.

Use the scenario on p114 to decide:

1 what misrepresentations, if any, have been made by Adam and, if so, what type?

2 whether any of the misrepresentations, if any, have become terms of the contract and, if so, why?

You should now be able to:

- understand the different types of misrepresentation

- apply the law to problem situations.

3 Examination techniques

Before any application of the law is used a statement of the relevant law of misrepresentation is essential. The answer must commence with the definition of misrepresentation and an explanation of any part of the definition that you consider may be of particular relevance to the question. For example, the question may refer to the representor making a statement which may be of fact or of opinion. Specific reference should be made to this area of the definition with case(s) used in support of the law.

The answer should then explain the three types of misrepresentation. You should be able to identify when reading the question which type or types of misrepresentation is or are involved. The exam scenario will rarely involve a question involving innocent misrepresentation. It is likely the representor will have made the statement intentionally knowing it was untrue or was careless as to the truth of the statement. You must therefore explain the rules about fraudulent misrepresentation and/or negligent misrepresentation in some detail with reference to cases. You must take particular care to differentiate between common law and statutory negligent misrepresentation and the shift in the burden of proof in the latter.

You should now be in a position to apply the law stated in your answer. The definition should be applied to ensure all the component parts of misrepresentation are present. For example, if there was confusion over whether the statement was one of fact or opinion then the rule and relevant case should be discussed and a justified conclusion reached.

You should then decide which type of misrepresentation applies, explain why and whether the claim is likely to succeed or not.

Even if the conclusion to the answer is that the claim will fail the remedies for misrepresentation must now be mentioned. Rescission and damages should be explained. Depending on the type of misrepresentation will decide whether both are claimable. Rescission may be unavailable if, for example, there has been a delay in making the claim and the test of foreseeability of loss must be mentioned.

The question will often refer to 'rights' and 'remedies' and you must ensure enough time is allowed for an explanation and application of appropriate remedies at the end of the answer.

The examiner is looking for a clear, concise and accurate explanation and application of the relevant law. It is worth spending a little time when reading the scenario to note those aspects of the law which strike you as important, for example which type of misrepresentation is involved. This makes the stating of the law more relevant and saves time overall.

You should now be able to:

- ▪ answer problem questions involving misrepresentation
- ▪ evaluate the law relating to misrepresentation
- ▪ describe proposals for reform of those areas
- ▪ construct an appropriate essay on these topics.

8 Discharge of contract

In this topic you will learn how to:

- state a definition of the term discharge of contract
- outline the different ways in which a contract may be discharged
- explain the effect of discharge of contract.

Key terms

Discharge of a contract: when it has come to an end. The contract will have created obligations with which the parties must comply and when completed the contract is discharged.

Frustrating event: one that makes completion of the contract 'radically different' from what was originally agreed between the parties. It must be an event that is unforeseen **and** is not the fault of either party.

1 Discharge of contract

Chapter 5, Formation of contract dealt with the formation of a contract, and this chapter deals with the end of a contract. The majority of contracts will end by the parties performing all their respective obligations in which case the law will not become involved.

However, sometimes a contract will be ended by one of the parties not performing some or all of their primary obligations. This may result in secondary obligations being imposed on the party at fault, for example by the payment of damages. This chapter will cover three ways a contract may end and explain and discuss the impact of each in turn.

The meaning of discharge of contract

Imagine Kurtis (a self-employed decorator) has contracted with Simon to paint Simon's conservatory for a fee of £1,000. It is agreed the painting will be completed by Friday. Apart from Kurtis completing the contract, there are three possible ways in which the contract may be **discharged**.

First, Kurtis commences painting the conservatory on the Monday, paints the ceiling and three of the walls but leaves the job incomplete on Friday. Kurtis arrives on Saturday morning and apologises to Simon for the non-completion of the contract. Kurtis asks for £800 as he has completed 80 per cent of the work. The contract has not been completed by Kurtis and the basic rule is that if a party has not completed their side of the bargain they are unable to claim *any* payment. This is called the strict rule of 'performance'. Kurtis is obviously not entitled to the £1,000 and may not be entitled to the £800. The contract would have been 'discharged' had Kurtis completed the entire contract.

Second, Kurtis has made the same contract as above. However, having commenced painting on the Monday through no one's fault and without warning the conservatory burns down so Kurtis is unable to complete the contract. Kurtis is now unable to claim full payment although he has done nothing wrong. This situation is called the 'frustration' of a contract. The **frustrating event** discharges the contract.

Third, Kurtis has made the same contract. The painting must be completed by the Friday as Simon is holding his engagement party on the Saturday and the conservatory is required. Kurtis has commenced the painting but has worked rather slowly so the work is not completed by Friday evening. Simon calls in another decorator to complete the work on Saturday morning. Kurtis has breached (broken) a term of the contract. If the breach is of a term fundamental to the contract then the term is a condition and Simon may sue Kurtis for damages (for example, the extra cost of employing the second decorator) and/or for repudiation (i.e. the contract is discharged and obligations under the contract are ended).

To summarise the above:

1 Complete *performance* discharges a contract.
2 A *frustrating* event discharges a contract.
3 A *breach* of a condition discharges a contract (if the victim so chooses).

The effect of discharge of contract and the link to remedies

The discharge of a contract ends the contract and the parties' respective obligations to each other are ended. The court regards the contract as valid from the date of creation up to the time of discharge.

If both parties complete the contract satisfactorily then the contract is discharged. This chapter is not concerned with that scenario. The three rules stated above will terminate a contract and because the contract has not been completed the court has to decide to what, if anything, the disappointed party (or parties, in the case of frustration) is entitled.

If Kurtis has only *performed part* of the contract to what, if anything, is he entitled? If Kurtis cannot complete the contract due to an *unforeseen incident*, to what are Simon and Kurtis entitled? Finally, if Kurtis *breaches* a condition of the contract, to what is Simon entitled?

Activity

Create three scenarios, each with one type of discharge of contract.

You should now be able to:

- ■ understand the meaning of discharge of contract.

2 Performance

When all parties have performed their obligations under a contract, that contract is completed and is therefore discharged (i.e. terminated).

The strict rule

The strict rule can be seen to be unfair.

In **Cutter v Powell (1795)**, Cutter was a crew member and was to be paid as second mate on a trip from Jamaica to Liverpool. The boat left Jamaica on 2 August and was due in Liverpool on 9 October. Cutter died on 20 September. His widow sued for his wages from 2 August to 20 September. The claim was dismissed as Cutter had signed up to complete the entire trip and clearly had not completed all his obligations.

The application of the strict rule does seem unfair but was confirmed in *Re Moore & Co.* v *Landauer & Co.* (1921), when tinned fruit was sold and described as being in cases of 30 tins per case. The purchaser received the correct number of tins in total but some cases contained 24 tins in a case. The seller had not completed the contract (i.e. there was incomplete performance) so the purchaser could reject the cases.

It should be noted that s15(A) of the Sale of Goods Act 1979 might now mean a different decision would be reached. A business purchaser is not entitled to reject goods which are only slightly different from the contractual description and it would be unreasonable to reject them.

As these cases show, the strict rule of performance can operate harshly and as a result the courts have developed exceptions to the strict rule.

Divisibility

If a contract can be seen as comprising separate parts then non-completion of one part is *not* a breach of the whole contract, e.g. a salary is described as yearly but is **divisible** into monthly payments so an employee leaving after three months is still entitled to three month's salary. The employee in this example may, of course, still be in a breach of contract if the contract was for a fixed period and the employee left early without authority, but that does not terminate the employee's right to the three-months' salary.

In **Ritchie v Atkinson (1808)** a ship-owner agreed to carry a specific cargo at an agreed rate per ton. He carried only a part of the cargo. The ship-owner was entitled to be paid for the part cargo carried (the contract was divisible as it specified a price to be paid per ton) but was liable in damages for breach of contract for not carrying the remainder of the delivery.

In this topic you will learn how to:

- ■ define the strict rule as to performance
- ■ distinguish between substantial and part performance
- ■ explain the importance of time for performance of a contract
- ■ state the remedies for failure to perform
- ■ apply the rules in a given situation.

Key terms

The strict rule: if the agreement is that payment will be made on completion of the contract then the strict rule for performance is that there must be 100 per cent completion of a party's obligations under the contract for that party to be entitled to payment.

Divisibility: if a contract specifies that payment is due from time to time as performance of a particular part of the contract is completed then this a 'severable' contract.

Key cases

Cutter v Powell (1795): if the contract has not been completed and some obligation(s) remain outstanding then no payment is due at all.

Ritchie v Atkinson (1808): the contract was divisible as it specified a price to be paid per ton.

Key terms

Quantum meruit: the basis for an award made by a court whereby one party claims reasonable payment for a benefit given or for work done.

Time of the essence: when time for performance of the contract is important.

Key cases

Hoenig v Isaacs (1952): a decorator contracted to decorate and supply furniture for £750 but supplied two pieces of defective furniture which could be repaired for £55; the contract was substantially completed on a financial basis (93 per cent) so the decorator was entitled to be paid for what he had done on a *quantum meruit* basis less the cost of repairing the furniture.

Bolton v Mahadeva (1972): as there was no substantial completion of the contract, the claimant was entitled to nothing.

Sumpter v Hedges (1898): if the innocent party has no option but to take the benefit of the work done then there is no consent to part performance.

Union Eagle Ltd v Golden Achievement Ltd (1997): a contract for the sale of a flat specified the time for completion of the contract as 5.00pm and time was expressly stated to be 'of the essence'; the purchaser delivered the purchase price at 5.10pm and the seller repudiated the contract; the seller was entitled to repudiate as the time for completion had been made a condition of the contract.

Charles Rickards Ltd v Oppenheim (1950): a party to the contract who has waived a term as to time can later make it of the essence again.

Substantial or part performance

There are two further exceptions to the strict rule:

1 If a party has completed a '*substantial*' amount of work under the contract then that party is entitled to be paid for the work done

2 If a party accepts a *partial* performance of the contract.

In both exceptions the party 'at fault' may be entitled to payment based on *quantum meruit*, as shown in the case of **Hoenig v Isaacs (1952)**.

The question arises as to what 'substantial' means and was considered again in **Bolton v Mahadeva (1972)** when a builder contracted to install a central heating system for £560. His installation was defective and repairs cost £170 (i.e. on a financial basis he had carried out 69 per cent of the work). The builder was entitled to nothing, as there was no substantial completion of the contract.

If one party has agreed the other party need not complete the entire contract then the strict rule will not apply. However, the consent must be in the form of a specific acknowledgement that the defaulting party is entitled to be paid for what they have completed so far.

In **Sumpter v Hedges (1898)** a builder contracted to build two houses for £565, completed some work then ran out of money so the customer completed the outstanding work. The builder was not entitled to be paid for the work he had done as the customer had no alternative but to complete the work himself and had not consented to the builder's part performance.

Time of performance

Generally, failure to complete a contract on time is treated as a breach of warranty so a claim can only be made for damages and the contract will continue. The court will regard time as a condition (known as making '**time of the essence**'), which allows the victim to claim the contract is repudiated (terminated) and/or damages if:

■ the parties have *expressly stated* in the contract that time is of the essence

or

■ *in the circumstances* time for completion is critical

or

■ one party has failed to perform on time and the other has insisted on a *new date for completion* as 'time of the essence'.

The **Union Eagle Ltd v Golden Achievement Ltd (1997)** case is an example of the first situation in which time is of the essence. However, what would happen if a contract specified time was of the essence but the parties agreed to extend the time for completion indefinitely? Could either party subsequently insist on a new date for completion as making time of the essence again? This occurred in the case of **Charles Rickards Ltd v Oppenheim (1950)**, when the original date for the supply of a car (date 1) was of the essence but the parties agreed to extend the date. The purchaser then became impatient with the continuing delay and gave twenty-eight days notice of a new date for completion (date 2), which the supplier failed to meet. The court held date 2 had made time of the essence again and the purchaser was entitled to reject the car when it was delivered after this new date.

Remedies for failure to perform

The innocent party in this type of case has to deal with a contract that is only partly performed or is performed but not in accordance with the terms agreed. Chapter 9, Remedies covers the different remedies available to a victim in detail but an outline of the remedies which may be appropriate for non-performance are set out below.

In the first scenario, Kurtis has only completed 80 per cent of the work within the agreed time span. Kurtis admits he is in the wrong but is demanding 80 per cent of his fee for the work completed (which is not defective in any way). The remedy for Kurtis is to seek damages to compensate him for the work done based on quantum meruit.

Simon meanwhile has been left with a partially decorated conservatory and a decorator who is unwilling or unable to complete the work. Simon may consider three possibilities.

First, he may try and insist Kurtis returns to complete the outstanding 20 per cent of the work. The court may order a party to complete a contract in limited circumstances – this is called an order for 'specific performance'. This type of order is not used to order the completion of personal services, as the court is unable to monitor the continuing situation in what is already a tense atmosphere.

Simon's more realistic alternative is to deny that Kurtis is entitled to any payment relying on the strict performance rule. No doubt Kurtis would argue that one of the exceptions applies – probably that he has 'substantially' performed the contract. An argument will then occur as to whether the work completed by Kurtis is substantial or not.

Finally, Simon may sue Kurtis for breach of contract as the work was not completed on time. This situation overlaps with the third scenario. If time is *not* of the essence then Simon may only claim a breach of warranty and damages as a remedy – probably the cost of another decorator completing the 20 per cent of uncompleted work less the balance of £200 Simon would have paid Kurtis for this work anyway. If time *is* of the essence, Kurtis has breached a condition so Simon may sue for damages and/or that the contract is repudiated. As Kurtis does not wish to return and it is unlikely Simon would want him to then repudiation is rather academic.

Activities

1. Define the strict rule of performance and explain why it may be an unfair rule.

2. Create a scenario where one exception to the strict rule may be applied.

You should now be able to:

- understand the importance of performance of a contract
- understand the consequences of failure to perform
- apply the law to problem situations.

Key cases

Paradine v Jane (1647): confirmed the common law rule that in the circumstances the contract must continue even though this might be unfair on one of the parties.

Taylor v Caldwell (1863): decided that there is an implied term in all contracts that if an unforeseen event occurs before completion of the contract that makes completion impossible, then the parties have no further obligations to each other; the contract will be valid and enforceable up to the frustrating event but after the event all future obligations are cancelled.

Denny, Mott & Dickson v James Fraser (1944): a government ban on contracts such as the one in existence – the ban being made after the contract is made – will frustrate the contract for subsequent illegality.

Krell v Henry (1903): if the main reason for the contract is based on a particular event or purpose and that event or purpose will not take place then the contract may be frustrated.

Herne Bay Steamboat Co. v Hutton (1903): unlike *Krell* v *Henry*, the main purpose of the contract still existed so the contract was not frustrated.

3 Frustration

Imagine a contract has been made but before the contract can be completed an event occurs (which is *not* the *fault* of either party *and* which is *unforeseen*) which makes completion of the contract impossible. This is now known as a *frustrating event*.

The general principle

In **Paradine v Jane (1647)** a tenant was evicted from his land due to an invading army. The landlord sued for rent arrears and the court held the rent had to be paid even though the tenant was no longer in occupation of the land and it was impossible for him to return.

The decision in *Paradine* seems harsh on the tenant. As a result the courts developed a principle called frustration to allow fairer decisions to be made in such circumstances.

In **Taylor v Caldwell (1863)** an owner contracted to rent out his music hall to a hirer so that musicals could be performed. Due to no-one's fault and before the musicals could take place the music hall burned down. The hirer had spent money advertising the musicals for which he would be paid on completion of the contract. The hirer wanted reimbursement of these expenses. The court decided it was now impossible to complete the contract, it was frustrated, the parties' future obligations to each other under the contract were terminated so the owner did not have to pay the hirer for the expenses.

The courts have now defined frustration as occurring when an event makes the performance of the contract 'radically different' from what was originally agreed between the parties.

Impossibility

If it is impossible for the contract to be completed, because for example the subject matter of the contract is destroyed, then the contract may be frustrated.

This applies to *Taylor* v *Caldwell* (1863), as can be seen from the facts described above, the contract was impossible to complete due to the destruction of the music hall.

Subsequent illegality

If, due to a change in the law the purpose for which the contract was made becomes illegal then the contract may be frustrated such as in **Denny, Mott & Dickson v James Fraser (1944)**, where a contract was made for the sale of timber, but before the contract was completed the government banned the sale of such timber. The court held the contract was frustrated as the main purpose for the contract was now illegal.

Radical change in circumstances

In **Krell v Henry (1903)**, a guest hired a hotel room in order to view Edward VII's coronation procession. The Prince became ill and the coronation was postponed. The room had to be paid for on the day of the coronation and the guest refused to pay. The court decided the contract was based on the viewing of the coronation procession and as this would not occur the contract was frustrated so the guest did not have to pay for the room.

In **Herne Bay Steamboat Co. v Hutton (1903)**, Hutton hired a boat in order to see the fleet when the King viewed it. Hutton claimed he did not have to pay for the reason set out in *Krell* above. However, the court held the contract was not frustrated as one reason for the contract still remained (to view the fleet). Hutton had to pay for the boat hire.

When frustration may not apply

Generally, courts wish parties to complete their contractual obligations and will only allow frustration to interfere with the contract in the three situations listed above. Other situations may arise when frustration seems applicable but is not accepted by the courts.

Self-induced frustration

In **Maritime National Fish Ltd v Ocean Trawlers Ltd (1935)** a fishing company owned two trawlers and contracted to hire a third for the purpose of commercial fishing. The company needed a licence for all fishing vessels and was only allowed two, which it allocated to its own trawlers. The company then claimed frustration of the hire contract, as it could no longer use the hired trawler (a radical change in circumstances). The court decided frustration did not apply and the contract was still valid. The 'frustrating' event was within the company's control, and classed as self-induced frustration, as it could have allocated one licence to the hired trawler.

The contract has become less profitable

In **Davis Contractors Ltd v Fareham UDC (1956)**, builders contracted to build houses for the UDC for £94,000 but then discovered it would cost £115,000 to complete the contract due to labour shortages. The builders claimed frustration of the contract but were unsuccessful as the contract was not radically different to what the parties had originally intended, just less profitable.

This decision should be compared with *Williams v Roffey Bros & Nichols (Contractors) Ltd* (1990) (Chapter 5, Formation of contract, Topic 3, Consideration) when an extra payment, caused by labour shortage problems, was enforceable. It is accepted there is inconsistency in the decisions but the cases do have subtle differences. For example, in *Davis* (1956) the houses had been built and the builder then asked for extra payment while in *Williams* (1990) the roofing work *had not been completed* and it was the builder who *offered* the extra payment to the sub-contractor.

The 'event' was either a 'foreseeable' risk or referred to in the contract itself

In **Amalgamated Investment v Walker Ltd (1977)** a buyer contracted to buy a building for redevelopment for £1.7m. Unknown to both parties the building then became listed by the government so its value dropped to £200,000. The court decided this was not a frustrating event as the listing of old buildings was a foreseeable risk and the original price had to be paid.

Fig. 1 *The listing of a building was judged to be a foreseeable risk prior to its purchase, and so was not classed as a frustrating event*

Key terms

Self induced frustration: when non-completion of the contract is due to an event which is under the control of that party.

Key cases

Maritime National Fish Ltd v Ocean Trawlers Ltd (1935): self-induced frustration is not frustration as where the defendant chooses which contract not to perform.

Davis Contractors Ltd v Fareham UDC (1956): merely because a contract becomes less profitable and/or more difficult to complete does not frustrate the contract.

Amalgamated Investment v Walker Ltd (1977): if the event was foreseeable or was specifically described in the contract then if that event occurs it does not frustrate the contract.

Remedies for frustration

At common law the frustrating event automatically terminates the contract at the time of the event. Obligations already existing must be completed but future obligations are terminated. This explains why the customer in *Krell* v *Henry* (1903) did not have to pay for the room, as the payment was an obligation that only had to be performed when the room was actually used.

This decision should be compared to *Chandler* v *Webster* (1904), when the facts are the same except the room had to be paid for in advance when the room was booked. The court decided the contract was frustrated but the man still had to pay for the room. His obligation to pay (when booking the room) arose before the frustrating event (the postponement of the coronation).

The courts felt there was unfairness between these two cases so in *Fibrosa Spolka Ackyjna* v *Fairbairn Lawson Combe Barbour Ltd* (1943) the House of Lords decided that if there had been a total failure of consideration then money already paid could be recovered (this case may be referred to as the *Fibrosa* case).

However, in a contractual situation it is rare for there to be a total failure of consideration. A party to a contract is likely to have provided something under the contract, no matter how negligible, which means the precedent of the *Fibrosa* case would not be commonly applicable.

Law Reform (Frustrated Contracts) Act 1943

The rule of frustration was created to help innocent parties but caused its own problems (see *Chandler* v *Webster* (1904) above). Parliament therefore passed the 1943 Act to cover what happens *once* a frustrating event has occurred, i.e. to help decide who would owe what and to whom.

The Act does *not* affect the law on the situations *when* frustration may occur; it *only* applies to situations where frustration is found to exist.

The Act covers three areas:

1 Money already paid over (e.g. a deposit) is recoverable, and money already due under the contract (as in *Chandler*) is not payable.

2 The court can use its discretion to order compensation to be paid for work done and expenses incurred under the contract before the frustrating event (provided there was an obligation to pay money before the frustrating event). The quantification of the amount due is based on the principle of *quantum meruit* (see p126 for the definition).

3 The court may order compensation to be paid for any valuable benefit one party may acquire under the frustrated contract.

Conclusion

A frustrating event may only occur if the event is not due to the fault of any party and the event is unforeseen. A frustrating event will terminate the contract immediately and future contractual obligations of the parties are cancelled. The 1943 Act allows the court some discretion to decide who may owe what and to whom.

In the scenario on p124, Kurtis is unable to complete the contract as the conservatory is destroyed. This event was the fault of neither Kurtis nor Simon, so it is a frustrating event. As a result the contract is discharged, Kurtis may be entitled to be paid for the work he has completed and may receive compensation for the expenses he has incurred so far, e.g. the cost of materials used while Simon does not have to pay for the remainder of the contract.

You should now be able to:

■ understand the importance of frustration of contract

■ understand the consequences of frustration of contract

■ apply the law to problem situations.

4 Breach

When a party fails to perform an obligation under a contract then that party may be sued for breach of contract.

The nature of breach

The victim will always be entitled to claim damages but the contract will only be terminated depending on the type of term that has been breached (see Chapter 6, Contract terms, Topic 1, Terms of a contract).

The different effects of breach of condition and warranty

Conditions

When a condition is breached (broken) the victim may repudiate (terminate) the contract if they wish and/or sue for damages, such as in the case of *Poussard* v *Spiers* (1876), seen in Chapter 6, Contract terms.

Warranties

When a warranty is breached the victim may sue *only* for damages and the contract continues, as seen in *Bettini* v *Gye* (1876), in Chapter 6, Contract terms.

A condition is an important term of the contract. A breach of condition by a defendant means the claimant may treat the contract as repudiated, i.e. terminated and/or make a claim for damages. Before repudiating the claimant *must* be sure that the breached term is a condition and not a warranty as if it is a warranty and the claimant tries to repudiate then the claimant will be in breach of contract as there was no right to repudiate! The defendant may then sue for breach by the claimant as the claimant has repudiated (terminated) the contract with no authority.

In this topic you will learn how to:

■ explain the nature of breach

■ distinguish between the effects of breach of condition and breach of warranty

■ explain the meaning of the term anticipatory breach and outline its effect

■ distinguish between breach and frustration

■ state the remedies for breach of contract

■ apply the rules in a given situation.

Anticipatory breach

An **anticipatory breach** occurs when a party to a contract gives notice in advance to the other party that they will not be performing/completing the contract. The claimant in this situation has a choice *either* to sue immediately for breach of a condition (i.e. to treat the contract as repudiated and/or to claim damages) *or* to wait for the time for performance of the contract and to sue then.

In **Hochster v de la Tour (1853)** the claimant agreed to work for the defendant as a courier on a tour which was to start in June. The defendant told the claimant he no longer required the claimant's services in May. The claimant was entitled to sue the defendant immediately and did not have to wait until the *actual* breach of contract (which would have occurred in June).

The choice the claimant has in this situation is of importance. The claimant may sue the defendant on receiving notice of the anticipatory breach (as in *Hochster* v *de la Tour*) or may choose to sue when the *actual* breach occurs (in the *Hochster* case this would be when the victim would have been taken on as the tour guide in June). However, what if the claimant chooses to delay suing but before the actual breach occurs the contract is discharged by a frustrating event? The claimant in this situation has no contract on which to sue as frustration ends the contract.

This is important as a common question will involve one party giving advance notice of a breach (anticipatory breach), the claimant choosing to wait for the actual breach to sue and in the meantime a frustrating event occurs. The claimant may then have lost the right to sue for breach.

In scenario on p124, what if, having made the contract with Kurtis, Simon warns Kurtis that he no longer requires the painting of the conservatory? In the meantime Kurtis has purchased materials for the job but decides to wait until the start date of the contract to sue Simon but before then the conservatory burns down. Kurtis is now in a dilemma. He can no longer sue for breach as the contract is discharged by the frustrating event and he may only claim under the Law Reform (Frustrated Contracts) Act 1943.

Remedies for breach

This topic must be read in conjunction with Chapter 6, Contract terms, Topic 1, Terms of a contract, which outlines the three types of term in a contract.

There are two possible remedies available to a victim of a breach of contract:

1 repudiation; and/or

2 damages.

Anticipatory breach

If the victim claims an *anticipatory breach* then the claimant may choose to repudiate the contract when the consequences are that the claimant is released from future contractual obligations and is no longer bound to perform any obligations under the contract. The claimant could also claim damages *immediately*. These damages are to put the claimant in the position he would have been, had the contract been completed.

Actual breach

The claimant may choose not to accept the anticipatory breach but to see if the defendant commits an actual breach at the time performance is due. Here, the claimant may claim repudiation and/or damages that would be assessed at the time when performance should occur and, if the losses have increased due to a change in market factors, the loss will be increased. Alternatively, an event may occur which discharges the contract (e.g. frustration), which results in the claimant losing their rights under the anticipatory breach (see the scenario above when Kurtis waited for the actual breach of contract by Simon).

It must be remembered that for a breach of *condition* the right of the claimant is to claim for repudiation and/or damages. Repudiation is defined above and contractual damages are based on putting the claimant in the position they would have been had the contract been completed.

For a breach of *warranty* the claim is limited to damages – again based on the above basis.

Activities

1. What are the three types of contractual term? Create examples of each.

2. Explain an anticipatory breach and how it is different to an actual breach, giving examples of both.

3. Under the heading 'Anticipatory breach' an example is given, from the scenario, of Kurtis choosing to wait for the actual breach by Simon. What danger does this raise for Kurtis?

4. In this scenario, Simon's anticipatory breach is clearly a breach of condition entitling Kurtis to repudiate the contract and/or claim damages. What if Simon's anticipatory breach was only a breach of warranty – what rights does Kurtis have?

You should now be able to:

■ understand when breach of contract occurs

■ understand the effect of breach of contract

■ apply the law to problem situations.

5 Overview of discharge of contract

How to attack a problem involving discharge of contract

The examination question will often specify the topic required by the examiner. For example, frustration will be referred to *and* breach. This usually involves an anticipatory breach (discussion of which must include the choice of the victim to sue immediately or wait for the actual breach) and then a frustrating event which would affect the victim's right to claim for actual breach as the contract is terminated by the frustrating event.

Frustration questions are usually identifiable as when a contract is made and then the contract becomes impossible, illegal or the purpose for the contract disappears. A definition of frustration is essential with examples of all three types of frustrating event. The Law Reform (Frustrated Contracts) Act 1943 must then be explained as to how the court will attempt to apportion loss. Anticipatory breach must be explained with a discuss of the remedies available to the victim of the breach and the effect the frustrating event has on these remedies.

Alternatively, one party may not have completed the entire contract.

In this topic you will learn how to:

■ apply the law to problem scenarios involving discharge of contract

■ construct an essay evaluating the law on discharge of contract.

Here, the examiner will be expecting a discussion of the strict rule of performance *and* breach. An exception to the strict rule may be possible (e.g. substantial performance) and this must be explained and discussed. The non-completion may also be a breach of contract (probably of a condition) so an explanation and application of relevant law is required.

Finally, the question may just involve parties who have made a contract and one, or both, have then failed to perform a respective obligation. The answer must explain the three types of term (condition, warranty and innominate) and then apply the law to each breach and explain and discuss the remedies available.

It is important to note the question will often ask about remedies as well as rights available to the parties. A discussion of damages, repudiation and/or the 1943 Act is required.

For example, one previous exam question in June 2008 was:

> Nick decided to set up in business on his own. He entered into a contract with Perry, who owned a fleet of taxis, to carry out repairs to all of Perry's current vehicles. The total price agreed was £5,000. Of this, £1,000 was to be paid immediately and the remainder on completion of the work. Nick spent £1,500 on materials and on other preparation for the work. However, shortly before the work was due to begin, the local authority removed Perry's licences for most of his taxis because of persistent problems with Perry's drivers. Perry refused to go ahead with the contract with Nick and demanded the return of the £1,000 already paid.
>
> Taking into account the rules on frustration and on breach of contract, consider the rights and remedies of Nick and Perry in relation to the contract for the repairs to the fleet of taxis.

You should have no difficulty identifying the topics involved as the question makes this clear.

A good answer would first deal with the breach of contract by Perry. The answer should explain that this is an anticipatory breach which entitles Nick to repudiate the contract and/or claim damages immediately or to wait for the actual breach to claim breach (with reference to cases as examples). Specific mention should be made of the danger to Nick of waiting for actual breach. Repudiation and damages should be defined and explained. There should be some discussion of whether Perry's breach is of a condition or warranty and the effect this has on Nick's position.

The good answer should then define frustration, explain its effect on the contract and *outline* the three situations when frustration may occur. The relevant situation should be chosen and the law applied to the question (probably 'radical change in circumstances'). There are various cases to which reference should be made and the answer should discuss whether there is frustration (as some of Perry's taxis are still in business). Mention should also be made that perhaps the frustrating event was self-induced as Perry did not control his drivers and this caused the removal of the licences.

As always, it is very important that explanation and application of *relevant* elements of breach and frustration are used. No credit will be given for a detailed discussion of other situations when frustration may occur. You *must* read the question carefully and take time to consider what are the relevant topics contained within the question.

The answer should also cover remedies and this is dealt with in Chapter 9, Remedies. For frustration, mention must always be made of the 1943 Act and the effect this will have on both the positions of Nick *and* Perry.

How to write an essay evaluating the law on discharge of contract

The (c) examination question is different to the questions (a) and (b) which are based on the scenario described in the question. The typical (c) question will ask you to 'critically analyse the law of [specific area of discharge] and to include any appropriate suggestions for reform'. There are 25 marks each for questions (a) and (b) and also 25 marks for question (c) so this question must be given the same consideration as the other two.

The examiner will be expecting an accurate *explanation* of the specific area of the law. There must also be a *discussion* of the fairness, relevance and clarity of this area. Inevitably, all areas of law are not perfect and a description of that law and a logical criticism of that law are required. The examiner will also be expecting to see sensible suggestions as to how the law could be improved or whether in all the circumstances reform is not appropriate or possible.

You should also explain areas of relevant law that work well, are clear and/or fair as 'critically analyse' does not mean all the analysis results in suggestions for reform of a bad law.

You should now be able to:

- answer problem questions involving discharge of contract
- evaluate the law relating to discharge of contract
- describe proposals for reform of those areas
- construct an appropriate essay on this topic.

Remedies

Key terms

Remedy: an award made by a court in favour of a claimant in relation to non-performance of a term, or all terms, of a contract by a defendant.

1 Remedies

The purpose of the law of contract is to fulfil the reasonable expectations of the parties. However, the contract may only be partly performed, or not at all, by one party. The other party will no doubt be very disappointed and may ask the court to rectify the situation. What that party is asking the court for is called a **remedy**. The court cannot award whatever remedy it considers appropriate but must be guided by the type of claim (e.g. is it a breach of contract or frustration?) and the range of remedies available in the circumstances of the dispute.

Legal and equitable remedies

There are various remedies available to the court and they may be defined as being either *legal* or *equitable* remedies.

Legal remedies

A claim for damages (compensation – see Topic 2) is *always* available, *as of right*, to the claimant when a contractual term has been broken. This means that if the claimant has not suffered any loss the court *must* still make an award of damages – but the amount ordered to be paid would be nominal (i.e. a small amount).

Equitable remedies

Equitable remedies are dealt with in detail in Topic 3. As a general rule, equitable remedies *may* be awarded by the court where damages alone would not prove an adequate remedy and justice would not be served.

Equitable remedies therefore are at the *discretion* of the court. Even though there may be a breach of contract or a misrepresentation the court will only award an equitable remedy (for example, specific performance or rescission) if it is fair in all the circumstances for it to do so.

Remedies relating specifically to goods

The Sale of Goods Act 1979 allows the buyer to sue for damages if the seller of the goods either fails to deliver the goods or breaches a contractual warranty. If the seller breaches a condition the buyer will be able to treat the contract as ended (repudiation), to *reject* the goods and/or claim damages. However, once the buyer has *accepted* the goods the right to treat the contract as ended and to reject the goods is lost and only the right to claim damages will remain.

The content below is a repeat of Chapter 6, Contract terms, Topics 3 and 4, but is essential knowledge. It is highly likely that an exam question will ask for an explanation and discussion of the possible remedy of repudiation in a sale or transfer of goods scenario (which may allow the victim to reject the goods and reclaim the purchase price and/or damages).

Under ss13, 14(2) and 14(3) of the 1979 Act the victim may repudiate the contract and/or sue for damages.

Repudiation

The victim may choose to terminate the contract due to the breach of the implied condition. In effect, the victim is entitled to the return of the price paid but must return the goods that do not fit their description, are not of satisfactory quality or are not fit for their purpose. This remedy may prove attractive to the victim as they may then recommence their search for the appropriate goods with their financial position restored to its original position.

The right to reject the goods may be lost if, for example, the goods have been *accepted* by the victim. Under s11(4) of the 1979 Act where a buyer has accepted goods a breach of condition will *not* allow the buyer to repudiate the contract and reject the defective goods. This could cause unfairness as the buyer may purchase an item and not use it for some time. If when used the item is found to be in breach of ss13 and/or 14 the buyer's only remedy would be damages as the buyer had the item for some time.

The 1994 Act amended the 1979 Act to redefine when the buyer is held to have 'accepted' goods. The 1994 Act defines acceptance as when:

- the buyer tells the seller the goods are accepted, or
- the buyer does something inconsistent with the seller's ownership of the goods, or
- the buyer keeps the goods without telling the seller they are rejected after a reasonable time.

A case showing the unfairness of the original section is *Bernstein* v *Pamson Motors Ltd* (1987), when Bernstein purchased a new car but only managed to drive it 142 miles before he fell ill and the car was not then used for three weeks. When next used the car was found to have serious defects and Bernstein was stranded in an isolated part of the country. Bernstein claimed a breach of the implied conditions under the 1979 Act and attempted to claim repudiation and to reject the car. The right to reject the car was lost as Bernstein had retained the car for three weeks and this was long enough for Bernstein to have accepted the car.

The decision in this case raised controversy. It was felt that the innocent victim was left unable to claim rejection of an expensive item that failed to meet any of the requirements of the implied conditions of the 1979 Act. The victim's only claim was for damages.

In **Clegg v Olle Anderson (2003)**, Clegg purchased a new yacht in August 2000 and was told immediately that the keel was substantially heavier than specified in the contract. Clegg negotiated with the seller and then rejected the yacht by letter in March 2001. The court confirmed that the *Bernstein* (1987) case was no longer good law and that Clegg was entitled to reject the yacht under the 1979 Act as amended by the 1994 Act.

As a general rule therefore, a victim with a claim under ss13, 14(2) or 14(3) should reject the goods as soon as possible so that repudiation has a practical and positive result and rejection is possible.

Similar principles and rules apply to claims made under ss3 and/or 4 of the Supply of Goods and Services Act 1982 in respect of the transfer of goods rather than their sale.

Damages

As an additional or sole remedy, the victim may choose to claim damages (i.e. compensation for the losses incurred due to the breach of one or more of the implied conditions).

Damages are explained in detail in Topic 2, Damages, but to summarise, the aim of contractual damages is to put the victim in the position they would have been had the contract been performed properly. In the scenario, if the moped is not delivered then James may elect to repudiate (reclaim the £1,500 paid to Mike) and then to claim the expense incurred

> **Key cases**
>
> **Clegg v Olle Anderson (2003)**: confirmed the amended rules on acceptance applied to a claim under ss13, 14(2) and 14(3) of the 1979 Act.

in purchasing an equivalent moped. For example, James may now have to pay an extra £250 for a similar moped.

In the Bernstein case, Bernstein recovered the cost of making his way home, the loss of a full tank of petrol, £150 for a 'totally spoilt day comprising nothing but vexation', and compensation until Bernstein purchased a replacement car.

■ Activity

Create one scenario where goods are 'accepted' by the buyer and another scenario where the goods are not accepted. Explain the reason(s) for the difference between the two results.

You should now be able to:

■ understand the purpose of remedies.

In this topic you will learn how to:

■ explain the purpose of damages in the law of contract

■ explain the rules relating to remoteness of damage

■ explain the way in which the law quantifies damages

■ state the basis for an assessment of damages

■ apply the rules in a given situation.

2 Damages

Damages is a technical expression in law for an award of money by the court to be paid by one party to another for losses suffered (i.e. compensation).

The purpose of damages in the law of contract

The purpose of damages in contract law is to put the injured party (the victim or claimant) in the position he would have been had the contract been completely performed by the defendant.

The court is therefore looking forward to what should have happened.

For example, James is a computer games creator and has contracted with Mike (a computer games manufacturer) that James will design a new computer game called 'The Whiz' for the computer games convention in London on 30 June. Mike has provided James with a design studio and all the computer hardware and software required. Unfortunately, James is distracted by his karate career and does not complete the design in time for the convention. James is in breach of contract and Mike may sue for damages. The court will try and estimate what profit Mike would have made from the game and order James to pay that amount as damages.

This scenario throws up a problem in the calculation of damages, which is dealt with under 'Bases of assessment'.

Remoteness of damage

In the scenario above, what do you think James should be responsible for?

What if Mike would have produced the computer game for say £400,000 and would have sold 50,000 units at £20 each leaving a net profit of £600,000? It probably seems reasonable that James should be liable for this loss as he caused it. However, what if, as a result of James' breach of contract, Mike was unable to expand his business empire into nightclubs and he lost the opportunity of buying suitable premises (which were available after June when the profit from 'The Whiz' should have been received)? Do you think James should also be liable for these losses?

A breach of contract may have far-reaching consequences and the court has developed a rule to restrict the defendant's liability. The leading case below sets out the principle of 'remoteness of damage' in contractual situations.

In **Hadley v Baxendale (1854)** a crankshaft in the claimant's mill broke so the claimant contracted for a carrier (the defendant) to take the shaft to the makers who would use it to model a new shaft. The carrier breached the contract by taking longer than agreed to deliver the shaft which meant the mill was out of action for longer than anticipated and the claimant lost profit over this extra period. The carrier had not been told the mill would be out of action until the new shaft arrived. The carrier was not liable for the loss of profit as he was entitled to assume the mill owner had a spare shaft or could borrow one.

This case outlined the two alternative tests available to a victim who, if *either is proved*, will satisfy the court the losses were not too remote and therefore the defendant should be liable.

The rules were considered and applied in **Victoria Laundry (Windsor) v Newman Industries (1949)** when the defendant was five months late in delivering a boiler to the laundry company (the claimant), which the defendant knew was needed by the claimant to run its business. The claimant sued for its usual loss of profits for this period (claim 1) and for the loss of profit on a special government contract it had just obtained which gave higher laundry fees (claim 2). The defendant was liable for claim 1 under the objective test but claim 2 failed under both tests.

It must be remembered that the application of the two alternative tests is *at the time when the contract is made*. What the reasonable person or the actual defendant may discover after the contract is made is irrelevant.

In the scenario with James and Mike it can be seen that James is liable to Mike for the loss of net profit of £600,000 as, at the time the contract was made, this loss would have been foreseeable to a reasonable person (and it may also have within the knowledge of James). However, Mike is unlikely to be able to prove either that a reasonable person (objective test) or James (subjective test) knew of the loss of profit from the potential nightclub business so James would not be liable for this loss.

Bases of assessment

Presume in the scenario above that James is in breach of contract and the loss suffered by Mike is foreseeable. The next question is how Mike's losses are calculated, i.e. the basis for assessment of the losses.

Assessment may be classed under three types:

Expectation loss (or loss of bargain)

This approach attempts to put the victim in the position they would have been had the contract been performed, i.e. in the position the victim *expected* to be. In Mike's case he expected to receive a net profit of £600,000 so that would be the basis for calculating his damages. In a case of non-delivery of specified goods (e.g. 12 apple trees) the loss is the *extra* cost of obtaining 12 apple trees elsewhere.

The calculation (assessment) in the two examples above is relatively straightforward. However, problems may occur in other situations. In the case of **Ruxley Electronics and Construction Ltd v Forsyth (1996)** there was a clear breach of contract, the loss was foreseeable but the assessment of the loss caused the court problems (see 'Quantification of damages' on p140).

Reliance loss

As a rare alternative to the expectation basis for loss, it is possible to claim compensation calculated on the expenses incurred by the victim before the breach.

Key cases

Hadley v Baxendale (1854): a defendant will be liable for losses caused if the victim can satisfy the court of either of the following two tests: (i) would a reasonable person foresee the loss as a consequence of the breach of contract (the objective test?); or (ii) what potential losses were in the minds of the parties when the contract was made (the subjective test?).

Victoria Laundry (Windsor) v Newman Industries (1949): the application of the two alternative tests of foreseeability is at the time when the contract is made.

Ruxley Electronics and Construction Ltd v Forsyth (1996): even where there is a clear breach of contract with foreseeable loss, assessment of the loss can be difficult, particularly where it is for loss of amenity.

In **Anglia Television Ltd v Reed (1972)**, Anglia TV spent a lot of money preparing for a film including fees paid to the director, designer and stage manager. Oliver Reed agreed to be the main actor but then pulled out and a suitable replacement could not be found so the film was not made. Anglia TV could not predict what its profit on the film would have been (the success of films is very problematic) so the court awarded damages based on reliance loss. Oliver Reed must have known that such expenditure would have been incurred and was liable for the expenses incurred by Anglia TV both before and after the contract with him was made.

Quantification of damages

The quantification (calculation) of the damages to be paid is closely related to the basis of assessment. Once the basis for assessment is decided then the quantification of damages may be obvious. However, in some situations the quantification of the loss is complicated or difficult. There are three examples of such complicated or difficult situations:

Non-pecuniary loss

On occasions a victim may suffer upset and distress caused by the breach of contract. In general, courts do not award compensation for injured feelings in contract cases. In **Addis v Gramophone Co. Ltd (1909)**, the victim was dismissed by his employer in a way that was described by the House of Lords as 'harsh and humiliating'. The victim's claim for distress failed.

The courts have developed some exceptions to this rule, for example if the contract is based on pleasure, relaxation and peace of mind, etc. In **Hamilton Jones v David & Snape (2004)** a solicitor acting for the mother failed to stop a father taking the children abroad permanently and the client suffered distress. This was a contract based on peace of mind so the client was awarded damages for her distress.

Loss of amenity (loss of a benefit)

On some occasions a victim may have suffered a breach of contract but the expectation loss (loss of bargain) basis of assessment will produce an unfair or absurd result. The court was faced with this difficulty in *Ruxley Electronics and Construction Ltd v Forsyth* (1996) where the contract for a swimming pool stated the depth as seven feet six inches, but the builder completed the pool with a depth of six feet nine inches. There was nothing wrong with the pool apart from the depth, it was still worth its cost, it did not affect the value of the property as a whole and F could still use the pool as he originally intended. The cost to correct the pool was £21,650, which was equivalent to the original cost. The House of Lords confirmed that in building contracts there are two bases for quantification of damages namely the 'cost of reinstatement' or the 'difference in value'. The cost of reinstatement was totally unreasonable in this case and there was no real difference in value so F was entitled to nothing. However, he had not received that which he had contracted for and so the court awarded him £2,500 for loss of amenity (i.e. loss of benefit).

There is no rule that assists the court to quantify the damages in such a case and the court appears to have discretion to award whatever amount it considers appropriate, providing it is modest. If, for example, the pool had been built for a developer, who was to sell the property in any event, then no award would be made for loss of amenity as the developer would not suffer any loss.

There was discussion that the *Ruxley* (1996) decision was another example of an exception to the 'non-pecuniary loss' rule (see above). However, the following case confirmed that was not the case.

In *Farley* v *Skinner* (2001) the prospective purchaser of a house instructed a surveyor and specifically asked about aircraft noise. The surveyor failed to investigate properly and the purchaser's enjoyment of the house was affected although there was no reduction in its market value. The House of Lords confirmed the award of £10,000 was for the loss of a benefit that had been contracted for rather than for discomfort and upset caused as in the *Ruxley* (1996) case.

Mitigation of loss

Once a breach has occurred the claimant is not entitled to sit back and allow the losses to increase. There is an obligation on the claimant to take *reasonable* steps to mitigate (reduce) the losses. For example, if James breaches the contract Mike should look in the market place to see if another computer games creator is able to create the product James did not. If Mike does not take that reasonable step then he may not recover some or all of his losses.

However, if there is an anticipatory breach (see Chapter 8, Discharge of contract, Topic 4, Breach) then there is no duty to mitigate.

The **White and Carter (Councils) v McGregor (1962)** decision is seen as harsh, but would not be repeated if the completion of the contract required any cooperation by the defendant (which is usually the case as most contracts are not as one-sided as this one).

Liquidated (fixed) damages

The parties may fix in the contract what the amount of damages will be if there is a breach of contract and the court will enforce that agreement such as in the case of **Dunlop Tyre Co. v New Garage and Motor Co. (1915)**. The court will only interfere with this agreed figure if the fixed amount is not an accurate estimation of loss *and* there is no justification for the figure – this is called a *penalty* and is not enforceable.

Activity

1. List the headings in this topic with a brief outline of the content of each.

2. Create a scenario where the victim has suffered losses part of which are recoverable under the *Hadley* v *Baxendale* tests and part of which are too remote.

You should now be able to:

- understand the law relating to an award of damages in contract
- apply the law to problem situations.

Key cases

White and Carter (Councils) v McGregor (1962): the defendant had contracted to buy advertising space on the claimant's litterbins; the defendant cancelled the contract, which was an anticipatory breach; the claimant did not accept the breach and went ahead with the contract for three years and then sued the defendant for its fee under the contract; the House of Lords (by a 3:2 majority) decided the claimant had no duty to mitigate.

Dunlop Tyre Co. v New Garage and Motor Co. (1915): the defendant agreed to pay £5 to the claimant for every tyre sold below list price; this was a valid fixed damages clause as it was a genuine attempt to estimate the losses that might occur.

In this topic you will learn how to:

■ explain the purpose of each of the remedies, apart from damages, in the law of contract

■ explain the rules relating to rescission

■ explain the rules in relation to rejection of goods

■ explain the rules with respect to remedies against the goods themselves

■ apply the rules in a given situation.

3 Other remedies

Apart from rejection these three remedies are 'equitable' remedies and are only awarded by the court exercising its discretion, i.e. if the court believes it correct to make the award in all the circumstances. Equitable remedies are not remedies available to a claimant as of right (as is an award of damages for breach of contract).

Rejection

As was discussed in Chapter 6, Contract terms and earlier in Topics 1 and 2 (Remedies and Damages respectively), if there is a breach of a term implied by ss13, 14(2) or 14(3) of the 1979 Act or ss3 and/or 4 of the 1982 Act the buyer/hirer has the right to treat the contract as ended (repudiation) and to return the goods, i.e. to *reject* the goods. The implied terms from the 1979 and 1982 Acts are conditions, the breach of which allows the claimant to repudiate the contract and/or claim damages.

However, under s15A of the 1979 Act if the buyer is *not* a consumer (i.e. is a business) and there is a breach of any of the terms mentioned above but 'the breach is so slight that it would be unreasonable for him to reject the goods' then damages are the only remedy available.

This section will affect a case on similar facts to those in *Re Moore & Co.* v *Landauer & Co.* (1921) (see Chapter 6, Contract terms, Topic 3). In this case the claimant was entitled to reject the goods for not fitting their description (a specific number of tins of fruit per case) but it is arguable that this breach would now be seen as insufficient to justify rejection of the goods.

It is emphasised that s15A does not affect those buying for personal use or consumption.

The following are all equitable remedies:

Rescission

This remedy is found mainly in cases of misrepresentation. The effect of this remedy is that the parties are placed in their pre-contractual position and if that is not possible then rescission is not granted. In the scenario, if James had made a misrepresentation then Mike may claim that any advance payments made by Mike to James would be repaid to Mike and any information or goods given by James to Mike would have to be returned to James.

Apart from the general rules that rescission will only be awarded if fair, and damages are not appropriate, there are other examples of when this remedy may not be awarded (for those examples see Chapter 7, Vitiating factors, Topic 2, Types of misrepresentation).

Other equitable remedies

Injunction

An **injunction** is usually awarded when damages are not an adequate remedy and the rights of the claimant need protecting.

For example, if James had contracted that all his development of the game 'The Whiz' would be owned by Mike and Mike discovered James was to sell the development to another competitor, Mike may be awarded an injunction to stop James releasing that information. Mike wants to acquire the development information rather than obtain damages against James on this point.

Key terms

Injunction: a court order instructing a party *not* to perform an action; occasionally, an injunction will order a party to perform an action.

An injunction will not be awarded for a party to complete a personal service, as the court is unable to supervise such an order. In **Page One Records Ltd v Britton (1967)** a pop group sacked their manager and were in breach of contract. The pop group's manager claimed an injunction to stop the group employing any other manager but failed as this would mean the group could only employ the manager, which was impractical. The court awarded the manager damages.

Specific performance

The court may order a party who is in breach to complete their side of the contract. This is a very rare remedy and will only be awarded when the subject matter of the contract is unique and an award of damages would be an inadequate remedy, e.g. a contract for the sale of land or a Picasso painting.

As described for an injunction, specific performance will *not* be awarded if damages are an adequate remedy, supervision of the contract would be required, the order would cause hardship or the contract involves the provision of personal services.

Specific performance must be a remedy available to *both* parties for it to be awarded to either party *and* the party claiming specific performance must have acted equitably (fairly) before and during the contract.

 Activity

Define injunction and specific performance and give examples of when they would, and would not, be granted by the court.

You should now be able to:

■ understand when the law relating to remedies, other than damages, in contract will apply

■ apply the law to problem situations.

4 Overview of remedies

How to attack a problem to include a discussion of remedies

It will be usual for the exam question to state the area of law to be explained and applied. The question will often, but not always, ask for an explanation and application of the relevant remedies that may be available to a named party in the question.

You will often answer the question based on the relevant law (e.g. misrepresentation) but then not continue to complete the answer by explaining and applying the remedies, e.g. damages and/or rescission. This is an easy omission to make as the excitement of knowing some or all of the relevant law blinds the student to continue with the possible remedies available.

Once the relevant law has been explained and applied then you must consider the suitable remedy or remedies. Even if you have concluded the victim has no claim, an explanation and application of the possible remedy or remedies is still needed. This part of the answer could commence:

> **Key cases**

> **Page One Records Ltd v Britton (1967)**: an injunction will not be awarded for a party to complete a personal service as the court is unable to supervise such an order.

In this topic you will learn how to:

■ apply the law to problem scenarios involving remedies

■ construct an essay evaluating the law on remedies.

However, if the victim did have a valid claim under fraudulent misrepresentation then rescission and/or damages could be claimed. Rescission is when the court will return the parties to their pre-contractual positions so in this case the purchaser will have the purchase price returned and the car will be returned to the seller.

Rescission is only awarded if …

Rescission is not awarded if …

Alternatively, the buyer could claim damages, which are to ….

The examiner will be expecting an explanation and application of the relevant remedy or remedies but a good discussion is sufficient and no definite decision need be reached as to whether a particular remedy would be successful or not.

How to write an essay evaluating remedies

The (c) examination question is different to the questions (a) and (b) which are based on the scenario described in the question. The typical (c) question will ask you to:

> … critically analyse the remedies available under contract and consumer law and to include any appropriate suggestions for reform of those remedies.

There are 25 marks each for questions (a) and (b) and also 25 marks for question (c) so this question must be given the same consideration as the other two.

The examiner will be expecting an accurate explanation of the different remedies discussed in this chapter. There must also be a discussion of the fairness, relevance and clarity of those remedies. Inevitably, all aspects of these remedies are not perfect and a description of each remedy with logical criticism is required. The examiner will also be expecting to see sensible suggestions as to how the remedies could be improved or whether in all the circumstances reform is not appropriate or possible.

You should also explain the remedies that appear to work well, are clear and/or fair as 'critically analyse' does not mean all the analysis results in suggestions for reform of weak or inadequate remedies.

Activities

1 Define contractual damages, rejection and rescission.

2 Outline two situations showing the inadequacy of damages and explain how another remedy would be preferable.

You should now be able to:

- answer problem questions involving remedies
- evaluate the law relating to remedies
- describe proposals for reform of those areas
- construct an appropriate essay on these topics.

3B   Review and examination techniques

Answering questions on contract law in Unit 3B.

To complete an examination paper on contract law successfully, you must both prepare carefully beforehand and deploy a range of skills when actually answering questions.

In preparing for an examination, you may find the following guidelines helpful:

- Make sure you have a thorough understanding of the key principles relating to each contractual topic. Be aware that each contract consists of terms that have been agreed by the parties or implied to the contract when they formed the contract. There may also be issues of discharge of contract and the remedies available for breach.

- Be prepared to illustrate key principles with the use of authority. Authority means a case or an Act of Parliament demonstrating the principle in question or a case explaining a point about the Act of Parliament.

- With respect to cases, you should be able to explain the principle that the case illustrates. It is helpful to have an outline knowledge of the facts of the case, as that gives a useful example, but it is not necessary to know the facts in great detail or to memorise the date of the case.

- With respect to Acts of Parliament, you need to be able to cite the relevant section number, as well as the name and date of the statute, and to be able to explain in your own words what the section says. It is preferable to quote the key extract from the section of an Act of Parliament so that you use the correct legal term.

- Make sure you frequently practise writing answers to past papers and similar examples, and ensure that you pay attention to the feedback that you receive. You do not want to be in the position of trying out your problem solving skills for the first time in the examination. No one gets everything right the first time and everyone benefits from experience.

- Pay attention to your written English. There are five marks awarded for using good English, organising information clearly and using legal vocabulary accurately and at appropriate places. Five marks may not sound very much but it could be the difference between two grades, especially as the other A Level Law examinations also carry marks for the quality of your written communication. When you practise exam answers, be aware of the need to produce organised answers (not random points churned out in the hope that something will be correct) and take the time to check spellings.

- When looking at a problem scenario, begin by identifying the characters involved. You need to know who the parties to the contract are. Be sure to read the question carefully and answer only what you are asked. If the question asks you about the contractual liability of Character A, you will waste time if you discuss what Character B's contractual liability might be.

- Then consider which aspects of contract are relevant. The examiner will often point you in the right direction, but you will still need to make decisions about the relevance of terms to a contract and in particular the listed implied terms in the specification.

■ Restrict yourself to discussing the law covered by the specification. You may well think that a character in a problem has committed a trade description offence but this is not being examined on this paper, and a discussion of it is unlikely to gain you marks.

■ When writing about a formation of contract problem, make sure you deal with all aspects of the offer and acceptance, but say very little about those parts that are not in question – there may well be no issue about intention to create legal relations. Concentrate on those where the application of the law to the problem is not clear and then conclude.

■ Give a concise explanation of the relevant legal principles. Do not waste time talking about related, but irrelevant, matters that you happen to know about. If, for instance, a question is clearly about offer and acceptance, but does not involve letters being sent, do not spend time on the posting rules.

■ Where you can, give the names of relevant cases to illustrate the legal principles you are discussing. You do not have to explain the fact of the case unless you think it helps your discussion.

■ Be aware that it is not enough just to explain the law. You need to go on to apply the law to the scenario. This means that you need to discuss what the position of the characters is, and make sure you do it at each stage of your answer.

■ When answering an evaluative question, make sure you focus on the area of law asked in the question.

■ Don't be worried if there doesn't seem to be a definite answer. Sometimes scenarios are written deliberately to pose awkward questions. Discuss both sides of an issue and consider the application of the law for both views.

You should now be able to:

■ complete an answer to a scenario question on contract law in an organised fashion with the purpose of gaining as high a mark as possible.

 Examination-style questions

Read this scenario, together with its questions, and then complete the activities that follow it.

Scenario 1

Martens, the publisher of a new magazine, *Sportlife*, placed advertisements in the press which read, 'Annual subscription for *Sportlife* delivered to your door, only £200. Special bonus – subscribe by 20 April and get £50 worth of free sports equipment.' In smaller print, the advertisement also said, 'Special bonus offer may be withdrawn at any time.' Nirmal sent a letter on 30 March, enclosing his £200 subscription. The letter was delayed in the post and was not delivered to Martens until 25 April. On 16 April, Owen was told by a friend that he thought that Martens was no longer offering the special bonus. Even so, Owen sent off a letter enclosing the £200 subscription and referring to the special bonus. Martens began to supply both Nirmal and Owen with *Sportlife*, but refused to supply the £50 worth of free sports equipment. Nirmal was told that his letter had not been received in time. Owen was told that Martens had published an advertisement in two national newspapers on 15 April, withdrawing the special bonus offer. Neither Nirmal nor Owen wanted the magazine without the special bonus of free sports equipment.

Paul was well-known for his service to sport over a period of 40 years. Ray arranged a football match to celebrate Paul's service, and agreed with Martens that Martens would print and supply programmes for the event at a cost of £1000. Ray paid £300 immediately and was expected to pay the remainder on supply of the programmes 14 days before the match was to take place. Paul was killed in a car accident 16 days before the date of the match. Ray chose to cancel the celebration football match and he informed Martens that he no longer required the programmes. By this time, Martens had printed the programmes at a cost of £600.

1 **(a)** Taking into account the rules on formation of contract, consider whether Nirmal and Owen are each bound by a contract for the subscription to *Sportlife*, and whether each has any rights against Martens in relation to the free sports equipment.

(25 marks)

(b) Taking into account the rules on frustration and on breach of contract, consider the rights and remedies of Martens and of Ray in connection with the contract for the supply of the programmes for the match.

(25 marks)

 Question (a):

1 In relation to Nirmal – discuss the formation issues: the status of the advertisement as offer/invitation to treat, acceptance by post and whether the postal rule applies, acceptance of the general subscription offer.

2 In relation to Owen – discuss the formation issues: the status of the advertisement as offer/invitation to treat, withdrawal of offer and effect of communication by a third party, possible offer by Owen to include free equipment, possibility of contract being formed for the magazine but not the free equipment.

3 Mark on your two plans where you might use cases to support the rules that you intend to discuss.

4 Finally, write full answers based on your plans. Use continuous prose, make sure your information is organised and that your spelling is accurate.

Question (b):

1   Discuss the issue of frustration or breach. Possible frustration of the common venture. Possible fault on Ray's part. Consideration of breach.

2   Discuss the issue of consequences of frustration or breach. Effect of the Law Reform (Frustrated Contracts) Act 1943 if the contract is frustrated – sums paid recoverable but subject to recompense for expenses incurred and benefit conferred. Effect of the rules on breach if the contract has been broken – damages for loss incurred.

3   As with question (a), prepare a paragraph by paragraph plan for each claimant, marking on where you will use cases to support your explanations. You need to consider the respective duties, whether Ray has breached those duties and any questions relevant to defences and remedies. Be careful to make sure that your plans reflect the ages of the claimants.

4   Finally, write a full answer based on your plans.

Now read this second scenario, together with its questions, and then complete the activities that follow it.

Scenario 2

Brightco owned a car park in the centre of town. They told Chris that he could rent one of the two remaining spaces for the year for £3000. Chris replied that he would take one of the spaces, but asked if he could rent it for nine months only, at reduced cost. Brightco then sent a letter to all local businesses offering 'the last two spaces' for the year at a rent of £3000 each. Dave sent an e-mail on Monday 'accepting' the 'offer' of one space. On Tuesday, Chris left a telephone message to say that he had changed his mind and would take the space for the full year at £3000. On Wednesday, Brightco received a letter from Elaine stating that she wished to rent both spaces for £6000.

Elaine engaged George to install a computer network in her offices, after making some brief enquiries about his claims to be an expert in computer networks. However, a week before George was due to start, Elaine changed her mind about the computer network and 'cancelled' the contract. She then discovered that George had very limited experience in computer networks.

(a)   Having regard to the rules on offer and acceptance, consider the rights and remedies, if any, of Chris and of Dave, if Brightco make both car parking spaces available to Elaine.   *(25 marks)*

(b)   Having regard to the rules on misrepresentation and breach, consider the rights and remedies of Elaine and of George.   *(25 marks)*

1   Identify the aspects of contract law relevant to each question. In question (a), note the requirement for offer and acceptance and rights and remedies. You must deal with all the stated aspects. In question (b) you must focus on the stated areas of law only.

2   Following the routine set out for the previous scenario, plan and write answers to questions (a) and (b).

3   Ask your teacher or lecturer for plenty of other past papers, and plan and write answers for those. The more you do, the better the answers you will write in the examination.

3B Critical evaluation and proposals for reform of contract law

This chapter aims to consider the areas of the law of contract that you have studied, apart from discharge of contract – that does not need to be evaluated in this AQA specification. For each part that you do need to evaluate, there are a number of points made that you can use to develop your arguments. You should remember that every aspect of the law has its good and bad points. Indeed, in contract law, these may well vary with the point of view of the person considering the law; a consumer may view the law differently to a business and a claimant may view the law differently to a defendant.

As you will appreciate, a great deal of time and care is taken by experts when drafting an Act of Parliament. Nevertheless, statutes have to be interpreted in the light of the infinite range of human behaviour, and according to the ever-changing nature of society and the way in which business operates. The common law, too, has developed to accommodate these changes. Over the years, judges refine and clarify the law to reflect the needs of the time. In many cases this is entirely successful, and adds to our understanding of what the law is on a particular point.

It also often happens, however, that a particular area of law is capable of ambiguity, and we find that conflicting decisions occur. There is a real risk that injustices might happen as a result. In these cases, there comes a point where it may be necessary to introduce reforms. These would take the form of new legislation, and their aim would be to:

- ▪ clarify existing areas of difficulty or ambiguity
- ▪ change the law where necessary
- ▪ introduce new laws to reflect present needs.

Each of the topics are evaluated in turn. You should be able to write an essay on each topic so as to be prepared fully for the exam.

1 Offer and acceptance

The current law of offer and acceptance can be critically evaluated in the following areas:

- ▪ The confusion between an offer and an invitation to treat.
- ▪ What comprises a 'course of action' in an advertisement.
- ▪ The unfairness of the rules of offer and acceptance and the difficulties created by the 'postal rule'.

The confusion between an offer and an invitation to treat

The differences between an invitation to treat and an offer can, on occasions, be very slight. As a result it may be difficult and confusing for the public. For example, most customers in a *Pharmaceutical Society of GB* v *Boots Cash Chemists* (1953) (item on shelf) situation will believe the availability of the goods and their status comprises an offer, which they are able to accept to make a valid contract. A suggestion is that all invitations to treat should be treated as offers so the law mirrors the public's belief in the situation. However, this would interfere with the process of opening and proceeding with negotiations and would also allow contracts to be created when against the wishes of a party, usually a seller of goods or services.

For example, in the Boots case if the item on the shelf had the status of an offer then once the item is placed in the customer's basket a contract would be made and the customer would then be bound to pay for the item. However, all customers wish to change their minds but in the suggested scenario this would be a breach of contract. Another problem would arise if the shop owner had made a mistake in pricing the item. If the contract were to be made at the shelf then the shop owner would have no opportunity to correct this mistake – which would be unfair. This is clearly inappropriate and so the only viable option is for such items to be classed as invitations to treat.

In the *Fisher* v *Bell* (1961) case the invitations to treat was the shop window display of the flick-knives. The justification for this decision is based on the traditional view in English law of 'freedom of contract', i.e. a party may choose with whom they wish to contract. To allow the shop window display to be classed as an offer would remove the shop owner's right to decide whether to contract with that particular customer or not. If an offer, the customer could enter the shop and accept the offer and create a legally binding contract. The shop owner may not wish to sell to that customer for many reasons (e.g. age, attitude) but would not have the opportunity to decline the sale.

The principle of freedom of contract is in conflict with the criminal law, however. Under s20 of the Consumer Protection Act 1987 it is an offence to 'mislead' a consumer as to the price of goods. Most shop owners will not insist on their right not to sell the goods at the advertised price in order to maintain good relations with their customers *and* so there is no criminal offence under the 1987 Act. There is, therefore, an argument justifying a change to the rule about shop window displays being invitations to treat on the basis that the rule is artificial and does not relate to the reality of commercial life.

What comprises a 'course of action' in an advertisement

The case of *Carlill* v *Carbolic Smoke Ball Co.* (1893) appears to be an invitation to treat but was given the status of an offer by the court. The advertisement is asking the potential customer to take a course of action and something is promised at the end of that action. There is no clear definition as to what comprises a 'course of action' and what will convert an invitation to treat into an offer. For example, what if there had been no mention of the £1,000 on deposit – would the promise of £100 be enough for the advertisement to be classed an offer?

The *Carlill* decision created a wide definition as to which situations may be classed an offer. There are now more statutory and common law safeguards to protect innocent purchasers of faulty goods and/or services so perhaps the case would be decided differently in modern times. Further, commerce and business have assimilated the principles of *Carlill*, and no advert will now contain specific promise(s) which result in a genuine advert (or 'advertising 'puff') becoming an offer capable of acceptance.

The unfairness of the rules of offer and acceptance and the difficulties created by the 'postal rule'

An offer may be stated to be open for acceptance for a set period, the offeree may rely on that statement and yet the offeror may withdraw the offer within the stated period – *Routledge* v *Grant* (1828). It may be argued this is grossly unfair on the offeree. The law could be reformed to ensure that an offer, expressed to be open for a set period, must remain open for acceptance for that entire period. A breach of that provision by an offeror would lead to a claim by the offeree for damages and/or specific performance.

The courts claim the law on formation of contracts will consider what the parties intended (a 'subjective' approach) however, what the courts actually consider is what the 'reasonable' person would think of the facts (an 'objective' test). The objective test may result in unfairness as, for example, in *Felthouse* v *Bindley* (1863) (see p81) the uncle (the offeror) and the nephew (the offeree) both wished for there to be a contract and there was independent evidence to confirm this – the nephew had contacted the auctioneer holding the horse to remove the horse from the auction. However, the court held against the uncle and nephew as, from an objective viewpoint, there was no evidence of an acceptance from the nephew. This is, of course, arguable, as there was evidence of the nephew instructing the auctioneer to withdraw the horse from the auction.

The justification for this decision is that for the court to declare there to be a valid and legally enforceable contract there should be clear and identifiable evidence. For example, the offer has to be communicated (see Chapter 5, Topic 1, Offer) so why not the acceptance? Silence as a form of acceptance could create many problems, which is partly why the Unsolicited Goods and Services Act 1971 states that, for example, where goods are received without request there can be no contract unless the acceptance is communicated by the sender. This will be so even if the letter accompanying the unsolicited goods states that the receiver will be liable to pay for the goods unless they are returned within a certain period.

It should be noted that the need to communicate an acceptance may be waived (see the *Carlill* case) but the uncle did not waive this need, he merely stated that the nephew's silence would be acceptance – which it cannot be.

Unless the contract involves the purchase of a simple item (a newspaper) or service (a train ticket) most contracts involve some form of negotiation about the contractual terms. There is often a small distinction between a counter-offer and a request for information. The former terminates the offer while the latter leaves the offer open for acceptance. It is unlikely that a party to negotiations (unless a commercial lawyer) would be able to draw such a fine distinction between the two, but the difference is crucial.

To create consistency, the law could be reformed so a counter-offer could have no affect on the existence of the original offer and negotiations would then continue, both parties knowing the original offer still existed. In a simple negotiation this may prove a fair result but in a complicated negotiation confusion would occur. Under the present law the parties terminate their previous offers by making counter-offers so there is only one offer in existence from one party at any one time. If all offers stayed open for acceptance despite counter-offers then a party could accept an offer that was made at the commencement of negotiations which may be minutes, hours or even days beforehand. An accurate record of all offers would be required to ensure there was no misunderstanding over what was being accepted. This would be an impractical way to run commercial life in the UK so the current law seems the only alternative.

The postal rule has always created argument as to whether it is fair or not. The rule appears to be unfair on an offeror who may never receive the letter of acceptance or it is late. The offeror is a party to a legally binding contract without realising so. The offeror may have contracted with another party in the meantime so the courts have to deal with three innocent parties and can make a decision that will only be satisfactory to two parties, or perhaps even just one party.

The postal rule is justified for the two reasons set out above. Further, the offeror is regarded as having the most power and ability to protect him/herself in this situation. If the offeror states the acceptance must, for example, be received or must be by face-to-face communication then the postal rule can never apply. The rule, therefore, seems a fair compromise as far as it relates to the post.

A further problem with the postal rule is whether it applies to any other method of communication. The *Entores* (1955), *Brinkibon* (1982) and *Mondial* (1995) cases indicate the courts' unwillingness to expand the rule to more modern methods of communication. This unwillingness may be due the courts' belief that an offeree should take reasonable steps to ensure the acceptance is received and that the postal rule is outdated in any event and should be restricted to the post. Clarification has been given that an offeree is entitled to assume the acceptance will be read within a reasonable time (for example, within office hours) and it is suggested this is a justifiable and fair rule.

2 Consideration

The current law on consideration can be critically evaluated in the following areas:

■ That consideration must be sufficient but need not be adequate.
■ The fairness of certain rules of consideration.
■ The willingness of the court to be flexible when interpreting. consideration in certain areas but not in others.

That consideration must be sufficient but need not be adequate

A rule of consideration is that it must be sufficient. As decided in the *Nestlé* (1960) case a chocolate wrapper is sufficient for consideration as it is real, tangible and has some value. However, in the view of a member of the public this would be seen as an unfair decision as the chocolate wrapper has no value in the real world. The justification for this rule is the courts' willingness to validate an agreement made by parties to an agreement. If a party wishes to give something to another party and this is to form the basis of the agreement then the court will always attempt to allow the agreement to exist and be enforceable. To do so, the consideration must have some value, and chocolate wrappers do represent value to Nestlé as evidence of their product being purchased.

The fairness of certain rules of consideration

A party to a contract may have made a bad bargain but the court will not be concerned to protect the party who has made that bad decision. If a party chooses to make a bad bargain (provided there is no illegality involved, for example, a misrepresentation) then that is the party's choice and risk. The court, rightly so, will not act as a mediator or arbitrator to decide what a *fair* consideration could or should have been. The decision in *Thomas* v *Thomas* (1842) is a fair decision as it supports the agreement made between the parties (the subjective test) and is not concerned with whether a reasonable person (the objective test) would see the consideration as a *fair* amount or not.

The willingness of the court to be flexible when interpreting consideration in certain areas but not in others

Re McArdle (1951) confirmed that promising to pay for something that has already occurred is not good consideration (known as 'past consideration is not valid consideration'). In this case, certain members of the family promised to contribute to work already completed by other members of the family.

Although this rule may seem unfair (allowing a party to break a promise) there is logic in the decision as, to enforce the promise would be to validate an agreement that does not have consideration from both parties. A contract is very important and may impose serious obligations on a party. To allow a contract to exist when there are no simultaneous promises of consideration would 'open the floodgates' to too many inappropriate claims.

Further, an exception does exist (see *Lampleigh* v *Braithwaite* (1615)) when, under certain conditions past consideration will be valid consideration. This exception is sufficient to cover any possible unfairness in the 'past consideration' rule.

In *Stilk* v *Myrick* (1809) the crew members did not receive the extra payment as they were only carrying out an existing duty. There is sense and fairness to this decision as in the background evidence to the case there is a hint of pressure from the crew on the captain for the extra payment or they would all desert. In *Williams* v *Roffey* (1990) there was no such pressure and, in fact, it was the defendant builder who offered the extra payment to the claimant roofer.

The decision in *Williams* v *Roffey* (1990) is to be welcomed as it shows the court is able to review the true realities of the situation and find consideration where previously it may have been ignored. The court is now not limited to looking just to the consideration within the contract but may now also consider factors outside the contract (e.g. the benefit to the builder of not being sued by the developer).

Again, as with promissory estoppel, the court is not keen to extend the principle from *Williams* v *Roffey* (1990) to other cases (again, see *Re Selectmove* (1995)).

If one party to an existing contract makes a promise to vary the contract but the other party provides no consideration for that promise then there can be no alteration. This does not seem fair as a party is being allowed in law to break a promise, which may seem immoral (does this conflict with *Re McArdle* (1951) above?). The case of *High Trees* (1947) attempts to take a moral view by allowing the promise to be enforceable despite the lack of reciprocal consideration (called 'promissory estoppel').

Lord Denning, who stated this principle in *High Trees* (1947) believed the rule should apply to all contractual situations. In effect, he was saying that consideration was not always a necessity for a valid contract. There is a conflict here between morality (of breaking a promise) and the strict rule of law (consideration is required for a valid contract).

The courts are not keen to extend the principle of promissory estoppel and it will certainly not apply it to cases based on pure debt (*Re Selectmove* (1995)).

3 Privity

The current law on privity in contract can be critically evaluated in that the 1999 Act, although a welcome addition to the law on privity, may have been unnecessary and may be non-effective in commercial situations.

1 The original rule was that a person who did not provide consideration to a contract could not enforce it, as they were not a party to that contract (see *Tweddle* v *Atkinson* (1861)). The decision in this case is, arguably, unfair on both the bride and bridegroom. The 1999 Act has attempted to make this aspect of contractual law fairer by

allowing third parties to the contract to enforce the contract in certain circumstances.

a However, the 1999 Act is open to criticism. First, the parties to the contract may specifically exclude the application of the 1999 Act. Potentially, a carefully drafted contract will not allow a third party to obtain the benefit of the contract so the law pre-*Tweddle* will apply.

b Second, it is believed that the majority of commercial contracts in the UK contain such an exclusion.

c Third, it could be argued the law was developing to allow third parties to enforce contract where necessary and/or appropriate. The exceptions referred to in Chapter 5, Topic 4, Privity of contract together with the decision in *Jackson* v *Horizon Holidays Ltd* (1975) would, arguably, cover any situation where a third party may wish to enforce a contract against one of the contractual parties.

2 The 1999 Act does not affect the common law rule that a contract cannot impose liabilities on a third party. This rule seems appropriate, as it does not appear fair to impose contractual obligations on a person who is not a party to the contract and who has not given consent.

4 Intention to create legal relations

The current law on intention to create legal relations can be critically evaluated in the following areas:

■ The overlap between the two presumptions.
■ The conflicting case law.
■ Whether this factor is required for a valid contract.

The overlap between the two presumptions

The two presumptions created by the courts have proved helpful when deciding if an agreement has legal validity or not. However, the court will always consider all the circumstances surrounding the case and, particularly in respect of social and domestic arrangements, the final decision will not always be clear. The case of *Jones* v *Padavatton* (1969) divided the Court of Appeal as to the existence of legal intent.

The conflicting case law

Sometimes, in similar cases there may be different results. This can be seen from the cases of **Hardwick v Johnson (1978)** and **Ellis v Chief Adjudication Officer (1998)**.

These cases show the fine difference as to whether an enforceable contract exists or not. The presumption against legal intent for social and domestic arrangements is understandable but by considering the surrounding circumstances the courts will, inevitably, reach inconsistent decisions. As a basis for precedent and an indication for future decisions the cases are of little use.

In a business or commercial setting there can still be uncertainty as to whether there is legal intent or not. In *Esso Petroleum Ltd* v *Customs and Excise* (1976) a minority of the House of Lords felt the offer of a gift of a free coin should *not* be regarded as a business matter. The majority considered that the context of the offer of the free coin was enough to allow the presumption for legal intent to remain. The situation of legal intent is not clear even in a commercial situation.

Key cases

Hardwick v Johnson (1978): a mother purchased a house as a residence for her son and daughter-in-law on the terms they should pay her £7 per week to pay off the purchase price; held: the agreement had legal intent so as long as the couple paid the money they had a right to remain in the property.

Ellis v Chief Adjudication Officer (1998): there was a gift of a flat by a mother to her daughter on condition the daughter would look after the mother; held: in this case there was not a legally binding contract, as the parties did not intend that to be the case.

It could be argued that by taking the case to court this would be evidence of at least one party's view that legal intent exists. This would not be conclusive evidence either way, however. On the contrary, there are certain contracts made in a commercial setting when neither party would consider taking the dispute to court (for example, a missed appointment at a hairdressing salon). The taking, or non-taking, of legal action is, of itself, little assistance in deciding the question of legal intent.

Whether this factor is required for a valid contract

There is an argument that there should be no need to prove legal intent. Offer, acceptance and consideration are the foundations on which a contract is made. If there are these three elements and *no* clear statement that the agreement is *not* to be legally binding then it should be a valid contract.

This principle could be linked in with an objective test as to the intention of the parties. Such a test would probably find most social and domestic arrangements not legally enforceable because the reasonable person would not find them so. This would allow the two 'presumptions' to be set aside and legal intent as an element of contract in itself to be ignored.

5 Implied terms aimed at consumer protection

There is overlap with the evaluation of remedies which can usefully be considered when looking at this topic.

There are three types of contractual term:

- Condition: breach of which allows the victim to repudiate the contract and/or claim damages.
- Warranty: breach of which only allows the victim to claim damages.
- Innominate: breach of which may permit repudiation, depending on the seriousness of the consequences of the breach.

These lead to confusion and unfairness, as will be seen below.

Implied conditions in respect of goods

The implied conditions in respect of goods under the 1979 and 1982 Acts allow the consumer to reject the goods and/or claim damages. This appears to be an effective and powerful remedy. However, the right in non-consumer sales is restricted under s15(A) of the 1979 Act to those cases where rejection is reasonable. This compromise seems to create a fair and justifiable system for dealing with dissatisfied customers whether they are consumers or businesses.

The right to reject for defective goods

The right to reject for defective goods is an important weapon in the consumer's hands and, to a lesser extent, businesses'. However, it may be argued that the party in default is prejudiced. Should not the seller be allowed a reasonable opportunity (as of right) to replace or fix the defective goods? This is certainly arguable if the defective is of a minor nature and is easily and quickly repairable. However, is a change in the law actually required as most consumers would expect and request a repair in any event? For businesses the right to reject is now restricted so the opportunity to repair and/or offer compensation is available to the seller.

Losing the right to repudiate the contract

An area of confusion for both sellers and buyers is when the right to repudiate the contract and, therefore, the right to reject the goods is lost. Section 11(4) of the 1979 Act states the right is lost when the buyer has 'accepted' the goods. The law was altered in the buyer's favour in 1994. The *Bernstein* (1987) case brought matters to a head and the court will now take a more lenient view of when goods have been accepted and the right to reject is lost. A case showing the development of the law in this respect is *Truk (UK) Ltd* v *Tokmakidis GmbH* (2000), when the owner of a Ford chassis contracted with Truk that Truk would fit appropriate lifting equipment. The lift was installed and was not checked for six months, when the defect in installation was discovered. The owner claimed a breach of condition, repudiated the contract and rejected the goods. The court held the owner was entitled to do so.

The law of repudiation (including the right to reject) has now been made clearer and is certainly more generous to the purchaser than previously, and this development is to be welcomed for consumers generally.

However, the detailed and overlapping rights and remedies available to both consumers and businesses in receipt of defective goods are confusing. It is recommended that there should be a consolidation and simplification of these matters, which would benefit all those involved in the sale and transfer of ownership of goods.

It should also be noted that there is concern that although there is more consumer protection than ever, members of the public are unaware of their basic rights, for example, under the implied terms of the 1979 and 1982 Acts. Further, consumers are either unwilling or financially unable to access good legal advice to pursue their valid claims.

Finally, the implied terms under ss13 and 14 of the 1982 Act are not automatically conditions, as for the implied terms in the Sale of Goods Act 1979, and are less effective. Further, they can even be excluded from a consumer contract if it is reasonable so to do – depriving consumers of protection.

6 Control of exclusion and limitation clauses

We can consider how these clauses are controlled by both common law and statute.

Common law controls

The courts have attempted to control the creation of such clauses by the rules of incorporation. These rules seem to work well and protect the unwary, whether a consumer or business. However, such a clause may still be created if, for example, notice is given in the required form but the victim does not read the relevant document or notice.

It is suggested that English law should include, from the principles of European contract law, a duty on *all* contracting parties to act 'in accordance with good faith and fair dealing' and that such a duty could *never* be excluded or limited.

Statutory controls

The Law Commission in its report on Unfair Terms in Contracts (LC No 298; SLC No 199) included a draft Bill to consolidate the law currently in force under UCTA and UTCCR. The report set out various criticisms of the current law with recommendations for reform. The summary of the report is only four pages and is very readable and would give more detail on the points below.

Criticisms in that report include:

■ UCTA and UTCCR contain inconsistent and overlapping provisions, using different language and concepts to produce similar but not identical results. UCTA only covers exclusion and limitation clauses while UTCCR apply to all terms but only for consumer contracts. Under UCTA some terms are automatically ineffective while under UTCCR no term is automatically unfair.

■ UCTA is written in a particularly dense style, which even specialist lawyers find difficult to follow.

■ UTCCR use European concepts which are unfamiliar to English lawyers.

■ UTCCR allows the Office of Fair Trading (OFT) to go to court to clarify a term, and this is very helpful for consumers and businesses.

To resolve this there are a number of proposals. These include:

■ A new Unfair Contract Terms Act to replace UCTA and UTCCR.

■ To maintain that terms excluding basic matters of quality, and fitness of goods are ineffective.

■ That in claims brought by consumers the burden of proof lies on the business to show the term was fair; this is justified as the business will have greater resources than the consumer.

■ The OFT will have additional powers to demand, for example, that a sign in a store car park saying 'no liability is accepted for injury' is taken down.

7 Misrepresentation

There are many criticisms of misrepresentation and these can be grouped together:

■ General principle.

■ Distinction between types of misrepresentation.

■ Remedies for a misrepresentation.

General principle

Misrepresentation imposes a duty on a representor not to tell untruths but does not impose a duty to tell the truth, i.e. it is a duty of a negative nature. In the scenario in Chapter 7, Vitiating factors, Tristan had a duty not to tell an untruth to Adam because he had been asked a specific question about reliability and service history. If Adam had never asked about these matters Tristan is under no duty to tell the truth.

There are some exceptions to this rule of silence not being a misrepresentation but could it not be argued that all parties negotiating should have a duty to disclose all relevant matters to the other – whether detrimental to that party's bargaining position or not?

There is a justification for this rule. The classical view of the English law of contract is that of 'freedom of contract'. This means parties who wish to negotiate and contract with each other should be left alone by the court and allowed to make whatever agreement they wish. The court should not intervene just because one party is poor at negotiation and makes a bad bargain. The court's view is that if the information not disclosed was of such importance then the party should have asked about it. If the truth followed then the representee could decide whether to proceed with the contract and, if an untruth followed, the representee would have a claim for misrepresentation.

This classical view of contract law should be compared to the law in other countries. For example, in the French Civil Code there is a positive obligation of 'good faith and fair dealing' when following a contractual term. Should not the English courts take a view that honest and unselfish behaviour should be expected from all parties both during and after negotiations are completed? For a party to conceal a fact which is known to have a negative impact on the other party's view of the potential contract should form some form of legal claim. Should not misrepresentation be extended to cover all silences?

Distinction between types of misrepresentation

In the scenario given in Chapter 7, Vitiating factors, Tristan may have known the moped was unreliable and there was an incomplete service history. Tristan would have made an untrue statement of fact intentionally and this would be classed as fraudulent misrepresentation. It is often difficult to ascertain if a representor has intentionally lied and the victim may have evidential problems in this respect. From the information provided in the scenario it would be unlikely Adam would succeed in such a claim.

Negligent misrepresentation exists in two forms:

1 The common law claim based on *Hedley Byrne & Co. Ltd* v *Heller & Partners Ltd* (1964)
2 The Misrepresentation Act 1967.

To succeed under the common law claim Adam must prove there was a 'special relationship' and 'proximity' between him and Tristan. Probably, the fact that they were negotiating a contract between them would be enough to satisfy these two conditions. However, if Adam fails to prove both conditions his claim for negligent misrepresentation under *Hedley Byrne* would fail, even if the statement were untrue. Adam would have to prove that Tristan was careless as to the truth of the statement, i.e. that Tristan did not act as the reasonable person would have done in those circumstances.

The 1967 Act does not require a 'special relationship' or 'proximity' between the parties, and Adam has only to prove that Tristan made an untrue statement to him. The burden of proof then shifts from Adam to Tristan, who is liable 'unless he proves that he had reasonable ground to believe, and did believe up to the time the contract was made, that the facts represented were true'. Obviously, this is more likely to prove successful for Adam than the common law claim.

Finally, Tristan may have believed his statements to be true and had reasonable grounds for that belief. Adam would be able to succeed in a claim for innocent misrepresentation but his remedies would be limited

The remedies available for a misrepresentation indicate the court is taking a moral view on the actions of the representor. If the representor has made a fraudulent misrepresentation (i.e. has lied about a fact to the victim), then the victim is entitled to claim damages without the limiting rule of reasonable foreseeability. One purpose of this rule is to make the award of damages a fair amount and to limit the defendant from potentially unlimited liability. It is generally considered that the purpose of damages in civil law is to compensate the victim for losses incurred, and it is not the purpose of damages to punish the defendant – that is regarded as the responsibility of a criminal court when passing sentence.

By allowing a successful claim under fraudulent misrepresentation, to ignore the rule of reasonable foreseeability is drifting into the area of punishment. This criticism has another factor, in that a claim for negligent misrepresentation under the 1967 Act does not specify whether the reasonable foreseeability rule applies to a successful claim and judicial decisions are unclear but indicate that the rule does not apply. As a result, a representor who has been careless will be ordered to pay compensation on the same basis as a representor who has lied – which seems inequitable.

Remedies for misrepresentation

There are two possible remedies for a misrepresentation – rescission and damages.

Rescission is to restore the parties to their original position before the contract. If Adam were successful in this claim he would return the moped to Tristan and in return receive the price he paid.

Damages under misrepresentation are unusual for a claim relating to a contractual situation. Contractual damages are usually based on the principle of compensating the victim by putting them, financially, in the position they would have been had the contract been properly completed. Damages under misrepresentation, however, are based on tort on the principle of compensating the victim by returning them, financially, to the position held before the misrepresentation was made.

Rescission and/or damages are available for fraudulent misrepresentation and negligent misrepresentation (both common law and under the 1967 Act). However, for innocent misrepresentation damages will be awarded in lieu of rescission if it is equitable to do so: s2(2) of the 1967 Act.

In the scenario if the claim were for fraudulent misrepresentation or negligent misrepresentation under the 1967 Act, Adam would be able to claim for losses even if not reasonably foreseeable to Tristan, e.g. for the cost of transport to and from Adam's new job until a replacement moped is purchased.

The test of foreseeability does apply to damages awarded under common law, negligent misrepresentation and innocent misrepresentation.

Under *Hedley Byrne* (1964), liability is difficult to prove, as there are various requirements to be met. The 1967 Act made the law easier for victims of a negligent misrepresentation as once the representee has proved the statement was untrue the burden of proof is transferred to the representor to prove they had reasonable grounds for making the statement. This reverses the traditional rule that in a civil claim it is for the claimant (the victim) to prove the case and losses on the balance of probabilities and the defendant does not have to prove anything. The same principle applies in criminal cases as the prosecution must prove the case beyond reasonable doubt (a higher standard than for civil cases). There seems no justification for the 1967 Act reversing this traditional rule for negligent misrepresentation. One argument may be that as society now recognises consumers should have protection when making a contract anyone who misleads another into making such a contract should be held responsible as the representor has superior knowledge and is abusing their position.

In *Bissett* v *Wilkinson* (1927) the representor was not liable for stating he believed the land could take 2,000 sheep. It could be argued this decision is unfair and the definition of misrepresentation should be altered to include statements of opinion as well as fact. The justification for this reform would be that if a representor is willing to make a comment to encourage a party to enter a contract then the representor should be liable for that comment if it proves to be untrue. It is sometimes difficult to differentiate between an opinion and a fact which may lead to unfairness for the representee. For example, in the scenario Tristan could argue that his statement that the moped was reliable was his opinion and not a fact. How would the court decide this? Tristan's standards may be different to those of Adam so whose definition of 'reliability' would the court use? Would it not be fairer that all statements, whether of fact or opinion, are caught by misrepresentation? A problem with this suggestion is that although the statement would now be classed as a misrepresentation Tristan could still argue the statement to be true as, under his standards, the moped was reliable.

Rescission (to put the parties in their pre-contractual positions) is a fair remedy but should still be allowed even when the innocent party has delayed in bringing the claim. In the case of *Leaf* v *International Galleries* (1950) the claim for rescission failed, as the innocent party only discovered the misrepresentation five years after the contract. The delay in bringing the claim was not the fault of the representee, so why should this delay prejudice the claim of the representee? One argument for the rule of delay is that for the court to hold a contract as void after a five-year delay would be unfair (even to a wrong-doer) as all parties are entitled to presume a contract is certain after a reasonable period of time. Of course, the representee will still be liable for damages. However, rescission is lost if the representee has affirmed the contract. In the case of *Long* v *Lloyd* (1958) the representee was penalised by returning the lorry for repair. This appears to be unfair as what difference has this made to the representor? If the representee chooses to allow the representor at least one chance to remedy the problem why should the representee then lose the opportunity to claim rescission?

There are some positive points to raise about the law of misrepresentation. For example, the three types misrepresentation now cover all possible eventualities in relation to the making of an untrue statement by a representor, i.e. lying, carelessness or innocence. There are two remedies usually available and rescission is a very satisfactory result for a representee as they are restored to their original pre-contractual position. The current definition of misrepresentation covers most situations where a claim should be allowed and the 1967 Act allows a claim for rescission to be made, even if the misrepresentation has become a term of the contract.

8 Remedies

Each of the remedies needs to be considered in turn.

Damages

English courts have decided that the purpose of contractual damages is:

> '… that where a party sustains a loss by reason of a breach of contract, he is, so far as money can do it, to be placed in the same situation, with respect to damages, as if the contract had been performed'. Parke B in *Robinson* v *Harman* (1848).

This basic principle supports the freedom of contract values on which our commercial world is based, i.e. the profit on a contract is as good as earned when the contract is made. It is not acceptable to have that *expectation* of profit disrupted by a breach of the contract. The court has developed principles to assist in the calculation of contractual damages and these need review.

The remoteness of damage

■ In *Hadley* v *Baxendale* (1854) it was confirmed that the innocent party's claim in respect of losses caused by the defendant's breach would be limited to those that are not too remote. This means if the innocent party would have made an exceptional gain if the contract had been performed or made an exceptional loss due to a breach of contract the party at fault is not liable.

■ This appears unfair as the defendant's breach has caused the victim's loss. The House of Lords has confirmed in *The Heron* (1969) that the party at fault should not be liable for consequential losses that are merely possible or pretty unlikely. The justification for this is that without the remoteness rule parties in the commercial world would be less inclined to enter contracts and even if they do the chance of obtaining adequate insurance to cover the risk of breach would either not be unavailable or unaffordable.

The basis of assessment of damages

■ The two main bases for assessment cover most of the situations where a claim for damages is made. As a general rule, the victim can choose whether to claim on loss of expectation (loss of bargain) or on reliance. Provided the victim avoids overlapping claims there is no reason why a claim for both cannot be made.

■ Reliance loss allows the court to award damages in an amount that may more accurately reflect the victim's losses than an award based on loss of expectation: see *Anglia Television Ltd* v *Reed* (1972).

The quantification of damages

The difficulty faced by the court when attempting to quantify a victim's claim was highlighted in the *Ruxley* (1996) case. Mr Forsyth was, without doubt, entitled to damages but was the calculation based on the cost of 'cure' (£21,560 being more than the original contract price) or a loss of market value (nil as the property suffered no loss due the shortfall in the depth of the pool). The House of Lords used its discretion and made the award of £2,500 based on loss of amenity, which is widely seen as the sensible decision.

However, the Court of Appeal had ordered damages in the full sum of £21,650. This shows the risks involved in allowing the court to make an award based on its discretion. If the parties had not been able to fund the appeal to the House of Lords, the Court of Appeal's decision would be the precedent to be followed today. This shows how arbitrary and random the courts' decisions may be, which creates uncertainty in the English legal system.

Further, with a few exceptions, no award is made for mental distress and upset following a breach of contract. In many cases, the worry of the consequences of a breach of a commercial contract may be devastating to an innocent party, especially if that party is a small business which may fail due to the breach.

Further, damages may be awarded in due course but are unlikely to take account of loss of business, which may be crucial to the victim. Damages do not cover all losses and harm caused by a breach. The cost and time required to achieve a successful outcome in court is exhausting and there is no guarantee that the defendant will be able to pay the damages awarded, especially if there is no insurance cover.

Finally, the Law Commission considered the question of damages when the party in default profited from the breach in its report *Aggravated, Exemplary and Restitutionary Damages* (1997). It concluded that the application of the law should be left with the courts rather than for Parliament to set out the law. The courts are therefore trusted to make awards of damages by applying the rules set out in this chapter and by using discretion despite the risks (as set in the discussion of the *Ruxley* (1996) case).

Injunction

If appropriate, the court may order a party in breach of contract *not* to do something. There is no 'balance of convenience' test between the parties, which there would be if the injunction were to order a party *to do* something.

The making of an injunction will be rare because, as for specific performance, the court will always consider damages as the first alternative. An injunction may be an appropriate remedy if the victim wishes the party at fault not to carry out a certain act when damages would not be a satisfactory remedy. In the scenario discussed above under 'Injunction', Mike does not want compensation but wants the protection of James being ordered by the court not to release the computer game to another.

The court treats the breach of an injunction very seriously, as it is a contempt of court. The final sanction for breach of an injunction is a custodial sentence. The impact and effect of an injunction may well provide the victim with a satisfactory resolution to the court proceedings.

Specific performance

There will be few situations when specific performance is required or is appropriate but as a remedy it does allow the court to achieve justice in a case.

As explained, specific performance covers those situations where damages are either inadequate or inappropriate. This allows the court to award the victim a remedy or remedies that adequately covers the victim's needs and requirements and does not allow the defendant to escape from responsibility for their breach.

For example, in *Beswick* v *Beswick* (1968) a nephew purchased his uncle's coal merchant's business and, as part of the contract, agreed to pay his uncle £6.50 per week until he died and then pay his aunt £5 per week if she survived her husband. After his uncle's death the nephew refused to pay his aunt. She could not sue him personally as she was not a party to the contract but sued him in her capacity as trustee of the uncle's estate. The estate's claim was for nominal damages (it made little difference to the estate if his widow received the money or not) but the Court of Appeal awarded specific performance of the contract. This would ensure the aunt would receive her full entitlement.

If severe hardship would be caused by the order of specific performance then it is unlikely to be granted even if the hardship arises after the contract is made. In the case of *Patel* v *Ali* (1984) there was a four-year delay after the making of the contract in the completion of the sale of a house, through no one's fault. The purchaser wanted specific performance rather than damages. However, during the delay the seller's wife had become disabled, and the sale would cause her serious hardship as she would lose her network of help, so specific performance was not ordered.

Remedies against goods

There are three types of contractual term:

1 Condition: breach of which allows the victim to repudiate the contrac and/or claim damages.

2 Warranty: breach of which only allows the victim to claim damages.

3 Innominate: breach of which may permit repudiation, depending on the seriousness of the consequences of the breach.

The implied conditions in respect of goods under the 1979 and 1982 Acts allow the consumer to reject the goods and/or claim damages. This appears to be an effective and powerful remedy. However, the right in non-consumer sales is restricted under s15(A) of the 1979 Act to those cases where rejection is reasonable (see Chapter 6, Contract terms, Topic 3). This compromise seems to create a fair and justifiable system for dealing with dissatisfied customers, whether they are consumers or businesses.

The right to reject for defective goods is an important weapon in the consumer's hands and, to a lesser extent, businesses'. However, it may be argued that the party in default is prejudiced. Should not the seller be allowed a reasonable opportunity (as of right) to replace or fix the defective goods? This is certainly arguable if the defective is of a minor nature and is easily and quickly repairable. However, is a change in the law actually required as most consumers would expect and request a repair in any event? For businesses the right to reject is now restricted so the opportunity to repair and/or offer compensation is available to the seller.

An area of confusion for both sellers and buyers is when the right to repudiate the contract and, therefore, the right to reject the goods is lost. Section 11(4) of the 1979 Act states the right is lost when the buyer has 'accepted' the goods. As stated in Chapter 6, Contract terms, Topic 3, the law was altered in the buyer's favour in 1994. The *Bernstein* (1987) case brought matters to a head and the court will now take a more lenient view of when goods have been accepted and the right to reject is lost. A case showing the development of the law in this respect is *Truk (UK) Ltd v Tokmakidis GmbH* (2000) when the owner of a Ford chassis contracted with Truk that Truk would fit appropriate lifting equipment. The lift was installed and was not checked for six months when the defect in installation was discovered. The owner claimed a breach of condition, repudiated the contract and rejected the goods. The court held the owner was entitled to do so.

The law of repudiation (including the right to reject) has now been made clearer and is certainly more generous to the purchaser than previously and this development is to be welcomed for consumers generally.

The detailed and overlapping rights and remedies available to both consumers and businesses in receipt of defective goods is confusing. It is recommended there should be a consolidation and simplification of these matters, which would benefit all those involved in the sale and transfer of ownership of goods.

Conclusion

With all the areas of contract law that need criticism, it should also be noted that there are positive aspects as well as negative aspects of that criticism. You should be aware of that in constructing your essay to the part (c) answers in the exam. You should also note that any question on evaluation of contract law is likely to focus on a single area.

You should now be able to:

- evaluate aspects of the law of contract

- understand proposals for reform of those aspects

- answer an exam question based on those found on p147.

Activities

1 Construct a chart of all the areas in the specification for this unit, listing positive and negative criticisms that you have learned.

2 Plan an essay based on evaluating each of the areas above.

Unit 4 gives you a choice between the study of criminal law and the law of tort. The unit constitutes 50 per cent of the overall marks for the A2 section of the qualification, and 25 per cent of the overall marks for the A Level qualification. The Unit 4 examination is of 2 hours' duration. Candidates must answer one question on tort and write an essay from the Concepts of law unit. The first part of the examination paper will include both criminal law and tort questions, Questions 1 and 2 being criminal law and Questions 3 and 4 being tort. Candidates who choose criminal law will have to select one question to answer, as will those who have chosen tort. Each question is divided into two parts, both of which must be answered. These questions are similar in style and expectation to those in Parts(a) and (b) of Unit 3. There are no questions involving critical evaluation of the substantive law studied in Unit 4, critical evaluation forming the basis of the separate essay on concepts of law.

Each question on criminal law is therefore worth 50 marks. Each part is worth 25 marks. These two parts will be a test of your ability to select and apply the law to the given scenario.

All questions require essay style answers. In Parts (a) and (b), attainment of high grades is dependent on correct identification of the issues raised by the question, sound explanation of each of the points and clear application of the law to the facts disclosed. This may involve some consideration of alternatives where the law lacks clarity in its application to the scenario. Further exam tips are provided throughout each topic and at the end of the chapter.

Unit 4A comprises four chapters:

10 Theft: concerned with the explanation of the law with respect to theft.

11 Robbery, blackmail, burglary, and criminal damage: explains the law on robbery, blackmail, burglary and criminal damage.

12 Fraud and making off without payment: considers the law on fraud and making off without payment.

13 Defences: concerned with the defences to the offences dealt with in Chapters 10–13.

10 Theft

In this topic you will learn how to:

- state the definition of theft
- explain the *actus reus* of theft
- explain cases that illustrate the *actus reus* of theft
- apply the rules to a given situation.

Key terms

Theft: the dishonest appropriation of property belonging to another with the intention of permanently depriving the other of it.

1 Theft 1: Definition and *actus reus* of the offence

Introduction

Theft is one of the most commonly understood crimes. Everybody recognises stealing as theft, and would include shoplifting as one of the examples of theft. However, there are other situations that may be theft, even though the crime is not always obviously committed. Compare the situation between finding a 10p piece on the pavement, a £20 note, and a diamond ring. When, and in what situations would you consider each finding to be theft? Or, is none of them theft? Is it theft to keep additional goods sent to you by mistake by a supplier? Can you steal your own property?

The definition of theft

Theft appears to be a straightforward offence. The law on theft clearly embraces a number of ideas, but is sometimes not as straightforward as simple theft appears to be.

Theft is defined in the Theft Act 1968, s1:

> 1 A person is guilty of theft if he dishonestly appropriates property belonging to another with the intention of permanently depriving the other of it; and 'thief' and 'steal' shall be construed accordingly.
>
> 2 It is immaterial whether the appropriation is made with a view to gain, or is made for the thief's own benefit.
>
> 3 The five following sections of this Act shall have effect as regards the interpretation and operation of this section (and, except as otherwise provided by this Act, shall apply only for purposes of this section).

There are five things to be proved to secure a conviction of theft: three of these form the *actus reus* of the offence and two the *mens rea*. They are summarised in the table below.

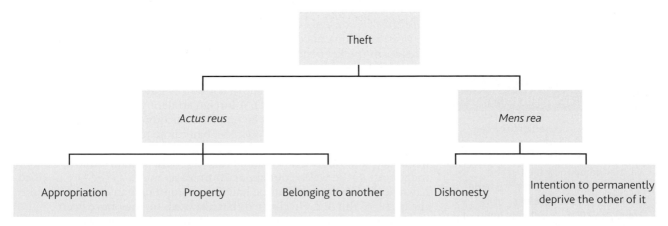

Fig. 1 *Elements of the offence of theft*

Actus reus: element 1 – appropriation

Appropriation is defined in s3 of the Theft Act 1968 as follows:

> 1 Any assumption by a person of the rights of an owner amounts to an appropriation, and this includes, where he has come by the property (innocently or not) without stealing it, any later assumption of a right to it by keeping or dealing with it as owner.
>
> 2 Where property or a right or interest in property is, or purports to be, transferred for value to a person acting in good faith, no later assumption by him of rights which he believed himself to be acquiring shall, by reason of any defect in the transferor's title, amount to theft of the property.

There are therefore, a number of aspects of appropriation that need to be investigated.

The general meaning of appropriation is to take something. More formally, this is the assumption of the rights of an owner. This does not, however, reflect the true meaning of appropriation in the context of theft. Theft can involve more than the mere taking of property; it can include taking the rights that someone has over that property. The Act makes this clear when it refers in s3(2) to right or interest in property. A person who owns property can do anything he likes with it (subject to the general law). For example, he can lend it to someone else, hire it to someone else, damage or destroy it. When a person has lent or hired something to someone, they retain the right of ownership. That right can therefore be the subject of theft by the person to whom the thing was lent. Appropriation can, therefore, occur in a variety of ways whilst doing something to the property that an owner can do such as possess it, use it, modify it, sell it or destroy it.

This has resulted in a number of cases. The case that confirms that a range of activities can amount to appropriation is **Morris (1984)**. In that case, the defendant dishonestly switched the labels on goods in a supermarket so as to show lower prices. He then acquired the goods by paying only the lower price at the check-out – this was his intention. The switching of the labels and placing the goods in the basket or trolley forms the appropriation.

Clearly there has been no criminal appropriation where the property has been taken with consent. There is appropriation when I put goods in my supermarket basket, but, as I intend to pay for them at the checkout, this is appropriation with consent, and is not criminal. It becomes part of the crime when I decide to leave without paying for the goods. The supermarket consents to my taking the goods off the shelf. The link between the elements of appropriation and dishonesty is very close and often form the key aspects of the crime. This idea of consent by the owner becomes a point of difficulty in some cases.

The first case involving the issue of consent is **Lawrence (1972)**. In that case Lawrence was a taxi driver. A foreign student got in his taxi and asked to be taken to a hotel. The real fare was quite small. The student had little spoken English and offered a bank note to pay for the trip. Lawrence said that it was not enough. The student then offered Lawrence his wallet, and indicated he should take the right amount. Lawrence took money out of the wallet, but about 20 times as much as the fare justified. Lawrence's defence was that he had not appropriated any money, within the terms of the Act. He claimed that although he may have been dishonest, there was no appropriation. However, Lawrence was guilty of theft, as the court decided that the appropriation need not be without the consent of the owner. This is clearly consistent with other cases and a sensible approach, even though there are alternative offences available under the Fraud Act 2006 and its predecessor legislation.

Another case on this point is **Gomez (1993)**. In that case, the defendant was an assistant manager at an electrical store. His accomplice asked to be supplied with £16,000 worth of goods, using two worthless cheques. The defendant, with full knowledge that the cheques were worthless, asked the manager to authorise the sale and the manager asked the defendant about the cheques. The defendant pretended to do this with the bank and returned to the manager stating that the cheques were 'as good as cash'. The cheques were later returned by the bank unpaid.

The defendant was convicted of theft, but there was an appeal on the grounds that there had been no 'appropriation' of the goods because the manager had willingly released them. (This would not have been a problem if he had been charged with a deception offence under what is now the Fraud Act 2006).

The House of Lords decided that there was a dishonest appropriation of the goods. The electrical store's manager was lead into giving his consent to the removal of goods by fraud, deception or a false representation. This made the appropriation dishonest. The House of Lords' judgement widens the scope of theft to overlap with deception in cases where fraud specifically operates to release the goods into the hands of the thief – the appropriation. The consent to remove the property is not 'true consent' so the property was dishonestly appropriated.

A twist on the idea of consent arose in the case of **Hinks (1998)**. In this case, Hinks, a single mother, became very friendly with Mr Dolphin, a naive, gullible, middle-aged man of low intelligence, a month after his father died. She effectively took over the running of his life. He withdrew sums of £300 (the maximum permissible under the rules for his account), almost every day. On each occasion he was accompanied by her. Hinks placed the money in her account. After seven months, £60,000 had been moved out of his account and into her account. This was almost all of his money he had inherited from his father. The House of Lords upheld Hinks' conviction for theft, even though all transactions appeared to be a voluntary gift. The House of Lords stated that the issue of consent was related to dishonesty rather than appropriation.

There have been problems with appropriation where a money transfer has been fraudulently requested. It seems that this will not amount to appropriation for theft, although there is likely to be an offence of fraud. The reason for this is that appropriation seems to require handling of physical items such as goods, banknotes or cheques.

Actus reus: element 2 – property

The Theft Act 1968 s4 deals with property. The general principle is set out in s4(1) as:

1 'Property' includes money and all other property, real or personal including things in action and other intangible property.

This means everything that you can own including money, land, belongings, cheques and other things of value where the value is not defined by the physical thing, for example rights of ownership of stocks and shares or forms of credit.

The Act itself, in s4, goes on to make some further explanation and exceptions. These are set out in s4(2), (3) and (4) as follows:

2 A person cannot steal land, or things forming part of land and severed from it by him or by his directions, except in the following cases, that is to say –

   a when he is a trustee or personal representative, or is authorised by power of attorney, or as liquidator of a company,

Key cases

Gomez (1993): the issue of consent occurred here in relation to releasing goods against worthless cheques; it was decided that there can be an appropriation even if the goods are released with the owner's consent.

Hinks (1998): appropriation can take place even where there is a voluntary gift.

or otherwise, to sell or dispose of land belonging to another, and he appropriates the land or anything forming part of it by dealing with it in breach of the confidence reposed in him; or

b when he is not in possession of the land and appropriates anything forming part of the land by severing it or causing it to be severed, or after it has been severed; or

c when, being in possession of the land under a tenancy, he appropriates the whole or part of any fixture or structure let to be used with the land. For purposes of this subsection, 'land' does not include incorporeal hereditaments; 'tenancy' means a tenancy for years or less period and includes an agreement for such a tenancy, but a person who, after the end of a tenancy, remains in possession as statutory tenant or otherwise is to be treated as having possession under the tenancy, and 'let' shall be construed accordingly.

This means, subject to exceptions, that you cannot steal land or part of it such as the soil, rocks, plants or buildings. The first exception occurs in s(2)(a): a person can commit theft of land where he has the ability to transfer the ownership (or other rights over land) to another person and the land or rights being transferred are not his to transfer. This can occur where he transfers the land in a way that he is not expressly authorised to do. The Act refers to a range of situations where this can occur but, using the *ejusdem generis* rule of statutory interpretation, the words 'or otherwise' means the list is not exclusive. An example of this occurs where I am the trustee of a house and other property; this could arise under a will, particularly where the dead person's assets are left to children under the age of 18 or to a very old and infirm person. As trustee I would manage the assets, including the house (land). I might well have the right to sell the house, but would have to do so for the benefit of the children or old person. If I were to sell it for a very low price to my wife, or keep some of the sale money for myself, it could form the basis of the offence of theft. Equally, it could be theft if I lived in the house rent free, although there is more likely to be an offence under the Fraud Act 2006.

The exception in s(2)(b) means that a person can commit theft of things forming part of the land that the owner of the land has not allowed the thief to possess. This, therefore, includes soil, rocks, gravel, buildings (or part of the building such as lead on a church roof) and crops. Clearly a tenant farmer (who rents the land to grow crops and perform other farming activities) can harvest the crops he has grown without it being theft, and the landowner or anyone else cannot. Thus, it is theft to take apples from an orchard or from someone's allotment or garden. This will apply even where the tree overhangs your land or a public road. If the apples fall off onto your land (without your help!), it is not theft.

The exception in s(2)(c) refers to tenants of land, whether a tenant farmer or a student in a rented house. The section also refers to other technical aspects of land law that we do not need to explore. The tenant can be guilty of theft where he removes 'fixtures'; this would include a shed or separate garage, and parts of a house such as plumbing, electrical cables or light fittings. This is one reason why a person should be very careful before signing an inventory on renting a house or flat, as if the items they have signed for are not there at the end of the tenancy there could be an offence of theft committed.

3 A person who picks mushrooms growing wild on any land, or who picks flowers, fruit or foliage from a plant growing wild on any land, does not (although not in possession of the land) steal what he picks, unless he does it for reward or for sale or other commercial purpose. For purposes of this subsection 'mushroom' includes any fungus, and 'plant' includes any shrub or tree.

Link

For more on the *ejusdem generis* rule see pp44–5 and 50–1 of *AQA Law AS*.

This means that a person foraging for wild food is not guilty of theft unless they do so to sell it to someone else or the person has been paid to collect the wild fruit or mushrooms. This is why people who collect wild mushrooms for restaurants need to get permission from the landowner first, but the person collecting blackberries from the hedgerow for himself is not guilty of theft of the blackberries. Foraging is just picking from a plant. Removal of the whole plant can still form the basis of the offence of theft. It should be noted that some wild plants are protected under other Acts of Parliament and their removal might amount to an offence.

> 4 Wild creatures, tamed or untamed, shall be regarded as property; but a person cannot steal a wild creature not tamed nor ordinarily kept in captivity, or the carcase of any such creature, unless either it has been reduced into possession by, or on behalf of, another person and possession of it has not since been lost or abandoned, or another person is in course of reducing it into possession.

This means that a person who traps a wild rabbit is not guilty of theft. However, once someone else has caught the wild animal, it can then be stolen. Thus it is theft to take away a deer shot by someone else that they are waiting to take away or a pet such as a cat or a zoo animal.

Despite the expansion of the potential for an offence in this section, there remain situations where the court has had to decide on the question of whether there has been theft as a result of the nature of the property involved. This has come up with some surprising results.

In **Oxford v Moss (1978)** a student 'borrowed' an examination paper for the purpose of obtaining the information on the forthcoming exam. He copied the paper and then returned it. The student was charged with theft of the information contained on the exam paper. (He was not charged with theft of the paper as there was insufficient evidence that he intended to permanently deprive the owner of the paper, merely have access to the information. However, it could be argued that there was theft of the paper as its value reduced when the information was no longer confidential.) The court decided that the confidential information was not property and so there was no offence of theft. This is similar to copyright issues such as have occurred in music file sharing and video streaming cases. There are, however, other potential offences committed here and the owner of the paper would have civil remedies available too.

Another problem arose leading to a controversial decision in the case of **Marshall (1998)**. In late 1996 the defendant (and others) were video-recorded obtaining London underground tickets or travel cards from members of the public passing through the barriers and reselling them to other potential customers. The travellers were asked if they had finished with their card and, if they had, were asked if the defendant might have the card. Where the traveller had finished with his card, he often handed it to the defendant rather than throw it away. The cards often had some value left on them being a day pass for a particular travel zone. The defendant then resold them at a reduced rate to persons intending to travel. London Underground Limited did not receive the revenue which it might have expected to receive from those persons who had bought the tickets. The court decided that the tickets belonged to London Underground and not to the travellers who merely used them as evidence of the right to travel. This principle could be applied to prepaid car park tickets.

An interesting problem arose in the case of **Kelly (1998)**. Kelly, an artist, had removed a number of human body parts from the Royal College of London without its permission and without the intention of returning them. Usually, there is no property in a corpse. However, in this case, the body parts had been preserved and most of them had been the subject of further dissection so as to reveal the inner workings of the body. The court decided that that the parts of a corpse could be 'property' if they had acquired different attributes by virtue of the application of skill, such as dissection or preservation techniques, for exhibition or teaching purposes. This has particular implications for those working in hospital mortuaries, undertakers and crematoriums and the potential use of donor organs.

Actus reus: element 3 – belonging to another

The Theft Act 1968 s5 deals with this element of the *actus reus* of theft. The general principle is set out in s5(1) as:

> **1** Property shall be regarded as belonging to any person having possession or control of it, or having in it any proprietary right or interest (not being an equitable interest arising only from an agreement to transfer or grant an interest).

This means that at the time the property is appropriated it must belong to another. This clearly involves rights that are less than ownership, as the Act refers to concepts such as possession and control. There are a number of areas of this section that have been the subject of cases with, usually, sensible results.

The first concepts to consider are of possession and control. A person who owns property has the fullest rights over it. Possession is the physical ability to enjoy the property. In the case of tangible property such as this book, it would be holding it and using it. With intangible property, an owner has the fullest rights to use the benefits of the property, such as spending a credit balance (money in an account) by transferring it to someone else. Possession of the intangible right is having the ability to access the use of the property.

Ownership of property may be separated from possession. If I lend you a book, I still own it but you will possess and control it. Your rights over the book are less than mine. I can still sell it (subject to any rights you may have as to possession), but you cannot sell it without my permission or it is likely to be theft. If I hire a car, I do not own it, but will have possession and control of it. This can be seen in the case of **Webster (2006)**. The case involved a medal, the Operation Telic medal for service in Iraq. The medal was awarded to Captain Gill, regional administration officer of the King's Royal Hussars, who received such a medal in early 2005. In September 2005 he received a duplicate medal. It was engraved with his name and details and was sent from the medals office which was responsible within the Ministry of Defence for the administration and issuing of medals. It is not known how the duplicate came to be sent, as Captain Gill had not applied for one. Webster was Captain Gill's staff support assistant. Captain Gill handed the medal over to Webster, who advertised it on eBay and sold it for £605.

The defendant accepted that the proper thing to do would have been to return to the medal to the medals office, though he did not believe that he was legally required to return it, believing he had a mere moral obligation to return it. It was argued that would be insufficient for a finding of ownership of the medal by the Secretary of State. There was no dispute that when a medal is given it becomes the property of the member of the forces to whom it is given. However, the court decided that the medal's office did retain a proprietary interest in the medal and was entitled to call for the return of the duplicate medal. Therefore, the defendant could be convicted of theft.

There are other rights less than ownership that a person can acquire in various ways. This can include the right to retain possession of goods

Key cases

Webster (2006): where duplicate property has been delivered to the defendant by mistake, the defendant cannot keep the second item; it remains the property of the person who sent it in error.

Fig. 2 *Operation Telic medal*

until a bill has been paid. This can be seen in the case of **Turner (No.2) (1971)**. In that case the defendant, using his spare keys, removed his car from outside the garage at which it had been repaired, so as to avoid having to pay for the repair. The garage was entitled to keep possession of his car until the repairs had been paid for, so the defendant was convicted of theft. It should be noted that making off without payment might be a more appropriate offence.

It is also the case that a person could be convicted of stealing stolen goods from a thief who had possession of the stolen goods. Whilst the original thief does not own the stolen goods, he is in possession of the goods. The court decided in *Kelly* (1998) (the body parts case discussed earlier) that s5(1) does not include the word lawful, so any form of possession, even unlawful, will suffice.

A person can be in control of property even though he does not know that he possesses it. In **Woodman (1974)**, the defendant took a van to a disused factory near Bristol and removed a quantity of scrap metal. The disused factory still belonged to a company and the scrap metal at the factory was sold to another company, who removed much of it. They left behind some metal that was difficult to remove, and it remained there for over a year behind a barbed wire fence and with warning notices, until the defendant removed it. Even though the owner of the disused factory did not know the metal remained on its premises, it was still in control of the site as could be seen from the barbed wire and warning notices, so the defendant could be convicted of theft of the metal that the factory owners did not know was there.

Where property is abandoned, there is no owner of that property. The real problem is as to what amounts to abandonment. If I lose my wedding ring, I have not abandoned it – I wish to keep it and will look for it, thus retaining ownership but not actual possession. A finder who keeps it could be guilty of theft. However, if I deliberately leave a magazine on a train, I will be abandoning it, as I do not want it any more and do not care what happens to it, but perhaps hope someone will find it and take it. However, just because I throw something out, it does not mean it has become abandoned property. Rubbish placed in a dustbin for the council to collect becomes owned by the council. This explains why assistants at household recycling sites cannot just take things left there for themselves, but, subject to council regulations, may ask if they may keep the item personally. This can be seen in the case of **Williams v Phillips (1957)** where refuse collectors were convicted of the theft of refuse as they removed it from commercial premises. Their employers had posted notices which provided that any proceeds from selling refuse had to be shared with the council, and warned of criminal prosecutions. The defendants had collected and sold on sacks of rags and wool they had collected without telling the council. Similarly, 'lost' golf balls on a golf course belong to the golf course owner and are not abandoned goods, so can be stolen. However, those lost on public land such as a road alongside the golf course are probably abandoned and have no ownership and therefore cannot be stolen.

Where property has been given to be dealt with in a particular way and that is not done there can be theft. This is seen from s5(3) of the Act, which states:

> 3 Where a person receives property from, or on account of another, and is under an obligation to the other to retain and deal with that property, or its proceeds in a particular way, the property or other proceeds shall be regarded (as against him) as belonging to the other.

Key cases

Turner (No.2) (1971): a person can be convicted of theft where he steals another person's rights over goods; in this case it was the right to retain possession of the goods until a repair bill had been paid: the defendant appears to have been convicted of stealing his own car, but in fact it was the right over the car that was stolen.

Woodman (1974): a person can be in control of property he does not know he possesses: in the case, scrap metal in a disused factory.

Williams v Phillips (1957): property that has been abandoned by its owner may become the property of those that remove it; in this case, the council owned rubbish left for collection.

Key cases

Davidge and Bunnett (1984): where money or cheques are given for a particular purpose, they must be used for that purpose or there can be a conviction for theft.

DPP v Huskinson (1988): where money or cheques are given for a particular purpose, there can be a conviction for theft only if there is a legal and not merely a moral obligation to use the proceeds for that purpose.

Wain (1995): where money is held in trust for someone, the money is money belonging to another.

This means that the Act recognises that there are obligations that are in existence that may not be quite as formal as a trust, but still give rise for the opportunity to commit the offence of theft. Cases on this usually involve money being given to someone for a particular purpose. One such case is **Davidge and Bunnett (1984)**. In that case, the defendant shared a flat with several others, who gave her cheques on the understanding that their communal gas bill would be paid with the proceeds of the cheques. In fact, she spent the proceeds on Christmas presents and left the flat without giving notice. As she was under a legal obligation to use the proceeds of the cheques for the payment of the gas bill they were regarded as property belonging to another under s5(3). She was convicted of theft.

However, it seems from the case of **DPP v Huskinson (1988)** that this will only apply if there is some form of legal rather than moral obligation to deal with the money in a particular way. In that case, the defendant was sent a cheque for housing benefit even though he stated he wanted his rent to be paid direct. He used some of the proceeds of the cheque to pay arrears of rent, but spent some on himself. As there was no legal requirement to use the money to pay rent arrears, he was not convicted of theft.

This confusion can perhaps be remedied by relying on s5(2) of the Act, which states:

> 2 Where property is subject to a trust, the persons to whom it belongs shall be regarded as including any person having a right to enforce the trust, and an intention to defeat the trust shall be regarded accordingly as an intention to deprive of the property any person having that right.

This means that money held in any form of trust is money belonging to another and this can be seen to occur where there is difficulty in showing a legal obligation rather than a moral obligation. This argument was used to secure a conviction for theft in the case of **Wain (1995)**. This case involved charity fundraising. People running an event were required to complete a registration form and return it to a television company. Once the form was returned to the charity (Telethon Trust), according to their usual practice, they send out a whole package of documents which provide help in organising events, a recommendation that the money be paid into a separate bank account and information on where to obtain collecting boxes, balloons and such like. In this case, the defendant said that he had never received such a package from Telethon Trust, but nonetheless he did in fact open a separate bank account in the name of the Scarborough Telethon Appeal. The amount raised was £2,833.25. He was invited along to Yorkshire Television Headquarters, where he presented a dummy cheque to a television celebrity. He did not in fact pay over the money, claiming he was still getting it in. When pressed for payment, he gave various cheques drawn on various accounts that were worthless. The court relied on the fact that the money collected was held by him on trust for the charity and therefore the *actus reus* of the offence had been committed and the jury would have to consider the *mens rea* of dishonesty for there to be a conviction. Following the case of *Dyke and Munro* (2001), this principle will apply even if there is no specific person who is to benefit from the trust.

The final aspect of this element of the *actus reus* of theft occurs where property is received by mistake such as an overpayment of wages or two items being sent instead of one ordered and paid for. The relevant part of the Act is s5(4) which states:

> 4 Where a person gets property by another's mistake, and is under an obligation to make restoration (in whole or in part) of the property or its proceeds or of the value thereof, then to the extent

of that obligation the property or proceeds shall be regarded (as against him) as belonging to the person entitled to restoration, and an intention not to make restoration shall be regarded accordingly as an intention to deprive that person of the property or proceeds.

This simply means that, where you are given something by mistake and have a legal obligation to give it back, keeping it may be theft.

Conclusion

There are three elements to the *actus reus* of theft: appropriation; property; belonging to another. All three elements have particular aspects that need to be considered when discussing liability under s1 of the Theft Act 1968. Despite the fact that the Act itself amplifies some aspects, the courts too have made an input to the meaning of these three elements.

Activity

Identify and consider the issues with respect to the *actus reus* of theft, so far as Alan is concerned, in the following situation:

Alan went into a newsagent's shop and picked up a copy of *Law* magazine. He was not sure if he wanted the magazine so put it down. Beth looked at the magazine and, thinking it was *Claw* magazine, decided she wanted it, but had no money, so stole it. When she discovered the content was about law and not cats she put the magazine in a rubbish bin. Alan saw the magazine in the bin and took it from the bin.

You should now be able to:

■ understand the *actus reus* of theft

■ apply the *actus reus* of theft to a given situation.

2 Theft 2: *Mens rea* of the offence

The *mens rea* of theft has two elements:

■ Dishonesty

■ **Intention to permanently deprive** the other of the appropriated property.

Both elements must be proved for the offence to be committed. It is this element of *mens rea* that distinguishes normal transactions from theft. It should be noted that the Theft Act 1968 points out in s1(2) that it is 'immaterial whether the appropriation is made with a view to gain, or is made for the thief's own benefit'. This means that a person could be convicted of theft when destroying another person's property, even though he would normally be prosecuted for criminal damage.

The prosecution must prove the elements beyond reasonable doubt and this can sometimes prove difficult. It is logical to consider the elements in the reverse order. Whilst the overriding element of theft is **dishonesty**, a person can intend to permanently deprive someone of an item honestly. It is therefore preferable to consider this element first.

In this topic you will learn how to:

■ explain the *mens rea* of theft

■ explain cases that illustrate the *mens rea* of theft

■ apply the rules relating to both the *actus reus* and *mens rea* of theft to a given situation.

Key terms

Intention to permanently deprive: occurs where a person's intention is to treat the thing as his own to dispose of, regardless of the other's rights.

Dishonesty: this is set out in the Ghosh test on page 176.

Mens rea: element 1 – intention to permanently deprive the other of the appropriated property

As a general rule, merely borrowing something does not form an intention to permanently deprive. However, every thief would always raise this as a defence and there would be very few convictions for theft once the accused said 'Oh, I would have given it back as soon as I realised I had it…' The offence of theft begins when that intention is formed. In most cases, intention can be inferred from the surrounding circumstances.

Section 6(1) helps explain the meaning. It states:

> 1 A person appropriating property belonging to another without meaning the other permanently to lose the thing itself is nevertheless to be regarded as having the intention or permanently depriving the other of it if his intention is to treat the thing as his own to dispose of regardless of the other's rights; and a borrowing or lending of it may amount to so treating it if, but only if, the borrowing or lending is for a period and in circumstances making it equivalent to an outright taking or disposal.

There are two aspects of this:

1 Disposing of the property regardless of the other's rights.
2 A borrowing or lending making it equivalent to outright taking or disposal.

This can be seen in the case of *Marshall* (1998), considered in the previous topic. In that case, the idea that the underground ticket remained the property of London Underground meant that the subsequent sale to another traveller was a disposal regardless of the other's rights. This would apply equally, for example, to re-using a cinema ticket that had not been collected.

In **DPP v J and others (2002)**, the defendant took and broke his victim's headphones and then gave them back. Here the question of whether there was an intention to permanently deprive arose and it is considered that there was such an intention.

The aspects of borrowing have lead to some difficulties. In **Lloyd (1985)** the defendant worked as a projectionist at a cinema and was responsible for looking after the films. He took films from the cinema to be copied, but the films were only out of the cinema for a few hours and were always back in time for their projection to take place at the advertised times to those people who attended the cinema to see them. Remarkably, he was not convicted of theft, although there are potentially other offences with which he could be charged.

In other cases, defendants have not been so fortunate. In **Velumyl (1989)**, the defendant, without any authority from the company and contrary to the company's rules, took £1,050 from the safe at his place of work on Saturday evening, and lent it to a friend. It was a condition of that private loan that his friend should return it on Monday. A spot check took place before the money was returned. The court asked whether he intended permanently to deprive the owner of the money and concluded that he had no intention of returning the objects he had taken. His intention – at best – was to return objects of equivalent value, so this part of the *mens rea* had been fulfilled.

This wider approach to the idea of depriving permanently was used again in the case of **Lavender (1994)**. In this case, the defendant lived with his girlfriend at 37 Royce Road, Spalding. His girlfriend was the tenant

Key cases

DPP v J and others (2002): the taking and destroying of property can amount to an intention to permanently deprive; in this case it was headphones that were taken and then returned.

Lloyd (1985): in this case, the removal of films from a cinema for a short time so they could be illegally copied did not amount to an intention to permanently deprive.

Velumyl (1989): the defendant had intended to permanently deprive the owner of his property as he clearly did not intend to return the same notes and coins, even if he returned items of a similar value.

Lavender (1994): the wider approach to the interpretation of intention permanently to deprive was taken here so as to convict a person who swapped internal doors from another council house to his council house.

of the council house. She asked the council to replace damaged doors at that property, but the council refused because she was responsible for any damage to the doors. The council would have replaced the doors if she paid £400, which she did not do. The council also owned 25 Royce Road which was unoccupied because it was undergoing repair. The defendant took two doors from 25 Royce Road to replace the damaged doors at 37 Royce Road. His intention was to use the doors at 37 Royce Road for so long as he remained there and leave them there when he eventually left that address. He argued that swapping the doors did not amount to theft because he was not permanently depriving the council of them. This argument failed and he was convicted, the court saying that the defendant intended to treat the doors as his own in dealing with the council regardless of their rights. There can be no doubt that what the respondent did was regardless of the council's right. Those rights included the right not to have the doors at 25 Royce Road removed, and to require the tenant at 37 Royce Road to replace or pay for the damaged doors.

Mens rea: element 2 – dishonesty

The meaning of dishonesty is not defined in the Theft Act 1968. It was assumed by the draftsmen of the Act that everyone would know what the word meant and therefore a jury or magistrates would be able to decide easily enough. The word was used so as to have no specific legal meaning other than its natural meaning. The Act did, however, give three specific situations where a person would be deemed not to be dishonest in s2, whilst noting in s2(2) that a person may still make a dishonest appropriation even though he is willing to pay for the property.

Section 2 is as follows:

1 A person's appropriation of property belonging to another is not to be regarded as dishonest –
   a if he appropriates the property in the belief that he has in law the right to deprive the other of it, on behalf of himself or a third party; or
   b if he appropriates the property in the belief that he would have the other's consent if the other knew of the appropriation and the circumstances of it; or
   c (except where the property came to him as trustee or personal representative) if he appropriates the property in the belief that the person to whom the property belongs cannot be discovered by taking reasonable steps.

Before discussing the meaning of dishonesty, we need to consider the exceptions in s2(1).

The first exception requires an honest, but not necessarily reasonable, belief in the defendant of his right to take the item. This is a subjective test, so the sole concern is for the defendant to convince a jury that he reasonably held that belief. An example of this is where an employee is instructed to collect certain goods from a third party. The employee honestly believes he has the legal right to do so (having been told to so by his boss) and therefore will not be dishonest in taking the goods even if, in fact, there is no such right to do so.

An example of this can be seen in the case of **Small (1987)**, where the defendant noticed an old and very scruffy car parked in the road for over a week with the key in the ignition. Parts were missing, and there was no petrol in it. The defendant thought the car had been dumped and therefore decided to get it going and drive it. His defence to stealing the car was that he believed it was abandoned by its owner and therefore

Key cases

Small (1987): this is an example of s2(1)(a) of the Theft Act 1968 operating to prevent the conviction of the defendant, who genuinely believed that the car he had taken was abandoned.

he had a legal right to take it, even though the owner could have been found from the registration number (this is why this case is different to one falling within the third exception). In fact this was not the case; nevertheless, he was not guilty of theft.

The second exception requires an honest belief that the owner of the goods would consent if he knew of the circumstances. An everyday example of this is borrowing a person's pen without asking, and later returning it, or continuing a normal practice of borrowing tools and machinery between neighbours.

The third exception most usually applies in situations of finding items and then keeping them. This again requires an honest belief by the defendant that the owner cannot be found by taking reasonable steps. An example of this would be finding a £1 coin in the street. There is usually an honest belief that the owner could not reasonably be found, but that would not be so if the defendant had just seen someone pull the coin out of their pocket along with a handkerchief. Clearly, the more valuable the item, the less likely the owner cannot reasonably be found – hence the volume of lost property that gets handed in!

Where these exceptions do not apply, the courts have developed a test for dishonesty. There is usually little argument about whether an act is dishonest – for example, shoplifting is obviously dishonest and a jury would have little difficulty with that. However, defendants from time to time claimed that they had not been dishonest and there was no standard test that should be applied. Examples include borrowing from the petty cash at work without permission and contrary to the company rules, but intending to replace the money the next day, or borrowing from the till and leaving an IOU.

The matter was resolved in the case of **Ghosh (1982)**. In that case, the defendant was a surgeon acting as a consultant at a hospital. He claimed that he had himself carried out a surgical operation to terminate a pregnancy and that payment for the operation was due to himself or an anaesthetist for such an operation, when in fact the operation had been carried out by someone else, and/or under the National Health Service provisions. His defence was that he had not been dishonest, as the sums paid to him were due for consultation fees which were legitimately payable under the regulations, or, alternatively, were the balance of fees already owed to him. In other words, he was alleged to have claimed money for work he had not done even though he was in fact owed money for work he had done.

The Lord Chief Justice set out the test for dishonesty:

> In determining whether the prosecution has proved that the defendant was acting dishonestly, a jury must first of all decide whether according to the ordinary standards of reasonable and honest people what was done was dishonest. If it was not dishonest by those standards, that is the end of the matter and the prosecution fails.
>
> If it was dishonest by those standards, then the jury must consider whether the defendant himself must have realised that what he was doing was by those standards dishonest. In most cases, where the actions are obviously dishonest by ordinary standards, there will be no doubt about it. It will be obvious that the defendant himself knew that he was acting dishonestly. It is dishonest for a defendant to act in a way which he knows ordinary people consider to be dishonest, even if he asserts or genuinely believes that he is morally justified in acting as he did.

Key cases

Ghosh (1982): this case set out the definitive test for what amounts to be dishonesty; the two-part test is: (1) Would the defendant's behaviour be regarded as dishonest by the standards of reasonable and honest people? (If the answer is 'no', the defendant is not guilty of theft as he has not been dishonest). If the answer is 'yes' the second question is: (2) Was the defendant aware that his conduct would be regarded as dishonest by reasonable and honest people?

Link

You can usefully link this test, and much of the law of theft, to Chapter 20, Law and morality.

This test is a two-part test, known as the Ghosh test, and can be stated as follows:

1 Would the defendant's behaviour be regarded as dishonest by the standards of reasonable and honest people?

(If the answer is 'no', the defendant is not guilty of theft as he has not been dishonest.)

If the answer is 'yes' the second question is:

2 Was the defendant aware that his conduct would be regarded as dishonest by reasonable and honest people?

It can be seen that the first part of the test is objective and the second part of the test is subjective. If both parts of the test are satisfied, the defendant fulfils the criteria for being dishonest.

Conclusion

The *mens rea* of theft is best considered in the order: intention permanently to deprive, followed by dishonesty. If there is no intention to permanently deprive, the honesty of the act is irrelevant. The intention permanently to deprive has two aspects: disposing of the property regardless of the other's rights; and issues with respect to borrowing or lending. The element of dishonesty has some statutory exceptions; if they do not apply, the two-part Ghosh test must be applied.

Application of the elements of theft to problems in the examination

In the examination, there are often questions involving the elements of theft. In such cases, the best practice is to outline the *actus reus* and *mens rea* of the offence, but concentrate on the application of the law to the problem that has been set. Where the problem does include theft, theft is likely to account for roughly one third of the issues that will need to be identified, have the law stated and applied. At A2 the application is more important than the statements of law and it is essential to focus on the issues that need discussion rather than those that are virtually self-evident from the facts in the scenario.

Consider this scenario from the AQA January 2007 examination:

> Uma and Violet were employed by Warren. One day at work, Uma discovered that Violet had left her purse in the toilets. Uma removed a fitness club membership card from the purse and then put the purse in the wastepaper bin (from which it was later removed and returned to Violet by a very alert colleague). Uma subsequently used the membership card to get herself a training session at the fitness club, for which she would normally have had to pay £10. She quietly dropped the card at the reception desk when she left.

There are a number of issues with respect to theft arising from this situation. The mark scheme refers to:

> Theft of the purse and the membership card – explanation, in particular, of *mens rea* issues involving dishonesty and intention permanently to deprive.

The mark scheme focuses on the *mens rea* issues, as the *actus reus* of the crime requires little explanation. The fact that under s1 of the Theft Act 1968 the *actus reus* involves the appropriation of property belonging to another must be stated in the answer. Because this is so obvious, the application needs only to state that when Uma took the purse from the toilet she was appropriating (taking) property (the purse and its contents) belonging to another (Violet). There is no need to spend a great deal of time explaining aspects of the law of theft relating any other aspect of the *actus reus* of theft.

With respect to the *mens rea*, however, much more needs to be said. Though discussion of dishonesty in the *mens rea* is certainly relevant, the fact that she removed the membership card and put the purse in a bin is clearly dishonest. Both parts of the Ghosh test are present – Uma's behaviour would be regarded as dishonest by the standards of reasonable and honest people, and Uma would surely be aware that her conduct would be regarded as dishonest by reasonable and honest people. The real issue is the meaning and application of intention permanently to deprive, given the contrast between the disposal of the purse and the disposal of the card.

Here, there needs to be a consideration of what deductions about intention permanently to deprive can be made from the way in which Uma disposed of the two different items. It is not really possible to deduce intention permanently to deprive from the *use* of the card to get the training session. The use of the card is much more relevant to appropriation, though not really needed as there was an assumption of the rights of owner involved in taking the card. The use of the card is relevant for offences involving fraud that will be considered in a later chapter.

With respect to intention permanently to deprive, the disposal of the purse in the bin shows no intention to return the item to the owner, who is clearly a known person from the contents of the purse. This therefore fulfils the criteria for theft. It is entirely fortuitous that the purse is found and returned.

Similarly with the membership card, it can be argued that there is an attempt to show no such intention by leaving it so it will be collected and returned, but its use and retention for a period of time permanently deprived the owner of the use of that card for that time. Uma is in possession and control of the property of another and deals with it dishonestly for her own purpose – using the fitness club. It could, however, be argued that no loss had been suffered with respect to the card as, presumably, Violet had not wished to use the fitness club whilst her card was missing, or had not needed it to access the club. In such circumstances, it could be argued that there is no liability for theft of the card.

Fig. 3 *The* actus reus *here is Uma taking Violet's purse*

Activities

1   Consider the elements of theft in relation to the scenario set out below for both Darren and Evan:

One day, Darren was in an open park when he came across a mountain bike, which was lying on the ground near a path. Although he waited for 15 minutes, he did not see anyone else, so he rode off on the bike. A week later, Evan saw the bike parked outside a house. Though there were significant differences in colour and other features, he immediately believed it to be his own bike, which had been stolen a few weeks before. He had just put his hands on the handlebars and was about to jump onto it when Darren came out of the house. Evan ran off. In reality, it was not Evan's bike.

2   Go back to the questions posed at the start of this chapter and reconsider your answers now you have studied the topic of theft.

You should now be able to:

■   understand the *mens rea* of theft

■   apply the *actus reus* and *mens rea* of theft to a given situation.

Robbery, blackmail, burglary, and criminal damage

In this topic you will learn how to:

■ state the definition of robbery

■ explain the *actus reus* and *mens rea* of robbery

■ explain cases that illustrate the law on robbery

■ apply the rules to a given situation.

Key terms

Robbery: if someone steals, and immediately before or at the time of doing so, and in order to do so, uses force on any person, or puts or seeks to put any person in fear of being then and there subjected to force, he or she is guilty of robbery.

Blackmail: an offence where there is a threat made so that a person does an act against his will, or in order to obtain the person's money or property.

Key cases

Dawson and James (1976): force is required for robbery, but the word has no special meaning; it is up to the jury to decide whether the defendant's actions amounted to force.

1 Robbery

Robbery can be seen very simply as theft with force. The traditional view of the bank robber with a mask over his face waving a sawn-off shotgun around is everyone's idea of robbery. But, can it be robbery if two people, holding their Oyster cards (the London travel pass), run into each other at a tube station and pick up each other's card after they have been dropped in the collision; one card has little credit on it, the other has a substantial credit balance? What circumstances might change the accident to a robbery?

The definition of robbery

The offence of robbery is defined in the Theft Act 1968, s8(1) as:

> A person is guilty of robbery if he steals, and immediately before or at the time of doing so, and in order to do so, he uses force on any person or puts or seeks to put any person in fear of being then and there subjected to force.

Robbery is, therefore, an aggravated form of theft. The *actus reus* is:

■ the *actus reus* of theft

■ use of force or putting or seeking to put any person in fear of subjection to force in order to steal immediately before or at the time of stealing.

The *mens rea* is:

■ the *mens rea* of theft

■ intent or recklessness as to the use or threat of force.

Therefore, all the limitations to the offence of theft, such as the limits on what can be stolen, are equally applicable. There are a number of points to be considered apart from the elements of theft discussed in the previous chapter. These are:

■ What amounts to force on a person?

■ What amounts to a threat of force on a person?

■ When does the force or threat of force have to take place?

■ What connection must there be between the force and the theft?

It is essential that the offence of theft has been committed before there can be a conviction for robbery.

What amounts to force or threat of force on a person?

The word 'force' is not defined in the Act. However, the force, or threat of force must be sufficient to be noticeable, but not necessarily to the victim. Thus, waving a knife at someone who is blind would probably be sufficient. What would not be sufficient would be the threat of future violence, as that would not fulfil the definition of 'fear of being then and there subjected to force'. Such activity may be the basis of a charge of **blackmail**.

There is no need to use any technical meaning to the term 'force'; indeed in the case of **Dawson and James (1976)**, the Court of Appeal specifically stated that the word was an ordinary word, and the jury could decide if what had occurred amounted to force. This could be jostling, as in that case where the defendants stood around the victim, one of them nudged the victim. This made the victim to lose his balance so that his wallet could be easily taken.

It appears that it does not matter whether the victim is actually put in fear or not: it is the defendant's intention that matters. The fact that the victim was not afraid does not mean that the defendant did not attempt to put him in fear. This is sufficient for the offence as can be seen from the case of **B and R v DPP (2007)**. In that case, five boys stopped the victim and asked if he had a mobile phone or some money. The victim said he did not, and was then asked which school he attended. He said where he went to school and he was then asked for his mobile phone and money. Whilst that was happening about five or six more males ran to join the group. The eleven or twelve boys all surrounded the victim and when he did not hand over his telephone and money, his drink was taken and a packet of crisps was snatched from his hands. A number of the boys went into his pockets and took his wallet from his inside pocket, his watch from an outside pocket and his travel card. A £5 note was removed from the wallet; the wallet was then thrown to the ground. The victim said he did not feel 'particularly threatened' or 'scared' and he was not physically assaulted. He said he was 'a bit shocked'. The boys were convicted of robbery

It also appears that there does not have to be direct force on the victim. The word force is all that is required, so the jury can decide if it was sufficient. In **Clouden (1987)**, the defendant was seen to follow a woman who was carrying a shopping basket in her left hand. He approached her from behind and wrenched the basket down and out of her grasp with both hands and ran off with it. This was sufficient force for a conviction for robbery.

It is also the case that the threat does not have to be as the victim imagines it if it is intended to cause fear. In the case of **Bentham (2005)** the defendant positioned his fingers, concealed within his jacket, in such a way as to give the appearance of a gun which he pointed at the victim. This amounted to force for the purposes of robbery, although not of possessing an imitation firearm.

When does the force or threat of force have to take place?

The importance of this question is that the definition requires the force or threat of force to take place immediately before or at the time of stealing. This deliberately makes the time when the force is used fairly fluid within the overall time that the crime took place. This has been made clearer by the case of **Hale (1978)**, where burglars entered a house and took a jewellery box. They then tied up the occupant before leaving. The court decided that appropriation (and therefore theft) was still continuing when the occupant was tied up. The court took the view that the appropriation and therefore the stealing was a continuing act and the jury could decide when the theft was complete.

In *Hale* (1978), Eveleigh LJ said:

> In the present case there can be little doubt that if the appellant had been interrupted after the seizure of the jewellery box the jury would have been entitled to find that the appellant and his accomplice were assuming the rights of an owner at the time when the jewellery box was seized. However, the act of appropriation does not suddenly cease. It is a continuous act and it is a matter for the jury to decide whether or not the act of appropriation has finished. Moreover, it is quite clear that the intention to deprive the owner permanently, which accompanied the assumption of the owner's rights was a continuing one at all material times. This court therefore rejects the

AQA Examiner's tip

Whenever there is the slightest push or jostle in a scenario where theft is present, you should also consider robbery.

Key cases

Corcoran and Anderton (1980):
knocking a handbag out of the
victim's grasp with force was
sufficient for there to be a robbery
even though the robber did not
take the bag.

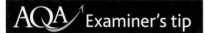

AQA Examiner's tip

Look for the continuing event and
raise the issue of when the theft is
complete following the principles
laid down in *Hale* (1978).

---

contention that the theft had ceased by the time the lady was tied
up. As a matter of common sense the appellant was in the course of
committing the theft; he was stealing.

In some cases the actual stealing and appropriation may be very brief. In
Corcoran and Anderton (1980) the robbery was committed at the point
of appropriation even though the robber failed. The court decided that a
robbery was committed where the victim's handbag was wrestled from
her grasp, even though it then fell to the ground and the robber ran off
without it.

At the other end of the scale, a line must be drawn even though
continuing possession of the goods stolen would appear to make it a
continuing act. Eveleigh LJ's common sense approach can be used to
come to a conclusion on this matter. In *Hale* (1978) the appropriation
would probably end when the robbers left the house and were in the
street outside. This is consistent with the theft case of *Atakpu* (1994),
where the defendant hired expensive cars abroad to sell in England. The
defendant successfully argued that no appropriation had taken place in
England and therefore the case was not triable in England. The theft was
complete long before the cars were brought into England.

What connection must there be between the force and the theft?

The force or threat of force must be used in order to steal. If the force or
threat of force is used for a different purpose (such as rape), then it is not
robbery. Where the force is used to allow the theft to happen, for example
to obtain the keys to a building or safe, then it can be robbery. This can
be seen from the case of *Hale* (1978), where tying up the victim allowed
the successful completion of the theft.

Conclusion

The offence of robbery requires consideration of the offence of theft.
If there has been no theft, there can be no robbery. The question then
remains whether there was force or threat of force that, immediately
before or at the time of stealing, was used in order to steal.

Application of the elements of robbery to problems in the examination

In the examination there are often questions involving the elements of
robbery. As with all problem questions, the key is to focus on the issues
that require discussion and analysis and minimise the time spent on
descriptions that do little to advance the issues. Consider this extract
from a past problem:

Andy went to the West Hotel to enquire about prices. Whilst the
reception area was unstaffed, Andy reached over the reception
counter to see what he could find in the drawer. He removed a
plastic card which could be used by the hotel to 'cut' a room key. He
then went to the bar and spent two hours drinking. To 'pay' for the
drinks, he claimed to be a guest by showing the barman, Barry, the
card and giving a room number. Barry made out the bill to the room
and did not ask for any money there and then.

Andy became quite drunk and began to attract attention by eating
all the free snacks placed at the bar for hotel guests. Eventually,
Barry tried to stop him taking yet another plate of snacks. Resisting
Barry's attempt, Andy threw a pint of beer at him, which missed
Barry and soaked the carpet. Andy then ran off with the plate of
snacks but without having paid for any of the drinks.

There are a number of offences that have been committed here as well as the issue of intoxication. At this stage we will just concentrate on the aspect of robbery. There is the possibility that Andy had stolen the bar snacks, as it can be argued that he had no right to eat them because he was not a *bona fide* guest and was deliberately not paying for his drinks. The snacks are provided for guests or those paying for drinks. Andy fell into neither category. Aspects of theft that need to be considered are, therefore, consent and appropriation and, briefly, dishonesty. If Andy was guilty of theft of the bar snacks, then his efforts to resist Barry's attempts to stop him by throwing beer at him could amount to the use of force for the purpose of committing the theft, and so introduce the offence of robbery. There then remains the question whether the force was used merely for the purpose of escape or actually to assist in the commission of the theft, thus leading to robbery.

Activity

Consider the following situation and consider whether Jason has committed robbery or not:

Jason was playing with a penknife whilst he repeatedly asked George, who was a couple of years younger, for a go on his bike. George let him. Jason rode off, was chased by an adult, dumped the bike and ran off.

George says he only let Jason have the bike because he was scared of him as he had a knife.

You should now be able to:

■ understand the law relating to robbery

■ apply that law to given scenarios.

2 Blackmail

Introduction

The term blackmail referred, originally, to a payment made by English people living along the border of Scotland to Scottish chieftains in exchange for protection from thieves and marauders. Today, blackmail involves a threat made so that a person does an act against his will, or in order to obtain the person's money or property. It is a threat from the blackmailer to do something for not agreeing to the demand. The threat doesn't have to be something illegal and doesn't even have to be true. An example would be a demand for money from someone if they did not want their previous criminal record publicised.

The definition of blackmail

Blackmail is defined in s21 of the Theft Act 1968 as:

> 1 A person is guilty of blackmail if, with a view to gain for himself or another or with intent to cause loss to another, he makes any **unwarranted demand** with menaces; and for this purpose a demand with menaces is unwarranted unless the person making it does so in the belief –
>
> a that he has reasonable grounds for making the demand; and
>
> b that the use of the menaces is a proper means of reinforcing the demand.

In this topic you will learn how to:

■ state the definition of blackmail

■ explain the *actus reus* and *mens rea* of blackmail

■ explain cases that illustrate the law on blackmail

■ apply the rules to a given situation.

Key terms

Unwarranted demand: a demand for something that the defendant is not legally entitled to.

> 2 The nature of the act or omission demanded is immaterial, and it is also immaterial whether the menaces relate to action to be taken by the person making the demand.

The *actus reus* of blackmail, therefore, has two aspects:

1 Unwarranted demand.
2 **Menaces**.

The *mens rea* of blackmail has three aspects:

1 An intention to make a demand with menaces.
2 Doing so with a view to gain for himself or another or with intent to cause loss to another.
3 Either –
   a not believing he has reasonable grounds for making the demand, or
   b not believing that the use of the menaces is a proper means of reinforcing the demand.

There are, therefore, a number of points that need to be considered for the offence of blackmail. These are:

■ What amounts to an unwarranted demand?
■ What amounts to 'menaces'?
■ The defendant's view to gain or loss.
■ The defendant's belief as to reasonable grounds for making the demands.
■ The defendant's belief that use of the menaces is a proper means of reinforcing the demand.

Key terms

Menaces: these can be threats of violence, including threats of any action detrimental to or unpleasant to the person addressed. It may also include a warning that, in certain events, such action is intended.

What amounts to an unwarranted demand?

The demand can be made either expressly or impliedly. Usually the demand is made expressly, such as an oral or written demand for a sum of money for not exposing some possible scandal. It also appears that the demand can be made impliedly. In **Collister and Warhurst (1955)**, the defendants were two policemen. They indicated to the victim that he would be reported for a sexual offence, but that they would hold back the report until they met him the next day. The next day the defendant policemen asked if he had anything for them, saying, 'Remember, sir, I am now making an appeal to your benevolence.' The victim handed over £5. Whether this amounted to a demand was a matter for the jury. The test is whether the evidence shows that, even though there was no express demand or threat, the attitude of the accused and the circumstances of the case were such that an ordinary reasonable man would understand that a demand for money was being made.

Key cases

Collister and Warhurst (1955): the demand in blackmail can be implied as well as expressed; it will be implied when a jury (the reasonable man) can see from the attitude, actions and circumstances that the defendant is making a demand.

Treacy v DPP (1971): a demand is made when the defendant has done all he can to communicate the demand.

The demand is made when the defendant has done all he can to communicate the demand. In the case of **Treacy v DPP (1971)**, this was when a letter was posted. This is presumably the same when an e-mail is sent (that does not bounce) or a text message is sent, assuming there is no evidence of a failure to deliver the message.

The demand made must be unwarranted. This means that it must be for something that the defendant is not legally entitled. Thus, a demand is not unwarranted if it is for money legally owing to the defendant. It would also not be unwarranted if the claimed debt turned out not to be legally enforceable. This is because the defendant would believe he had reasonable grounds for making the demand.

What amounts to 'menaces'?

The word 'menaces' has always had a broad interpretation. In **Thorne v Motor Trade Association (1937)**, Lord Wright said:

> I think the word menace is to be liberally construed, and not as limited to threats of violence, but as including threats of any action detrimental to or unpleasant to the person addressed. It may also include a warning that, in certain events, such action is intended.

It is also the case that the effect of the demand must be that the reasonable person would be influenced or fearful so that the demand was likely to be met. However, if the person to whom the threat is made is known by the defendant to be particularly timid, then threats which do not affect the reasonable person can still be taken as menaces. This can be seen from the case of **Garwood (1987)**, where the defendant was unusually timid and the defendant knew that fact.

An example of threats that do not amount to menaces can be seen in the case of **Harry (1974)**, where the defendant was a member of a university rag week committee who had written to shopkeepers on the route of a rag procession that they could be excluded from 'inconvenience' by supporting the rag week charities. This was seen to be essentially trivial and, at the time, was probably standard practice during rag weeks.

The defendant's view to gain or loss

In s34(2) of the Theft Act 1968 there are definitions:

> **2** For purposes of this Act –
>
> **a** 'gain' and 'loss' are to be construed as extending only to gain or loss in money or other property, but as extending to any such gain or loss whether temporary or permanent; and –
>
> **i** 'gain' includes a gain by keeping what one has, as well as a gain by getting what one has not; and
>
> **ii** 'loss' includes a loss by not getting what one might get, as well as a loss by parting with what one has.

This means that the intended result of the blackmail involves some money or property rather than something of no monetary value such as a kiss. Things of economic value, such as a morphine injection to get pain relief from a doctor, are sufficient for blackmail. This was seen in the case of **Bevans (1988)**.

The defendant's belief as to reasonable grounds for making the demands, and that the use of the menaces is a proper means of reinforcing the demand

The key thing about these defences to a charge of blackmail is that the defendant believed there were reasonable grounds for making the demand or believing that the use of menaces is a proper means of reinforcing his demand. The belief must be genuinely held and can be a moral rather than a legal belief, but a belief that would generally be viewed as immoral is no defence. This can be seen from the case of **Harvey (1981)**, where a drug deal had left the defendant having paid £20,000 for something worthless. He then kidnapped the seller's wife and child and threatened to maim and rape them if the money was not returned. He was convicted of blackmail even though he believed he was justified in making the threats.

Key cases

Thorne v Motor Trade Association (1937): this case provides an explanation as to the meaning of the word menaces; it includes violence, but also threats of any action detrimental to or unpleasant to the person addressed or warnings of such action.

Garwood (1987): in this case the defendant was very timid; as the defendant knew that was the fact, then his threat could amount to menaces even though the reasonable person would not be affected by the threat.

Harry (1974): this is an example of threats so mild as not to amount to menaces; the case involved a letter to shopkeepers on a rag week procession route that sought contributions to the charities to avoid 'inconvenience'.

Bevans (1988): gain or loss requires something of some economic value; in this case it was a painkilling injection.

Harvey (1981): the defendant's belief as to whether his use of menaces is proper can be a moral belief, but not, as in this case one that is not generally considered moral: maiming and raping.

Conclusion

The offence of blackmail is one that requires a consideration of situations where a person makes unwarranted demands with menaces. There is a specific defence within the Theft Act 1968 s21 that can be used to avoid conviction.

Application of the elements of blackmail to problems in the examination

In the examination, there can now be questions involving the elements of blackmail, it having been outside the scope of the AQA specification until the 2010 examinations. The questions may well focus on the issues surrounding the making of the demand and whether it was, in fact, unwarranted. As with other areas of the specification, answers need to concentrate on the areas that are less clear in the scenario, rather than those that are almost self-evident.

Activity

In the following situation, consider whether Ahmed has committed blackmail or not:

Ahmed is interviewed on suspicion of dealing in cannabis. He tells the interviewing officer that he knew some nasty people who could harm him or make trouble for him, and that he pays £300 a month for 'protection'. He suggests that he should not be charged with any offence on this occasion.

You should now be able to:

■ understand the law relating to blackmail

■ apply that law to given scenarios.

In this topic you will learn how to:

■ state the definition of burglary

■ explain the *actus reus* and *mens rea* of burglary under s9(1)(a) and (b) of the Theft Act 1968

■ explain cases that illustrate the law on burglary under s9(1)(a) and (b) of the Theft Act 1968

■ apply the rules to a given situation.

Key terms

Burglary: entry as a trespasser with intention to commit one or more of the stated offences or whilst trespassing, committing one of the stated offences.

3 Burglary under s9(1)(a) and (b) of the Theft Act 1968

Burglary is a well-known crime, although many people do not recognise the range of activities that can amount to burglary; it is not just entering a house and stealing something. Consider this situation which arose a few years ago: a man, with many previous convictions for burglary, was questioned by police when he was found on the roof of a house where a burglary had taken place. He was next to an open roof light. He had his shoes on but no socks as he was wearing his socks on his hands. He explained his presence on the roof as follows:

> I realised the house had been burgled and was concerned for the safety of the occupant. I did not want to disturb any evidence, so was going into the house by a different route to the burglars to check on the person who lives there. I had my socks on my hands so I did not leave any confusing fingerprints. The occupant is not present. Perhaps you could give back this ring I found on the path outside.

Do you think he could be charged with burglary? Do you think a jury would believe him?

The law on burglary is divided into two parts: s9(1)(a) of the Theft Act 1968 is concerned with going into a building as a trespasser with intent to commit one or more of a number of specified offences; s9(1)(b) of the Theft Act 1968 is concerned with committing one of a specified range of offences after an entry has been made to a building as a trespasser. There are a number of aspects of the definitions that need to be discussed.

The definition of burglary in s9(1) of the Theft Act 1968

The Theft Act 1968 defines the offence of burglary as follows:

1 A person is guilty of burglary if:

   a he enters any building or part of a building as a trespasser and with intent to commit any such offence as is mentioned in subsection (2) below; or

   b having entered any building or part of a building as a trespasser he steals or attempts to steal anything in the building or that part of it or inflicts or attempts to inflict on any person therein any grievous bodily harm.

2 The offences referred to in subsection (1) (a) above are offences of stealing anything in the building or part of a building in question, of inflicting on any person therein any grievous bodily harm therein, and of doing unlawful damage to the building or anything therein.

There are, therefore two distinct offences, the first under s9(1)(a) and the other under s9(1)(b).

Burglary under s9(1)(a)

The offence has a number of elements that need to be considered:

The *actus reus* has three elements:

1 enters
2 a building or part of a building
3 as a trespasser.

The *mens rea* has two elements:

1 knowledge or recklessness as to his entering as a trespasser
2 with intent to commit theft, grievous bodily harm or damage to the building or its contents.

Burglary under s9(1)(b)

The *actus reus* has four elements:

1 enters
2 a building or part of a building
3 as a trespasser
4 *actus reus* of theft or grievous bodily harm, or attempt theft/grievous bodily harm therein.

The *mens rea* has two elements:

1 knowledge or recklessness as to his entry as a trespasser
2 *mens rea* for theft or grievous bodily harm or attempt theft/grievous bodily harm therein.

The basic distinction between the two offences is that the first offence entry with an ulterior intent – to steal, cause grievous bodily harm or cause damage; the second offence is the commission of theft or grievous

Fig. 1 *Do you think he can be charged with burglary?*

AQA Examiner's tip

Whenever someone enters any premises or goes somewhere he would not normally be allowed, you should consider the prosecution of burglary.

Collins (1973): entry, for the purpose of burglary, needs to be effective; this means that it enables the crime to be committed, not that the defendant's body was wholly inside the building.

Brown (1985): the defendant was seen with his head and shoulders inside a broken shop window; this was enough for effective entry to the shop.

Ryan (1996): entry is effective even if the crime intended cannot be committed; in this case a would-be thief got trapped in a window, but he was still convicted of burglary.

bodily harm (or an attempt to do so) once entry as a trespasser has taken place.

There are, therefore, a number of common elements to theft: enters; building or part thereof; as a trespasser; knowledge or recklessness as to his entering as a trespasser.

The first common element – enters

Entry is done when what is called 'effective' entry has taken place. This is a question of fact and depends on whether enough of the defendant is in the building to achieve the ulterior intent (s9(1)(a)) or commit the crime or attempt crime (s9(1)(b)). Three cases illustrate this point.

The first case is **Collins (1973)**, where the defendant, having discovered that a woman was lying asleep and naked on her bed, stripped off his clothes (apart from his socks) and climbed up a ladder on to the window sill of the bedroom and leaned in. At this moment the woman awoke and, mistakenly believing that the naked form at the window was her boyfriend, beckoned the defendant in. The defendant then got into her bed and it was only after the defendant had intercourse with her that the woman realised her error. The defendant's conviction for burglary (entering as a trespasser with intent to commit rape (this was an ulterior offence for burglary until the Sexual Offences Act 2003), contrary to s9(1)(a)). One question the court had to decide was whether there was entry as he lent in the window before being beckoned to come in. The court decided that he had made an effective entry.

The second case is **Brown (1985)**. In that case, the defendant was seen partially inside a shop window. The top half of his body was inside the

shop window, as though he were rummaging inside it. The witness assumed that his feet were on the ground outside, although his view was obscured. The defendant was convicted of burglary as he had effective entry – he could handle the goods inside the shop window.

The third case is that of **Ryan (1996)**. Here the victim, an elderly householder, found the defendant stuck in a downstairs window of his house in the early hours of the morning. The defendant's head and right arm were inside the window which had fallen on his neck and trapped him. The rest of his body was outside the window. He was convicted of burglary because there was effective entry for his intention to steal, even though he could not actually reach anything. There is no requirement of a successful theft, etc. to have taken place for there to be a conviction under s9(1)(a).

One final point to note is that it is probably the case that standing with a fishing rod through a letter box or using some other remote device to steal will amount to burglary as the device is likely to be considered as an extension of the defendant's body.

The second common element – building or part thereof

There is no formal definition of a building, but it must be a fairly permanent structure. This would appear to exclude a tent, so theft from a tent at a music festival remains theft and not burglary. The Theft Act 1968, s9(3) expands a little on this:

Fig. 2 *Ryan (1996)*

3 References in subsections (1) and (2) above to a building shall apply also to an inhabited vehicle or vessel, and shall apply to any such vehicle or vessel at times when the person having a habitation in it is not there as well as times when he is.

This effectively means that burglary only applies to fixed structures or substantial portable structures that are designed for living in. It seems that a motor caravan would be capable of being burgled whilst being used to live in, but not when simply used as a vehicle or parked up over winter. It remains to be seen whether a sleeper cab of a lorry is classified as a caravan and whether theft from an attached trailer would be burglary!

For the purposes of burglary it is only necessary to enter part of a building as a trespasser. This is because a person often has permission to enter parts of a building but not others – this can be seen with signs in shops stating 'staff only'. In the case of **Walkington (1979)**, the defendant went into Debenhams department store in Oxford Street, London, during opening hours. He moved around the shop and then went into a three-sided partition that surrounded a till on the middle of the shop floor. He stood inside the partitioned area and opened the till drawer to see if it contained any money for him to steal. The defendant was convicted under s9(1)(a) of entering part of a building as a trespasser with intent to steal as he entered the sectioned-off part as a trespasser as it was impliedly a staff-only area.

The third common element – as a trespasser

As has been seen in *Walkington* (1979), entry to a part of a building that is clearly not one to which the defendant has express or implied permission to enter is trespass. Trespass can be defined as occurring when a person intentionally or recklessly enters a building in the possession of another without permission or a legal right to do so. This entry must be voluntary, not forced or purely accidental. Thus, in *Collins* (1973), he could not be guilty of burglary if he was outside the building when the offence took place, that is, before the permission to enter was given. It is a different matter whether the permission was given by mistake in that case.

Permission is given either expressly ('go into my garage and get my tools') or impliedly from the circumstances. A pupil at a school has implied permission to enter the common areas of the school, designated classrooms at designated times and other areas with permission. A sign on a staff room door 'Knock and wait' suggests no general permission to enter the staff room. A pupil who has been suspended from school has his permission to enter also suspended, so entry on the school premises would be entry as a trespasser.

A person who is given permission to enter for one purpose but in fact enters for another purpose is entering as a trespasser. A person who has a key to my house to come in and feed the cats enters as a trespasser if that person uses the key to gain entry to steal my computer. This can be seen from the case of **Jones and Smith (1976)** where the defendants took two television sets from Smith's father's house without his knowledge or consent. In the early hours of 10 May 1975, a police officer saw a car with the two appellants inside and a television set protruding from the boot of the car, and another officer saw Jones sitting on the back seat with a second television set behind him. In the front of the car was Smith. The defendants were convicted of burglary contrary to s9(1)(b) Theft Act 1968, despite evidence given by the father that his son 'would never be a trespasser in my house'.

> ### Key cases
>
> **Walkington (1979):** part of a building may include a partitioned-off part of a shop; in this case the partition sectioned off the till and that was sufficient to make it burglary.
>
> **Jones and Smith (1976):** the defendants were convicted of burglary because they had knowingly exceeded their permission to be in the house; permission was not given to enter and steal things.

The underlying principle is that if a person enters a building with intent to steal, cause grievous bodily harm or criminal damage, he does so as a trespasser except in the unlikely event of the occupier giving him permission to do so.

The fourth common element – knowledge or recklessness as to his entering as a trespasser

We have already seen that trespass is defined as occurring when a person intentionally or recklessly enters a building in the possession of another without permission or a legal right to do so. This entry must be voluntary, not forced or purely accidental. For this purpose, the recklessness is *Cunningham* (1957) – subjective recklessness that is where the defendant knows there is a risk, is willing to take it and takes it deliberately.

The different elements of s9(1)(a) and (b) of the Theft Act 1968

The first difference between the two sections is that for the offence under s9(1)(a) the defendant does not have to have committed that offence, only that he had the *mens rea* of intention to commit either theft, grievous bodily harm or damage to the building or its contents. The essential feature is that the defendant formed the intention before he entered the building as a trespasser. This intent can be a conditional intent, for example to steal jewellery if there is some jewellery inside the building.

For the offence under s9(1)(b) to be committed, the defendant must commit or attempt to commit theft or grievous bodily harm. Thus the offence requires the full *actus reus* and *mens rea* of those offences to be committed. So far as grievous bodily harm is concerned, this can be either s18 or s20 of the Offences Against the Person Act 1861, and, presumably, would by implication include murder if that were to occur. This means that the *mens rea* of s20 (maliciously) can suffice. As Lord Diplock stated in *Mowatt* (1968), it is enough that the defendant foresaw that some physical harm to some person, albeit of a minor character, might result.

Conclusion

The offence of burglary is one that requires a consideration of two possible situations where a person enters a building as a trespasser. The Theft Act 1968 s9 divides the offence into two: the first offence being committed where the defendant forms the intention to commit the ulterior crime before entry, and the second where the intention is formed after entry.

Application of the elements of burglary to problems in the examination

In the examination, there are often questions involving the elements of burglary. The time spent in the exam on identifying the issues is well spent as it avoids wasting time describing irrelevant offences. You should identify the offences that require discussion before applying pen to paper! Consider this extract from a past problem:

> Neville's daughter, Pam, learned that Martin had been given £5,000 by her elderly father. Because of his mental state, her father did not realise what he was doing. She asked Martin to return it. When he refused, she went round to his house with the aim of getting in to find it. She managed to force open a window but could not find any money. Angry and frustrated, she hid Martin's DVD player under a pile of rubbish in his wheelie bin and had just gone back inside

when Martin returned. As she tried to rush past him, he stopped her and hit her in the face. She then pushed him and he fell and badly damaged his ankle.

There are three main offences to discuss here: theft of the DVD player, burglary under s9(1)(a) and burglary under s9(1)(b). In view of the fact that analysis of the burglary offences depends, in part, on analysis of the theft offences, the most efficient strategy is to discuss the possible theft offences first, and then move on to burglary.

If Pam had found and taken any money from Martin's house, there is a question as to whether she would have been guilty of theft. She would have appropriated with intent permanently to deprive but could argue that her conduct was not dishonest within the Ghosh test. If dishonesty is present, then there is an intention to commit theft. The fact that she did not find the money is irrelevant as she only has to intend to steal to fulfil the requirements of s9(1)(a).

The theft aspects of Pam's actions with the DVD player require analysis of proving an intention permanently to deprive and the effect of it being hidden under the rubbish in the wheelie bin. There needs to be an analysis of the meaning of 'intention of permanently depriving'. This is relevant to a potential offence under s9(1)(b).

Whilst in Martin's house, Pam was confronted by Martin himself. When he hit her, she pushed him and he fell and badly damaged his ankle. This does not require a detailed discussion of personal injury offences as the question is limited to property offences. It can be queried whether the damage to Martin's ankle amounted to grievous bodily harm, particularly given the possible defence of self-defence (discussed in Chapter 13, Defences). However, if she has inflicted grievous bodily harm, Pam could be guilty of burglary. This would be under s9(1)(b) as she did not enter with any such intention.

Activity

Consider the following situation:

Chereem dismissed David from his employment without notice and without paying him for work he had done. David was very angry about this, so the day after he left work, he returned on the excuse of collecting some possessions and photocopied important information about Cherreem's business, intending to sell it to one of Chereem's rivals. As David was leaving the building, he pushed over a security guard who was trying to see what documents David had with him.

You should now be able to:

- understand the law relating to burglary under s9 of the Theft Act 1968
- apply that law to given scenarios.

4 Criminal damage

Criminal damage consists of three separate offences that cover a range of activities from minor vandalism to arson. All the offences are dealt with in the Criminal Damage Act 1971. The law has been subject to scrutiny recently as there have been a number of well publicised cases of arson where the fires have been started by a young person, and the fires rapidly spread causing damage worth millions of pounds, and more importantly death or injuries to firefighters.

The three offences are basic criminal damage, aggravated criminal damage (correctly called destroying or damaging property with intent to endanger life) and arson.

The basic offence of criminal damage

The basic offence is set out in s1(1) of the Criminal Damage Act 1971 as:

> 1 A person who without lawful excuse destroys or damages any property belonging to another intending to destroy or damage any such property or being reckless as to whether any such property would be destroyed or damaged shall be guilty of an offence.

The *actus reus* of the offence has the following elements:

■ destroy or damage

■ property

■ belonging to another

■ without lawful excuse.

The *mens rea* of the offence is either:

■ intention to destroy or damage property belonging to another

or

■ recklessness as to whether such property is destroyed.

Fig. 3 *Criminal damage*

The *actus reus* – destroy or damage

Destruction or damage is a question of fact and degree including temporary or permanent physical harm to property, reduction in value or usefulness. Damage is not defined by the Act. The courts have construed the term liberally. In one case, smearing mud on the walls of a police cell was considered to be criminal damage. What constitutes damage is a matter of fact and degree and it is for the court, using its common sense, to decide whether what occurred is damage. It is also the case that the damage need not be visible or tangible if it affects the value or performance of the property.

There are a number of aspects to this. One case is **Hardman v Chief Constable of Avon and Somerset (1986)**, which decided that there was criminal damage where a pavement had been painted with water-soluble paint and chalks, even though the natural elements would eventually remove all trace of the paint on the pavement.

In **Morphitis v Salmon (1990)**, a scaffold pole was used to block an access road. A scratch on a metal scaffolding bar could not amount to criminal damage because it did not reduce its usefulness or value. However, the removal of the scaffold bar impaired the usefulness of the roadblock, and that would amount to criminal damage.

Dumping of rubbish on land may amount to criminal damage if the owner of the land will be put to expense in removing it. However, spitting on a person's clothing is not criminal damage, however unpleasant it might be, unless the clothing is damaged by the spittle. Many of the problems associated with damage to computer data is now covered by the Computer Misuse Act 1990, and, under the Police and Justice Act 2006, criminal damage to computers is limited to physical damage to the computer.

Destruction of property includes removing parts from a car, killing an animal or killing plants or crops.

The *actus reus* – property

Section 10(1) of the Criminal Damage Act 1971 defines property as:

> … property of a tangible nature, whether real or personal, including money and –
>
> a including wild creatures which have been tamed or are ordinarily kept in captivity, and any other wild creatures or their carcasses if, but only if, they have been reduced into possession which has not been lost or abandoned or are in the course of being reduced into possession; but
>
> b not including mushrooms growing wild on any land or flowers, fruit or foliage of a plant growing wild on any land.
>
> For the purposes of this subsection 'mushroom' includes any fungus and 'plant' includes any shrub or tree.

This is therefore wider than the definition of property that we considered under the Theft Act 1968 s4 in the previous chapter as it includes land itself, but excludes wild plants.

The *actus reus* – belonging to another

This is much the same as in the Theft Act 1968 s5 and is set out in s10 of the Criminal Damage Act 1971. The main difference is that criminal damage requires custody and control of property rather than possession or control. The effect is that there can be an offence of criminal damage whenever some person has any rights over property, but it is not possible to cause criminal damage to abandoned property.

Key cases

Hardman v Chief Constable of Avon and Somerset (1986): the meaning of damage within the Criminal Damage Act 1971 includes temporary damage that will naturally disappear; in this case it involved water-soluble paint on a pavement.

Morphitis v Salmon (1990): this case decided that there must be some reduction in usefulness or value of an item to amount to criminal damage; a scratch to a scaffold pole was, therefore, insufficient.

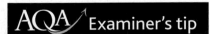

AQA Examiner's tip

Every time something gets damaged or destroyed in a scenario, consider the prosecution of criminal damages.

The *actus reus* – without lawful excuse

This is set out in s5 of the Criminal Damage Act 1971. Section 5(2) defines lawful excuse where there is belief in consent or belief in the immediate necessity to protect property. Section 5(3) makes it clear that the belief is subjective and must be honestly held. This has led to some interesting cases involving this defence to a charge of criminal damage.

In **Jaggard v Dickinson (1980)**, the defendant, having been drinking, took a taxi to 67 Carnach Green, South Ockendon, a house occupied by Mr RF Heyfron, with whom she had a relationship such that, in the words of the magistrates, she had his consent at any time to treat his property as if it was her own. She got out of the taxi, entered the garden but was asked to leave by a Mrs Raven, whom she did not know. She carried on trying to get into the house and in doing so broke the glass in the hallway of the house. She then went to the back door, where she broke another window and got into to the house, damaging a net curtain in the process. She then realised that the house was not 67 Carnach Green but 35 Carnach Green, a house which looked identical, occupied by Mrs Raven. There was lawful excuse here as she honestly believed she had consent.

In the case of **Denton (1982)**, the defence was successfully used where the defendant set fire to his employer's factory, having been asked to do so as part of an insurance fraud. The way that the employer put it was: 'There is nothing like a good fire for improving the financial circumstances of a business'! Denton was not guilty of criminal damage (arson) despite causing £40,000 of damage to the premises. He could have been found guilty of other offences relating to the fraud.

With respect to protection of property, this covers events such as emergency services damaging property to get in to fight a fire as where they push a badly parked car out of the way with a fire engine. The main problem here is not the defendant's belief in the means used were reasonable, but the immediacy of the necessity which is objective. Thus, removing a wheel clamp on a car which has been illegally parked is criminal damage as in the case of *Lloyd v DPP* (1985), where Lloyd had parked in a private car park without permission, and returned to find his car clamped. He refused to pay the £25 fee to have the clamp removed, instead returning later that night to remove it with a disc cutter. He was subsequently prosecuted, and convicted of criminal damage.

In *Hill and Hall* (1989), the judge had to determine whether, on the facts as stated, there was any evidence on which it could be said that the defendant believed there was a need of protection from immediate danger. This means evidence that immediate action had to be taken to do something which would otherwise be a crime in order to prevent the immediate risk of something worse happening. In this case the something worse was nuclear war, as the defendants were protesting at a naval base for nuclear submarines.

The *mens rea*

This is straightforward – either intention to destroy or damage property belonging to another or recklessness as to whether such property is destroyed. In both cases, the recklessness is *Cunningham* (1957) subjective recklessness.

Key cases

Jaggard v Dickinson (1980): the defence to a charge of criminal damage of lawful excuse is effective if the defendant honestly believes that he has consent of the owner to carry out the damage; in this case, it was damaging property to get into a house.

Denton (1982): here the defendant's employer asked him to set fire to his business premises as part of an insurance fraud; this raised the defence of lawful excuse because he was asked to do it and the fact that the outcome was intended by the person making the request to be unlawful is irrelevant.

The aggravated offence of criminal damage

This offence is set out in s1(2) of the Criminal Damage Act 1971 as:

> 2 A person who without lawful excuse destroys or damages any property, whether belonging to himself or another –
>
>   a intending to destroy or damage any property or being reckless as to whether any property would be destroyed or damaged; and
>
>   b intending by the destruction or damage to endanger the life of another or being reckless as to whether the life of another would be thereby endangered;
>
> shall be guilty of an offence.

The key aspects of this more serious offence are the intention or recklessness as to endanger life. It should also be noted that a person can be guilty if he destroys or damages his own property with intent to endanger life, for example, cutting the brake lines of your car before someone else borrows it. There is no need to prove that a life was in fact endangered.

The *mens rea* is not just the intention to damage or destroy property or be reckless thereto, the defendant must also be shown to have intended or been reckless thereto by that damage. This can be seen in the case of **Steer (1987)** where, in the early hours of the morning, the defendant went to the bungalow of his former business partner, David Gregory, against whom he bore some grudge. He was armed with an automatic .22 rifle. He rang the bell and woke Mr and Mrs Gregory, who looked out of their bedroom window. The defendant fired a shot aimed at the bedroom window. He then fired two further shots, one at another window and one at the front door. Fortunately no one was hurt. It was never suggested that the first shot had been aimed at Mr or Mrs Gregory.

The prosecution had to prove that the danger to life resulted from the actual destruction of, or damage to, property. In this case, the shooting, not the broken window, endangered life, so the defendant was not guilty of the aggravated offence.

However, the defendant may be guilty, either if he intended to endanger life by the damage, which was intended to be done, or was reckless that life would be endangered by the damage. This can be seen from the case of **Warwick (1995)**, where the defendant was a passenger in a stolen car. He threw bricks at a pursuing police car, smashing a window and showering a policeman with glass. As this could cause the driver to lose control it would endanger the life of the driver and any passengers. Therefore, there was a conviction under s1(2) of the Criminal Damage Act 1971.

Thus, if a person drops something from a bridge onto cars passing below, or throws missiles at, or rams, police cars there can be a conviction for the aggravated offence. If the intent is to break the windscreen or window, a jury is entitled to infer that there was an intention to shower the driver or passengers with glass and that as a result control could be lost, thereby endangering life. The danger would be caused, and intended to be caused, by the broken glass.

Finally, it should be noted that the defence of lawful excuse does not apply to the aggravated offence.

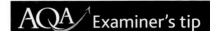
Examiner's tip

When any criminal damage sets up a potentially dangerous situation, consider the aggravated offence.

Key cases

Steer (1987): the aggravated criminal damage offence must arise from the damage caused rather than the cause of the damage.

Warwick (1995): the aggravated criminal damage offence requires that the defendant's act was done with the intention or recklessness as to endanger life by the damage done.

Arson

This offence is set out in s1(2) of the Criminal Damage Act 1971 as:

> **3** An offence committed under this section by destroying or damaging property by fire shall be charged as arson.

This offence is the same as the basic offence but requires that the damage is caused by fire. As this offence is related to the basic offence, the lawful excuse defence is available as was seen in the case of Denton (1982).

Conclusion

The offences of criminal damage are all related, one that requires a consideration of the intention or recklessness as to endanger life, the others being the basic offence and arson. The main reason for the separate offence of arson is the potential seriousness of the consequences.

Application of the elements of criminal damage to problems in the examination

In the examination, there are sometimes questions involving the elements of criminal damage, but these questions are usually a relatively minor part of the whole question. Even so, these questions should be looked for and dealt with appropriately. A typical part of a scenario is:

Dave got into a race with another car and threw a bottle at it as it passed. The bottle broke the car's windscreen, causing the driver to swerve across the road and into the grass verge on the opposite side.

Here, you need to be able to differentiate between basic and aggravated criminal damage and explain precisely how damaging a car windscreen might endanger life, so that a charge of aggravated criminal damage might be made against Dave. This would require proof that he foresaw the risk of endangering life by the damage.

Activity

Consider the following situation:

Gary had a grudge against Henry. Whilst Henry was busy, Gary loosened the wheel nuts on a bicycle that Henry frequently used. When Henry next rode the bicycle, the wheel worked loose and Henry fell off the bicycle, narrowly avoiding a serious accident.

You should now be able to:

■ understand the law relating to criminal damage

■ apply that law to given scenarios.

12 Fraud and making off without payment

In this topic you will learn how to:

- outline the law relating to fraud

- distinguish between fraud by false representation and obtaining services dishonestly.

Key terms

False representation: a false or misleading statement of fact or law which may also be done by conduct.

1 Distinguishing the areas of fraud in the specification

The Fraud Act 2006 came into being as a direct result of the need to overcome problems with the old law and to simplify the law. In February 1998, the Institute of Chartered Accountants suggested that business fraud was a growing problem that affected everyone both as individuals and corporately in the country. The cost was huge, and the damage to the country's business reputation was increasing. Individual fraud was (and is) on an alarming scale, with billions of pounds being defrauded from credit companies, insurance companies and the state benefits system. Fraud trials tended to be long and complex, with some suggesting that jurors could not understand the evidence. There were few successful major fraud trials.

This background is surprising as everyone can recognise dishonest behaviour that is not theft, burglary or robbery. It is dishonest to claim an item of property has been lost or damaged to an insurance company when it has not. It is dishonest to claim the cost of goods supplied as part of building work is more than the real cost. It is dishonest for your solicitor to bill you for more hours worked than was in fact the case. It is dishonest for a garage to claim to have fitted new parts to a car when that is not the case. It is dishonest to walk out of a restaurant without paying for a meal.

The Fraud Act 2006 creates a general offence of fraud with different ways of committing it. The AQA Law specification includes fraud by **false representation** and obtaining services dishonestly only. Making off without payment continues under the Theft Act 1978 and is retained from the previous AQA specification. There are, therefore, three statutory offences to understand:

- Fraud by false representation (s2 Fraud Act 2006).
- Obtaining services dishonestly (s11 Fraud Act 2006).
- Making off without payment (s3 Theft Act 1978).

The offences can be outlined as follows:

The elements of the offence under the Fraud Act 2006 s2 are that the defendant:

- makes a false representation
- dishonestly
- knowing that the representation was or might be untrue or misleading
- with intent to make a gain for himself or another, to cause loss to another or to expose another to risk of loss.

The elements of the offence under the Fraud Act 2006 s11 are that the defendant:

- obtains for himself or another
- services
- dishonestly
- knowing the services are made available on the basis that payment has been, is being or will be made for, or in respect of, them or that they might be and
- avoids or intends to avoid payment in full or in part.

This offence replaces obtaining services by deception in s1 of the Theft Act 1978.

The elements of the offence of making off without payment under s3 of the Theft Act 1978 are:

■ makes off
■ without having paid as required or expected
■ knowing payment on the spot is required
■ dishonesty
■ intent to avoid payment.

Each of these will be considered in separate topics.

Where statutory interpretation is needed, as much of the law is new, the courts will use cases decided under the previous law to help interpret the Fraud Act 2006. This is reflected here.

Conclusion

These three offences have some overlapping concepts, the most obvious of which is dishonesty. There are circumstances where the offences will overlap. In such cases, the Crown Prosecution Service will choose the most appropriate offence. In the exam, you should discuss all offences that might be relevant and decide whether or not the elements of each relevant offence are fulfilled.

You should now be able to:

■ understand the scope of the specification

■ understand the basic differences between the areas of the specification.

In this topic you will learn how to:

■ state the definition of fraud by false representation

■ explain the *actus reus* and *mens rea* of fraud by false representation

■ explain cases that illustrate the law on fraud by false representation

■ apply the rules to a given situation.

2 Fraud by false representation: Fraud Act 2006, s2

This offence is part of a suite of three offences that come under the general offence of fraud found in s1 of the Fraud Act 2006; the others are failure to disclose information when there is a legal duty to do so (s3) and abuse of position (s4). We only need to consider s2, fraud by false representation.

Trading standards officers have now got more ammunition for their work.

Kent County Council made this statement in reaction to the Fraud Act 2006:

> Traders who prey on the elderly and vulnerable, claiming that building work is necessary when it isn't, claiming to have carried out work that wasn't done and charging huge sums of money, inferring a certain price and then charging much more, could be dealt with using the Fraud Act. It would not be necessary to prove that a victim had been deceived or that a gain or loss had been made. It could be an equally effective way of dealing with other scams such as bogus charity collections and may even extend to some of the more traditional trading standards offences such as car clocking and counterfeiting.

A typical charge of fraud by false representation can be seen from the following news item from Merseyside police:

MERSEYSIDE Police in St Helens arrested an 18-year-old man on 16 January 2008, following reports of a man in the Parr and Newton area claiming to be a local window cleaner and taking payment, without returning to carrying out the window cleaning service.

Lee Stuart, from Moss Lane, Derbyshire Hill, has subsequently been charged with 4 counts of Fraud by false representation.

He is due to appear at St Helens Magistrates' Court on 4 February 2008.

The Act itself helps clarify the definition:

2 Fraud by false representation

1 A person is in breach of this section if he –

   a dishonestly makes a false representation, and

   b intends, by making the representation –

      i to make a gain for himself or another, or

      ii to cause loss to another or to expose another to a risk of loss.

2 A representation is false if –

   a it is untrue or misleading, and

   b the person making it knows that it is, or might be, untrue or misleading.

3 'Representation' means any representation as to fact or law, including a representation as to the state of mind of –

   a the person making the representation, or

   b any other person.

4 A representation may be express or implied.

5 For the purposes of this section a representation may be regarded as made if it (or anything implying it) is submitted in any form to any system or device designed to receive, convey or respond to communications (with or without human intervention).

Fig. 1 *Benefit fraud is a very common form of fraud by misrepresentation*

There are four elements to consider:

1 makes a false representation

2 dishonestly

3 knowing that the representation was or might be untrue or misleading

4 with intent to make a gain for himself or another, to cause loss to another or to expose another to risk of loss.

Let us look at each element of the offence in turn.

1 Makes a false representation (the *actus reus*).

This is explained in subsections (2)–(5) of s2 of the Act, set out earlier. A number of aspects of this definition need to be considered. The first point is that fraud is a conduct crime. This means that no particular end result has to be proved. Therefore, no one has to believe the false representation that has been made. Just making the false representation is enough. It is complete as soon as the defendant makes the false representation provided that it is made with the necessary dishonest intent (the *mens rea*). It differs from the old deception offences in that it does not matter whether or not any one knows of the representation, is deceived, or any property is actually gained or lost.

The Act, in s2(2) makes it clear that false means untrue or misleading, but the word 'representation' is not defined. The Act does, however, explain what the representation must be about and how it may arise. In the law of contract the word 'misrepresentation' is defined; the 'mis-' merely means it is false. We may therefore explain the word 'representation' as a factual statement made by one party in order to induce another party to do something.

Section 2(3) helps by stating that a 'representation' means any representation as to fact or law. This means that the argument as to whether something is a statement of fact or law is irrelevant; both suffice for fraud. A statement of fact is straightforward. It could be something such as the statement that a piece of jewellery is silver when it is in fact silver plated only. A statement of law may be a statement about the effect of a legal document such as a loan agreement that is in fact a mortgage and not an unsecured loan.

A difficulty arises where the representation is a statement of opinion. If the statement is not the genuine opinion of the person making it, it can amount to fraud, but often the victim will prefer to take civil action to recover his money, only resorting to criminal law when there is little prospect of succeeding. Thus, a statement that a car is in good condition is often made by car sales persons. This will only give rise to legal rights when the seller knows that is not the case or could not possibly have held that view. In such cases, the victim will have rights under the law of contract, but there may also be the offence of fraud by false representation.

However, it should be noted that where the representation was true when made, but later becomes false, the offence can be committed by not telling of the change. Thus, in the example of selling the car which is stated to be in good condition, the potential purchaser who returns later must be told of any change that would make the car no longer in 'good condition'. This can be seen in the cases of **DPP v Ray (1974)** and **Rai (2000)**.

In *DPP v Ray* (1974), 30 September 1971, the defendant was a student. He and his friends went to the Wing Wah Restaurant in Gainsborough, Lincolnshire, and ordered a meal. At the time he entered the restaurant the defendant had only 10p on him but one of his friends had agreed to lend him some money to pay. He ate the meal and they then decided not

Key cases

DPP v Ray (1974): a representation can be a continuing representation and therefore any change of the situation must be notified if the previously true representation is not to become false and the offence committed; in this case the representation was the intention to pay for meals ordered at a restaurant.

Rai (2000): a material part of an application that becomes false can be a representation and form the basis of the offence of fraud by false representation; in this case the representation was as to the continuing existence of the defendant's mother, for whom a grant was being obtained to modify a house to cope with her infirmities.

to pay and to run out of the restaurant. They did so some 10 minutes later. No payment was offered or made, and no money was left, for the meals served. The court decided that there was an implied representation that payment would be made when the meal was ordered and that, so far as the waiter was concerned, the original implied representation made to him must have been a continuing representation so long as the defendant remained in the restaurant. (Note this case is also one of making off without payment).

In the case of *Rai* (2000), the defendant was the owner of a property, 20 Sandwell Road, Handsworth, Birmingham. On about 7 June 1996, he applied to Birmingham City Council for a grant towards providing a downstairs bathroom at his room for the use of his elderly and infirm mother. The council approved a grant and on 29 July 1997, the defendant was told of this. Two days later, on 31 July, his mother died. He did not tell the council of the changed circumstances, and used the grant of £9,500 for the agreed modifications to his house. Here the representation that was true when made, became false and was a continuing representation, so could be the basis of an offence which, today, would be fraud by false representation.

The representation as to the state of mind of a person can also be sufficient for criminal liability. Section 2(3) states '…including a representation as to the state of mind of the person making the representation or any other person.' If you were to go to your father to ask for £10 to help buy this textbook, but you really want the £10 to go the pub, you would be falsely representing your state of mind. If you were to go to your father to ask for £10 to help your brother buy this textbook, but you really want the £10 to go the pub, you would be falsely representing the state of mind of 'any other person'.

Under s2(4), a representation may be express or implied. It can be expressly made in many ways; the Act puts no limit on this. It could, for example, be written or texted, spoken directly or by phone or radio, posted on a website, put on a podcast or sent by e-mail. A representation can be implied by conduct. This could occur when a person uses a credit card or purports to make a payment from his bank account, for example, by cheque or debit card. By using the card, a person represents that he has the authority to use it for that transaction. He would not do so if it was stolen or over its credit limit. This can be seen from the cases of **MPC v Charles (1976)** and **Lambie (1982)**.

In *MPC v Charles*, on 2 January 1973, the defendant went to the Golden Nugget club, a gaming club, and in the course of the night he used all the cheques in his new cheque book for the purchase of chips for gaming. He used his cheque card in relation to each cheque. The bank had consequently to honour all the cheques with the result that he went hugely over his overdraft limit. This was sufficient for him to be convicted under an offence equivalent to fraud by false representation. In the House of Lords, Viscount Dilhorne said:

> The reality is in my view that a man who gives a cheque represents that it will be met on presentment, and if a cheque is accepted by the payee, it is in the belief that it will be met … His use of a cheque card to secure acceptance of his cheque can in my opinion amount to a representation that he has the authority of the bank to use it in relation to that cheque for that purpose, and as a matter of fact will ordinarily do so. He is authorised by the bank to give its undertaking to pay … a cheque if the stipulated conditions are fulfilled. But the authority given to him is not unlimited. … He is not authorised to use it to secure the acceptance of a cheque which he knows would not be met by the bank if the cheque card had not been used.

Key cases

MPC v Charles (1976): giving a cheque makes the implied representation that he has the authority to use the cheque; in this case the cheque was to a casino and backed by a cheque guarantee card; as the account was overdrawn beyond its agreed limit, this could be fraud.

Lambie (1982): the use of a credit card is an implied representation that the user has authority from the credit company to use the card; in this case, the fact that the transaction would take the card over its limit meant there was no such authority from the credit card company, so an offence of fraud could be committed.

This principle was extended to cover credit cards in *Lambie* (1982). In that case, the defendant had a Barclaycard (a credit card) which was issued subject to the Barclaycard current conditions of use. It was an express condition of its issue that it should be used only within the given credit limit. She knew her credit limit was £200. As it had been notified to her in writing when the card was issued and appears on each statement. Between 18 November 1977 and 5 December 1977 she used the card for at least 24 separate transactions amounting to £533. The bank became aware of this debt and requested the card be returned. On 6 December 1977 she agreed to return the card on 7 December 1977, but she did not do so. By 15 December 1977 she had used the card for at least 43 further transactions, incurring a total debt to the bank of over £1,000. The House of Lords decided that the representation arising from the presentation of a credit card is a representation of actual authority to make the contract with the shop or to whom the payment is to be made.

A representation can be made through a gesture such as a nod of the head or by presence in a restricted area which implies the right to be there. This would include presence within a secure computer system or being dressed or wearing an identification badge that implies a certain status or right to be present. A representation can also be about a person's identity and will be relevant for identity fraud. All these become possible because of the meaning of false being untrue or misleading.

This is all confirmed in the explanatory notes to the Act, which state:

> 15. A representation may also be implied by conduct. An example of a representation by conduct is where a person dishonestly misuses a credit card to pay for items. By tendering the card, he is falsely representing that he has the authority to use it for that transaction. It is immaterial whether the merchant accepting the card for payment is deceived by the representation.
>
> 16. This offence would also be committed by someone who engages in 'phishing': i.e. where a person disseminates an e-mail to large groups of people falsely representing that the e-mail has been sent by a legitimate financial institution. The e-mail prompts the reader to provide information such as credit card and bank account numbers so that the 'phisher' can gain access to others' assets.

Finally, s2(5) makes it clear that the offence can be committed by making a representation to a machine such as an ATM (automated ticket machine).

2 Dishonestly (first part of the *mens rea*)

This is the crucial element of the offence. Throughout the passage of the Fraud Act 2006, it has been considered that the Ghosh test applies. This has been studied in Chapter 10, Theft, Topic 2 and you should review the details now.

This test came from the case of **Ghosh (1982)** and is a two-part test, known as the Ghosh test, and can be stated as follows:

1 Would the defendant's behaviour be regarded as dishonest by the standards of reasonable and honest people?

(If the answer is 'no', the defendant is not guilty of theft as he has not been dishonest.)

If the answer is 'yes' the second question is:

2 Was the defendant aware that his conduct would be regarded as dishonest by reasonable and honest people?

Key cases

Ghosh (1982): this case set out the definitive test for what amounts to be dishonesty; the two-part test is: (1) Would the defendant's behaviour be regarded as dishonest by the standards of reasonable and honest people? (If the answer is 'no', the defendant is not guilty of theft as he has not been dishonest). If the answer is 'yes' the second question is: (2) Was the defendant aware that his conduct would be regarded as dishonest by reasonable and honest people?

It can be seen that the first part of the test is objective and the second part of the test is subjective. If both parts of the test are satisfied, the defendant fulfils the criteria for being dishonest.

It should be noted that the examples of things that are not dishonest in s2 of the Theft Act 1968 do *not* apply to fraud offences.

3 Knowing that the representation was or might be untrue or misleading (second part of the *mens rea*)

As we have seen, a representation is defined as 'false' if it is untrue or misleading. The person making the false representation must know that it is, or might be, untrue or misleading, but makes a decision to make it anyway. The words 'might be' do not mean recklessness. Actual knowledge that the representation might be untrue is required rather than an awareness of a risk that it might be untrue. The first point is that the statement must, in fact, be untrue or misleading. The defendant cannot be convicted if the statement is, in fact, true. If it is the case that the statement is untrue or misleading, then the defendant must know that is the case.

The Crown Prosecution Service make the point in their commentary on the Fraud Act 2006 that the same type of evidence as was used to prove the nature of the deception in cases of obtaining by deception will be sufficient for fraud by false representation. They then give the example of the situation where, for example, a debit or credit card has been used fraudulently, evidence of the rightful owner and that he or she did not carry out the transaction in question will suffice as the illicit user must know that any statement he makes about his authority to use the card is (or might be) untrue. You can consider this in the light of exceeding authority in use of a company credit card or authority to place an order on behalf of a business.

4 With intent to make a gain for himself or another, to cause loss to another or to expose another to risk of loss (third part of the *mens rea*)

This part of the *mens rea* has the key words 'with intent to'. This means that there is no need for anyone to have suffered any actual loss or be exposed to any loss or even that the defendant makes a gain. This is all about what the defendant intends by carrying out his act. It is very similar to the definition of 'blackmail', as discussed in Chapter 11, Topic 2, Blackmail. In the case of *Parkes* (1973), a blackmail case, the defendant was using the threats to get money that was lawfully owing to him. The court decided he was making a gain because he was getting the money owed now rather than merely having the legal right to claim for money owed through the courts.

Conclusion

In many cases fraud will also be theft. However, the *actus reus* requirement for fraud is not as difficult to prove. It is also not necessary to prove or demonstrate any consequences of fraud and fraud does not require any intent permanently to deprive. In some cases there will also be making off without payment. The offence is, therefore, fairly straightforward and much simpler than the previous offences of deception.

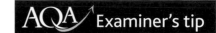

AQA Examiner's tip

Make sure you apply the meaning of the word 'dishonestly' in the different manner for Theft Act 1968 offences and Fraud Act 2006 offences.

Application of the elements of s2 Fraud Act 2006 to problems in the examination

In the examination, there are often questions involving the different offences of fraud and making off without payment. Given the overlap between some offences and the need to apply defences, past examination questions often have several interlinked themes. As with all problem questions, the key is to focus on the issues that require discussion and analysis and minimise the time spent on descriptions that do little to advance the issues. Consider this problem:

> Carlos was in a hotel where a conference was being held, but he was not part of that conference. He helped himself to some coffee and biscuits. Later, when the delegates at the conference went to the restaurant to get some lunch, he went into the restaurant as the delegates went in and said to the food server – 'I am with them' and was given a plate of food, which he ate.

Here we find Carlos has committed two offences: theft and fraud by false representation. The theft relates to the coffee; note also that if the coffee was in a room reserved for delegates at the conference only, there could be an offence of burglary too. When he goes into the restaurant he fulfils the elements of fraud by false representation:

- makes a false representation – that he is a delegate at the conference
- dishonestly – he fulfils the Ghosh test
- knowing that the representation was or might be untrue or misleading – he knows it is untrue to imply that he is a part of the conference
- with intent to make a gain for himself or another, to cause loss to another or to expose another to risk of loss – the intention is to get free food.

You should now be able to:

- understand the law relating to fraud by false representation
- apply that law to given scenarios.

Activity

Consider the following situation and consider the offences that have been committed:

Daffyd knows that there is a large party taking place at a large country house near where he lives. He has not been invited and decides to gatecrash the party. When he gets to the door he tells the security person 'I am with Ellie' (one of the hosts). He is let into the party and, whilst there, consumes a large quantity of drinks that are provided for the guests.

In this topic you will learn how to:

- state the definition of obtaining services dishonestly
- explain the *actus reus* and *mens rea* of obtaining services dishonestly
- explain cases that illustrate the law on obtaining services dishonestly
- apply the rules to a given situation.

3 Obtaining services dishonestly: Fraud Act 2006, s11

The offence of obtaining services dishonestly is a direct replacement for the offence under the Theft Act 1978, s1 of obtaining services by deception. Examples include: someone who climbs over the wall of a football ground to watch the match without paying, or someone who seeks free NHS treatment to which they are not entitled. Elements of the offence under the Fraud Act 2006, s2 are that the defendant: obtains for himself or another services dishonestly knowing the services are made available on the basis that payment has been, is being or will be made for or in respect of them or that they might be and avoids or intends to avoid payment in full or in part.

Section 11 of the Act itself helps clarify the definition:

1 A person is guilty of an offence under this section if he obtains services for himself or another –
   a by a dishonest act, and
   b in breach of subsection (2).

2 A person obtains services in breach of this subsection if –
   a they are made available on the basis that payment has been, is being or will be made for or in respect of them,
   b he obtains them without any payment having been made for or in respect of them or without payment having been made in full, and
   c when he obtains them, he knows –
      i that they arc bcing made available on the basis described in paragraph (a), or
      ii that they might be,
   but intends that payment will not be made, or will not be made in full.

It should be noted that, in many cases, the defendant will also have committed an offence under s2 of fraud by making a false representation, the false representation being that payment will be made or, where only part payment has been made, will be made in full.

Let us look at each element of the offence in turn.

1 Obtains for himself or another

Unlikc thc offcncc under s2, this offence is a result crime, as there must be proof that the services have actually been obtained. No act of deception is needed, and there is no need to prove that the service provider has been deceived. This is why climbing the wall to see the football match can form the offence. He is accessing a service (the football match, entertainment) that is normally provided only on payment of a fee (the ticket price).

It should also be noted that the offence can be committed where the person performing the act does not do so for his own benefit. This could, therefore, possibly include lifting someone over a fence to get into a music festival.

2 Services

The offence applies to services that are 'made available on the basis that payment has been, is being or will be made for or in respect of them'. This means that where a service is being provided without charge, there cannot be an offence under this section. The word 'services' is not defined within the Act, but the Crown Prosecution Service give a number of examples of services that would fall within this section:

- Obtains chargeable data or software over the internet without paying.
- Orders a meal in a restaurant knowing he has no means to pay.
- Attaches a decoder to his TV to enable him to access chargeable satellite services without paying.
- Uses the services of a members' club without paying and without being a member.

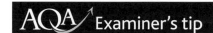

AQA Examiner's tip

Note that ss2 and 11 of the Act sometimes overlap. It would be better to discuss both where that is the case.

These examples raise some interesting points. Chargeable data would include music or video downloads; ordering the meal without the means to pay would also suggest an offence under s2; accessing the chargeable satellite services would presumably mean there was a separate offence each time a service was accessed; if a person got access to the club, but did not use the services (for example a gym), would there still be an offence if the sole purpose of access was to get warm on a cold day?

There is one case that helps with respect to banking services – **Sofroniou (2004)**. This is a case of identity theft. The defendant falsely pretended to be Andrew Cole, John Groves or Andrew Narramore to deceive or attempt to deceive banks into providing him with banking services, credit card companies into providing him with credit cards, and retailers into providing him with goods. The Court of Appeal decided that for there to be a service within the meaning there had to be 'an agreement or sufficient understanding that an identifiable payment or payments have been or will be made by or on behalf of the person receiving the services to the person providing them'. This understanding would not automatically exist between a bank and its account holders. It would not apply to free banking. On the actual facts the court found that there was a sufficient understanding as to payment, as interest would be payable on the loans and credit card balances that went beyond any interest free period. This seems a rather artificial distinction in terms of the reality of what has gone on. In any event, since the whole purpose of identity fraud is to leave interest accruing on loans and credit cards, etc, it seems likely that identity fraudsters could be prosecuted under s11.

It should, therefore, be noted that if the banking services obtained are free, s11 cannot be the appropriate offence. However, the same restriction does not apply to s2.

3 Dishonestly

This is exactly the same use of the *Ghosh* test as there was for s2. It is worth repeating that the examples of things that are not dishonest in s2 of the Theft Act 1968 do *not* apply here.

4 Knowing the services are made available on the basis that payment ...

In most cases, this will not be a problem as it is self-evident that the service is one for which payment is normally made either in advance of the service, at the time of the service or afterwards. The defendant must get the service either by not paying for it or not paying in full if there is to be a conviction under s11.

5 Avoids or intends to avoid payment in full or in part

The key aspect here is that whilst avoiding payment is the gist of the offence, it is sufficient that the defendant intends to avoid payment. This means that the defendant must intend to avoid payment for the service provided in full or in part and have that intention at the time that the service is obtained. Presumably, with banking services, this is a continuing act and so a later intention, whilst the service continues, will be sufficient.

It would appear that the intent must be never to pay the sum involved. This means that an honest belief that credit is being given will mean the offence is not being committed. This would be consistent with the existing law with respect to making off without payment and the case of **Allen (1985)** (for definition, see Chapter 4, Defences). In that case, Allen booked a room at a hotel and finally left on 11 February 1983 without

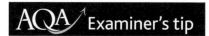

paying his bill of over £1,200. He telephoned two days later to explain that he was in financial difficulties because of some business transactions and arranged to return to the hotel on 18 February 1983 to remove his belongings and leave his Australian passport as security for the debt. He was arrested on his return and said that he genuinely hoped to be able to pay the bill and denied he was acting dishonestly. On 3 March 1983, he was still unable to pay the bill. He said he had acted honestly and had genuinely expected to pay the bill from the proceeds of various business ventures. The House of Lords agreed, and stated:

> Anyone who knows that payment on the spot is expected or required of him and who then dishonestly makes off without paying as required or expected must have at least the intention to delay or defer payment. It follows, therefore, that the conjoined phrase 'and with intent to avoid payment of the amount due' adds a further ingredient – an intention to do more than delay or defer – an intention to evade payment altogether.

Conclusion

This offence is quite straightforward but has some subtle distinctions between it and s2.

Application of the elements of s11 Fraud Act 2006 to problems in the examination

Consider this problem:

> Janet and John decided to go an art gallery in the city where they were having a break. When they got there, they discovered that this was a private art gallery, and, unlike public art galleries, there was an entry fee. As they were short of money, Janet claimed to be a student and showed an old, out-of-date student card whilst holding her fingers over the date and said that John was unemployed although, in reality, he was in full-time employment. On the basis of this, the art gallery gave them concessionary tickets which were half the normal price.

Fig. 2

Look at the elements of the offence:

- obtains for himself or another – Janet for herself and for another (John)

In this topic you will learn how to:

■ state the definition of making off without payment

■ explain the *actus reus* and *mens rea* of making off without payment

■ explain cases that illustrate the law on making off without payment

■ apply the rules to a given situation.

■ services – entry to the art gallery

■ dishonestly – this is self-evident

■ knowing the services are made available on the basis that payment has been, is being or will be made for or in respect of them or that they might be – whilst there might often be no payment required at art galleries, Janet knows that payment is required and still decides to go in

■ avoids or intends to avoid payment in full or in part – the lies about their status are designed to avoid full payment

Note also that there is the offence of fraud by false representation.

You should now be able to:

■ understand the law relating to obtaining services dishonestly

■ apply that law to given scenarios.

4 Making off without payment

This offence occurs in situations such as where the defendant fills up his car with petrol and drives off without paying or has a meal in a restaurant and walks out without paying. It is a crime that commonly takes place at petrol stations and has been the focus of police targets. Despite this, offences still take place such as the one reported below.

Banned customer drove off without paying

ANNOYED staff had switched off the fuel supply to a diesel pump he was using, Oliver Pidgley drove off without paying for £3.11 worth of fuel, magistrates heard.

Pidgley, 25, of Krattigen, Eastville Road, Toynton St Peter, admitted making off from Partney Filling Station without making payment. He also admitted using his mother's vehicle without insurance.

Skegness magistrates fined him £50 for making off and ordered him to pay £3.11 compensation.

He was fined £200 for the no insurance offence and ordered to pay £60 costs and a £15 surcharge. Six penalty points were endorsed on his licence.

Prosecutor Jim Clare told the court Pidgley had previously been barred from using the filling station because of a previous incident and so the fuel supply was switched off.

Later, in a police interview he said he had planned to put £10 worth of fuel in his mother's car but when the pump was switched off he was annoyed and drove off without attempting to pay.

Liz Warwick, representing Pidgley, said her client had been on his way to football training. He was low on fuel and did not believe he had enough diesel to get to another garage.

Pidgley had an insurance policy for his own vehicle and had believed he was covered to drive his mother's car, said Miss Warwick. It had been a genuine mistake, she said.

The offence is defined in the Theft Act 1978, s3 as:

1 Subject to subsection (3) below, a person who, knowing that payment on the spot for any goods supplied or service done is required or expected from him, dishonestly makes off without having paid as required or expected and with intent to avoid payment of the amount due shall be guilty of an offence.

2 For purposes of this section 'payment on the spot' includes payment at the time of collecting goods on which work has been done or in respect of which service has been provided.

3 Subsection (1) above shall not apply where the supply of the goods or the doing of the service is contrary to law, or where the service done is such that payment is not legally enforceable.

This has the following elements:

- Goods supplied or services done.
- Makes off from the spot.
- Fails to pay on the spot as required or expected.
- Dishonesty.
- Knows that payment on the spot is required or expected.
- Intention to avoid payment permanently.

The first three of these are the *actus reus* and the last three form the *mens rea* of the offence.

Let us look at each element of the offence in turn:

1 Goods supplied or services done

The key point here is that the goods must be supplied. This requires the goods to be delivered to the defendant or the defendant being allowed to take the goods – as at a petrol filling station or from a self-service shop. If that is not the case, the offence is theft. Where the goods are taken from the self-service shop both theft and making off without payment are committed.

Where services are involved, the services must be done. This includes examples such as repairing a bicycle, supplying a meal or renting a car. In the case of *Allen* (1985), considered in the previous topic, it was the provision of a hotel room. This, therefore, includes the use of a facility such as a car park. The offence is not, however, committed where 'the supply of the goods or the doing of the service is contrary to law, or where the service done is such that payment is not legally enforceable'. This is s3(3) of the Act. This refers to illegal transactions such a supplying alcohol to the under-18s and also to transactions that are not legally enforceable. This refers to contract law where contracts with minors (under 18) for goods that are not 'necessaries' are unenforceable. If that was the case, there would be no offence of making off without payment, but there would be an offence of theft.

2 Makes off from the spot

The idea of making off is just one of departing. There is no need to be seen to be running away or surreptitiously leaving when no one is looking, even though that behaviour often occurs. The important thing is that the departure is dishonest. This can be seen from the case of **Brooks and Brooks (1983)**, where it was said the words 'dishonestly makes off' are words easily understandable by any jury. In that case, the defendants had a meal in the upstairs room of a restaurant. The first defendant left the restaurant in a hurry. The second defendant also tried to leave but was caught by the manager. There was clearly making off in that case.

> **Key cases**
>
> **Brooks and Brooks (1983):** the expression 'making off' is an expression that should be treated as departing; the manner of the departure is what is important.

In **McDavitt (1981)**, the defendant and three friends had a meal at a restaurant. The friends left, but the defendant stayed at the table. The bill was presented by a waiter and an argument started and the defendant refused to pay. He went to the door, to try and leave, but the exit was blocked and he was kept in the restaurant until the police arrived. It was decided that 'making off' refers to 'a departure from the spot where payment is required or expected'. Where that spot is, is a matter for the jury to decide, depending on the circumstances. Here the defendant did not actually leave the spot, but merely attempted to do so. This is why shoplifters are usually arrested outside the shop as the offence of making off without payment (and theft) will definitely be complete then, rather than being an attempt to commit the crime.

It is therefore clear that 'the spot' covers a wide range of places, but usually means the area controlled by the person to whom payment should be made.

3 Fails to pay on the spot as required or expected

Normally this is at the end of a meal in a restaurant or before leaving a shop with goods. The key point is that the departure is made without paying as required or expected. This, therefore, depends on the normal relationship between the defendant and the victim.

However, if the defendant makes a false representation to get the victim to agree to payment later, this is no longer making off without payment but fraud by false representation under s2 of the Fraud Act 2006. This can be seen from the case of **Vincent (2001)**, where the defendant, in the autumn of 1998, stayed for a week at the Langton House Guest House in Windsor and shortly afterwards for a month at the Bricklayers' Arms, Windsor. He left both hotels without paying his bill in full, the bill being almost £300 at Langton House and almost £1,000 at the Bricklayers' Arms. In the course of his stay he had made a part-payment at the Bricklayers' Arms. The expectation normally is that hotels will be paid before the customer leaves the premises. In this case, there were discussions between the defendant and the hotels as to when payment would be made. In circumstances where an agreement is made a considerable time before payment would normally be expected, that agreement is capable of defeating the expectation of payment on the spot and so no offence of making off without payment is committed.

4 Dishonesty

This is the first part of the *mens rea* and relates to the making off. The test is the *Ghosh* test, as previously discussed. Thus, a defendant who honestly believed he had been given credit for the goods supplied or service done would not be guilty.

5 Knows that payment on the spot is required or expected

We have seen in the previous element that dishonesty relates to the making off. The idea that credit is not available is merely something that the defendant must know and, as in s2 of the Fraud Act 2006, is usually self-evident. Dishonesty is not part of the method of payment element. If payment is no longer expected (however that may have been achieved) the suspect is not dishonestly making off when he leaves as we have seen in the case of *Vincent* (2001).

It should be noted that in *Vincent* (2001), the bill was a reasonably substantial bill for hotels. It would be much more difficult to show an agreement had been reached to defer payment of a taxi fare, petrol at a filling station or for a meal in a restaurant. It could happen as, perfectly innocently, people get caught out by not having enough money with them, or realising they have lost their wallet. They then have to make an agreement to pay the next day. Indeed it happened to the author who filled up his car with petrol, only to discover that his credit and debit cards had been removed from his wallet by a thief at the hotel at which he had been staying!

6 Intention to avoid payment permanently

Here the intent must be never to pay the sum involved. This means that an honest belief that credit is being given will mean the offence is not being committed. This has already been seen in the case of *Allen* (1985).

Conclusion

There are six elements of this offence that is a relatively straightforward offence. Most of the cases suggest that a common-sense approach is taken. There are, however, alternative offences where the defendant's behaviour does not fall within the requirements of the offence.

Application of the elements of the offence of making off without payment to problems in the examination

Here is a sample question:

> Wayne was walking down the street when someone suddenly said to him, 'You have just dropped this', thrust a piece of paper into his hand and walked off. Wayne put the piece of paper into his pocket without looking at it and did not discover until two hours later that it was actually a ticket for a seat at that evening's football match between City and United. Feeling a little guilty about using a ticket that he had not paid for, Wayne went to the football stadium and used it to gain entry.

Consider how this scenario contains elements of the offences of:

- theft of the ticket – initial and subsequent appropriation, property, dishonesty
- liability under the Fraud Act – fraud by false representation, obtaining services dishonestly
- making off without payment – the spot, payment as required or expected.

Activity

Consider the following situation and consider the offences that have been committed:

Farah had a row with her boyfriend and ran out of the flat she shared with him, intending to go to her mother's house. She knew she had very little money in her purse. She flagged down a passing taxi and asked to be driven to the local cinema complex. When the taxi stopped at traffic lights opposite the railway station, she leapt out of the taxi without paying and ran into the station. She used her credit card that had already reached its credit limit to buy a ticket to the town where her mother lived.

You should now be able to:

- understand the law relating to making off without payment
- apply that law to given scenarios.

Key terms

Duress: this occurs where the defendant is forced to perform the criminal act by someone else.

1 Introduction to defences in criminal law

The AQA Law specification for Unit 4 sets out the defences that will be included. The defences are: intoxication; duress by threats; duress of circumstances; self-defence/prevention of crime. Defences become relevant when the *actus reus* and *mens rea* of an offence have been committed. Therefore, in your answers to the scenario-based questions you are well-advised to discuss the offences and then consider the application of any relevant defence.

The defence of intoxication through drink or drugs is sometimes said not to be a defence at all, but incapacity to form the *mens rea* of the crime. If this is considered as an idea, then it is obvious that the defence will not be of universal application. In any event, since some offences involve intoxication (being drunk in a public place or driving whilst unfit through drink or drugs), it is logical that the defence of intoxication will be of limited application.

Duress occurs where an individual carries out the crime unwillingly, but because of either threats made to him (the lesser of two evils in the defendant's mind), or because the circumstances in which he finds himself suggest to the defendant that he has no other option. There are obviously going to be limits as to the application of these defences too. These defences are known as duress by threats and duress of circumstances.

Self-defence/prevention of crime are a mixture of defences that largely apply to crimes involving violence, and so have limited, but important, application in the offences within this unit.

You should now be able to:

- outline the range of defences available in the AQA specification

- understand the effect of a defence to a crime

- understand how to approach problem questions involving a defence.

2 The defence of intoxication

Intoxication can be either voluntary or involuntary. In general, where the intoxication is voluntary, a person should not be excused from the consequences of their actions. This is because that person is responsible for being in the state of intoxication that impairs their judgment. Intoxication, however, can be used to show that the defendant could not form the necessary *mens rea* for the offence with which he has been charged. In that sense, it can provide a defence.

The law distinguishes between voluntary and involuntary intoxication and the effect that has on different offences, the offences being divided into those of basic intent and those of specific intent. The result that will be discussed below can be seen in Fig. 1 opposite.

Voluntary and involuntary intoxication

Voluntary intoxication is where the defendant takes the drink or drugs of his own free will. Involuntary intoxication is where a person does not know he was taking alcohol or an intoxicating drug. In such cases, there will only be a defence if the *mens rea* for a crime was not formed.

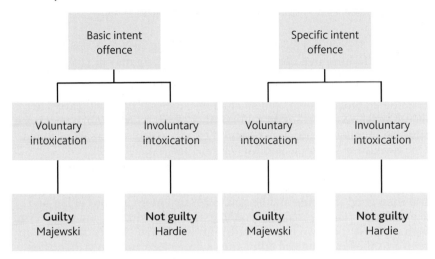

Fig. 1 *The effect of intoxication*

Involuntary intoxication can arise where:

- the defendant's drinks were spiked with alcohol or drugs, such as where a drug is slipped into a soft drink or alcohol is added without the defendant's knowledge
- the defendant takes drugs prescribed by his doctor in accordance with the instructions
- the defendant takes a non-dangerous drug, although not prescribed to him, in a non-reckless way.

If involuntary intoxication is to be a defence, it must be shown that the effect of the intoxication is that the defendant was, as a result of the intoxication, unable to form the *mens rea* of the offence. This is not always possible, as can be seen in the case of **Kingston (1994)**. In that case, at a trial in Lewes Crown Court in March 1992, the defendant, Barry Kingston and a man named Penn were jointly indicted on a count of indecent assault on a youth aged 15. The defendant, who had paedophiliac homosexual tendencies (which he normally controlled fully), was blackmailed by two former business associates, who arranged for Penn to photograph and audio-tape him in a compromising situation with the boy. Sedative drugs were found in Penn's flat when it was searched, and the prosecution claimed that Penn had laced the boy's drink. Kingston's defence was that Penn had also laced his drink. Kingston said that he had seen the boy lying on the bed but had no recollection of any other events that night and had woken in his own home the next morning. He said that he would never have committed the offence had he not been affected by the drug. The House of Lords stated that involuntary intoxication was not a defence to a charge if it was proved that the defendant had the necessary intent when the offence was committed, even though he was not to blame for the intoxication. Lord Mustill saw this case as one of disinhibition – the taking of the drug (whatever it was) lowered his ability to resist temptation, so that his desires overrode his ability to control them.

Key cases

Kingston (1994): a defendant can only use the defence of involuntary intoxication if the court is convinced that, because of being intoxicated, the defendant lacked the required *mens rea* for the offence; in the case, the court said that an intoxicated intent was still an intent.

Key cases

Allen (1988): intoxication remains voluntary even where the defendant claims he did not know the drink's or drug's strength.

Hardie (1985): the voluntary consumption of dangerous drugs might be conclusive proof of recklessness; this is not the case with non-dangerous drugs and a jury should have been directed to consider whether the defendant had been reckless in consuming the Valium.

Majewski (1977): this case made the distinction between crimes of basic intent and crimes of specific intent.

Where the defendant does not realise the strength of the alcohol or drug he has taken, it does not make the intoxication involuntary. The fact that the intoxication remains voluntary can be seen from the case of **Allen (1988)**, where the defendant was charged with buggery and indecent assault following an evening drinking in the pub and some wine given later by a friend. His claim that he did not realise the alcoholic strength of the wine that he had been given did not make the intoxication involuntary.

Where the defendant takes a non-dangerous drug, although not prescribed to him, in a non-reckless way, the taking may be treated as involuntary and may therefore provide a defence. This can be seen in the case of **Hardie (1985)**. In this, the defendant's relationship with Mrs Hardie had broken down, and she had insisted that he must leave. He did not wish to do so, but on the morning of 2 January 1982, he packed a suitcase. At about lunchtime he found two bottles of tablets in a cabinet. One contained Valium which Mrs Hardie had had in 1974.

Whilst he had never taken Valium before, he took one about 12 o'clock to calm him down but it did not have much effect. He and Mrs Hardie had then gone shopping and he had taken two more in front of her and she had said, 'take as many as you like, they are old stock and will do you no harm'. He took two more shortly afterwards and shortly thereafter on return to the house he had fallen into a deep sleep and could thereafter remember only periods.

It was not disputed that he must have started the fire, for he was alone in the bedroom when it started. Having started it, he emerged, returned to the sitting room to be with Mrs Hardie and her daughter, Tonia, and stayed there. Shortly afterwards Mrs Hardie heard sounds from the bedroom, went there, and found smoke and flames coming from the wardrobe. There was evidence that before, at the time of and after the fire the defendant was showing signs of intoxication, and that such signs might have resulted from the taking of Valium some hours earlier.

The court decided that this did not necessarily amount to voluntary intoxication. The jury should be directed that, if they came to the conclusion that, as a result of the Valium, the defendant was, at the time, unable to appreciate the risks to property and persons from his actions, they should then consider whether the taking of the Valium was itself reckless. The courts later decided that there was a distinction between 'dangerous' drugs including those where it is 'common knowledge' that the taker 'may become aggressive or do dangerous or unpredictable things' or make the defendant incapable of appreciating risks (amphetamines and LSD being well-known examples), and non-dangerous drugs such as Valium. Where the drugs can be said to be dangerous, there may be recklessness in self-administering it which would be the case when the drug was well known for causing the effects.

The distinction between crimes of basic intent and specific intent

The principle is that intoxication is a defence to crimes of specific intent and not those of basic intent. The key case with respect to this is **Majewski (1977)**. In that case during the evening of 19 February 1973 the defendant and his friend, Leonard Stace, who had also taken drugs and drink, went to The Bull public house in Basildon. Stace became involved in a disturbance. Glasses were broken. The landlord asked Stace to leave and escorted him to the door. As he did so, Stace called to Majewski: 'He's putting me out.' Majewski got up and prevented the landlord from getting Stace out and abused him. The landlord told them both to go. They refused and a brawl followed. Majewski was violent and abusive and spat in the landlord's face. When the police came, a fierce struggle took place to get him out. He shouted at the police: 'You pigs, I'll kill you all, you f — pigs, you bastards.'

The House of Lords considered the whole aspect of intoxication and came to the conclusion that self-induced intoxication can only be raised as a defence to crimes of specific intent, but not to crimes of basic intent.

The difficulty arises in that whilst the term 'specific intent' had been used in previous cases, 'basic intent' had not. Indeed it was not wholly clear what was meant by specific intent. It seems that a crime of basic intent is one where there is a general criminal intent rather than a sort of ulterior intent that the defendant wishes to achieve from his *actus reus*. Self-induced (voluntary) intoxication is no defence to a crime of basic intent, as the defendant's actions in becoming intoxicated voluntarily is in itself reckless behaviour — he knows there is a risk he will behave badly or criminally, but goes ahead anyway.

For many crimes, there are variations that have the specific intent crime as the more serious offence, with a lesser offence of basic intent. An example is basic criminal damage under s1(1) of the Criminal Damage Act 1971 and aggravated criminal damage which is destroying or damaging property with intent to endanger life under s 1(2) of the Act. The 'with intent to endanger life' is the specific intent crime. Thus, a defendant who had the *actus reus* and *mens rea* for both offences, but was voluntarily intoxicated at that time, might be able to show that he was so intoxicated that he could not form the specific intent of the aggravated crime and thus only be convicted of the lesser, basic offence. However, not all 'specific' intent offences have a corresponding 'basic' intent offence. A typical example of this is theft.

The offences that we have considered in this unit can be categorised as follows:

Table 1 *Specific and basic intent offences*

Basic Intent Crimes	Specific Intent Crimes
Offences Against the Person Act 1861 s47	Offences Against the Person Act 1861 s18
Offences Against the Person Act 1861 s20	Murder
Assault	
Battery	
Involuntary manslaughter	

It should also be noted that if the *mens rea* is formed before the intoxication, as in 'Dutch courage', there will be no defence of intoxication. This can be seen in the case of **Attorney-General for Northern Ireland v Gallagher (1963)**. In this case the defendant decided to kill his wife. He went out and bought a bottle of whisky and a knife. He drank the whisky and became so drunk that he could not form the *mens rea* for murder (an intention to kill or cause really serious harm); then he killed his wife. As he had formed the intention to kill her before he became intoxicated, he had no defence of intoxication.

Key cases

Attorney-General for Northern Ireland v Gallagher (1963): if the *mens rea* is formed before the intoxication, as in Dutch courage, there will be no defence of intoxication; here the intention to kill his wife was formed before he got drunk.

Conclusion

The first distinction is between voluntary and involuntary intoxication. Involuntary intoxication is a defence, but only where the intoxication is completely involuntary. The defence of intoxication applies differently to offences of specific intent and those of basic intent. It is essential, therefore, to understand the distinction between the two.

Application of the defence of intoxication to problems in the examination

In the examination, there are often questions involving the defence of intoxication. Discussion of this defence is suggested whenever a character in the scenario takes an alcoholic drink or drugs, whether illegal or legal. It may well be the case that you decided, after due consideration, that the defence will be unsuccessful. Nevertheless, you must make that discussion.

Consider the following scenario and the offences and the defence involved:

> Andy went into a park and drank a half bottle of whisky. By now, he was reeling around and finding it difficult to stand up. He tried to thumb a lift home from passing cars and was relieved when Charles stopped and picked him up. In reality, Charles was a taxi driver who expected to be paid. When the taxi stopped at traffic lights, Andy got out and began to walk away, unable to understand what Charles was shouting at him. He stumbled into Dora, an elderly lady, and knocked her bag out of her hand. He picked it up and walked off with it. When he woke up next day, he discovered the bag, but did nothing with it.

The scenario has three aspects to be dealt with:

1 In relation to the taxi ride – possible offences of fraud by false representation and/or dishonestly obtaining services and of making off without payment – ignore the issue of intoxication to start with.

2 In relation to Dora – possible offences of theft and robbery.

3 In relation to both of the above, the possible relevance of intoxication – issues of basic and specific intent given that theft is a specific intent crime.

In relation to the taxi ride Andy has committed offences of fraud by false representation, and of dishonestly obtaining services and of making off without payment. In relation to the incident with Dora, he was possibly guilty of theft and robbery. His intoxication means he might have been able to plead intoxication to the specific intent elements in those offences. In relation to the theft aspect of the incident with Dora, however, it was possible to argue that, even if the initial appropriation was not dishonest and so not theft, a later appropriation occurred when, having sobered up next morning, he found the bag but did nothing with it. With respect to robbery, the requirement for the force to be inflicted for the purpose of committing the theft is unlikely to be present given the accidental nature of the collision with Dora.

You should now be able to:

■ answer problem questions which include the defence of intoxication.

Activity

Consider the criminal liability of in the situation below:

Whilst drinking from a bottle of whisky in a garden centre, Charles took a steel tape-measure from a shelf to measure some concrete blocks. Finding the calculations difficult, he put the tape-measure into his pocket. He then tried to reach some heavy plant pots stacked on higher shelves, even though a notice warned customers to seek help from staff. He disturbed the stack and many pots fell and broke, narrowly missing a small child walking by. As he ran out of the garden centre, Charles realised that he still had the tape-measure. He left it on a wall in a nearby car park.

3 The defence of duress by threats

Duress occurs where the defendant is forced to perform the criminal act by someone else. Duress is now split into two parts: duress by threats, such as is explained above, and also duress of circumstances. The courts tend to discuss duress alongside the idea of necessity, and therefore some of the cases seem to have little to do with duress! Originally, the only defence was duress by threats as the law took the view that, because of the level of threat compared to the crime, the defendant's act became one that, whilst voluntary, was not one that he should be held responsible for. Duress is a defence available to all crimes except murder; therefore it is available to all crimes within the AQA specification for this unit. The more recent legal development of duress of circumstances is dealt with in the next topic.

The test for duress can be stated:

1 Was the defendant impelled to act as he did because he feared death or serious physical injury?

2 If so, did he respond as a sober person of reasonable firmness sharing the characteristics of the defendant would have done?

This test comes from the case of **Graham (1982)**. In that case, the defendant was the victim's husband. He was a practising homosexual who lived with his wife and another homosexual called King. King was known to be violent. Previously, King had tipped the defendant and his wife off a settee because they were embracing and he was jealous. He had also broken another woman's ribs. On 27 June 1980, the day before the killing, King attacked the wife with a knife. The defendant intervened, and cut his finger when he tried to grab the knife.

As a result of this incident the wife left. King then suggested getting rid of the wife once and for all. The two of them hatched a plan. The defendant telephoned his wife in the small hours, told her falsely that he had cut his wrists and asked her to come home at once. When the wife arrived, she knelt down beside the defendant to see how he was. King had the flex from a coffee percolator in his hands. He attempted unsuccessfully to put it round the wife's neck while she was kneeling. The appellant and his wife then both got up and King said: 'What's it feel like to know that you are going to die, Betty?' That remark was repeated. King then put the flex round the wife's neck and pulled it tight, hauling her off her feet onto his back as if she were a sack of coals. She put her hands up to the flex at her neck, whereupon King told the defendant to cut her fingers away. The appellant said in evidence that he picked up a knife but could not bring himself to use it. King thereupon put the wife on the floor, still holding the flex. He told the defendant to take hold of one end of it. The defendant said in evidence that he did so. He added that it was only in fear of King that he complied with the order. He said that, in any event, the plug at the end of the flex which he was holding came off as he exerted pressure on it. Thereafter he helped King to dispose of her body by wrapping it up, carrying her out of the flat and dumping it over an embankment.

There are a number of aspects of this defence to consider:

▉ The nature of the threat.

▉ The threat must be made in connection with the offence committed.

▉ The characteristics of the defendant.

▉ The effect of intoxication.

▉ The immediacy of the threat and possible escape.

▉ Self-induced duress.

In this topic you will learn how to:

▉ state the definition of the defence of duress by threats

▉ explain how the law balances the seriousness of the harm threatened and the offence committed

▉ explain how the law deals with the issues of immediacy, means of escape and self-induced duress

▉ apply the rules to a given situation.

▉ **Key cases**

Graham (1982): this case set out the test for duress as: (1) Was the defendant impelled to act as he did because he feared death or serious physical injury? (2) If so, did he respond as a sober person of reasonable firmness sharing the characteristics that the defendant would have done?

The nature of the threat

The *Graham* test states 'feared death or serious physical injury'. Thus, the threats must be as to serious physical harm however minor the offence committed. Thus, 'I will kill you if you do not break Emma's pencil', could give rise to a defence of duress to a charge of criminal damage. 'I will tap you on the hand with my pen if you do not break Emma's pencil' will not give rise to the defence against a charge of criminal damage arising from breaking the pencil. There is no defence if the threat is to damage or destroy property, although there can be a defence of self-defence relating to this which we shall consider in Topic 5 of this chapter.

What exactly amounts to serious physical injury is unclear. Certainly, psychological harm will not suffice as in *Baker and Wilkins* (1997). Similarly, in the case of *Quayle* and others: *Attorney-General's Reference* (No. 2 of 2004), a case about the self-medicating use of cannabis, it was suggested that the threat of severe pain would be insufficient.

Threats which do not form part of the defence are merely mitigating factors that come into play when sentence is being passed. These include threats to expose a sexual affair or a person's particular sexual practices. These aspects are to be disregarded in any consideration of duress even when they appear to be increasing the pressure caused by the threat. This can be seen from the case of **Valderrama-Vega (1985)**, where a cocaine smuggler for Colombian drug dealers had been threatened with death or serious injury to himself and his family if he did not take part in importing drugs. He was also under financial pressure and had been threatened with disclosure of his homosexuality. This later part could not be used as a defence.

It should also be noted from *Valderrama-Vega* (1985) that the threat can be made to a member of his immediate family. The same applies in the case of a person for whose safety he would reasonably regard himself as responsible. This can be seen in the specimen directions to juries set out by the Judicial Studies Board which were specifically approved in **Hasan (2005)**.

The threat must be made in connection with the offence committed

The defence can only be relied on where there is a connection between the threats made to the accused and the offence committed in response to the threats. Thus, it is no defence to say I was threatened with death if I did not burn down a factory to a charge of breaking a totally unconnected person's arm. In the case of **Cole (1994)**, the defendant robbed several building societies. He claimed moneylenders had threatened to harm him and his girlfriend if he did not repay money he had borrowed from them. The threat related to consequences if the money was not repaid, not if he did not commit the armed robberies.

It should be noted that the case does not establish the closeness of the connection required. It could be that a demand to rob a bank would still be too unconnected, but to take part in a robbery on Tuesday at HSBC, Leyburn, to get the money for the debt is probably close enough.

The characteristics of the defendant

The second leg of the test, 'If so, did he respond as a sober person of reasonable firmness sharing the characteristics of the defendant would have done?', requires a consideration of the effect of the threats on the reasonable man sharing the characteristics of the defendant.

Key cases

Valderrama-Vega (1985): the only relevant factors are threats of death or serious personal injury; in this case, financial pressure and the fact that he had been threatened with disclosure of his homosexuality were irrelevant factors to the defence of duress.

Hasan (2005): the defence of duress can be used where the threats are made with respect to a person for whose safety he would reasonably regard himself as responsible.

Cole (1994): there must be a connection between the threats made to the accused and the offence committed in response to the threats; there was no sufficient connection between armed robberies committed by the defendant and failure to repay a debt to a moneylender.

The key case on characteristics with respect to duress is **Bowen (1996)**. Here, the defendant pleaded the defence of duress to charges of obtaining services by deception. On some forty occasions the appellant had visited shops selling electrical goods and obtained a large number of them by applying for 'instant credit'. On all occasions he had paid a proportion of the cost by way of deposit. He had not completed payment of any of the goods concerned. On all occasions he had given his correct name and bank details. On some occasions he had given his correct address; on others not. The total amount of credit obtained was about £20,000.

After some initial prevarication he told the officers that he had obtained a large number of goods that he subsequently sold and that, although he had made some payments for them, he stopped paying the finance company. He said that he had stopped paying for the credit because he could see little point in doing so when it was so easy, and he had sold the goods as a way of making a 'quick buck'. He said that he had not realised that what he was doing was a criminal offence; he thought he was just getting himself into debt.

He claimed that throughout the period he had acted under duress. He said that two men had accosted him in a public house, and he had been threatened by them that he and his family would be petrol-bombed if he did not obtain goods for them. On each occasion he was told what goods the men required. He was told that if he went to the police his family would be attacked.

Evidence was given by a psychologist that he had a low IQ (68) and was abnormally suggestible. The court decided that the low IQ had no bearing on how the defendant was able to respond to the threat. They said, 'we do not see how low IQ, short of mental impairment or mental defectiveness, can be said to be a characteristic that makes those who have it less courageous and less able to withstand threats and pressure'.

What is more important in the case is that the court set out the characteristics that would be relevant.

Extract from *R* v *Bowen* as to relevant characteristics of the defendant

> It seems clear that age and sex are, and physical health or disability may be, relevant characteristics. But beyond that it is not altogether easy to determine from the authorities what others may be relevant ... In the case of duress, the question is: would an ordinary person sharing the characteristics of the defendant be able to resist the threats made to him? What principles are to be derived from [the] authorities? We think they are as follows:
>
> 1 The mere fact that the accused is more pliable, vulnerable, timid or susceptible to threats than a normal person are not characteristics with which it is legitimate to invest the reasonable/ordinary person for the purpose of considering the objective test.
>
> 2 The defendant may be in a category of persons who the jury may think less able to resist pressure than people not within that category. Obvious examples are age, where a young person may well not be so robust as a mature one; possibly sex, though many women would doubtless consider they had as much moral courage to resist pressure as men; pregnancy, where there is added fear for the unborn child; serious physical disability, which may inhibit self-protection; recognised mental illness or psychiatric condition, such as post traumatic stress disorder leading to learned helplessness.

Bowen (1996): this case sets out the characteristics that can be relevant for the defence of duress.

3 Characteristics which may be relevant in considering provocation, because they relate to the nature of the provocation itself will not necessarily be relevant in cases of duress. Thus, homosexuality may be relevant to provocation if the provocative words or conduct are related to this characteristic; it cannot be relevant in duress, since there is no reason to think that homosexuals are less robust in resisting threats of the kind that are relevant in duress cases.

4 Characteristics due to self-induced abuse, such as alcohol, drugs or glue-sniffing, cannot be relevant.

5 Psychiatric evidence may be admissible to show that the accused is suffering from some mental illness, mental impairment or recognised psychiatric condition provided persons generally suffering from such a condition may be more susceptible to pressure and threats and thus to assist the jury in deciding whether a reasonable person suffering from such a condition might have been impelled to act as the defendant did. It is not admissible simply to show that in the doctor's opinion an accused, who is not suffering from such illness or condition is especially timid, suggestible or vulnerable to pressure and threats. Nor is medical opinion admissible to bolster or support the credibility of the accused.

This means that the following are characteristics which *can* be put forward:

- Age and sex.
- Physical health or disability.
- The defendant may be in a category of persons whom the jury may think less able to resist pressure than people not within that category.
- Psychiatric evidence may be admissible to show that the accused is suffering from some mental illness, mental impairment or recognised psychiatric condition provided persons generally suffering from such a condition may be more susceptible to pressure and threats.

This also means that the following are characteristics which *cannot* be put forward:

- The mere fact that the accused is more pliable, vulnerable, timid or susceptible to threats than a normal person.
- Characteristics which may be relevant in considering provocation, because they relate to the nature of the provocation itself will not necessarily be relevant in cases of duress unless they make the person more susceptible to threats.
- Characteristics due to self-induced abuse, such as alcohol, drugs or glue-sniffing.

The effect of intoxication

It would appear from the previous paragraph that intoxication is not relevant to the defence, but, as we have seen, may be a defence in itself. If the intoxication is involuntary, then it may be that the defence can be affected by the intoxication as the extract from *Bowen* (1996) only refers to self-induced abuse.

The immediacy of the threat and possible escape

The defendant can only successfully plead the defence of duress where the threat was operating on his mind at the time and he feared death or serious harm would follow immediately if he did not commit the crime. In *Hudson and Taylor* (1971), a fight took place in a Salford public house between two men with the result that one was charged with wounding the

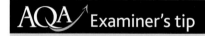

AQA Examiner's tip

Be aware of scenarios where there is a combination of involuntary intoxication and duress by threats. In such cases you should consider both defences and suggest that the court might be persuaded to accept the defendant's susceptibility to threats is lowered because of the involuntary intoxication, bearing in mind the result of the case of *Kingston* (1994).

other. The defendants, aged 19 and 17, gave statements to the police and they were the principal prosecution witnesses at the trial but when called to give evidence they failed to identify the attacker resulting in an unjust acquittal. They were charged with perjury.

At their trial they admitted that the evidence which they had given was false but set up the defence of duress. The basis of the defence was that, shortly after the fight, Hudson had been approached by a group of men including a man called Farrell who had a reputation for violence and was warned that if she 'told on Wright in court' they would get her and cut her up. Hudson passed this warning to Taylor who said that she had also been warned by other girls to be careful or she would be hurt. They were frightened and decided to tell lies in court in order to avoid the consequences which might follow if they identified the attacker. Their resolve was strengthened when they arrived at court for the trial and saw that Farrell was in the gallery. The jury had to decide whether this was an immediate threat. Whilst the girls were safe in court, the fact that the person making the threat was in court and could follow them out was important. It was also shown that the defendants had little or no police protection offered or given.

However, this case has been disapproved in *Hasan* (2005), as the defendants had the opportunity to go to the police. It has also been seen in **Abdul-Hussain (1999)**, a case about aircraft hijackers who were Shiite Muslims who had fled from Southern Iraq, and the persecution by Saddam Hussain, to Sudan, but had overstayed in Sudan and feared being returned to Iraq, tortured and executed. Despite the lack of immediacy of the threat, the court decided that the possibility of death could overbear their minds and therefore might be available to the defendant as a defence.

It should be remembered that duress is an excuse so its existence does not necessarily result in a not guilty verdict; it will depend on the jury's view. The defendant can always not commit the crime. The defendant is more concerned with avoiding implementation of the threat. A case where the defendant would be expected to contact the police and could not rely on duress was *Gill* (1963). Here, the defendant was told to steal his employer's lorry and was threatened with violence if he failed to do so. Gill would not have had the defence because he had time to go to the police in between the threat and the commission of the crime. However, the more recent cases seem to have relaxed this rule a little.

Self-induced duress

Where the defendant voluntarily puts himself in a position in which he was likely to be subjected to threats made to persuade him to commit an offence, then the defence of duress is less likely to be available. This is consistent with other defences such as intoxication, where the voluntary nature of the defendant's behaviour usually means he has no defence. This can occur where the defendant joins a criminal group likely to subject him to such threats, or gets involved with crime and thus with other criminals likely to subject him to such threats if he lets them down or came to owe them money. From the defendant's point of view, the problem often arises when he wishes to end the association.

This can be seen in a number of cases. For example in **Sharp (1987)**, in August 1984 the defendant and two others, both of whom were armed with sawn-off shotguns, held up a sub-post office in Hounslow. They wore wigs. One of the others threatened the wife of the postmaster, whereupon the postmaster himself pressed the alarm. All three then ran off to the getaway car empty-handed. One of the others tried to fire his gun in the air in order to discourage anyone who was minded to pursue them.

Key cases

Abdul-Hussain (1999): even though there was a lack of immediacy of the threat, the court decided that the possibility of death could overbear their minds and therefore might be available to the defendant as a defence; this was the case of the Shiite Muslim hijackers avoiding being returned to Iraq.

Sharp (1987): where a person has voluntarily, and with knowledge of its nature, joined a criminal organisation or gang which he knew might bring pressure on him to commit an offence and was an active member when he was put under such pressure, he cannot use the defence of duress.

In September 1984 the sub-post office at Wraysbury, near Staines, was the subject of an attack by them. The others again carried loaded sawn-off shotguns. Sharp was responsible for locking the post office door after the three of them had entered. Unfortunately the postmaster was shot and killed. Sharp admitted that he had been invited to take part in these robberies and had willingly done so. He regarded one of the others as a 'nutcase'. He did not wish any weapons to be used, or so he said. He claimed that he panicked when he saw the guns being loaded into the car, because he knew from the first robbery that the others were prepared to fire them. He wanted to pull out, but he lost his nerve and he carried on despite his wish to withdraw because one of the others pointed a gun at him and threatened to blow his head off if he did not carry on with the plan to rob the post office. The court did not allow the defence of duress because he had voluntarily got into the situation by his association with the other criminals.

The defendant does not have to join a gang as such; just association with the others can suffice. This is particularly likely when doing business with drug dealers as in the cases of *Heath* (2000) and *Harmer* (2000), although the later case of *Hasan* (2005) perhaps states the situation better. This can be said to be that a defendant could not plead duress when he had foreseen or ought to have foreseen that his voluntary association with a known criminal involved the risk of being subjected to any compulsion by acts of violence. This is not restricted to compulsion to commit crimes of the kind with which he was charged. The defendant loses the benefit of a defence based on duress if he ought reasonably to have foreseen the risk of coercion. A person voluntarily associating with known criminals should foresee the risk of future coercion. As a matter of policy, the law must discourage association with known criminals.

Conclusion

Duress applies to excuse a defendant where his crime has been committed so as to avoid death or serious injury threatened to him or others if he did not commit the crime. The courts attempt to limit the scope of the defence by limiting the category of persons against whom the threats must be made. There are also limits set where the defendant has the opportunity to escape from the threats, but does not do so when he could, and when he puts himself in a position in which he was likely to be subjected to threats, usually by his criminal association.

Application of the defence of duress by threats to problems in the examination

In the examination, there are often questions involving the defence of duress. Discussion of this defence is suggested whenever a character in the scenario is put under some sort of pressure by threats.

Consider the following scenario and the offences and the defence involved:

> Until recently, Dave had been Gina's partner, and he was very upset that Gina had now begun to live with Fred. When he discovered that Eric had been invited to Fred and Gina's engagement party at Fred's house, Dave threatened to 'beat up' Eric unless Eric took the opportunity to smash the engagement presents brought by guests. Eric was very frightened of Dave and he agreed to do so. At the party, Fred thought that Eric was behaving strangely and followed him upstairs to a bedroom where the presents had been left. Realising that he was being watched as he was about to begin smashing the presents, Eric tried to rush past Fred. In the struggle that followed, Fred fell downstairs and broke his leg.

The scenario has three aspects to be dealt with:

1 Burglary under s9(1)(a) – this raises issues of entry as a trespasser and the intention to cause criminal damage.
2 Burglary under s9(1)(b) – this again raises issues of entry as a trespasser and subsequent infliction of grievous bodily harm.
3 Duress as a defence to both charges above – possible prior association between Dave and Eric; threat of death or serious injury; possibility of avoiding implementation of the threat; application of the objective test.

Eric's initial entry into the house was as a trespasser, notwithstanding his invitation to the party, because he intended from the outset to exceed the scope of any permission he had been given. It could also be argued that Eric entered the bedroom as a trespasser, on the basis that it was a part of a building into which he had no permission to go. Thus, s9(1)(a) burglary had been committed because Eric entered (the house or the bedroom) intending to commit criminal damage.

The broken leg suffered by Fred when he fell downstairs in consequence of the struggle with Eric could itself have amounted to grievous bodily harm which would raise the issue of s9(1)(b) burglary. Eric might be able to assert a defence of duress on account of the threats made to him by Dave.

You should now be able to:

- answer problem questions involving the defence of duress by threats.

4 The defence of duress of circumstances

Duress of circumstances differs from duress by threats in that in duress by threats the defendant claims he is forced to commit an offence, whereas in duress of circumstances the defendant believes he, or those with him (for example, in a car) would suffer death or serious injury if he did not escape by doing what he did. In this sense, it is a little like self-defence considered in the next topic.

In **Martin (1989)** Simon Brown J summarised the position as follows:

First … duress … can arise from other objective dangers threatening the accused or others. Arising thus it is conveniently called 'duress of circumstances'.

Secondly, the defence is available only if, from an objective standpoint, the accused can be said to be acting reasonably and proportionately in order to avoid a threat of death or serious injury.

Third, assuming the defence to be open to the accused on his account of the facts, the issue should be left to the jury, who should be directed to determine these two questions: first, was the accused, or may he have been impelled to act as he did because as a result of what he reasonably believed to be the situation he had good cause to fear that otherwise death or serious physical injury would result? Second, if so, may a sober person of reasonable firmness, sharing the characteristics of the accused, have responded to that situation by acting as the accused acted. If the answer to both those questions was 'yes', then the jury would acquit: the defence of necessity would have been established.

The case of *Martin* (1989) involved a charge of driving whilst disqualified. His wife had suicidal tendencies and had attempted suicide on a number of occasions. Her son had overslept, was bound to be late for work, and

Activity

Consider the following scenario and discuss the offences and defences involved:

Helen ran the finances for Irma's art gallery and had authority to sign cheques drawn on Irma's account. Jamal told her that if she did not write out a cheque payable to him for £1,000 that he believed Irma owed him, he would make sure she never saw her children again. Helen, a very timid person, was so frightened that she gave Jamal a cheque for £1,000. Jamal was still very angry despite getting the cheque and unscrewed the rear light covers of Irma's car, removed the bulbs, and then replaced the covers. He put the light bulbs in Irma's bin.

In this topic you will learn how to:

- state the definition of the defence of duress of circumstances
- explain how the law balances the seriousness of the harm threatened and the offence committed
- explain how the law deals with the issues of immediacy and means of escape
- apply the rules to a given situation.

Key cases

Martin (1989): this case set out the principles behind duress of circumstances.

was at risk of losing his job unless, so it was claimed, the defendant drove him to work. The defendant's wife was distraught. She was shouting, screaming, banging her head against a wall and she was threatening suicide unless he drove the boy to work. The defence had a statement from a doctor which expressed the opinion that in view of her mental condition it is likely that Mrs Martin would have attempted suicide if her husband did not drive her son to work. The defendant believed that his wife would carry out that threat unless he did as she demanded. Despite his disqualification he therefore drove the boy to work. He was in fact stopped by the police within about a quarter of a mile of the house!

From this case it can be seen that the test is very similar to that of duress by threats. There are a number of elements to consider:

- The objective nature of the threat.
- Reasonable and proportionate action.
- The nature of the test.
- Limits to the defence.

The objective nature of the threat

The fact that the threat must be seen objectively means that this is the view that a reasonable man – in other words the jury – would take. This is the same as in the defence of duress by threats and therefore requires consideration of the same characteristics of the defendant as we considered in the previous topic and the case of *Bowen* (1996).

Reasonable and proportionate action

This acts to limit the circumstances in which the defence may be pleaded. This is not just proportionate action, but action that would only be taken given the very serious nature of the threats made. This can be seen in the case of **Conway (1989)**, where the defendant, having been attacked by two men whilst he was in a vehicle a fortnight previously, saw two men approaching his car. He drove off recklessly as, he claimed, he feared another attack. In fact, the two men were plain clothes policeman about to arrest a passenger in his car. The jury would then have to consider whether his behaviour was proportionate.

The nature of the test

The test is exactly the same as the test for duress by threats, with the obvious changes:

1 Was the accused, or may he have been impelled to act as he did because as a result of what he reasonably believed to be the situation he had good cause to fear that otherwise death or serious physical injury would result?

2 If so, may a sober person of reasonable firmness, sharing the characteristics of the accused, have responded to that situation by acting as the accused acted?

An application of the test can be seen in the case of **Rodger and Rose (1997)**. In that case, the defendants were serving terms of life imprisonment for murder. Their original tariff set by the trial judge, of 12 and 20 years respectively, had since been increased to 17 years and indeterminate respectively. They claimed they became angry and depressed and had begun to consider suicide. This, they claimed, prompted them to break out of prison. The defence was not allowed as the circumstances which caused the action were internal to themselves and not extraneous circumstances as in all the other cases.

Key cases

Conway (1989): the defendant, fearing a repeat attack, drove off recklessly; the court could consider whether this was a proportionate and reasonable behaviour so as to amount to the defence of duress of circumstances.

Rodger and Rose (1997): the defence is not available where the circumstances are internal to the defendant; to do so would be a license for anyone to commit a crime based on some evidence of 'suicidal thoughts'.

Limits to the defence

The defence has the same limitations on it as duress by threats. This was specifically stated in the case of **Pommell (1995)**, where the Court of Appeal made it clear that the defence was not just limited to driving offences. In that case, the police entered the defendant's house at about 8.00am on 4 June 1993 to execute a search warrant. He was found lying in bed with a loaded gun in his right hand. He was asked if the gun was his and he replied, 'I took it off a geezer who was going to do some people some damage with it'. In the same bedroom police officers found a bag containing ammunition. When interviewed he was asked to explain his possession of the gun, and he said:

> Last night someone come round to see me, this guy by the name of Erroll, and he had it with him with the intention to go and shoot some people because they had killed his friend and he wanted to kill their girlfriends and relatives and kids, and I persuade him, I took it off him and told him that it's not right to do that.

The defendant went on to say that Erroll had called between 12.30am and 1.00am and, after he left, he took the gun upstairs and kept it from his girlfriend and took the bullets out of it. He then decided to wait until morning and decided to put the bullets back into it. He was lying in bed with the gun against his leg because, he said, he did not want his girlfriend to see it. He said that he was going to hand the gun to his brother so that he could hand it to the police because his brother gets on with the police and had handed in guns in the past.

The question then remains whether the jury would believe the story and excuse the defendant by finding him not guilty.

Conclusion

Duress of circumstances now has very similar principles as duress by threats but you still need to be able to distinguish the two and apply them accurately.

Application of the defence of duress of circumstances to problems in the examination

In the examination, there are often questions involving the defence of duress. Discussion of this defence is suggested whenever a character in the scenario is put under some sort of pressure by the circumstances in which he finds himself.

Consider the following scenario and the offences and the defence involved:

> David cycled into the countryside with his 12-year-old daughter, Ellie, who suddenly suffered serious breathing problems. Fred was passing in his car but, though he stopped, he refused to take David and Ellie to a hospital because he had an important appointment. Whilst Fred was standing holding the car door, David jumped in with Ellie and slammed the door shut, causing Fred to stumble and fall. David then drove Ellie to hospital, abandoning the car on yellow lines outside. The journey used a quarter of a tank of petrol.

The scenario has three aspects to be dealt with:

1 *Actus reus* issues in theft and robbery – property (the car, the petrol), appropriation, the use of force, purpose.

2 *Mens rea* issues in theft and robbery – dishonesty, intention permanently to deprive (applied to the car and to the petrol), intention or recklessness as to the use of force.

Key cases

Pommell (1995): the Court of Appeal specifically extended the defence of duress of circumstances to all crimes as in duress by threats.

3 Duress of circumstances issues – subjective and objective tests, involving imminent threat of death or serious injury and reasonableness of response.

This question raises issues of theft (Theft Act s1) and of robbery (s8) by David in connection with the taking of Fred's car and the use of the petrol during the journey. However, it was also very important to note that David's actions were prompted entirely by his concern for the safety of his daughter, Ellie. Thus, the defence of duress of circumstances can be offered in order to justify or excuse his conduct.

It should be noted that robbery applies not only in relation to the theft of the car but also to the theft of the petrol. The whole question of dishonesty is raised as it must be shown that David would be regarded as dishonest according to the ordinary standards of reasonable and honest people. This might not be the case if his motive in taking the car was to get treatment for his daughter when she was experiencing serious breathing problems.

The requirement of an intention permanently to deprive can be seen from the abandoning of the car, although the fact that it would readily be found, identified and returned might counteract that. This is not an issue with the petrol.

These facts give rise to a possible defence of duress of circumstances as there is ample evidence on which David could argue that he reasonably feared that Ellie might suffer serious injury or death, that no other course of action was open to him to avert that risk, and that a sober person of reasonable firmness would have responded in the same way.

■ Activity

Consider the case of *Backshall* (1998), set out below and decide whether the defendant could successfully plead duress of circumstances. What could Howell be charged with?

Backshall had been driving his car (a Ford Mondeo) when his co-accused, Howell, attempted to overtake. It was alleged that Backshall drove his vehicle from side to side and applied his brakes several times before Howell overtook him. That was the first driving incident.

Both vehicles stopped and a fight ensued during which it seemed Howell was the aggressor. Howell went to his car and returned with a hammer. He smashed the Mondeo's windscreen and front side windows while Backshall sat in the driver's seat.

Backshall drove away at speed pursued by Howell. Backshall reversed from a side street into a major road and stopped, facing the wrong direction in traffic. That was the second incident. Backshall was charged with dangerous driving.

You should now be able to:

■ answer problem questions involving the defence of duress of circumstances.

5 The defence of self-defence/prevention of crime

This topic is sometimes called public and private defence. This is because the common law defence of self-defence is extended, and to some extent superseded, by the statutory defence of public defence (prevention of crime) under the Criminal Law Act 1967 s3. As the two do overlap, the idea of self-defence is still relevant as it may be that a person is defending themselves from someone who is not, in fact, committing a crime, for example because that person is insane.

The Criminal Law Act 1967 s3

This section provides:

> A person may use such force as is reasonable in the circumstances in the prevention of crime, or in effecting or assisting in the lawful arrest of offenders or suspected offenders or of persons unlawfully at large.

The following points need to be considered:

- The necessity of force.
- The reasonableness of force.

The necessity of force

The basic principle is that the use of force is not justified if it is not necessary. It will be necessary if it is seen to be so in the circumstances which exist or which the defendant genuinely believed existed. This can be seen from the case of **Gladstone Williams (1987)**, where a man saw a women become the victim of a robbery by a youth. This man struggled with the robber with a view to stopping him and handing him to the police. At this point the defendant appeared and took the view that the man was attacking the youth and stepped in to protect the youth. The defendant was successful in pleading prevention of crime, even though he was mistaken as to the actual facts. His defence is based on what he genuinely believed was happening.

The defence comes into operation even if the attack has not yet taken place providing it is imminent. In other words, the defendant does not have to wait for an attack to start but can get in the first blow. The difficulty with this is establishing that the force he uses is reasonable. However, it is clear that the defendant does not have a duty to retreat as far as possible before using force which was the case under the old law. This can be seen from the case of **Bird (1985)**. The facts of the case were that on 10 March 1984 the defendant, Debbie Bird, was celebrating her 17th birthday. There was a party at a house in Harlow. There was a guest at the party called Darren Marder, who became the victim. He and the defendant had been friendly and had been going out together between about January and the middle of 1983. That close friendship had come to an end, but Marder arrived at the party with his new girlfriend and an argument broke out. The defendant told Marder to leave, and he did.

A little later he came back and a second argument took place. The defendant poured a glass of Pernod over Marder, and he retaliated by slapping her around the face. When she was later held up against a wall she lunged at Marder with her hand, which was the hand which held the Pernod glass. The glass hit him in the face, broke, and took out his eye. The court decided that it was unnecessary to show an unwillingness to fight and there were circumstances where a defendant might reasonably react immediately and without first retreating as in this case. The force was not reasonable in terms of what had happened, but was reasonable with respect to what she thought might happen when pinned against the wall.

In this topic you will learn how to:

- state the definition of the defence of self-defence/ prevention of crime
- distinguish between self-defence and prevention of crime
- apply the rules to a given situation.

■ Key cases

Gladstone Williams (1987): the defence under s3 Criminal Law Act 1967 is based on the genuine belief of the defendant rather than the actual facts; in this case the defendant believed a youth was being attacked when in fact his victim was trying to arrest the youth.

Bird (1985): the defendant does not have to wait for an attack to start but can get in the first blow.

The reasonableness of force

The jury have the task of deciding whether, in all the circumstances, the defendant used reasonable force. The jury, of course, can take as long as they need to balance the facts, the facts as the defendant believed them, the circumstances of the attack, the time available to the defendant to decide on his course of action, and balance the risk to himself against the risk of harm to the victim. The defendant usually does that in a split second so he may use excessive force. If that is the case, that excessive force is unlawful.

Lord Morris of Borth-y-Gest said, in the case of **Palmer (1971)**:

> It is both good law and good sense that a man who is attacked may defend himself. It is both good law and good sense that he may do, but may only do, what is reasonably necessary. But everything will depend upon the particular facts and circumstances … It may in some cases be only sensible and clearly possible to take some simple avoiding action. Some attacks may be serious and dangerous. Others may not be. If there is some relatively minor attack it would not be common sense to permit some action of retaliation which was wholly out of proportion to the necessities of the situation. If an attack is serious so that it puts someone in immediate peril then immediate defensive action may be necessary. If the moment is one of crisis for someone in imminent danger he may have to avert the danger by some instant reaction.

> If the attack is all over and no sort of peril remains then the employment of force may be by way of revenge or punishment or by way of paying off an old score or may be pure aggression. There may no longer be any link with a necessity of defence. Of all these matters the good sense of a jury will be the arbiter. If there has been no attack then clearly there will have been no need for defence. If there has been attack so that defence is reasonably necessary it will be recognised that a person defending himself cannot weigh to a nicety the exact measure of his necessary defensive action.

The famous cases of Corporal Clegg, a soldier on a checkpoint in Northern Ireland in the 1990s faced with what might be a terrorist attack, and Tony Martin in 2001, who shot and killed a 16-year-old intruder with a pump-action shotgun, demonstrate the extremes to which a jury must go when considering what amounts to reasonable force.

Conclusion

The defence of self-defence and prevention of crime is available to a person who may use such force as is reasonable in the circumstances in the prevention of crime, or in effecting or assisting in the lawful arrest of offenders or suspected offenders or of persons unlawfully at large. The key aspects of the defence are the necessity of force and the reasonableness of force.

Application of the defence of self-defence/prevention of crime to problems in the examination

In the examination, there are occasional questions involving the defence of duress. Discussion of this defence is suggested whenever a character in the scenario is put under some sort of pressure by the circumstances in which he finds himself.

Consider the following scenario and the offences and the defence involved:

> Andy wanted to see a controversial film at his local cinema so he could start a protest and run riot in the auditorium. As he had little money, he joined the drinks queue in the foyer and then entered the auditorium with a group of people who had come out to get their drinks. When the film had been running for some time he had become so incensed at what he saw that he threw his drink to the front of the cinema. This soaked some seats and the clothing of some customers. During a row that followed his outburst, Andy violently pushed Bob, another customer who was trying to hold him whilst someone else punched him and grabbed his drink and threw that to the front as well. Bob broke his arm when he fell awkwardly.

The scenario has these aspects to be dealt with:

- Obtaining services dishonestly.
- Fraud by false representation.
- Burglary under s9(1)(a) – entry as a trespasser to commit criminal damage.
- Burglary under s9(1)(b) – entry as a trespasser and subsequent GBH (the broken arm).
- Criminal damage to the seats and clothing.
- Theft and robbery of the second drink.

There are many offences that have been potentially committed here – rather more than would be expected in the examination. The key point to this is the fact that self-defence is most likely to occur where robbery is involved.

Activity

Review all the defences and list the key requirements of each.

You should now be able to:

- answer problem questions involving the defence of self-defence/ prevention of crime.

4A Review and examination techniques

In this topic you will learn how to:

■ prepare for an examination in criminal law

■ identify key areas for revision

■ plan and write answers to scenario questions.

Answering questions on criminal law in Unit 4A

To complete an examination paper in criminal law successfully, you must both prepare carefully beforehand and deploy a range of skills when actually answering questions.

In preparing for an examination, you may find the following guidelines helpful:

■ Make sure you have a thorough understanding of the key principles relating to each crime and defence. Be aware that each crime consists of rules relating to the existence of an *actus reus* and *mens rea*. There may also be issues of causation and there may be a defence available.

■ Be prepared to illustrate key principles with the use of authority. Authority means a case or an Act of Parliament demonstrating the principle in question or a case explaining a point about the Act of Parliament.

■ With respect to cases, you should be able to explain the principle that the case illustrates. It is helpful to have an outline knowledge of the facts of the case, as that gives a useful example, but it is not necessary to know the facts in great detail or to memorise the date of the case.

■ With respect to Acts of Parliament, you need to be able to cite the relevant section number, as well as the name and date of the statute, and to be able to explain in your own words what the section says. It is preferable to quote the key extract from the section of an Act of Parliament so that you use the correct legal term.

■ Make sure you frequently practise writing answers to past papers and similar examples, and ensure that you pay attention to the feedback that you receive. You do not want to be in the position of trying out your problem-solving skills for the first time in the examination. No one gets everything right the first time and everyone benefits from experience.

■ Pay attention to your written English. There are five marks awarded for using good English, organising information clearly and using legal vocabulary accurately and at appropriate places. Five marks may not sound very much but it could be the difference between two grades, especially as the other A Level Law examinations also carry marks for the quality of your written communication. When you practise exam answers, be aware of the need to produce organised answers (not random points churned out in the hope that something will be correct) and take the time to check spellings.

■ When looking at a problem scenario, begin by identifying the characters involved. You need to know who the victims and possible defendants are. Be sure to read the question carefully and answer only what you are asked. If the question asks you about the criminal liability of Character A, you will waste time if you discuss what Character B's criminal liability might be.

■ Then consider which crimes are relevant. There are actually only a limited number of crimes on the specification, and you should be able to run through them in your mind. You might consider whether there are several possible offences arising out of the same incident. If the question relates to theft, has it also involved burglary or robbery? If threats are involved, is it robbery or blackmail? Where property is damaged, which type of criminal damage is it? Which type of fraud is involved?

- Restrict yourself to discussing the law covered by the specification. You may well think that a character in a problem has committed offences against the person or a breach of contract, but these things are not being examined on this paper, and a discussion of them is unlikely to gain you marks.

- When writing about a particular crime, make sure you deal with all aspects of the *actus reus* and *mens rea*, but say very little about those parts that are not in question. Concentrate on those where the application of the law to the problem is not clear and then conclude (taking into account any defences that might be apparent).

- Give a concise explanation of the relevant legal principles. Do not waste time talking about related, but irrelevant, matters that you happen to know about. If, for instance, a question is clearly about s9(1)(a) burglary only, do not discuss s9(1)(b) burglary.

- Where you can, give the names of relevant cases to illustrate the legal principles you are discussing. You do not have to explain the fact of the case unless you think it helps your discussion.

- Be aware that it is not enough just to explain the law. You need to go on to apply the law to the scenario. This means that you need to discuss what the position of the characters is, and make sure you do it at each stage of your answer.

- Don't be worried if there doesn't seem to be a definite answer. Sometimes scenarios are written deliberately to pose awkward questions. Discuss both sides of an issue and consider the application of the law for both views.

You should now be able to:

- complete an answer to a scenario question on criminal law in an organised fashion with the purpose of gaining as high a mark as possible.

Read this scenario, together with its questions, and then complete the activities that follow it.

Scenario 1

Adrian sold computers from a shop in the high street. Bill paid £500 for a computer which Adrian promised would be available in four weeks' time. After taking the order and putting the money into his business account, but before it had been spent, Adrian learned that his supplier was threatening not to deliver any more computers because of unpaid bills. Subsequently, Craig also paid Adrian £500 for a computer which Adrian promised would be available shortly. Bill complained that, after five weeks, he had still not got his computer. Adrian said that he would refund the £500 as soon as he had sorted out his bank accounts. He made the same promise to Craig on a number of occasions. In fact, Adrian's business had gone bankrupt, and he was unable to supply the computers or to refund the money paid, because it had been used to pay other debts.

Bill brooded on the loss of his £500 and on how he could get it back. Having drunk a great deal of wine one night, he went round to Adrian's house. Though the house was in darkness, Bill began to bang on a window. To his surprise, the glass broke and Bill climbed in through the window. Once inside, he wandered aimlessly through the house, pushing over a small table which was in his way and breaking an ornament which had rested on it. Eventually, he looked through some bookshelves and put a book in his pocket, which he then completely forgot about. When he woke up in his own house next morning, he discovered that he had the book, but did nothing with it.

(a)	Discuss Adrian's possible liability for property offences arising out of his dealings with Bill and Craig.	*(25 marks)*
(b)	Discuss Bill's possible criminal liability for property offences arising out of his visit to Adrian's house.	*(25 marks)*

Question (a):

1 Fraud issues need to be discussed – offence of fraud by false representation under the Fraud Act 2006, with particular reference to *mens rea* aspects in distinguishing between Bill and Craig in respect of the obtaining of the money.

2 Discussion of theft issues – consideration of the difficulties in establishing theft of the money from Bill at the time of payment (lack of dishonesty) and at the time that the money is used to pay creditors (possible operation of s5(3)); consideration of the dishonest appropriation of Craig's money at the time when it is appropriated.

3 Mark on your two plans where you might use cases to support the rules that you intend to discuss.

4 Finally, write proper answers based on your plans. Use continuous prose, make sure your information is organised and that your spelling is accurate.

Question (b):

1 Discussion of criminal damage and theft offences: the broken window, the broken ornament and issues of recklessness; possible theft of the ornament, and theft of the book in the house or at his own house.

2 Discussion of burglary issues: entry as trespasser (but without intent?), possible subsequent theft of ornament and/or of book

3 Defence of intoxication issues: specific and basic intent offences and effect in relation to the offences criminal damage and theft.

4 As with question (a), prepare a paragraph by paragraph plan for each defendant, marking on where you will use cases to support your explanations.

5 Finally, write a full answer based on your plans.

Now read this second scenario, together with its questions, and then complete the activities that follow it.

Scenario 2

Des, who had a violent and unpredictable personality, saw Eddie in the street and called him over. Eddie, who was 16 years old and who knew Des, was very frightened when Des showed him a knife and told him to 'get some money for me from a few old ladies'. Des also said that he would be watching Eddie all the time. Eddie managed to get money from a number of old people in the street, either by telling them that he was homeless and needed money for food, or, if they refused his request, by persistently asking in an increasingly aggressive manner. Des took the money with him to a bar where he drank a large amount of beer. He managed to get his last pint of beer without paying by allowing the barman to believe that he was part of a larger crowd who had ordered a lot of drinks.

Des left the bar to visit a female friend. However, he had only been to her house once before and he became confused between a number of houses. Finally, though he was wrong, he was certain that he had found his friend's house. No one seemed to be in, but he managed to go through an unlocked door from the garage into the house. Inside, he began to play about lighting paper with his cigarette lighter. Eventually, the carpet was set alight, and he hastily smothered it with a cushion. The cushion was badly damaged. When Des woke up in the house next morning, he was confronted by the owner, Fred, who was returning from work. Des ran out, barging into Fred on the way. Fred was knocked down and suffered a broken arm.

(a) Discuss the possible criminal liability of Eddie for property offences arising out of his collection of money from the old people, and of Des arising out of the way in which he got his last pint of beer without paying. *(25 marks)*

(b) Discuss the possible criminal liability of Des arising out of the incidents at the house. *(25 marks)*

1 Identify the crimes relevant to each question, paying particular intention to the *actus reus* and *mens rea* of the offence you have identified.

2 Consider the effect of any defences that might appear to be present.

3 Following the routine set out for the previous scenario, plan and write answers to questions (a) and (b).

4 Ask your teacher or lecturer for plenty of other past papers, and plan and write answers for those. The more you do, the better the answers you will write in the examination.

Introduction

Unit 4 gives candidates a choice between the study of criminal law and the law of tort. The unit constitutes 50 per cent of the overall marks for the A2 section of the qualification, and 25 per cent of the overall marks for the A Level qualification. The Unit 4 examination is of 2 hours' duration. Candidates must answer one question on tort and write an essay from the Concepts of law unit. The first part of the examination paper will include both criminal law and tort questions, Questions 1 and 2 being criminal law and Questions 3 and 4 being tort. Candidates who choose criminal law will have to select one question to answer as will those who have chosen tort. Each question is divided into two parts, both of which must be answered. These questions are similar in style and expectation to those in parts (a) and (b) of Unit 3. There are no questions involving critical evaluation of the substantive law studied in Unit 4, critical evaluation forming the basis of the separate essay on concepts of law.

Each question on the law of tort is therefore worth 50 marks. Each part is worth 25 marks. These two parts will be a test of your ability to select and apply the law to the given scenario.

All questions require essay style answers. In Parts (a) and (b), attainment of high grades is dependent on correct identification of the issues raised by the question, sound explanation of each of the points and clear application of the law to the facts disclosed. This may involve some consideration of alternatives where the law lacks clarity in its application to the scenario. Further exam tips are provided throughout each topic and at the end of the chapter.

The nature and method of response for the concepts of law question is described before Chapter 20, Law and morality.

Unit 4B comprises six chapters:

14 The tort of negligence: general principles relating to physical damage and medical negligence: looks at the principles of negligence in the context of a claim for physical loss (personal injury and damage to property). The chapter also considers the principles of negligence in the context of a claim for clinical negligence.

15 The tort of negligence: claiming psychiatric damage and economic loss: considers the principles of negligence in relation to losses other than straightforward physical damage.

16 Product liability: liability in tort for defective goods: looks at the contribution of tort law to compensating the consumer for losses caused by defective goods.

17 Occupiers' liability: examines the duty which an occupier of premises owes to both his lawful visitors and to his unlawful visitors (trespassers).

18 The tort of nuisance and the rule in *Rylands* v *Fletcher*: considers the liability of those whose activities interfere with the smooth running of the lives of others. The chapter considers both public and private nuisance and the rule in *Rylands* v *Fletcher*.

19 Vicarious liability: examines the nature of an employer's liability for the torts of his employees committed during the course of employment

14

The tort of negligence: general principles relating to physical damage and medical negligence

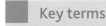

Introduction

If one person is injured or suffers physical damage to his property through the carelessness of another, he may be able to bring an action in negligence. Negligence is a tort (or civil wrong) and it is one of the commonest and most important civil actions.

To win a claim for negligence, the claimant must show that:

- the defendant owed a duty of care to the claimant – examined in Topic 2 of this chapter
- the defendant breached that duty of care – examined in Topic 3 of this chapter
- by breaking the duty of care, the defendant caused loss to the claimant – examined in Topic 4 of this chapter.

Once the claimant has established his claim in negligence, it is open to the defendant to show a defence, and we consider this in Topic 5 of this chapter before examining remedies open to the claimant in Topic 6.

Finally, Topic 7 of this chapter considers the principles of negligence – duty, breach and the causation of damage – in the context of medical negligence.

In this topic you will learn how to:

- explain what is meant by the term 'duty of care'
- identify and explain the 'neighbour test' and the *Caparo* three-part test for identifying when a duty of care exists
- identify an omission.

Key terms

Duty of care: a duty which the law says one person owes to another to take proper care of the other.

Key cases

Donoghue v Stevenson (1932): a person owes a duty to anyone who is his 'neighbour'; a neighbour is a person the defendant should reasonably be thinking of when considering his actions.

1 When does a duty of care exist?

'**Duty of care**' is a legal phrase which means that one person has a responsibility to take proper care not to injure or cause loss to another.

Although the idea of negligence has been around for a very long time, there was originally no single test to decide when one person owed a duty of care to another. Instead, the law contained a limited set of individual liabilities based on specific relationships or circumstances. Examples included the relationship between a ferry company and its passengers, the responsibilities of an innkeeper and the duty owed by those handling weapons and ammunition. This state of affairs became increasingly difficult to manage, not least because there was no good reason why some categories of people were able to claim while others were not.

The House of Lords therefore developed a single test to decide when one person should owe a duty to another. This step was taken in the case of **Donoghue v Stevenson (1932)**, when Lord Atkin stated:

> The rule that you are to love your neighbour becomes in law: You must not injure your neighbour; and the lawyer's question: Who is my neighbour? receives a restricted reply. You must take reasonable care to avoid acts or omissions which you can reasonably foresee would be likely to injure your neighbour. Who, then, in law is my neighbour? The answer seems to be persons who are so closely and directly affected by my act that I ought reasonably to have them in contemplation as being so affected when I am directing my mind to the acts or omissions which are called in question.

The effect of this test is that a person owes a duty to take care of another whenever it is reasonable for them to think about the consequences of their actions on others, and the importance of *Donoghue* v *Stevenson* (1932) in the development of English law is that it effectively established a single action for negligence.

The courts were quick to recognise that this new duty of care existed in a number of commonly occurring circumstances. These include:

■ A manufacturer of goods owes a duty to the ultimate consumer of the goods. This, of course, was established by the decision in *Donoghue* v *Stevenson* (1932) itself. The claimant had fallen ill after drinking ginger beer bought for her by her friend. The ginger beer was poisoned because it contained a decomposed snail, but the claimant had not seen this, as the bottle containing the drink was made of opaque glass. The House of Lords decided that, assuming the facts could be proved, the claimant could sue the manufacturer of the ginger beer as the manufacturer owed a duty to ensure that its products were safe to drink. Chapter 16, Product liability examines consumer protection law in more detail.

■ A user of the road owes a duty to other users of the road. This means that drivers, passengers, cyclists and pedestrians should all behave to keep each other safe, and a common consequence of a road traffic accident is an action in negligence against the person whose carelessness caused it.

■ A professional person, such as a solicitor, an accountant or a surveyor, owes a duty to his client to practise his profession properly. Professional negligence is an expanding area of liability, and most professional people are required to have appropriate insurance. Frequently, there is an overlap with contract law as the client will have engaged the services of his adviser, but this is often not the case with doctors, whose services are provided by the state. Negligence therefore is particularly important in this respect, and we examine the liability of doctors later in this chapter in Topic 5.

■ An employer owes his employees a duty to keep them safe in the workplace. This duty has been largely supplanted by health and safety legislation, but a claim for an accident at work usually includes a claim for negligence.

Establishing a duty of care in new sets of circumstances

While most claims in negligence will fall into one of the established categories, the courts have made it clear that the duty of care can be extended to cover new circumstances. However, after a period when liability risked expanding too quickly, the courts have adopted a more restrictive (albeit flexible) approach, following the decision of the House of Lords in **Caparo v Dickman (1990)**. The case itself concerned the negligent preparation of a set of accounts, and we examine it more fully in Chapter 16, Product liability, where we consider liability for economic loss; but for present purposes, the importance of the decision is the test which it laid down for considering when a duty of care exists in a new situation. The House of Lords stated that a duty of care exists if:

1 it is reasonably foreseeable to the defendant that his negligence will cause injury, damage or loss to the claimant;

2 there is a relationship of sufficient proximity between the two; and

3 it would be fair, just and reasonable to impose liability.

It is possible to criticise the three-part test in *Caparo* v *Dickman* (1990). First, it is not precise, as it is difficult to know what terms such as 'fair', 'just' and 'reasonable' mean. Secondly, some of the elements overlap, for instance if two people have a relationship of close proximity it is almost

> **Key cases**
>
> **Caparo v Dickman (1990)**: the modern test for establishing when a duty of care exists in a new set of circumstances is based on reasonable foreseeability, proximity and fairness.

inevitable that it is reasonably foreseeable that the actions of one might injure the other. In reality, the test is a set of guidelines to help the court to reach a sensible decision as to when a duty should be introduced to a new area of liability. The court will consider questions of policy such as:

- which party is in the better position to buy insurance
- whether it is likely that a new duty will prevent accidents in the future or whether it will simply discourage people from undertaking normal activities for fear of being sued
- whether the claimant should have a responsibility to look after himself.

In particular the House of Lords has emphasised that the approach in *Caparo v Dickman* (1990) is 'incremental'. This means that liability will only be extended to new areas step by step and by comparison with existing areas of similar liability. This should therefore prevent a future litigation 'free for all', leading to large increases in the types of loss that can be claimed for.

One example of this type of reasoning is the decision in **Watson v British Boxing Board of Control (2001)**. The claimant was a boxer, whose injuries, following a fight organised by the defendant, were made worse because proper medical equipment and doctors trained to use it were not immediately available at the ring side. The court decided that the defendant owed a duty to provide proper medical back-up because injuries in a boxing match were foreseeable, the defendant both promoted and profited from the activity and the defendant controlled the organisation of the event.

By contrast, the court was not prepared to find that a duty of care existed in **Sutradhar v National Environment Research Council (2006)**. The claimant lived in Bangladesh and had fallen ill after drinking water poisoned by arsenic. He sued the NERC on the ground that one of its agencies had produced a report on water resources in Bangladesh and, he claimed, had given the impression that the water was safe to drink. The court held that no duty existed for a variety of reasons: the defendant had not in fact said that it was declaring the water safe, the defendant had no responsibility for the water supply, the information was publicly available and therefore there were many potential claimants and the effect of any liability would be to discourage anyone from making information generally available.

A final example is **Calvert v William Hill (2008)**. The claimant suffered financial ruin after his gambling addiction ran completely out of control. He sued the defendant, a well-known bookmaker, for damages, saying, among other claims, that it owed a duty to 'problem' gamblers to offer them help and to prevent them from further gambling. The court rejected this argument on the grounds that it was impossible for a bookmaker to identify from among its customers the small number of gamblers with an uncontrollable habit, and that for a bookmaker to take such steps would be an interference with the gambler's personal liberty and freedom of choice.

Omissions

In most cases when a duty of care exists, it is because the person concerned has chosen to undertake a particular activity, such as drive a car or manufacture ginger beer. The duty is then a duty not to cause harm to others, such as other road users or the consumer of the ginger beer, while undertaking that activity. In these circumstances, the person carrying out the activity will be liable for both his acts (such as pulling out of a side road or mixing in dangerous ingredients) and his omissions (such as not stopping at a red light or failing to check the bottling process for snails).

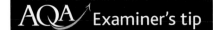

AQA Examiner's tip

When discussing whether a duty of care exists, use the three-part framework laid down in Caparo v Dickman (1990) as a guideline for your answer.

■ **Key cases**

Watson v British Boxing Board of Control (2001): a duty of care will exist where loss is foreseeable and the defendant both controls and profits from the activity.

Sutradhar v National Environment Research Council (2006): no duty of care exists when the defendant has not taken on a responsibility and where there were a very large number of potential claims.

Calvert v William Hill (2008): no duty of care exists when it is impracticable for a defendant to take action and when any claimant has a responsibility towards himself.

However, negligence does not normally impose a general duty of care whereby a person is under a duty to look out for everyone around him and to prevent harm coming to them. In these circumstances, if a person fails to act there is no liability for this **omission**. If a person is walking through the park and sees a small child in danger of drowning in a paddling pool or a teenager about to climb an electricity pylon, he has no obligation to intervene, even to save life at no risk to his own.

Thus, in **Ancell v McDermott (1993)**, when the claimant was killed in a road accident caused by an oil spillage on the road, of which the police were aware, there was no liability, as the police owed no general duty of care to warn motorists. The exception to this rule is where there is some sort of existing relationship between the claimant and the victim so that the defendant does owe a general duty to prevent harm. One example is a school which owes a general duty of protection to its children: whereas a member of the public can walk past and not assist a child drowning in a paddling pool, the teacher in charge of the class should act. An example is **Barnes v Hampshire County Council (1969)**, where a school was liable when it released the children early, before the parents arrived, and one of them was injured on the road. A member of the public would have had no duty to ensure the children's safety on the road, but the school did.

Topic illustration

Consider this scenario:

> Malcolm, in order to celebrate passing his driving test earlier in the day, drove to his local pub and drank four pints of beer. He then set off for home driving at speeds in excess of 50mph although it was a built-up area, but collided with a car being driven by Nina. The police accident investigation established that Malcolm was over the drink-drive limit, that Nina had been using her mobile telephone at the time of the accident and that both vehicles had strayed into the middle of the road. Malcolm has stated that he did not realise the effect the alcohol would have on him, and Nina is particularly upset because she had to abandon her car by the roadside overnight, thus allowing an unknown person to steal her wheels.

Should Nina want to sue Malcolm in negligence, she must first show that Malcolm owes a duty of care.

This should be straightforward. The fact that one road user owes a duty of care to others is one of the best examples of a duty of care under the principles *Donoghue* v *Stevenson* (1932).

If there is any doubt, Nina should be able to establish the existence of a duty under the principles in *Caparo* v *Dickman* (1990), including, for instance, the fact that injury was reasonably foreseeable and that Malcolm and Nina had a sufficient degree of proximity as they were using the same road.

Fig. 1 *Malcolm and Nina*

Activities

1 Thinking about omissions, consider why it is that the law does not require a person to take care of those around him. Ideas might relate to cost, freedom of action and proximity to the claimant. Do you think a person should be required to intervene to save another's life when there is no risk to himself?

2 Consider this scenario, which has been adapted from a past exam paper:

Maxbuild, a construction company, was demolishing a building and two of its employees, Tim and Vic, were working on the site. Tim was removing brick rubble from an upper floor. To save time, he did not set up a chute for the rubble, as he had been instructed to do. Thinking that workers below had gone for a break, he did not check before throwing bricks down. In fact, Vic was still below and his eyesight was severely damaged when a brick shattered and fragments entered his eyes. Discuss whether Tim owes a duty of care to Vic, and give reasons for your answer.

You should now be able to:

- identify situations in which a duty of care exists

- explain the reasoning used by judges when deciding whether a duty of care exists in new circumstances.

2 Breaching the duty of care

Once the claimant has established that a duty of care exists, he must then go on to show that the defendant has breached the duty. The court will use the 'reasonable person' test: did the defendant's actions fall below those of the reasonable person in the same circumstances? The famous, and slightly more formal, statement of this test is found in *Blyth* v *Birmingham Waterworks* (1856):

> Negligence is the omission to do something which a reasonable man, guided upon those considerations which ordinarily regulate the conduct of human affairs, would do, or doing something which a prudent and reasonable man would not do. (Alderson B)

Note, however, that if the defendant did act as the reasonable person would have done, then he is not liable even though the claimant has suffered an injury or a loss. English law recognises that there can be a genuine accident for which no one is to blame.

The **'reasonable person' test** is objective: in other words the defendant's actions are measured against the standard of the reasonable person (objective), and not against his own personal standards (subjective). It is not a defence for the defendant to say that he was doing his best, if his best is below what the reasonable person would have done. In **Nettleship v Weston (1971)**, a learner driver was held liable when she caused an accident, as her driving was not up to the standard of the reasonable qualified driver, even though the court accepted that she had been driving to the best of her ability. This decision may seem harsh, given that all drivers are beginners at some point and given that the defendant could do no more than she did, but it is the right decision, as it ensures that the claimant was not left without compensation just because he had the bad luck to be injured by a learner.

In this topic you will learn how to:

- identify and explain the test for establishing when a duty of care has been breached

- describe the characteristics of the reasonable person

- explain how the reasonable person behaves.

Key terms

The **'reasonable person' test**: in deciding whether a defendant has broken a duty of care that he owes, the court will ask whether he did all that the reasonable person would have done in the same circumstances.

Key cases

Nettleship v Weston (1971): the reasonable person test is objective; this means that the defendant will be measured against the standard of the reasonable person rather than against his own person standard.

AQA Examiner's tip

Remember that the rule in *Bolton v Stone* (1951) can be used both ways: just as a reasonable person does not take precautions against unlikely risks, so he does take precautions against risks that may well occur.

The 'reasonable person' test raises two questions: who is the reasonable person, and how does he act?

Who is the reasonable person?

The law has the following to say about the identity of the reasonable person:

The reasonable person is of average intelligence and self-control, and he possesses average skill and experience. The defendant cannot escape liability by saying either that he cannot make a proper decision because he is not very bright or, as we saw in *Nettleship* v *Weston* (1971), that he is a learner or beginner. In addition, the reasonable person has knowledge of other people, and will take into account their reasonably foreseeable frailties. In **Haley v London Electricity Board (1964)**, the claimant, a blind man, was injured when he fell in a trench dug by the defendant who had left it unfenced. The court decided that the reasonable electric company would have fenced the hole as blindness was not so uncommon as to be unforeseeable.

The 'reasonable person' test accepts a lower standard in two instances. If the defendant is disabled, the law requires a standard of behaviour that is reasonable for a person with that disability. In return, however, a disabled person must not exceed the reasonable limits for a person with that disability. In addition, if the defendant is either very old or very young then the court will measure his behaviour against a reasonable person of the same age. In **Mullin v Richards (1998)** the claimant and the defendant were fifteen-year-old schoolgirls engaged in a mock sword fight with plastic rulers. One of the rulers splintered and the claimant was injured in the eye. The defendant was not liable as she had shown the standard of care of the reasonable fifteen-year-old, even though the reasonable adult might have been more careful.

By contrast, the 'reasonable person' test expects a higher standard from a professional person practising his profession. Such a person must use the skill of a reasonable member of that profession. In **Philips v Whiteley (1938)** the defendant, a jeweller, was held not to be liable after his client contracted blood poisoning after having her ears pierced. The jeweller's instruments were clean by the standard of the reasonable jeweller even though that might be below the standard expected in, for instance, a clinic.

How does the reasonable person behave?

In deciding how the reasonable person will behave in a given situation, the court considers the interests of the parties and the interests of society generally, and how any decision will have an impact in the future. The court will be careful not to impose too high a standard of care as it knows that society has limited resources. The following are examples of factors which the court may take into account:

1 Likelihood of injury

The less likely an accident is to happen, the more justified the defendant is in ignoring the risk. In contrast, if an accident is more likely to happen, then the reasonable person will take precautions against it. In **Bolton v Stone (1951)**, the claimant was injured when she was struck on the head by a cricket ball that had been hit over a 17-foot-high fence, 78 yards from the wicket. The evidence was that in 28 years only six balls had gone over the fence, and that this was the first to have hit someone. The claimant's case failed, as the defendants had acted reasonably in not taking further precautions against such an unlikely risk.

2 The seriousness of the consequences

The more serious the consequences, the higher the defendant's duty of care. In **Paris v Stepney Borough Council (1951)**, the defendant employer was liable when the claimant was blinded in one eye when a splinter flew up from his work. The job was not normally one which an employer would supply goggles for, but because the claimant only had the sight in one eye to begin with the defendant should have taken greater care as to lose an eye in those circumstances is very much more serious.

3 The value of the conduct

If what the defendant is doing is socially valuable then that may justify him taking extra risks. In **Watt v Hertfordshire County Council (1954)** the claimant fireman was injured when, on his way to a road traffic accident to rescue a woman trapped under a bus, the lifting gear shifted and squashed him. The accident happened because the lorry was not the correct vehicle for the lifting gear, but the claimant failed because the court decided that the reasonable fire brigade would respond to an emergency quickly rather than waste time trying to find the correct lorry. In the long run more people would be protected.

4 Cost of precautions

The easier, cheaper and more practicable it is for the defendant to minimise or eliminate a risk, the more likely he is to be negligent if he does not. In **Latimer v AEC (1953)**, the claimant, an employee of the defendant, broke his leg when he slipped at work on floors made wet by overnight flooding. The defendant was not liable because they had carried out all reasonable precautions such as sweeping away surface water and putting down straw.

Topic illustration

Consider again the scenario concerning the collision between Malcolm and Nina:

> Malcolm, in order to celebrate passing his driving test earlier in the day, drove to his local pub and drank four pints of beer. He then set off for home driving at speeds in excess of 50mph, although it was a built-up area, but collided with a car being driven by Nina. The police accident investigation established that Malcolm was over the drink-drive limit, that Nina had been using her mobile telephone at the time of the accident and that both vehicles had strayed into the middle of the road. Malcolm has stated that he did not realise the effect the alcohol would have on him, and Nina is particularly upset because she had to abandon her car by the roadside overnight thus allowing an unknown person to steal her wheels.

Having established that Malcolm owes her a duty of care, Nina now needs to show that he breached the duty. She should perhaps take the following factors into account:

- The test is based on what the reasonable person would do. This test is objective: the fact that Malcolm does not know of the effects of alcohol is irrelevant, as the reasonable person would.

- Equally irrelevant is the fact that Malcolm is a very inexperienced driver. The standard of care required is that of the reasonable driver. The reasonable driver does not drive too fast and does not stray into the middle of the road.

- Nina will be able to use cases such as *Bolton* v *Stone* (1951) (the reasonable person takes precautions against foreseeable risks) and *Paris* v *Stepney Borough Council* (1951) (the reasonable person takes extra care if any damage is likely to be serious).

Activities

1 Thinking about the facts of *Haley* v *London Electricity Board* (1964), consider the advantages and disadvantages of imposing liability in that case. Did the benefits outweigh the costs?

2 Remind yourself of the facts of the scenario relating to Tim and Vic (Activity 2 on p239). Assuming that Tim does have a duty to Vic, consider whether he broke the duty. Which cases might be relevant?

You should now be able to:

- understand the role of the reasonable person test

- explain the factors which govern how the reasonable person acts.

- identify and explain the difference between causation and remoteness

- explain the 'but for' test in relation to causation, and the reasonable foreseeability test in relation to remoteness

- identify and explain the effect of an intervening cause.

Key terms

Causation: the relationship between two events, whereby the first caused the second to happen.

The 'but for' test: the test for determining whether causation exists. If the defendant had not acted negligently would the damage still have occurred? If so, then something other than the negligence caused it, and there is no causation.

Remoteness of damage: a defendant is not liable for those losses which are too far removed from his actions.

Reasonable foreseeability: the test for remoteness of damage. If an item of damage is not a reasonably foreseeable consequence of the defendant's negligence, then the claimant cannot claim for it.

Key cases

McWilliams v Arrol Ltd (1962): a defendant will not be liable, even though he has breached a duty of care that he owes, if the claimant would have suffered the same loss even if the defendant had done everything he should have.

The Wagon Mound (No. 1) (1961): the test for remoteness of damage is reasonable foreseeability.

3 Causation and remoteness of damage

The claimant must prove that the breach of duty by the defendant and the loss suffered as a result are sufficiently closely linked. This must be answered in two parts:

- Causation: was the damage caused by the defendant's breach of duty, or was it actually caused by something else?
- Remoteness of damage: is the loss suffered too far removed from the defendant's breach of duty as to be unforeseeable?

Causation

Causation is decided by the **'but for' test**: but for the defendant's breach, would the loss have occurred? A different way of putting this is to ask whether, if the defendant had done all that he should have, the loss would still have occurred. If the answer is that the loss would still have occurred, then it must have been caused by something other than the defendant's negligence, and the defendant is therefore not liable. In **McWilliams v Arrol Ltd (1962)** the claimant, a scaffolder who had not been supplied by his employer with the correct safety harness, fell and was killed. The defendant employer clearly owed a duty of care (the duty owed by an employer to an employee) and had equally clearly breached the duty by not supplying the harness. Nevertheless, the claim failed because the employer was able to show that that claimant would not have worn the harness even if it had been supplied, as experienced workers in the industry usually did not. In other words, had the employer done all that it should have, the claimant would still have been killed.

Occasionally, a strict interpretation of the 'but for' test would deny damages to a claimant who should, by any standard of fairness, be compensated. In these circumstances, the courts adapt the test. One such example is *Fairchild* v *Glenhaven Funeral Services* (2002). The claimant, across his working life, had worked for a number of employers each of which had negligently exposed him to asbestos fibres. One such exposure caused mesothelioma, a lung disease, but it was impossible to say which employer was responsible for that exposure. On a strict reading of the 'but for' test, the claimant would receive no damages, as each individual employer could show that, even if they had acted responsibly, the claimant would probably still have contracted the disease, as the chances were that the exposure occurred while working for one of the others. The court therefore adapted the 'but for' test, so that the claimant could take action against any employer that had materially contributed to the risk of contributing to the disease.

Remoteness of damage

Only losses which are not too remote, or too far removed from the original negligence, are recoverable. The test for **remoteness of damage** is whether a loss is a **reasonably foreseeable** consequence of the defendant's negligence. If a loss is not reasonably foreseeable then it is not recoverable. This approach was established by the decision in **The Wagon Mound (No. 1) (1961)**. Due to the defendant's negligence, oil had been spilled in the water of a harbour, and the oil had drifted across to the claimant's wharf where welding work was being carried out. Having taken advice that it was safe to do so, the claimant continued welding secure in the knowledge that oil in the sea at sea temperature is not flammable. Nevertheless, the oil ignited, and the ensuing blaze badly damaged the claimant's property. However, the claimant's action failed as, although pollution damage is a reasonably foreseeable consequence of spilling oil in the sea, fire damage is not.

There are, however, three instances when damage can be claimed even if it is not entirely reasonably foreseeable. These are when:

- a claimant may recover damages when the specific losses that occurred are not foreseeable as long as the general category or type of loss is foreseeable
- a claimant may recover damages if the loss is foreseeable, but the precise manner in which it happened is not
- a claimant may recover damages if the type of loss is foreseeable but the full extent of the loss is not.

1 Kind of damage caused

If the general type of damage is reasonably foreseeable then it does not matter that the precise form which occurred was not. In **Bradford v Robinson Rentals (1967)** the claimant was a van driver sent out by his employer on a very cold day. His van was unheated and he suffered frostbite. Although frostbite in this country is not reasonably foreseeable, the claimant's action succeeded as some sort of cold weather harm was reasonably foreseeable.

2 Sequence of events is not foreseeable

If the damage which occurred was reasonably foreseeable, it is not necessary to foresee the precise sequence of events that led to the damage. In **Hughes v Lord Advocate (1963)** the defendant left unguarded an open manhole surrounded by paraffin lamps. The claimant, a young boy, while investigating, knocked one of the lamps into the hole and was burned in the subsequent explosion. His claim succeeded because burn injuries caused by an unattended lamp were foreseeable even if what actually happened was not. A similar outcome occurred in **Jolley v Sutton London Borough Council (2000)**. The defendant council, in breach of is duty, left a derelict boat on waste ground for more than two years. The claimant, a child, was badly injured when he propped up the boat in order to try and repair it and the boat collapsed on him. His claim succeeded because it was reasonably foreseeable that children would be injured in some manner if they played on the boat, even if what actually happened was not.

3 Extent of the damage

Provided that some of his damage is reasonably foreseeable, the claimant can claim for the full extent of his loss. In **Vacwell Engineering v BDH Chemicals (1970)** the defendant negligently supplied a chemical to the claimant without a warning that the chemical was liable to explode if it came into contact with water. The claimant placed some of the chemical in a sink and the resulting explosion extensively damaged its premises. The claimant was able to claim for its full loss as the explosion was foreseeable even if the scale was not. This rule applies if, in a personal injury case, the extent of injuries is made worse by a hidden and unforeseen frailty on the part of the claimant (the 'thin skull' rule). In **Smith v Leech Brain & Co. (1962)** the claimant, through his employer's negligence, suffered a burn to his lip. This caused a cancer, due to a medical condition which made him vulnerable to this sort of illness. The claimant died as a result, and his estate was able to claim both for the burn and for the death.

Intervening causes

Sometimes the law will not impose liability for negligence, even though damage is reasonably foreseeable, because the defendant's negligence does not cause the loss directly but instead sets the scene for something or someone else to inflict the loss. The something or someone else is called an **intervening cause**, and the law has to decide which intervening causes are sufficiently significant as to free the defendant from liability, in other words which intervening causes break the chain of causation.

Key cases

Bradford v Robinson Rentals (1967): as long as the type of damage is reasonably foreseeable it does not matter that the specific loss is not.

Hughes v Lord Advocate (1963) and **Jolley v Sutton London Borough Council (2000):** the specific sequence of events leading to a loss does not have to be foreseeable as long as the nature of the resulting damage is.

Vacwell Engineering v BDH Chemicals (1970) and **Smith v Leech Brain & Co. (1962):** provided that some damage is foreseeable, then the full extent can be claimed.

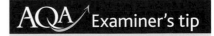
Examiner's tip

When discussing remoteness of damage, think carefully about the three rules outlined. Usually, at least one will be relevant.

Key terms

Intervening cause: something or someone forming a link between the actions of the defendant and the loss suffered by the claimant.

A natural event as an intervening cause will normally free the claimant from further liability. In **Carslogie Steamship Co. v Royal Norwegian Government (1952)**, the defendant negligently caused damage to the claimant's ship. The ship's schedule was therefore changed to bring it home for repairs, and this meant that it was at sea when it would otherwise not have been. While at sea, the ship sustained further damage in a severe storm, but the claimant, while liable for the original damage, was not liable for the storm damage.

If the intervening cause is the actions of a third party, whether the defendant is freed from further liability normally depends on how blameworthy the third party is. If the third party is a criminal, then the chain of causation is normally broken and the defendant is not liable for further losses. In **Lamb v Camden London Borough Council (1981)** the defendant council's negligence led to the claimant's house being flooded. The claimant vacated the property, but squatters moved in and caused considerable damage. The defendant, however, was not liable for this damage as causation had been broken. Equally, a grossly negligent third party can also break the chain. In **Knightley v Johns (1982)** the defendant negligently caused a road accident in a tunnel. The police attended, and a police motorcycle rider was instructed to drive against the flow of traffic in the tunnel to close it from the other end. Not surprisingly, the motorcyclist caused a second accident, but the defendant was not liable for the losses caused by that accident as the negligence of the police had broken the chain of causation. By contrast, the actions of a third party acting without blame or even instinctively will not free the defendant from the further consequences. In **Scott v Shepherd (1773)** the defendant threw a lit firecracker into a crowded market. The firework was thrown on by two further people, before exploding and injuring the claimant. The defendant was liable for the injuries of the claimant, even though he had not thrown the firecracker at him directly, because the two middlemen were acting instinctively in an effort to protect themselves.

A final example of an intervening cause is when the claimant suffers damage over and above that caused by the defendant's negligence because of his own subsequent actions. The claimant will be able to claim for such further damage but only if his own actions were reasonable. In **McKew v Holland Hannen and Cubitts (1969)** the defendant's negligence injured the claimant's leg in such a way that the leg was liable to give way without warning. The claimant was furthered injured when he attempted to walk down some stairs that had no handrail and he fell because his leg gave way. The defendant was not liable for the second set of injuries because it was unreasonable for the claimant to have acted in the way that he did, given his injuries.

Topic illustration

Consider again the scenario concerning the collision between Malcolm and Nina:

> Malcolm, in order to celebrate passing his driving test earlier in the day, drove to his local pub and drank four pints of beer. He then set off for home driving at speeds in excess of 50mph although it was a built-up area, but collided with a car being driven by Nina. The police accident investigation established that Malcolm was over the drink-drive limit, that Nina had been using her mobile telephone at the time of the accident and that both vehicles had strayed into the middle of the road. Malcolm has stated that he did not realise the effect the alcohol would have on him, and Nina is particularly upset because she had to abandon her car by the roadside overnight thus allowing an unknown person to steal her wheels.

Given that Malcolm both owed a duty of care, and breached that duty, Nina now needs to consider the issues of causation and remoteness:

- Causation should not be a problem: Malcolm's actions led to the accident.
- With respect to remoteness, Nina can claim all reasonably foreseeable losses. Some damage to her car and to the contents of the car is foreseeable, as is some personal injury. Nina should therefore be able to claim all her losses, even though they were not specifically foreseeable, using the rules from cases such as *Hughes* v *Lord Advocate* (1963) and *Smith* v *Leech Brain & Co.* (1962).
- However, it is unlikely that Nina can claim for the stolen wheels. Although Malcolm's actions led to the loss of the wheels, there was an intervening cause in the form of a criminal third party.

Activities

1 Make two lists of intervening causes: one where the cause does break liability and one where it does not. Consider each list – do its members have anything in common?

2 Thinking again about the scenario relating to Tim and Vic (Activity 2 on p239), apply the tests for causation and remoteness of damage and decide whether each is satisfied in relation to Vic's injuries. Are Vic's injuries entirely foreseeable, and does it affect his claim if they are not?

You should now be able to:

- understand the concepts of causation and remoteness
- apply the 'but for' and reasonable foreseeability tests
- identify situations where causation may not be broken.

4 Defences to a claim in negligence

A defence allows a defendant to escape liability even where all the elements of the tort in question exist. Two possible defences to a claim in negligence are contributory negligence, which allows the court to apportion blame between the two parties, and consent (sometimes known as *volenti non fit injuria*) which is a complete defence thus resulting in the defendant paying nothing by way of damages.

Contributory negligence

Contributory negligence in its modern form was introduced by the Law Reform (Contributory Negligence) Act 1945. To set up the defence, the defendant need not show that the claimant owed him a duty of care, but he must show both that the claimant's behaviour was below the standard of the reasonable person and that this behaviour contributed to the claimant's loss. In deciding these issues, the court will look to the principles discussed above relating to breach of duty (for instance a lower standard of behaviour might be expected of a careless claimant who was a child) and causation (for instance whether the damage caused was a reasonably foreseeable consequence of the claimant's own negligence).

Contributory negligence can be applied in two different ways. The first is where the claimant is partly to blame for the accident happening. An example is **Brannon v Airtours (1999)**. The claimant, a holidaymaker, was at a party night organised by the defendant. The claimant was injured when he climbed onto a table in order to get out, and collided with a low fan hanging from the ceiling. The defendant was held to be negligent in arranging the room in such a way as to make it difficult for people to get out without climbing over the furniture, but the claimant was found to be partly to blame for actually standing on a table despite warnings not to.

In this topic you will learn how to:
- identify and explain the defence of contributory negligence
- identify and explain the defence of consent.

Key terms

Contributory negligence: the claimant's loss is caused in part by his own actions and not solely by the actions of the defendant.

Key cases

Brannon v Airtours (1999): ignoring warnings can amount to contributory negligence.

AQA Examiner's tip

Never, in your answer to a legal problem, jump straight to the defence, however obvious it may seem. Always describe the liability of the defendant first, because without that there is nothing for the defence to be a defence against.

Key cases

Froom v Butcher (1975) and **O'Connell v Jackson (1971)**: failing to take basic precautions can amount to contributory negligence.

The second way in which contributory negligence can be applied is where the claimant was not to blame for the accident, but his actions made his injuries or losses worse than they should have been. Two obvious examples are not wearing a seatbelt in a car (**Froom v Butcher (1975)**) and not wearing a crash helmet on a motorbike (**O'Connell v Jackson (1971)**).

If the defendant is successful in establishing contributory negligence, then the court will reduce the claimant's damages to reflect his own carelessness. The basic principle is that if the court feels that the claimant is say 30 per cent to blame for the losses which he suffered, then his damages will be reduced by 30 per cent. The claimant in *Brannon* v *Airtours* (1999) thus lost 50 per cent of his damages, and in *Froom* v *Butcher* (1975) it was stated that someone who does not wear a seatbelt can typically expect to lose 15–25 per cent of their damages.

Consent

Consent, as a defence, applies when the claimant knows that there is a risk of the defendant acting in a negligent way and freely consents to take that risk. This is illustrated by **Morris v Murray (1990)**. The claimant and the defendant had spent several hours drinking, and then decided to go for a trip in the defendant's light aircraft. The plane crashed, the defendant was killed and the claimant badly injured. The claimant's subsequent action against the estate of the pilot for his undoubted negligence failed, as the claimant was fully aware of the risk of negligence on the part of the defendant, yet decided to get into the plane anyway.

The fact that consent must be freely given can lead to the defence failing. In **Smith v Baker (1891)** the claimant was an employee working on a railway line when he was injured by material falling from a crane that swung overhead. The defendant argued the defence of consent, on the ground that the crane had been swinging overhead in such a fashion for many weeks, but that the claimant had continued to work and had therefore consented to the risk. The court rejected this because simply knowing of the risk did not amount to consent particularly where the claimant had little choice but to continue to work as he needed the job. In **Haynes v Harwood (1935)** the defendant's negligence had allowed a horse to run amok in a busy street. The claimant was injured when he tried to stop the horse. The defence of consent, made on the ground that the claimant had chosen to get involved, failed because the consent was not freely given as the claimant had felt morally obliged to try and help people in danger.

If consent is successfully pleaded by the defendant its effect is to act as a complete defence so that the claimant receives no damages. This 'all or nothing' outcome is one reason why the defence is less commonly used today as judges much prefer the flexibility of contributory negligence and the opportunity it gives to them to apportion blame between the parties.

Key terms

Consent: a defence that can be used when a claimant is aware that the defendant may act negligently but agrees to the risk.

Key cases

Morris v Murray (1990): the defence of consent will be established if the claimant knows that there is a risk that the defendant will act in a negligent way and consents to that risk.

Smith v Baker (1891): a defendant cannot establish the defence of consent on the basis of the claimant's knowledge of the risk alone: he must show that the claimant freely consented to the risk.

Haynes v Harwood (1935): the defence of consent is not available if the claimant felt morally obliged to act.

Topic illustration

Consider once again the scenario concerning the collision between Malcolm and Nina:

> Malcolm, in order to celebrate passing his driving test earlier in the day, drove to his local pub and drank four pints of beer. He then set off for home driving at speeds in excess of 50mph although it was a built-up area, but collided with a car being driven by Nina. The police accident investigation established that Malcolm was over the drink-drive limit, that Nina had been using her mobile telephone at the time of the accident and that both vehicles had strayed into the middle of the road. Malcolm has stated that he did not realise the

effect the alcohol would have on him, and Nina is particularly upset because she had to abandon her car by the roadside overnight thus allowing an unknown person to steal her wheels.

It is likely that Nina can successfully bring an action in negligence against Malcolm as she can show that he owed a duty, that he breached it and that this led to reasonably foreseeable damage. However, Nina too is at fault, and Malcolm may wish to raise the defence of contributory negligence.

■ Malcolm needs to show that Nina was also below the standard of the reasonable driver. Presumably he can do this as Nina was using a mobile telephone and had strayed into the middle of the road.

■ Malcolm also needs to show that Nina's actions were, at least in part, the cause of the accident. It might be that if Nina had been concentrating fully she could have braked sooner thus ensuring that the collision was less severe.

■ If Malcolm is able to show contributory negligence, then Nina's damages will be reduced in proportion to her contribution to the accident.

Activities

1 Consider whether the decision in *Haynes* v *Harwood* (1935) was correct.

2 Referring back to the accident involving Tim and Vic (Activity 2 on p239), consider whether Tim can raise either the defence of contributory negligence or the defence of consent against Vic.

You should now be able to:

■ explain when a defence to a claim in negligence applies

■ identify the behaviour on the part of a claimant which may allow the defendant to establish such a defence.

5 Claiming damages for negligence

The basic rule governing the calculation of damages for a claim in negligence is that the damages should restore the claimant to the position that he was in before the accident happened, at least as far as money can.

Damages for loss to property

Compensation for damage to property is usually straightforward to calculate. A court will normally award the cost of repairing the property unless this exceeds the value of the property in which case that will be paid instead. Thus, if the claimant's car is damaged in an accident, the defendant will be liable for the cost of the repairs or for the value of the car – whichever is the less. The claimant can also recover any associated losses, provided that they are foreseeable. If, for instance, the claimant's taxi is damaged and needs to spend a week in a garage for repairs, the claimant should be able to recover a week's lost fares.

Damages for personal injury

Although damages for personal injury caused by negligence use the same basic principle, the rules are more complex. This is because of the complicated nature of the loss, and because some categories of loss are difficult to translate into money terms. Damages for personal injury are divided into special damages and general damages.

In this topic you will learn how to:

■ identify and explain the principles relating to the calculation of damages in a claim for negligence.

Special damages cover the claimant's out-of-pocket expenses from the date of the accident to the date of the judgement. These can normally be calculated exactly. Examples include loss of wages, medical expenses, such as prescriptions or the hire of a wheelchair, and cost of travel to medical appointments.

General damages cover the claimant's injury and his losses for the future. These can be complex to calculate, but examples of categories of loss for which the claimant might receive damages include: pain, suffering and loss of amenity; future medical care and personal assistance; and loss of future earnings.

Pain, suffering and loss of amenity

The award for **pain, suffering and loss of amenity** compensates the claimant for his actual injury and for his physical and mental suffering. To ensure consistency, the Judicial Studies Board has laid down a framework detailing how much compensation each type of injury attracts, and factors the court should also consider include length of time in hospital, loss of life expectancy, cosmetic injuries and depression. Loss of amenity is also included in the award. This means the reduction in the quality of life of the claimant, and can include any impact on both the claimant's ability to look after himself and his hobbies and interests.

Future medical care and personal assistance

This heading covers the cost of future care required by the claimant. It can include a claim for loss of wages by a relative who gives up their job to care for the claimant.

Loss of future earnings

This heading can lead to very awkward calculations, but the basic principle is that the claimant is awarded the amount of the reduction in his annual net earnings multiplied by the number of years he had left before he retired. Reductions are made if the claimant is receiving certain types of social security payments and also for the fact that he is receiving a lifetime's earning in one lump sum and therefore can earn extra money by investing his compensation. Whether the claimant would, for instance, have received promotions (and therefore pay rises) in the future is, of course, speculative, but the court must make the best decision that it can, using such evidence as is available.

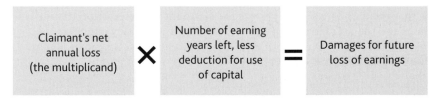

Fig. 2 *Loss of earning calculator*

Key terms

Pain, suffering and loss of amenity: that part of an award for damages which compensates a claimant for his injuries and for the consequent reduction in the quality of life.

Activity

Thinking one last time about Vic's accident on the building site (Activity 2 on p239), make a list of the items of special and general damages he might be able to claim.

You should now be able to:

■ explain briefly the principles governing an award of damages in a negligence claim

■ explain how those principles apply in a case of personal injury.

6 Medical negligence

Medical or clinical negligence refers to carelessness on the part of medically qualified practitioners such as nurses, family doctors or consultants at a hospital. Examples might include failing to diagnose an illness properly or at all, prescribing or administering the wrong drugs, failing to follow correct procedures during an operation, or failing to give proper advice to a patient so that he could make an informed choice. Such negligence can lead to personal injury, and, as such, is governed by the ordinary principles of negligence – duty of care, breach and causation – discussed in this chapter. What follows is an application of those principles in a medical context.

Duty of care and omissions

There is no doubt that a doctor treating a patient owes the patient a duty of care to practise his profession properly. By agreeing to take the patient, the doctor assumes responsibility for the patient, and it is reasonably foreseeable that a failure to exercise reasonable care could lead to personal injury. The existence of a duty of care promotes medical safety, minimises the risk of injury and gives a patient an opportunity for compensation. In response to the duty, doctors, like most professionals, take out professional insurance so that a claimant can be sure that he will receive his damages.

As explained in Topic 2, having chosen to take on a patient, a doctor is liable both for what he does (for instance prescribing the wrong drug) and for what he does not do (for instance failing to consider an X-ray). However, a doctor, like anyone else, is not under a duty, as a member of the public, to assist if he should come across someone in need of help.

One exception to this appears to be the casualty department of a hospital. In **Barnett v Chelsea and Kensington Hospital Management Committee (1968)** the claimant presented himself in the defendant's casualty department, vomiting and feeling extremely unwell. The doctor on duty refused to examine him because he too was feeling unwell, and sent him away. The court decided that the hospital did owe a duty to anyone arriving in casualty. This presumably means that a hospital cannot pick and choose which casualty patients to treat and therefore which patients to whom they owe a duty.

Breaching the duty of care

In order to satisfy the duty of care to his patient, a doctor must display the standard of care of a normal person practising his profession. The standard, therefore, will be different for a family doctor and for a consultant at a hospital. In both cases, the duty is to exercise reasonable competence and skill: if a doctor makes an error of judgement then there is no liability if a reasonable member of the profession would have made the same error.

In **Bolam v Friern Hospital Management Committee (1957)** the claimant received electric shocks as part of a treatment for psychiatric problems and had sustained fractures as a result. The risk of fractures would have been all but eliminated if the claimant had been given relaxant drugs beforehand and some doctors would have done so, but the defendant, in line with a different body of medical thought, had chosen not to because the drugs carried their own risks. The trial judge explained that:

> A doctor is not negligent, if he is acting in accordance with a practice accepted as proper by a responsible body of medical men skilled in that particular art, merely because there is a body of such opinion that takes a contrary view.

This test has two consequences. The first is that if the medical profession is split, as in the *Bolam* case, the court will refuse to choose between the two sides. As long as some reasonable practitioners would follow the defendant's course of action then the defendant is not negligent even if his side of the profession is in a minority. This is because a judge does not have the necessary knowledge to be able to make a decision, and he cannot simply choose whichever side is in the majority as that would stifle innovation given that every new technique starts as a minority. The defendant doctor in *Bolam* thus was not liable.

The second consequence appeared to be that a doctor could escape liability if he could show that he had complied with the generally accepted practice of reasonable members of his profession. This raised the question of what happened if the whole profession was acting below what should be an acceptable standard. The issue was addressed in **Bolitho v City and Hackney Health Authority (1997)**, when the House of Lords said that a court should enquire as to whether a generally accepted practice had a logical basis and whether the profession had weighed up the risks and benefits of the practice and reached a proper conclusion. In theory, therefore, it is possible for a court to find a doctor liable in negligence even though he did what any other doctor would have done, but in practice it will be rare for the court to hold that an entire profession is acting below a proper standard not least because if the leading experts in a particular field believe that a practice is the correct thing to do then that in itself suggests that the practice is a reasonable one.

A different issue relating to whether a medical defendant has broken his duty of care is the problem of medical technology advancing between the date of an alleged instance of negligence and the date of the resulting trial in court. The courts have decided that the relevant standard of care to apply is reasonable practice as it was at the time of the facts of the case. In **Roe v Minister of Health (1954)** the claimant was paralysed when he was given an injection that had been contaminated by a chemical leaking into the syringe. Medical technology at the date of the trial was able to explain how the accident had happened and how to prevent it, but the defendant escaped liability as the court judged him by the standard of the reasonable doctor who, at the time of the original incident, would not have known of the danger.

A final issue relating to breach of duty in a medical context is evidence of negligence. The normal rule is that a claimant has a burden of proof to show what happened and what actions or omissions on the part of the defendant breached the duty of care. However, in practice this can sometimes be awkward: the details of the accident are unclear and it is very difficult for the claimant formally to prove the sequence of the events. In these circumstances, the claimant may be able to use the principle of *res ipsa loquitur* ('the thing speaks for itself'). The principle applies if:

- the thing that caused damage was under the defendant's control at the relevant time
- what happened would not normally happen unless negligence was involved somewhere.

The effect of the principle is to establish a preliminary case in negligence against the defendant on the ground that, although the claimant cannot prove negligence, the very facts of the case suggest that negligence must have been present. The defendant must then show an alternative explanation for the events: if he can do this then the claimant must show negligence in the ordinary way, but if he cannot then he is unlikely to escape liability.

■ **Key cases**

Bolitho v City and Hackney Health Authority (1997): a court should enquire whether a medical practice can be justified on the basis of relevant risks and benefits.

Roe v Minister of Health (1954): when judging the standard of care of a doctor, a court should consider the state of medical knowledge at the time of the events of the case rather than at the time of the trial.

■ **Key terms**

Res ipsa loquitur: the facts of a case themselves suggest that negligence must have occurred.

The principle was explained in **Scott v London and St Katharine Dock (1865)**. The claimant was hit by some bags of sugar which had fallen from the defendant's warehouse. He was able to recover damages, even though he could not prove the sequence of events which had led to bags falling, as the bags were under the control of the defendant, bags do not normally crash onto the street without negligence and the defendants were unable to offer an alternative explanation. The principle can be very useful in a medical context, where a patient has little idea of what actually happened, perhaps because he did not understand what was happening or because he was unconscious or too ill at the relevant time, but its application is likely to be limited to clear-cut cases such as removing the wrong kidney or amputating the wrong leg. Three case law examples are **Mahon v Osborne (1939)**, in which a swab was left inside a patient after an operation, **Cassidy v Ministry of Health (1950)**, in which the claimant, having been treated for a condition of the hand that had restricted movement in two fingers, was unable to use any of the four fingers on that hand properly, and **Saunders v Leeds Western Health Authority (1984)**, in which a child with a healthy heart suffered a cardiac arrest during a routine anaesthetic.

However, the principle is likely to be of less relevance where the facts are not clear-cut and where it is not obvious that negligence is the only realistic explanation. In **Ratcliffe v Plymouth and Torbay Health Authority (1998)** the claimant, after a successful operation on his ankle, had been given a spinal injection to relieve pain, but the injection had led to neurological problems. Neither side was able to prove what had actually happened or why this injury had occurred. However, the defendant was able to show by way of expert evidence that the state of the claimant's back was such that the injury might have occurred even if there had been no negligence. Given that the defendant had now shown that there was a possible alternative explanation, it was down to the claimant to prove actual negligence, which he was unable to do, and thus his claim was unsuccessful.

Causation

Like any other negligence case, the claimant in a medical negligence case must be able to show that his claim satisfies the 'but for' test, in other words the negligence on the part of the defendant was the thing which caused the loss rather than something else. We illustrated this with the decision in *McWilliams* v *Arrol Ltd* (1962) in Topic 3 (see p242). A further example, in a medical context, is provided by *Barnett* v *Chelsea and Kensington Hospital Management Committee* (1968), which we discussed earlier in this topic. In that case, the doctor, in breach of the duty owed a duty to treat anyone presenting himself in the casualty department of the hospital, had sent the claimant home. The claimant died, but the legal action against the doctor for his negligence failed because even if the doctor had done all that he should, the claimant would still have died as he was suffering from an untreatable arsenic poisoning. In other words, it was not the negligence that caused the death.

The courts have taken a strict approach in their application of the 'but for' test in situations where there are a number of possible causes. In **Wilsher v Essex Area Health Authority (1988)**, the claimant suffered blindness as a result of events surrounding his birth. There were six possible causes: five relating to various medical conditions, and the sixth relating to the negligence of the hospital. The House of Lords sent the case to be tried again, stating that the claimant, using the normal civil standard of balance of probabilities, had to prove that it was more likely than not that it was the negligence rather than the medical conditions which had caused the blindness.

Key cases

Scott v London and St Katharine Dock (1865): negligence was established because the facts of the case themselves suggested that at some point the defendant must have been negligent.

Mahon v Osborne (1939), Cassidy v Ministry of Health (1950) and **Saunders v Leeds Western Health Authority (1984)** all demonstrate that negligence can be established, even in the absence of clear evidence, if the facts of the case suggest that negligence must have occurred at some point.

Ratcliffe v Plymouth and Torbay Health Authority (1998): the principle of *res ipsa loquitur* is likely to be of limited use where any alleged negligence is not clear-cut.

Wilsher v Essex Area Health Authority (1988): if a loss suffered by a patient could have been caused by a number of things, not all of which are negligence on the part of the doctors, the claimant needs to prove that it was more likely than not that it was the negligence that was the cause.

Hotson v East Berkshire Health Authority (1987) and **Gregg v Scott (2005)**: courts are reluctant to award damages on the basis that medical negligence may have reduced a patient's chances of recovery.

Chester v Afshar (2004): a doctor has a duty to explain risks of surgery to a patient.

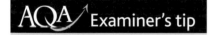

Examiner's tip

When considering medical negligence, it is important to discuss the normal rules of negligence first before trying to apply them in a medical context.

A similarly strict approach has been taken in the 'loss of chance' cases, in other words incidents where medical negligence increased the chances of permanent damage in circumstances where there was already a risk because of the nature of the medical condition. In **Hotson v East Berkshire Health Authority (1987)**, the claimant fell and was taken to hospital, but an injury to his hip was not discovered for five days by which time there was permanent damage. The evidence was that there was a 75 per cent chance that the damage would have occurred even if the injury had been properly diagnosed, and on that basis the House of Lords refused a claim for damages as the claimant was unable to show, on the balance of probabilities, that it was more likely than not that the negligence had contributed to the loss. A similar approach was taken in **Gregg v Scott (2005)**. The defendant's negligence led to a cancer going undetected for nine months longer than it should have done. The result was that the claimant's chances of being alive and disease-free in ten years' time were reduced from 42 per cent to 25 per cent, but again the House of Lords refused to allow a loss of chance to form the basis of liability.

A different scenario is illustrated by **Chester v Afshar (2004)**. The defendant operated on the claimant's spine having failed to warn her that there was a 1–2 per cent risk of paralysis. Although the operation was carried out with proper care, the claimant was left paralysed. She sued for negligence, not in the carrying out of the medical procedure, but rather in the failure to warn, saying that if she had known of the risk she would not have had the operation at that time (although she may have had the operation at a later date when she would have faced the same risk). Using the normal 'but for' test, her claim would fail as, even if the doctor had done all that he should, the claimant could still have been left paralysed. However, the House of Lords allowed the claim for damages on the ground that if they refused the claim then the doctor's duty to inform his patients of any risks would have no practical effect as there would be no consequence if it were broken.

Topic illustration

Consider the following scenario:

> Shortly after undergoing abdominal surgery at the Royal Foxton Hospital, Gertrude began to suffer stomach pains. An investigation revealed that one of the clips used in her operation had been left inside when it should have been removed. Gertrude was booked in for surgery the next day, and given some tablets to take overnight to help her symptoms. Gertrude did not take the tablets as directed with the result that the operation was more difficult than it should have been, and Gertrude took longer to recover. In addition, she also suffered some further temporary, but unusual, complications.

Gertrude has a potential claim in negligence against the hospital, but in order to be successful she will need to have regard to each of the following points:

■ Firstly, she needs to establish that the hospital owes a duty of care. This should be straightforward using a simple application of the principles in *Donoghue* v *Stevenson* (1932) and *Caparo* v *Dickman* (1990).

■ Secondly, she needs to show that the hospital breached the duty of care. Presumably, the reasonable hospital does not leave clips inside a patient, and we can illustrate this by citing cases such as *Paris* v *Stepney Borough Council* (1951), which states that where any damage is likely to be severe, the reasonable person takes extra care. In this case, Gertrude may have to rely on the principle of *res ipsa loquitur* if she is unable to prove the actual sequence of events which led to the accident.

- There is little doubt that causation is satisfied: the hospital's breach of duty caused Gertrude's problems. With respect to remoteness of damage, Gertrude will need to prove that her problems were a reasonably foreseeable consequence of the hospital's actions, and she will perhaps rely on the rule in *Smith v Leech Brain & Co.* (1962) that, provided some damage is foreseeable, she will be able to recover damages for the full extent of her injuries, including the unusual complications.

- Finally, there is the issue of the defence of contributory negligence. The hospital will want to show that Gertrude's own actions made her problems worse than they might have been.

Activities

Damages in most successful claims for medical negligence are paid by the taxpayer. Consider whether this a good use of public funds.

Simon was admitted to Leafytown General Hospital to have his tonsils removed. Due to a mix-up, the surgeon actually removed Simon's appendix. In the confusion surrounding the accident, the hospital's team failed to notice for four days that Simon had picked up a serious infection since being admitted. The delay meant that his chances of making a full recovery from the infection were reduced from 40 per cent to 10 per cent. Advise Simon on his chances in making a claim for negligence against the hospital.

You should now be able to:

- explain when a doctor will have broken the duty of care that he owes to his patients

- identify, in a medical context, examples of the rules relating to causation.

15

The tort of negligence: claiming psychiatric damage and economic loss

Introduction

In Chapter 14 we discussed the principles of ordinary negligence in relation to a claim for physical damage, in other words personal injury and damage to property.

Negligence also allows claims for psychiatric damage and economic loss. As with any claim in negligence, the claimant must show that:

- the defendant owes a duty of care;
- the defendant has breached the duty of care; and
- the breach of the duty has caused reasonably foreseeable loss to the claimant.

However, for a variety of reasons, the courts are much more reluctant to allow claims for psychiatric damage and economic loss than for straightforward physical damage. Consequently, in both cases, the courts have adopted a **restrictive approach** as to when a duty of care is owed, and the range of potential claimants is much narrower than for physical damage.

This chapter considers the narrow rules relating to the duty of care in these two instances. It does not discuss breach and causation as they remain the same as for physical damage and need to be demonstrated by the claimant in the normal way.

> **Key terms**
>
> **Restrictive approach**: the idea that the courts will only allow a duty of care in respect of a narrower range of claimants than is the case for physical loss.

In this topic you will learn how to:

- explain what is meant by the term 'psychiatric damage'
- identify and explain the categories of claimant that can claim for psychiatric harm
- define and discuss the qualifying criteria required by someone who wishes to claim as a secondary victim.

> **Key terms**
>
> **Psychiatric damage**: the long-term mental consequences of being involved in, or witnessing, a horrific event.

1 Claiming psychiatric damage

What is psychiatric damage?

Psychiatric damage, which is also known as nervous shock, means a recognised psychiatric illness that can be independently verified on the basis of the medical evidence. It represents the long-term psychiatric consequences of a shocking event that was experienced by the claimant. The most common example is post traumatic stress disorder. This occurs when the claimant is involved in, or witnesses, an event which is so disastrous or catastrophic as to be outside the normal range of human experiences. Typically, the event threatens death or serious personal injury to the claimant or another, and leaves the claimant feeling extreme fear or helplessness. Symptoms are very diverse, but examples are irritability, sleep problems, flash-backs, and problems with memory and concentration. Symptoms are persistent and leave the claimant unable to carry out ordinary work, family or social activities in a normal way.

By contrast, the definition excludes grief, emotional distress and ordinary shock.

But, in order to bring a claim, it is not enough for the claimant to show that he is suffering psychiatric damage. He also needs to show that he is either a primary victim or a secondary victim, as it is only to those two categories that a duty of care in relation to psychiatric damage is owed. These two categories are defined very narrowly, and if the claimant is unable to show that he falls within either then there is no duty and the claim fails.

There are a number of reasons why the courts have taken such a restrictive approach as to who can claim for psychiatric damage. They include a traditional unwillingness to treat mental injuries as seriously as physical injuries, difficulty of diagnosis and the risk of fraudulent claims. In addition, there is a fear of 'floodgates': the idea that a single accident can lead to an unknown and unpredictable amount of liability. Whereas there is normally only a limited number of people who might be physically injured by an act of negligence, the number of people who might suffer psychiatric damage by witnessing a dreadful event or hearing about it might be very much larger especially given modern media such as television. This is illustrated by the Hillsborough Stadium disaster. The police negligently managed the crowd at a football match with the result that several dozen fans were crushed to death, and many more were injured. In addition to the claims for death and personal injury, there were a large number of claims for psychiatric damage suffered not only by those who witnessed the events in and around the stadium but also by those who had followed events through live television coverage. The subsequent litigation led to two appeals reaching the House of Lords: *Alcock* v *Chief Constable of South Yorkshire* (1991), which dealt with claims brought by family members of those killed or injured, and *White* v *Chief Constable of South Yorkshire* (1998), which dealt with claims brought by individual police officers on duty in the stadium that day. We discuss these two cases in the following paragraphs, and we will see that in both the House of Lords took the opportunity to define the rules narrowly in order to avoid nearly impossible levels of liability in respect of the thousands of people affected by the incident.

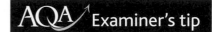

Examiner's tip

In an A Level Law exam, you cannot be expected to comment in detail on psychiatric illnesses. Briefly outline what is required and continue with your answer.

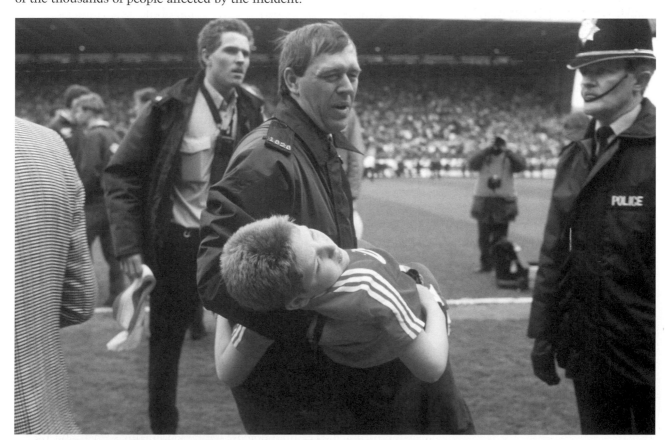

Fig. 1 *Claims were brought by individual police officers who were on duty in the stadium on the day of the Hillsborough disaster*

We now turn to the question of which claimants might qualify as either a primary or a secondary victim.

Primary victims

A **primary victim** is someone who is injured or fears he will be injured and who suffers psychiatric harm as a result. In the former case, of course, he can claim for both his physical loss and his psychiatric damage.

There are two key examples of a primary victim: someone who is directly involved in an accident and someone who goes to help those involved in an accident (a **rescuer**).

a Those involved directly in an accident

A person involved directly in an accident can claim for psychiatric damage, even though he escaped physical injury, provided that he feared for his own safety. In such circumstances it does not matter that psychiatric harm specifically was not reasonably foreseeable, as long as some sort of harm, either physical or psychiatric, was reasonably foreseeable. In **Page v Smith (1996)**, the claimant was involved in a road traffic incident caused by the defendant's negligence. He escaped physical injury, but the accident re-triggered the ME (myalgic encephalomyelitis, or chronic fatigue syndrome) from which he had suffered in the past and which rendered him unable to work. The House of Lords decided that his psychiatric damage was claimable, even though psychiatric damage itself was not reasonably foreseeable, as injury of some sort was a reasonably foreseeable consequence of the defendant's negligence in causing the road accident. The case is also an illustration of the 'thin skull' rule (see p243). The accident was comparatively minor (which is why the claimant probably escaped physical injury), and most people would probably not have suffered long-term psychiatric consequences as a result. But the claimant, although he had a 'thin skull' personality, was able to claim for all his injury, even though the full extent was not reasonably foreseeable.

Although most cases of this type will relate to a claimant who is directly involved in an accident, the courts have made it clear that a primary victim can exist in other situations. One example is **Donachie v Chief Constable of Greater Manchester (2004)**. The claimant was a police officer who was required to attach a tracking device to the underside of a car belonging to a suspected gang of criminals while the gang members were inside a public house, drinking. Through the negligence of the police force, the tracking device was defective, and the claimant had to make nine trips to the car before the device would work. He suffered psychiatric damage, because the risk grew greater on each occasion he returned to the car that he would be discovered and would suffer serious injury at the hands of the gang.

b Rescuers

The House of Lords confirmed in **White v Chief Constable of South Yorkshire (1998)** that someone who is not involved in an accident but who attends the scene as a rescuer can qualify as a primary victim if they suffer psychiatric damage as a result of their experiences. In order to claim, such a person must be engaged in rescue activities and must fear for their own safety during such activities.

In *White v Chief Constable of South Yorkshire* (1998) itself, the claimants were police officers attending the scene of the Hillsborough stadium disaster. Although they undoubtedly witnessed horrific scenes, and suffered psychiatric damage as a result, their claims failed as they themselves never feared for their own safety.

A similar example is **McFarlane v EE Caledonia Ltd (1993)**. The claimant was onboard a supply ship near to the Piper Alpha oil rig on the night that there were a series of catastrophic gas explosions which killed 164 men, and injured many others. The claimant helped prepare his ship to receive the injured, for instance by bringing blankets, but his claim for psychiatric damage caused as a result of what he saw and experienced failed: he was neither a rescuer or in immediate physical danger himself.

A contrasting example is **Chadwick v British Railways Board (1967)**. The claimant, a member of the public, attended the scene of a fatal train crash which occurred near his home. His claim for psychiatric injury succeeded: he was engaged as a rescuer and he had placed himself in danger.

Secondary victims

A **secondary victim** is someone who was not in personal physical danger, but who witnessed the accident or its aftermath. Because of the scope for multiple claimants from a single incident, the rules on who qualifies as a secondary victim are very tightly drawn, and any claimant must satisfy the following four controls, namely: (a) the rules in *Alcock*'s case; (b) the injury must be caused by a sudden shock; (c) reasonable fortitude; and (d) a primary victim owes no duty to a secondary victim.

a The rules in Alcock's case

The leading case on the definition of a secondary victim is **Alcock v Chief Constable of South Yorkshire (1991)**. The case was actually a series of cases brought by relatives and friends of football fans killed or injured at the Hillsborough Stadium disaster. The House of Lords was acutely aware of the potential for unlimited liability arising from this type of case, and it therefore established three qualifying criteria all of which a claimant must satisfy before being able to claim as a secondary victim.

1 The claimant must have a close tie of love and affection

The claimant must have a sufficiently **close tie of love and affection** with the person killed, injured or endangered, such that it is reasonably foreseeable that they would suffer psychiatric harm. As a result of *Alcock*, the courts are prepared to assume that the parent, child or spouse of a victim will have such a close tie, but it is possible that a judge might find that such a tie did not exist if the evidence suggests otherwise. One example might be a married couple who have lived apart for many years.

It is open to a claimant who has a relationship with the victim other than that of parent, child or spouse to prove that he had an equally close tie of love and affection. However, this is very hard to do and in *Alcock* (1991) itself grandparents, siblings, uncles and close friends all failed in their claims. It may be that a fiancé(e), a grandparent who has brought up a grandchild, or an identical twin might succeed.

Clearly, therefore, a bystander who has no link at all with the victim is very unlikely to succeed in claiming damages. In **Bourhill v Young (1943)**, the claimant heard a crash in which a motorcyclist was killed. Although she was never in any personal danger, she suffered, among other things, psychiatric damage. However, her claim failed as it was not reasonably foreseeable that someone in her position would be affected by the negligence of the motorcyclist. However, the House of Lords in *Alcock* (1991) did leave open the possibility that even an unrelated bystander could claim if he witnessed something truly and unimaginably horrific. One example given was a petrol tanker careering into a playground full of small children and exploding.

 Examiner's tip

When identifying whether the characters in a problem are primary or secondary victims, be careful to consider whether they went to help a victim of any accident.

Key cases

Alcock v Chief Constable of South Yorkshire (1991): in order to qualify as a secondary victim, a claimant must satisfy a series of conditions.

Bourhill v Young (1943): a witness with no connection to an accident victim is unlikely to be able to claim for psychiatric damage.

Key terms

Secondary victim: a person who witnesses a horrific event, but who is not personally endangered.

Close tie of love and affection: a relationship between the claimant and another that is so close that if that other person is injured it is reasonably foreseeable that the claimant will suffer psychiatric damage.

2 The claimant must be close to the accident in time and space

The claimant should be present at the scene of the accident in order to claim. In *Alcock* (1991) itself it was decided that this requirement excluded both a claimant who had been in a different part of the stadium at the time, and a claimant who was sitting in a coach outside the ground, following events on a television in the vehicle, and who went to look for his son when he realised what was happening.

The courts are prepared to relax this rule slightly to allow a claim by a person who did not witness the event itself, but who did witness its **immediate aftermath**. In **McLoughlin v O'Brian (1983)**, the claimant was a mother who was told that her husband and three of their children had been involved in a serious road accident. She went straight to the hospital to be told that one child had been killed, and that her husband and the two other children were seriously injured. She saw the surviving members of her family in various states of great distress and covered in blood and dirt. She suffered psychiatric damage as a result of what she had seen and heard, and her claim was allowed by the House of Lords on the ground that, although she had not witnessed the accident itself, she has witnessed the immediate aftermath, in other words, consequences of the accident that were so close to the accident, so reminiscent of the scene of the accident, that her shock and upset were as if she had witnessed the accident.

One difficulty is that the words 'immediate aftermath' have an uncertain definition: which consequences count as immediate aftermath and which do not? In *Alcock* (1991), for instance, the House of Lords decided that identifying a body in a mortuary was not sufficiently close to the scene to allow a claim for psychiatric damage. By contrast, in **Galli-Atkinson v Seghal (2003)**, the claimant was a mother who, having realised that her daughter had not come home, went out to look for her. She came across the scene of a road traffic accident at which the emergency services were already in attendance. The claimant realised that the victim was her daughter, but did not see her until she was asked to identify her daughter's body in the mortuary a little later. Her claim for psychiatric harm was successful, as what she had seen, from the police cordon at the scene of the accident to her daughter's body in the mortuary, amounted to the immediate aftermath of the accident.

3 The accident must be perceived by the claimant with his own senses

The claimant must directly perceive the accident with his own senses. This can include sight, hearing and even touch. However, it is not enough to be told about the offence or to hear about it on the television or the radio, and some of the claimants in the Alcock case failed in their claims as they had learned about the disaster from those who had been there and through the media rather than witnessing it for themselves.

One possibility which remains unclear is a claimant who witnesses events as they unfold by being in touch via mobile 'phone, particularly a 'phone with video images.

b The injury must be caused by a sudden shock

A secondary victim must show that any psychiatric damage was caused by a **sudden shock** (an 'assault on the senses'). This will occur if the claimant witnesses a single, sudden event such as an accident, rather than experiencing a growing realisation that something dreadful is happening ('slow shock'). In **Sion v Hampstead Health Authority (1994)**, the claimant suffered psychiatric damage as a result of watching his son die over a period of days from road traffic injuries which it was alleged had been negligently treated by the defendant hospital. The claim failed as there was no sudden shock, but rather a growing awareness. One of the Court of Appeal judges in that case had this to say on the definition of shock.

> I understand 'shock' in this context to mean the sudden sensory perception – that is, by seeing, hearing or touching – of a person, thing or event, which is so distressing that the perception of the phenomenon affronts or insults the plaintiff's mind and causes a recognisable psychiatric illness. (Staughton LJ)

The courts are, however, prepared to take a realistic view of the meaning of the word 'event' when deciding if there was a single shocking incident that led to psychiatric damage. In **Walters v North Glamorgan NHS Trust (2002)** the claimant was the mother of an infant who had been negligently misdiagnosed by a hospital in South Wales. The baby suffered a fit, and was transferred by ambulance to a hospital in London, where he died. The court decided that, although it had been 36 hours from the initial fit to the death, this amounted to a single event with one step leading inevitably to the next and which had led to the claimant's psychiatric damage.

c Reasonable fortitude

A secondary victim must show that his psychiatric damage was reasonably foreseeable and that a person of **reasonable fortitude** ('customary phlegm') would have sustained the injury. He cannot claim if he has a 'thin skull' personality and consequently suffers psychiatric damage when a person of reasonable fortitude would not have done.

However, a person with a 'thin skull' personality can claim for the full extent of his injury if the circumstances are that a person of reasonable fortitude would have suffered some psychiatric damage.

d A primary victim owes no duty to a secondary victim

In the cases we have looked at so far in relation to secondary victims, the claimant is suing for the psychiatric damage caused when the defendant's negligence harmed, or put at risk of harm, some third person. However, it might be that the negligent defendant and the individual harmed or put at risk of harm are the same person. In these circumstances the defendant owes no duty, and any claim will fail. The reason for this is that an individual does not owe a duty to anyone to look after himself so as to avoid predicaments which might cause distress to another: it would infringe personal liberty and the right of an individual to do with his life as he wishes.

In **Greatorex v Greatorex (2000)** the defendant was badly injured in a road traffic accident caused by his own negligent driving. By chance, his father was one of the fire and rescue officers attending at the scene, and he suffered psychiatric damage as a result of realising that the victim of the accident was his own son. His claim however failed as the defendant owed no duty to look after himself in case it caused distress to another.

Who else might claim for psychiatric damage?

At the fringes of the law relating to psychiatric damage, there are a number of cases which are, at best, difficult to fit into the established categories of primary victim and secondary victim, but the courts have made it clear that they will allow claims in appropriate circumstances.

One example is a person who is an unwilling participant in causing an accident, in other words, someone who mistakenly believes that his actions have led to the death, injury or endangerment of others, and who suffers psychiatric harm as a result. This situation occurred in both **Dooley v Cammell Laird (1951)**, where the claimant, a crane operator, feared he had injured his colleagues when, through no fault of his own, the crane dropped its load into the hold of a ship where he knew they were working, and *Salter* v *UB Frozen and Chilled Foods Ltd* (2003), where the claimant, the driver of a fork-lift truck, wrongly

Key cases

Walters v North Glamorgan NHS Trust (2002): for the purposes of psychiatric damage, a shocking event need not be an instantaneous occurrence, but can be prolonged over several hours.

Greatorex v Greatorex (2000): a person does not owe a duty of care to look after himself so that those close to him do not suffer psychiatric harm in the event that he is injured because of his own carelessness.

Dooley v Cammell Laird (1951): a claimant may be able to claim for psychiatric loss if he believes that his own actions have injured a work colleague when in fact the accident occurred because of the employer's negligence.

Key terms

Reasonable fortitude: the strength and resilience shown by an ordinary person.

blamed himself for the death of a colleague who had been riding in an observation cage fitted to the vehicle's lifting gear. In both cases, the claimant was able to recover for psychiatric damage. In the *Salter* case, the judge decided that the claimant was a primary victim, even though he had not been in danger, as he was actively involved in the accident.

Another difficult case is **W v Essex County Council (2000)**. The claimants, who had four children of their own, fostered a teenager, having been assured, wrongly, by the defendant council that he was not a known or suspected sexual abuser. The foster child seriously abused the claimants' own children, and the parents suffered psychiatric damage, not least because they felt responsible for having brought their own children into contact with someone who would abuse them. The defendant asked the courts to strike out the claim on the ground that there was no arguable chance of success given the definitions of primary and secondary victims. The House of Lords refused to do this: they felt that the definitions were sufficiently uncertain that there was a possibility that a trial court, having established the facts, might find that the claimants qualified as secondary victims or even primary victims (perhaps because the claimants felt personal responsibility for the harm to their children much as the claimant felt personal responsibility for the accident in the *Dooley* case). In the event, the case settled out of court, but the comments of the House of Lords will almost certainly give rise to future litigation in unusual sets of facts.

A final example of psychiatric damage in unusual circumstances is **Attia v British Gas (1987)**. The claimant had contracted with the defendant to install gas central heating. Due to the defendant's negligence, the house caught fire, and it and its contents were severely damaged. The claimant was uninjured and had not been in personal danger, but she suffered psychiatric harm and was successful in her claim for damages for this. It might seem surprising that she was able to claim, although she only witnessed property being destroyed, when others have failed in their claims, even though they witnessed people being injured, but the explanation might be that the claimant and the defendant had a legal link before the negligence was committed in that they had a contract.

Topic illustration

Consider this scenario, adapted from a recent exam paper:

> Nabeela (aged 11) had been trespassing in a derelict building owned by Lister Properties when she fell from an upper floor and became trapped in debris. She suffered serious back and leg injuries, and her screams were heard by Oliver, a police officer who was walking past the building. As soon as he saw her, he telephoned for an ambulance, and then tried to remove rubble from her and to comfort her. Meanwhile, other children had run to tell Nabeela's aunt, Pat, who lived close by. Pat arrived just in time to see paramedics sedating Nabeela and putting her into the ambulance. Both Oliver and Pat found it very difficult to recover from the experience and both were away from work for prolonged periods of time with anxiety and depression. Discuss the rights available to Oliver and to Pat against Lister Properties.

Any claim will be against Lister Properties for their negligence in allowing Nabeela to play in the building in the first place. However, Oliver and Pat have not suffered any kind of physical loss, whether personal injury or damage to property, and therefore we need to consider the rules relating to psychiatric damage.

■ The first element is a discussion of whether Oliver and Pat have suffered psychiatric damage. In an exam, you are unlikely to get beyond describing the rules.

The second element is to discuss whether either Oliver or Pat qualifies as a primary victim. There might be an argument for Oliver, as he is a rescuer, but only if he placed himself in personal danger. It is difficult to see how Pat can be a primary victim, as she only arrived later and when the ambulance was leaving.

We then need to discuss if either Oliver or Pat are secondary victims, and this requires a discussion of the rules in *Alcock* (1991). Key issues include whether either has a close enough relationship to Nabeela, whether either was at the scene of the accident or (in Pat's case) at the immediate aftermath, and whether either suffered psychiatric damage through sudden shock.

Activities

1 What reasons might there be for allowing recovery for psychiatric damage in the case of a rescuer who is unconnected to any of the victims? Should professional rescuers, such as fire crew or ambulance staff, be able to claim even if they are not in personal danger?

2 The rules relating to recovery for psychiatric damage in the case of secondary victims have been widely criticised for being too narrow. Would you reform the rules? If so, how would you do so in order to prevent unlimited liability?

3 Malcolm was driving to work in an absent-minded way as he was worried about some of that day's meetings. His car mounted the pavement and struck some scaffolding around a building. Part of the scaffolding collapsed, narrowly missing Norma, but trapping her behind the debris. Oscar, a bystander rushed across to help Norma even though he could see that the remainder of the scaffolding was wobbling dangerously. Peter, Norma's brother, who had been shopping with Norma and had gone on ahead, heard the crash and dashed out of a shop to see scaffolding collapsing where Norma had been standing. Norma, Oscar and Peter all suffered long-lasting mental problems as a result of their experiences. Discuss Malcolm's liability in connection with these mental problems.

You should now be able to:

- explain the nature of psychiatric damage and discuss how liability for it differs from liability for physical damage

- identify situations when a defendant owes a duty of care to a claimant for psychiatric damage

- explain whether a claimant satisfies the requirements for a primary victim or a secondary victim.

2 Claiming economic loss

What is economic loss?

Economic loss is 'damage to the wallet' of the victim of negligence, in other words the claimant is less well off than he would have been if the negligence had not occurred. Examples include a loss in profits, an unwise investment, a loss of a financial benefit or payment and a loss in value of items.

There are two types of economic loss: consequential economic loss and pure economic loss. The distinction is important because, subject to exceptions, a claimant can recover for consequential economic loss, but not for pure economic loss.

Consequential economic loss occurs when the claimant suffers a money loss because he has suffered an item of physical loss, in other words the economic loss is consequential on the physical loss. Examples include a worker who loses wages because he has been injured by the defendant's negligence or a taxi driver who loses fares because his taxi has been damaged by the defendant's negligence. In both cases, the defendant's

In this topic you will learn how to:

- explain what is meant by the term 'economic loss'

- identify and explain the requirements needed in a claim for negligent misstatement.

Key terms

Economic loss: any loss which leaves a claimant financially less well off.

Consequential economic loss: economic loss that occurs because the claimant has also suffered physical loss.

Key terms

Pure economic loss: when a claimant suffers an economic loss but no physical loss.

Key cases

Spartan Steel and Alloys Ltd v Martin and Co. (Contractors) Ltd (1972): an economic loss caused by a physical loss can be recovered, an economic loss that stands alone cannot be.

Cattle v Stockton Waterworks (1875) and **Weller v Foot and Mouth Disease Research Institute (1965):** a claimant cannot recover for a pure economic loss.

negligence causes physical loss or injury which in turn leads to a money loss for the claimant.

By contrast, **pure economic loss** is a stand-alone economic loss: there is no item of physical loss. An example would be if the defendant's negligence causes a traffic accident which closes the road, thus preventing people getting to the claimant's café and the claimant, as a result, loses several hours' worth of takings. The claimant has suffered a money loss, but no physical loss or injury and therefore his loss is a purely economic loss.

The difference between consequential economic loss and pure economic loss is illustrated by the facts of **Spartan Steel and Alloys Ltd v Martin and Co. (Contractors) Ltd (1972)**. The defendant was carrying out road works when, negligently, it severed the electricity cable which supplied power to the claimant's smelting works. At the time the power was shut off, the claimant was producing a consignment of ingots (in a process called a 'melt'). In order to protect its furnace, the claimant had to remove the metal by prematurely cooling it, but this in turn meant that the metal was damaged. The claimant suffered three losses:

- Damage to the metal: this was a physical loss in the form of damage to property.
- Loss of profit, because the damaged metal could not now be sold: this was an economic loss consequential on the physical loss to the metal.
- Loss of profit on four further melts that had been planned for the period when the electricity was off: this was an economic loss not associated with any physical loss (a pure economic loss) as the metal that was scheduled to be used was undamaged by the incident.

The rule relating to the recovery of economic loss

The rule relating to the recovery of economic loss is that consequential economic loss is always recoverable, as long as the claimant can satisfy the normal rules on causation and remoteness, but that pure economic loss is not recoverable, although there are a number of exceptions, notably loss caused by a negligent misstatement.

In the modern era, this rule is often traced back to the decision in **Cattle v Stockton Waterworks (1875)**. The claimant was building a tunnel for a fixed price for a third party, when the tunnel was flooded due to the defendant's negligence. The claimant lost money on his building contract because it was now more difficult and more expensive to complete the tunnel, but he could not pass the cost on to the third party because of the fixed price clause in the contract. The court refused his claim as the claimant had suffered an economic loss without any physical loss.

Similarly, in **Weller v Foot and Mouth Disease Research Institute (1965)**, the defendant's negligence caused an escape of the foot and mouth virus. To prevent the disease from spreading, the authorities banned the movement of animals which in turn damaged the business of the claimant who were livestock auctioneers. The claimants sued for their losses, but they were refused as the losses were purely economic: they had suffered no physical loss.

A final example is *Spartan Steel and Alloys Ltd v Martin and Co. (Contractors) Ltd* (1972) itself. The claimant successfully recovered for the first two of its losses: the damage to the metal (physical loss) and the loss of profits that should have been made on the sale of the metal (consequential economic loss). But the claimant failed in its third claim, as the loss of profits on the planned melts was a pure economic loss.

As with liability for psychiatric damage, there are a number of reasons why the courts are said to take such a restrictive approach to the recovery of pure economic loss. The principal explanation is, again, the fear of 'floodgates' and the danger that a single accident can lead to an unknown and unpredictable amount of liability. A good example is if the contractor in the Spartan Steel case had negligently severed the electricity cable supplying an entire city, then it would be virtually impossible to work out the economic losses that would be suffered by all the city's businesses during the time that the power was off. By contrast, in those instances where pure economic loss is recoverable, the courts have drawn the rules in such a way that there is only likely to be liability to a limited class of claimants. Other reasons include the difficulty in calculating future loss of profits and the fact that a claimant may be suing in negligence to avoid a clause in a contract between the two parties restricting liability.

We now consider the exceptions to the general rule that pure economic loss cannot be recovered. The most important of these is a loss caused by a negligent misstatement on the part of the defendant, and we discuss this first. We then look briefly at some of the other instances when the courts have been prepared to allow the recovery of a purely economic loss.

The principal exception: negligent misstatement

A defendant is liable if he makes a statement to someone to whom he owes a duty of care but, due to his negligence, the statement is inaccurate and it causes the claimant a reasonably foreseeable pure economic loss. Such a statement is a **negligent misstatement**: it can be written or verbal, and can be in any form which conveys information to the claimant. Examples include a report, a reference, professional advice, a survey, a set of accounts and a map.

The possibility of liability existing for a negligent misstatement was first recognised in **Hedley Byrne v Heller (1964)**. The claimant was an advertising agency which was about to book, at its own financial risk, a large amount of advertising space on behalf of a client. The claimant asked the defendant, the client's bank, for a financial reference relating to the client as the claimant wanted reassurance that the client would be able to pay for the advertising space. The financial reference was negligently prepared: it suggested that the client was in a much stronger financial position than was actually the case. As a result, the claimant booked the space, but the client never paid for it as it went into liquidation shortly afterwards, and the claimant lost its money. The claimant therefore sued the bank for its negligence in preparing the reference. In the event, the defendant won the case because it had included in the reference a clause excluding liability, but the House of Lords made it clear that, in the absence of such an exclusion clause, liability for a negligent misstatement could exist.

As with any other example of pure economic loss, negligent misstatement raises the risk of an unknown and unpredictable liability, for instance a newspaper publishing careless investment advice which many thousands of readers then rely on. Therefore, in *Hedley Byrne* v *Heller* (1964), the House of Lords made it clear that, for the purposes of negligent misstatement, a defendant owes a duty of care only to someone with whom he has a '**special relationship**'. The effect of this is to greatly restrict the number of potential claimants and thus avoid the risk of unlimited liability.

The case law is not entirely clear as to what the precise requirements for a special relationship are, but it is possible to identify five key elements.

Key terms

Negligent misstatement: a statement which is inaccurate because of the negligence of the person who made the statement.

Special relationship: a link of sufficient closeness between a defendant and a claimant that liability for a negligent misstatement can be imposed.

Key cases

Hedley Byrne v Heller (1964): a claimant can recover pure economic loss caused by a negligent misstatement if there is a special relationship between him and the defendant.

Key cases

Lennon v Metropolitan Police Commissioner (2004): a person need not be a professional adviser in order to possess the skill or expertise necessary for liability in negligent misstatement.

Chaudhry v Prabhakar (1988): a special relationship for the purposes of negligent misstatement may exist in a social setting.

Caparo v Dickman (1990): with reference to 'known user', liability for negligent misstatement only exists if the maker of the statement can identify the person or class of persons who will be relying on the statement.

Goodwill v British Pregnancy Advisory Service (1996): a defendant will not be liable for negligent misstatement when he cannot know to whom his statement will be passed.

Key terms

Voluntary assumption of responsibility: the defendant chooses to take responsibility for advising the claimant.

a The defendant possesses a skill or expertise

The defendant is in possession of a skill or an expertise which the claimant needs. Normally the defendant in a negligent misstatement case will be a professional adviser. Good examples are an accountant preparing a set of accounts, a surveyor writing a report on a building, and a solicitor giving legal advice. However, liability can be extended to a non-professional adviser. In **Lennon v Metropolitan Police Commissioner (2004)** the claimant, a policeman transferring between forces, asked a clerical officer in the defendant's personnel department for advice on his eligibility for a housing allowance. Liability was established, as the clerk gave wrong information with the result that the claimant lost financial payments to which he would otherwise have been entitled.

Liability has even been extended to a social setting. In **Chaudhry v Prabhakar (1988)**, the defendant, who had some knowledge of cars, helped the claimant, a friend, choose a second-hand car, but failed to notice that the car had been in an accident. He was held liable for the money the claimant wasted purchasing the car when shortly afterwards the car was found to be unroadworthy and therefore valueless.

b The defendant voluntarily assumes responsibility for his statements

If the defendant **voluntarily assumes responsibility** for his statements, it means that he is effectively saying to the claimant that he is prepared for the claimant to rely on any advice and that he (the defendant) will take responsibility for the advice. As was pointed out in *Hedley Byrne* v *Heller* (1964), a defendant does not have to give advice: he can either decline altogether or give any advice subject to a disclaimer as to liability (as of course happened in *Hedley Byrne* itself).

c Known user

A defendant will normally only be liable if he knows or should know, when making a statement, the identity of the particular person or class of persons who will rely on the statement. In **Caparo v Dickman (1990)**, an accountant prepared a company's annual accounts. One of the shareholders, on the basis of the accounts, took the company over and then discovered that it had lost a lot of money as the company was not worth what the accounts had suggested that it was. The claimant's action for negligent misstatement failed as the accounts were prepared for the shareholders as a class to use in the interests of the company, rather than for an individual shareholder to use in his own interests. A similar case, but with a different result, is *Morgan Crucible* v *Hill Samuel Bank* (1990). The claimant was bidding to take over a company, and based its plans on accounts and other financial statements prepared by the defendant accountant. This time, however, the defendant was liable for the negligent misstatements contained in the accounts because the defendant knew, when it made its misstatements, that there was a confirmed bidder and that it would be relying on the accounts.

A very different example is **Goodwill v British Pregnancy Advisory Service (1996)**. The defendant charity had carried out a vasectomy on a client, but had not warned him that there was a small chance that the procedure could reverse itself naturally. Three years later, the client entered into a relationship with the claimant, who fell pregnant. She sued for the economic losses caused by the costs of bringing up a child, but her claim failed. The defendant did not owe a duty to someone who was not their client, particularly when the defendant could not know that its statements would be passed to the claimant or how she would use them.

d Known purpose

Similarly, a defendant will normally only be liable if he knows or should know, when making a statement, what purpose his statement will be used for. This was another reason why the claim failed in **Caparo v Dickman (1990)**: the accounts were drawn up for the purposes of complying with company law and of allowing the shareholders as a group to exercise control over their company. The accounts were not drawn up for the purpose of a takeover.

A second example is *Reeman* v *Department of Transport* (1997). The claimant had bought a boat on the strength of a seaworthiness certificate issued by one of the defendant's inspectors. The certificate had been negligently prepared, and the boat was unsafe and therefore of little value, particularly compared with what the claimant had paid for it. However, the claim for negligent misstatement failed on the ground that the certificate had been produced for the purpose of complying with regulations designed to promote safety at sea, not for the purpose of putting a commercial value on the boat.

A contrasting example is **Law Society v KPMG Peat Marwick (2000)**. The defendant was a firm of accountants that had prepared the annual accounts for a firm of solicitors. The accounts did not pick up the fact that large amounts of client money were being stolen. When the true picture emerged, the claimant's compensation fund had to pay out to the victims of the fraud, and the claimant sued to recover the loss from the defendant. The claim succeeded because, although the accounts were prepared for the solicitors, the defendant knew first that they would be passed to the claimant, as that was part of the regulations governing the solicitors' profession, and secondly that the purpose of the accounts being passed to the claimant was to allow it to make a decision as to whether to intervene in a particular solicitors' practice to stop fraud and minimise claims against the compensation fund.

e Reasonable reliance

Finally, the claimant must demonstrate that he actually did rely on the misstatement and that it was reasonable in the circumstances for him to do so. One common example is the contrast between a business appointment and a drinks party: it is reasonable to rely on advice given by a professional person at a formal consultation; it is not reasonable to take advice given by someone late in the evening and after several drinks.

In **Smith v Bush (1990)**, the claimant was the purchaser of a house who had approached a lender for a mortgage. As is common practice, the lender asked the defendant, a surveyor, to prepare a report on the house, and then passed the resulting survey to the claimant. The claimant relied on the survey, rather than paying for her own, and subsequently suffered an economic loss when the house partially collapsed because of defects the survey had negligently failed to identify. The House of Lords decided that it was reasonable for the claimant to have relied on the survey: the defendant knew that the survey would be passed to her, there was not an unknown liability as both the identity of the claimant and the amount of any loss were known in advance and the alternative was to insist that the claimant should also get a survey at the same time as the lender, which was an unnecessary duplication of effort.

Miscellaneous exceptions: other examples of pure economic loss

There are a small number of narrow instances where the courts have been prepared to award pure economic loss other than for a negligent misstatement. It may be that each example was designed to address a

specific problem, or to give a remedy where it was right to do so, but it may be that they form the basis for a future expansion of liability for pure economic loss. We will briefly discuss three examples.

a Beneficiaries of a will

If a solicitor prepares a will negligently so that the assets are left to someone other than the intended beneficiary, there is a problem in liability in that the estate cannot sue, as it has lost nothing, and the intended beneficiary cannot sue in contract as he is not the client of the solicitor. One solution is to allow the intended beneficiary to sue the solicitor in negligence, even though he is suing for a pure economic loss (the bequest he should have received).

This type of liability was recognised by the House of Lords in **White v Jones (1995)**. Following a family argument, the testator had cut his two daughters, the claimants, out of his will. The family then settled its differences, and the testator gave instructions to his solicitor, the defendant, for a fresh will, leaving bequests to both the claimants. The solicitor was negligent in that he delayed drawing up the will so that the testator died before he could execute it. The claimants thus lost their gifts, as effect was given to the existing will which excluded them, but they recovered their loss as the House of Lords allowed their action for negligence against the defendant.

This type of case does not pose a threat of unlimited liability: the negligent solicitor would know which beneficiaries would lose and by how much.

b Providing services

In **Henderson v Merrett Syndicates Ltd (1994)**, the House of Lords extended the principles relating to negligent misstatement to cases where a defendant has negligently carried out services (in the Henderson case itself, the negligent management of specialised investments in the insurance market). Provided there is a special relationship between the two parties, based on the defendant assuming responsibility to perform professional services and the claimant relying on the defendant, then the claimant can claim for any pure economic loss caused by the defendant's negligence in providing the services.

The House of Lords also decided that if the services in question were performed under a contract between the two parties, then liability in negligence could exist side-by-side with liability for breach of contract, unless the contract specifically excluded liability in negligence. The reason why a claimant, in these circumstances, might want to sue in negligence rather than for breach of contract is that the time limits for bringing an action in negligence can be more generous.

c Job references

In **Spring v Guardian Assurance (1994)**, the House of Lords decided that an employer owes a duty of care to his employee when preparing a reference for a potential future employer, and that the employer is liable for any economic loss resulting from a negligently written reference. In these circumstances, the employer assumes responsibility towards the employee because the employer has access to specialised information (his knowledge of the employee) and the employee has to rely on the employer's skill and care in drawing up the reference.

This is similar to the rules relating to negligent misstatement (and a reference is a good example of a statement), but the difference is that in negligent misstatement cases the claimant suffers an economic loss because he himself relies on the defendant's statement, but in this case, the claimant suffers an economic loss because a third party (the prospective employer) relies on the defendant's statement.

Key cases

White v Jones (1995): a beneficiary to a will who loses his bequest because of a solicitor's negligence can sue for the resulting pure economic loss.

Henderson v Merrett Syndicates Ltd (1994): if a special relationship exists, a claimant can sue for pure economic loss caused by the negligent performance of a professional service.

Spring v Guardian Assurance (1994): an employer can be liable for pure economic loss caused by a negligently prepared reference.

There is, of course, a further problem for the claimant in this sort of case: he needs to be able to prove that he would have got the job if the reference had been correct, and that is likely to be difficult.

Topic illustration

Consider this scenario, taken from a recent exam paper:

> An article in the IT pages of the *Herald*, a national newspaper, described and recommended Safestore, a security software package. After reading the article, Gordon bought a copy of Safestore and installed it on his computer's hard disk, hoping to protect his clients' confidential business information. In fact, the article had failed to explain that the version of Safestore on public sale was less comprehensive than the version reviewed. Gordon's security was breached two months later while he was online. In consequence, he had to pay a total of £30,000 to clients affected by the breach and he stopped receiving orders for his services.

Fig. 2

Gordon has suffered a loss as a result of the *Herald*'s article, and any discussion of his claim against the paper would need to cover the following points:

- First, we would need to discuss the nature of Gordon's loss. He has suffered no physical loss, whether personal injury or damage to property, but rather his loss is purely economic.

■ We might then discuss the fact that pure economic loss cannot be claimed unless it is the result of a negligent misstatement. An article in a newspaper is a statement.

■ To claim for negligent misstatement, Gordon needs to establish a special relationship between himself and the newspaper, and this will require a discussion of the various factors. Particularly relevant will be whether the newspaper has a skill or expertise, whether it knew that Gordon would rely on the article and whether it was reasonable for Gordon to rely on the article.

Activities

1 Consider the cases discussed earlier in relation to the elements required to establish the special relationship needed for a negligent misstatement. To what extent is each element present in every case?

2 Amelia writes a weekly financial column which she sells to various newspapers and journals, and which is widely respected for its accurate assessment of investment opportunities. One column was very positive about an investment in a new mining company, and Bart, having read the article, invested heavily in the mining company. Callum also read the article and telephoned Amelia to speak to her directly about the mining company, after which he too invested heavily. Both Bart and Callum lost all the money they had invested when the mining company collapsed because of a fundamental but obvious flaw in its business plan which Amelia had failed to spot. Meanwhile, Dirk, an internet engineer, while carrying out work in the office next door to Amelia's, reconnected various cables wrongly with the result that Amelia's column for that week, unknown to her, was not sent to her subscribers and she was therefore not paid for it. Consider Amelia's liability to both Bart and Callum, and Dirk's liability to Amelia for the losses suffered.

You should now be able to:

■ distinguish between consequential economic loss and pure economic loss and explain the significance of the difference

■ explain the purpose of a special relationship in the context of a negligent misstatement

■ identify the elements which a claimant must demonstrate in order to show a special relationship.

16

Product liability: liability in tort for defective goods

Introduction

In a modern economy, countless numbers of goods, of every possible type, are bought and sold, usually by large companies with great economic power. The consumer, an ordinary person buying or using goods, is unable to stand up to these big businesses because he does not have the knowledge or the resources to negotiate appropriate contracts to protect himself against the risk of faulty goods.

There, therefore, exist a number of laws to protect the consumer and to ensure fairness in the market place. Some are criminal laws, such as the offences relating to unsafe products or food unfit for consumption. Others originate in contract law, such as the protection offered by the Sale of Goods Act 1979 which automatically implies into every contract, by which goods are sold in the course of a business, terms relating to description, satisfactory quality and fitness for purpose.

This chapter though is concerned with the contribution of tort law to consumer protection. This takes two forms: an action in negligence and an action brought under the Consumer Protection Act 1987.

In this topic you will learn how to:

- identify the duty of care in negligence in the context of defective goods

- explain factors the court might use when deciding if the duty has been broken

- consider which types of loss might be recoverable.

Key cases

Donoghue v Stevenson (1932): a manufacturer owes a duty of care to the consumer of his goods.

Key terms

Duty of care: a duty which the law says one person owes to another to take proper care of the other.

1 Negligence

A claimant suing in negligence in respect of defective goods must show, as with any action in negligence, that the defendant owes a duty of care, that the defendant has breached the duty of care and that reasonably foreseeable damage has resulted. In doing this, the claimant will use the same principles that we discussed in Chapter 14, Negligence: physical damage and medical negligence, and we now turn to consider these as they apply in a claim for defective products.

The duty of care

Donoghue v Stevenson (1932) itself was, of course, a case about defective goods. Having considered the general principles as to when a **duty of care** might exist (the neighbour test), Lord Atkin went on to consider the position with specific reference to manufacturers. His conclusion was that a manufacturer of goods owes a duty of care to the consumer of those goods when he intends those goods to reach the consumer in the form that they left the factory and without further examination or preparation by any intermediate person. Thus, in relation to the facts of the case, a manufacturer of ginger beer, which is supplied in a sealed bottle made of opaque glass, owes a duty of care to the consumer of the drink to take reasonable care to ensure that the ginger beer does not injure the consumer or damage her goods.

The claimant

Donoghue v *Stevenson* (1932) stated that the duty of care was owed to the consumer of the defective goods, and the case itself is an example of a consumer who was able to recover damages, even though she had not bought the ginger beer. Subsequent cases have widened the scope of the duty to cover any person who buys or uses the goods, or who is affected by them.

In *Grant* v *Australian Knitting Mills* (1935), the claimant was a purchaser who bought for himself woollen underpants manufactured by the defendant. The fabric of the garments contained sulphites, and this contamination caused the claimant to suffer dermatitis when he tried to wear them. The defendant was held to be negligent as the underpants contained a hidden defect which could not be reasonably discovered by a purchaser or wearer.

In **Stennett v Hancock (1939)** the defendant was a garage that had repaired the wheel of a lorry. Two hours later, while the lorry was being driven along the road, part of the wheel came off and hit the claimant, a pedestrian, who was injured. The claimant was not the owner or user of the wheel, and had not asked the defendant to repair it. Nevertheless, as a bystander affected by the defendant's negligence in repairing the goods, she was able to claim.

The defendant

Donoghue v *Stevenson* (1932) stated that the duty of care is owed by the manufacturer of goods. This too has been widened by subsequent cases so that today anyone who is involved in supplying goods, and whose actions might reasonably foreseeably affect the consumer, owes the duty of care.

Donoghue itself provides an example of a manufacturer being found liable, but in *Stennett* v *Hancock* (1939), above, the defendant was not a manufacturer but a repairer.

A different example is **Fisher v Harrods Ltd (1966)**. The claimant attempted to open a bottle of jewellery cleaning fluid given to her by a friend who had bought it from the defendant's store. The fluid contained a mixture of chemicals which caused pressure to build up in the bottle so that when the claimant removed the screw cap, the stopper underneath flew out and some of the fluid squirted into the claimant's eye, injuring it. The defendant, as retailer, was liable, as they were aware that there had been problems with the bottles and therefore they should have investigated further, as that is what the reasonable retailer would have done. Had they done so, they would have discovered that the manufacturer was inexperienced in preventing leaks and had created the hazard by putting a stopper in the bottle.

Finally, we can note that the duty of care exists in respect of all types of goods and the packaging in which they come.

Fig. 1 *Fisher v Harrods Ltd* (1966)

Breaching the duty of care

The test for whether a manufacturer has breached the duty of care he owes to the consumer is the normal negligence test of the standard of the **reasonable person**. To decide whether the manufacturer has breached the duty of care he owes, the court will consider all the circumstances of the case, and we now need to discuss examples of those circumstances.

Faulty manufacturing process

A common cause of faulty goods is that a defect occurs because of a lack of care in the manufacturing process. Under the normal rules relating to the burden of proof, it would be the responsibility of the claimant to prove how the defendant had fallen below the standard of the reasonable manufacturer. This clearly is very difficult for an ordinary person who has no knowledge or experience of the relevant manufacturing process. The courts have therefore stated that they are prepared to find liability where it is clear from the facts of the case that carelessness must have been involved even though it is very difficult to pinpoint precisely where.

An example of this is **Grant v Australian Knitting Mills (1935)**, which we discussed earlier. The very fact that the underpants left the defendant's factory containing the sulphites indicated that negligence was present somewhere in the manufacturing process, as a reasonable manufacturer would have taken proper care to ensure that his goods were not sent out from the factory in such a state.

A more modern example is **Carroll v Fearon (1998)**. The claimants were injured in a car accident caused by a tyre manufactured by the defendant. Liability was found to exist, even though the claimants were unable to demonstrate how the defendants were negligent. The court found that the very fact that the tyre was defective was enough to demonstrate negligence on the part of the defendant in the absence of an alternative explanation. This is an application of the principle of *res ipsa loquitur* that we discussed in Chapter 14, Negligence: physical damage and medical negligence.

Intermediate examination

The defendant should take reasonable steps to protect any person into whose hands goods might come if he knows that there is no reasonable expectation that any third party will check the goods before they reach the hands of the claimant. One example of this is **Donoghue v Stevenson (1932)** itself: the manufacturer of the ginger beer should have taken reasonable precautions to ensure that the drink was safe as he knew that it would not be checked by any intermediate third party before it reached the hands of the person who would drink it.

A second example is *Griffiths* v *Arch Engineering* (1968). The defendant hired out a grinding machine that had been fitted with a wheel that was too large for the speed at which the machine was set. The hirer lent the machine to the claimant, an employee of another company, who was injured when he attempted to use the machine and the wheel shattered. The court decided that the defendant was liable for failing to take reasonable precautions to protect any person into whose hands the machine might come on the ground that they had no reason to believe that any third person would check the machine before it was used.

Instructions and warning labels

If goods present a danger unless used in a particular way then the manufacturer should give proper instructions for use and an appropriate warning. Common examples include labels on goods which state that they should not be allowed to come into contact with the eye or that they should not be eaten. If an appropriate warning is not given, then

Key terms

The **'reasonable person'** test: in deciding whether a defendant has broken a duty of care that he owes, the court will ask whether he did all that the reasonable person would have done in the same circumstances.

 AQA Examiner's tip

Your discussion as to whether the duty of care has been broken will be one of the more important parts of your answer. Often it is obvious that a duty is owed and that the actions of the defendants have caused the losses complained of. What is more difficult is deciding whether the defendant acted as the reasonable person would have done.

Key cases

Grant v Australian Knitting Mills (1935) and **Carroll v Fearon (1998)**: where it is clear from the facts of a case that there was negligence at some point in the manufacturing process, liability will exist even though the claimant is unable to prove the exact nature of the negligence.

Donoghue v Stevenson (1932): a defendant manufacturer owes a duty to the ultimate consumer of his goods when it is clear that no third party will check the goods before they are delivered to the claimant.

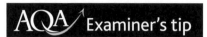 Examiner's tip

the manufacturer may be liable in negligence. One example is *Fisher v Harrods Ltd* (1966), in which the cleaning fluid represented a foreseeable hazard to eyes. In addition to being found negligent for not carrying out proper investigations, as discussed above, the defendant was also found negligent for not having attached an appropriate label warning of the danger.

A second example is **Kubach v Hollands (1937)**. A manufacturer of chemicals had supplied them to a shop with a warning that they should be tested before use. The shop resold the chemicals to a school for use in a chemistry class, but without passing on the warning. The chemicals in fact were not what they were supposed to be, and they exploded injuring the claimant, a pupil at the school, when she attempted to heat them. The claimant recovered damages against the shop because they had acted negligently in supplying chemicals without the relevant warning. However, the claimant failed in her action against the manufacturers because they had given an appropriate warning when selling the goods and had acted as the reasonable manufacturer would have done.

Causation

As with any negligence case, the claimant must demonstrate that the breach caused the damage complained of. This might be difficult if there are multiple explanations for an accident, only one of which is defective goods, as the claimant may be unable to show on the civil balance of probabilities that it was the defect which caused the accident.

One example of this is **Evans v Triplex Safety Glass (1936)**. The claimant, who had bought his car a year earlier, was injured when his car windscreen, which had been manufactured by the defendant, shattered through no obvious cause. He sued the defendant for his injuries but was unable to show on the balance of probabilities that it had been any negligence on the part of the defendant which had caused the accident. Factors which the court took into account included first the length of time between the purchase of the car and the accident, secondly the possibility that the glass may have been put under strain when it was screwed into its frame, and thirdly something other than a defect in the manufacture may have caused the glass to break.

Damage

A claimant suing in respect of defective goods can recover damages for his personal injuries and for damage to other property of his caused by the defective goods. However, in contrast with contract law, he cannot recover the value of the defective item itself (or for the cost of repairs to the defective item). This illustrates a key principle of tort law: a claim exists only when damage has actually been caused. If defective goods cause no damage but simply sit there not working properly then there is no action in negligence.

Thus, if I buy a toaster which does not work when I take it home, I have an action for breach of contract against the shop, and I can recover the value of the toaster. However, I have no action against the manufacturer of the toaster, even if the defect was caused by negligence in the manufacturing process. If I am given a toaster as a birthday present, and the toaster does not work, I have no action in either contract or negligence. The situation is different if the toaster's defects are so serious that, when I try to use it, it burns me and causes a fire in my kitchen. Even if I have no contract, because the toaster was a gift, I can sue the manufacturer, as long as I can demonstrate negligence on their part. I will recover damages for my injuries and for the damage to the kitchen, but even then I will not recover the value of the toaster.

The reason why the value of the defective goods themselves cannot be claimed is that it is a pure economic loss, and, as we discussed in Chapter 15, Negligence: psychiatric damage and economic loss, a claimant cannot normally recover damages for pure economic losses in negligence (unless the rules relating to a negligent misstatement are satisfied). The lost value is counted as a pure economic loss because the claimant has suffered a reduction in the value of his assets and he is therefore worth less than he should have been.

An illustration of this is **Muirhead v Industrial Tank Specialties (1985)**. The claimant was a fish farmer who had installed pumps, made by the defendant, to his lobster tank to ensure a flow of oxygenated water. The pumps did not work properly because they were fitted with French motors which were not compatible with British voltages, and as a result the claimant lost an entire consignment of lobsters. The claimant did not have a contract with the manufacturer, but was able to bring an action against them in negligence in respect of defective goods. The court found that there was a duty of care to ensure that electrical products would work properly in the UK, and that the defendant had breached that duty. In the relevant part of the claim, the claimant was able to recover damages in respect of the lost lobsters, as that was damage caused by the defective goods to other property, but he could not claim for the money he had spent on buying the pumps in the first place.

Given that a claimant can sue for damage to other property but not for the loss of the defective item itself, the law needs to be able to draw a line between the two. This is straightforward in both the toaster example and the Muirhead case, but not all examples are as easy. The issue was raised in **Aswan Engineering v Lupdine Ltd (1986)**. The claimant had bought a quantity of a waterproofing compound, contained in plastic pails, which had been manufactured by the defendant. The waterproofing compound was lost because the pails had been stacked on a quayside in Kuwait and had collapsed in the heat. The claimant brought an action against the manufacturer in negligence for defective goods, but the action failed on the general ground that the damage suffered was not reasonably foreseeable.

However, if the damage had been foreseeable then that would have raised the question whether the claimant could recover the value of the waterproofing compound on the ground that the defective goods were the plastic pails and that the pails were separate from the waterproofing compound which could then be sued for as other property. The judges of the Court of Appeal were unable to agree, even though they discussed a number of similar examples. These examples can be divided into two categories: components and packaging. With components, the basic question is whether a claimant can recover for physical damage to an assembled item caused by a single defective component within that item. One example discussed was a defective car tyre: if I replace a tyre on my car and the new tyre is defective and causes an accident which damages my car, can I claim for the car as being other property? If so, is the position the same if I buy a brand new car and one of the tyres is defective? A similar question would have arisen on the facts of *Muirhead* if the electrical motors in the pumps had caught fire and had caused physical damage to the pumps themselves. It is not clear if the claimant could then have claimed for the pumps as being other property. With respect to packaging, the basic question is whether defective packaging is separate from the goods contained in the packaging thus allowing a claim for the contents. This of course was the problem in *Aswan* itself, and other examples discussed by the judges (with no agreed conclusions) were whether a manufacturer of a cork would be liable if a defect in the cork contaminated a bottle of wine or whether a manufacturer of a carrier

Key cases

Muirhead v Industrial Tank Specialties (1985): an action in negligence for defective goods does not allow the recovery of damages for the value of the defective goods themselves.

Aswan Engineering v Lupdine Ltd (1986): it is unclear whether a claimant can claim for the value of goods supplied with the defective item.

bag supplied at a supermarket or a jeweller's shop would be liable for the contents of the bag if the bag gave way and damaged the goods inside.

Defences

The normal negligence defences, contributory negligence and consent, apply to an action in respect of defective goods. One example from the cases above is **Griffiths v Arch Engineering (1968)**. The claimant lost 20 per cent of his damages on the ground that his injuries may well have been less severe if he had gripped the grinding machine with both hands given that it was clearly a two-handed tool.

Topic illustration

Alf was given a new television set, manufactured by Consumer Electricals Ltd, as a birthday present, by his mother, Bertha. When Alf unpacked the television, he found that the set was slightly dusty, so he wiped it down with a wet cloth. Alf then plugged the television in and switched it on. The set exploded, injuring Alf and damaging various items of furniture in the vicinity. An investigation revealed that the explosion occurred because some of the wires had not been properly fitted, but that the situation had been made worse because of water which had leaked into the back of the set from Alf's cloth. There was a users' manual at the bottom of the box in which the television had been packed warning users not to use a wet cloth, but Alf had not read it.

Fig. 2

Alf has a potential claim in negligence against Consumer Electricals Ltd, and a discussion of that claim would cover the following points:

■ First, we need to identify the duty of care that Consumer Electricals owes to Alf, and to be able to explain why the former is the defendant and the latter is the claimant. This is a straightforward application of *Donoghue* v *Stevenson* (1932).

■ Secondly, Alf needs to establish a breach of that duty. This requires an application of the standard of the reasonable manufacturer of electrical equipment, and might involve a discussion of factors such as a faulty manufacturing process, the likelihood (or otherwise) that someone would inspect the television before it was first plugged in and the lack of a more prominent warning against wet cloths.

■ Causation and remoteness of damage are straightforward, but there is the possibility of a defence of contributory negligence. We need to discuss whether Alf acted as a reasonable person in wiping an item of electrical equipment with a wet cloth and whether he should have read the users' manual as a very first step.

Activities

1 In order to illustrate the wide nature of product liability in negligence, and in order to produce a revision tool, compile a table showing, for each of the cases in this section, what type of person each claimant was (for instance a consumer or a bystander), what type of person each defendant was (for instance a manufacturer or a repairer) and which factors the courts took into account when deciding whether the duty of care was broken.

2 Sylvia owns a large casserole dish, the handle of which was recently replaced by a local hardware store with a new handle that they had made themselves. Sylvia warned her cleaning lady, Tanya, that the dish, which was sitting on top of the stove, contained a very hot stew which Sylvia had just taken out of the oven. When Tanya, who was talking to her sister on her mobile phone at the time, came to move the dish, in order to clean the top of the stove, the handle snapped and hot stew spilled out scalding Tanya and damaging the kitchen floor. The casserole dish itself was badly dented in the accident.

Discuss whether the hardware store owes a duty of care in respect of the handle to Sylvia, Tanya or both, whether it broke that duty, which losses might be claimed by either lady and whether there is any defence.

You should now be able to:

- identify situations in which a duty of care exists

- explain the reasoning used by judges when deciding whether the duty of care has been broken.

2 Consumer Protection Act 1987

As an alternative to negligence, a person suffering loss caused by defective goods may be able to bring an action under the provisions of Part I of the **Consumer Protection Act 1987** (CPA 1987). The CPA 1987 was enacted in order to bring UK law into line with the requirements of a European Union directive concerning product liability. The key difference between the two types of action is whether the claimant needs to prove fault on the part of the defendant. In the case of an action in negligence, which is fault based, the claimant needs to show that the defendant fell below the standard of the reasonable person. But in the case of an action brought under the CPA 1987, liability is strict and the claimant does not have to prove any fault at all on the part of the defendant.

An example of this is **Abouzaid v Mothercare (2000)**. The claimant, a child, suffered a serious eye injury when he was hit in the face by a buckle. The buckle was part of a pram accessory and it was attached to an elastic strap that had sprung back when it had slipped from the grasp of the claimant. The defendant argued that there should be no liability because at the time that the product has been supplied no one, including child safety experts, was aware of the risk posed by the accessory. The court, however, found the defendant strictly liable under the Act on the ground that the accessory was clearly unsafe, but found no liability in ordinary negligence because the defendant had done all that the reasonable supplier of children's products would have done given that the risk was unknown at the time.

In this topic you will learn how to:

- identify the liability for defective products under the Consumer Protection Act 1987

- define the categories of defendant under the Act

- explain what is meant by 'defect' and 'damage'.

Key terms

Consumer Protection Act 1987: an Act which imposes strict liability for defective goods as an alternative to any action in negligence.

Key cases

Abouzaid v Mothercare (2000): actions in negligence and under the Consumer Protection Act 1987 for defective goods require the claimant to prove different levels of fault.

Nature of the liability under the CPA 1987

By s2(1) of the CPA 1987, a claimant may sue if he suffers damage which is caused wholly or partly by a defect in a product.

We now turn to consider who can be liable under the Act, and what is meant by the words 'product', 'defect' and 'damage'.

Defendant

The CPA 1987 imposes liability on four different classes of defendant:

1 By s2(2)(a), the producer of a product. 'Producer' is defined by s1(2) as:

    a The person who manufactured the product. In **Bogle v McDonald's Restaurants (2002)**, which we discuss later, a restaurant was held to be the producer of cups of coffee which it served.

    b The person who won or abstracted a substance (such as sand, gravel, coal or minerals).

    c The person who carried out a process which gave a product one of its essential characteristics (such as canning or freezing fruit and vegetables, cooking meat or dyeing cloth).

2 By s2(2)(b), a person who holds himself out to be the producer of a product by putting his name on the product or by using a trademark or other distinguishing mark in relation to the product. The best example is a supermarket which sells own-brand products, which were actually made by a different company.

3 By s2(2)(c), a person who has imported a product into the European Union in order to supply that product as part of a business.

4 By s2(3), a supplier of a product who, when asked by a claimant, fails to identify any person falling within the first three classes of defendant. Any request by the claimant must be made a reasonable time after the damage occurs and at a time when it is not reasonably practicable for the claimant to identify the defendant for himself.

If more than one person is liable, then, by s2(5), each is liable for the full amount, and the court will need to apportion liability between them.

Product

By s1(2), a **product** is any goods (including electricity), and includes any product within a product such as a component or raw materials. The Act states in s45(1) that 'product' includes substances, crops, things attached to land, and ships, vehicles and aircraft. Buildings are included if any damage or injury is caused by defective materials but are excluded if the loss is caused by poor workmanship.

In **A v National Blood Authority (2001)**, the court decided that human blood to be used in transfusions is a product covered by the Act. Presumably this would extend to body parts, such as hearts and corneas, to be used in transplant operations.

Defect

By s3 CPA 1987, there is a **defect** in a product if the safety of the product is not such as persons generally are entitled to expect in the circumstances.

In **Richardson v LRC Products Ltd (2000)**, a condom failed at just the moment when one would hope that a condom would not fail, and the claimant became pregnant as a result. The claimant failed in her action for the cost of bringing up the resulting child because, among other reasons, the condom was held not to be defective. Its safety was of a standard that people are entitled to expect, as it is widely known that such a product does not offer a complete guarantee.

The meaning of 'defect' was also considered in **A v National Blood Authority (2001)**. The claimant contracted the hepatitis C virus from contaminated blood given during a blood transfusion. The court decided that people generally expect a blood transfusion to be entirely safe, and in the event that it causes injury or loss then the supplier of the blood is liable under the Act.

Section 3 goes on to outline a number of factors which the courts should take into account when deciding if a product is defective.

- The marketing of the product: relevant factors might include the target of any advertising (such as products for children or for those with diabetes) and any claims made by the advertising (for instance, that goods have been tested to a higher standard than is normal).

- Instructions provided with goods: there are many examples of goods that are safe only if used properly. In those cases, whether the courts decide that an item is defective will depend on whether any instructions as to use or warning labels provide adequate information as to the dangers and how to avoid them. Examples include household medicines, DIY tools and chemicals used for clearing drains. In **Worsley v Tambrands (2000)**, the defendant, a manufacturer of tampons, was not liable for the consequences of toxic shock syndrome suffered by the claimant, a user of its products, because the box carried a clear warning.

- Reasonable expectations as to how the product is used: a properly constructed bath is suitable for taking baths, but no action would exist for losses caused if the bath were used in an attempt to cross the English Channel.

- Time of supply: as technology progresses, products will become safer. The Act is therefore careful to say that just because subsequent versions of a product are safer that does not mean that older versions are necessarily defective.

Another factor which might be taken into account is the consumer's reasonable care for his own safety. In **Bogle v McDonald's Restaurants (2002)**, the claimants were scalded by very hot drinks which were packaged in strong paper cups with lids, but which were knocked over on trays or on tables so that the lids came off allowing the hot liquid to pour out and cause injuries. The court held that the drinks were not defective as they were of a safety that people generally are entitled to expect in the circumstances, even though the lids came off. This was because sufficient precautions had been taken (the cups and their lids were of adequate strength and the staff had been trained to put the lids firmly on the cups) while still allowing customers to receive what they wanted (drinks served at near boiling temperatures and removable lids so that they could sip from the cups). In these circumstances, people knew that there was a risk, and that extra care should be taken particularly around children.

The Act, however, does not cover products which are faulty but which do not cause any damage or injury. If my new radio does not work, but is otherwise harmless and causes no damage, then I have no action.

Damage

By s5 of the CPA 1987, a claimant is able to sue for the following categories of damage caused by a defective product:

- Death or personal injury.
- Damage to property, including damage to land.

Key cases

A v National Blood Authority (2001): an item is defective if there is a general expectation that goods of that type will always be entirely safe.

Worsley v Tambrands (2000): instructions, labels and warnings will be taken into account when deciding if a product is defective.

Bogle v McDonald's Restaurants (2002): what a consumer might reasonably be expected to do to look after himself will be taken into account when deciding if a product is defective.

However, the following may not be claimed:

- Damage to property when the damage is worth less than £275.
- Damage to the defective item itself, or any item supplied with the defective item.
- Damage to any goods which are being used other than for personal use, for instance, a business use.

The Act, therefore, would not have helped the claimant in *Muirhead* v *Industrial Tank Specialties* (1985) which we discussed on p273.

Defences

The CPA 1987 sets out a number of defences to an action for a defective product. The most controversial of these is the development risks defence, which we will consider first before moving onto other defences covered by s4(1) and, finally, contributory negligence.

The development risks defence

By s4(1)(e) CPA 1987, it is a defence to a claim brought under the Act in respect of a defect in goods if the defendant can show that the state of scientific and technical knowledge at the time of the supply of the product was not advanced enough to allow a producer of goods of that type to discover the defect.

The **development risks defence** is controversial because it dents the Act's strict liability. Strict liability should mean that, in order to protect a claimant, a defendant is liable even if he is not at fault, but the defence allows the defendant to escape liability. If, therefore, a claimant suffers injury or loss as a result of something like a new medicine, cosmetic or food item which turns out to have unforeseen and harmful effects, he may not have a legal action. He cannot use negligence because if the defect is undiscoverable then the defendant will have done all that he reasonably could, given the state of scientific and technical knowledge; and he cannot use the Act because of the existence of the defence.

In applying the defence, the key issue is what is meant by 'the state of scientific and technical knowledge'. The following three cases give some guidance.

In **European Commission v UK (1997)**, the European Court of Justice (ECJ) said that only scientific and technical knowledge that was accessible should be taken into account. If knowledge is not accessible, then a defendant will escape liability. This raises the question as to what 'accessible' means. One example given during the case was that research published in Chinese in an obscure journal in Manchuria would not be accessible. Presumably, therefore, research published in the West would be accessible, and a defendant would not be able to use the defence even though he himself was unaware of the research.

The case reached the ECJ because it was thought that the version of the defence which appears in the UK Act was wider than the version in the original EU directive. The UK Act allows the defence when scientific and technical knowledge in the relevant industry is unaware of the defect, whereas the EU directive allows the defence only when general scientific and technical knowledge, whether inside the industry or elsewhere, is unaware of the defect. The court decided that the UK version was not necessarily incompatible with the directive, but any future case should interpret the defence according to EU law principles including the accessibility test.

Key terms

Development risks defence: a defence that allows a defendant to escape liability when a defect in a product is unknown and cannot be discovered given the current state of scientific and technical knowledge.

Key cases

European Commission v UK (1997): for the purposes of the development risks defence, scientific and technical knowledge only includes information which is accessible.

The defence was raised in **Abouzaid v Mothercare (2000)**, discussed earlier. The defendant's argument was that the defence should apply as even child safety experts had not identified the risk posed by a buckle attached to an elastic strap. The court rejected this argument on the ground that the defence was available only where the fault was undiscoverable by existing scientific and technical knowledge rather than simply because no one had thought to test for this particular problem.

The defence also failed in **A v National Blood Authority (2001)**, in which the claimant had contracted the hepatitis C virus from contaminated blood given during a blood transfusion. The defendant argued that although the risk of such an infection was known, there was no known way to test individual batches of blood to see which were infected. The court rejected this argument, saying that the development risks defence is only available when a risk is unknown not when it is known but cannot be identified in individual products.

Other defences available under s4(1) of the CPA 1987

There are five further defences listed by s4(1) CPA 1987. They are:

1   Compliance with the law (s4(1)(a)): it is a defence if a product is defective because the law said that it had to be made in a particular way. One example might be that a warning label on a dangerous product has to be in a particular form to comply with regulations, but the warning is in fact inadequate.

2   Non-supply of the product (s4(1)(b)): a defendant will escape liability if he can show that he has never supplied the product in question. One example may be if experimental goods are stolen, and sold on by the thieves.

3   Any supply was non-commercial (s4(1)(c)): there is no liability if the defendant supplied the goods without a view to a profit. Examples include donating items to a jumble sale and giving a prize to be used in a charity raffle.

4   The defect did not exist when the goods were put into circulation (s4(1)(d)): there is nso liability if the defendant can show that any defect only came into existence after the goods were supplied by him. Examples would be a third party deliberately adding a contaminant to a jar of jam after it had left the factory or a toaster becoming dangerous because someone has accidentally dropped it down the stairs.

5   Subsequent products (s4(1)(f)): a defendant will escape liability if he supplies a component to a manufacturer who incorporates the component into a larger product and the larger product is defective, provided that the defect has appeared either because of the design of the larger product or because the defendant followed the instructions of the manufacturer of the larger product.

Contributory negligence

Section 6(4) CPA 1987 preserves the defence of contributory negligence in relation to liability under the Act, so that if injury or damage to property occurs partly as a result of the actions of the claimant, the court will be able to reduce the amount of damages payable by the defendant to reflect the level of the claimant's contribution to his losses.

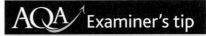
Examiner's tip

Once you have considered whether the defendant is liable, don't forget to go on to think about possible defences. However, you should not jump straight to the defences in your answer. Make sure you establish the main liability first.

Topic illustration

Consider again the scenario concerning Alf and his new television:

> Alf was given a new television set, manufactured by Consumer Electricals Ltd, as a birthday present, by his mother, Bertha. When Alf unpacked the television, he found that the set was slightly dusty, so he wiped it down with a wet cloth. Alf then plugged the television in and switched it on. The set exploded, injuring Alf and damaging various items of furniture in the vicinity. An investigation revealed that the explosion occurred because some of the wires had not been properly fitted, but that the situation had been made worse because of water which had leaked into the back of the set from Alf's cloth. There was a users' manual at the bottom of the box in which the television had been packed warning users not to use a wet cloth, but Alf had not read it.

In addition to any claim in negligence, Alf might also be able to claim under CPA 1987. Any discussion of that claim would cover the following points:

- The first step is to explain why Alf will be the claimant and why Consumer Electricals will be the defendant.
- Secondly, Alf needs to show that his case satisfies the rules relating to the definition of 'product' and 'defect'. This will require a discussion of the rules in respectively s1(2) and s3 of the CPA 1987.
- We then need to discuss which losses Alf can claim. Clearly he can claim for the injury to himself, but he will not be able to claim for the value of the television itself and he will only be able to claim for damage to other property if it exceeds £275.
- Finally, as with the claim in negligence, there is the issue of the defence of contributory negligence.

Activities

1 Compile a table to compare and contrast the rules governing liability for defective products in negligence and under the Consumer Protection Act 1987. Entries might include: rules relating to the identity of the claimant and the defendant, the definition of a defective product, the level of fault the claimant must prove, the types of damage which can be claimed and defences available.

2 Carla bought a bottle of own-brand drain cleaner from her local supermarket, which she poured down the plughole of her bath. The chemicals reacted with water in the drain causing the plughole to erupt in Carla's face burning her skin and damaging some towels.

Discuss whether Carla might have an action under the Consumer Protection Act 1987. Issues you may need to consider include the identity of the defendant, the packaging of the bottle, and what Carla might be able to claim for.

You should now be able to:

- consider the reasoning a court might use when deciding if liability under the Consumer Protection Act 1987 exists
- identify and explain defences which might exist to a claim under the Act.

17 Occupiers' liability

Introduction

The occupier of premises owes a duty to keep safe lawful visitors to those premises. The duty is imposed by the Occupiers' Liability Act 1957, which we will abbreviate in this chapter to 'OLA 1957'.

The occupier may also owe a second (and different) duty to protect trespassers who enter his premises. This duty is contained in the Occupiers' Liability Act 1984, and we will abbreviate the name of that Act to 'OLA 1984'.

As a first step, therefore, it is important to know whether an entrant to premises is a lawful visitor or a trespasser.

In this topic you will learn how to:

- define a lawful visitor and a trespasser

- identify and explain these concepts where a visitor has implied permission to enter or exceeds his permission to enter.

Key terms

Lawful visitor: a person who enters premises with either express or implied permission.

Key cases

Lowery v Walker (1911): a frequent entrant, to whom the occupier does not object, may have implied permission to be on the premises.

Jolley v Sutton London Borough Council (2000): if premises contain something which is an attraction to children, then the children will have implied permission to enter if the occupier does nothing to prevent them from investigating.

1 Lawful visitors and trespassers

Lawful visitors

A **lawful visitor** is someone who has permission to enter, and this can be either express or implied. If a person has express or stated permission to enter, there is normally no doubt that he is a lawful visitor. More difficult is when a person appears to be a trespasser, but the law implies permission for him to enter thus ensuring that he is a lawful visitor and one who is covered by OLA 1957. Four examples can be given:

1 Repeated visits

If the occupier knows, or should know, that people are repeatedly visiting his land, and he does nothing about it, then permission may well be implied. In **Lowery v Walker (1911)**, villagers were in the habit of taking a shortcut across the defendant's field to reach the railway station. The defendant, without warning, placed a wild horse in the field and it attacked one of the villagers. The court held that the villager was a lawful visitor, and therefore owed a duty by the defendant, as the defendant had known of the shortcut but had done little to discourage people from using it.

2 The doctrine of allurement

The doctrine of allurement states that a child will not be a trespasser if he wanders on to land to investigate something which is both dangerous and attractive to children. In *Cooke* v *Midland Great Western Railway* (1909), the allurement was a railway turntable and in **Jolley v Sutton London Borough Council (2000)** the attraction was an abandoned boat left on waste ground. In both cases, the child was able to claim, as a lawful visitor, for injuries sustained on the attractive item.

3 Entry in order to communicate

There is implied permission to walk up the front path of a house to the front door with the purpose of communicating with the occupants (*Robson* v *Hallett* (1967)). This permission does not extend beyond the front door, even if it should be open, and it does not cover any person who is forbidden to enter by a notice on a gate (for instance hawkers, canvassers and salesmen). If asked to leave, the visitor remains a lawful visitor as long as he leaves within a reasonable time and by a reasonable route.

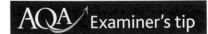
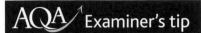
Key terms

Trespasser: someone other than a lawful visitor; he or she has no permission to enter.

Key cases

Pearson v Coleman Bros (1948): if it is unclear where on premises a visitor may go, the visitor will be given the benefit of the doubt.

Tomlinson v Congleton Borough Council (2003): if a lawful visitor exceeds the permission he has to enter, then he becomes a trespasser.

4 Statutory powers of entry

There are a large number of circumstances when a person is authorised by a statutory power to enter the premises. Examples include an electricity meter reader, a postman, a fireman and a policeman with a search warrant. In such a case, the entrant will be a lawful visitor even if the occupier objects to his presence.

Trespassers

A **trespasser** is:

■ a person who enters without an invitation; and

■ either whose presence is unknown to the occupier, or, if known, is objected to by the occupier in some actual practical fashion, for example, a sign, a locked gate or a verbal warning.

Trespass is a strict liability tort: it is irrelevant that the trespass is inadvertent or unintentional. The motive is also irrelevant: a child on an adventure or a walker who has lost his way are trespassers in the same way as a burglar or a poacher.

Sometimes a person who begins his visit as a lawful visitor can become a trespasser. This will occur if the visitor's permission to enter the land is limited or restricted in some way and he oversteps that limit. Three examples can be given:

1 Limit as to area

It is commonplace for a visitor to premises not to have permission to wander at will throughout those premises. A student at school probably should not enter the staffroom or the head teacher's study without an invitation, and a visitor to a stately home or a museum should not go through a door marked 'Authorised Personnel Only'.

If the limits of the permission are unclear, the court will give a claimant the benefit of the doubt. In **Pearson v Coleman Bros (1948)**, the claimant, a young girl, was visiting a circus with her family. While looking for the toilet, she wandered into the zoo area and was mauled by a lion. She was able to claim as a lawful visitor as it was not at all clear that she should not have been where she was, for instance there was a lack of signs and barriers.

2 Limit as to time

A visitor who stays longer than they should becomes a trespasser. A student at school or someone visiting a museum will become a trespasser if they linger after closing time.

3 Limit as to purpose

A visitor, who is invited to premises for a particular purpose but then chooses to undertake a different activity, also risks becoming a trespasser. The most famous judicial statement to this effect is as follows (although the case itself was about navigation and the proper use of a shipping channel):

> When you invite a person into your house to use the staircase, you do not invite him to slide down the banisters, you invite him to use the staircase in the ordinary way in which it is used. (Scrutton LJ The Carlgarth (1927))

In **Tomlinson v Congleton Borough Council (2003)**, the claimant visited a country park owned by the defendant council. He chose to dive into a lake despite the presence of a sign forbidding swimming. At that point the claimant became a trespasser as he had moved from activities he was permitted to undertake to an activity he was not permitted to undertake. Consequently, when he was injured in the lake, his claim was brought under OLA 1984, as a trespasser, even though he had started as a lawful visitor.

Activities

1 Given that trespassers can include everyone from playing children to burglars, consider the advantages and disadvantages of a legal duty to safeguard those entering without permission. Should occupiers be allowed to maintain defences such as broken glass embedded in the top of a wall or barbed wire?

2 How is the difference between a sign that says 'Keep Out' and one that says 'Slippery Footpath – Be Careful' relevant to the decision whether an entrant is a lawful visitor or a trespasser?

You should now be able to:

- identify which entrants to premises are owed the duty under the Occupiers' Liability Act 1957 and which are owed the duty under the Occupiers' Liability Act 1984

- explain the difference between express permission to enter and implied permission to enter.

2 Occupiers' Liability Act 1957

A claim under OLA 1957 operates in much the same way as a claim for negligence: the claimant must show that a duty of care exists, that the defendant has breached the duty and that the breach has led to damage. In turn, the defendant can establish one or more of a number of defences, and there are issues relating to remedies for a successful claimant.

The duty

Establishing the existence of a duty of care is straightforward. By s2(1) of OLA 1957, an occupier of premises owes a duty of care to all his lawful visitors.

The duty of care

According to s2(2) of OLA 1957, the duty of care is:

> a duty to take such care as in all the circumstances of the case is reasonable to see that the visitor will be reasonably safe in using the premises for the purposes for which he is invited or permitted by the occupier to be there.

This definition makes heavy use of the idea of 'reasonableness'. The occupier should act only with reasonable care and he should ensure that his visitor is simply reasonably safe. The duty is also a duty to keep visitors safe and not premises. This is because sometimes the economic cost of making premises safe would be unreasonable. If land contains dangerous cliffs, crumbling archaeological ruins or deep wells, it is more sensible to put up fences and warning notices than to try to eliminate the danger.

Occupier

OLA 1957 does not define who an **occupier** is, but it is clear from the cases that an occupier is any person who controls the premises (or the

In this topic you will learn how to:

- explain what is meant by the term 'duty of care' in the context of the Occupiers' Liability Act 1957

- define key terms such as 'occupier' and 'premises'

- consider when a duty of care has been breached and when the occupier might have a defence.

Key terms

Occupier of premises: a person whose control of those premises is such that his actions can prevent or cause risk to visitors.

relevant part of the premises) to such an extent that his carelessness could lead to a visitor suffering loss. The obvious example is the owner of the premises, but others might include a tenant, the organiser of a stall at a fairground, the main contractors in a large building project and a local authority that has taken possession of a house.

Possession need not be exclusive, and it is possible for premises to have more than one occupier. In **Wheat v Lacon (1966)**, the first defendant was the manager of a pub owned by the second defendant. The first defendant lived in a flat over the premises and, with the permission of the owner, took in paying guests in his private accommodation. One guest was killed when he tripped and fell down the back stairs. The court decided that both the manager and the brewery owed the guest a duty under OLA 1957 (although in the event the claim failed as the claimant was unable to show negligence against either). When more than one person is an occupier, the duties of the different occupiers may vary according to the degree of control they exercise, perhaps as to different parts of the building including different parts of the fabric of the building.

Premises

Premises include land and any buildings on the land. By s1(3)(a) of OLA 1957, the term also includes any fixed or moveable structure, for instance a shed, a bridge or scaffolding, and any vessel, vehicle or aircraft.

Discharging the duty

The standard of care to be shown by the occupier is the same as the standard of care in ordinary negligence. This means that the occupier should act as the reasonable occupier would have done in the same circumstances, and that the court will refer to the same cases and rules as in negligence. We referred to these on pp240–1, and you should be particularly aware of the rules in cases like *Bolton* v *Stone* (1951), *Paris* v *Stepney Borough Council* (1951), *Watt* v *Hertfordshire County Council* (1954) and *Latimer* v *AEC* (1953).

Warnings

The duty of care is to keep the visitor safe rather than the premises. To this end, s2(4)(a) of OLA 1957 states that the occupier may be able to carry out his duty by providing **reasonable warnings**. These might be implied warnings, such as a fence or a locked door, or express warnings, such as a notice warning of dangers. Any notice should be clear in explaining the danger and should be visible. In **Woollins v British Celanese (1966)**, the defendant was liable as, although it had put up a notice warning of a dangerous roof, the notice was behind a door so that it was not easily visible to anyone working in the area.

The occupier's duty is varied in two particular circumstances:

Children

By s2(3)(a) of OLA 1957, an occupier must be prepared for children to be less careful than adults. Consequently, it is not a defence for an occupier to say that any precautions he took would have been adequate to protect an adult if the reasonable occupier would have taken further precautions to protect a child. In **Moloney v Lambeth London Borough Council (1966)**, a four-year-old child slipped through the banisters lining a staircase in a block of flats. The defendant council was liable as it was foreseeable that small children would be using the staircase and it was no defence that the gaps in the banisters were too small for an adult to fall through.

Young children present a particular difficulty to occupiers: almost anything can be dangerous to them and they rarely understand written notices warning of danger. However, when deciding what precautions need to be taken, an occupier is entitled to expect that parents will take appropriate care of young children. In **Phipps v Rochester Corporation (1955)**, a five-year-old boy fell into a substantial trench dug by the defendant on its own land. The child was held to be a lawful visitor, as the defendant knew children played on the site but had done nothing to prevent them from doing so, but his claim failed on the ground that reasonable parents would not allow their children to be placed in a dangerous situation without proper supervision and protection.

A specialist visitor undertaking his job

By s2(3)(b) of OLA 1957, an occupier may expect that a specialist visitor will be aware of and will protect himself against risks within his own specialism. If an occupier knows that the electrics in his house are unsafe, and he calls out an electrician to deal with the problem, then the occupier may take fewer precautions with respect to the danger as the electrician should know what he is doing. In **Roles v Nathan (1963)**, two chimney sweeps died after they were overcome by carbon monoxide fumes when cleaning out part of the defendant's heating system. The claim brought under OLA 1957 failed, as they had been properly warned about the danger and the risk was one they should have been familiar with and known how to have dealt with.

Causation and remoteness

As with any negligence based action, once the claimant has shown that a duty of care exists and that it has been broken, he must then go on to show that the defendant's actions caused his loss and that any loss is not too remote a consequence of the negligence. These rules were described in Topic 4 of Chapter 14, Negligence: physical damage and medical negligence.

Defences

An occupier may use the following defences to a claim brought under OLA 1957.

Independent contractors

By s2(4)(b) of OLA 1957, the occupier is not liable if the visitor is injured by something dangerous that was created by faulty workmanship on the part of an outside contractor, provided that it was reasonable for the occupier to have brought in an **independent contractor**, and provided that the occupier took reasonable steps to ensure that the contractor was competent and that the work had been properly done.

This means that an occupier will not be liable if his property is dangerous because of work done by an outside contractor if the work is beyond the knowledge and expertise of an ordinary reasonable person either to complete for himself or to check. Examples might include rewiring the electrics or fitting a satellite dish. In **Haseldine v Daw (1941)**, the claimant was injured when, while visiting the defendant's premises, the lift he was travelling in fell to the ground. The defendant was not liable because a reasonable person would ask a reputable contractor to maintain a lift and would not be in a position to check the work.

However, if the work could have been completed or checked by the occupier himself, then he will be liable even if he chooses to ask an outside contractor to do it. Examples might include cleaning a floor so that it is not left in a slippery state, or fitting a carpet so that the edges are loose and there is a danger of someone tripping over. In **Woodward v Mayor of Hastings (1944)**, an outside contractor swept snow from the steps of a school, but failed to deal with the frozen snow underneath so that the steps were left in a slippery condition. The claimant, a pupil of

Key cases

Phipps v Rochester Corporation (1955): an occupier of land is entitled to assume that small children will be properly supervised.

Roles v Nathan (1963): a specialist visitor to premises can be expected to guard against risks related to his specialism.

AQA Examiner's tip

Having identified that an occupier owes a duty under the Occupiers' Liability Act 1957, make sure that you discuss whether he has breached the duty, and make sure you focus on relevant factors: there is little point in giving a full discussion of children if the entrant is an adult.

Key terms

Independent contractor: someone who is not an employee but who is carrying out a service in exchange for a fee.

Key cases

Haseldine v Daw (1941): an occupier is not liable for risks created by an independent contractor provided that the risk is something which the occupier could not be expected to check for himself.

Woodward v Mayor of Hastings (1944): an occupier will be liable for the actions of an outside contractor if he could have completed or checked the work for himself.

the school, fell and was badly injured. The defendant was liable, because a reasonable person ought to be able to check whether steps are safe even if they had asked someone else to sweep them.

Contributory negligence

Section 2(3) states that when considering a claim brought under OLA 1957, the court should consider both the care and lack of care which would ordinarily be looked for in a visitor. This is the defence of contributory negligence, and it works in the same way against an action brought under OLA 1957 as it does against an action in ordinary negligence. You should therefore be familiar with the principles relating to the defence, which we discussed in Topic 6 of Chapter 14, Negligence: physical damage and medical negligence, and be prepared to use them when discussing OLA 1957.

Consent

Similarly, s2(5) of OLA 1957 states that the defence of consent is available against an action brought under OLA 1957, where the visitor consents to the risk of negligence on the part of the occupier. The defence uses the same principles as in ordinary negligence, and again we discussed these in Topic 6 of Chapter 14, Negligence: physical damage and medical negligence. However, the defence is unlikely to be used often, as a visitor will not normally consent to such a risk.

Excluding liability

By s2(1) of OLA 1957, an occupier may restrict or exclude altogether the duty of care owed to his visitors. This might be done by putting up a sign saying that he does not accept responsibility for the safety of anyone visiting the premises, although any such sign should be clearly worded and clearly visible. In **Ashdown v Samuel Williams & Sons Ltd (1957)**, the claimant was in the habit of taking a shortcut to her workplace across the railway goods yard belonging to the defendant. She was hit by some railway trucks that were being shunted negligently, but her claim under OLA 1957 failed because there were clear signs saying that people took the shortcut at their own risk.

The rule allowing exclusion of liability has been substantially modified in the case of business premises by the provisions of the Unfair Contract Terms Act 1977 (UCTA 1977). By s2(1) of that Act, liability cannot be excluded for the death or personal injury of a visitor where that loss is caused by negligence; and by s2(2) liability for other types of loss caused by negligence can only be excluded if it is reasonable for the occupier to do so.

However, by s1(3)(b) of UCTA 1977, the occupier of business premises is able to exclude liability in respect of visitors admitted for a recreational or educational purpose which is outside the occupier's business. An example might be a farmer who allows a class from the local school to conduct a nature trip in one of his fields.

Remedies

A successful claimant can claim damages for death and personal injury. By s1(3) of OLA 1957, he can also claim damages for damage to property (including damage to the property of someone other than himself) and any consequential economic loss resulting from damage to property such as the costs of recovery.

AQA Examiner's tip

This defence is often relevant. Ask yourself whether the visitor himself acted reasonably and sensibly at all times.

Key cases

Ashdown v Samuel Williams & Sons Ltd (1957): an occupier may exclude any liability he might have under the Occupiers' Liability Act 1957 by giving proper notice to the visitor.

Topic illustration

Consider this scenario, taken from a recent exam paper.

> Gordon engaged Ian to repair damage to a wall in his house. While doing so, Ian cut through an electricity cable and fused the power supply. Gordon was out, so Ian opened the locked door to the cellar with a key hanging from a nail on a nearby wall. As he went down the cellar stairs to find the electricity unit, a rotten stair gave way under his weight and he fell, breaking his leg and ripping his clothes.

In discussing Ian's possible claim under OLA 1957, we would need to consider the following issues:

- The first issue is whether Ian is a lawful visitor. He was clearly an invitee to the premises when he arrived to repair the wall, and we can argue that he remained a lawful visitor when he entered the cellar as it was a necessary, if unexpected, part of his job.

- Assuming Ian is a lawful visitor, we need to establish whether Gordon owed a duty of care to Ian on the ground that he is an occupier and that the house is within the definition of premises.

- The next issue is whether Gordon broke the duty he owes to Ian. Did he act as the reasonable occupier would have done? We can discuss issues such as whether there was a need for a warning in the circumstances and whether the presence of a locked door was adequate protection.

- There is little to discuss on the issues of causation and remoteness: Ian's losses are reasonably foreseeable. However, there may be an issue of contributory negligence given that Ian went somewhere unusual without checking and perhaps with no light.

- Finally, there is the issue of remedies. As this is OLA 1957, Ian can claim both for personal injury and for damage to property (his clothes).

Activities

1 In *Searson* v *Brioland* (2005), the claimant was an 82-year-old lady attending the wedding reception for her granddaughter at the defendant's banqueting venue. As she was leaving through the exterior door, she tripped over the raised threshold which had a height of 2.8cm. The Court of Appeal allowed her claim for damages for the injuries she had sustained on the grounds that the claimant's mind was on other matters, there was no warning of a raised step and it is unexpected to step *up* when leaving a building (as distinct from entering a building). Do you agree that liability should exist in such circumstances?

2 Consider this scenario, which has been adapted from a recent exam paper:

Jarvis opens his large house and gardens to the public. On one particular day, despite torrential rain, Liam visited the house and paid the entrance fee. Jarvis's gardens were laid out on a number of levels, the path between two levels consisting of steep steps. Down one side of the steps was a low spiked fence, to which a handrail was attached. A notice at the top of the steps warned that extra care was necessary in wet weather. Liam slipped and overbalanced while running down the steps holding the handrail, and was jerked round onto the spikes of the fence badly cutting his face.

Why is Liam a lawful visitor? What factors might the court take into account when deciding whether Jarvis breached the duty he owed under the Act? If Jarvis is found to have breached the duty, can he rely on any defence?

You should now be able to:

- identify factors which a court might take into account when deciding whether an occupier has breached the duty of care he owes to a visitor

- identify and explain possible defences to an action brought under the Occupiers' Liability Act 1957.

In this topic you will learn how to:

■ identify the limited circumstances in which the duty under the Occupiers' Liability Act 1984 is owed

■ explain the nature of the duty and the standard expected of an occupier.

3 Occupiers' Liability Act 1984

A trespasser is not a lawful visitor and is therefore not protected by OLA 1957. Originally, the law offered such a person little, if any, protection, but this was a harsh approach and could be very unfair if for instance a wandering child was involved. The House of Lords therefore modified the law in *British Railways Board* v *Herrington* (1972). The claimant, a child aged six, was badly injured when he trespassed onto an electrified railway line owned by the defendant. The railway line ran next to a field open to the public and where the defendant knew that it was common for children to play. The fence between the field and the line had been trodden down for some time, but the defendant had done nothing about it. The House of Lords held that the defendant was liable because common sense and common humanity suggested that if a company were to build something as dangerous as an electric railway line in the vicinity of an area in which children played they should take measures to protect the children, particularly where the danger, as here, was not obvious to a small child. However, this duty of 'common humanity' was uncertain in its scope, so Parliament clarified the position with the enactment of the Occupiers' Liability Act 1984.

When is the duty under OLA 1984 owed?

A potential claimant under OLA 1984 must overcome two preliminary hurdles before he can show that the occupier of premises owes him a duty under the Act at all.

The first is that the claim must arise out of the dangerous state of the premises rather than the dangerous activities of the claimant himself. If the premises are safe, but the accident was caused by the claimant acting unwisely, then the duty under OLA 1984 does not arise. In **Keown v Coventry NHS Trust (2006)**, the claimant was an 11-year-old boy playing with other children on land around a building owned by the defendant. At that stage, the claimant was a lawful visitor, as the defendant knew that children played there, but he became a trespasser when he overstepped the limit of any implied permission by climbing 'monkey fashion' up the underside of a metal fire escape attached to the outside of the building. The claimant fell and was badly injured, but his claim failed as the accident happened through his own dangerous activities and not because of any fault with the building. A similar example is *Tomlinson* v *Congleton Borough Council* (2003), discussed on pp282–3. The defendant owed no duty as the premises in question, the lake, were not unsafe as far as lakes go.

Key cases

Keown v Coventry NHS Trust (2006): an occupier does not owe a duty under the Occupiers' Liability Act 1984 when the risk is created by the dangerous activities of the entrant rather than the state of the premises.

Fig. 1 *In* Keown *v* Coventry NHS Trust *the claim failed as the claimant fell as a result of his own activities and not because of a fault with the building*

The second hurdle is the provisions of s1(3) of OLA 1984, which states that an occupier owes a duty in respect of a danger on his premises if:

- he is aware of the danger or has reasonable grounds to believe that it exists

- he knows or has reasonable grounds to believe that someone else is in the vicinity of the danger or may come into the vicinity of the danger

- the danger is one which, in all the circumstances, he may reasonably be expected to offer some protection against.

If the claimant cannot show that these three conditions all exist, then the defendant owes no duty of care and the claim fails. One illustration of this is **Donoghue v Folkestone Properties (2003)**. In the middle of a winter's night, the claimant dived into a harbour owned by the defendant and broke his neck when he collided with an underwater piling. The claimant was a trespasser, but the defendant was held not to owe a duty under OLA 1984 as it had no reasonable ground to believe that anyone would be in the vicinity of the danger as it could not be anticipated that anyone would want to dive into a harbour at that time of the night and at that time of the year.

A more complex example is **Scott v Associated British Ports (2000)**, in which the defendant was the occupier of a railway line. There had been two instances of 'train surfing' (youngsters attempting to jump onto goods trains as they moved slowly past) both of which had led to the participant losing a limb. The accidents were a number of years apart. With respect to the first, the defendant did not owe a duty under OLA 1984 as they had not known that trespassers were present. In the second case, this was not so because of the defendant's knowledge of the first incident. (In the event, the defendant was not liable as the court decided that even if the area had been properly fenced, the claimant would still have got in and thus causation was not proven.)

Fig. 2 Scott v Associated British Ports (2000) *demonstrates the rules of the OLA with regard to trespassers train surfing*

The Duty under OLA 1984

By s1(4) of OLA 1984, the duty owed by an occupier to a trespasser is to take such care as is reasonable in all the circumstances to see that the trespasser does not suffer injury on the premises because of the danger.

By s1(2) of OLA 1984, the terms 'occupier' and 'premises' have the same meaning as they do for the purposes of OLA 1957. Similarly, a

Key cases

Donoghue v Folkestone Properties (2003): an occupier will not owe a duty under s1(3) Occupiers' Liability Act 1984 if he cannot be expected to know that trespassers will be in the vicinity of a danger at that time.

Scott v Associated British Ports (2000): a court may decide that a defendant has the relevant knowledge because of previous incidents on the premises.

AQA Examiner's tip

Unlike the duty under the Occupiers' Liability Act 1957, the duty under the 1984 Act is not automatic. There will be instances where the occupier owes no duty at all.

trespasser is someone who is not a lawful visitor for the purposes of OLA 1957. (The protection offered by OLA 1984 also covers someone entering under the National Parks and Access to the Countryside Act 1949 and the Countryside and Rights of Way Act 2000, and someone exercising a private right of way. There is a different duty for people on a public right of way.)

Discharging the duty

Case law suggests that the courts are prepared to take a reasonable, not to say, fairly brisk approach when considering whether an occupier has done enough to protect unlawful visitors on his premises. Factors which the judge might take into account include likelihood of trespass, seriousness of the injury risked, the cost and practicality of precautions, the likely age of any trespasser, common sense and the fact that an occupier should not have to guard against an irresponsible minority. In **Platt v Liverpool City Council (1997)**, the claimant, a child, was killed when the derelict building in which he was trespassing collapsed. The defendant was held not liable on the ground that there was nothing more that they could reasonably have done: they had secured the building with an eight-foot-high metal fence with wooden posts secured in concrete. The court recognised that it is impossible to guard against a determined and irresponsible minority.

As with OLA 1957, the occupier may be able to discharge his duty by taking such steps as are reasonable in all the circumstances of the case to give warning of the danger concerned or to discourage persons from incurring the risk (s1(5) of OLA 1984). This might include clear and visible warning signs, fences and secured entrances. In **Tomlinson v Congleton Borough Council (2003)**, we have already discussed why the occupier did not owe a duty. However, the House of Lords stated that even if a duty had been owed, the occupier, by putting up signs forbidding swimming, had done enough to discharge the duty.

With respect to what an occupier might need to do to discharge his duty, *Tomlinson* is also interesting for further remarks made by the House of Lords. The defendant had made known its plans to prevent such an accident happening again by turning the beach, from which the claimant had dived, into marshy ground so that people would be unable to get close to the lake. The House of Lords said that such action was unnecessary: it would be very expensive; it would be a measure needed to stop only a small number of irresponsible people; and it would deprive the vast majority of visitors of the use of a beach.

Defences

Contributory negligence

Although OLA 1984 makes no specific mention of a defence of contributory negligence, it is clear that judges will accept the defence. As with OLA 1957, the defence works in the same way as it does for a claim in ordinary negligence.

Consent

Section 1(6) of OLA 1984 states that the defendant owes no duty in respect of risks willingly accepted by the trespasser.

In **Ratcliff v McConnell (1999)** the claimant, an adult student at the defendant college, dived one night into an outdoor swimming pool owned by the defendant, but misjudged his actions and suffered very serious injuries when he broke his neck. The claimant was a trespasser as he had ignored signs prohibiting use of the pool and had clambered over a

> ### Key cases
>
> **Platt v Liverpool City Council (1997)**: an occupier may have done all that is reasonable even if he cannot guard against a determined and irresponsible minority.

> ### Key cases
>
> **Tomlinson v Congleton Borough Council (2003)**: clear and visible signs warning of a danger may be all that an occupier needs to do to satisfy his duty under the Occupiers' Liability Act 1984.
>
> **Ratcliff v McConnell (1999)**: an occupier owes no duty in respect of risks willingly accepted by the trespasser.

fence to get to it. The court decided that the defendant did not owe a duty under OLA 1984 as the claimant was aware of the risk of diving into a pool in the dark and had accepted that risk.

Excluding liability

The law is not clear whether an occupier of premises can exclude any duty he might owe under OLA 1984 by, for instance, putting up a sign stating that people enter at their own risk. The question is not dealt with in either the Occupiers' Liability Act 1984 or the Unfair Contract Terms Act 1977, and there appears to be no case law decision either.

It might be that an occupier can exclude the duty, but within the same limits relating to business premises as exist for OLA 1957. Alternatively, given that OLA 1984 was a result of the House of Lords establishing a duty of common humanity in the *British Railways Board* v *Herrington* (1972) case, it might be that the duty is an unexcludable minimum: it is owed in all circumstances because common decency and humanity suggests that it should be. If this latter approach is correct, then it is probably also correct to say that in those circumstances where an occupier is able to exclude his duty under OLA 1957, he will in fact be unable to exclude his liability altogether but will instead owe the lower duty under OLA 1984, otherwise lawful visitors would be left in a worse position than trespassers.

Remedies

A successful claimant can claim damages for death and personal injury, but, by s1(8) of OLA 1984, he cannot claim damages for any loss to his property.

Topic illustration

Consider again the scenario concerning Ian and Gordon:

> Gordon engaged Ian to repair damage to a wall in his house. While doing so, Ian cut through an electricity cable and fused the power supply. Gordon was out, so Ian opened the locked door to the cellar with a key hanging from a nail on a nearby wall. As he went down the cellar stairs to find the electricity unit, a rotten stair gave way under his weight and he fell, breaking his leg and ripping his clothes.

On this occasion, we are discussing Ian's possible claim under OLA 1984:

- The first issue remains whether Ian is a lawful visitor. Although he first entered Gordon's house as a lawful visitor, there is an argument that he became a trespasser when he exceeded his permission to be there, either by trying to do something he wasn't engaged to do (switching off the electricity) or by going somewhere Gordon did not expect him to go (the issue of the locked door and the key is relevant).
- Assuming Ian is an unlawful visitor, we need to establish whether Gordon owed a duty of care to Ian under OLA 1984. Our discussion would focus on s1(3), and on questions such as whether Gordon knew that Ian would go into the cellar and whether he knew that the step was rotten.
- If Gordon does owe the duty, we need to define the duty, and discuss whether Gordon did take such care as is reasonable in all the circumstances.
- Finally, as with OLA 1957, there is the issue of a possible defence in contributory negligence and the question of remedies (damages for personal injury only).

Activities

1 Several of the cases discussed in this section involve people diving into shallow water and sustaining extremely serious and permanent injuries. Can anything realistically be done to prevent such accidents?

2 Consider this scenario, which has been adapted from a recent exam paper:

Following recent embarrassing revelations, Andrew was being pursued by investigative journalists from the national press. He retreated to his weekend cottage, and engaged Charles, a local joiner, to fit shutters to the outside of all windows to protect his privacy. While doing so, Charles fell from a ladder and broke his arm, when a rotten window sill on which he had placed his foot gave way under his weight. David, one of the reporters, climbed a wall at night to get into the grounds of the cottage. When he jumped down, he landed on an old glass frame left under the wall and suffered a very bad cut to his leg.

In relation to both Charles and David, consider the issues of whether Andrew owed a duty, whether he breached any duty owed and whether any defences and remedies may be available.

AQA Examiner's tip

When referring to the Occupiers' Liability Act, make sure you always state whether it is the 1957 or 1984 Act to which you refer.

You should now be able to:

■ explain the duty contained in the Occupiers' Liability Act 1984 and when it might apply

■ consider factors which a court might take into account when deciding if an occupier has breached the duty owed to trespassers

■ identify possible defences.

18

The tort of nuisance and the rule in *Rylands* v *Fletcher*

Introduction

This chapter is about liability for activities which interfere with another person's land or which cause a nuisance to the public at large. Such liability exists in four types:

1 Private nuisance: an activity which interferes with a person's ability to use his own land in a reasonable way.

2 Public nuisance: an activity which impacts on the public at large.

3 The rule in *Rylands* v *Fletcher* (1868): a specific type of nuisance which covers an escape of a dangerous substance.

4 Statutory nuisance: there are a number of statutes covering matters such as clean air, an escape of oil or chemicals, water pollution, radioactive substances and public health and hygiene.

We consider only the first three, as statutory liability is outside the scope of the A Level specification.

In this topic you will learn how to:

- explain and define what is meant by private nuisance

- outline the factors a court will use when deciding if an activity is lawful

- identify defences and remedies appropriate to a claim in private nuisance.

Key terms

Private nuisance: an activity which interferes for a substantial length of time with the claimant's right to enjoy his land in a reasonable way.

Legal interest: formal ownership or control of land, for instance the freehold or a tenancy.

Key cases

Hunter v Canary Wharf (1997): to sue in private nuisance, a claimant must have a legal interest in the land affected.

1 Private nuisance

A **private nuisance** is an unlawful interference for a substantial length of time with a person's right to enjoy or use his land in a reasonable way and is actionable as a tort.

A claimant in an action for private nuisance must show that:

- he has the right to bring an action and that the person he is suing is capable of being a defendant

- there is an interference in the form of either physical damage to the land or a loss of amenity (convenience) in using the land

- the interference is sufficiently serious in all the circumstances to be unlawful.

If the claimant is successful in all of these, the defendant may show one of the defences available in any action for private nuisance, but if that fails the claimant will be entitled to a remedy from the court usually in the form of damages or an injunction or both.

The parties to an action for private nuisance

Claimant

To be able to bring an action in private nuisance, a claimant must be someone with a **legal interest** in the affected land, such as an owner or a tenant. This rule was confirmed by the House of Lords in **Hunter v Canary Wharf (1997)**. The case was brought by a number of claimants who were complaining about things such as dust and interference with television reception caused by the building works relating to the Canary Wharf development in London's Docklands. Some of the claimants were unable to pursue their claims because they lacked any legal interest in the affected land, one example being a wife who did not jointly own the family home with her husband.

The reason for this rule is that private nuisance is a tort relating to interference with land and the possible impact that that might have on the value of the land, and therefore the proper claimant is the person who might suffer a financial loss. In addition, if the law protected people other than owners (for instance, lodgers), it might be very difficult for someone who is creating a nuisance to reach an out of court settlement with all the various interested parties.

Defendant

The obvious defendant is the creator of the nuisance.

In addition, the occupier of the land, if he is a different person from the creator of the nuisance, can also be a defendant if he adopts or continues the activities of the creator. One example is **Sedleigh-Denfield v O'Callaghan (1940)**, where a trespasser installed a pipe in a ditch on the defendant's land. Three years later, the pipe became blocked and the subsequent flooding damaged the claimant's land. The defendant was liable, even though he had not installed the pipe, as he knew of its existence.

Finally, it is possible for a landlord to be liable for the activities of a tenant if he authorised or approved those activities. In **Tetley v Chitty (1986)**, a local council was liable for the noise and disturbance caused by a go-kart club after the council had leased land to the club for the express purpose of developing a race track.

Interference

Claims in private nuisance cover two types of interference with, or loss to, the affected land.

1 Physical damage

Private nuisance covers **physical damage to land**, to plants and crops growing in the land and probably damage to goods stored on the land. However, private nuisance does not allow the recovery of damages for personal injury, and in those circumstances, a claimant should bring an action in negligence.

Examples of physical damage include gases from a factory killing or damaging flowers, oil smuts from a refinery covering washing pegged on a line or damaging paintwork, water damage if a drain overflows and damage to foundations caused by vibrations from a generating plant.

2 Loss of amenity/enjoyment

Nuisance also covers cases where there is no physical damage, but where the claimant's ability to use or enjoy his land is restricted by the activities of the defendant. This is known as **loss of amenity**. Examples include excessive noise preventing the claimant from getting a good night's sleep, or unpleasant smells and fumes preventing the claimant from opening his windows.

Unlawfulness

When will an interference be unlawful?

The function of private nuisance is to balance the conflicting interests of neighbours. In general, people do have the right to use their own land as they wish, and it might be that their neighbours have to put up with the occasional late night party or with the noise from the building of a conservatory.

However, there is a limit beyond which activities become unlawful. The test that the courts use in deciding when this limit has been reached is whether the nuisance interferes with ordinary existence, in other words

---

Key cases

Sedleigh-Denfield v O'Callaghan (1940): a person can be liable for a private nuisance which he did not create, if he adopts the activity in question.

Tetley v Chitty (1986): a person can be liable for a private nuisance which he does not create but which he authorises.

Key terms

Physical damage to land: actual damage to land or the buildings and plants on the land.

Loss of amenity: interference with the claimant's ability to use his land in a reasonable way.

whether the impact on the claimant is so unreasonable that he should not be expected to put up with it.

To help them make this decision the court will consider a number of factors when balancing the conflicting interests of the claimant and the defendant. One interesting result of this balancing of the factors is that certain activities will be lawful in some sets or circumstances but not in others, so that we can say that nuisance has a variable standard. One example is that playing very loud music through the night is not a problem in an isolated farmhouse but would be a problem in a block of flats.

The following are factors which the court might take into account when balancing the conflicting interests of neighbours:

- The locality of the events.
- The duration of the nuisance.
- The degree to which the activity interferes with neighbours.
- The sensitivity of the claimant.
- The reasons for the defendant's activities and whether they have a useful function.
- The motive behind the defendant's activities and whether he is acting simply out of malice.

1 Locality

The location of the nuisance is important as a wider range of activities are acceptable in, for instance, industrial zones than in residential areas. In **Halsey v Esso (1961)**, for instance, the defendant oil company was found liable for the activities of its oil depot which was located in the middle of a housing area. Part of the nuisance was the constant coming and going of oil tankers by day and by night, which would have been less of a problem on an industrial estate.

However, locality is irrelevant where the nuisance causes physical damage. This can be seen in **St Helens Smelting v Tipping (1865)**. The claimant complained that fumes from the defendant's copper smelting works were damaging trees and crops on the claimant's land. The claimant was successful, even though the location was a manufacturing area, because the courts will act to prevent physical damage.

2 Duration

The more often something happens, the more likely it is to be nuisance. However, in the right circumstances, even a single event can amount to nuisance. In **Spicer v Smee (1946)** the defendant was held liable in nuisance when a fire on her premises, caused by defective wiring, spread to and destroyed the claimant's house, and in **Crown River Cruises v Kimbolton Fireworks (1996)**, the defendant was liable in nuisance for burning debris that originated in a 20-minute firework display and which damaged the claimant's river boats.

3 Degree of interference

The more serious or worse an interference, the more likely it is to be a nuisance. How serious an interference is can depend on the time of day. Building works which are acceptable at three o'clock in the afternoon might not be acceptable at three o'clock in the morning.

If physical damage is involved, then relatively small nuisances are actionable. If a loss of enjoyment is involved, the threshold is higher: the court must decide if the nuisance materially interferes with ordinary existence. In **Murdoch v Glacier Metal (1998)**, the claimant complained that the constant low level droning noise from the defendant's factory was keeping her awake at night, but the court held that there was no

Key cases

Halsey v Esso (1961): industrial activities are more likely to be a nuisance in a residential area.

St Helens Smelting v Tipping (1865): even in an industrial zone, a defendant does not have the right to carry out activities which inflict physical damage on his neighbours' properties.

Spicer v Smee (1946) and **Crown River Cruises v Kimbolton Fireworks (1996)**: even a single incident can amount to a nuisance.

Murdoch v Glacier Metal (1998): a claim in private nuisance will fail if the activity does not interfere with ordinary existence.

nuisance as no one else had complained and that in any event there was a considerable amount of noise from a nearby road so that any noise from the factory would not interfere with ordinary existence.

4 Sensitivity

If the claimant is using his property for an extra-sensitive use he is not entitled to sue in circumstances where a reasonable use would not need protection. In **Bridlington Relay v Yorkshire Electricity (1965)** the claimant's complaint was that the defendant's overhead electric power cables were interfering with transmissions from the claimant's television mast. The court dismissed the claim on the ground that the power cables would not have interfered with any ordinary user of the land, and that the only reason that the claimant had suffered damage was because of the very sensitive nature of his activities.

If the defendant's activities would have interfered with an ordinary use of the claimant's land, then the claimant can claim for the full extent of his loss even though the loss was partly caused by the extra-sensitive nature of his use. In the Canadian case of **McKinnon v Walker (1951)**, the claimant could claim for the full damage caused to delicate orchids by gas emitted from the defendant's factory, as even flowers of ordinary sensitivity would have been affected.

5 Social utility of the defendant's conduct

The usefulness to society of the defendant's conduct has a bearing on whether it is reasonable for the claimant to have to put up with it. One example is that the noise and dust from a building site over a limited period of time is allowable because it is useful to have new buildings, whereas in other circumstances the noise and the dust might be a nuisance.

Often, social utility does not prevent what is a clear nuisance from being a nuisance, but it does have a bearing on remedies. In **Dennis v Ministry of Defence (2003)**, the claimant lived in a large house in the country, but his peace was regularly destroyed by RAF training jets flying overhead. The court found that the noise did amount to a nuisance and awarded damages, but it was not prepared to grant an injunction as the flights were a necessary part of this country's defence preparations.

6 Malice on the part of the defendant

If a defendant deliberately does something with no purpose other than to annoy the claimant, the defendant's **malice** can make unlawful something which might not otherwise be a nuisance. This can be most clearly seen in **Hollywood Silver Fox Farm v Emmett (1936)**. The claimant farmed silver foxes. The defendant, as part of an ongoing feud, deliberately fired shotguns within the boundaries of his own land so as to startle the foxes and cause them to miscarry. In normal circumstances, firing a shotgun in the countryside would probably not amount to a nuisance, but the malicious motive in this case made it unlawful.

A second example of malice is **Christie v Davey (1892)**. The defendant lived next door to a house in which various people gave piano and singing lessons. To show his annoyance, he began to whistle, shriek and bang tin trays on the walls whenever a lesson was taking place. The court imposed an injunction against him because it was clear that his activities where done deliberately to disrupt and to upset. After a careful consideration of evidence relating to number, length and timings of lessons, the judge also found that the original music-making was not a nuisance.

> ### Key cases
>
> **Bridlington Relay v Yorkshire Electricity (1965):** a claim in private nuisance will fail if the claimant's use of his land is so sensitive that even ordinary activities on the part of the defendant create an interference.
>
> **McKinnon v Walker (1951):** a claimant can sue for the full extent of his loss, even though his use of his land is extra-sensitive, if the defendant's activities would have disturbed even a normal use.
>
> **Dennis v Ministry of Defence (2003):** if an activity is in the public interest, the claimant may fail to win an injunction.
>
> **Hollywood Silver Fox Farm v Emmett (1936)** and **Christie v Davey (1892):** malice on the part of the defendant can convert a lawful activity into an unlawful activity.

> ### Key terms
>
> **Malice:** deliberate intent to cause some sort of injury or upset.

Fig. 1 Christie *v* Davey (1892)

Defences to an action in private nuisance

There are two specific defences available to an action for private nuisance, statutory authority and prescription.

Statutory authority

Statutory authority means that the nuisance is created by a public body acting under a legislative duty or power. As long as the activity is carried out without negligence and with reasonable regard to, and care of, the interests of others, a person affected will not be able to sue in nuisance as the nuisance has effectively been authorised by Parliament. An example is **Allen v Gulf Oil (1981)**: the House of Lords decided that the defence was arguable in the case of an oil refinery, that had been built under powers contained in an Act of Parliament, and which was causing a nuisance to its neighbours in the form of fumes and noise.

It is also a defence for a public body to show that the Parliament has created an alternative remedy. In **Marcic v Thames Water (2003)** the claimant sued for private nuisance as a result of the flooding of his land caused by inadequacies in the defendant's drainage systems. The House of Lords ruled that there could be no action in nuisance as Parliament had established a statutory framework of remedies for people who had been affected by the defendant's activities.

Prescription

A second defence is **prescription**. This means that the defendant's activities become lawful because he has been carrying them out for the last twenty years.

Non-defences: arguments not open to the defendant

By contrast, there are a number of possible arguments which the courts will not accept as a defence to a claim for private nuisance. The defendant, for instance, cannot rely on the fact that he was creating the nuisance before the claimant moved to the area and that the claimant knew of the activity before he arrived. In **Sturges v Bridgeman (1879)**, a doctor was able to bring an action for private nuisance when he built a consulting room in his garden on land adjacent to a confectioner. The noise from the latter interfered with the doctor's ability to see his patients, and it was no defence that the confectioner had been established first.

It is also not a defence to say that the claimant could have helped himself, for instance by shutting his windows; that the defendant was using reasonable care and skill; or that the nuisance was partly caused by someone else.

Key terms

Statutory authority: permission given by Parliament to create a private nuisance.

Prescription: gaining a right to do something not otherwise permitted on the basis of the length of time which the activity was carried out unlawfully but without objection.

Key cases

Allen v Gulf Oil (1981): a defendant will escape liability in private nuisance if his activities have been authorised by Parliament.

Marcic v Thames Water (2003): a defendant will escape liability in private nuisance if Parliament has created an alternative remedy for any claimant.

Sturges v Bridgeman (1879): a defendant will not escape liability in private nuisance simply because he was there before the claimant.

Examiner's tip

In an exam, do not forget to conclude your answer with a discussion of possible remedies.

Key terms

Injunction: a court order (usually) forbidding a party to do something on pain of a criminal penalty.

Key cases

Miller v Jackson (1977) and Kennaway v Thompson (1981): whether an injunction is granted to stop a private nuisance will depend in part on balancing the interest of the parties and of the community.

Hunter v Canary Wharf (1997) and Dennis v Ministry of Defence (2003): damages for loss of use and enjoyment will be equivalent to the loss in value to the affected premises.

The Wagon Mound (No. 2) (1966): only damages which are reasonably foreseeable can be claimed.

Key terms

Abatement: the claimant taking steps himself to remove or minimise a nuisance.

Remedies in an action for private nuisance

1 Injunction

An **injunction** is an order prohibiting or strictly controlling an activity. Frequently, a claimant will seek this remedy instead of, or as well as, damages because what he really wants is for the offending activity to stop. However, the courts will not grant an injunction for trivial matters or where it is in the public interest for the activity to continue. An injunction might impose a complete ban, or it might allow the activity to continue but within defined limits as in *Kennaway* below.

In **Miller v Jackson (1977)** the claimant sought an injunction to stop cricket being played on a pitch adjacent to his house as occasionally a ball would land on his property causing damage. The court refused because the cricket club was a focus of village life and it was in the interest of the community that the activity should continue. That interest outweighed the relatively minor inconvenience to the claimant.

In **Kennaway v Thompson (1981)**, the defendant was a powerboat club that was organising an ever increasing number of races and other events with ever noisier boats. The defendant admitted that they were causing a nuisance to the claimant, who lived nearby, but they argued that, because their activities were of great interest to the public, damages only should be awarded. The court disagreed stating that, unlike *Miller* v *Jackson* (1977), the nuisance was substantial and that it was not part of English law that a defendant could effectively turn an unlawful activity into a lawful activity by paying over a large sum of money. The court went on to impose a partial injunction limiting the number of races.

2 Damages

In the case of physical damage, damages are awarded for consequential damage to land, plants, buildings and goods. In the case of loss of use and enjoyment, the damages are equal to the loss in value to the land: **Hunter v Canary Wharf (1997)**.

A good example is the case of **Dennis v Ministry of Defence (2003)**, discussed above. Having found that the noise from the training flights amounted to a nuisance, the court awarded damages for the reduction in value of the land, but refused an injunction to stop the flights as activities preparing the defence of the country were necessary.

When claiming damages, any loss must be reasonably foreseeable as the rules on remoteness are identical to those in negligence: **The Wagon Mound (No. 2) (1966)** as confirmed by *Cambridge Water* v *Eastern Counties Leather* (1994).

3 Abatement

Abatement is a self-help remedy and it means the right of a claimant to take reasonable steps to deal with any nuisance himself. Two examples might be chopping off the branches of a tree overhanging a boundary and unblocking a drain that is threatening to spill over.

In using abatement, the claimant must be careful not to overstep the limits of what is reasonable in the circumstances. For instance, if he needs to enter the defendant's land he should do so only having given proper notice or in an emergency, and if he needs to chop off the branches of any overhanging tree, he should only do so from the point at which they overhang the boundary, and he should return any branches. The courts are wary of the remedy because of the possibility of confrontation and a resulting breach of the peace.

Topic illustration

Consider this scenario, taken from a recent exam paper:

> Residents living in the vicinity of the Johnsons factory had been complaining for some time of noise and vibration coming from the factory, especially at night. When an explosion occurred in the factory one morning, a thick cloud of smoke spread rapidly across the town, leaving a dirty, oily deposit on houses and other buildings.

Using the rules described in this topic, we can say that a discussion of any claim by the residents in private nuisance should identify the following elements:

- Many of the residents will own their properties, and thus qualify as claimants. Similarly, Johnsons, as the creator of the nuisance, will be the defendant.

- The damage suffered by the residents may be both physical loss (for instance if the vibrations have shaken buildings) and a loss of amenity (for instance sleepless nights).

- There are a number of factors relevant to any discussion on the unlawfulness of Johnsons' activities, for instance locality, duration, degree of interference and social usefulness of the activity.

- On the facts, it is difficult to identify a relevant defence for certain, but remedies in the form of damages and an injunction are clearly relevant.

Activities

1. Consider whether you, your family or your friends have recently experienced anything, either at home, at school or in the workplace, which may amount to a private nuisance.

2. Consider this case study, which has been adapted from a recent exam paper:

    Matt lived in a house with very substantial grounds. Once isolated, his property now backed onto newly built houses on an estate, from which it was screened only by a fence and a row of trees. Matt enjoyed a range of hobbies, including building and flying model helicopters. He was very eccentric, and often flew them late into the evening and early in the morning in the summer months. They were very noisy and disturbed the residents in their houses and their pet animals. His response to complaints seemed to be to fly them at even more unpredictable hours.

    With reference to the tort of private nuisance, discuss the rights and remedies, if any, available to the residents of the estate aring out of Matt's pursuit of his hobby.

You should now be able to:

- explain the nature of private nuisance

- analyse the reasoning processes used in deciding whether an activity amounts to a private nuisance.

In this topic you will learn how to:

■ explain the meaning of public nuisance

■ identify the elements needed for a claim in public nuisance.

Key terms

Public nuisance: an activity which interferes with the safety or convenience of a section of the general public.

Key cases

Attorney-General v PYA Quarries (1957): a public nuisance is one which affects a class of Her Majesty's subjects

R v Madden (1975): a telephonist and a group of police officers and security guards do not amount to a class of Her Majesty's subjects.

R v Rimmington (2005): a public nuisance requires a common injury, in other words interference with a public right.

AQA Examiner's tip

When considering a case study in an examination, do not forget the possibility of a liability in public nuisance. Ask yourself whether a large number of people have been affected by the activities of the defendant.

2 Public nuisance

Despite the similarity in name, private nuisance and public nuisance have little in common, although an unlawful activity on the part of the defendant can amount to both.

Definition of public nuisance

Public nuisance has very uncertain boundaries, and has been used to cover a wide variety of activities, many of which are now in fact covered by legislation. It is both a crime and a tort, and it seeks to protect the health, safety, morals and convenience of the public and to prevent the obstruction of any right held by every member of the public.

Case law examples of public nuisance include:

■ A pop festival causing noise, traffic congestion and general inconvenience: *Attorney-General for Ontario* v *Orange Productions* (1971).

■ Selling contaminated water: *AB* v *South West Water* (1993).

■ Obstructing a canal by mooring a boat across the navigation channel: *Rose* v *Miles* (1815).

■ Emitting large clouds of smoke so as to endanger the highway: *Holling* v *Yorkshire Traction* (1948).

■ Placing a golf tee so that players frequently hit golf balls onto the adjoining public road: *Castle* v *St Augustine's Links* (1922).

In order to establish a public nuisance, it is necessary to show that a class of people have been affected, and that the members of that class have suffered a common harm.

Class of people

Unlike private nuisance, it is not enough that the defendant's activities affect a particular claimant. A public nuisance is any nuisance:

> which materially affects the reasonable comfort and convenience of life of a class of Her Majesty's subjects. (Romer LJ in Attorney-General v PYA Quarries (1957))

What constitutes a 'class of Her Majesty's subjects' is a question of fact, and has to be decided case by case. It should consist of a section of the public rather than individuals, and should involve a considerable number of people. In **Attorney-General v PYA Quarries (1957)** itself, a group of about 30 houses was enough to amount to a class, and consequently the noise, vibrations and dust thrown up by the defendant's quarry blasting were held to be public nuisance. In **R v Madden (1975)** a hoax bomb call was held not to amount to a nuisance because it only affected the telephonist who took the call, the police, and the security guards who spent an hour looking for the device before it was realised that it did not exist. The court in that case said that a public nuisance was one where 'a considerable number of persons or a section of the public, as distinct from individual persons, had been affected'.

Common injury

A public nuisance is one which affects a right, a protection or a benefit enjoyed in common by the members of the affected class. Thus, obstruction of a road is a public nuisance because it interferes with the public's ability to make use of a right of way, but the actions of the defendant in **R v Rimmington (2005)** in sending packages containing racially offensive material to a wide variety of recipients was not a public nuisance because although the packages may have caused an injury to each individual's personal rights there was no injury to a public right.

Actions and remedies for public nuisance

Public nuisance, like private nuisance, is about balancing the competing interests of different people. It is not public nuisance if a road or a pavement is partly and temporarily blocked by a vehicle that has broken down or a van that is unloading goods outside business premises. However, it is different if the defendant is regularly blocking the highway for no good reason. In **Lyons v Gulliver (1913)**, the defendant committed a public nuisance as he regularly allowed large queues of people seeking cheap seats to build up on the pavement outside his theatre thus impeding access to the claimant's shop.

A case of public nuisance can reach the courts in one of three ways.

The first, and most common, is as a criminal case. Public nuisance is a **common law crime**, and will be investigated by the police and prosecuted by the Crown Prosecution Service like any other offence. Secondly, if a criminal case is not sufficient to deal with the problem, then the Attorney-General has the power (but not a duty) to seek an injunction in the civil courts on behalf of the public.

The third route into the courts is a civil action brought by an individual. This option is not open to a person just because he is a member of the class affected, as to allow all those affected to sue would lead to multiple cases from a single incident. In order to be able to sue, an individual must show that he has suffered a special or particular damage, in other words a loss or injury over and above the rest of the members of the class. Examples include:

- In *Castle* v *St Augustine's Links* (1922), the defendant placed a golf tee so that golf balls regularly landed on the road thus causing a public nuisance, but the claimant was able to claim damages as it was his car, of all the cars on the road, that was hit.
- In *Halsey* v *Esso* (1961), the activities of the oil depot amounted to a public nuisance in that they affected the neighbourhood, but the claimant suffered special damage as it was the paintwork of his car that was damaged by acidic smuts.
- In **Tate & Lyle Industries v Greater London Council (1983)**, the defendant caused a public nuisance by causing a river to become silted, thus interfering with public navigation rights. The claimant suffered special loss as it had to pay for dredging works to allow ships to reach its jetty.

Remedies, as in private nuisance, include damages and an injunction.

Comparing private nuisance and public nuisance

As we said earlier, private nuisance and public nuisance have little in common, although an unlawful activity on the part of the defendant can amount to both. Differences between the two include:

- Public nuisance is both a crime and a tort, whereas private nuisance is actionable only in the civil courts as a tort.
- Private nuisance protects a claimant's interest in his land (remember that only someone with an interest in land can sue), whereas public nuisance can protect those without any relevant interest in land.
- Private nuisance may only affect a single individual, whereas public nuisance must affect an entire class.
- Public nuisance allows recovery for damages for personal injury, whereas private nuisance does not.
- Prescription can be used as a defence to an action in private nuisance, but not as a defence in an action for public nuisance as a defendant cannot acquire the right to commit a crime.

 Key cases

Lyons v Gulliver (1913): in an action for public nuisance, a court will consider the interests of the different parties.

Tate & Lyle Industries v Greater London Council (1983): an individual can sue for damages in public nuisance if his injury or loss is over and above the injury or loss suffered by the public.

Key terms

Common law crime: a crime whose elements are defined in case law rather than by statute.

Topic illustration

Consider again the scenario concerning Johnsons and their neighbours:

> Residents living in the vicinity of the Johnsons factory had been complaining for some time of noise and vibration coming from the factory, especially at night. When an explosion occurred in the factory one morning, a thick cloud of smoke spread rapidly across the town, leaving a dirty, oily deposit on houses and other buildings.

A discussion of public nuisance in relation to this scenario is likely to be briefer than any discussion relating to private nuisance, but we can probably identify the following elements:

■ Given that the whole town is affected, there would appear to constitute a class of Her Majesty's subjects.

■ Equally, there appears to be a common injury in the form, for instance, of a threat to health from the lack of sleep and the thick smoke.

■ Concluding remarks would include a discussion of who could bring an action (probably only the Attorney-General in the absence of an individual householder suffering damage over and above everybody else) and what remedies might be granted.

Activities

Given the wide definition of public nuisance, consider which events you may have seen in the media recently might give rise to such a liability?

Clara lives on a farm just outside a small village, and she runs an art studio in one of the barns. In each of the last several years, she has organised a country arts fair which has become steadily more popular and well attended. Last year's event attracted so many visitors that the road in the village was partially blocked by parked cars, and people were coming and going throughout the weekend. One of the villagers, Debbie was particularly inconvenienced as the normal access to her animal feeds business was blocked and she had to use an old farm track at great inconvenience and expense. Consider Clara's liability, if any, in public nuisance.

You should now be able to:

■ explain the nature of public nuisance

■ examine the differences between a claim in private nuisance and a claim in public nuisance.

In this topic you will learn how to:

■ identify when the rule in *Rylands* v *Fletcher* applies

■ identify and explain the elements needed to claim under the rule in *Rylands* v *Fletcher*

■ identify defences and remedies appropriate to a claim under the rule in *Rylands* v *Fletcher*.

3 The rule in *Rylands* v *Fletcher*

The rule in *Rylands* v *Fletcher* originates in an 1868 House of Lords case of that name. It states that a defendant is liable if, on his land, he accumulates a dangerous thing in the course of a non-natural use of that land, and the thing escapes and causes reasonably foreseeable damage.

In **Rylands v Fletcher (1868)** itself, the defendant was the owner of a water mill who contracted with builders to construct a reservoir to guarantee a water supply to the mill. The builders sealed the bottom of the reservoir carelessly so that when it was filled water leaked into the mine shafts below and from there escaped through connecting tunnels into the claimant's mines causing considerable damage. The defendant was held liable for the escape.

There are two aspects to this liability which should be mentioned at the beginning. The first is that the rule in *Rylands* v *Fletcher* is one of strict liability. In *Rylands* v *Fletcher* itself, the defendant was liable for the actions of his independent contractors even though there was no fault on his part.

The second aspect is that the House of Lords confirmed in **Transco plc v Stockport MBC (2003)** that the rule is a sub-species (type) of nuisance. The significance of this is that a number of the rules which apply to private nuisance should therefore also apply to the rule in *Rylands* v *Fletcher*, and we will see this as we discuss some of the elements required to establish liability.

The Transco case itself involved a water pipe which was owned by the defendant and which supplied water to a block of flats. The pipe leaked, and the water washed away the earth supporting a gas pipe owned by the claimant, who then had to spend a considerable amount of money making the pipe safe. In the event, the claim in *Rylands* v *Fletcher* failed as the claimant, as we will see, was unable to show a number of the necessary elements.

Bringing an action under the rule in *Rylands* v *Fletcher*

To establish liability in *Rylands* v *Fletcher*, a claimant needs to show each of the following elements:

1 Claimant's legal position

Following the Transco case, discussed above, if it is the case that *Rylands* v *Fletcher* is a sub-species of private nuisance then a claimant should have a legal interest in the land affected by the escape. This follows from the decision in *Hunter* v *Canary Wharf* (1997), which we discussed under private nuisance above.

2 Accumulation

The defendant must voluntarily bring onto his land an **accumulation** of the substance which escaped. This requirement covers an artificial accumulation of material (whether the material itself is natural or not) but not a natural accumulation such as a lake (unless the escape occurs because of non-natural processes, e.g. rock-blasting as against rock erosion). In **Giles v Walker (1890)**, the defendant ploughed up his land, which then became self-sown with thistles, which in turn spread to neighbouring land. The defendant was not liable as the accumulation of thistles was natural and not artificial.

Liability exists only if the accumulation is on land the defendant controls, perhaps as an owner or a tenant. 'Land' has a relaxed meaning: various cases have suggested it can include the public highway, leaking pipes belonging to the defendant but running across the claimant's land, and a boat moored on a river that was being used for storing fireworks.

3 A dangerous thing

The substance accumulated must be dangerous, in other words something likely to do mischief if it escapes. This includes obviously hazardous materials, such as chemicals and explosives, but also less threatening substances, such as water, if they are stored in bulk (as, of course, was the case in *Rylands* itself). Other case law examples include gas, electricity, oil, and sparks. An unusual example is **Hale v Jennings Bros (1938)** in which the escaping object was a chair from a 'chair-o-plane' fairground attraction which had flown away from its moorings mid-ride.

An alternative definition of this requirement, discussed by the House of Lords in **Transco plc v Stockport MBC (2003)**, is that the accumulated substance should be something which poses an 'exceptional risk'. In that case, the water flowing through a pipe was not something which posed

Key cases

Rylands v Fletcher (1868): a defendant is liable if, on his land, he accumulates a dangerous substance during the course of a non-natural use of that land, and the substance escapes and causes damage.

Transco plc v Stockport MBC (2003): *Rylands* is a type of nuisance.

Giles v Walker (1890): a defendant is not liable for the escape of a substance that had accumulated naturally.

Key terms

The rule in *Rylands* v *Fletcher*: an action available to a person who has suffered losses because of an escape of a dangerous substance from the defendant's land.

Accumulation: the gathering together of a large amount of a material. In *Rylands* v *Fletcher*, any accumulation should be man-made.

A dangerous thing: something likely to do a mischief if it escapes.

AQA Examiner's tip

Use the elements discussed in the text as a framework for an answer in an exam. Consider each in turn, citing cases where possible.

Key cases

Hale v Jennings Bros (1938): a 'dangerous thing' can consist of many and varied items, in this case the chair from a 'chair-o-plane' fairground ride.

Transco plc v Stockport MBC (2003): a 'dangerous thing' is one which poses an exceptional risk if it escapes.

an exceptional risk should it escape and this was one of the grounds on which the claimant failed.

4 Non-natural use

A non-natural use does not mean a use which is artificial or man-made, but rather a use which is not commonplace. In **Rickards v Lothian (1913)**, a tap overflowed in a part of the building leased by the defendant, and the water escaped to a lower level damaging the claimant's goods. The defendant was not liable, as a tap supplied by a pipe was an ordinary and reasonable use of a building.

The same point was made in *Transco plc* v *Stockport MBC* (2003), where some members of the House of Lords rephrased the requirement as a use which is 'extraordinary and unusual'. Thus, the claimant in that case failed to satisfy the requirement as supplying water to a block of flats was an ordinary use.

An example of a non-natural use is provided by **Cambridge Water v Eastern Counties Leather (1994)**. The defendant was a long-established tannery. Chemicals from the process seeped through the concrete floor of the defendant's premises, and down through the earth until they reached a non-permeable layer of rock. At that point, the chemicals ran along the top of the layer, for about a mile and a half, until they reached the rock strata from which the claimant pumped water through a borehole. The chemicals contaminated the borehole, and the claimant was unable to use it and sued for substantial damages. The House of Lords stated that the bulk storage of chemicals to be used in an industrial process was almost the classic example of a non-natural use. (The claim ultimately failed on another ground.)

5 Escape

The claimant must show that the substance in question escaped, in other words it has moved from land the defendant controls to land that he does not. In **Read v Lyons (1946)**, the claimant was an inspector visiting the defendant's munitions factory. She was injured by an exploding shell, but her claim in *Rylands* failed, as she was still on the defendant's premises at the time and therefore there had been no escape.

6 Reasonably foreseeable damage

Only damage which is reasonably foreseeable is recoverable. This requirement was introduced by the House of Lords in **Cambridge Water v Eastern Counties Leather (1994)**, the facts of which we discussed above. The claimant's action in that case failed because it was not reasonably foreseeable that the defendant's activities would contaminate its springs.

As we have already said, the Transco case confirmed that *Rylands* v *Fletcher* is a sub-species of nuisance. Presumably, therefore, as in private nuisance, only damage to land and goods stored on the land can be recovered, and that damage elsewhere and personal injury cannot be claimed. Not all of the older cases fit in with these ideas and in particular some of them, such as *Read* v *Lyons* (1946) (above), appear to assume that personal injury is recoverable.

Defences to a claim made under the rule in *Rylands* v *Fletcher*

There are a number of specific defences to a claim made under the rule in *Rylands* v *Fletcher*.

Act of a stranger

A defendant is not liable if the escape is caused by the deliberate and unforeseen **act of a stranger**, in other words someone over whom the defendant has no control. In *Rickards* v *Lothian* (1913), discussed above,

---

Key cases

Rickards v Lothian (1913): for the purposes of *Rylands*, a non-natural use does not include an ordinary use of the land.

Cambridge Water v Eastern Counties Leather (1994): the bulk storage of chemicals is the classic case of a non-natural use.

Read v Lyons (1946): there is no escape if the substance does not leave the land controlled by the defendant.

Cambridge Water v Eastern Counties Leather (1994): only loss or damage which is reasonably foreseeable as a consequence of an escape can be claimed.

Key terms

A non-natural use: a use which is man-made and which is unusual.

Escape: for the purposes of *Rylands* v *Fletcher*, an escape is when the dangerous substance leaves land controlled by the defendant.

Act of a stranger: a defence to a claim in *Rylands* v *Fletcher*, when the escape has been caused by the actions of a third party which the defendant neither foresaw or could control.

the defendant would not in any event have been liable for the damage caused by the overflowing water, because it was caused by the actions of a third party in turning on a tap and blocking the drain. Similarly, in **Perry v Kendricks Transport (1955)**, the defendant was not liable for the consequences of an explosion caused by a third party placing a lit match in the petrol tank of one of the defendant's coaches.

Act of God

An **act of God** is a natural event so enormous that it cannot be either foreseen or guarded against. If an escape is caused by such an event, then the defendant is not liable as there is nothing he could have done to stop it. In **Nichols v Marsland (1876)**, the defendant was not liable when water escaped from an artificial lake after a prolonged and violent rainstorm, the worst in living memory, caused the embankment of the lake to collapse under the pressure of the extra water.

Statutory authority

A defendant is not liable if the escape occurs during activities authorised by an Act of Parliament, provided negligence is not involved. In **Green v Chelsea Waterworks Company (1894)**, the defendant was not liable when one of its water pipes burst and flooded the claimant's land. The defendant had a statutory duty to maintain a supply of water, and, given that it was not negligent, it was not liable for the results of carrying out that duty.

Further defences

A defendant will avoid liability if the escape relates to something that was being maintained for the common benefit of the defendant and the claimant. A good example is a system of water pipes to different parts of a large building. A defendant will also avoid liability if the escape is due to the fault of the claimant. Finally, a claimant's damages will be reduced if the escape was partly his fault or if his damage is made worse because of the highly sensitive nature of his own property.

Topic illustration

Consider for a third time the scenario concerning Johnsons and their neighbours:

> Residents living in the vicinity of the Johnsons factory had been complaining for some time of noise and vibration coming from the factory, especially at night. When an explosion occurred in the factory one morning, a thick cloud of smoke spread rapidly across the town, leaving a dirty, oily deposit on houses and other buildings.

Clearly, there is the possibility of a claim under the rule in *Rylands* v *Fletcher*. Any discussion of this liability will probably cover the following points:

- As with private nuisance, many of the residents will qualify as claimants as they own their own properties. Similarly, Johnsons is the defendant, as it is its activities that caused the explosion.
- The elements necessary for a claim need to be identified: accumulation (although we do not know exactly what, something must have been brought into the factory to cause an explosion), a dangerous substance (it has exploded), a non-natural use of the premises, an escape (an oily deposit has been left on buildings) and reasonably foreseeable damage.
- Finally, we need to discuss defences (it is not easy to identify one on the facts of this case) and remedies (damages, to put right any loss, but not an injunction as presumably the explosion was an isolated event that will not happen again).

Activity

Read this case study, which was taken from a recent past paper, and then consider the rights and remedies of the owners of the cottages, including Irene, in connection with the problems caused by the leisure activities and the oil spill.

Previously a quiet lake overlooked by a few cottages, Greenwater has recently been developed by its owner, Highlife Sports, to provide extensive leisure facilities, including swimming and powerboating. In consequence, the owners of the cottages, including Irene, have experienced a large increase in noise, especially at weekends and during frequent competition weeks, when traffic and parking problems have also made it difficult for them to leave or return to their properties. Additionally, damage to a diesel storage tank owned by Highlife Sports resulted in a leak which caused extensive contamination of Irene's vegetable garden.

You should now be able to:

■ explain the nature of *Rylands* v *Fletcher* in relation to isolated escapes

■ identify and apply the requirements for a claim under the rule in *Rylands* v *Fletcher*.

19 Vicarious liability

Introduction

Vicarious liability is when the law makes one person liable for a tort committed by another. In order for this to happen, there should be some sort of legal relationship between the two people, and the tort should in some way be connected to that relationship.

The most important example of vicarious liability is that an employer is liable for any tort committed by one of his employees during the course of employment. Other examples include business partners, who can be liable for each other's torts, and a principal, who can be liable for a tort committed by his agent. The A Level specification requires an understanding of vicarious liability only in the employer/employee context, and that therefore is the example that this chapter will focus on.

Justification for vicarious liability

Vicarious liability is a form of **strict liability** because an employer remains liable for the actions of his employees even though the employer is not at fault in any way. This might seem harsh, but there are a number of reasons why vicarious liability can be justified. These include:

- Protecting the claimant: an employer is much more likely than an employee to have the resources, including insurance, to meet any claim. In addition, a claimant may not be able to identify the precise employee involved, but this does not matter if he can sue the employer instead. One example of this is medical negligence, where it may be difficult to identify which hospital employee was to blame for an accident, but the patient can sue the hospital itself.
- Protecting the employee: vicarious liability ensures that an unscrupulous employer cannot escape liability by forcing his employees to take risks rather than himself.
- Improving safety standards: vicarious liability encourages an employer to take responsibility towards his employees, for instance in checking qualifications, training, supervision and equipment.

Liability of the employee

Vicarious liability does not extinguish the employee's liability, and he remains **jointly liable**, with his employer, for his actions. In theory, the claimant can choose to sue the employee, but, as we have said, he is much more likely to sue the employer because the employer has the resources to pay any damages awarded.

In addition, an employer, having been sued, can sue the employee in turn under the provisions of the Civil Liability (Contributions) Act 1978. There is usually little point in doing this as, again, the employee does not have the personal resources to meet a major claim, but the employee may be subject to disciplinary procedures or even dismissed.

Establishing vicarious liability against an employer

To establish vicarious liability against an employer, a claimant must show three things.

The first is that the employee has committed a tort. The claimant must show the existence of the elements of whichever tort is alleged, as if he was suing the employee himself, so if, for instance, the claimant was

---

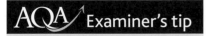

suing for negligence, he would need to show the normal negligence requirements of duty, breach and causation. Note that if the employee could have used a defence, such as contributory negligence, then the employer will be able to use the same defence.

Having established the relevant tort, the claimant must then show secondly that the worker concerned has employee status, and thirdly that the employee committed the tort during the course of his employment. We now turn to discuss these second and third requirements.

Topic illustration

Consider this scenario, taken from a recent exam paper:

> A year after Gita bought a new car, the manufacturer announced that the paint finish on certain models of that car would not maintain its desired appearance. The manufacturer offered, for three months, to fund the cost of a respray. The retailer from whom Gita bought her car was no longer in business and so she took her car to Frank. Frank asked Henry to find out whether Gita's model of car was affected. Henry consulted the manufacturer's list and decided that Gita's model was not affected. However, he had not realised that there was a more recent, amended list which did not include Gita's model. By the time that the mistake was discovered, the manufacturer's offer had ended and Gita's car was worth £2,000 less than it should have been.

If Gita is to make a claim against Frank in vicarious liability, we first need to establish the framework of the case:

- The first step is to identify the person who made the mistake, and to consider whether that person is liable. In this case, Henry gave wrong information to Gita, and this caused her a financial loss. To decide whether Henry is personally liable for his actions we would need to apply the rules relating to economic loss in the context of a negligent misstatement.
- If Henry is liable, the issue is then whether Gita can sue Frank. This requires a discussion of whether Henry is an employee and whether he was acting in the course of his employment, and that is what this chapter now turns to.

☐ Who is an employee?

A worker is someone who performs services in return for payment. There are two types of worker: **employees** and **independent contractors** (those who are self-employed). The distinction is critical because an employer is vicariously liable for an employee but not for an independent contractor.

The basic definition is that an employee works under a contract of service (an employment contract), and an independent contractor works under a contract for services. In most circumstances, the difference between the two will be obvious, for instance a teacher at a school or an assistant in a shop are employees of the school and the shop respectively, whereas a plumber or a decorator working in someone's house are independent contractors and are not employees of the householder. Equally, there is a clear difference between a taxi driver, who is an independent contractor, and a chauffeur, who is an employee, even though both are performing the same service as drivers.

However, there are a number of awkward examples where it is less clear whether a worker is an employee or an independent contractor. Examples include casual workers (people who only work irregularly), those

In this topic you will learn how to:

- identify the difference between an employee and an independent contractor
- explain the approaches that are open to a court when identifying an employee and an independent contractor.

Key terms

Employee: a worker who is employed and has a contract of employment.

Independent contractor: a worker who is self-employed.

working on commission (who may therefore be working for themselves), consultants, freelance workers (people who work for a number of different employers) and agency workers (staff such as secretaries and cleaners who are supplied by an agency to a business which has a temporary shortage). In order to decide whether the employer is vicariously liable for such workers, the courts need to determine their status, but there is no single, simple test to decide this.

Employee or independent contractor – the traditional approaches

The original approach used by the courts to decide if someone was an employee or an independent contractor was the **control test** is the original test and it dates back to Victorian times. It states that an independent contractor is someone who is told only what to do, whereas an employee is told not only what to do but how to do it.

An example is **Walker v Crystal Palace Football Club (1909)** in which the court held that a professional footballer was an employee because his employer maintained a high degree of control over training schedules and procedures, play on the field and personal discipline.

Although this test works for many categories of worker, its major fault is that it does not deal adequately with professional or highly skilled workers. A lawyer employed by a local authority or a doctor employed by an NHS Trust are clearly employees, but, given that they were employed for their expertise, they would not be told how to do their job.

One attempt to solve this problem raised by the control test was the **integration test**. It states that the more closely a worker is involved with the core business of the employer, the more likely he is to be an employee. The doctor employed by the NHS is clearly central to the purpose of the NHS and therefore is an employee. However, the test has problems of its own not least that it is not always certain who is integral to the employer's business and who is not, or even what the employer's business is.

Neither the control test nor the integration test therefore provides an answer to every case, but the courts still use both control and integration as factors when applying the multiple test.

Employee or independent contractor – the multiple test

The **multiple test** is the modern approach to classifying a worker, and it reflects the reality that there is no single way of telling employees and independent contractors apart. In those cases where it is not clear which a particular worker is, because some factors suggest that he is an independent contractor and some suggest that he is an employee, the courts weigh up the two sets of factors and decide which set outweighs the other.

Factors that the court might look at include whether the worker is paid a regular salary or is paid on commission, whether the worker pays income tax and national insurance contributions as an employee or as a self-employed person, whether the contract describes the worker as an employee or not and whether the worker has the ability to delegate his work to another without permission. In addition, an independent contractor is more likely to work from his own premises, have his own equipment, hire his own helpers and to be personally affected by his own investment and management decisions.

A good example of the business approach is **Ready Mix Concrete v Minister of Pensions (1968)**. The workers in question were lorry drivers for the employer. A number of factors suggested that they were

AQA Examiner's tip

Sometimes an examiner will tell you that a worker is an employee. If that happens, do not spend much time discussing the rules in this section, but concentrate instead on the tort that the employee has committed and whether it was in the course of his employment.

Key terms

Control test: an employee is a worker who is told not only what to do but how to do it.

Integration test: an employee is a worker who is closely involved with the main business of the employer.

Multiple test: an approach whereby the court, having considered all the facts of a case, decides whether the overall picture of a worker is closer to an employee or to an independent contractor.

Key cases

Walker v Crystal Palace Football Club (1909): a worker is an employee if he satisfies the control test, in other words his employer tells him both what to do and how to do it.

Ready Mix Concrete v Minister of Pensions (1968): the multiple test involves the court considering all the facts of a case before deciding whether a worker is an employee or an independent contractor.

employees: they wore a company uniform; their lorries were painted in company colours; they had to follow instructions given by the company; and they could not work for anyone else. Against that, the drivers owned their own lorries, were responsible for keeping them repaired, paid the running costs of the lorries and could employ a substitute driver to carry out their deliveries. The court decided that the drivers were independent contractors because the fact that they owned their own major assets (the vehicles) and the fact that the amount of profit they made depended on their own decisions (for instance where to buy petrol, where to get repairs carried out and whether to employ substitute drivers) effectively made them small businessmen trading for themselves.

The multiple test can be uncertain because each case is different and because of the variety of factors the courts take into account, and sometimes it is difficult to predict the outcome of a case. However, there appear to be three factors which must exist before a worker can be classified as an employee, and if one is missing then a worker is an independent contractor. (The reverse however is not true: even if all three are present the courts might decide that other factors indicate that a worker is nevertheless an independent contractor.)

The first is control. This does not mean the degree of control required by the old control test, but it does mean that the employer is, to some degree, in charge of the worker and the work being carried out.

The second is that under the contract the worker gives **personal performance**, in other words he cannot delegate his job to someone else. In **Echo and Express Publication v Tanton (1999)**, therefore, the Court of Appeal decided that a van driver who was able to employ someone else to do his job if he was unavailable was an independent contractor.

The third is **mutuality of obligation** between the employer and the worker. This means that the employer has a legal obligation to pay the worker and the worker has a corresponding obligation to be available to work within the terms of the contract. Neither can choose on a particular day not to be an employer or a worker. In **Carmichael v National Power (1999)**, the worker worked as a tour guide at a power station. However, the company only contacted her when her services were needed, she was able to refuse to attend on a particular day and she was paid by the hour for the work she actually did. Thus, neither side had a legal obligation to the other and, on that basis, the House of Lords decided that she was an independent contractor even though she wore a company uniform and was entitled to shares under the company's employee share scheme.

Topic illustration

Consider again the scenario concerning Frank, Henry and Gita:

> A year after Gita bought a new car, the manufacturer announced that the paint finish on certain models of that car would not maintain its desired appearance. The manufacturer offered, for three months, to fund the cost of a respray. The retailer from whom Gita bought her car was no longer in business and so she took her car to Frank. Frank asked Henry to find out whether Gita's model of car was affected. Henry consulted the manufacturer's list and decided that Gita's model was not affected. However, he had not realised that there was a more recent, amended list which did not include Gita's model. By the time that the mistake was discovered, the manufacturer's offer had ended and Gita's car was worth £2,000 less than it should have been.

Assuming Henry is personally liable for negligent misstatement, Gita needs to know whether he is an employee of Frank's before she can proceed against Frank for vicarious liability.

- Unhelpfully, if deliberately on the part of the examiner who set the paper, we are told nothing about the status of Henry. We have no information on, for instance, how he is paid or even if he is paid at all, how many hours he does and whether his work is regular.

- In these circumstances, we can only describe the rules relating to the identification of employees and independent contractors and explain the consequences of Henry being one or the other.

You should now be able to:

- explain and discuss the control test, the integration test and the multiple test

- identify factors which a judge might use when considering whether a worker is an independent contractor or an employee.

2 Course of employment

Authorised acts

An employee is acting within the course of his employment if he is carrying out an act authorised by his employer and if that act amounts to a tort then the employer is vicariously liable for it. This applies even if the employee is carrying out his duties in an unauthorised manner.

A good example of this is **Century Insurance v Northern Ireland Road Transport Board (1942)**. The worker, a petrol tanker driver, was making a delivery to a petrol station when he lit a cigarette and discarded the match. This caused a fire, then an explosion and there was considerable damage to property. The employer was vicariously liable for this damage because the employee was carrying out his authorised duties, albeit in a highly negligent way.

An employer can also be vicariously liable for an act of his employee even if the authorisation for that act is implied and the act is one which benefits only the employee rather than furthering the employer's work. In *Harvey* v *RG O'Dell Ltd* (1958), the employee had been sent out on a repair job that would last all day. At lunch time, he rode his bike into the nearest town to get lunch, but his negligence caused an accident during the return journey. The employer was vicariously liable for the employee's negligence, even though it happened at a time when the employee was not actually working on his tasks, because on a day-long assignment it would be necessary to travel out to find lunch.

An authorised act using an expressly forbidden method

An employer is vicariously liable for an authorised act carried out by his employee, even when the authorised act has been carried out in a manner which the employer has expressly forbidden. In **Limpus v London General Omnibus (1863)**, the defendant bus company had expressly told its drivers not to obstruct or race buses from rival companies. In contravention of this instruction, the driver in question manoeuvred his bus in such a way as to obstruct a rival bus and in so doing injured one of the horses drawing the other vehicle. The employer was vicariously liable because at the time of the accident the driver was acting for his employer's business and the fact that he was doing so in a forbidden way was irrelevant.

In this topic you will learn how to:

- distinguish between authorised acts and unauthorised acts

- consider the term 'course of employment' in relation to a variety of scenarios.

AQA Examiner's tip

Even if you conclude that a worker is not an employee, you should nevertheless go on to discuss the rules relating to course of employment.

Key terms

Authorised act: an act carried out by the employee on the instructions of the employer.

Key cases

Century Insurance v Northern Ireland Road Transport Board (1942): an employee acts within the course of his employment even if he carries out his duties negligently.

Limpus v London General Omnibus (1863): as long as an act of the employee has been authorised by the employer, the employer is vicariously liable for that act even if the act is carried out using a method which has been expressly forbidden by the employer.

An unauthorised act

If an employee undertakes an act which is not part of his job the employer is not vicariously liable as the act is unauthorised and is not part of the job which the employee was employed to do. In **Beard v London General Omnibus (1900)**, the conductor of a bus took it upon himself to turn a bus around, during the course of which he injured a member of the public through his negligent driving. The employer was not vicariously liable as the conductor was not employed to drive, and his acts were therefore unauthorised. This contrasts with the *Limpus* case, where the worker was employed as a driver and was therefore carrying out an authorised act although he was doing it in an unauthorised manner.

Road traffic accidents

A common example of vicarious liability is when an employer is liable for the negligent driving of one of his employees. Journeys to and from work are generally outside the course of employment, but road journeys made during working hours will normally be covered. Two specific issues commonly arise: giving a lift to an unauthorised person and making a detour. In both instances, whether the driver is acting in the course of his employment will depend on the individual facts of the case.

Dealing first with unauthorised lifts, an example is **Conway v Wimpey (1951)**. The defendant building company was a contractor in a major construction project, and its employees were driven around the site in the company's own lorries. However, there were notices in the cab of each lorry stating that drivers were not allowed to give lifts to employees of other companies and the drivers had received verbal instructions to the same effect. On the day in question, the driver gave a lift to another company's employee who was injured during the course of the journey by the driver's negligence. The defendant was not vicariously liable as the driver was carrying out an unauthorised act, an act that was not part of his job, namely giving a lift to someone he should not have.

A contrasting example is **Rose v Plenty (1975)**. The employer, a dairy, specifically forbade its milkmen, by means of prominent notices, to employ children when out making deliveries or to give them lifts on the milk floats. The milkman in question, in direct contravention of these instructions, employed the claimant, a thirteen-year-old boy, to help him make milk deliveries, and the claimant was injured through the milkman's negligent driving of his float. The defendant was held to be vicariously liable for these injuries because the court felt that, unlike Conway, the driver was carrying out an authorised act (delivering milk) albeit in an unauthorised way (using a forbidden assistant). A further factor which influenced the court is that the claimant in *Rose* was effectively contributing to the defendant's business (by delivering milk) whereas the claimant in *Conway* was not.

The other issue is deviation from a set route. Whether the driver remains in the course of employment depends on the degree of deviation and whether he remains on his employer's business or is setting about something quite different ('on **a frolic of his own**' to use the Victorian phrase). In **Storey v Ashton (1869)**, for example, the driver and a clerk were asked to deliver wine, but on the return journey, they deviated significantly from the route in order to carry out a personal errand for the clerk. During the detour, a member of the public was injured due to the driver's negligence. The employer was held not to be vicariously liable as the detour amounted to a new and independent journey and was not made for the employer's business.

A different result was reached in **A&W Hemphill v Williams (1966)**. The driver of a lorry was transporting some boys back home after a camping expedition. At the request of the boys, the driver made a detour from the normal route home, and during the deviation an accident happened in which the claimant, one of the boys, was seriously injured. The employer of the driver was held to be vicariously liable because the driver was still carrying out his central task, taking the boys home, even though he had deviated from the proper route.

Criminal offences

If the employee's tort also amounts to a criminal offence, an employer is still vicariously liable if he authorised the acts either expressly or impliedly. In **Poland v Parr (1926)**, the employee hit a twelve-year-old boy on the back of the neck in order to stop him stealing sugar from the employer's cart. The employer was vicariously liable as the employee had implied authority to act in his employer's interest and to make reasonable efforts to protect its property. A contrasting example is *Warren v Henlys Ltd* (1948). A petrol pump attendant had a heated argument with a customer over paying for petrol. The customer stated that he would report the attendant to his employer, whereupon the attendant punched the customer on his nose. The employer was not vicariously liable as the act was one of personal vengeance and was not connected to protecting his employer's interests.

However, the rules relating to an employer's vicarious liability for a criminal offence now have to be considered in the light of more recent developments. The key case is **Lister v Hesley Hall Ltd (2001)**. The employee, a warden of a children's home, subjected a number of the boys in his care to systematic sexual abuse. Using traditional principles, the employer would not be vicariously liable: the abuse was not an authorised act and nor was the warden acting in the interests of his employer. However, the House of Lords introduced a new test: were the acts of the employee so closely connected with his employment that it was fair and just to hold the employer liable? Applying that test, the employer was vicariously liable for the abuse as the warden's job as a carer was inseparable from his acts as an abuser.

The House of Lords were probably influenced by a wish to make sure the boys received compensation, but the new test represents an extension of liability in this area, and it has been used in a number of subsequent cases. In **Mattis v Pollock (2003)**, a doorman at a nightclub was involved in a heated and violent row with a group of customers including the claimant. The doorman escaped to his flat nearby and armed himself with a knife. Returning to the scene, set on revenge, the doorman stabbed the claimant several times paralysing him. The nightclub was vicariously liable as it had encouraged the doorman to be aggressive, and the stabbing, although it took place outside the club, was the conclusion of a sequence of events that had begun in the club and which was closely connected to the doorman's employment. On the other hand, in **Attorney-General of the British Virgin Islands v Hartwell (2004)**, a policeman removed a gun from the police station locker, abandoned his post and went looking for his ex-girlfriend in a bar in a completely different location from the area he was responsible for. When he found her, he started shooting, and the claimant was badly injured by a stray bullet. The police were not vicariously liable for the policeman's activities as they were unconnected with his duties and were instead part of a personal vendetta. (The claimant in fact received compensation by a different route: the police themselves were negligent in employing a man with the record that this policeman had and letting him have access to weapons.)

Key cases

A&W Hemphill v Williams (1966): an employer is vicariously liable for a deviation by a driver from the normal route as long as the detour is connected to the employer's business and is not too great in extent.

Poland v Parr (1926): an employer is vicariously liable for a criminal act on the part of one of his employees if he authorised the act either expressly or impliedly.

Lister v Hesley Hall Ltd (2001): an employer is vicariously liable for the criminal acts of an employee if those acts are so closely connected to what the employee was employed to do that it is fair and just to hold the employer responsible.

Mattis v Pollock (2003): an employer will be vicariously liable, even for actions strictly outside the place of work, if the sequence of events had begun at work and the employee had been encouraged to act in a particular way.

Attorney-General of the British Virgin Islands v Hartwell (2004): an employer will not be vicariously liable for activities that had no connection with an employee's job.

Topic illustration

Consider for a third time the scenario relating to Frank, Henry and Gita:

> A year after Gita bought a new car, the manufacturer announced that the paint finish on certain models of that car would not maintain its desired appearance. The manufacturer offered, for three months, to fund the cost of a respray. The retailer from whom Gita bought her car was no longer in business and so she took her car to Frank. Frank asked Henry to find out whether Gita's model of car was affected. Henry consulted the manufacturer's list and decided that Gita's model was not affected. However, he had not realised that there was a more recent, amended list which did not include Gita's model. By the time that the mistake was discovered, the manufacturer's offer had ended and Gita's car was worth £2,000 less than it should have been.

At this stage, we are assuming both that Henry is personally liable for negligent misstatement and that he is an employee of Frank. Gita now needs to establish whether Henry's actions were in the course of his employment.

■ The first step is to ask whether Henry's acts were authorised. They would appear to be so, as Frank asked him to find out the position in relation to Gita's car.

■ There may be a place for a discussion of whether Henry carried out an unauthorised act but in an unauthorised manner as Frank presumably did not mean Henry to use an out-of-date manufacturer's list.

■ However, one way or the other, Frank would appear to be vicariously liable as Henry's acts were authorised. We simply now need to explain the consequences for Frank, namely that he is liable for Gita's financial loss.

Activities

1 Do you think that it is fair that the employer in *Lister* v *Hesley Hall Ltd* should be liable given that it was unaware of the warden's activities?

2 Consider this problem, which raises the issue of vicarious liability:

Andrew was a historian engaged as a consultant by a national newspaper, *The Recorder*. He was shown diaries alleged to have been written in the 19th century by a famous soldier. The diaries were not previously known to exist. After extensive research, Andrew concluded that the diaries were genuine and *The Recorder* publicised his conclusions in a front page story. This was read by Beth who then bought the diaries at an auction for £50,000. Soon afterwards, Beth allowed other historians to examine them, and it was very rapidly discovered that the diaries were definitely not genuine and were, in fact, worthless forgeries. By that time, the forger had disappeared with the money. Consider the following questions:

a Which tort has Andrew perhaps committed? Do you think that he is in fact liable for that tort?

b Is Andrew an employee, and who is the employer? What reasons would you give for your conclusions?

c Was Andrew acting within the course of his employment? Give reasons for your answer.

You should now be able to:

■ identify the rules which govern when an act is part of an employee's course of employment

■ explain how the rules operate in relation to both negligent and criminal acts of employees.

In this topic you will learn how to:

- prepare for an examination in the law of tort

- identify key areas for revision

- plan and write answers to scenario questions.

Answering questions on tort in Unit 4B

To complete an examination paper in the law of tort successfully, you must both prepare carefully beforehand and deploy a range of skills when actually answering questions.

In preparing for an examination, you may find the following guidelines helpful:

- Make sure you have a thorough understanding of the key principles relating to each tort. Be aware that each tort consists of rules relating to the existence of a duty, breach of that duty, causation of damage, defences and remedies.

- Be prepared to illustrate key principles with the use of authority. Authority means a case or an Act of Parliament demonstrating the principle in question.

- With respect to cases, you should be able to explain the principle that the case illustrates. It is helpful to have an outline knowledge of the facts of the case, as that gives a useful example, but it is not necessary to know the facts in great detail or to memorise the date of the case.

- With respect to Acts of Parliament, you need to be able to cite the relevant section number, as well as the name and date of the statute, and to be able to explain in your own words what the section says.

- Make sure you frequently practise writing answers to past papers and similar examples, and ensure that you pay attention to the feedback that you receive. You do not want to be in the position of trying out your problem-solving skills for the first time in the examination. No one gets everything right the first time and everyone benefits from experience.

- Pay attention to your written English. There are five marks awarded for using good English, organising information clearly and using legal vocabulary accurately and at appropriate places. Five marks may not sound very much but it could be the difference between two grades, especially as the other A Level law examinations also carry marks for the quality of your written communication. When you practise exam answers, be aware of the need to produce organised answers (not random points churned out in the hope that something will be correct) and take the time to check spellings. It is not very impressive if, at the end of two years' law study and when answering a paper on the law of tort, you cannot spell words like 'claimant', 'defendant', 'negligence' and 'nuisance'.

When writing your exam answers, you may find these further guidelines helpful:

- Begin by identifying the characters involved. You need to know who the claimants and defendants are. Be sure to read the question carefully and answer only what you are asked. If the question asks you what rights Character A might have, you will waste time if you discuss what Character B's rights might be.

- Then consider which tort is relevant. There are actually only a limited number of torts on the specification, and you should be able to run through them in your mind. You might consider what type of loss is involved; is it physical, economic or psychiatric? If the question relates to nuisance, ask yourself whether it has affected a large number of people (public nuisance) or whether something has escaped across a boundary (the rule in *Rylands* v *Fletcher*). If you are asked to consider the position against two different defendants, it could be that one is an employer, in which case you need to think about vicarious liability.

■ Restrict yourself to discussing the law covered by the specification. You may well think that a character in a problem has committed a driving offence or a breach of contract, but these things are not being examined on a law of tort paper, and a discussion of them is unlikely to gain you marks.

■ When writing about a particular tort, make sure you begin at the beginning (duty), then progress through the stages (breach, causation of damage) and then conclude (defences and remedies).

■ Give a concise explanation of the relevant legal principles. Do not waste time talking about related, but irrelevant, matters that you happen to know about. If, for instance, a question is clearly about private nuisance only, don't waste time talking about public nuisance. Similarly, if a question on occupiers' liability does not involve children, don't waste time discussing the rules which specifically relate to children.

■ Where you can, give the names of relevant cases to illustrate the legal principles you are discussing. You do not have to explain the fact of the case unless you think it helps your discussion.

■ Be aware that it is not enough just to explain the law. You need to go on to apply the law to the scenario. This means that you need to discuss what the position of the characters is, and make sure you do it at each stage of your answer.

■ Don't be worried if there doesn't seem to be a definite answer. Sometimes scenarios are written deliberately to pose awkward questions. Discuss both sides of an issue. One example is that it is not always clear whether a claimant in a problem relating to psychiatric loss satisfies the rules relating to secondary victims or whether what they witnessed amounts to the immediate aftermath of an accident.

You should now be able to:

■ complete an answer to a scenario question in the law of tort in an organised fashion with the purpose of gaining as high a mark as possible.

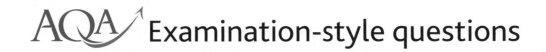

AQA Examination-style questions

Read this scenario, together with its questions, and then complete the activities that follow it.

Scenario 1

John built an extension to his house, including a bedroom for himself, which brought it much closer to the house of his neighbour, Karl. In consequence, John was frequently disturbed by loud music being played late into the night by Karl's son Lee. When he politely asked whether the sound level could be reduced, he was met with abuse from Lee, and the music was played even more loudly. Additionally, John discovered that nothing would grow on a patch of his land. This patch was next to Karl's land, where a number of rusty, leaking tin drums containing some chemical had been left for a long time.

John had built a tree-house for his children in a corner of his land close to a lane. The tree-house was recently damaged in a storm and John told his children not to play in it. Even so, Mary, and his niece, Nasma, who were both 12 years old, decided that they would repair the tree-house whilst John was at work. Part of the tree-house collapsed whilst Nasma was climbing around it, and she fell and broke her leg. Following this, John roped off an area around the tree. However, a few days later, Peter, who was 9 years old and well known in the area for mischievous behaviour, got over the hedge from the lane onto John's land and suffered head injuries when the tree-house fell onto him as he was climbing up the tree.

(a) Discuss the rights and remedies available to John in connection with the noise and the apparent damage to his land from the chemical. *(25 marks)*

(b) Consider whether Nasma and Peter have any rights and remedies against John in connection with the injuries that each suffered. *(25 marks)*

Question (a):

1. John's actions are in private nuisance and under the rule in *Rylands* v *Fletcher*. Explain first why these two torts are relevant, and secondly why public nuisance is not relevant.

2. John is clearly the claimant. State the identity of the defendant and give reasons for your answer.

3. With respect to the action in private nuisance, plan an answer paragraph by paragraph. Make sure you include somewhere in your plan a definition of private nuisance, an explanation of the losses which can be claimed in private nuisance (physical damage and loss of amenity), the factors which a court might take into account when deciding whether the defendant's activities were reasonable (be careful not to waste time on irrelevant factors), defences (if any) and remedies.

4. Complete a similar plan for your answer relating to the rule in *Rylands* v *Fletcher*. Make sure that your paragraphs include a definition of the rule, the elements of the rule, defences (if any) and remedies.

5. Mark on your two plans where you might use cases to support the rules that you intend to discuss.

6. Finally, write proper answers based on your plans. Use continuous prose, make sure your information is organised and that your spelling is accurate.

Question (b):

1   The question has identified the claimants and the defendant. Identify the torts for which Nasma and Peter respectively will be able to sue. Give reasons for your answer, and in particular be careful to explain fully why the two claimants will be using different liabilities.

2   As with question (a), prepare a paragraph by paragraph plan for each claimant, marking on where you will use cases to support your explanations. You need to consider the respective duties, whether John has breached those duties and any questions relevant to defences and remedies. Be careful to make sure that your plans reflect the ages of the claimants.

3   Finally, write a full answer based on your plans.

4   As with question (a), prepare a paragraph by paragraph plan for each defendant, marking on where you will use cases to support your explanations.

5   Finally, write a full answer based on your plans.

Now read this second scenario, together with its questions, and then complete the activities that follow it.

Scenario 2

TV10 broadcast a very popular do-it-yourself programme which included advice on viewers' problems provided by Richard, who did a lot of work for TV10, as well as writing a column for a local newspaper. During one such broadcast, Richard was asked by Susan about a suitable form of wooden flooring for her house and, by mistake, named 'Woodblox' when he meant to say, 'Blockwood'. Both Susan and another viewer, Tom, bought 'Woodblox', only to discover that the product was totally unsuitable and that they subsequently had to buy 'Blockwood'.

Whilst William was walking through town, he became curious about work being carried out on a new building site by Unibuild. He squeezed through a gap in a high wooden fence around the site, and had been watching the work for about ten minutes when he was suddenly struck by, and trapped underneath, a mobile crane which was being driven on the site. In the accident, the crane also partly demolished the fence. Vince, a passer-by, spent some time at the scene, trying to help William but was constantly afraid that the crane might topple over onto him. Zara, William's partner, saw a news item about the incident on TV10 and became hysterical when she realised, from some of the details mentioned, that the victim was William. William suffered severe permanent injuries, and both Vince and Zara found it very difficult to recover psychologically from their experiences.

(a)   Discuss the rights and remedies, if any, available to Susan and to Tom against Richard and TV10.   *(25 marks)*

(b)   Discuss the rights and remedies, if any, available to William, to Vince and to Zara in connection with the incident at the building site.   *(25 marks)*

1   Identify the torts relevant to each question. If, in question (a), the mistake was Richard's, why might TV10 be liable? How, in question (b), do William's injuries differ from both Vince and Zara's?

2   Following the routine set out for the previous scenario, plan and write answers to questions (a) and (b).

3   Ask your teacher or lecturer for plenty of other past papers, and plan and write answers for those. The more you do, the better the answers you will write in the examination.

Introduction

1 The specification

The final section of Unit 4 is entitled 'Concepts of law'. This requires you to review from a different perspective the areas of law you have already studied at AS and at A2. The AQA specification identifies five topics available for study. These are:

1 law and morality
2 law and justice
3 judicial creativity
4 fault
5 balancing conflicting interests.

2 Your study

The number of topics you study will be influenced very much by considerations of time, teacher preference and your own workload. You need to study a minimum of three topics to ensure that you can answer at least one question in the examination. The study of four topics will guarantee a choice of question, whereas coverage of all five topics will enable you to answer any question. Remember, however, that you are marked only on the question you choose to answer and not on knowledge, or ignorance, of the other questions on the examination paper. Therefore consider carefully the appropriate number of topics to study and revise.

In your coverage of these topics you will be drawing upon areas of law that you have already studied, as you are required to provide illustrative material from these. It is perhaps wise to draw much of the material from units that you are sitting at the same time, as this will 'kill two birds with one stone', especially if you are re-sitting AS papers. There is no prescribed material that must be covered. The only requirement is that the material you select is relevant to the argument being developed.

You will notice that the following five chapters contain a lot of information, too much for any individual student to be expected to cover. Don't worry. These chapters have been designed to be relevant for students who have specialised in contract, in crime and in tort. Select from these chapters the material that is relevant to your study. You will not be expected to cover all the areas in the examination.

3 The examination

In the examination, you will be asked to write one essay question from a choice of three. It is not possible to predict with any degree of certainty which three topics will appear on any one paper. The fact that a topic is not asked one year is no guarantee that it will appear on the paper the following year. As the paper is two hours long, you will have time to reflect on the questions before deciding which one to answer. You will also have time to plan your answer for your selected question.

When planning and writing the essay, you should be conscious of the need to ensure that it contains some theory, usually by reference to the thoughts or writings of philosophers, academics and judges. The answer should normally contain reference to a range of topics, or, where possible, a range of areas of Law (remember you have studied criminal and civil liability in Unit 2). This should be supported by reference to appropriate statutes and cases to illustrate the points being made. Refer to the facts of cases where these develop your discussion, but avoid merely writing detailed narratives of the cases without explaining their relevance. In addition try to make reference to current affairs. Every week issues arise that are relevant to this paper. Incorporate some of these into your answer. Finally, in your discussion you should address the particular question that is asked, and not merely reproduce a prepared answer.

The essay will be marked according to its legal content and according to the quality of discussion. It is possible to score highly under the first category by referring widely and in detail to relevant areas of law. The required content for each topic does not significantly change from one question to the next. Therefore it is possible to prepare this material with confidence in advance. The quality of the discussion will be assessed by its relevance to the question, by its reference to theories of law, and sometimes by your personal response to the issues. It is possible that the question in the examination will be very different from any question you have already considered on the topic. Therefore be prepared to take time to reflect on the particular nuance of the question in the examination.

20 Law and morality

In this topic you will learn how to:

- explain theories of law and morality
- explain the characteristics of legal rules
- explain the characteristics of moral rules.

1 An introduction to law and morality

Law

Law is not a term that lends itself to easy definition. For a start the term is used in a general sense, in phrases such as English law, to mean all those rules of the state that govern our lives. It is also used in a narrower sense to describe specific areas, such as the law of contract which is concerned with agreements made between people, generally for the provision of goods or services, or the law of succession, which is concerned with the passage of a person's belongings upon his death. However, these terms describe the substance, not the nature, of law. To discover what men believe law is, we need to look at two distinctive theories. These are legal positivism and natural law.

Legal positivism

The first of these theories is known as **legal positivism**. Positivists believe that a law is a legal rule which, if made in the manner recognised by the legislative power in the state, is valid irrespective of its content. But each legal positivist has his own individual explanation of this theory, and these can diverge significantly, as we can see with the theories of John Austin and **H.L.A. Hart**.

Early in the 19th century, John Austin was appointed to the first chair of Jurisprudence at London University. He believed that once laws are made, or posited (put in place), they are binding upon people, whatever the morality of their content. In his own words: 'The existence of law is one thing, its merit or demerit is another. A law which exists is a law, though we happen to dislike it.' Thus, we might find a law highly offensive, but that does not affect its validity.

Austin is perhaps best known for developing the **command theory of law**. He argued that a law is a command from a sovereign whom the population at large is in the habit of obeying, and it is reinforced by the availability of a sanction. Put simply, laws are orders backed by threats. A law, therefore, is the expressed wish of the sovereign and as such is distinguishable from other commands such as those from God or from an employer. The sovereign is the person or body whom others habitually obey, and who is not in the habit of giving obedience to anyone else.

Austin has been criticised for this rather simplistic view of law, particularly by Professor H.L.A. Hart, partly because it is difficult to identify a sovereign in many states, but also because many areas of law such as contract, which grant powers to people, do not fit neatly into such a definition. As a legal positivist, he insisted on the separation of law and morality. However, he developed a much more sophisticated model than Austin's to explain the nature of law. There are, he argued, two categories of rules, called primary and secondary rules, which, in combination, form the basis of a functioning legal system.

Primary rules either impose legal obligations, as in criminal law, or they grant powers, as in the power to make a will in the law of succession, or the power to enter into a contract.

Secondary rules are concerned with the operation of primary legal rules. Hart identified three specific secondary rules. Firstly, the rule of recognition sets criteria for identifying primary legal rules. These criteria would include reference, for example, to Acts of Parliament and judicial decisions. Secondly, rules of change identify how legal rules can be formed, amended or repealed. For example, in the case of an Act of Parliament, reference would be made to the various readings in the House of Commons and the House of Lords, and to the need for royal assent. Thirdly, rules of adjudication enable the courts not only to settle disputes, but also to interpret the law.

Hart argues that a legal system is established by the union of these two sets of rules. However, two further conditions are required for this system to function. Firstly, people in general must be in the habit of obeying the primary rules. Secondly, public officials must accept the rules of recognition, change and adjudication.

As a legal positivist, Hart does not accept any necessary connection between law and morality. In other words, the validity of a law is not dependent upon its moral acceptability. Even a morally repugnant law may be legally valid. However, that does not mean we must obey laws that are morally repugnant. Obedience remains a matter of personal decision or conscience.

Natural law

Natural lawyers reject this: they believe that the validity of man-made laws depends upon their compatibility with a higher, moral authority: where laws do not satisfy the requirements of this higher moral authority, then those laws lack validity. There are, though, different views advanced on the precise nature of this higher moral authority. We shall explore two examples.

Thomas Aquinas was a 13th-century Catholic philosopher and theologian, who devoted his life to scholarship, in particular to the study of Aristotle. His major work, the *Summa Theologica*, contains his explanation of four different types of law. The highest is eternal law: this governs everything within the universe, such as the law of gravity (although this was not known at the time of Aquinas), and includes general moral rules of conduct. Although we do not enjoy direct access to it, we can acquire partial knowledge of it by reasoning upon the way that nature operates.

Divine law is concerned with the standards man must conform to in order to attain salvation. These are revealed to mankind by inspiration or revelation, as for example the Ten Commandments contained within the Bible. Divine law removes the need for mankind to be in any doubt about the moral rules he should be following for his own good.

Natural law is derived from eternal law and deals with general rules of conduct that govern the behaviour of 'beings possessing reason and free will', i.e. humans. It is implanted in us by God as part of our nature, and so we have a natural inclination to behave in a way that fulfils our purpose in life. These include the inclination to preserve life, procreate, and live within society. By reasoning upon natural law, certain general rules of conduct can be developed. The first of these is to '**do good and avoid evil**'. Some others are 'not to commit suicide', reflecting the inclination to preserve life; to 'rear and care for offspring', reflecting the inclination to procreate; and to 'develop our rational and moral capacities'.

Human law is derived by reason from natural law. It is the result of a process of applying the principles contained within natural law to particular geographical, historical and social circumstances. Thus, human laws may differ from society to society, but they should always conform to the spirit of natural law. Where they fail to achieve this, human laws are a perversion of law: they are laws in name only, and do not require obedience. In other words, human laws lack validity where they fail to conform to a higher authority, this authority being, for Aquinas, natural law. This illustrates a key general point: posited law, human law in Aquinas' case, is dependent for its validity upon its conformity to a higher authority.

Lon Fuller was Professor of Jurisprudence at Harvard Law School. He is known as a natural lawyer in that he rejected legal positivism: he refused to accept the belief that law has no higher authority than that of a sovereign authority. Fuller, though, is not a natural lawyer in the tradition of Aquinas: for Fuller, law is earth-based.

Like Aquinas, Fuller views law as serving a purpose. In his case, that purpose is to 'achieve social order through subjecting people's conduct to the guidance of general rules by which they may themselves orient their behaviour'. For laws to be able to achieve this purpose, they must satisfy eight particular principles. These principles make up an '**inner morality of law**' which Fuller describes as a procedural version of natural law.

According to these eight principles, laws should be:

1 in existence, not ad hoc
2 promulgated, i.e. published
3 prospective, rather than retrospective
4 clearly stated and comprehensible
5 consistent with each other
6 possible for people to obey
7 constant, i.e. relatively long-lasting and not constantly changing
8 applied and administered as stated.

Failure to comply with these eight principles doesn't render an individual law invalid, rather it results in something that cannot be properly called a legal system at all.

Professor Hart, while not critical of the eight principles themselves, argued that Fuller was not justified in calling them a morality. He illustrates his objection by reference to the art of poisoning. Like law-making, poisoning is an activity with a purpose. The poisoner will develop principles to render his art effective. However, nobody would consider calling these principles the 'inner morality of poisoning'. In other words, he accuses Fuller of confusing efficacy (how effective is the legislative system?) with morality (is it good or bad?).

Morality

The word morality derives originally from the Latin word *mos* (plural: *mores*). The standard meaning of this word is a custom, habit or usage that is determined by man's will rather than by law. The Roman statesman and orator Cicero once wrote that law and custom (*mos*) must both be obeyed, illustrating their parity. Custom formed the bedrock of Roman society in Cicero's day, with duties and obligations balanced by rights and privileges. One example neatly illustrates this point: within the Roman patron-client system, leading men were regularly, often daily, attended by men of humbler origins. In return for assistance in humble matters, such as escorting them to the forum, and voting for them when they stood for public office, these leading men would reciprocate by granting their protection, advice and occasional acts of kindness. Often this relationship passed from one generation to the next, in this way forging strong family bonds between the leading families on the one hand and plebeians or freedmen on the other. This patron-client system was a significant factor in providing the integration between the social classes that gave the Roman Republic stability for many centuries.

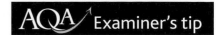

AQA Examiner's tip

These notes provide detailed explanations of various philosophies. In the examination, you need to identify and explain only the key points from these.

Key terms

Inner morality of law: describes the eight principles adopted by Lon Fuller. Laws must satisfy these eight principles, otherwise the legal system lacks validity.

This custom, like others, had a number of distinctive features. First of all it had no identifiable origin: rather it developed into an accepted practice over a long period of time. Secondly, it constituted a course of conduct willingly practised by the majority. Thirdly, value was attached to it: it concerned not merely how people did behave, but also how they should behave. Fourthly, adherence to it was a matter for public judgement: reputations were damaged by failure to comply with its standards. Fifthly, being a custom it was not enshrined in law, but it was no less binding for that, even though enforcement was by social disapproval rather than by formal sanctions.

In short, this custom formed the basis of a code of conduct which reflected the expressed wishes of that society, and which members of that society accepted in large measure. It was therefore part of the morality of that age.

The Roman Republic was an example of what the 19th century sociologist **Emile Durkheim** would later refer to as a traditional society. In such a society people had much in common. However, by Durkheim's day, society was becoming more fragmented. First, labour was becoming specialised, with workers developing expertise in increasingly narrow fields, thereby becoming alienated from each other. Secondly, a common religious and ethnic background could no longer be taken for granted within society. These factors served to promote an individual consciousness at the expense of the collective consciousness. The speed of change, Durkheim argued, led to confusion in moral outlooks, and to the breakdown of traditional norms of behaviour. Durkheim used the word '**anomie**' to describe this result. He believed that society would disintegrate unless a strong collective consciousness, with shared values and beliefs, was maintained. One of the functions of education, therefore, is to strengthen the common morality and reduce individual consciousness. This can in part be achieved by a pledge of allegiance to the state, an idea recently promoted for all school leavers in Britain.

Durkheim therefore identified a range of factors as potentially contributing to the breakdown of a common morality. These included the increasing specialisation of labour, ethnic diversity within society, and the fading influence of religious belief. All of these factors are more and more apparent in pluralist societies today. Under Durkheim's analysis, therefore, we should not be surprised to discover a parallel growth in the diversity of moral outlook and in norms of behaviour in modern Britain.

Characteristics of legal and moral rules

Both legal rules and moral rules have certain characteristics that help to identify them and distinguish them from each other. These characteristics relate not only to formal issues such as their means of creation, change and enforcement, but also to their nature and the extent of their influence.

Their origins

It is generally possible to trace legal rules back to a source. For centuries the most creative source of legal rules was the common law. Areas of law, such as tort, contract, and crime, have been developed incrementally by judges. For example, the principle that occupiers can owe a duty of care to trespassers comes originally from the decision made by the House of Lords in *British Railways Board* v *Herrington* (1972) as recently as 1972. During the 20th century Parliament became increasingly active as a source of law. For example, the Occupiers' Liability Act of 1984 established new rules concerning the liability of occupiers for trespassers. In recent times, the European Union has become a major source of

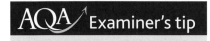

Examiner's tip

In the examination you are not expected to cover all of these points in the detail provided here. You can either cover a wide range of issues in outline, or a more limited number in depth.

law-making through treaties, directives, regulations and decisions. For example, a 1993 directive established a 48-hour maximum working week and lay down requirements for rest periods.

Moral rules are usually more difficult to trace back to a precise origin. For many, morality is based upon religious teaching: thus the Ten Commandments (which can be dated to 1513 BC) will form the basis for their moral outlook. This code will inform their attitudes towards issues such as pre-marital sex, petty theft and the discovery of lost property. For others, morality is based upon upbringing, upon peer views, or upon the leanings of their own consciences.

Their date of commencement

Legal rules generally have a date of birth. Cases have a year attached to them. Acts of Parliament come into force on midnight of the day on which they receive royal assent, or at a specified later date. For instance, the Human Rights Act 1998 came into force on the 1 October 2000, and provisions under the Equality Act 2006 have been introduced by stages. Similarly, European law becomes operative on a given date.

Moral rules are less straightforward. For example, western attitudes towards pre-marital sex have undergone significant change since World War II. However, it is not possible to attach a date to this change, as it is part of a wider change in social attitudes towards matters of sexual morality.

Their enforcement

Legal rules can be enforced. In criminal law, sanctions are available, ranging from life sentences for serial killers like Steve Wright, to an absolute discharge for an ambulance driver who caused a collision while speeding in response to an emergency. In tort, damages are available for those whose interests are harmed. These are generally compensatory, where the purpose is to restore the victim to his pre-tort position. The equitable remedy of injunctions is available when the claimant seeks to put an end to the commission of the tort, for example to put an end to a private nuisance. In contract law, the award of damages is the normal remedy sought by the claimant. These seek to place the claimant in the position he would have been in had the contract been performed.

Sanctions may also be available for those who breach moral codes. A religious group might excommunicate a wayward member, and a member who uses offensive language may be excluded from his golf club. More often, though, moral rules are enforced through disapproval or social ostracism. A guest who uses his hands to rip apart his joint of beef, an acceptable habit in another age, may soon find himself short of invitations. Or a youth who takes drugs within the family home may be required to leave the family home to avoid harming his younger siblings. Often, however, moral rules are unenforceable.

Their ease of change

In theory, legal rules are relatively easy to change as Parliament has the authority to pass laws whenever it wants. This may be in response to distasteful court judgments (e.g. the War Damage Act 1965), to proposals from a law reform body (e.g. The Supply of Goods and Services Act 1982), or to public pressure (e.g. the Dangerous Dogs Act 1991). In practice, however, Parliament is often slow to respond to the need for change. The courts also have the power to change legal rules. The decision in **Williams v Roffey (1990)** limited the avoidance of obligations for lack of consideration; and the house of Lords in *R* v *G and R* (2003) reinstated the subjective test of recklessness for the offence of criminal damage.

Key cases

Williams v Roffey (1990): in the law of contract an agreement must be supported by both parties giving something of value in exchange for the benefit they receive; this is known as consideration; carrying out an existing obligation does not provide consideration; however, following the decision in *Williams v Roffey*, the performance of an existing obligation may now be taken as consideration.

Moral rules tend to change gradually, perhaps over decades or centuries. It is often only in hindsight that we are aware of such change. For example, it has taken decades for the attitude to cigarette smoking to harden. This has been encouraged by health warnings, by restrictions upon advertising, by bold 'Smoking kills' notices, and by an increasing intolerance of the nuisance smoking causes to others. And yet it is not possible to identify a particular date, or even a particular decade, when intolerance towards smoking became the dominant attitude.

Their certainty of content

It is normally possible to discover the precise content of legal rules. For example, reference to s9 of the Theft Act 1968 will show the requirements for the *actus reus* and *mens rea* of burglary. The law can also be discovered by reading judgments in cases. Reference to **Partridge v Crittenden (1968)**, for instance, will show that newspaper advertisements are generally considered an invitation to treat rather than an offer. A measure of uncertainty may arise where an Act has been amended. For example, following the Sexual Offences Act 2003, intent to rape will no longer provide the *mens rea* for a burglary conviction. Uncertainty may also arise where there are apparently conflicting authorities, such as *Lefkowitz* v *Great Minneapolis Stores* (1957), where the newspaper advertising coats for sale to the first three customers was regarded as an offer.

The content of moral rules may also be clear: for example, rules on etiquette and table manners are available in books; rules on sexual morality are often available within the written teachings of religious organisations; and rules on acceptable conduct within schools are often displayed on classroom walls. However, knowledge of the content of moral rules can often only be acquired informally through exposure to them in the setting where they are applied, whether that is the family home, the school playground, or the golf course. Each setting will have its own mores, and strangers will take time to acquaint themselves with the rules and standards of what is acceptable conduct: what is acceptable at Glastonbury might not be tolerated at Gleneagles.

Their range of application

Legal rules generally apply to everyone. Thus, everyone in this country, including the prime minister, is obliged to drive on the left hand side of the road, to stop at red traffic lights, and not to park on double yellow lines. It is true that diplomats enjoy a measure of immunity. Many embassies in London, for example, refuse to pay the congestion charge, claiming that they enjoy diplomatic privilege. This, however, is a minor exception to the general rule that the laws of the country apply to all who live here.

Moral rules, on the other hand, range in application from enjoying almost universal adoption to having only marginal acceptance. For example, the wedding guest wearing only a fig leaf would probably be quietly escorted from the premises, whoever the bride and groom were. However, perhaps only a small minority of people today regard themselves as required to give up their seat on a busy train to an elderly person. Other moral issues polarise public opinion: stem cell research, assisted suicide and gay adoption are all areas where it is possibly difficult to determine a prevailing public morality.

> **Key cases**
>
> **Partridge v Crittenden (1968)**: an advertisement in a newspaper will normally be regarded as an invitation to treat; the person responding to the advert will then be making an offer, which the advertiser is free to accept or reject.

Fig. 1 *The congestion charge aimed to relieve the pressure on London's roads*

Activity

Read the following hypothetical situation:

'Under their unwritten constitution the citizens of Brownland have always enjoyed freedom of speech. However, in 1984 the Parliament of Brownland duly passed a law declaring that all natural blondes are barred from voicing political opinions in private. The penalty for disobedience is a fixed five-year prison sentence. In 1988 Joe reported his wife, Marilyn, for criticising the government. She was given the mandatory five-year sentence. In 1995, the 1984 law was repealed. Joe was then charged with the common law offence of 'depriving an innocent person of his liberty'.

How might natural lawyers and legal positivists decide the outcome of Joe's case?

You should now be able to:

- understand the main distinction between different theories of law
- understand the key differences between legal rules and moral rules.

2 The relationship between law and morality

The coincidence of legal and moral rules

Legal and moral rules, though distinctive, share certain characteristics. They are both concerned with setting standards, which are essential for governing the behaviour of individuals within society. For example, in order to avoid unnecessary death and injury, the law requires us to drive on the left. However, it is a long-established custom, part of our mores, that drivers slow down to allow ambulances to pass when their emergency lights are flashing. Both rules are concerned with the behaviour of drivers and the saving of life.

Legal and moral rules therefore employ similar language: they distinguish between right and wrong, and they speak of duties, obligations and responsibilities. For example, murder is regarded as wicked under both the legal and moral codes of conduct; parents have a legal duty and a moral duty to ensure that their young children are provided with shelter and nourishment; and getting emergency medical help for someone for whom you have responsibility is regarded as morally virtuous as well as legally binding.

Law and morality often coincide or overlap: for example, the Ten Commandments, given to Moses on Mount Sinai, continue to serve as a moral code for many today. Indeed, these commandments contain a number of prohibitions which are to be found in the laws of even the most primitive societies. In our age, the order: 'Thou shalt not kill', is reflected in the common law on murder; the command: 'Thou shalt not steal', is currently contained within ss1–6 of the Theft Act 1968; and the principle of the virtue of honesty, which lies behind the command not to give false witness, can be seen in the development of the law in areas such as fraud (crime), misrepresentation (contract), and defamation (tort).

Legal rules are strengthened by this convergence, and their enforcement can more readily be justified. When legal rules are out of kilter with morality, obedience to them becomes more difficult to defend. Often, though, legal rules possess no obvious moral content. Parking a car on a double yellow line in a town centre at four o'clock in the morning does not seem to infringe any moral code (other than the act itself of breaking

In this topic you will learn how to:

- explain where legal and moral rules coincide
- explain the influence of legal and moral rules upon each other.

AQA Examiner's tip

As in the previous section, you need to introduce examples to illustrate the points you are making. Try to think of some examples of your own to make your essay distinctive, rather than relying exclusively on those in the textbooks.

the law). Similarly, it is morally neutral whether public houses (under the licensing laws introduced in November 2005) close at 12 o'clock rather than 11 o'clock.

It might be argued that strict liability offences are like this. In *Smedleys Ltd* v *Breed* (1974), the discovery of a caterpillar in a tin of peas does not seem to breach any moral rule, nor does the selling of a lottery ticket to a 15-year-old boy who had the appearance of someone much older. It is therefore not surprising that the principle of strict liability is controversial: legal rules are given greater validity by their moral content.

Conversely, there are many moral rules which are not enshrined in law. The commandment: 'Thou shalt not commit adultery' was part of the Mosaic Law (i.e. the law of Moses) for the people of ancient Israel, and is the law in many countries of the world today. Indeed, such importance is attached to it that it is punishable by death. In Britain, however, there is no legal prohibition against the commission of adultery, although it has provided a common ground for divorce under the Matrimonial Causes Act 1973. This, though, does not reduce the possible moral outrage felt at its commission.

On a similar point, there is no liability in English criminal law for omissions, unless the failure falls within one of the recognised exceptions where there is a duty to act, such as a duty to children (*R* v *Gibbons and Proctor* (1918)), or a duty through a contract of employment (*R* v *Pittwood* (1902)). In other words, there is no requirement in English law to act as the 'good Samaritan'. Interestingly, this term is derived from a parable where a despised foreigner came to the aid of a man beaten and left for dead. The parable was designed to answer the question: who is my neighbour? Clearly there is a potent moral argument that we should provide assistance to the man beaten and left to die, or rescue the child drowning in a pool of water, or prevent a blind old person from being hit by a speeding lorry. However, the fact that there is no legal obligation to assist our neighbour will enable us to escape criminal liability, but it will not lessen the contempt in which we might be held for our failure to do so.

Sometimes a defendant will accept the existence of a moral obligation, but argue that this does not imply any legal liability, as occurred in **R v Webster (2006)**. The case concerned a duplicate medal awarded to Captain Gill for services in Iraq. Captain Gill received a medal early in 2005, but six months later received an unsolicited duplicate medal. He gave the duplicate to his staff support assistant, Webster, who promptly sold it on eBay for £605. Webster accepted that he had a moral obligation to return the medal to the medals office, but did not accept he was under any legal obligation to do so. However, the court decided that the medals office retained a proprietary interest in this particular duplicate medal and was therefore entitled to call for its return.

The influence of law and morality upon each other

Changing moral values can lead to developments in the law. In the History of the Pleas of the Crown (published in 1736, although Hale had died 60 years before this date), Sir Matthew Hale had declared that 'a man cannot rape his wife'. This was based upon the doctrine of implied consent, i.e. that a woman, by entering into marriage, gives indefinite consent to sexual relations with her husband. During the 20th century the courts succeeded in removing this immunity where there was a legal separation order (*R* v *Clarke* (1949)), where a decree nisi had been issued (*R* v *O'Brien* (1974)), and where a non-molestation order had been imposed (*R* v *Steele* (1977)). In these decisions the courts were eager to limit the moral outrage that an acquittal would arouse.

Key cases

R v Webster (2006): this case illustrates the coincidence of moral and legal obligations.

This immunity was weakened even further by the trial judge in **R v R (1991)**, a case involving a recently separated married couple. Owen J declared: 'I find it hard to believe that it ever was common law that a husband was in effect entitled to beat his wife into submission to sexual intercourse.' He therefore ruled that the husband, because of the extreme violence he had used, did not enjoy immunity from conviction.

Before the case arrived at the House of Lords on appeal, the Law Commission had produced a report recommending that 'the present marital immunity be abolished in all cases'. The House of Lords followed this recommendation. Lord Lane declared that 'the idea that a wife by marriage consents in advance to her husband having sexual intercourse with her whatever her state of health or however proper her objections is no longer acceptable'. In this way the law eventually caught up with perceived public morality.

The Abortion Act 1967 represents an area of statutory reform introduced as a result of public concern over the existing law. Under s58 of the Offences against the Person Act 1861, abortion was punishable by up to life imprisonment, even if performed for good medical reasons. The Infant Life Preservation Act 1929 allowed a limited exemption from this general prohibition in cases where the abortion was carried out in good faith for the sole purpose of preserving the life of the mother. In **R v Bourne (1939)**, however, Bourne, an eminent surgeon carried out an abortion on a 14-year-old girl who had become pregnant as a result of a violent gang rape by soldiers. At his trial, Bourne argued that the operation had been necessary to preserve the mental health (but not the life) of the girl. The trial judge proved sympathetic to this argument. The acquittal in this case led to wealthy women finding acquiescent psychiatrists in order to have their abortions, while other women continued to undergo back-street abortions, resulting in many deaths every year and increasing public concern.

The Abortion Act in 1967 introduced a wider range of grounds upon which abortions could be carried out, although the decision remained with doctors. Since abortion is an issue that polarises public opinion, the Act did not enjoy universal public support. However, the law had changed in response to changing public concerns.

Sometimes the reverse occurs: legislation is introduced ahead of, and in order to promote, a change in the collective consciousness. Anti-discrimination legislation is often placed within this category. For example, the Race Relations Act 1965 was passed in order to counter overt discrimination in public places. Prior to this Act, colour prejudice, as it was then called, was widely practised in Britain, with signs such as 'No Blacks' seen on the fronts of guest houses, and non-whites turned away from some restaurants and public houses.

The 1965 Act, passed in spite of fierce opposition within Parliament, forbade discrimination 'on the grounds of colour, race, or ethnic or national origin'. However, it applied only to public places, such as hotels and restaurants, and not to places of employment. The powers of enforcement were also minimal: a Race Relations Board was empowered to listen to complaints, and to attempt to negotiate with the parties to stop further discrimination. Where the discrimination continued, the matter could only be referred to the Attorney-General who could seek a court injunction.

Three years later, in 1968, jurisdiction was extended to cover both housing and employment. Although these two Acts did not eliminate discrimination, they made a robust official statement about the values of British society. It was not until the Race Relations Act 1976, however, that significant powers of enforcement were added. This Act established the Commission for Racial Equality to replace the Race Relations Board,

Key cases

R v R (1991): this case is the culmination of a series of cases in which judges attempted to avoid an outdated precedent generally regarded as morally repugnant.

R v Bourne (1939): this case illustrates the willingness of judges to develop the law to avoid a conviction where the defendant is deemed to have acted morally.

Key terms

Wolfenden Report 1957: the report of a 14-member committee appointed to examine the law on homosexuality and prostitution, and to make recommendations for law reform.

and gave it extensive powers. It distinguished between direct and indirect discrimination: direct occurring where a person is treated less favourably than another in similar relevant circumstances on the grounds of colour, race, nationality, ethnic or national origins. Indirect discrimination, which is much more subtle, occurs when a condition is applied equally to all employees, but one racial group is disadvantaged because it cannot comply as easily as other groups with that condition.

These provisions have done much to mitigate harsh, overt racism. On the fortieth anniversary of the passage of the 1965 Act, Trevor Phillips, chairman of the Commission for Racial Equality, stated, 'The fact that we have strong anti-discrimination laws has led to the near disappearance of commonplace practices which disfigured our society. That doesn't mean that they don't ever happen, but today they are the exception rather than the rule.' Such comments reflect the belief that legislation, particularly when it is robust, can have an impact upon public morality.

Often it is difficult to assess whether changing attitudes or changes in the law came first. It is even possible that the two march alongside each other, though not necessarily in step all the way. One of the most heavily legislated areas in the last 50 years has been the law on homosexuality. In 1957, the **Wolfenden Report** (see later for more details of this) recommended that 'homosexual behaviour between consenting adults in private should no longer be a criminal offence'. The committee further recommended that the age of consent be fixed at 21, which at that time was the age of majority in Britain.

Ten years were to pass before the Sexual Offences Bill was presented to Parliament, time enough for many to reflect on the principles underpinning Wolfenden, and time perhaps for Parliamentarians to muster up the boldness required to secure the passage of the Bill in the face of some earnest opposition. The Bill contained the two most significant recommendations of the Wolfenden Committee: first, that homosexuality be decriminalised for private consensual homosexual activity; and secondly, that the age of consent be set at 21.

A quarter of a century was to pass before the age of consent was reduced to 18 in the Criminal Justice and Public Order Act 1994, but only six years until it was further reduced to 16 under the Sexual Offences (Amendment) Act 2000, thereby equalising the age of consent for heterosexual and homosexual activity. This last reform attracted determined opposition within the House of Lords, and the powers of the Parliament Acts had to be invoked to secure passage of the measure. It is difficult to gauge whether those promoting or those opposing these Acts more accurately reflected public opinion on this issue, but what is evident is that the years since 1957 have seen not only substantial legislative activity, but also a major shift in public attitudes in this area.

Activity

Consider the following hypothetical situations. What point about the relationship between law and morality would they illustrate?

1. After World War I there was a shortage of men of marriageable age in Britain. As a result many young women's hopes of marriage were dashed. Parliament therefore passed an Act making polygamy compulsory for all men between the ages of 20 and 40.

2. Ivor Camm, a former member of the North Wales mountain ranger service, was scrambling over the ridge known as Crib Goch, when he met a party of inexperienced walkers. He ignored their pleas for help, as he was going to be late home for lunch. Two members of the party fell to their deaths.

You should now be able to:

■ understand how legal and moral rules coincide, and how they influence each other.

3 The enforcement of morality

Britain is a pluralist society containing a diversity of moral views. This section explores the questions of whether, and to what extent, the law should seek to enforce any particular moral views. This is not merely a subject of academic debate: judges are often forced to consider these questions before determining the law. There are two starting points for this debate: the first is that the law, as the guardian of public morals, should intervene to ensure the continuation of the dominant morality within the state. The second is diametrically opposed: individuals should be left free to decide their own morality. In practice, both these positions are modified so that they tend towards convergence.

John Stuart Mill

In his book *On Liberty*, John Stuart Mill, a 19th-century philosopher, explored 'the nature and limits of the power which can be legitimately exercised by society over the individual'. He began by tracing the historical development of liberty as a protection against the rule of tyrants. Over a period of centuries, limits began to be imposed upon governmental power first by the recognition of certain immunities, called rights or liberties, and secondly by the establishment of constitutional checks. Later, when tyrants were replaced by elected, temporary rulers who served as representatives of the people, the need for protection should have disappeared, as, in theory at least, people should not need protection against themselves. However, protection was still necessary against suppression by the elected majority: limitations on the power of the government were still needed to prevent the '**tyranny of the majority**'.

Mill went on to argue that such tyranny could be exercised by society collectively and not just by governments, and that this 'social tyranny' was more formidable than many forms of political repression. He therefore declared that it was necessary to protect individuals against the tendency of society to impose its own ideas and practices upon dissenters. There is, he asserted, 'a limit to the legitimate interference of collective opinion with individual independence'.

Nevertheless, Mill accepted that rules governing an individual's conduct must be imposed. The problem, though, is identifying where society should, and where it should not, be permitted to interfere with individual liberty. Mill developed the '**harm principle**' as the appropriate test to be used when considering this issue.

He wrote:

> The only purpose for which power can be rightfully exercised over any member of a civilised community, against his will, is to prevent harm to others. His own good, either physical or moral, is not a sufficient warrant .... Over himself, his own body and mind, the individual is sovereign.

Under this principle, an individual should be allowed to harm himself: society can only intervene where his conduct harms others.

Mill limits the application of the harm principle in one significant way: it does not apply to those who are not 'in the maturity of their faculties'. In other words, it does not apply to children, over whom society enjoys 'absolute power'. They must be protected against their own actions as well against the actions of others. Nor, interestingly, does the principle apply to barbarian states: benevolent despotism is seen as good for them.

Mill provided a broad definition of harm. He argued that, as a general rule, harm will be caused by commissions rather than by omissions

In this topic you will learn how to:

■ explain different theories about whether the law should be used to enforce morality, including the Hart–Devlin debate

■ discuss recent cases and legislation that reflect this debate.

Key terms

Tyranny of the majority: a term used by Mill to describe the situation where the elected majority in government, or the majority within society as a whole, force their views upon others, thereby restricting their freedom.

Harm principle: Mill's belief that an individual's private conduct can be restricted only where it brings harm to other people. Otherwise an individual is sovereign over his own mind and body.

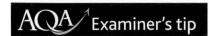

(a familiar concept from Unit 2). However, he recognised that harm may also in certain circumstances be caused by a failure to act, such as a failure to give evidence in court, a failure to bear a fair share in the common defence, and a failure to save a fellow creature's life. In these and similar situations, an individual may rightfully be held accountable for his failure to act, and deserves society's disapproval. In the most severe cases, he also deserves to be punished under the law.

Mill recognised that others might refuse to admit this distinction between that part of a person's life which concerns only himself and that which concerns others. One such objector was the 19th century judge, Sir James Stephen, who opposed the liberalism of Mill. Stephen argued that there is no distinction between acts that harm others and acts that harm oneself. He wrote: 'There are acts of wickedness so gross and outrageous that they must be punished at any cost to the offender'. He went on to argue that the prevention of wickedness and immorality is a proper end in itself and justifies state action. The law, he argued, has a duty to proscribe behaviour condemned by society at large.

Mill answered such objections by making a distinction between the harmful act itself and its particular consequences. For example, society has no right to interfere with drunkenness itself. However, it does have the right to interfere where a man, through his drunkenness, is in breach of his duty to his family or his creditors, or if he was a soldier or a policeman on duty. In Mill's words: 'Whenever there is definite damage to an individual or to the public, the case is taken out of the province of liberty, and placed in that of morality or law'. However, where there is no such breach of duty to society and the damage affects only the individual himself, then 'the inconvenience is one which society can afford to bear, for the sake of the greater good of human freedom'. In other words, the liberty of the individual is too precious to be sacrificed merely to ease another's feeling of revulsion or repugnance.

The Hart–Devlin debate

This argument has endured. In the 20th century it blossomed in the debate between an eminent Law Lord, **Patrick Devlin**, and the academic H.L.A Hart, a debate sparked by the publication in 1957 of the Wolfenden report on homosexuality and prostitution. The committee had concluded that the law has a role in preserving public order and decency, but 'it is not, in our view, the function of the law to intervene in the private life of citizens, or to seek to enforce any particular pattern of behaviour'. Furthermore, there 'must remain a realm of private morality and immorality which is, in brief and crude terms, not the law's business'. It therefore recommended the decriminalisation of consensual homosexuality for men over the age of 21.

In 'The Enforcement of Morals', published in 1965, Lord Devlin wrote that a society means a community of ideas: 'without shared ideas on politics, morals, and ethics, no society can exist'. Society, therefore, is constituted in part by its morality. In language reminiscent of Durkheim, Lord Devlin argued that the fabric of society is dependent upon a shared or common morality: where the bonds of that morality are loosened by private immoral conduct, the integrity of society will be lost, and society will be liable to disintegrate. Society therefore has the right to defend itself against immorality. Even private wickedness and immorality may be punished because they are harmful to society. In Lord Devlin's own words, 'The suppression of vice is as much the law's business as the suppression of subversive activities.'

However, Lord Devlin recognised that there are limits to the right of society to interfere with private immoral conduct: 'there must be toleration of the maximum individual freedom that is consistent with the integrity of society'. He accepted that personal preferences, or likes and dislikes, should not form the basis for decisions about what immoral conduct should be outlawed. He therefore developed an apparently objective test, that of the reasonable or ordinary man, to help decide where the boundaries are to be drawn: only where immoral conduct is regarded by this ordinary man with 'intolerance, indignation or disgust', should it be prohibited by law.

It is worth noting that Lord Devlin's morality is based upon convention: in other words, it is based upon what is generally regarded by society at large as being the acceptable and desirable state of affairs. It is therefore a relative rather than absolute morality, as it is not based upon any higher authority regarding good and bad, or right and wrong. **Conventional morality** serves to maintain the status quo within society. Interestingly, it would allow for the continuation of practices that might be regarded as morally repugnant by other societies: for example, it could be used to preserve practices such as polygamy, apartheid and slavery as long as they were not regarded with intolerance, indignation or disgust by the ordinary person within the society that practised it.

Professor Hart proposed a more limited role for the law in the enforcement of morality. Whereas Lord Devlin started from the general principle that society has a duty to enforce its dominant morality, and then limited the application of this general principle to acts that the ordinary man regards with intolerance, Professor Hart started from the opposite end of the spectrum, that society should not interfere with private moral or immoral conduct. However, Hart then limited the application of this general principle by sanctioning the enforcement of morality in certain situations. First of all, he accepted that enforcement is permitted when one of society's dominant moralities is being eroded by a true threat to the cohesion of society. Such a threat, though, has to be more than merely a challenge to society's code of conduct: there must be evidence that it creates a genuine public nuisance.

Hart's discussion of the offence of bigamy illustrates this approach. He wrote that, in a country where deep religious significance is attached to monogamous marriage and to the wedding service, the law against bigamy should be accepted as an attempt to protect religious feelings from offence by a 'public act desecrating the ceremony'. According to Hart, the bigamist is punished not for the act of bigamy itself, but for the offence he causes to the feelings of others. Hart applied the same reasoning to public sexual intercourse between a man and his wife. The act of intercourse, he states, is not in itself immoral, but if it takes place in public, it is an affront to decent people, and, as a nuisance, deserves to be punished under the law.

Devlin accused Hart of being inconsistent. He challenged Hart, saying: 'Bigamy violates neither good manners nor decency. When committed without deception, it harms no one.' Although Devlin is not necessarily arguing here in favour of legalising bigamy, it is at least ironic that he seems to be adopting a more liberal stance than Hart on this issue.

Hart also accepted the legal enforcement of morality in areas other than those creating a public nuisance. On some issues he adopted a paternalistic approach. The taking of drugs and consensual euthanasia are two areas where he believed people need to be protected against themselves. This stance seems less liberal than that adopted by Mill.

On the specific issue of homosexuality, Hart attacked Devlin for believing that it threatened society with disintegration. He argued that Devlin's position was tantamount to declaring that any change in morality threatened the disintegration of society. Furthermore, he pointed out that Lord Devlin's approach would cause society's values to stagnate, to become permanently fixed at one point in time.

Key terms

Conventional morality: morality that is based upon a commonly agreed view of what is acceptable.

AQA Examiner's tip

Lord Devlin's approach to morality could be described as 'conservative'. This might provide useful discussion in an essay on judicial creativity. Always be aware of the possibility that material covered in one topic may also be relevant in another.

Some issues reflecting the Hart–Devlin debate

Judges and Parliament are often forced to confront complex moral issues. In **Shaw v DPP (1962)**, which concerned a magazine advertising the services of prostitutes, Shaw was convicted of 'conspiracy to corrupt public morals' a previously unknown offence. The House of Lords confirmed the existence of this new common law offence. Viscount Simonds declared: 'there remains in the courts a residual power to enforce the supreme and fundamental purpose of the law, to conserve not only the safety and order, but also the moral welfare of the State'. Lord Devlin would have approved.

In *R v Gibson* (1990), an artist was convicted under the common law offence of outraging public decency for exhibiting earrings made from freeze-dried human foetuses. No doubt Devlin would maintain that this is exactly the type of immoral conduct that would arouse the intolerance, indignation and disgust of the ordinary person, and so should be subjected to the full rigour of the criminal law. Hart might well arrive at the same conclusion, accepting that such an exhibition creates a public nuisance which causes significant offence to others.

In the celebrated case of **R v Brown and Others (1993)**, the defendants were convicted under s47 and s20 of the Offences against the Person Act 1861 after engaging in violent sado-masochistic activities. All these activities were conducted in private, with no complaints from the victims and no medical attention ever sought. There were no permanent injuries. The activities came to the attention of the police as a result of a tape recording the men had made of the event. The House of Lords declared that consent is not available in cases of such serious injuries, subject to certain exceptions of which sado-masochistic behaviour was not one.

Speaking for the majority, Lord Templeman declared that the issues of policy and public interest must be taken into account before deciding whether the defence of consent should be extended to sado-masochistic activities. Then, in words resonant of Lord Devlin, he expressed his own opinion: 'Society is entitled and bound to protect itself against a cult of violence. Pleasure derived from the infliction of pain is an evil thing. Cruelty is uncivilised.' He dismissed the men's appeal.

Lord Mustill, dissenting, declared, in words reminiscent of Professor Hart, that:

> the state should interfere with the rights of an individual to live his or her life as he or she may choose no more than is necessary to ensure a proper balance between the special interests of the individual and the general interests of the individuals who together comprise the populace at large.

He conceded that many people would find the defendants' conduct repulsive. Nevertheless, that feeling of repulsion did not, in his view, justify the men's conviction.

The defence of consent was also considered in the case of *R v Wilson* (1996). At his wife's request, Alan Wilson branded his initials ('AW') on her buttocks. Hearing the appeal against conviction for ABH, Russell LJ explained:

> Consensual activity between husband and wife, in the privacy of the matrimonial home, is not, in our judgment, a proper matter for criminal investigation, let alone criminal prosecution.

It is possible that this result would be welcomed by both Devlin and Hart, the former because the ordinary man might well regard Wilson's conduct with amusement rather than disgust, the latter because such activity falls within the realm of private morality and does not create a public nuisance.

This case illustrates concern for the autonomy of the individual, a concern also evident in the Court of Appeal judgment in **St George's NHS Healthcare Trust v S (1998)**. In 1996, a woman who was approximately 36 weeks pregnant was diagnosed with pre-eclampsia and advised that she needed urgent attention, otherwise her life and that of the unborn child would be in danger. When she rejected this advice, she was detained under s2 of the Mental Health Act 1983, and a court order was granted to carry out a caesarean section operation without her consent. The Court of Appeal ruled that an adult of sound mind is entitled to refuse medical treatment, and this entitlement is not reduced because her decision might appear morally repugnant, bizarre or irrational.

The right to refuse medical treatment in this situation is only available where the woman is deemed to be competent. This language is reminiscent of the decision of the House of Lords in *Gillick v West Norfolk and Wisbech Area Health Authority and the DHSS* (1985). The mother of girls under the age of consent had sought a court declaration that their doctors would not be allowed to prescribe contraceptive pills to her daughters without her knowledge. The House of Lords declared that a 'competent child', who had sufficient understanding of the issues involved, could decide for herself without her parents being informed.

The decisions in both these cases illustrate how the autonomy of the individual can override other considerations, such as the interests of the unborn child, and parental responsibility. However, such autonomy is not absolute. Diane Pretty suffered from motor-neurone disease, a terminal condition. She wanted her husband to be allowed to help her to end her life peacefully and with dignity. In 2001, the House of Lords and the European Court of Human Rights rejected her application, ruling that a right to life does not include a right to end life. Her application conflicted with broader issues of public morality.

Parliament must also confront issues of public morality.

The Human Fertilisation and Embryology Act 1990 introduced regulations for the creation, storage and use of human embryos outside of the human body. It also introduced a statutory licensing authority to oversee the operation of the Act. In 2004, as a result of advances in reproductive medicine and changes in public morality, the government began a review of the 1990 Act, leading to the Human Fertilisation and Embryology Bill 2008. Among its features are:

- a new concept of parenthood for a mother's female partner:
- statutory approval to be given to 'saviour siblings', i.e. children born from embryos that have been genetically screened to ensure they share the same tissue type as the sick, live sibling
- in relation to children born after surrogacy arrangements, same sex couples and unmarried opposite sex couples to enjoy the same rights to parenthood as married couples now
- an increase in the type of embryo research that will be permitted, including the use of hybrid embryos.

This Bill has been described in Parliament as 'a pragmatic fusion between science and the social mores of today'. Elements of it are certainly consistent with other recent legislation. In 2004, the Civil Partnership Act allowed partners of the same biological sex to enter into a civil partnership giving them the same rights and responsibilities as heterosexual married couples. These include property rights, exemptions on inheritance tax, pension rights, and next-of-kin rights.

In 2006, Parliament passed the Equality Act. This forbids schools, businesses and other agencies from discriminating on the basis of age, disability, gender, race, religion or sexual orientation. Under the terms of this Act, adoption agencies have to consider applications for adoption

Key cases

St George's NHS Healthcare Trust v S (1998): a case illustrating the autonomy of the individual in refusing a particular medical treatment.

Fig. 2 *Diane Pretty*

In this topic you will learn how to:

■ identify what material questions require

■ provide the required range of information and discussion.

from homosexual couples. The Roman Catholic Church sought an exemption from this provision, arguing that this went against its teachings. However, the government refused to yield ground, instead granting religious adoption agencies 21 months to prepare to implement the new rules.

Professor Hart accused Lord Devlin of attempting to cause the development of society's moral values to stagnate at a fixed point in time. Clearly, he need not have worried. The law continues to be developed as it is used to enforce the dominant public morality.

You should now be able to:

■ understand the main points in the Hart–Devlin debate

■ illustrate this debate by reference to recent cases and judicial comment.

4 Answering questions on the topic of law and morality

Essays on the topic of law and morality are extremely popular among students. The titles usually call for discussion of some or all of the following issues:

■ An explanation of what is meant by the terms law and morality.

■ Discussion of the relationship between law and morality.

■ Consideration of whether the law should enforce morality.

To answer the first part successfully, you need to introduce some theory regarding what law is. Reference for example to the distinction between legal positivism (e.g. Austin and/or Hart) and natural law (e.g. Aquinas and/or Fuller) would satisfy this requirement. You also need to identify and explain the characteristics of legal and moral rules, with appropriate examples to illustrate.

To answer the second part successfully, you need to identify and discuss the common factors that unite law and morals, e.g. their concern with standards, and their use of similar terminology. You then must try to demonstrate how they influence each other, with examples of law promoting changes in moral attitudes, and vice-versa, or areas where such judgments are hard to make.

To answer the third part successfully, you need to refer to relevant theories. Discussion of the main arguments employed in the Hart–Devlin debate would satisfy this requirement. It is important that you then introduce some areas of law to illustrate how the points raised in this debate have been the subject of judicial reflection and Parliamentary activity. Although it is perfectly acceptable to refer to events of fifty years ago (e.g. the Wolfenden Report; *Shaw* v *DPP* (1962)), remember that this must be offset by reference to recent legislation (e.g. the Civil Partnership Act 2004; the Equality Act 2006), and to current or recent issues (e.g. gay adoption, stem cell research).

Overall, the essay should contain theory (e.g. positivism v natural law; the Hart–Devlin debate), explanation of relevant material (e.g. characteristics of legal and moral rules), relevant authority (e.g. cases and statutes), and thoughtful discussion. The discussion makes the necessary links between the other elements.

You should now be able to:

■ understand what is required in an essay on the topic of law and morality.

21 Law and justice

In this topic you will learn how to:

- explain and distinguish between various theories of justice

- provide material to illustrate these theories.

1 Theories of law and justice

Theories of law are discussed in the chapter on law and morality. For the purpose of this chapter the term 'law' refers not only to the substantive law, whether developed in the courts, by Parliament or from other sources, but also to procedural rules and principles by which the laws themselves are made and the legal system administered. For the most part, examples of substantive law are drawn from the A Level syllabus.

Justice is a concept that can be described simply by a synonym such as fairness, equality or even-handedness. It is something for which we develop a 'feel' at a young age. It clearly includes treating like cases in a like manner, showing impartiality, and acting in good faith. However, the term has occupied the minds of some of the greatest thinkers across the ages. As a result there is a wide range of theories available to explain its meaning and application. Some of these are described below.

Justice as harmony

Plato

Plato was a 4th-century Greek philosopher. In his major work, *The Republic*, he uses Socrates as a mouthpiece to develop his own view of justice. Socrates begins by asking others what they think justice is. Cephalus, a wealthy man, suggests that justice is 'speaking the truth and paying one's debts'. Socrates quickly counters this view by asking whether it would be just to return a deadly weapon to a friend who has become insane. Clearly not. Polemarchus then proposes that justice is 'giving to each what is owed', that is to help one's friends and harm one's enemies, a popular Greek view. Socrates also rejects this, pointing out that harsh treatment of one's enemies makes them even more unjust.

After rejecting further suggestions, Socrates outlines his (i.e. Plato's) view of justice, both for the individual and for society. Dealing with the individual first: a man's soul has three elements, i.e. reason (the mind, responsible for decision-making), spirit (the human will, responsible for carrying out decisions made by the mind), and appetite or desire (the emotions, over which self-control must be exercised). A man is just when each of these three elements fulfils its appropriate function, and there is a harmonious relationship between them. If appetite/desire takes control, harmony and justice are lost.

Within society there are also three groups: the ruling class, made up of philosophers, corresponds to reason; the warrior class corresponds to spirit; and artisans, farmers and merchants correspond to appetite or desire, over which control must be exercised. Society is just when each class fulfils its appropriate function, and there is a harmonious relationship between them. Socrates compares an unjust city to a ship at sea which has a drunken captain and an unruly crew. The only way the ship will be able to reach land safely is by returning control to the navigator (the philosopher).

For both the individual and the state, therefore, Plato views justice as harmony between the warring elements.

Fig. 1 *Scarecrow, Lion and the Tin Man. How do they relate to Plato's theory of justice?*

Distributive justice

Distributive justice is concerned with the fair allocation of the benefits (e.g. money, property, family life) and responsibilities (e.g. taxes, civic duties) of life within an organisation.

Aristotle

Aristotle was a pupil of Plato. It is no surprise, therefore, that he also describes justice as referring to individuals in their dealings with each other, and to the state in making and enforcing laws. He often stressed the need for proportionality, and for achieving the middle way, i.e. a proper balance between extremes.

He identifies particular examples of justice which apply to different situations. Among these is distributive justice, which is concerned with the fair distribution of society's wealth. Aristotle argues that a just state will distribute its wealth on the basis of merit, giving to each according to his virtue and to his contribution to society. This is a proportionate system: the worthiest, rather than the neediest, receive the greatest share. To allocate resources on the basis of people's needs would be unjust, as it would reward the lazy at least as much as the hard-working. We might consider how this would apply today to paying for care for the elderly.

Corrective justice is needed to ensure that individuals can keep their entitlement. It is applied where one person, by his greed and self-interest, causes a loss to another person, for example by stealing his property. The role of the court is to ensure that the gains and losses of each party are equalled out so that the offender doesn't benefit from his wrongdoing and that the victim doesn't suffer loss. In this way balance, the middle way he so often sought, is achieved.

Thomas Aquinas

Thomas Aquinas, the 13th-century theologian, described justice in language similar to that of Aristotle. In general terms, justice governs our relationships with other people: it is the constant willingness to deal with other people as they deserve. The end result of justice is the common good, for the individual and for the community.

Aquinas identified particular forms of justice that govern our dealings with others, which help put into practice the general principle that people are given what is due to them. First of all, distributive justice concerns the fair allocation of goods and responsibilities throughout the community. This is governed by 'due **proportion**': people receive what they are due in accordance with their merit, rank and need. Concerning merit, it would be wrong to pay workers an equal amount for unequal work, or an unequal amount for equal work; concerning rank, people of higher social status will require a greater proportion of society's benefits; and concerning need, there is a moral obligation to look after the poor. Clearly these principles may conflict when put into practice.

Aquinas also spoke of commutative justice, which concerns the exchange of goods or services between people. This is governed by '**equality**': in a contract, for example, on the one hand the value of a product is what one should pay for it; on the other hand the vendor should receive the true worth of the goods.

Karl Marx

Karl Marx, widely regarded as the founder of communism, developed a radically different model of distributive justice, embodied in his slogan, 'from each according to his ability, to each according to his need'. This enshrines two principles of the ideal of communism: first, each will maximise his contribution to the common wealth by making full use of his abilities. Secondly, each will receive according to his need, irrespective of the personal contribution he has made to the production process. No doubt Aristotle would have regarded this model of distribution as unjust in that it has the potential for giving the greatest rewards to the least productive, and therefore least deserving, members of society.

Chaim Perelman

These models of distributive justice are among those identified by Chaim Perelman, a Polish-born philosopher who lived in Belgium. In 1944, he produced a study of justice, entitled *De la Justice*. He concluded that justice cannot be studied logically, as each attempt to define it is based upon a person's subjective values.

In *De la Justice* he discusses different understandings of justice. The first, 'to each according to his merits' is reminiscent of Aristotle: each person is treated in the manner he deserves. The good are rewarded, the bad deprived or punished. This view is consistent with the practice of the criminal courts, meting out punishment in the measure that is warranted by the offence committed. It is also consistent with many people's religious beliefs about life after death.

'To each according to his needs' is reminiscent of Marx's slogan. This approach is consistent with social democracy, in which a welfare system allocates resources such as social housing, tax allowances and benefits payments according to a means tested system. Those in greatest need receive a proportionately higher share of the common wealth. This was the dominant philosophy behind the development of the welfare state in the United Kingdom in the years following World War II, and still enjoys a significant measure of consensus among political parties today.

An alternative view of justice is 'to each according to his works', a liberal, individualistic approach favoured by supporters of the enterprise culture as it measures an individual's rewards according to the contributions he has made. Under this system a highly skilled worker will receive considerably greater rewards than an unskilled worker. This approach is claimed to provide incentives for people to better themselves.

A fourth approach, 'to each equally' has a superficial attraction, and in some situations will be the fairest system of allocating scarce resources. For example, when food was in short supply during and after World War II, ration books were issued to each person. These contained tokens which had to be removed by the shopkeeper when scarce items

Key terms

Proportionality and **equality**: two principles adopted by Aquinas for allocating society's benefits and responsibilities (proportionality), and for the exchange of goods and services (equality).

of food and clothing were purchased. Even here, though, there were some exceptions: pregnant women were issued with more food tokens, and nursing mothers were allowed more milk. An equal distribution of resources would often be wasteful, and an equal sharing of burdens, such as tax contributions, would be unfair unless all resources were equally shared.

'To each according to his rank' may sound anti-democratic, but is widely practised. Rank may refer to social status: deference continues to be shown to members of the royal family and even to celebrities. It may refer to a position of authority: the quarters of army officers are superior to those of their troops. It may refer to age: the over 75s do not require a TV licence, irrespective of the ability to pay, and little sister is well aware that big sister enjoys more privileges.

Finally, 'to each according to his legal entitlement' is a rights-based system, and is not dependent upon merit. Thus, the vilest serial killer will be entitled to protection from attack by his fellow-inmates in prison; and the most disloyal, undeserving child will inherit under the rules of intestacy.

Utilitarianism

Jeremy Bentham

Jeremy Bentham was a social reformer, inventor, wordsmith and philosopher. As well as designing a new type of prison, promoting animal rights, and introducing new words to the language, he developed the theory known today as **utilitarianism**. From observing that people act out of self-interest, pursuing happiness by seeking pleasure and avoiding pain, he developed the legal and moral principle of utility: what makes an action right or wrong is the usefulness, or value, of the consequence it brings. The more an action increases overall happiness, the more valuable it is; and the more it decreases happiness, the more reprehensible. For example, by visiting *The Spotted Rat* tonight I can add to my own happiness by enjoying a glass or two of India Pale Ale. I will also be bringing pleasure to the landlord because of the boost I provide to his business. And if I help my team to win the pub quiz, I am adding immeasurably to the happiness of my colleagues. Clearly I must go there.

Maximising happiness is the object of justice. To help measure this, Bentham developed a mathematical formula, known as the 'felicific calculus', which enables us to assess whether our conduct increases happiness. This formula identifies a range of factors concerning the pleasurable activity itself, for example its intensity, its duration, and its extent. It then identifies and grades different kinds of pleasures, for example those relating to the exercise of power, or to friendship, and different kinds of pain, for example regret or grieving. These factors help to introduce some objectivity into what would normally be regarded as a subjective issue. Before deciding upon a course of action, a person is therefore able to judge whether it will add to or subtract from the sum of happiness.

One of the criticisms of utilitarianism is that the interest of an individual may be sacrificed on the altar of greater community happiness. For example, when Stefan Kiszko was convicted in 1976 of the murder of Lesley Molseed, an 11-year-old Rochdale girl, the parents of other young girls in the area will have felt enormous relief believing that the killer was off the streets. The fact that he was innocent will have brought considerable misery to Kiszko himself and to his immediate family. Under the felicific calculus, though, the greater happiness brought to the larger community by a conviction might outweigh the pain of a few individuals. Does this possibly make such an outcome just? Rawls rightly criticises utilitarianism on this point.

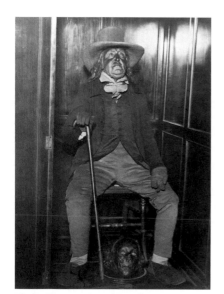

Fig. 2 *The remains of Bentham on exhibition in University College, London*

■ **Key terms**

Utilitarianism: the doctrine that all actions should be judged in terms of their utility in promoting the greatest happiness for the greatest number.

Yet utilitarianism does at least attempt to provide a route to resolving difficult problems. For example, managers and doctors in the National Health Service have to prioritise resources. The felicific calculus will necessarily result in outcomes that are not pleasing to everyone; however, it will provide a rational justification for deciding priorities.

John Stuart Mill

John Stuart Mill was a 19th century liberal, an ardent advocate of freedom of speech, a sponsor of Irish land reform and a supporter of equal rights for women. His pamphlet *Utilitarianism*, published in 1861, supported the basic principles of utilitarianism put forward by Bentham. In Chapter 2 of *Utilitarianism*, he wrote that actions are right 'in proportion as they tend to promote happiness, wrong as they tend to produce the reverse of happiness'. However, he focused upon the quality of happiness rather than merely upon its quantity. He wrote: 'Better to be a human being dissatisfied than a pig satisfied; better to be a Socrates dissatisfied than a fool satisfied'.

For more information on the writings of John Stuart Mill, see Chapter 20, Law and morality.

Mill also linked utilitarianism to justice. Justice, he explained, includes respect for people, for property and for rights, as well as the need for good faith and impartiality. All of these are consistent with the principle of utility, since their application brings the greatest happiness to the greatest number. It could also be argued that punishing wrongdoers also brings happiness to the greatest number. However, Mill argued that punishment is in itself an evil as it involves inflicting harm or pain, and can only be justified where it brings a greater benefit, such as public order.

Act and rule utilitarianism

The theory of utilitarianism has developed since Bentham and Mill. Under act utilitarianism, the rightness of an act is judged in isolation to see whether it adds to, or subtracts from, the sum of human happiness. For example, if I drive my Harley Davidson at 130mph on an empty motorway at three o' clock in the morning, I am considerably increasing my own happiness and causing pain to nobody else: the sum of human happiness is increased. According to rule utilitarianism, the rightness of an action is judged according to whether the sum of human happiness would be increased if everyone acted in the same way. Developing the example, if all Harley Davidson owners tried to drive along the same stretch of motorway at the same speed and at the same time, chaos would probably ensue, resulting in pain and misery: the sum of human happiness would decrease.

Social justice

John Rawls

John Rawls, a professor of political philosophy at Harvard, published *A Theory of Justice* in 1971. It sets out the concept of **social justice**. Rawls' starting point will be familiar to parents with only one bar of chocolate. They ask the first child to cut the bar, and allow the second to choose the larger piece. Fairness is guaranteed! Rawls described justice as fairness, and then presented a hypothetical society where each member would distribute its resources in a disinterested manner. To make this possible, nobody would know in advance what their position in that society would be, nor what stage of that society's development he would be born into: he would operate behind a 'veil of ignorance'. In Rawls' own words: 'No one knows his place in society, his class position or social status, nor does anyone know his fortune in the distribution of natural assets and abilities, his intelligence, strength, and the like'. Rawls believed that, on this basis, benefits and burdens would be distributed justly, i.e. fairly.

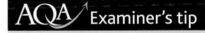

AQA Examiner's tip

Examples such as this (the motorcyclists) can be effective to illustrate how theories work in practice.

Key terms

Social justice: a key term used by John Rawls to describe a system where the burdens and benefits of society would be distributed in an equitable manner.

Rawls argued that two basic principles of justice would be evident within this society: first, each person would have 'an equal right to the most extensive scheme of basic liberties compatible with a similar scheme of liberties for others'. This would include certain basic freedoms, such as the right to own property, freedom of speech, freedom of association, and freedom from arbitrary arrest.

Secondly, social and economic inequalities may exist, but only: (a) where they benefit the least-advantaged members of society; and (b) provided all offices and positions are open to everyone. In other words, under (a), it is acceptable for a neurosurgeon to earn four times the average wage, live in a large detached house, drive a Mercedes S class, and go to the Yorkshire Dales for his holidays because his work benefits disadvantaged members of society, and others are encouraged to imitate his example, further benefiting the disadvantaged. It is also acceptable under (b), provided that everyone with skills and abilities comparable to those of the neurosurgeon have a reasonable opportunity to pursue a similar path.

In employing the fiction of the 'veil of ignorance' to develop a society based upon consent, Rawls was promoting a rights-based system: basic rights such as freedom of speech and association are '**inalienable**': they can never be sacrificed for the common good. The state must always respect the autonomy of the individual. He wrote: 'Each person possesses an inviolability founded on justice that even the welfare of society as a whole cannot override. Therefore, in a just society the rights secured by justice are not subject to political bargaining or to the calculus of social interests.' This distinguishes Rawls from Bentham and the utilitarianists, against whom the final comment is directed, for utilitarians might allow individual freedoms to be sacrificed where this is considered necessary to promote wider benefits for the greater number.

Robert Nozick

Robert Nozick was a Harvard colleague of Rawls. In *A Theory of Justice*, Rawls had provided a philosophical basis for the welfare state and the redistribution of wealth to help the disadvantaged. In *Anarchy, State and Utopia*, Nozick developed an entitlement theory of justice, which consisted of three principles:

1 A principle of justice in acquisition, dealing with how property is initially acquired.
2 A principle of justice in transfer, dealing with how property can change hands.
3 A principle of rectification of injustice, dealing with injustices arising from the acquisition or transfer of property under the two principles above. This third principle would not be required if the world was entirely just.

Where a person obtains property in accordance with the principles of acquisition or transfer, he is entitled to keep that property. Where people obtain property by fraud or theft or other unjust means, the third principle provides a remedy.

This is fundamentally different from Rawls, who argued that inequalities may exist only where they benefit the most disadvantaged members of society. Nozick places no such limits upon private ownership: property justly acquired may not be appropriated simply as a form of redistribution of wealth, to reduce inequalities. He wrote: 'No one has a right to something whose realisation requires certain uses of things and activities that other people have rights and entitlements over'. Therefore, those in possession of property have an inalienable right to keeping it, and no competing authority can justly deprive them of their property, no matter how just their cause may appear. This is a free-market, libertarian form of justice.

Following the publication of *Anarchy, State and Utopia*, Nozick became closely associated in people's minds with conservative economists such as Milton Friedman, who influenced the policies of the conservative government of Margaret Thatcher in Britain in the 1980s. However, unlike other libertarians, Nozick did not restrict his principles to the field of economics: he also adopted a **libertarian** approach on social issues such as gay rights.

Activities

1. How would these philosophers react to the following situations?
   - Plato and Bentham to: Tamsin eating a trayful of chocolate muffins?
   - Aristotle and Mill to: Soft J, giving an absolute discharge to Robin Hood for robbing the rich to give to the poor?
   - Rawls and Aquinas to: the Chancellor of the Exchequer withdrawing the 10 pence in the pound tax band, thereby disadvantaging the lowest paid workers?
   - Rawls and Nozick to: a government Act confiscating all private property that has lain derelict and unused for at least 20 years?

2. You have been appointed as chief executive of the Dunedinglas NHS Trust, with responsibility for determining spending priorities for the next three years. Combating the rise in obesity-related diabetes is your most urgent health-related issue, as it affects tens of thousands of people in your area, significantly reducing their quality and length of life. However, this will require diverting funds from existing programs, including the introduction of expensive equipment to enable the Trust to support the life-support systems of babies born at 22 weeks. How can you argue that it is just to deny vulnerable babies the equipment they need to survive, particularly when the money is to be spent on what some regard as self-inflicted ill health?

You should now be able to:

- explain and illustrate various theories of justice.

2 Justice in procedural and substantive law

So much for the different theories. It is now time to examine the law and test out these theories. Is the law just? You will probably come to the view that, by and large, it is, although you are likely to have certain reservations. If you look at the law through the eyes of Plato, looking for justice in the form of harmony between the different groups in society, you may well be disappointed at the conflict between the legislature and the judiciary. Alternatively, if you look at the law through the eyes of Marx, you will probably seethe with rage at the way society's benefits have been distributed, and at how the law is used to enforce inequalities. Or, if you put yourself in the position of Robert Nozick, you will be disappointed to observe how much the social justice model promoted by Rawls has influenced policy makers since World War II.

A distinction is often made between procedural law and substantive law. Hart referred to justice 'according to law' and justice 'of the law'. The former term relates to how laws are made and how the legal system operates; the latter to the laws themselves, such as those studied in crime, in contract and in tort. It is a useful distinction upon which to

In this topic you will learn how to:

- recognise elements of the theories of justice in procedural and substantive law
- assess the extent to which procedural and substantive law are just.

AQA Examiner's tip

When evaluating whether the law is just, try to examine it through the eyes of one or two philosophers, as well as through your own eyes.

base this topic. Under each heading we shall examine a range of issues to help us to reflect on whether the law is just. Our conclusions, however, are likely to be personal, depending upon our view of justice.

Procedural justice

Social justice: legal aid

The Access to Justice Act 1999 established the Legal Services Commission (LSC), with responsibility for administering the annual **legal aid** budget of about £2 billion. Under the umbrella of the Legal Services Commission are two parallel organisations: the Community Legal Service, with responsibility for funding civil law issues such as asylum, domestic violence and community care; and the Criminal Defence Service, which provides professional advice and representation to those under investigation or facing criminal charges.

Legal aid is regarded as an important element in promoting social justice. In a democratic society all citizens have a right to access justice, to receive a fair hearing, and to understand their legal rights and obligations. Many people need help with this. Legal aid is the most significant vehicle through which this help is provided, to over two million people per year according to figures produced by the LSC.

However, the budget is no longer demand led: it is fixed by the Treasury, and responsibility passed to the LSC to administer it efficiently. Managing a fixed budget inevitably places limits upon the operation of the LSC. By franchising its services to firms of solicitors and to advice agencies, it hands over the risks associated with variations in demand. It also restricts its operation to priorities identified by the Lord Chancellor: it does not offer a comprehensive advice service. Also, funding is means tested. Under Perelman's analysis, the budget is distributed to each according to his legal entitlement, but also according to his needs.

Demand for the service continues to grow. The budget, however, does not. The LSC, therefore, is caught between a rock and a hard place. To meet this dilemna, it is endeavouring to make more of its budget available for civil legal aid (for example, family, housing and debt problems), but also seeking to ensure that funding is being spent 'where it is most needed and can make most difference to people's lives'. This utilitarian approach will inevitably lead to many needs not being met.

Corrective justice: sanctions and damages

When judges or magistrates pass sentence upon an offender, they take into consideration a number of factors. These include the aim of the sentence: this may simply be to punish the offender for breaking the rules or to deter others from committing the same offence. Balanced against these may be the desire to rehabilitate the offender. The court will also consider aggravating and mitigating factors relating to the offence and to the offender. As a result, the sentence should then be just. But in what way just? Well, it will more likely be 'proportionate' to the offence committed and to the relevant surrounding circumstances.

This is a more sophisticated model than Aristotle's. He argued that the role of the court is to ensure that the gains and losses of each party are equalled out so that the offender doesn't benefit from his wrongdoing and that the victim doesn't suffer loss. This would be applicable to offences such as theft, but even then would not take into consideration surrounding circumstances.

By contrast, John Stuart Mill did not accept the validity of a retributive approach, regarding all punishment as evil in itself. However, he did accept that imposing sanctions could be justified under the principle of utility if it corresponded to a greater benefit that measurably increased the happiness of others. Aims of sentencing such as rehabilitation, protection of the public, and reparation would therefore fall within the utility model.

Aristotle's model is probably more amenable to the award of damages in civil law. In the tort of negligence the aim of compensation is to restore the claimant to his pre-tort position, in so far as money can achieve this. The award would include payment for any specialist medical treatment required, for future loss of earnings, for any loss of enjoyment of life, and for pain and suffering. To balance this, any contributory negligence on the part of the claimant will reduce his award. For example, in **Jebson v Ministry of Defence (2000)**, 75 per cent of the claimant's award was deducted for his contributory negligence. The claimant had been with a party of about 20 drunken soldiers returning to their barracks in an army lorry after a night out in Portsmouth. He was standing on the lorry's tailgate when he fell out and was injured. This reduction is just because it is proportionate: it reflects that the claimant was largely responsible for his own harm.

In contract law, the basis of assessment of damages is loss of bargain: the claimant is placed in the position he would have been in had the contract been performed. However, only losses that are reasonably within the contemplation of the parties may be recovered. In **Victoria Laundry v Newman (1949)**, the defendant had been late in fitting a boiler. As a result the claimant had suffered not only normal business losses, but also exceptional losses through losing a special contract with the Ministry of Supply. As the latter were not within the contemplation of the parties at the time of the contract, they were not recoverable.

The judgments in these two cases reflect the 'middle way' that Aristotle promoted. They also illustrate Aquinas' concept of due proportionality in that damages are awarded pro rata according to the merits of the claim, and not automatically in relation to the harm suffered. Under these tests they are just.

The criminal process

The trial

Trial by jury enables the case against a defendant to be determined by his peers, who are free to apply their view of justice rather than adhere strictly to the rules of law. In **R v Ponting (1985)** a civil servant was charged with breaching the Official Secrets Act for releasing privileged information about the sinking of the General Belgrano. The judge told the jury that public interest in the information did not provide a defence. And yet the jury acquitted him. No doubt they felt differently about the public's right to have this information!

The rules of evidence adopted in criminal trials seek to balance the interests of the parties to the action. In *R v Sang* (1979), Lord Diplock stated: 'A trial judge in a criminal trial has always a discretion to refuse to admit evidence if in his opinion its prejudicial effect outweighs its probative value.' For this reason evidence of previous convictions is not generally admissible unless the facts are strikingly similar to those in the instant case.

On the other hand, even illegally obtained evidence may be admissible. In **Jeffery v Black (1978)**, the police arrested a student for the theft of a sandwich, and then conducted an illegal search of his flat, where they discovered some drugs. The magistrates threw out the case after ruling the evidence inadmissible. However, the Divisional Court ruled that the illegality of the search did not justify excluding the evidence it had exposed. This may at first seem to be unjust. However, if the police had discovered plans and materials to blow up Heathrow Airport, they would surely be justified in relying upon it in court.

Key cases

Jebson v Ministry of Defence (2000): contributory negligence allows the court to apply the principle of proportionality, an aspect of justice.

Victoria Laundry v Newman (1949): where a contract is breached, the claimant may only recover damages for losses that were in the thoughts of the parties at the time of their agreement.

R v Ponting (1985): this case either illustrates the theory of jury equity, or serves as an example of a perverse decision, depending upon your point of view.

Jeffery v Black (1978): evidence will not be ruled inadmissible merely because it was obtained through an illegally conducted police search.

Appeals

In criminal cases heard in the magistrates' court, the defendant may appeal either to the Crown Court against conviction or sentence, or to the High Court by way of case stated on a point of law. In Crown Court cases the relevant appellate court is the Court of Appeal. For example, in *R v Arobieke* (1988) the appellant successfully appealed against his conviction for unlawful act manslaughter, arguing that his behaviour had not amounted to an assault. In **R v Thornton (1992)**, by contrast, a retrial was ordered when the appellant introduced new evidence that would support one of the partial defences to murder. Note that permission is first needed from either the trial judge or the Court of Appeal itself. This was refused to those convicted of the 21/7 London bomb plot: one of the judges hearing the application described as 'ludicrous' the men's defence that the bombs were a hoax. The need for permission may seem difficult to justify: however, refusal is not an arbitrary decision. It is based upon realism: does the appeal have any merit? If not, why waste time pursuing it?

Under the Criminal Justice Act 1998 the prosecution may also appeal against 'unduly lenient' sentences. This may result in significantly increased sentences, as occurred in the case of a woman who was originally sentenced to probation and community service for killing another woman in a row over a parking space at a car boot sale. She was sentenced on appeal to four years in prison. In addition, under the Criminal Justice Act 1972, the Attorney-General may appeal on a point of law to the Court of Appeal where he wishes to question the judge's direction which has led to an acquittal. For example, in *Attorney-General's Reference* (No. 2 of 1992) the Court of Appeal declared that the defence of automatism is not available where awareness is merely reduced: a total destruction of voluntary control is required.

In spite of this system of appeals, injustices arise: innocent men and women still serve long prison sentences for crimes they have not committed. The Birmingham Six, the Guildford Four, the Maguire Seven, Judith Ward and Stefan Kiszko are among those whose innocence took years to establish. The publicity these miscarriages of justice have provoked led to the establishment in 1997 of the **Criminal Cases Review Commission** (CCRC) whose role is to review the cases of those they feel have been wrongly convicted of criminal offences, or unfairly sentenced.

Fig. 3 *Gerard Hunter, one of the Birmingham Six, released after being sentenced to life imprisonment in 1975 for two pub bombings on November 21, 1974. The justice decision was overturned by the Court of Appeal on 14 March 1991*

Fig. 4 *Gerry Conlon, the best known from the 'Guildford Four', speaks to the media outside the Houses of Parliament. Three decades after being falsely jailed for detonating IRA bombs at English pubs, the British government apologized to 11 people in one of the nation's worst miscarriages of justice*

They do not consider innocence or guilt, but whether there is new evidence or argument that may cast doubt on the safety of the original decision. Derek Bentley and Sally Clark are among those who have had their convictions quashed by the Court of Appeal following reference from the CCRC.

All of these cases involved gross miscarriages of justice, often where the evidence needed to prove the defendant's innocence was available at the time of the original trial. It is perhaps naïve to believe that some of these convictions would be less likely to occur today as a result of safeguards introduced under the Police and Criminal Evidence Act 1984, and the separation of the investigation and prosecution of crime introduced with the establishment of the Crown Prosecution Service. The only comfort in terms of justice is the fact that systems exist which can bring miscarriages of justice to the attention of the appeal courts. However, procedural justice relies very heavily upon the integrity of those responsible for the investigation and prosecution of crime.

Rules of natural justice

Natural justice is often described as containing two basic principles. The first is that the tribunal must not only be impartial, but also be seen to be so. Judges should have no personal interest in a case. In the **Pinochet** case (1998), the House of Lords ruled that Senator Pinochet, the former dictator of Chile, could be extradited to Spain to stand trial for his alleged involvement in the torture and death of Spanish citizens in Chile.

One of the judges hearing the case was Lord Hoffman, a director of Amnesty International, a human rights group which had been given permission to take part in the appeal. Clearly this infringed the principle of impartiality, a doctrine supported by Mill and others, and ignored the rule that a man should not be a judge in his own case (*nemo iudex in causa sua*).

The second principle is that each party to the dispute must have a fair opportunity to present his own case and to answer the case of his opponent. In **Ridge v Baldwin (1964)**, the House of Lords ruled that the decision by a police authority to dismiss its chief constable without a personal hearing contravened natural justice. In the words of Lord Hodson, the police authority 'had acted without jurisdiction'.

The rules of natural justice are designed to protect the interests of individuals against arbitrary decisions. In both the *Pinochet* case and *Ridge* v *Baldwin*, the original decision may have been correct. However, each was unreliable because of the breach of the rules of natural justice. Thus, we can see that justice is not necessarily concerned with the rights and wrongs of the decision, rather it is with the procedure followed in reaching the decision. The application of justice must be fair.

Substantive justice

Crime

The mandatory life sentence

The principle of proportionality, an attribute of justice under Aristotle and Aquinas, generally governs the sentencing practice of judges and magistrates. This satisfies our expectations that the more serious the offence, the harsher the sanction that will be imposed. However, those convicted of murder, and certain repeat offenders, are subject to a mandatory life sentence. Some murderers, though, are far less culpable than others: the setting of a minimum tariff does not allow for proportionality, and so may lead to harsh decisions. In *R* v *Cocker* (1989) the defendant suffocated his wife, at her insistence, with a pillow: she had been terminally ill and in much pain. The trial judge

Key terms

Natural justice: this generally refers to the rules that those sitting in judgment must be free from bias, and that each party to the dispute has the opportunity to state his case.

Key cases

The **Pinochet** case **(1998)**: this illustrates the need for judges not only to be impartial, but also to appear impartial.

Ridge v Baldwin (1964): the rules of natural justice require that an accused has the opportunity to state his case.

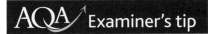

AQA Examiner's tip

It is useful to provide some material from both procedural and substantive law to illustrate the operation of justice. However, the two do not need to be equally balanced.

denied him the partial defence of provocation, leaving the jury with little alternative other than to convict him of murder. In such circumstances a life sentence may seem a disproportionate punishment. Perhaps justice would be better served by allowing judges to pass the sentence they feel to be most appropriate.

Defences

Life is sometimes said to be our most valued possession. The premeditated killing of another human being must therefore be considered one of the greatest acts of injustice man can commit. And yet the law recognises that not all premeditated killing is equally culpable. Hence the defences of provocation and diminished responsibility have been created to limit liability, and the defences of self-defence and automatism will, where successful, excuse liability altogether. However, there are anomalies within the current law that have the potential for creating injustice.

One of the generally accepted characteristics of justice is that like cases are treated in like manner. Yet the law gives more favourable treatment to those who kill while suffering diminished responsibility or while under provocation, than it does to those whose free will is overpowered by an external threat. The decision of the House of Lords in *R* v *Howe* (1987) clearly established that the defence of duress is not available on a charge of murder. Yet one feels much more sympathy for the defendant in *R* v *Gotts* (1991), a boy whose life was threatened by his own father, than one does for the defendant in *R* v *Byrne* (1960). The Law Commission has proposed adding duress to diminished responsibility and provocation as defences that would attract conviction for second degree murder. This would introduce parity of treatment under the law, and satisfy a basic requirement of justice that like cases are treated in like manner.

Objective recklessness

In the famous case of Caldwell, objective recklessness was introduced as the appropriate test for recklessness for those charged under the Criminal Damage Act 1971. In **Elliot v C (1983)** a young girl of low intelligence was convicted of criminal damage for setting fire to a neighbour's shed. She had been playing with white spirit and matches, without realising the danger involved. The fact that she had not appreciated the risk was of no relevance, as the test was purely objective. Fortunately the injustice of this outcome will not occur again following the decision in *R* v *G and R* (2003).

Contract

Exclusion clauses

Parties to a contract may try to limit their liability by relying upon exclusion clauses. The traditional rule of caveat emptor (let the buyer beware) could operate harshly against the interests of the weaker bargaining party. The courts have therefore sought to provide some measure of protection to consumers. In **Olley v Marlborough Court Hotel (1949)**, a fur coat belonging to the claimant was stolen from her hotel room. The hotel tried to disclaim liability, pointing to an exclusion clause on a notice on the door of her room. The court held that this exclusion clause was invalid: it had not been brought to Mrs Olley's attention when she booked in at reception.

In *Spurling* v *Bradshaw* (1956), Lord Denning observed that some exclusion clauses were written in 'regrettably small print', and the more harsh or unusual the term was , the more it needed to be brought to the attention of the person signing it, for example by being 'printed in red ink, with a red hand pointing to it'.

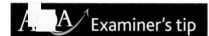

Examiner's tip

R v *Howe* (1987) and *R* v *Gotts* (1991) illustrate how the obiter dicta in an earlier case may form the ratio decidendi of a later one. Their facts may also be used to discuss whether the law operates justly.

Key cases

Elliot v C (1983): objective recklessness may lead to gross injustice.

Olley v Marlborough Court Hotel (1949): to be valid, an exclusion clause must be available at the point of agreement.

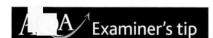

Examiner's tip

When considering justice in substantive law, you are advised to focus principally upon those areas of law which you have studied in depth in Units 2, 3 and 4.

In 1977, Parliament passed the Unfair Contract Terms Act to restrict the use of exclusion clauses. Under s2(1) a person cannot exclude liability for death or personal injury resulting from his negligence, and other exclusion clauses are subjected to the test of reasonableness. This Act prevents those with strong bargaining power from taking unfair advantage of weaker parties, and provides a reasonable degree of protection to consumers. In this way a fairer, more equitable balance is achieved between the bargaining parties.

Third party rights

Parliament has also intervened in protecting the rights of third parties to a contract. Traditionally, beneficiaries could not sue unless they were a party to the contract. Again the courts tried to erode the injustice this caused. In **Jackson v Horizon Holidays (1975)** the Court of Appeal ruled that the claimant would succeed in seeking damages for himself and for members of his family after a package holiday failed to match the advertised description, even though only he, and not his family members, had signed the contract. In 1999, Parliament passed the Contract (Rights of Third Parties) Act, allowing third parties to make a claim where the contract expressly provided for this, or where the contract purported to confer a benefit on them. These provisions should avoid in future the obvious injustices caused in cases such as *Tweddle* v *Atkinson* (1861), where a man was not enable to enforce an agreement between his father and father-in-law conferring a financial benefit on him.

Frustrated contracts

Parliament again was responsible for legislating to ensure that, where a contract is frustrated through no fault of either party, a just outcome can be reached. Traditionally, under the common law the losses lay where they fell: thus money paid in full in advance for a holiday was not recoverable. However, the Law Reform (Frustrated Contracts) Act 1943 enabled the courts to apportion the losses more fairly between the parties: the court may order 'a just sum' to be paid where either expenses have been incurred or a valuable benefit obtained.

Tort

Duty and breach in negligence

Within the tort of negligence a duty of care will not be imposed unless it is fair, just and reasonable to do so. In *Hill* v *Chief Constable for West Yorkshire* (1988), the mother of the Yorkshire Ripper's final victim sued the police for damages for not keeping their daughter's killer in custody. The House of Lords decided that it would not be fair or just for the police to owe a duty of care to every potential victim of crime, as it could lead to defensive policing practices. This may seem hard on the claimant.

The decision in **Nettleship v Weston (1971)** might also be regarded as rough justice: a learner driver was judged according to the objective standard of a competent driver, and so was liable for injuries caused to her instructor. However, leaving an innocent victim without a remedy is probably the cause of an even greater injustice. In such situations, justice can only be achieved where the potential for injustice to each party is weighed in the balance.

Occupier's liability

The decision in *British Railways Board* v *Herrington* (1972) illustrates how justice is achieved when the claims of the two parties to the dispute are weighed in the balance. Using the powers under the Practice Statement, the House of Lords ruled that an occupier may be liable for harm caused to trespassers. The fact that the victims were children was a significant factor: the railway company had 'failed to act with due regard

> ### Key cases
>
> **Jackson v Horizon Holidays (1975)**: in the interests of common sense and justice, the courts often seek to mitigate the harsh application of the law.
>
> **Nettleship v Weston (1971)**: a learner driver is judged by the same standard as a competent driver; this principle applies to other dangerous activities, for example a surgeon performing his first operation.

to humane considerations' and owed a 'common duty of humanity' to the children. Businesses, as well as individuals, bear responsibility for the consequences of their actions. The railway company had been aware of the weaknesses in its fencing, and of the habit of trespassing, but had taken no precautionary measures. The imposition of liability in such circumstances seems, on balance, to be fair.

Strict liability

However, in *Rylands* v *Fletcher* (1868) liability was imposed where the defendant was unaware of the danger. On the one hand it seems rough justice to impose strict liability where the offending party may have taken all known precautions. On the other hand, however, it is arguably justifiable that individuals should be held responsible for the consequences of their actions, even when these consequences are unforeseen. Furthermore, potentially greater injustice is caused by the victim being left without a remedy. On balance, justice may have been achieved.

Activities

1 The payment of damages is the normal common law remedy for breach of contract. However, this will occasionally be unsuitable, particularly where unique goods or services are being provided. Equity therefore has provided the remedy of specific performance, forcing the defendant to carry out his part of the contract. However, the claimant must have acted in good faith. What do you think would be the just outcome in the following case (*Falcke* v *Gray*)?

An art dealer had agreed to buy a pair of vases for £20 each. However, the owner suspected they were worth much more, so consulted another dealer, and managed to sell them for £200. The original dealer now sought specific performance (i.e. to be awarded the vases for £20 each).

2 In the tort of negligence, a duty of care will be imposed where it is fair and just to do so. Why would it not be fair and just to impose a duty in the following case (*Ashton* v *Turner*)?

The claimant and defendant, after a night's heavy drinking, decided to commit a burglary. Using a borrowed car, they drove around until they came to a shop selling radios. They threw a brick through the window, helped themselves to some radios, and then began to drive off. Two taxi drivers tried to prevent their escape. While attempting to get away, Kevin Turner took a corner at high speed. The car crashed, and Philip Ashton was seriously injured. Ashton now sued for damages in negligence.

You should now be able to:

■ refer to appropriate supporting material to examine whether the law is just.

In this topic you will learn how to:

■ identify what material questions require

■ provide the required range of information and discussion.

3 Answering questions on the topic of law and justice

Essays on the topic of law and justice provide considerable scope for students to draw upon the areas of law in which they have specialised. The questions: Is it fair? Is it just? can be asked of any material studied throughout the course. Therefore there is no prescribed content that must be included in an answer. Two equally deserving answers may contain no overlapping content.

Generally, a question will require you to provide:

■ an explanation of what is meant by the terms law and justice, with some reference to theory
■ discussion of justice within areas of procedural and substantive law
■ evaluation.

In the examination, you will have approximately 1 hour available for this section of the paper. This includes time to reflect on the specific issues raised in the question and to plan an answer.

As always, it is important for you to tailor your discussion of the material to the particular question that has been set, rather than to reproduce a prepared essay.

To answer the first part successfully, you need to introduce some explanation of what you understand by the terms law and justice. Emphasis will probably focus upon justice, and in particular upon some of the theories, not all of them in detail, explained in Topic 1. Some explanation of your understanding of the term 'law' is also required, as there will be reference made to considerable areas of law later in the essay.

To answer the second part successfully, you need to select a range of appropriate material, and to explain its relevance to the issue of justice. The selection of appropriate material is largely a matter of individual choice: you will be expected to draw it from your own specialised areas of study. It is not the choice of material, but rather the way that it is treated, that distinguishes between students in an examination. Whatever material is selected should be examined in the context of justice, with reference back to the theoretical framework provided earlier. Often it will be possible to identify a controversial area of law, where a matter would be regarded as just under one theory, but unjust under another. The ability to draw such distinctions would show a welcome level of sophistication.

Needless to say, the evaluation should focus on the question that is set. This will be designed to stretch and challenge you, to force you to adapt your material to an unexpected slant. Credit is always given for the selection of appropriate material. However, the higher grades cannot be reached without evaluation of the material in the light of the actual issues addressed in the wording of the question. The evaluation ought to be personal: you, as well as philosophers, have different views of justice, and these should be reflected in your answers.

Activity

Consider how the change of word in the middle of the following questions may influence the selection of material and focus of discussion.

1 To what extent does the law promote justice?

2 To what extent does the law achieve justice?

You should now be able to:

■ understand what is required in an essay on the topic of law and justice.

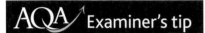
In this topic you will learn how to:

- explain the operation of the doctrine of judicial precedent
- explain the scope for judicial creativity in the operation of the doctrine.

Key cases

Re A (2000): the courts retain a residual power to establish new points of law.

Attorney-General for Jersey v Holley (2005): in deciding whether the partial defence of provocation is available on a charge of murder, the jury may consider characteristics of the defendant that relate to the gravity of the provocation, but not those that relate to his powers of self-control.

1 Creativity within the doctrine of judicial precedent

This topic deals with the role of judges when operating the doctrine of judicial precedent and when interpreting statutes, material that is familiar from Unit 1. However, the emphasis is no longer merely on the rules adopted by judges when engaging in these two activities, but rather on the degree of flexibility, or creativity, they enjoy. It therefore examines the extent to which they are bound by existing rules on the one hand, and the extent to which they are free to change and develop the law on the other.

The operation of judicial precedent

The basic principles

When hearing cases, judges apply existing law where it is available. However, they often have to develop it to fit new circumstances. This adds to the body of law, which can then be used by other judges in later cases. Known as the doctrine of precedent (or as *stare decisis*, meaning 'standing by decisions') this has certain key features:

- *Ratio decidendi* is the 'reason for the decision'. It is the legal principle upon which the outcome of a case is decided. This then sets a precedent for future judges to follow, such as the neighbour principle established in *Donoghue* v *Stevenson* (1932); or the point of law established in *R* v *G and R* (2003) that the test for recklessness in criminal damage is subjective, not objective; or the decision in *Williams* v *Roffey* (1990) that the completion of an existing obligation on time, thereby avoiding consequential loss to the other party, can provide sufficient consideration.

- *Obiter dicta* means 'other things said'. This refers to all other legal arguments and comments made by a judge that were not central to deciding the case before him. For example, he might consider a range of possible outcomes had the facts of the case been different. As a result, it is often difficult to draw a clear line between the *ratio decidendi* and the *obiter dicta* contained within the judgment.

Types of precedent

Precedents are described as original whenever the court addresses a point of law for the first time. For example, in **Re A (2000)** the court established a new precedent when it declared that the operation to separate conjoined twins was lawful, even though it would result in the immediate death of one of the girls.

Precedents are binding when they must be followed by a court in a later case. This will occur when the precedent was set by a higher court, or set by a court with limited powers to overrule its own previous decisions.

Precedents are persuasive when they are not binding on future cases. Judges, however, are free to adopt persuasive precedents. There are many reasons why precedents are merely persuasive. They may have been set in a lower court; or were part of the *obiter dicta* of the case; or they were set by the Privy Council, such as the decision of a nine-man Privy Council in **Attorney-General for Jersey v Holley (2005)**.

The hierarchy of the courts

Judicial precedent operates within the **hierarchy of the courts**. Decisions of the House of Lords are binding on all lower courts, including the Court of Appeal. Since issuing its Practice Statement in 1966, the House may depart from its own previous decisions 'when it appears right to do so'. However, it will bear in mind the danger of disturbing retrospectively the basis on which contracts, settlements of property and fiscal arrangements have been entered into and also the need for certainty in the criminal law. This new freedom would therefore be used sparingly.

The Court of Appeal is bound by decisions of the House of Lords, and it is generally bound by its own previous decisions. The justification for this is that the House of Lords exists to provide a remedy in cases where the Court of Appeal cannot. The Court of Appeal has limited powers to depart from its own previous decisions. Both divisions may take advantage of the three exceptions identified in *Young v Bristol Aeroplane* (1944), and the criminal division is free to depart from its own earlier decision in cases where the freedom of an individual is at stake, as in *R v Gould* (1968) CA.

Law reporting

Reports of the facts and judgments of cases are required for judicial precedent to operate successfully. Since 1865, **law reports** have been published under the auspices of the Incorporated Council of Law Reporting for England and Wales, which is a joint society of the Inns of Court, the Law Society and the Bar Council. In 1953, the Council began publishing the Weekly Law Reports, which are available either weekly or in annual bound volumes. The All England Reports are also published weekly, by LexisNexis Butterworths. Some newspapers publish summaries of important cases, and computerised law reporting systems are increasingly available.

Means of avoiding precedent

At first sight judicial precedent seems to operate restrictively, preventing judges from creative development of the law. The very name *'stare decisis'* implies rigidity and inflexibility, and the use of terms such as 'binding precedent' and 'hierarchy of the courts' reinforces this point. Furthermore, the fact that the House of Lords is often reluctant to use its powers under the Practice Statement, and the fact that the Court of Appeal has only limited powers to overrule its own previous decisions, confirm the impression that judicial precedent straightjackets judges.

However, further examination reveals that judges are able to perform a delicate balancing act between the undoubted advantages of consistency and fairness on the one hand, and flexibility and creativity on the other. Within the operation of the doctrine, a range of factors provide judges with flexibility, enabling them to avoid precedents that they deem inappropriate, or to develop new precedents when the situation requires.

Distinguishing

A precedent set in Case A should be followed in the later Case B where the facts of the two cases are similar. However, where the facts are **distinguishable**, the judge in Case B may choose not to apply the precedent set in Case A. For example, a contract is not formed unless the two parties intended to enter into a legally binding agreement. Where an agreement is made in a domestic setting, such as a husband promising to buy his wife an eternity ring for their silver wedding, the courts presume that it was not intended to be legally binding. In the case of **Balfour v Balfour (1919)**, Mr Balfour agreed to pay his wife monthly maintenance while he was posted to Ceylon. Soon after, they separated, and the payments ceased. Mrs Balfour then took action to hold him to his promise. However, her action failed: the court decided that this was a domestic arrangement rather than a legally enforceable contract..

Key terms

Hierarchy of the courts: the organisation of the courts into order of seniority.

Law reports: summaries of the details of decided cases.

Distinguishing: the court finds sufficient factual difference between two apparently similar cases that they are able to reach different decisions.

Key cases

Balfour v Balfour (1919); Merritt v Merritt (1971): where the facts of a case are materially different from those in the case establishing the precedent, the court may distinguish between them.

However, the presumption in favour of a domestic arrangement can be rebutted by evidence showing that the parties had intended to enter into a legal relationship. This occurred in **Merritt v Merritt (1971)**. After moving out of the family home, Mr Merritt made a signed, written agreement with his wife. Under this agreement he would pay his wife maintenance, and she would continue the mortgage repayments. Furthermore, he would eventually transfer the home into her name. When he later refused to do so, Mrs Merritt brought a court action to seek enforcement of this part of their agreement. The court decided that the facts were distinguishable from those in *Balfour* v *Balfour* (1919), and therefore the presumption in favour of a domestic arrangement had been successfully rebutted. Their agreement, therefore, was legally enforceable as there had been an intention to enter into a legal relationship.

The key differences between the two cases were that in *Merritt* v *Merritt* (1971), the husband and wife had separated before making their agreement, and secondly that their agreement had been written down and signed. These points allowed the court to distinguish the precedent set in *Balfour* v *Balfour* (1919). Theoretically, at least, the power to distinguish offers judges unlimited discretion to avoid existing precedents.

Reversing

Sometimes the higher court will decide that a lower court reached the wrong decision in a case. The higher court will then alter the decision made by the lower court. This is known as **reversing** the decision of the lower court. This famously occurred twice in **R v Kingston (1994)**. The case concerned the defence of intoxication: Kingston, a known paedophile, was drugged by blackmailers and lured into abusing a 15-year-old boy. His conviction for indecent assault was overturned by the Court of Appeal on the grounds of involuntary intoxication. However, the House of Lords reinstated a guilty verdict: Kingston's inhibitions had been severely impaired by the drugs he had involuntarily taken, but he was still capable of forming the *mens rea* of the offence. In the words of Mustill LJ: 'mere disinhibition' is insufficient to found a defence.

Overruling

In reversing, only one case is involved. In **overruling**, at least two cases are involved. In Case B, the court decides that the point of law decided previously in Case A was wrong and so changes it. In **Addie v Dumbreck (1929)** a four-year-old trespasser wandered onto the defendant's land and was crushed in the wheel of a machine operated by a colliery. The colliers had 'No Trespassing' signs in place, but were aware that these were regularly ignored by children. Nevertheless, the House of Lords decided that there was no general duty of care to trespassers.

Forty years on, attitudes had changed. In **British Railways Board v Herrington**, the claimant was a six-year-old boy who suffered serious burns and injuries on an electrified railway line. He had stepped over a damaged fence running alongside the line. The House of Lords decided that, in the years since the decision in *Addie* v *Dumbreck* (1929), social and physical conditions had changed dramatically: in particular the growth of towns had brought about a lack of play areas for children, leading to an increased temptation to trespass. In view of this, it would now be right for an occupier to owe a duty of care to trespassers.

Other features offering flexibility

Other features within precedent also provide flexibility for judges. Decisions of the judicial committee of the Privy Council are not binding upon judges. Dissenting judgments may also establish an argument about a point of law that is later adopted as a *ratio decidendi*. *Obiter dicta* are persuasive rather than binding. And new situations arise which allow judges to establish original precedents.

Privy Council decisions

Decisions of the **Judicial Committee of the Privy Council** are outside the UK court structure, and so are merely persuasive. Students of negligence will be familiar with **The Wagon Mound (1961)**.

Prior to this decision, damages in negligence were available for all damage 'directly traceable to the negligent act' (*Re Polemis* (1921)). In *The Wagon Mound* (1961), the Privy Council limited damages to harm that was reasonably foreseeable. In the words of Lord Simonds: 'After the event even a fool is wise. Yet it is not the hindsight of a fool; but it is the foresight of the reasonable man which alone can determine responsibility.' In *Doughty* v *Turner Manufacturing Co. Ltd* (1964) the principle of reasonable foreseeability was adopted into English law. According to Lord Justice Harman: 'We ought to start with the premise that the criterion in English law is foreseeability. I take it that whether *The Wagon Mound* is or is not binding on this court we ought to treat it as the law'.

Criminal law students will be familiar with the Privy Council decision in **Attorney-General for Jersey v Holley (2005)**. Dennis Holley was taunted by his girlfriend into killing her with an axe. The nine law lords who sat on the Privy Council had to decide between two conflicting authorities, one being the Privy Council's own decision in *Luc Thiet Thuan* (1997), the other the House of Lords' decision in *R* v *Smith* (2000). In following *Luc Thiet Thuan* (1997), they ruled that individual characteristics such as the defendant's alcoholism are not relevant when considering whether the reasonable man would have lost his self-control.

This decision, though technically persuasive, was followed by the Court of Appeal in the joined cases of *R* v *James*; and *R* v *Karimi* (2006). Lord Phillips CJ, though, reflected on the dilemma faced by the court: 'While there was some doubt as to the circumstances in which the Court of Appeal could depart from one of its own decisions, there was no doubt that it was bound to follow a decision of the House of Lords.' However, the circumstances of Holley were unusual: the case was decided by nine law lords, who had agreed that the result should 'clarify definitively the present state of English law' (Lord Nicholls). Interestingly, the Court of Appeal refused the appellants permission to take their cases to the House of Lords as the outcome of any such appeal was a foregone conclusion.

Dissenting judgments

Dissenting judgments arise where judges are split on the outcome of the case. In *R* v *Brown and Others* (1993) Lords Mustill and Slynn disagreed with the decision reached by the majority, and both provided speeches to explain their position. These were dissenting judgments. In his speech, Lord Mustill argued that 'the state should interfere with the rights of an individual to live his or her life as he or she may choose no more than is necessary to ensure a proper balance between the special interests of the individual and the general interests of the individuals who together comprise the populace at large'.

Dissenting judgments may be resurrected by judges in later cases, as in **Candler v Crane, Christmas and Co. (1951)**. Some investors had lost money through relying upon a negligent misstatement in a company's accounts. The court refused to recognise the existence of a duty of care. Lord Denning disagreed. In his minority judgment he argued that a duty of care is owed where accountants are aware of the particular person and purpose for which their reports are being prepared. This dissenting judgment was later followed by the House of Lords in *Hedley Byrne* v *Heller* (1964), and approved by Lord Bridge in *Caparo* v *Dickman* (1990).

 Key terms

Judicial Committee of the Privy Council: the court of final appeal for the UK overseas territories, Crown dependencies, and some Commonwealth countries.

Dissenting judgments: a minority of the judges on a panel disagree with the majority decision; this minority judgment might be used in later cases to change or develop the law.

Key cases

The Wagon Mound (1961): in the tort of negligence, the payment of damages is restricted to losses that are reasonably foreseeable.

Attorney-General for Jersey v Holley (2005): although technically persuasive rather than binding, a decision of the Privy Council will sometimes be followed.

Candler v Crane, Christmas and Co. (1951): a dissenting judgment may be applied by the courts in a later case.

You should now be able to:

- explain how judicial precedent operates
- understand the scope for judicial creativity available within the operation of judicial precedent.

Obiter dicta

Often judges reflect upon possible scenarios not directly relevant to the case before them. Such statements are part of the *obiter dicta* of a judgment, and are not binding. However, they may have persuasive authority. In *R v Howe* (1987), a murder case, Lord Griffiths declared: 'duress is not available as a defence to a charge of murder, or to attempted murder. Attempted murder requires proof of an intent to kill, whereas in murder it is sufficient to prove an intent to cause really serious injury. It cannot be right to allow the defence to one who may be more intent upon taking a life than the murderer.'

Since attempted murder was not at issue in Howe, Lord Griffiths' remarks were *obiter dicta*. However, when *R v Gotts* (1991), a case involving attempted murder, appeared before it, the House dismissed the boy's appeal against his conviction. In language reminiscent of Lord Griffiths, Lord Jauncey said: 'the intent required of an attempted murderer is more evil than that required of a murderer'. Thus the *obiter dicta* of Howe proved highly persuasive to the court in *Gotts*.

Original precedents

Original precedents establish new points of law on issues that have not been decided in previous cases. Some introduce important new principles, such as the decision in *Re A* (2000), referred to earlier; others merely refine or extend well-established existing principles. When faced with the responsibility of deciding a new point of law, judges would seem to enjoy considerable discretion. However, in practice, they are mindful of existing legal principles, and of public policy issues, and of the need for the body of law as a whole to remain coherent.

In **Airedale NHS Trust v Bland (1993)**, a civil case, the courts were asked for a declaration whether it would be lawful to discontinue life-sustaining treatment. Anthony Bland was a victim of the Hillsborough disaster. As a result of the crush injuries he had sustained, he was in a persistent vegetative state, with no hope of recovery. He was being kept alive by life-sustaining medical treatment, and by artificial feeding and hydration. Without this treatment he would die either within a few days as a result of infection or within a week or two as a result of the withdrawal of artificial feeding.

Because of its importance, the case was appealed to the House of Lords, where Lord Goff provided the leading speech. He recognised the existing law, that a failure to treat a patient will normally constitute an omission for which there is potential criminal liability. However, he acknowledged that the termination of treatment would not be a breach of the duty owed to the patient because it was no longer in the patient's interests to continue the treatment. It was this part of the judgment that established an original precedent.

Activities

1 Review the case of *Sweet v Parsley* (1970). What was the basis of the House of Lords' decision to reverse the decision of the Queen's Bench Division?

2 In Units 1, 2 and 3 you may have encountered the following cases. What point of law was overruled in them?

    R v Shivpuri (1981)

    Hall v Simons (2000)

    R v G and R (2003)

    Miliangos v George Frank Textiles (1976)

2 Creativity within statutory interpretation

The operation of statutory interpretation

The basic principles

The responsibility of Parliament for the legislative process has ended by the time that the Bill receives royal assent. Members of Parliament have no further influence over the Act. Under the doctrine of the separation of powers, it is the role of the judiciary to interpret and apply that legislation. To ensure that they manage this responsibility effectively, judges have developed a range of approaches. Although many of these approaches are called rules, they are not necessarily binding upon judges: discretion exists in the selection of approach to adopt, and the outcome of a case may depend entirely upon the approach selected.

The literal rule

Under this rule judges follow the literal meaning of the words used in the statute rather than seeking to discover the intention of Parliament behind the legislation. Lord Simonds argued that it is the duty of the court to interpret the words used and even if these words are ambiguous, judges should not go on a 'voyage of discovery' to find their intended meaning. In **Whiteley v Chappell (1868)** the defendant had voted twice in an election, first using his own name, and secondly masquerading as someone who had died. He was charged with impersonating a person entitled to vote in an election. Using the literal rule the court found him not guilty: he could not be guilty of impersonating someone entitled to vote, since dead people are not entitled to vote.

The golden rule

The golden rule is used to mitigate the harshness of the literal rule. However, it is restricted to cases where the key word has more than one meaning. If one meaning would result in a 'manifestly absurd' outcome, another is to be preferred. Lord Reid once declared: 'You may not for any reason attach to a statutory provision a meaning which the words of that statute cannot possibly bear. If they are capable of more than one meaning then you can choose between those two meanings, but beyond that you cannot go.'

This approach was adopted in *Adler* v *George* (1964). Under s3 of the Official Secrets Act 1920 it was an offence to be found 'in the vicinity of a prohibited place'. The accused was arrested inside Marham Royal Air Force station, and argued that the phrase 'in the vicinity of' implied being 'outside of' a prohibited place. Lord Parker used the golden rule: 'in the vicinity of' could mean 'being in or in the vicinity of' the prohibited place. To have acquitted the defendant would have been a manifestly absurd outcome.

The mischief rule

A very different approach can be seen in the mischief rule. Here the courts identify the mischief or problem with the old common law, and then examine the remedy provided by Parliament. They then try to ensure that they give effect to this remedy. This approach was adopted in **Smith v Hughes (1960)**. Under the Street Offences Act 1958 it was an offence for prostitutes to solicit in the street. In this case the prostitutes were soliciting men from the open window of a house. Using the mischief rule, the courts identified the problem with the old common law (harassment), and looked at how Parliament tried to overcome this (by preventing soliciting in the street). They gave effect to this by finding the women guilty, even though they could have argued under the literal rule that they were not in the street at the time of the offence.

In this topic you will learn how to:

- explain the operation of the doctrine of statutory interpretation
- explain the scope for judicial creativity in the operation of statutory interpretation.

AQA Examiner's tip

Any explanation of the rules of interpretation should be quite brief, so that you can pass quickly on to the more important issue of the opportunity for judicial creativity.

Key cases

Whiteley v Chappell (1868): adopting the literal rule can defeat the purpose of the legislation.

Smith v Hughes (1960): the mischief rule may be adopted to ensure that effect is given to the remedy Parliament was seeking to impose in its enactment.

The purposive approach

This approach is becoming increasingly popular in UK courts. Here, judges examine not only the words used on the pages of the Act, but also the intention of Parliament when using these words. In the case of **Jones v Tower Boot Company (1997)** the claimant had suffered constant harassment by fellow workers at the Tower Boot Company. The Race Relations Act 1976 stated: 'Anything done by a person in the course of employment shall be treated for the purposes of this Act as done by his employer as well as by him, whether or not it was done with the employer's knowledge or approval.' The employers argued that these activities were not authorised, and therefore not done 'in the course of employment'. The Court of Appeal adopted a purposive approach: the purpose of the Race Relations Act 1976 was to prevent in the workplace the discriminatory conduct to which the victim had been subjected. Therefore the employers were liable.

Creativity within the operation of statutory interpretation

Approaches that restrict judicial creativity

The literal approach is inflexible. It is argued in its favour that it promotes consistency and encourages Parliamentary draftsmen to be precise. However, neither of these two arguments carries great weight. Firstly, consistency is not a virtue in itself: it needs to be allied to justice and fairness. Secondly, it is unreasonable to expect Parliamentary draftsmen to be able to anticipate every conceivable interpretation, and misinterpretation, of their words. The argument in favour of the literal rule that carries most weight is that it respects a clear demarcation between the legislative function of Parliament and the interpretative function of the courts, thereby maintaining the doctrine of the separation of powers.

The main criticism of the literal rule is that it can defeat the legislative intention of Parliament. Clearly the defendant in *Whiteley* v *Chappell* (1868) was guilty of committing the very offence which Parliament had been mindful to outlaw. However, due to unfortunate draftsmanship and literal interpretation, he was acquitted. When Acts fail to meet their obvious and stated purpose, the law becomes discredited. Unfortunately, the golden rule provides only a limited safety valve, as its operation is restricted to cases where words have more than one meaning.

Approaches that promote judicial creativity

The mischief rule and the purposive approach both require judges to examine the intention of Parliament when introducing the legislation. To achieve a proper understanding of Parliament's intention they seek to appreciate the circumstances leading to the introduction of the Bill. This appreciation enables them to give effect to the declared intentions of Parliament. For example, in the case of *Jones* v *Tower Boot Company Ltd* (1997), if the Court of Appeal judges had adopted the literal approach, they may have agreed with the Employment Appeal Tribunal that racial harassment was not 'in the course of employment' as it was neither a wrongful act authorised by the employer, nor an act, though authorised, carried out in an unauthorised way, the familiar definition used in vicarious liability in tort.

Rather than relying upon this interpretation of 'course of employment', the Court of Appeal adopted a purposive approach to the meaning of this phrase in s32(1) of the Race Relations Act 1976. This allowed a broader understanding of its meaning, and one that was more consistent with the natural meaning of the words. Furthermore, the Act was designed to prevent racial harassment at work: this was better achieved by holding employers responsible for the actions of their employees. Where

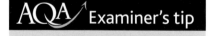

employers had taken reasonable steps to ensure that such harassment did not arise, a defence would be available to them. Where they had not, it would not be reasonable to excuse them. The purpose of the 1976 Act could only be achieved by holding employers responsible for the conduct of their employees.

External aids

When the courts are seeking to discover the intention of Parliament, they are prepared to refer to external sources of information. Although this is time-consuming, it is necessary if judges are to give effect to the intentions of Parliament. **Hansard** is the record of Parliamentary debates, and since the decision of the House of Lords in *Pepper* v *Hart* (1993), judges are able to refer to the speech of the government minister proposing the Bill in Parliament.

> **Key terms**
>
> **Hansard**: the edited verbatim report of proceedings in both Houses. Commons Hansard covers proceedings in the Commons Chamber, Westminster Hall and Standing Committees. Lords Hansard covers proceedings in the Lords Chamber and its Grand Committees. Both contain Written Ministerial Statements and Written Answers.

The Earl of Erroll: My Lords, I thought Pepper v Hart only applied if there was ambiguity on the face of the Bill or a conflict with European law? Otherwise, what is in the Bill applies and you cannot look at Pepper v Hart.

Baroness Hollis of Heigham: My Lords, as far as concerns Pepper v Hart, if there is any ambiguity or division of opinion as to what may be the situation, then, as I understand it, you may refer to the columns of Hansard in so far as they clarify the policy intent of Parliament.

Earl Ferrers: My Lords, before the Minister sits down, could she also clarify one point for me? It relates to what my noble friend Lord Tebbit said. He said that when you go down to inspect the register, if the birth certificate has been changed, why keep the original? The Minister says there are reasons for that, but does that not mean that there are then two birth certificates—the original one and the amended one? If so, what is the point of saying that nobody must refer to the original if it is still there?

Baroness Hollis of Heigham: My Lords, this is all about privacy and the right to privacy circumscribed by certain considerations—national security, crime, public health—that may impinge on that. There are indeed two birth certificates. People would have access to the acquired gender birth certificate. It would not be distinctive in any way. But the original one would exist in the same way as when studying the maps of Nottingham, I found that streets that later got called Corporation Street were originally known as Asylum Lane. I did not, as a result, suggest to my students that they got rid of the original maps. They kept both sets.

Lord Swinfen: My Lords, surely the birth certificate is a certified copy of the entry in the register of births. Is the Minister saying that that original entry is to be changed?

Fig. 1 *A Hansard report*

However, clear limits have subsequently been placed upon reference to Hansard. In **Wilson v Secretary of State for Industry (2003)**, the House of Lords ruled that Hansard may be consulted to discover the meaning of a word used in the legislation, but should not be consulted to try to unearth the reasons for the legislation. Warnings were also issued about the reliability of ministerial speeches as indicating the intention of Parliament. This judgment will reduce the fishing expedition approach to the use of Hansard, and will limit reference to it in future cases.

Law Commission reports help judges to identify the thinking behind an Act. When Parliament legislates in response to their reports, the courts have ready access to a reliable critique of the failings of the previous law, and to the principles behind the proposed remedies. *R* v *G and R* (2003) illustrates this point well. The case concerned the *mens rea* for criminal damage. In *R* v *Caldwell* (1982) the House of Lords had introduced an objective test for recklessness. This had proved controversial. In *R* v *G and R*, Lord Bingham reviewed the historical development of the *mens rea* for criminal damage, starting with s51 of the Malicious Damage Act 1861. He referred in detail to the initial working report of the Law Commission, in which it was stated: 'We assume that the traditional elements of intention, knowledge and recklessness (in the sense of foresight and disregard of consequences or awareness and disregard of the likelihood of the existence of circumstances) will continue to be required for serious crime.'

>
>
> **Key cases**
>
> **Wilson v Secretary of State for Industry (2003)**: judicial access to Hansard should operate within narrowly defined limits.

>
>
> **Key terms**
>
> **The Law Commission**: according to its own website, the Law Commission is the statutory independent body created by the Law Commissions Act 1965 to keep the law under review and to recommend reform where it is needed.

He then referred to a Law Commission definition of recklessness produced one month before its final report on criminal damage. According to the first limb of this definition a person is reckless if 'knowing that there is a risk that an event may result from his conduct or that a circumstance may exist, he takes that risk'. By reference to these proposals from the Law Commission, Lord Bingham was able to establish that the test for recklessness at the time of the 1971 Act was presumed to be subjective. In this way he laid the foundation for overruling the decision in *Caldwell*, and reimposing a subjective test for recklessness in criminal damage.

Activity

Research the facts of the following cases. Identify the approach or rule adopted by the courts in them. Consider the likely outcomes if different rules had been adopted.

> *Corkery* v *Carpenter* (1951)
>
> *Fisher* v *Bell* (1960)
>
> *Cheeseman* v *DPP* (1990)

You should now be able to:

■ explain how the rules of statutory interpretation operate

■ understand the scope for judicial creativity within the operation of the rules of statutory interpretation.

In this topic you will learn how to:

■ explain the constitutional relationship between Parliament and the judiciary

■ discuss the arguments for and against the exercise of judicial creativity.

Key terms

Relationship between Parliament and the Judiciary: according to the unwritten constitution, Parliament is responsible for making law, and judges for interpreting and applying law.

Key cases

A and Others v Secretary of State for the Home Department (2004): the courts may rule statutes to be incompatible with human rights legislation.

3 The creative role of judges

The constitutional relationship between Parliament and the judiciary

According to constitutional convention, Parliament is the supreme legislative authority in the United Kingdom, and no other body can challenge this position. In the words of Lord Radcliffe: 'It is unacceptable constitutionally that there should be two sources of law-making at work at the same time'. In recent years, however, Parliament has chosen to place some limits upon its own sovereign legislative authority, through membership of the European Union and through the passage of the Human Rights Act 1998.

Through membership of the European Union, Parliament has allowed primacy to be given to European law over conflicting national law, as seen in the series of cases known as Factortame. The law lords declared part of the Merchant Shipping Act 1988 invalid as it conflicted with European Union law, demonstrating not only the subordination of primary national legislation to European law, but also, and of more immediate relevance, the ability of the judiciary to set aside the clearly expressed will of Parliament.

The passage of the Human Rights Act 1998 also confers greater power on the judiciary. Where judges rule that part of an Act of Parliament has breached one of the human rights contained within the European Convention on Human Rights as enshrined in the 1998 Act, they have the power to make a declaration of incompatibility. This occurred in **A and Others v Secretary of State for the Home Department (2004)**. The House of Lords ruled that s23 of the Anti-Terrorism, Crime and Security Act 2001, in permitting the indefinite detention of foreign nationals without charge, was incompatible with article 5 of the European Convention of Human Rights. Parliament felt obliged to comply with this judgment, and so the Prevention of Terrorism Act 2005 was passed.

The impact of the HRA 1998 is explored in more depth Chapter 24, Balancing conflicting interests.

Subject to these two exceptions, the judiciary is constitutionally bound to remain obedient to the expressed will of Parliament in its legislative capacity. In other words, the courts should not act in a way that frustrates the stated will of Parliament. It is worthwhile in this regard to examine parts of the speech of Lord Nicholls in the Privy Council decision in *Attorney-General for Jersey* v *Holley* (2005).

The case of *Holley* (2005) concerned the partial defence of provocation. In *R* v *Smith* (2000), the House of Lords ruled that psychological characteristics of the defendant could be considered when asking whether the reasonable man would have reacted in the same way under the same provocation. Lord Hoffman explained that a jury 'may think that there was some characteristic of the accused, whether temporary or permanent, which affected the degree of control which society could reasonably have expected of him and which it would be unjust not to take into account'. Following this guideline, a jury could presumably now be asked to consider whether a short-tempered, irascible, jealous, possessive alcoholic could reasonably be expected to retain his self-control under provocation.

This judgment significantly diluted the objective test, but it proved short-lived. In 2005, a nine-member Privy Council heard the appeal of Holley, a drunken and violent chronic alcoholic who had killed his girlfriend after provocation. Delivering the opinion of the majority, Lord Nicholls was critical of the approach of the House of Lords in *Smith*. The main target of his criticism was not so much the diluted test adopted in *Smith*; rather it was the attempt by the House of Lords to depart from the law as declared by Parliament in the Homicide Act 1957. In his words: 'It is not open to judges to change the common law and thereby depart from the law as declared by Parliament.' He then went on to explain how the judgment in *Smith* conflicted with the 1957 Act.

Underpinning this judgment is recognition by Lord Nicholls of the constitutional position of Parliament as the supreme legislative authority. Judges cannot develop the common law either to rival or to replace the declared will of Parliament in its enactments. Nor can they interpret statutes to the point of extinction by imposing their own judgment of what the law should be because of their distaste for what it actually is.

Public policy issues

As the supreme legislative authority, Parliament is responsible for determining issues of policy. The anti-discrimination legislation of the Labour government in the 1960s and 1970s, for example, clearly concerned significant policy issues about race and gender, and set new standards for employers, public bodies, service providers and others in their treatment of disadvantaged or minority groups. The Civil Partnership Act 2004 and the Equality Act 2006 extended earlier provisions, demonstrating a new policy direction.

According to convention, the judiciary leaves matters of policy to Parliament. **Ronald Dworkin** distinguishes between principles and policy. Principles are concerned with rights, and with standards of fairness and justice, for example: justice is blind (impartial); people are equal before the law; defendants are presumed innocent until found guilty. These should always be applied by judges. Policies, on the other hand, are concerned with achieving social or political goals, such as the

> **Key terms**
>
> **Ronald Dworkin**: an American legal philosopher who was, until 2008, a professor of Jurisprudence at UCL; he argues that judges should apply legal principles, and leave matters of policy to the legislature.

Fig. 2 *Ronald Dworkin argues that judges should apply legal principles, and leave matters of policy to the legislature*

redistribution of wealth, or the protection of the environment. These, Dworkin argues, are the responsibility of the legislature rather than of the judiciary. He condemns judges who stray from principles into areas of policy.

When interpreting statutes, judges often stray into areas of policy. For example, the case of **Royal College of Nursing v DHSS (1981)** involved interpretation of the Abortion Act 1967. Under the Act, abortions had to be carried out by a 'registered medical practitioner'. Since 1967, various drugs have been developed making it possible for nurses to carry out this operation. The court had to decide whether a nurse was a 'registered medical practitioner'. In a dissenting judgment, two law lords argued that the matter should be left to Parliament since it would be a significant policy change to allow nurses to carry out abortions. This argument failed to persuade the majority, who applied the mischief rule. However, it can be argued that by adopting the mischief rule they are showing deference to the will of Parliament.

In developing the common law judges also stray into matters of policy. In **Shaw v DPP (1961)** the House of Lords recognised the new offence of conspiracy to corrupt public morals. In the words of Viscount Simonds: 'there remains in the courts a residual power to enforce the supreme and fundamental purpose of the law, to conserve not only the safety and order, but also the moral welfare of the State'. In his dissenting judgment, Lord Reid argued that Parliament is the proper place for deciding whether the law should intervene further in the enforcement of morality: 'Some think that the law already goes too far, some that it does not go far enough. Parliament is the proper place, and I am firmly of the opinion the only proper place, to settle that.' This view was echoed by Lord Simon in *DPP for Northern Ireland v Lynch* (1975) where he argued that 'the collective wisdom of Parliament' is better suited to solving matters of social policy.

Shaw v *DPP* is covered in more depth in Chapter 20, Law and morality.

The third limb of the *Caparo* v *Dickman* (1990) test for duty of care in the tort of negligence encourages the judiciary to consider policy issues. In *Hill* v *Chief Constable of West Yorkshire* (1988) the House of Lords declined to impose a duty of care upon the police as it would inhibit their judgment and encourage defensive policing strategies. In contrast, it was held in **Ashton v Turner (1980)** that a duty of care was not owed by one criminal to another while engaged in criminal activity.

Judges also engage in policy considerations when examining human rights under the Human Rights Act 1998. In *A and Others* v *Secretary of State for the Home Department* (2004) the courts declared existing counter-terrorism legislation to be incompatible with rights contained within the European Convention on Human Rights, as enshrined in the 1998 Act. Although the decision of the courts was based upon established principles such as *habeas corpus*, it has continued to have a serious effect upon the implementation of government policy.

In judicial review of the decisions of government ministers, judges inevitably have to consider matters of government policy. In **Council of Civil Service Unions v Minister for the Civil Service (1984)**, ('**The GCHQ Case**') the House of Lords upheld, on the grounds of national security, the ban on trade union membership imposed upon employees of the government surveillance headquarters in Cheltenham by the prime minister. This decision was seen by many as pro-government and anti-trade union. However, it was based upon an interpretation of established law and not upon policy considerations.

Key cases

Royal College of Nursing v DHSS (1981): a wide interpretation of the words used in an Act may be applied by the courts in order to give effect to the remedy devised by Parliament.

Shaw v DPP (1961): under common law, the courts retain a residual power to develop new offences.

Ashton v Turner (1980): where two parties are engaged in criminal activity, the law will not allow the first party to claim damages for harm suffered due to the negligence of the other party.

The GCHQ Case (1984); **DPP v Hutchinson (1990)**: this combination of cases may be used to illustrate that the courts decide matters concerning public policy in an impartial manner, without due deference to the government of the day.

In **DPP v Hutchinson (1990)** the House of Lords ruled that protesters at Greenham Common, a US airbase housing nuclear missiles, had the right to protest outside the base even though the Minister of Defence had banned them by issuing a bylaw denying them access to the land. Although this decision thwarted government policy, it was based upon existing principles of law and not upon policy issues.

Judicial attitudes

Judges openly acknowledge their law-making role. In the words of Lord Reid: 'We do not believe in fairy tales any more, so we must accept the fact that, for better or worse, judges do make law.' However, he recognised the demarcation between the judiciary and Parliament. In *Knuller* v *DPP* (1973), another case concerned with the offence of conspiracy to corrupt public morals, he declared: 'I said in Shaw's case and I repeat that Parliament and Parliament alone is the proper authority to change the law with regard to the punishment of immoral acts. Rightly or wrongly the law was determined by the decision in Shaw's case. Any alteration of the law as so determined must in my view be left to Parliament.'

Other judges have proved to be more ready to embrace a creative approach. Lord Denning was driven by the basic principle: 'The judge should make the law correspond with the justice that the case requires.' In *High Trees House* (1947), he developed the doctrine of promissory estoppel to prevent claimants going back on a promise on which the defendant had relied. In *Davis* v *Johnson* (1979) he ignored a binding precedent set by the Court of Appeal only days earlier, and extended the protection available under the Domestic Violence and Matrimonial Proceedings Act 1976. In *Schorsch Meier GmbH* v *Hennin* (1974), he ignored a binding precedent set in the *Havana* case (1961) by the House of Lords. He declared that damages may be paid in currencies other than sterling, and that the old rule had run its course.

In *Magor and St Mellons* (1950), Lord Denning made the following declaration in support of this creative role: 'We sit here to find out the intention of Parliament and carry it out, and we do this better by filling in the gaps and making sense of the enactment than by opening it up to destructive analysis.' He expressed his criticism of the 'ultra-legalistic' interpretations that would deprive claimants of their rights. A cynic might conclude that this does more to give power to the judiciary than to carry out the intention of Parliament. Viscount Simonds described filling in the gaps as a 'naked usurpation of the legislative function under the thin disguise of interpretation'.

This tension within the judiciary is not novel. **Karl Llewellyn**, a leading figure in the school of **American Legal Realism** of the 1920s and 1930s and a keen observer of judicial methods, argued that the law is indeterminate: in other words, cases are capable of more than one possible outcome. Judges merely use legal rules and reasons to justify decisions they have already reached for non-legal reasons. Therefore, when interpreting statutes they may either stick closely to the text, or look beyond it, to justify their decisions. When considering precedents, they may either view them as loose (broad in application) and so follow them, or as strict (narrow in application) and so distinguish them. Lord Denning would clearly belong to the class of judges who looks beyond the text of the statutes, and who views precedents narrowly. Lord Reid and Viscount Simonds would belong to those who look at the text closely, rather than beyond it, and who view precedents as being broad in application.

> ### Key terms
>
> **Karl Llewellyn (1893–1962):** an American legal scholar, Llewellyn argued that judges are influenced by a range of factors that are unrelated to the law; he was therefore critical of those who viewed the law as something that operated simply as a system of objective rules.
>
> **American Legal Realism:** legal realists believe that the outcome of cases is decided not by the law in the textbooks but by other factors. Jerome Frank once declared that a case might be decided by what the judge had for breakfast.

Should judges make law?

The benefits

The judiciary is responsible for the development of the common law. Crime, contract and tort contain large elements of judge-made law. Even topics governed by statute, such as theft, occupiers' liability, and consumer protection, have generated considerable case law as the legislation has been subjected to scrutiny in the courts. There is no doubt that judges play a significant role in creating and developing the law. The question arises: should they?

There are clear benefits to be derived from an active judiciary. First, it provides flexibility. Appropriate precedents may be followed, and inappropriate ones may be distinguished or overruled. *British Railways Board* v *Herrington* (1972), and **R v R (1991)** demonstrates the willingness of the judiciary to adapt the law to changing social circumstances. *Attorney-General for Jersey* v *Holley* (2005) shows its readiness to recognise past errors of judgment and amend the law accordingly.

Secondly, the judiciary is able to provide practical solutions to real-life situations. The decision of the House of Lords in *R* v *R* (1991) provided an instant solution to the problem of the law on marital rape that had been festering for many years. In the Court of Appeal hearing in *Davis* v *Johnson* (1979), Lord Denning pointed the way to providing a remedy for a cohabitee, as opposed to a married woman, suffering domestic violence at the hands of her partner. Similarly, in *Jackson* v *Horizon Holidays* (1975), he sought to limit the strictness of the rule of privity of contract. In *Re A* (2000) the courts were faced with an application to sever conjoined twins in the sure knowledge that one would immediately die. And yet they were able to apply existing principles to establish a new point of law.

Thirdly, judges are able to address problems created by advancements in technology. In *Royal College of Nursing* v *DHSS* (1981) the House of Lords, in the light of technical advancements in drug-induced abortions, had to address the interpretation of a section of the Abortion Act 1967, and the use of the term 'medical practitioners'. In 2004, in the case of Natalie Evans, the Court of Appeal had to decide whether, under the terms of the **Human Fertilisation and Embryology Act 1994**, a young woman could have her frozen embryos implanted once her former boyfriend had withdrawn his consent.

Fourthly, judges are able to devote the required time to due consideration of a case. This contrasts with Parliament, which may see the need for legislation in a particular field, but not be able to prioritise it because of competing interests. For example, the need for wholesale reform of the law on non-fatal offences has been recognised for many years, with reports and draft bills being produced. However, Parliament has failed to provide the necessary time to introduce legislation. During the same period of time the courts have been active in developing the law. In **R v Savage (1992)**, the House of Lords overruled *Spratt* (1990) and reversed *Parmenter* (1991) in declaring that the *mens rea* for s47 occasioning actual bodily harm does not require intention or recklessness as to the harm caused. In *Chan-Fook* (1994) the Court of Appeal declared that actual bodily harm includes psychiatric injury, and in *DPP* v *Smith* (2006) it was decided that cutting off a significant part of a person's hair satisfies the *actus reus* of actual bodily harm. Similarly the *actus reus* of grievous bodily harm has been incrementally developed in *Burstow* (1997) to include serious psychiatric harm, and in *Dica* (2004) to include inflicting the HIV virus.

The problems

Leaving aside constitutional issues and the proper relationship between Parliament and the courts, which were discussed earlier, there are other problems with the judiciary exercising a law-making role. First, judges are not elected. Nor are they representative of society as a whole in terms of gender, ethnic origin, social class or age. In May 2006, Lord Falconer, the Constitutional Affairs Secretary and Lord Chancellor, issued a ministerial statement giving details of a strategy to increase the diversity of the judiciary. This was to include widening the range of people eligible to apply for judicial office, encouraging a wider range of applicants, and promoting an open and fair selection process. Meanwhile, the senior ranks of the judiciary remain predominantly white, middle-aged and male, promoting a suspicion, whether well-founded or not, that the judiciary lacks understanding and accountability.

Secondly, laws made by Parliament generally apply to the future. Acts come into force either at midnight on the day they receive royal assent, or at some time in the future specified in the Act. For example, the Human Rights Act was passed in 1998, but came into force on 1 October 2000. In contrast, judge-made law is by its nature **retrospective**: it applies to the past. This makes a person a criminal for an offence that, arguably, did not exist at the time it was committed. For example, in *R* v *R* (1991) the bar on marital rape was removed. However, the offence was committed before this bar was removed, when the old law still applied. The European Court of Human Rights has ruled that this does not contravene Article 7 of the European Convention on Human Rights, which states that no one should be found guilty of an offence which was not an offence when it was committed. Retrospective law prevents the law being used as a guide to future conduct, and therefore breaches one of the eight principles identified by Lon Fuller as essential for a valid legal system.

Thirdly, judge-made law can only be made when cases come to court. Therefore it is patchy, random, unstructured, and dependent upon the willingness and ability of the parties to pursue the matter on appeal. As a result, some areas of law remain unclear for many years. The decision in **Jackson v Horizon Holidays Ltd (1975)** clearly breached the doctrine of privity of contract, but to what extent and in what circumstances remained unclear. Further cases were needed before clarification could be provided.

The law on involuntary manslaughter is a prime example of judicial ping-pong, with subjective recklessness and gross negligence apparently striving for supremacy in those cases which are not suitable for unlawful act manslaughter. The elements of gross negligence manslaughter continue to attract debate, and the existence of subjective recklessness manslaughter is still questioned. In contrast, the elements of voluntary manslaughter are clear as they have been determined by statute, the Homicide Act 1957: it is only the interpretation of those elements by the courts that has led to confusion.

Finally, judges are often pressurised into making hasty decisions. In **Re S (1996)** an application to force a heavily pregnant woman to undergo a Caesarean section operation against her wishes was heard by the court within hours of its receipt, and the application granted. Later, at leisure, the Court of Appeal was able to give due consideration to the principles involved, and ruled that the woman's rights were paramount: the fact that her decision seemed unreasonable or bizarre was of no relevance. However, the Court of Appeal ruling was too late for the outcome to be changed.

Fig. 3 *Lord Falconer, the final traditional Lord Chancellor*

 Key terms

Retrospective law-making: all judge-made law is necessarily retrospective; statute law is only occasionally retrospective; the War Crimes Act 1991 is such an example.

Key cases

Jackson v Horizon Holidays Ltd (1975): a remedy was provided to a claimant and to his family when their holiday had failed to live up to its advertised description, even though the claimant was the only member of his family to have contracted with the travel agent.

Re S (1996): a declaration of the law by a higher court may arrive too late to prevent an injustice occurring.

You should now be able to:

■ understand the constitutional relationship between Parliament and the judiciary

■ provide a balanced discussion of the arguments for and against the exercise of judicial creativity.

In this topic you will learn how to:

■ identify what material questions on judicial creativity require

■ provide the required range of information and discussion.

4 Answering questions on the topic of judicial creativity

Questions on judicial creativity are centred on judicial precedent and statutory interpretation, two topics covered in Unit 1. However, the descriptive elements concentrated upon at AS merely provide the context for a more sophisticated level of discussion at A2.

Knowledge is needed of the operation of judicial precedent, and of the rules of statutory interpretation, with a range of appropriate examples to illustrate the points being made. Areas of flexibility within each of these processes should be identified and explained, with some evaluation of the significance and importance of each. Where possible, draw the illustrative material from across the syllabus, and not merely from one area of substantive law. It should be possible to reach a coherent judgment about the extent to which judges are able to develop the law within the parameters set for them.

The most challenging and interesting part of the topic is the discussion of the relationship between the judiciary on the one hand, and the legislature (Parliament) on the other. There is plenty of recent material upon which to draw to illustrate the tensions that exist here. Students should also be able to provide a thoughtful, balanced discussion of the arguments for and against judicial creativity.

This discussion should be informed by judicial comments taken from the judgments in cases, and by the opinions of academics. It is essential to be able to support this discussion with illustrative material, and to demonstrate how this material is relevant to the question being addressed.

Those responsible for setting the question are keen to avoid the situation where you simply write out prepared answers. Although these may score highly on Assessment Objective 1 (knowledge and understanding), they are unlikely to score highly on Assessment Objective 2 (evaluation). To gain one of the higher grades, you need to be able to consider carefully the particular nuance, or shade of meaning, contained within the question. You will have most success if you take time to reflect on the wording of the question, and identify the particular issue being raised. Five or ten minutes spent in this way before embarking on the answer will usually be well rewarded. The same is true for all the essay titles.

For example, the June 2007 question paper contained the following question: 'Critically assess the extent to which judges can display creativity in developing and interpreting common law and statutory rules.'

A sound answer would probably contain the following elements:

1   A brief explanation of the operation of the doctrine of judicial precedent; consideration of areas of flexibility, e.g. distinguishing, overruling, and the House of Lords Practice Statement; evaluation of the extent of creativity, possibly including reference to restrictive factors as part of the discussion.

2   A brief explanation of the approaches to statutory interpretation; consideration of how flexibility is afforded, e.g. the choice of approach to follow, the availability of external aids; evaluation of the extent of creativity, including reference to factors that limit creativity.

The essay would certainly contain detailed reference to cases, and would benefit from the introduction of some theory such as the opinions of academics (e.g. Llewellyn) and/or of judges (e.g. Viscount Simonds).

It would then conclude with an overall assessment of the question, where personal judgment would predominate.

Activities

Consider the different issues that you might address in these two past questions on this topic.

1   Consider the extent to which a judge can develop the law through the operation of the doctrine of judicial precedent **and** by different approaches to statutory interpretation. (June 2006)

2   Write a critical analysis of the role of judges in interpreting and developing both the common law *and* statutory rules. (June 2004)

You should now be able to:

■   understand what is required in an essay on the topic of judicial creativity.

Introduction

The notion of fault conveys a range of distinct thoughts. Firstly, it can indicate a blemish or imperfection, such as a small scar on the human face, or a character weakness. Secondly, it can refer to an error or failing, such as a miscalculation in an arithmetical problem. Thirdly, it can denote an offence or wrongdoing. This would include offences such as theft in criminal law, and negligence in civil law. Fourthly, the term is used to describe the idea of culpability or blameworthiness, in other words the responsibility borne by a person for committing an offence. It is in this last sense that the term is generally used within this topic. We are concerned with the relationship between two distinct elements: the first is the degree of responsibility or culpability that people have for their actions; the second is their liability under the law. The topic examines the extent to which a person's liability under the law is dependent upon his being 'at fault', i.e. blameworthy or culpable.

1 Liability depending upon fault

Criminal law

In criminal law there is a general presumption that liability is based upon fault. This is consistent with our sense of justice: individuals should not be held liable for a criminal offence unless they are to some extent blameworthy, or at fault. The *mens rea* of a criminal offence is often thought to be the fault element, since it examines the state of mind of the defendant at the time of committing the offence. Generally speaking it is what is in a person's mind that distinguishes between a mere accident and a criminal offence. For example, breaking another's collarbone in a game of rugby will not normally incur criminal liability. However, breaking another's collarbone with an iron bar inside his home is probably a premeditated act, carried out with intention, and therefore rendering the offender liable for a conviction under s18 of the Offences against the Person Act. The injury is the same: conviction depends upon the state of mind.

The *actus reus* and *mens rea* are not entirely disconnected concepts, as the *actus reus* may also contain elements of fault. As with *mens rea*, these elements also relate to the level of responsibility the defendant has for the outcome. Thus, there is a general rule that the *actus reus* must be voluntary, that it was willed by the defendant. Secondly, in result crimes, the defendant must have caused the outcome.

A voluntary actus reus

The *actus reus* of the offence must be voluntary: in other words the defendant must be in control of his actions. For example, a waiter might suffer a sudden sneezing fit and spill hot tea over a customer, or a crash of thunder might startle a child causing him to step back and knock over an old woman. Or, to use the example quoted in **Hill v Baxter (1958)**, a driver might be attacked by a swarm of bees, and crash. In all of these examples, the *actus reus* would be involuntary as the defendant had no control over his conduct. He would not be regarded as being at fault. As a result, there would be no liability.

In this topic you will learn how to:

■ explain elements of criminal law where there is a close relationship between fault and liability

■ explain elements of civil law where there is a close relationship between fault and liability.

AQA Examiner's tip

In your essay you are not expected to introduce material from crime, and tort and contract. Concentrate on the areas you have studied in depth.

Key terms

Voluntary *actus reus*: voluntariness requires that the defendant is in control of his actions at the time of committing the *actus reus* of the offence. It has nothing to do with *mens rea*.

Key cases

Hill v Baxter (1958): Lord Goddard restated the general principle that no criminal liability is incurred unless the *actus reus* is voluntary.

Causation in result crimes

In result crimes the defendant will not be criminally liable if he did not in fact cause the outcome. In the case of *R* v *White* (1910), the victim died from natural causes rather than from the poison fed to her by her son. Although morally reprehensible, White was not the cause of his mother's death. Contrast this with *R* v *Pagett* (1983): here the defendant started the sequence of events that led directly to the death of his girlfriend. He was responsible for her death, and therefore held liable.

Nor will the defendant be liable unless he was responsible in law for the outcome. Where the chain of causation is broken, the defendant ceases to incur liability. In *R* v *Jordan* (1956) the victim was recovering from his stab wound when he was given 'palpably wrong' treatment by doctors. He died from the treatment, not the original injury. Jordan therefore was not responsible for his death, and so his conviction was overturned. In *R* v *Smith* (1959), however, the victim died directly from the original injury: the appalling medical treatment did not break the chain of causation. Smith was therefore held responsible for his victim's death. In this way, causation maintains the link between fault and liability.

Defences

The availability of defences recognises that the defendant may have committed the *actus reus* of an offence, with the appropriate *mens rea*, but still not be blameworthy. This may arise where he uses reasonable force to defend an innocent third party, or where the victim has consented to, or even requested, the harm caused. In recent years the courts have developed duress of circumstances, enabling defendants to escape liability where they reasonably believe that they face imminent death or serious injury if they do not commit the offence. In *Abdul-Hussain* (1999) the defendants were all Shiite Muslims who had escaped Iraq because of fears of persecution. They had fled to the Sudan, but were afraid of being sent back to Iraq. They therefore hijacked a plane and forced it to land at London. They had the required *mens rea* for the offence. Nevertheless, the Court of Appeal allowed the defence of duress because of the 'peril of death' which impelled the men to act as they did.

Partial defences

Conviction for murder requires proof of intention. However, there are degrees of culpability, and these are reflected in the availability of special defences for murder, that, if successful, will reduce conviction to manslaughter.

Under diminished responsibility the defendant seeks to rely upon an abnormality of mind that substantially impairs his mental responsibility for his conduct. In the case of *Byrne* (1960), the defendant had strangled a woman and mutilated her body. Evidence that he was a sexual psychopath who could exercise little control over his actions was adjudged to be an abnormality of mind. This reduced his responsibility for his behaviour, and allowed a corresponding reduction in liability.

Under provocation the defendant seeks to rely upon the fact that he was provoked beyond reasonable endurance. The defence was successful in *Humphreys* (1995): the defendant had been subjected to prolonged provocation that was cumulative in its effect. This reduced her culpability, allowing a conviction for manslaughter instead of murder, and enabling the judge to impose a sentence that fairly reflected her degree of blame.

Mens rea *is generally required for criminal offences*

Mens rea is an essential element of all serious criminal offences. Unless the offence is one of strict liability, the absence of *mens rea* will secure an

---

AQA Examiner's tip

Using the facts of two contrasting cases (e.g. Pagett and White; or Jordan and Smith) can help to clarify a point.

Key terms

Partial defences: where a defendant succeeds with a partial defence, he does not escape liability altogether. For example, a successful plea of provocation reduces murder to manslaughter.

acquittal. In *R* v *Clarke* (1972) a woman transferred some items from her shopping basket into her own bag before paying for them. She was able to show that she suffered from absent-mindedness due to depression. She therefore lacked *mens rea* for theft.

A person cannot be convicted of serious criminal offences without proof of either intention or subjective recklessness. Generally, the more blameworthy the offence, the higher the degree of *mens rea* that is required. In other words, crimes are graduated according to the level of fault. So, grievous bodily harm under s18, with a possible life sentence, requires proof of intention to cause serious harm, whereas s20, with a maximum of five years imprisonment, requires either intention or recklessness, and only as to causing some harm.

Some recent decisions of the House of Lords have emphasised the need for subjectivity in deciding the appropriate degree of fault needed for criminal liability. Think of *B* v *DPP* (2000), and *R* v *(Morgan) Smith* (2000). In *R* v *G and R* the House of Lords reintroduced subjective recklessness as the appropriate alternative to intention for the *mens rea* of criminal damage. This judgment ensures that liability is based upon fault, and will avoid the obvious injustice caused by cases such as *Elliott* v *C* (1983). Here, a 14-year-old girl of low intelligence began to play with matches and white spirit in a neighbour's shed. Unwittingly she set fire to the shed. She was clearly incapable of appreciating the risk of fire created by her conduct. Nobody would consider her to be at fault. And yet liability was imposed, as the risk was obvious to a reasonable man.

R v *G and R* (2003) is also relevant to the topic of precedent within the chapter on judicial creativity.

Sentencing

In most cases judges are free to impose a sentence that fairly reflects the culpability of the defendant. For example, two defendants may have been separately convicted of grievous bodily harm under s20 of the Offences Against the Person Act 1861. The first may have been racially provoked, have acted on the spur of the moment, and without a weapon. Further, it may be his first offence, for which he has shown remorse, been cooperative with the police and pleaded guilty. The second may have been part of a gang on the lookout for causing trouble, have hit his victim repeatedly and left him unconscious in the street. He may have previous convictions for similar offences, and threatened his victim with further violence later. Such **aggravating and mitigating factors** reflect the different levels of blameworthiness of the two defendants. This will in turn be reflected in the sentence passed on each: the sentence should match the crime.

Sometimes, however, judges are obliged to pass a particular sentence. This is particularly true for murder, where the life sentence is mandatory. Even here, though, judges enjoy certain flexibility: they are required to impose a tariff which the murderer should serve, ranging from a minimum of fourteen years to actual life. This range will allow judges to match the length of sentence to the particular circumstances of the offence. In practice, serial killers such as Peter Sutcliffe and Steve Wright, receive an actual life sentence; serious killers using firearms may receive 30 years; most domestic murderers, by contrast will receive nearer the minimum.

Civil law

Civil law is concerned with weighing the interests of the two parties to the action and, where appropriate, providing the most suitable remedy. As a general rule, liability will only be imposed where a party is at fault.

AQA Examiner's tip

The issues raised in *Elliott* v *C* (1983) are relevant to a number of other Concepts of law topics, for example Judicial creativity and Law and justice. If using it elsewhere, tailor the discussion to fit the context.

Key terms

Aggravating and mitigating factors: aggravating factors are likely to increase the severity of the sentence; mitigating factors to reduce it.

Admittedly, the courts often require the wisdom of Solomon to decide which of the competing parties is more, or less, to blame and hence where to impose liability. In *Lewis* v *Averay* (1971) a student (Lewis) sold a car to a man masquerading as the famous actor Richard Greene. He accepted a cheque for the car, but by the time he discovered that the cheque had bounced, the car had already been sold to a third party (Averay) for cash. The only remaining item of value was the car, which both victims of the same crook claimed was rightfully his. Whoever won, the other party would feel justifiably aggrieved. Fortunately, most cases present fewer dilemmas in identifying the more, or less, culpable party.

Lewis v *Averay* (1971) is also relevant to the issue of 'mistaken identity' in Chapter 24, Balancing conflicting interests.

The tort of negligence

For liability to be established in the tort of negligence, three tests must be satisfied. Firstly, the defendant must owe a duty of care to the claimant. **Caparo v Dickman (1990)** set out three requirements for this: the harm must be reasonably foreseeable; there must be a close relationship between defendant and victim, and it must be fair and just to do so. In *Bourhill* v *Young* (1943), a pregnant woman heard a motorcyclist crash. She hurried to the scene to view the aftermath. On her arrival she witnessed such a traumatic sight that she suffered a miscarriage. She sued the dead motorcyclist's estate. It was decided that the defendant did not owe a duty of care to the claimant: he could not reasonably have foreseen the likelihood of the outcome which occurred, nor was there a close relationship between the claimant and defendant.

Secondly, the defendant must fall below the standard of the reasonable man. In *Blyth* v *Birmingham Waterworks* (1856) it was stated: 'Negligence is the omission to do something which a reasonable man would do, or doing something which a prudent and reasonable man would not.' When deciding how the reasonable man would have behaved, the court will consider the size of the risk he was taking, the practicality of taking precautions, the likelihood of serious harm, and the social value of his activity. In **Bolton v Stone (1951)**, the defendants had taken all reasonable precautions and the likelihood of the harm occurring was minuscule. As a result, they could not be considered blameworthy, and so were not liable to Miss Stone for the injury she had sustained.

Thirdly, the defendant must be the factual and the legal cause of the damage. In **Barnett v Kensington and Chelsea Hospital (1969)** a man died from arsenic poisoning. His widow claimed compensation against the hospital because the doctor had failed to treat her husband with due care. Her claim failed: it was the arsenic, not the doctor's breach, which killed her husband. Even if the doctor had acted properly, he could not have saved the man. Thus, liability will only be imposed where the defendant caused the outcome. Even where the defendant was the initial link in the chain, liability will not be imposed unless the type of harm suffered was reasonably foreseeable (*The Wagon Mound* (1961)).

Award of damages in negligence

Damages are compensatory: they are intended to restore the claimant to his pre-tort position, in so far as money can achieve this. Thus, liability is closely linked to the extent of harm caused. However, where the defendant contributes to his own harm, there will be a corresponding reduction in the award granted to him to reflect his own share of responsibility. This occurred in *Jebson* v *Ministry of Defence* (2000). A soldier had been in town drinking. At the end of the evening he rang the barracks asking for a lift. A driver was sent with an open-backed van. The claimant fell out of the back of the van and was hurt. The driver clearly owed a duty of care to his passengers. However, in the circumstances,

> ### Key cases
>
> **Caparo v Dickman (1990)**: this case established the modern three-part test for establishing duty of care in the tort of negligence.
>
> **Bolton v Stone (1951)**: where the defendant has taken reasonable precautions against a small risk, he will not be in breach of his duty of care.
>
> **Barnett v Kensington and Chelsea Hospital (1969)**: even the most serious breach of duty will escape liability if the defendant did not in fact cause the damage suffered by the claimant.

it was reasonable to reduce the payment because of the significant contribution made by the defendant to his own injuries.

The opposite may also arise: if the defendant has been particularly contemptuous, **exemplary damages** may be awarded. In *Treadaway* v *Chief Constable of West Midlands* (1994) the claimant had been tortured by the police into making a confession to a crime, and subsequently sentenced to 15 years. Exemplary damages were awarded against the police, as they had shown total disregard for the law. These rules seek to ensure that the actual compensation paid properly reflects the fault of the parties.

Occupiers' liability

Under the Occupiers' Liability Acts 1957 and 1984 an occupier owes a duty of care to lawful visitors and trespassers respectively. His liability depends upon his failure to take proper precautions to ensure their safety. In *Cotton* v *Derbyshire Dales DC* (1994) a walker was injured after falling from a path running along the top of a dangerous cliff. There were no signs to warn of the danger. In this case there was no liability, as the risk was obvious to any visitor exercising reasonable care: there was no need for the council to take any further steps to alert visitors to the danger.

By way of contrast, in **British Railways Board v Herrington (1972)** a six-year-old boy had stepped over a damaged fence and walked onto an electrified railway line. He suffered severe burns and injuries. The British Railways Board had known of the damaged fence, but had failed to take steps to prevent trespassers entering onto the line. They were therefore held liable for the injuries suffered by the boy.

Misrepresentation in contract law

A misrepresentation is an untrue statement of fact made by one party to the contract which induced the other party to enter into the contract. Sometimes statements are recognised as no more than advertising slogans, and so do not create liability. This occurred in *Dimmock* v *Hallett* (1866), where land was described as 'fertile and improvable'. By contrast, where an opinion is regarded as authoritative and reliable, any falsehood it contains will be considered a misrepresentation. In *Smith* v *Land and House Property* (1884) a tenant was described by the defendant as 'most desirable'. In fact the tenant was completely unreliable. As this misrepresentation was relied upon by the other party, it was actionable.

Generally silence will not amount to misrepresentation. In **Fletcher v Krell (1973)** a governess was not guilty of misrepresentation when she failed to inform her employer at interview that she had previously been married, a fact which would at that time have jeopardised her chances of being appointed to the post. This seems fair: why should she volunteer information that is not sought? However, liability will be imposed for silence where there is a deliberate attempt to conceal an important fact. This occurred in *With* v *O'Flanagan* (1936): a doctor failed to disclose to a prospective purchaser the tumbling value of his medical practice due to illness. In this case the doctor knew that his original statement about the value of his practice was now untrue, yet he allowed it to stand. Clearly the law is right to hold him liable, as he is responsible for misleading the prospective purchaser.

Breach of contract

A major term in a contract is known as a condition. A minor term is known as a warranty. Where a condition is breached, the other party can either treat the contract as over (known as repudiation) or sue for damages. Where a warranty is breached, the other party may only sue for damages. The fairness of this distinction is well illustrated by two similar cases. In **Poussard v Spiers and Pond (1876)** the lead singer (the claimant) fell ill and missed the rehearsals and four performances. The defendant was entitled to treat the contract as over: the claimant had failed to fulfil the main part of her contract – the performances. In **Bettini v Gye (1876)** the claimant missed the rehearsals through illness, but recovered in time for the performances. This was merely a breach of a warranty which could be settled by the payment of damages.

In *Poussard* the degree of fault on the part of the claimant was significantly higher than that in *Bettini*. Therefore, the extent of legal liability was correspondingly higher, with repudiation of the contract available as a remedy, and not merely the award of damages. This illustrates a close correspondence between fault and liability.

Activities

1. Compile a list of those recently convicted of murder. Identify the minimum tariff given to each. What are the distinguishing features that account for the range in the sentences given?

2. Consider how the House of Lords emphasised the need for subjectivity in criminal liability in their decisions in *B v DPP* (2000); *R v (Morgan) Smith* (2000); and *R v G and R* (2002).

You should now be able to:

■ explain and illustrate the idea of fault-based liability.

2 Liability not depending upon fault

There are many areas where a person can be held liable, in both criminal and civil law, even though he does not appear to have been at fault. At first sight this seems to be a dreadful injustice, but often other considerations are adjudged to outweigh the interests of the individual involved.

Criminal law

Liability for negligence

Negligence occurs where a person falls below the standard of a reasonable man. This is an objective test that takes no account of the state of mind of the defendant. It occurs in the criminal offence of gross negligence manslaughter. In **R v Adomako (1995)**, an anaesthetist was in charge of an operation on a detached retina. One of the tubes supplying oxygen to the patient became disconnected. Adomako took six minutes to notice this. The patient suffered cardiac arrest and later died. At Adomako's trial, medical experts said that a competent anaesthetist would have noticed the disconnected tube within 15 seconds, and that his failure to do so was abysmal. However, the fact that the defendant can be found liable without intention or recklessness is partially mitigated by the fact that he can only be liable where he owes a duty of care to his victim, the negligence is gross, and there is a risk of death.

The mens rea of ss20 and 47 under the OAPA 1861

The *mens rea* for inflicting grievous bodily harm under s20 of the Offences against the Person Act is intention or recklessness to cause some harm. No *mens rea* is needed for the grievous (serious) harm that results: the defendant doesn't require *mens rea* for the critical element of

In this topic you will learn how to:

■ explain elements of criminal law where there is not a close relationship between fault and liability

■ explain elements of civil law where there is not a close relationship between fault and liability.

Key cases

R v Adomako (1995): where the defendant owes a duty of care, he may be criminally liable for manslaughter where he causes the death of someone as a result of gross negligence.

Fig. 1 *The case of* Harrow LBC *v* Shah *(1999) involved an employee in a corner shop selling a lottery ticket to a minor*

the offence. Similarly with s47: the *mens rea* is intention or recklessness for assault or battery. No additional *mens rea* is needed for the resulting harm. As a result, a person can be convicted of actual bodily harm even though he didn't even see the risk of causing harm (*Savage* (1992)). In both ss20 and 47 the *mens rea* is therefore relatively easily satisfied. The Law Commission has recognised the injustice this may cause, and recommended replacing these two offences with reckless serious injury, and intentional or reckless injury respectively. This would establish a closer relationship between fault and liability.

Strict liability offences

Some offences (offences of **strict liability**) require no *mens rea* for at least one of the elements of the *actus reus*. Liability is thereby imposed without the need for fault on the part of the defendant. These tend to be regulatory offences, dealing with matters of social concern, such as food hygiene (*Smedleys Ltd* v *Breed* (1974)), pollution of the environment (*Alphacell Ltd* v *Woodward* (1972)), and selling alcohol, cigarettes, lottery tickets, etc. to under-age children (*Harrow LBC* v *Shah* (1999)). In cases which are truly criminal, however, *mens rea* is required (*Sweet* v *Parsley* (1970)).

In *Gammon (HK) Ltd* v *Attorney-General of Hong Kong* (1985), Lord Scarman spoke of a presumption in favour of *mens rea*. As noted earlier, the House of Lords has, in recent years, promoted subjectivity in criminal law. In other words, it is increasingly looking for the element of fault in the part of the defendant. In *B* v *DPP* (2000), a 15-year-old boy was convicted under the Indecency with Children Act 1960 of inciting a 14-year-old girl to commit an act of gross indecency with him. She had refused. There was no mention of *mens rea* in the Act. The Divisional Court ruled that no *mens rea* was required with regard to the age of the girl. The House of Lords, however, decided that *mens rea* was required for this element of the offence, emphasising the link between fault and liability.

Absolute liability offences

We saw earlier the requirement that the *actus reus* be voluntary. However, where there is **absolute liability**, this requirement is waived: the defendant may be convicted even though he had no control over his conduct. The case of *R* v *Larsonneur* (1933) concerned a French woman. When her permission to remain in the UK expired on 22 March, she travelled to Ireland. However, she was refused entry and brought back to Britain by the Irish police. On arrival she was charged under the Aliens' Order 1920 with being 'an alien to whom leave to land in the United Kingdom had been refused'. The Court of Appeal decided that she had been rightly convicted, even though she had been brought into the country by force against her will.

A similar situation arose in *Winzar* v *Chief Constable of Kent* (1983). The defendant, who was drunk, was escorted out of a hospital by the police and then promptly arrested for 'being found drunk on the highway' contrary to s12 of the Licensing Act 1872. Clearly the *actus reus* was involuntary: the police had placed him on the highway. Some may argue that Larsonneur gave insufficient thought to whether she would be allowed entry into the Republic of Ireland, and Winzar was reckless in becoming drunk, thereby exposing himself to the risk of committing criminal offences. However, imposing liability for involuntary acts forced upon the defendants by the police seems particularly distasteful.

Typical examples of absolute liability offences are: being in possession of drugs, firearms and explosive substances.

People with good motives

Sometimes a person will be convicted of a criminal offence even where his motives are considered morally blameless. Think of Robin Hood, who stole from the rich to give to the poor. His motives might have been good, yet he still had the *mens rea* for theft. This is because a distinction exists between legal liability, which Robin Hood certainly had, and moral culpability, which some would argue he lacked. In some people's view the case of *R v Cox* (1992) also illustrates this distinction. Cox, a doctor, was asked by an elderly, terminally ill woman to end her life painlessly. He did so, but was then convicted of attempted murder. (He could not be charged with murder as the body had been cremated and there was no evidence to prove that his injection had caused her death.) Many might regard his actions as praiseworthy, yet he still had the necessary *mens rea* for attempted murder. Presumably the judge had considerable sympathy for him as he suspended his prison sentence.

Fig. 2 *Robin Hood's motives might have been good, yet he still had the* mens rea *for theft!*

Civil law

Strict liability

Strict liability also operates in tort. The best example of this is **Rylands v Fletcher (1868)**. In this famous case a landowner decided to build a reservoir on his land. The contractors failed to seal the entrances to some disused mine shafts. When the land was flooded, water escaped through these shafts and into the claimant's mine. In this case, no proof of fault is needed: not even negligence is required on the part of the defendant. In the words of Lord Cranworth, he is liable 'however careful he may have been and whatever precautions he may have taken'.

Vicarious liability

Vicarious liability arises where one person is liable for the tort of another. This usually occurs in the field of employment: the employer may be liable for the torts of his employees, even where he has taken all reasonable steps to prevent their misconduct. In *Limpus v London Omnibus Co.* (1862) a driver of the defendants' bus company deliberately drove across the path of a rival company's bus, causing it to topple over. Although the bus company had issued strict instructions to its drivers not to drive dangerously, it was still held responsible for the damage caused. As a result even the most cautious employer may find himself liable to pay damages for the wilful misconduct of his employees.

The employer will only escape liability where the employee was engaged in a 'frolic' of his own. In *Twine v Bean's Express* (1946) the driver had ignored his employer's instructions and given a lift to a hitchhiker. The employer was not liable for the driver's subsequent negligent driving, as it was outside the scope of his employment.

Key cases

Rylands v Fletcher (1868): the original rule in this case is: 'the person who for his own purposes brings on his lands and collects and keeps there anything likely to do mischief if it escapes, must keep it at his peril, and, if he does not do so, is answerable for all the damage which is the natural consequence of its escape.'

Key terms

Vicarious liability: the defendant is liable for the wrongdoing of another person for whom he is responsible.

AQA Examiner's tip

The ability to discuss the rationale for the different outcomes in *Limpus* and *Twine* will provide useful evaluation of this topic.

Negligence

The standard of care required in the tort of negligence is that of the reasonable man. This is a purely objective test, and does not make allowances for the particular circumstances of the individual. In **Nettleship v Weston (1971)** a learner was judged against the standard of the competent driver: inexperience is no defence. This seems harsh, but is justified on the ground that the driver is insured and therefore should bear the responsibility. The relationship between liability and fault is rather tenuous here..

The relationship between liability and fault is similarly tenuous under the 'thin-skull rule'. In *Smith* v *Leech Brain* (1962) an employee was scalded on the lip by molten metal. The burn was not severe, but it triggered a dormant cancer and he died. The burn was a foreseeable injury, but the death was not. Nevertheless the company, which had been negligent, was liable for all the consequential harm suffered by the victim due to any particular vulnerability of his. This has the potential for unlimited liability: a small act of negligence may result in extensive unforeseeable damage.

Contract: the postal rule

In contract law the court often has to decide between two apparently innocent parties. When it finds in favour of one party, it does not necessarily regard the other party as blameworthy. For example, under the postal rule an offer is accepted as soon as the letter of acceptance is posted. *Household Insurance* v *Grant* (1879) confirmed that this is true even if the letter never arrives. Suppose that Stanley offers to sell his bicycle to Oliver. Two days later Oliver posts a letter accepting this offer, but it never arrives. Three weeks later, thinking that Oliver isn't interested in the bicycle, Stanley sells it to someone else. Do you think that Oliver has a right to claim damages? What could Stanley have done to protect himself in such circumstances?

Contract: unilateral mistake

Earlier in this chapter, reference was made to *Lewis* v *Averay* (1971). This case was decided following the legal principle set in **Phillips v Brooks (1919)**, a case which involved a crook called North. Posing as Sir George Bullough, North entered Phillips' shop and persuaded him to accept a cheque as payment for a ring. By the time Phillips discovered that the cheque was valueless, the ring had been sold for cash to the defendant, Brooks. The court was asked to consider who owned the ring.

Both parties were innocent victims of the same crook. Neither was morally blameworthy. And yet the ring could only be awarded to one of them. In examining the initial dealings between Phillips and the crook, Horridge J referred to the reasoning of a judge in an American case: 'The minds of the parties met and agreed upon all the terms of the sale, the thing sold, the price and time of payment, the person selling and the person buying ... it does not defeat the sale because the buyer assumed a false name.'

The contract between Phillips and the crook was therefore binding. If the ring had not passed to a third party, Phillips would be entitled to its return. However, as it had been sold on, it belonged to Brooks. It could be argued that Phillips was in some measure at fault for not ensuring the identity and creditworthiness of the man before him. Yet, in reality he was an innocent man who had done no wrong. Nevertheless, the court decided against him. However, the court didn't regard him as culpable: rather it simply found in favour of the other party.

Consumer Protection Act 1987

This Act places strict liability upon a producer for death, personal injury or property damage over £275 suffered by a consumer as a result of a defective product. However, the harshness imposed by strict liability is mitigated by certain defences which are available under the Act, including the producer not being in business; the defect not existing at the time of manufacture; and the fact that the defect could not have been discovered under scientific or technical knowledge existing at the time.

Activities

1 Consider the use of implied malice in the *mens rea* of murder. Does it necessarily reflect a close relationship between fault and liability? How do the Law Commission proposals on homicide deal with implied malice for murder?

2 Consider the case of the terrorist who plants a small bomb in a busy shopping centre. He issues a warning to the police, but the bomb explodes prematurely, killing a policeman who was evacuating the centre. The terrorist will argue that he was trying to attract publicity for his cause, and not wanting to harm anyone, hence the warning. Most people would accept that he is morally more culpable than the defendant in *Cox* (1992). But does he have the *mens rea* for murder?

You should now be able to:

- explain and illustrate the idea of non fault-based liability.

3 Should liability depend upon fault?

Arguments in support of liability not based upon fault

The arguments supporting no-fault liability may be summarised under the following three points:

1 Sometimes no-fault liability is essential in order to protect the public interest.

2 Individuals bear responsibility for the consequences of their actions.

3 It encourages businesses and property owners to exercise greater vigilance.

The public interest

The law seeks to protect and promote the wider interests of the public, and sometimes these are given priority over the requirement for fault in individual offenders.

Many strict liability offences concern the running of businesses. In **Smedleys v Breed (1974)** the producers of tinned vegetables were held liable for the presence of a caterpillar in a tin of peas. The House of Lords ruled that there was no defence of reasonable care: liability was strict. A similar principle operated in *Alphacell Ltd v Woodward* (1972), another criminal case, and in *Rylands v Fletcher* (1866), a tort case. Underpinning these decisions is a presumption that those who run a business must be prepared to accept the risks, as well as the benefits, associated with that business. This argument is also used to justify vicarious liability: just as an employer profits from the activity of his employee, so he should accept any risks. Additionally, businesses and employers are in a stronger

In this topic you will learn how to:

- discuss arguments in support of non fault-based liability and fault-based liability.

Key cases

Smedleys v Breed (1974): in the interests of public health, producers will be held liable for contaminated food, even where all possible precautions were taken.

Link

For a different discussion of public interest, look at Chapter 24, Balancing conflicting interests.

Key cases

Sweet v Parsley (1970): where an offence is 'truly criminal', *mens rea* is more likely to be required.

Rylands v Fletcher (1868): a landowner will be held liable for the damage caused by the escape of a substance which he has stored on his land.

financial position either to insure against the risk or to meet claims made against them. This promotes a better level of protection for innocent members of the public.

Serious criminal offences require not only evidence of *mens rea* (and the more serious the offence the higher the level of *mens rea* that is generally required), but also proof beyond reasonable doubt. In this way the interests of the defendant are protected. However, the imposition of strict liability for less serious crimes may be justified on the ground that the public interest weighs heavily in the scales of justice. The public has an interest, for example, in road safety, in preventing pollution, in maintaining reasonable standards of hygiene and in protecting children from the dangers associated with alcohol, smoking and gambling. It is argued that these public interests are better served by restricting liability to questions of fact (Was the driver speeding? Did the pollutant material come from the factory? Was the meat infected? Was the customer under age?), which are relatively straightforward to prove, and avoiding questions concerning the mental element of the offender.

Additionally, no-fault offences tend to attract less serious penalties. Offences such as polluting the environment (*Alphacell Ltd* v *Woodward*), producing contaminated food (*Smedleys Ltd* v *Breed* (1974)), creating a public nuisance (*Shorrock* (1994)), and possession of cannabis (*Marriot* (1971)) are more likely to lead to fines than to custodial sentences. The guidelines issued by Lord Scarman in *Gammon (HK) Ltd* v *Attorney-General of Hong Kong* (1985) also point out that the presumption in favour of the need for *mens rea* is particularly strong in 'truly criminal' offences, these presumably being offences where the defendant is liable to be given a custodial sentence. **Sweet v Parsley (1970)** illustrates this point: the appellant's conviction was overturned by the House of Lords: the offence was so serious that *mens rea* should be required.

Strict and vicarious liability make it far less likely that an innocent victim will be left without a remedy in the courts. Supporters of no-fault liability argue that to leave a victim without a remedy is a greater injustice than to penalise a blameless defendant. For example, in *Limpus* v *London General Omnibus Co.* (1862), it was preferable to provide a remedy to the innocent claimant than to allow the equally innocent employer to escape liability for the wrongdoing of his employee. In **Rylands v Fletcher (1868)** it was preferable to grant the mine owners a remedy than to allow the landowner, albeit innocent, to escape liability for the harm he had caused.

For many strict liability offences, for example speeding, it would be almost impossible to prove a mental element in order to secure a conviction. Moreover, without vicarious liability, it would often be difficult to secure compensation because of difficulties in identifying the offending employee. No-fault liability clearly overcomes these problems. Where the claimant doesn't have to prove fault, the outcome of a claim is more predictable; and this in turn encourages defendants to admit their responsibility, thereby saving court time and costs. These are significant advantages.

Individual responsibility

There is a biblical principle that 'we reap what we sow'. No-fault liability promotes this principle in criminal and civil law. Strict liability in criminal law holds individuals or businesses responsible for the harm they cause, even where they are unaware of it. In *R* v *Howells* (1997) the defendant had failed to obtain a firearms certificate for his gun, falsely believing it was an antique and therefore not requiring a certificate. As an individual choosing to possess a gun, it is his responsibility to ensure that he complies with the necessary regulations. His failure to do so makes him guilty: what he believes is irrelevant.

We saw earlier that the *mens rea* for occasioning actual bodily harm is intention or recklessness for the assault or battery: no additional *mens rea* is required for the harm caused. This may seem harsh. However, examination of the facts of *R v Savage* (1992) from the victim's perspective may soften this view. The victim would no doubt believe that the law should hold individuals responsible for the harm they actually cause, and therefore expect that her assailant be punished for the cuts to her wrist (actual bodily harm) as well as for the soaking (battery).

Civil law also provides evidence of the principle of **individual responsibility**. In *Rose v Plenty* (1976) a milkman allowed a 13-year-old boy to assist him with his round, even though this was expressly forbidden by his employer. When the child was injured due to the milkman's negligence, the employer was held liable: he bore responsibility for the conduct of his employees.

Section 2(2) of the Consumer Protection Act 1987 contains a list of those who will be held strictly liable for death, personal injury or damage to property caused by a defective product. This list includes the manufacturers, those who abstract products, those involved in the production of the product, and suppliers. Any or all of these may be sued as they bear responsibility for the quality and safety of their products.

Deterrence

No-fault liability encourages higher standards of care among businessmen and property owners. In **Cundy v Le Cocq (1884)** the defendant was convicted of selling intoxicating liquor to a drunken person, contrary to the Licensing Act 1872. This verdict will encourage other landlords to exercise greater diligence when serving alcohol. In *Gammon (HK) Ltd v Attorney-General of Hong Kong* (1985) the defendants were held responsible for the collapse of part of a building, even though they were unaware that their plans were not being followed by the builders. Lord Scarman was convinced that strict liability would serve as a **deterrent**. He argued: 'Their Lordships are satisfied that strict liability would help to promote greater vigilance in the matters covered by the two offenders with which this appeal is concerned (the material deviation and the risk of injury or damage)'. In *Harrow LBC v Shah and Shah* (1999) the defendants, who were shopkeepers, were convicted of selling a lottery ticket to an under-aged boy. No doubt other shopkeepers will take greater care in the future. Sixth-form students working in supermarkets are no doubt aware of the greater vigilance being shown in selling alcohol to under-age customers.

Arguments in support of liability based upon fault

There are two broad lines of reasoning adopted by supporters of fault-based liability. First, they simply reject most of the above arguments. They deny that it better protects the public, and that its deterrent value helps to raise standards. Secondly, they argue that it is inherently unjust to impose liability without establishing fault on the part of the defendant.

Rejection of claims for no-fault liability

First of all, it is not true to say that strict liability in criminal law is restricted to offences that attract fines rather than custodial sentences. In *R v Howells* (1977) the defendant was convicted under s1 of the Firearms Act 1968, which carries a maximum penalty of five years in prison.

Secondly, no-fault liability cannot be justified merely to provide a body to compensate innocent victims. If priority should be given to ensuring that all victims of crime and tort are compensated, then it would be fairer and more efficient to introduce either wider insurance schemes or a no-fault government-sponsored compensation system. Victims will then be compensated according to their needs.

If the difficulty in establishing *mens rea* is the main argument in favour of no-fault liability, then an extension of the *res ipsa loquitur* rule, or a reversal in the burden of proof could serve as an alternative to the imposition of strict liability: there is no need to convict defendants merely on the basis of their actions.

Finally, there is little evidence to suggest that no-fault liability encourages the adoption of higher standards: how can shopkeepers or businesses prepare against unforeseeable outcomes? In **Callow v Tillstone (1900)** a butcher had some meat inspected by a vet to ensure that it was fit for human consumption. Unfortunately, the vet was negligent and passed the meat, even though it was unfit for humans. It was the butcher, though, who was convicted of exposing unsound meat for sale. Following this decision, butchers are probably less likely to have their meat inspected.

Vicarious liability is equally unlikely to promote higher standards. Where an employer has issued clear instructions to his drivers not to overtake competitors' buses (*Limpus* v *London General Omnibus Co.* (1862)), or to carry children on their milk floats (*Rose* v *Plenty* (1976)), it is hard to see how imposing liability on him will alter his employees' conduct.

Justice

The view that individuals and businesses may be held responsible for the unforeseen, or even unforeseeable, consequences of their conduct conflicts with our sense of justice and fairness. In criminal law it seems morally offensive to punish a person who is blameless, and in civil law it seems distasteful to impose liability upon a person who has taken all reasonable care to prevent an undesired outcome. This is because the notion of fault is central to people's idea of justice and fairness.

The law enforces society's rules and values. The conviction of blameless people fosters a sense of grievance within the offender, and promotes a more widespread lack of confidence in the fairness of the criminal justice system. It reflects badly upon the values of a free society that people may be punished, even deprived of their liberty, when they are morally guiltless. In **R v Storkwain (1986)**, a pharmacist was the victim of fraud: and yet he was convicted of supplying prescription drugs. People may even be convicted where the offence was procured by the police. In *Winzar* (1983), the defendant was removed by the police to the place where he was committing the offence. Even if it were true that no-fault liability offences attract only minor penalties, it is still unjustifiable that blameless people should be punished at all.

A conviction has lasting consequences: not only does the offender undergo the immediate sanction imposed by the court, but he also has to suffer society's condemnation, a point recognised in *Sweet* v *Parsley* (1970). A criminal record might act as a barrier to much employment, tarnish the offender's reputation and expose him to suspicion and prejudice. Such consequences should not have to be endured by the blameless.

Finally, one of the functions of law is to serve as a guide to behaviour, enabling people to amend their conduct to comply with society's requirements. No-fault liability does not allow for this: a defendant who has not been malicious, negligent, or even careless cannot avoid reoffending no matter how much more care or thought he applies. The pharmacist in *Storkwain* could be duped a second or even a third time by a convincingly forged prescription, but would be no more culpable than on the first occasion. The law requires public trust. This cannot be achieved where no distinction is made between the blameless and the blameworthy.

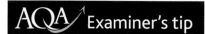

Key cases

Callow v Tillstone (1900): it is debatable whether the imposition of strict liability promotes higher standards of food hygiene.

R v Storkwain (1986): how may it be possible to justify the conviction of someone who is morally innocent of any offence?

AQA Examiner's tip

These arguments are enhanced by the inclusion of relevant illustrative material.

Activity

Make a list of the cases used in this chapter where you think that the wrong decision was reached. By looking at your reasons for criticising the decisions in these cases you will be able to work out where you stand on the issue of fault-based liability.

You should now be able to:

- understand and discuss arguments relating to fault-based and non fault-based liability.

4 Answering questions on the topic of fault

Questions on the topic of fault will inevitably require you to explore the relationship between fault and liability, and to provide some evaluation of the importance of fault in establishing liability. Usually this will require you to begin by providing some definitions of what is meant by the term 'fault'.

In providing an explanation of the relationship between fault and liability, you will be expected to provide a balanced discussion, identifying areas of fault-based and non fault-based liability. It is important that appropriate examples from the law are used throughout this part of the answer. Often you will be allowed to choose between criminal and civil law, but a more complete answer can normally be produced by reference to both areas of law. In Unit 2, both criminal and civil liability have been covered: this should provide a range of material in addition to whichever specialism has been followed at A2.

Sometimes the question will invite students to focus upon fault-based or non fault-based liability. This reduces the scope of the question. Even here, however, you might feel that you can better explain your argument by some reference to the other side of the argument. Thus, if the question was on non fault-based liability, it could still be useful to point out the general expectation of the need for fault to prove liability, supported by some illustrative material. Clearly, though, the main focus would then be on non fault-based liability.

The evaluation is often the most challenging part of the question. It will usually have a specific focus. The principal examiner setting the paper will be keen to force you to 'think on your feet', rather than to allow you to regurgitate a prepared answer. You should concentrate your arguments on a particular focus, and avoid simply repeating the whole range of arguments to which you have been exposed. Evaluation also needs to be supported by reference to relevant authority. It can be productive to develop the facts of cases to illustrate the point being made.

The topic of fault contains a lot of balanced discussion. You should show an awareness of this in your evaluation. It is not a black and white topic that lends itself to easy solutions. The arguments are complex, and involve conflicting principles. An awareness of this complexity will be reflected in the better answers.

In this topic you will learn how to:

- identify what material questions on 'fault' require

- provide the required range of information and discussion.

Activity

Consider the appropriate content for addressing the issues identified in the following question, set in June 2004.

'It is a principle of fundamental importance in English law that there should be no liability without fault.'

Consider how far fault is an essential requirement of liability in English law, and discuss the suggestion that fault should be an essential requirement.

You should now be able to:

- understand what is required in an essay on the topic of fault.

Balancing conflicting interests

In this topic you will learn how to:

- describe some theories about the nature of legal interests
- illustrate these theories with examples.

1 Theories about interests

Rudolph von Jhering

Rudolph von Jhering, a 19th-century legal theorist, regarded law as the end result of a permanent struggle between individuals and groups, each selfishly pursuing its own interests. Laws do not depend upon force of reason, but come about as a result of the relative strength of the competing parties. Jhering regarded this struggle in a positive light: it promoted healthy legal change, and prevented anarchy. This is a pragmatic interpretation of the development of the law. It recognises that not all interests can be satisfied, and that the law reflects the interests of the dominant group. If alive today, Jhering would have pointed to the considerable power of the media and of pressure groups to influence the law (for example, the Dangerous Dogs Act 1991, the Hunting Act 2004, and the Equality Act 2006).

Roscoe Pound

Roscoe Pound, an early 20th-century American judge, distinguished between individual interests, such as the right to own property and to privacy, and social interests such as public order, security and freedom of speech. He warned against balancing these interests against each other. Individual interests should only be weighed against other individual interests, and social interests likewise. Otherwise individual interests would be in danger of always being subordinated to social ones. For example, a householder may desire to grow 40 foot leylandii in his front garden in order to preserve his right to privacy. Under Pound's analysis, this should be balanced against his neighbours' right to sunlight in their garden, and not against the social interest in promoting the cultivation of indigenous trees such as oaks and elms.

Fig. 1 *A householder's desire to grow a large tree in their garden must be balanced against the neighbour's right to sunlight in his*

Wesley Hohfeld

A Professor of Law at Yale during the early 20th century, Wesley Hohfeld tried to introduce some intellectual rigour into the language used when discussing interests or rights. First he distinguished between rights and liberties. A right can be claimed as an entitlement, and can therefore be viewed as a 'claim-right': this imposes a corresponding duty on the other party to honour it. For example, if Aimee has a claim-right to freedom of speech, then Bethany has a duty to allow Aimee to exercise that right. She cannot, for example, put a gag on Aimee, or rip up all her letters to the local newspaper, or drown her opinions with deafeningly loud music. Note this point, however: the existence of a large number of rights, with their corresponding duties, limits other people's freedom to act as they choose.

A liberty (or privilege), on the other hand, is the freedom to act in the way that one chooses. It ensures that individuals have control over their choice of action. Unlike a right, a liberty enjoyed by Aimee does not impose any duties upon Bethany. For example, Aimee is at liberty to catch the number 528 bus from Rochdale to Halifax. However, if there is only one place left on this bus, Bethany is under no obligation to give up her place to Aimee. Note this point: if all legal interests were regarded as liberties rather than as rights, then there would be greater freedom of choice available to people in their legal relationships with others.

Activity

Identify the interests of the parties in the following cases. Which do you think should take priority, and why?

1. A development company built a tower block to provide office accommodation. Unfortunately this interfered with the television reception in nearby homes.

2. A doctor ran his practice from a smart London street. He later built an extension at the bottom of his garden, adjoining a factory with heavy machinery. As a result of the noise he couldn't use his new consulting rooms.

3. Bill accepted a cheque as payment for his car. When the cheque bounced he discovered that the car had been sold on for cash to Ben. Bill sued Ben for the return of the car.

4. Two sailors deserted ship. The captain promised to share their wages among the remaining crew. When the ship arrived home, he refused to pay.

You should now be able to:

■ explain and illustrate different theories about the nature of interests.

2 Balancing interests in procedural law

Throughout the criminal and civil processes an attempt is made to ensure that the parties' interests are given due consideration. This can be seen in the rules on disclosure of evidence, in the impartiality of magistrates and juries, in the opportunity for the prosecution/claimant and defendant to state their cases, and in the avenues for appeal.

Section A: The criminal justice system

Criminal law provides citizens with a code of conduct to guide their behaviour. Where individuals are accused of breaking that code, the

In this topic you will learn how to:

■ explain how the criminal and civil justice systems balance the interests of the opposing parties

■ illustrate with a suitable range of cases.

law will investigate that accusation and put it to the test. The criminal process keeps in balance the interest of society in ensuring that wrongdoing is properly dealt with, and the interest of the defendant in ensuring that any investigation, trial or sentence is properly conducted. The following examples illustrate this balancing exercise.

The right to legal advice

Under s58 of the Police and Criminal Evidence Act 1984, a person arrested and held in custody has a right to consult privately with a solicitor and to have a solicitor present during interview. The Police Code of Practice requires the custody officer to inform the suspect of this right, to issue him with a written notice with the arrangements for obtaining legal advice, and to invite him to sign the custody record to acknowledge receipt of this notice. This would be classified as a claim-right under Hohfeld's analysis as it imposes a corresponding duty upon others, particularly the custody officer.

In the case of a serious arrestable offence, access to a solicitor may be delayed for up to 36 hours. This is allowed where there are reasonable grounds for believing that contact with a solicitor will:

- lead to interference with the evidence, or interference with other people
- lead to alerting other suspects still at large
- hinder the recovery of stolen property.

The Act and the Codes of Practice strive for a fair balance between the need to enable the police to investigate crime and question suspects, and the right of suspects to be free from undue influence in an intimidating environment. Where the right to legal advice is unfairly delayed, the proper balance between the interests of the parties is temporarily lost, introducing scope for considerable injustice.

R v *Samuel* (1988) concerned a man who had been arrested and interviewed four times over two days. He was denied access to a solicitor on the ground that it would lead to the alerting of other suspects. At his fourth interview he confessed to two offences of burglary, and was charged with these. He continued to be denied access to his solicitor. He was then interviewed a fifth time, and confessed to a robbery. The Court of Appeal quashed his subsequent conviction for robbery. It described the right to legal advice as 'one of the most important and fundamental rights of a citizen'. This fired a warning shot across the bows of the police, who had acted in breach of their duty in denying the suspect his legal right.

Bail

The police and the courts perform a similar balancing of interests when deciding whether to grant **bail** to a suspect while further enquiries are made or while awaiting trial. The custody officer can refuse to grant bail if he does not have the suspect's name or address, if he doesn't believe the name or address given, or if any of the conditions of the Bail Act 1976 applies. Where bail is refused, the suspect must appear before magistrates at the first available opportunity. The magistrates will then decide whether bail should be granted. Their decision will be based on the Bail Act.

Under the Bail Act 1976, a person can be refused bail if:

- he is charged with an offence for which he could be imprisoned if found guilty, *and* the court believes that he would not turn up, commit an offence while on bail, or interfere with witnesses
- he is already serving a custodial sentence

Key terms

Bail: the conditional release of a suspect.

- he needs to be kept in prison for his own safety, or, if a juvenile, for his own welfare
- he has already been bailed during the same proceedings, but has absconded.

Where bail is granted, conditions may be attached. These include:

- sureties (a fixed payment which is forfeited if the suspect absconds)
- reporting to the local police station at regular times
- a residence order
- restrictions such as a curfew, or a ban on speaking to a certain witness.

The Act seeks to protect the right to liberty of suspects, but balances this against the need to ensure that victims are not intimidated, the public is protected, and the criminal process can operate without undue interference. Each application for bail, therefore, is determined on its merits. Bail is awarded or denied once the court has performed this balancing act.

Hearsay evidence

Once a case arrives in court, the judge must decide what evidence may be admitted. Evidence of previous convictions, for example, is generally not admissible as it is prejudicial, and is not in itself evidence that the defendant committed the offence in question. Another type of evidence generally not admitted is **hearsay evidence**. For example, Fred tells Wilma that he saw Betty hit Barney with a frying pan. Fred can give first-hand evidence in court of what he saw. But Wilma's evidence would be second-hand: it is hearsay, as she is stating what Fred told her. Traditionally the courts have barred hearsay evidence, as it prejudices the interests of the defendant, whose counsel cannot cross-examine Wilma to test the truth of her claim.

However, the Criminal Justice Act 2003 enables judges to admit hearsay evidence where the interests of justice require it. This shifts the balance between the interests of the defence and prosecution. In *Maher* v *DPP* (2006) the appellant reversed her BMW into an Astra in a supermarket car park, and drove off. An eye-witness observed the registration of the BMW and placed a note in the windscreen of the damaged vehicle. The owner of the Astra reported this to the police, who recorded it in the incident log. The original note was then lost. The prosecution was allowed to rely upon the log as evidence of the contents of the note, even though this was 'multiple' hearsay, as the information had passed through various hands before being recorded in the log.

Multiple hearsay evidence may be admitted where 'the court is satisfied that the value of the evidence in question, taking into account how reliable the statements appear to be, is so high that the interests of justice require the later statement to be admissible for that purpose'. Few, other than the appellant, would probably argue against the justice of this decision: the interests of the injured party should not be sacrificed on the altar of technical rules of court.

Sentencing

Before passing sentence, magistrates and judges consider a range of issues. These include **aggravating and mitigating factors** relating to the offence as well as to the offender. The following diagram illustrates aggravating and mitigating factors that might apply to a conviction for ABH under s47 of the OAPA 1861.

> ### Key terms
>
> **Hearsay evidence**: this is evidence contained in an out-of-court statement made by someone, and now offered in court to prove the truth of its contents.
>
> **Aggravating and mitigating factors**: aggravating factors increase the seriousness of the offence and lead to a more severe sentence; mitigating factors have the opposite effect.

Table 1 *Aggravating and mitigating factors that could relate to a conviction for ABH*

	Aggravating factors	Mitigating factors
Factors relating to the offence	1 The use of a weapon	1 Severe provocation
	2 A joint enterprise	2 Spur of the moment attack
	3 Attack racially motivated	3 Lone assailant
	4 Vulnerable victim	4 Single blow
Factors relating to the offender	1 Previous convictions	1 Early guilty plea
	2 On bail at time offence committed	2 First offence
	3 Resisting arrest	3 Show of remorse
	4 Lack of cooperation with the police	4 Offer of reparation to the victim

Where magistrates or judges fail in achieving an appropriate balance, both the defendant and the prosecution may lodge an appeal. Thus, an appropriate balance may be restored.

Section B: The civil justice system

The civil justice system seeks to ensure that those who believe that their rights have been infringed may test their claim before an impartial tribunal, and that the opposing party may reply to that claim. The claimant will seek some form of remedy, ranging from a declaration of the law, to injunctions and damages. Throughout the civil justice process, the law considers the interests of both parties to the dispute. Below are examples of how the delicate balancing act is maintained.

The burden and standard of proof

In the civil justice system the burden of proof falls upon the one who makes the assertion. This is normally the claimant. One exception arises in frustration in contract law. Here, the defendant is asserting that he couldn't carry out his obligations under the contract because of third party interference. For example, in *Taylor* v *Caldwell* (1863), the burden fell upon the defendant, Caldwell, to establish that he couldn't complete the contract because a fire had burned down the venue. This general rule, 'he who asserts must prove', treats both parties in an impartial, balanced manner.

The civil standard of proof required is 'on the balance of probabilities', or 'more probable than not'. This is easier to establish than the criminal standard of 'beyond reasonable doubt'. In May 2008, the General Medical Council adopted the civil standard of proof for its Fitness to Practise panel hearings. This tightening of control is seen as an attempt to regain public confidence in the regulatory system after the case of Harold Shipman. The British Medical Association, the body that represents the interests of doctors, opposed this change, arguing that the higher criminal standard should be used in cases where doctors are likely to lose their livelihoods. In this instance, however, the public interest in restoring public confidence in the medical profession has clearly outweighed the interests of doctors.

Contributory negligence in the award of damages in tort

Prior to 1945, a person who was partly responsible for harm done to him could not recover damages in tort. In the light of this injustice, the Law Reform (Contributory Negligence) Act 1945 was passed. This allows a claimant who contributes to his own injuries to succeed in his claim, but have his award reduced to the extent of his own contribution. For example, a passenger injured due to the driver's negligence will have his award reduced if he was not wearing a seat belt.

Jebson v *Ministry of Defence* (2000) concerned a soldier who was injured returning to camp after a night out in Portsmouth. He had fallen out of an army truck while attempting to clamber over the tailgate and onto the canvas roof. The MOD, as the provider of the vehicle and driver, did owe a duty of care to the soldier. Furthermore, since it was reasonably foreseeable that drunken soldiers might engage in dangerous activities, the defendants had breached their duty of care by not providing adequate supervision. However, in the words of Potter LJ: the claimant was 'largely the author of his own misfortune. On any view his actions were foolish and dangerous in the extreme.' As a result the Court of Appeal upheld the trial judge's ruling that the claimant should receive only 25 per cent of his award. This apportionment fairly reflected the contribution of each party to the injuries.

Activities

1 Apply the law relating to bail to the following situations:

   a Donald had badly beaten his wife, Mavis, before leaving the country. On his voluntary return two months later he handed himself over to the police, and has been charged under s20 of the OAPA 1861.

   b Angela's car ran out of fuel. As she tried to siphon some petrol from a car in a supermarket car park, she caused it to ignite. Nearly twenty cars were badly damaged, one of which had a baby sleeping in the back seat. The baby suffered minor burns. An angry crowd is waiting outside court.

2 Julie has been sentenced to three years in prison under s18 of the OAPA 1861. Provide her with written advice on whether to appeal against her sentence. The facts are as follows:

   Julie worked as a seamstress from home. She had been married for six years when her husband began a series of affairs with women from work. He twice left home, but each time Julie accepted him back. However, he became uncommunicative and violent. Whenever Julie questioned him about his late nights, he behaved threateningly towards her. This continued for over two years. One evening, while drunk, he smashed her sewing machines and threw them at her when she protested. Later that evening, when he fell asleep in an armchair, she threw a pan of boiling chip fat over him, blinding him in one eye and causing very serious burns to his face, neck and arms.

3 How would you decide how much, if any, you would deduct for contributory negligence in the following scenario?

   A lifeguard at the council baths left the pool unattended while he went outside for a cigarette. During this time Dwain ran and dived into the pool at the shallow end. He cracked his head on the floor, breaking his neck. He is now a paraplegic. Dwain had seen the warning signs and been told of the dangers by the lifeguard, but he chose to ignore this when he saw the lifeguard leave the pool.

You should now be able to:

■ explain and illustrate how opposing interests are balanced in the criminal and civil justice systems.

3 Balancing interests in substantive law

1 Criminal law

The substantive criminal law similarly seeks to provide an equitable balance between the interests of the parties. However, this balance is constantly shifting. For example, the development of the defence of duress of circumstances, and the increasingly subjective approach adopted by the House of Lords in cases such as *B* v *DPP* (2000), *R* v *Smith* (2000), and *R* v *Gemmell and Richards* (2003) indicate a shift towards the interests of the defendant. By contrast, the introduction of mandatory life sentences for repeat offenders, and the decision in *Attorney-General for Jersey* v *Holley* (2005) encroach upon their interests. The elements of offences and defences also demonstrate the law's concern to achieve an equitable balance between the interests of the parties involved in an adversarial process. The following examples illustrate this point.

'Belonging to another': theft

For someone to be guilty of theft, the property appropriated must '**belong to another**'. In *R* v *Turner* (1971), the defendant took his car to a garage for repairs, to be paid for later when he picked up the car. However, seeing the car on the road next to the garage, he used a spare key and drove it away without paying. When charged with theft of the car, he argued that it belonged to him. The Court of Appeal, however, upheld his conviction for theft: the garage had a proprietary interest in the car which was protected under the law.

In this case, the court did not seek to balance the interests of the two parties in the same property, or to discover which party had a stronger interest in it. It merely asked: did the garage have an interest in the property? Since it did, it was irrelevant that the defendant might have a stronger claim on the car.

'Belonging to another': criminal damage

Section 1(1) of the Criminal Damage Act 1971 creates the basic offence of damaging or destroying property belonging to another. Individuals cannot be convicted of damaging or destroying their own property. Clementine Churchill therefore merely attracted notoriety, rather than criminal charges, for destroying the 1954 portrait of her husband, Sir Winston, by the artist Graham Sutherland.

However, under the aggravated offence of endangering life under s1(2), and under arson in s1(3), the defendant can be convicted even where he damages or destroys his own property. This is logical. The basic offence is simply concerned with safeguarding people's interest in protecting their property. Where people damage or destroy their own property, they are merely setting aside this personal interest. Others may regard this as perverse or tasteless, but their interests are not affected. However, a powerful new interest is introduced under the aggravated offences: people's interest in their very lives. When this is placed in the scales it is rightly adjudged to outweigh the interest of the owner in dealing with his property as he chooses.

Self-defence

The defence of self-defence protects the interest of a defendant who has some justification in using force against another person. At common law a person may use reasonable force to defend himself, or another person, or property. Under the Criminal Law Act 1967 he may use reasonable force to prevent crime, or to assist the arrest of offenders or those unlawfully at large.

To succeed, the defendant must first have believed he needed to use force. In *R* v *Williams (Gladstone)* (1987), the defendant made an honest mistake about the need to use force. In the Court of Appeal Lord Lane made allowance for this: the defendant, he explained, 'must be judged against the mistaken facts as he believes them to be.' On the other hand, no such allowance is made if the mistake was induced by alcohol (*O'Grady* (1987)).

Secondly, the force used must be reasonable. In *R v Palmer* (1971), Lord Morris conceded that 'a person defending himself cannot weigh to a nicety the exact measure of his defensive action.' However, this would not extend to using a gun on burglars already heading towards the exit (*Martin* (2002)). Many argue that this balance between the interests of the householder and of the burglar needs to be realigned, allowing the householder to decide the appropriate degree of force to be used when confronting burglars.

Consent

Where the victim consents to an assault, the defendant may escape liability. Two cases illustrate how the courts balance the interests of the defendant against those of their victims. In *Wilson* (1996), the defendant, at his wife's request, had branded his initials on her buttocks. His appeal against conviction for ABH was allowed: it was not in the public interest for the courts to interfere with consensual activity occurring between married couples in private.

In *Brown* (1993) the defendants were convicted under ss47 and 20 of the OAPA 1861 after engaging in sadomasochistic practices. These were consensual and conducted in private. The House of Lords decided that consent is not available in cases of serious injury, subject to certain exceptions, of which sadomasochistic homosexual violence was not one.

The main distinction between these two cases is circumstantial. On the one hand was a married couple, engaging in a form of tattooing, where the pain was incidental to the desired outcome. On the other hand was a group of sadomasochists, engaged in forms of torture, where inflicting pain was their purpose. In *Brown*, Lord Templeman spoke of the need for issues of policy and public interest to be weighed in the balance. Lord Mustill, however, spoke of the rights of an individual to live his life as he chooses. Clearly these judges had different views about which considerations should form part of the balancing exercise they were performing.

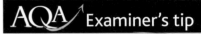

Fig. 2 *As shown in* Brown *(1993), different judges may have different attitudes when it comes to the balancing of interests*

2 Contract law

In contract law, the courts are often confronted with the interests of two innocent parties, both of whom have a plausible legal argument. The following issues illustrate the problems which they have faced when balancing the interests of the parties.

The postal rule

For a contract to be formed, A makes an offer to B which B then accepts. In *Adams* v *Lindsell* (1818) the defendant wrote to the claimant offering to sell him some wool, and asking for a reply by post. Due to postal delays, the letter of acceptance sent by the claimant arrived later than expected. By this time the defendant had sold the wool to another party. The question arose whether a valid contract had been formed between the claimant and defendant: if it had, the claimant was entitled to the wool; if not, the defendant had been free to sell the wool to someone else.

The court decided in favour of the claimant: a valid contract was formed at the moment the letter of acceptance was posted. In arriving at this judgment the court recognised that the offeror could protect his interests by insisting that the acceptance must be effectively communicated to him personally by a stated date.

Third party rights

In *Tweddle* v *Atkinson* (1861) the father and prospective father-in-law of the claimant contracted to provide the claimant with a future payment. When the father-in-law defaulted, the claimant sued. The claim failed: as he was not a party to the contract, he had no legal interest in the case. The rigidity of this rule was recognised in *Jackson* v *Horizon Holidays* (1975). The House of Lords awarded the claimant damages on his own behalf and on behalf of his family for their disappointment over a package holiday that failed to match the advertised description. This award was made even though Mr Jackson was the only member of his family who contracted for the holiday.

The Contract (Rights of Third Parties) Act 1999 gave wider recognition to the interests of third parties, allowing them to make a claim where a contract expressly provides for them (as it had in *Tweddle* v *Atkinson* (1861)), or where it purports to confer a benefit on the claimant. This recognises that the traditional approach unfairly disadvantaged the legitimate interests of innocent parties, and shifts the balance of power in the relationship between the defaulting defendant and the intended beneficiary. As a result, there is now formal legal recognition of set circumstances in which the interests of third parties become what Wesley Hohfeld would call 'claim-rights'.

Remedies for frustration

A contract becomes **frustrated** when, due to the fault of neither party, it becomes impossible to fulfil. In *Taylor* v *Caldwell* (1863) a music hall burned down, making it impossible for Caldwell to hire it to Taylor as promised. As Taylor had spent money advertising a programme of concerts, he sought damages from Caldwell. The court decided that the contract was frustrated, and both sides were therefore released from their obligations under the contract.

This decision does nothing to remove the potential for injustice. In *Chandler* v *Webster* (1904) the claimant made full advance payment for a room to watch the coronation procession of Edward VII. This could not be recovered when the coronation was cancelled and the contract frustrated. In *Krell* v *Henry* (1903), however, no money had been paid in advance, so the hotel bore the full loss when the contract was frustrated.

A better balance in apportioning losses between the parties was introduced in the Law Reform (Frustrated Contracts) Act 1943. This allows for the recovery of money paid in advance of a contract, and for the payment of a just sum for either expenses incurred or benefits obtained. This enables the court to apportion the losses fairly between the parties and not simply allow the loss to remain where it happens to fall. In this way the interests of both parties are afforded some measure of protection.

Mistaken identity

In frustration, the courts may arrive at a compromise decision, where the interests of both parties are to some degree protected. In cases of 'mistaken identity', however, this is not possible: the courts must decide in favour of one party. In reaching their decision they weigh in the balance the legal interests of the two parties, but in their judgment there will clearly be a winner and a loser.

'Mistaken identity' cases arise where a rogue, R, pretending to be someone else, buys (perhaps with a false chequebook) an item of value from A. By the time A realises that R is a rogue and is not going to pay, R has already sold the item to B. A has no alternative than to try to recover the item from B. To succeed, A must prove that the contract he signed with R was void from the start, and so title in the goods never transferred to R.

In *Shogun Finance Ltd* v *Hudson* (2003) a rogue obtained a new car from a dealer by paying a 10 per cent deposit and signing a hire purchase agreement under a false name. The credit company, Shogun Finance Ltd, conducted a credit search of the name they had been given before releasing the car. The rogue then sold the car to Mr Hudson. The House of Lords ruled that the contract between the credit company and the rogue was void, and therefore the credit company was entitled to the return of the car from Mr Hudson.

This seems to be harsh on Mr Hudson, an innocent third party. However, the court was obliged to decide in favour of one party or the other. Compromise was impossible: a car cannot be split into two. The court, therefore, balances the weight of legal argument of both parties, but the decision is one-sided.

Key terms

Frustration: a contract is frustrated when it becomes commercially sterile, when an intervening event makes performance impossible, or when performance becomes illegal.

Activity

Look at the facts and judgments in *Poussard* v *Spiers* (1876), and in *Bettini* v *Gye* (1876). Identify the interests of the parties in the two cases. Explain why the courts reached different outcomes even though the facts and interests were so similar.

3 Tort

Tort is concerned with obligations or duties owed by one party to another. It seeks to provide a remedy, usually damages, for the harm that is caused by the wrongdoing of another. Often it is difficult to decide which party's interest should take precedence. The following issues illustrate the courts' concern to find the appropriate balance between the interests of the claimant and defendant.

Negligence: breach of duty of care

In negligence, the fictional 'reasonable man' is used to establish whether a duty of care is breached. A variety of factors will be considered. One of these is the magnitude of risk. In *Bolton* v *Stone* (1951) a woman was struck by a cricket ball hit out of the ground. The club had erected a high fence, minimising the risk. The court decided that, although the risk was foreseeable, the likelihood of injury was so small that the defendants were not unreasonable in playing cricket without taking additional precautions.

Contrast this with *Haley* v *London Electricity Board* (1965). Workmen had dug a trench in a London pavement. They had positioned a pick and shovel at the far end, and a long handle with a weight attached at the near end. This handle sloped up from ground level on the road side, to two feet high on the inside of the pavement. The claimant, a blind man, tripped over the handle. He fell forward, and cracked his head on the pavement, causing deafness. The House of Lords held that the precautions taken were sufficient for able-bodied pedestrians, but not for blind ones. The likelihood of harm to someone blind was high.

Both claimants suffered harm. Both had a similar interest in pursuing a claim. However, damages were awarded in one case but not the other. This did not depend upon the seriousness of the harm caused, but upon the likelihood of harm occurring at all.

Vicarious liability

Under vicarious liability the defendant is held responsible for the actions of another party, such as an employer for the actions of his employees. In *Limpus* v *London General Omnibus Co.* (1862) the employer was held liable for the dangerous driving of his employee. In *Rose* v *Plenty* (1976) the employer was similarly liable when his employee allowed a boy to ride on its milk float. The boy was subsequently injured. However, in *Twine* v *Bean's Express* (1946) the employer was not liable when his employee gave a lift to a hitchhiker and negligently injured him.

In these cases the driver was ignoring clear instructions given by his employer. In *Twine* v *Bean's Express* (1946) the forbidden activity conferred no benefit upon the employer: it was totally outside the scope of his employment. The interests of the employer therefore outweighed those of the innocent, injured claimant. By contrast, in *Limpus* and in *Rose* the wrongful conduct of the employees was of benefit to the employer. In both cases the employee was engaged in his employer's work. The balance of interests, therefore, changed in favour of the claimant: the interests of the innocent, injured victim outweighed those of the employer.

Nuisance

Nuisance is defined as unlawful interference with a person's use or enjoyment of land. It generally deals with the conflicting claims of neighbours. The courts expect neighbours to tolerate a measure of inconvenience from each other, but will intervene where the interference becomes unreasonable.

In *Christie* v *Davey* (1893) the claimant used his home for private music lessons, to the annoyance of his neighbour, the defendant, who retaliated by banging on trays. The court granted the claimant an injunction. The malice behind the defendant's behaviour was a critical factor in the decision. However, it is not difficult to sympathise with the defendant: the strings of a violin in untutored hands is capable of causing great offence. Would the court have granted an injunction to the defendant if he had made a counter-claim for the nuisance caused by the music lessons?

In *Christie* v *Davey* (1893), the interests of the two parties were the same, the peaceful enjoyment of their land. In *Miller* v *Jackson* (1977) the parties' interests were very different. The claimant bought a house near a cricket ground to discover that balls were regularly hit into her garden. She sought an injunction to stop cricket being played. The court weighed up her interest in the peaceful enjoyment of her own home against the defendant's enjoyment of a valuable recreational activity. Roscoe Pound had warned against this balancing of a private with a social interest. Two Court of Appeal judges accepted that there was a nuisance, but refused to grant an injunction as there was a strong community interest in the playing of cricket. The claimant was merely awarded damages for the inconvenience. Was this judgment a sensible compromise between two interests of considerable merit? Or was it an abdication of responsibility towards the householder? The cricket club was found liable for creating a nuisance, but will have felt relieved at the remedy. The householder won the case, but will have regarded the award of damages as a Pyrrhic victory.

Defamation

The tort of defamation protects a person's interest in his reputation. It is committed where the defendant has published a defamatory statement referring to the claimant. For example, in *Cornwell* v *Daily Mail* (1989), the description of an actress as 'having a big bum' and 'the kind of stage presence that blocks lavatories' was held to be defamatory.

However, this tort places limits upon the competing right of freedom of speech. In order to introduce a proper balance between one person's interest in his reputation and another's in his freedom of speech, the courts allow a variety of defences to a defamation action. For example, 'justification' is available where the defamatory statement is true; 'consent' where the claimant invited the publication; and 'fair comment' where the statement is an opinion based on true facts on a matter of public interest.

The case of *Reynolds* v *Times Newspapers* (1999) concerns the defence of qualified privilege, which covers the reporting of Parliamentary proceedings. *The Sunday Times* wrote a report claiming that Albert Reynolds, the former Irish Prime Minister, had misled Parliament. In his speech Lord Nicholls recognised the freedom to disseminate information on political matters as essential for the proper functioning of parliamentary democracy. However, this needed to be balanced against the defendant's interest in his reputation, and the efforts made to ensure accuracy in reporting. In this case, the statements were highly damaging, and no effort had been made to seek comment from the claimant.

This language is not in the least conciliatory. When weighing the interests of the parties, the House of Lords did not seek a middle ground, a compromise solution. The majority decision robustly supported the interest of the claimant in his reputation, and was scathing about irresponsible political reporting. The scales of justice often fall heavily in favour of one party.

Fig. 4 Lord Hobhouse said: *'Misleading people and the purveying as facts statements which are not true is destructive of the democratic society and should form no part of such a society. There is no duty to publish what is not true: there is no interest in being misinformed.'*

> **Activity**
>
> Do you think that the defendant breached his duty of care in the following cases? Consider the 'risk factors' to help you decide, on balance, whether the defendant was unreasonable.
>
> **1** The defendants owned some land close to a road. They allowed some small boys to play football there. One of the boys kicked the ball onto the road, causing an accident that resulted in the death of the claimant's husband.
>
> **2** The defendants owned a tearoom run by a manageress. She had given permission for a church party to use the room. They made some tea in an urn and were carrying it along a narrow corridor into the tearoom when it was accidentally dropped. Scalding hot tea injured six of the children.

4 Human rights

The European Convention on Human Rights (ECHR) was signed by the Council of Europe in 1950. The United Kingdom government ratified the ECHR in 1951, and it came into force in 1953. In 1966, the United Kingdom government allowed 'individual petitions' to be made to the European Court of Human Rights in Strasbourg. Finally, in 1998, the Human Rights Act was passed, allowing individuals to seek redress under the ECHR in British courts. The following examples illustrate the fine balancing act in which the courts must engage.

Article 8 and the rights of prisoners to IVF treatment

Under Article 8 of the ECHR, everyone has the right to respect for his private and family life, his home and his correspondence. The case of *Dickson* v *UK* (2007) concerned a prisoner serving a life sentence for murder for kicking a drunk to death. While in prison he met and married his wife. Upon his earliest release date his wife would be 51 years old, and too old to conceive a child naturally. The couple had been refused their application for IVF treatment on the grounds that the relationship had yet to be tested in a normal environment, that there was insufficient provision for the welfare of any child, and that it was inconsistent with the public's expectation of how a violent killer should be punished.

The couple applied to the European Court of Human Rights under Article 8, arguing that the refusal of IVF treatment contravened their right to family life. The court upheld their complaint: prisoners did not forfeit their rights under the convention. The court argued that the wife was able to look after any child until her husband's release and that the interest of the state in wishing to avoid giving offence to public opinion was not a relevant consideration. Key to the decision was the fact that UK policy placed an impossible burden upon the complainants: they could not under any circumstances meet the criteria for IVF treatment. This prevented the secretary of state and the domestic courts from properly balancing the individual and public interests.

This case was heard in Strasbourg. The following two cases were heard before British courts using jurisdiction granted under the Human Rights Act 1998.

Article 5 and the prevention of terrorism

Under Article 5, everyone has the right to liberty and security of person. This is subject to certain exceptions, including lawful detention after conviction by a court, lawful arrest or detention for the purpose of bringing someone to trial, and lawful detention pending deportation. In the case of *A and Others* v *Secretary of State for the Home Department*

(2004) the House of Lords was asked to consider the case of foreign nationals who were being held indefinitely under the Anti-Terrorism, Crime and Security Act 2001. The House declared that s23 of the Act, in allowing the men's indefinite detention, was incompatible with Article 5 of the ECHR.

Lord Bingham, one of nine judges who heard the case, recognised the nature of the threat imposed by terrorists. However, he argued that if the threat presented to the security of the United Kingdom by UK nationals suspected of being terrorists could be addressed without infringing their right to personal liberty, then why did the same not apply to foreign nationals resident in the United Kingdom? He continued: 'Since the right to personal liberty is among the most fundamental of the rights protected by the European Convention, any restriction of it must be closely scrutinised by the national court.'

As a result of this judgment the government, in the Prevention of Terrorism Act 2005, limited the detention of foreign nationals to 28 days. However, there is continuing debate about the extent to which civil liberties should be subordinated to the need to fight the threat of terrorism.

The European Convention on Human Rights

The Convention is divided into sections, with s1 listing the rights as Articles. These include:

Article 2 Everyone's right to life shall be protected by law. No one shall be deprived of his life intentionally save in the execution of a sentence of a court.

Article 3 No one shall be subjected to torture or to inhuman or degrading treatment or punishment.

Article 4 No one shall be held in slavery or servitude.

Article 5 Everyone has the right to liberty and security of person.

Article 6 In the determination of his civil rights and obligations or of any criminal charge against him, everyone is entitled to a fair and public hearing within a reasonable time by an independent and impartial tribunal established by law.

Article 7 No one shall be held guilty of any criminal offence on account of any act or omission which did not constitute a criminal offence at the time when it was committed.

Article 8 Everyone has the right to respect for his private and family life, his home and his correspondence.

Article 9 Everyone has the right to freedom of thought, conscience and religion.

Article 10 Everyone has the right to freedom of expression.

Article 11 Everyone has the right to freedom of peaceful assembly and to freedom of association with others, including the right to form and to join trade unions for the protection of his interests.

Article 12 Men and women of marriageable age have the right to marry and to found a family.

Article 13 Everyone whose rights and freedoms as set forth in this Convention are violated shall have an effective remedy before a national authority.

Article 14 The enjoyment of the rights and freedoms set forth in this Convention shall be secured without discrimination on any ground.

Article 6 and witness anonymity

Under Article 6 of the ECHR, everyone is entitled to a fair and public hearing within a reasonable time by an independent and impartial tribunal established by law. Included within this is the right to examine or have examined witnesses against him.

In *R* v *Davis* (2008) the House of Lords was asked to consider whether this right was breached in the case of Iain Davis, who had been convicted in 2004 for murdering two men at a party in Hackney. The trial judge had granted **anonymity** to seven witnesses, three of whom identified Davis as the gunman. It was argued that this prevented defence counsel from performing an effective cross-examination of the witnesses, as they could not ask any questions that might lead to disclosing their identity.

The House found in favour of the appellant. Lord Bingham declared that the protective measures adopted by the trial judge 'hampered the conduct of the defence in a manner and to an extent which was unlawful and rendered the trial unfair'. He ruled that anonymity should not be granted where the testimony is the decisive evidence in a case, or where it prevents the defence from effectively cross-examining the witness.

What is the balance to be struck here? On the one hand the granting of witness anonymity promotes the public interest in securing the conviction of violent offenders who resort to intimidation. Without the promise of anonymity many cases will never reach court. On the other hand, the granting of anonymity increases the risk of people with ulterior motives 'setting-up' innocent men as part of a campaign of vengeance, and lying or exaggerating in order to achieve their purpose. Also, the mere presence of a screen and electronically distorted voices is prejudicial to the defendant.

Following the decision in *R* v *Davis* (2008), the Justice Secretary declared that 'there is a difficult balance to strike here, between giving witnesses who fear for their safety the confidence to give evidence in court, and ensuring that innocent people are not convicted'. However, Article 6 grants the defendant an absolute right to have witnesses examined. This cannot be balanced against other considerations. Should any legislation impose restrictions upon the operation of this right, doubtlessly the House of Lords will declare it incompatible with the defendant's rights under Article 6. Other solutions will have to be found to counter the problem of witness intimidation.

> ### ■ Key terms
>
> **Witness anonymity**: in an attempt to persuade members of the public to come forward with evidence that will help to secure the conviction of violent offenders, courts allow witnesses to remain anonymous in court; these witnesses are hidden behind a screen, visible to judge and jury, but not to the defendant or to the public gallery; their voices are electronically distorted so that their race, age and gender cannot be told.

> ### ■ Activity
>
> Consider the details of the following case and then answer the question beneath.
>
> Under Article 3 of the Protocol to the ECHR, member states 'undertake to hold free elections at reasonable intervals by secret ballot, under conditions which will ensure the free expression of the opinion of the people in the choice of the legislature'. Three prisoners, one serving ten years for importing drugs, another life for committing arson with intent to endanger life, and the third life for manslaughter, used this Article to challenge the Home Office ruling that prisoners are barred from participating in elections. They argued in addition that having the chance to vote would help them to become responsible citizens and increase their chances of going straight when released. The Home Office argued that prisoners forfeited their right to vote while in prison.
>
> How would you weigh the interests of the two parties in this claim?
>
> If you wish to discover the actual judgment by the European Court of Human Rights, look up *Hirst* v *UK* (2005) on a search engine.

You should now be able to:

- explain and illustrate how opposing interests are balanced in substantive law.

4 Answering questions on the topic of balancing conflicting interests

Questions on this topic call for less theoretical background than other topics. However, it is useful to make some reference to theories about the nature of interests and to intersperse later discussion with reference to these. It is also worthwhile to focus upon the meaning of the word 'balance'. There are different ways in which the term may be used. In procedural law, it means giving equal consideration to the interests of the different parties to the action. This can be seen in criminal and civil trials where both parties are granted the opportunity to state their cases and to influence the tribunal.

Substantive law may also provide balance in reflecting the competing interests of the parties. The defence of self-defence, for example, provides a measure of protection to both parties: the defendant is not denied the defence if he was honestly mistaken about the need to use force. In this way the interest of the defendant is recognised. However, if the mistake was alcohol-induced, the defence is not available. In this way the interest of the victim and of the prosecution is recognised.

Judges also perform a balancing act when applying the law. However, they do not necessarily attach equal weight to the opposing arguments. In cases such as *Reynolds* v *Times Newspapers* (1999) they may come down very firmly on one side of the argument. Imagine two children on a see-saw, with both of them trying to stay as near to the ground as possible. Other children then jump on one end or the other. Eventually one side or the other is likely to win this contest. Only rarely will the two sides be in perfect equilibrium. The law operates in a similar manner: the two parties to the action seek to add weight to their legal argument until they have the weight of evidence on their side. Only rarely will there be equilibrium. If the judges cannot distinguish between the interests of the parties in a civil case, then they must decide in favour of the defendant as the claimant has not proved his case on the balance of probabilities.

The question on this topic will require you to introduce a lot of illustrative material as the basis for discussion. You should refer in your answer to both procedural and substantive law. When dealing with the former, seek to include reference to the criminal and civil justice systems. When dealing with the latter, select areas of law you have studied in depth. Use cases and topics with which you are familiar. Every topic on the syllabus is capable of being analysed in the light of balancing interests. Where possible, introduce contrasting cases (such as *Williams* (1987) and *Owino* (1987) in self-defence; *Twine* v *Bean's Express* (1946), and *Rose* v *Plenty* (1976) in vicarious liability; or *Poussard* v *Spiers* (1876), and *Bettini* v *Gye* (1876) in contract terms), as drawing distinctions between them will help you to discuss the question of balance.

If the question asks you to consider whether individual interests may be sacrificed for the sake of public interests, refer to the human rights cases which demonstrate that the answer to that question is increasingly 'no'. However, if the question asks you whether individual interests should be sacrificed for the public good, you are at liberty to argue your own point of view, but still refer to decided cases.

Finally, when using cases, identify the interests of the parties, explain how these conflict with each other, and discuss how the law balances this conflict. Remember that balance does not necessarily mean compromise.

Activity

Select six cases that you might include in an essay on this topic. Refer briefly to the relevant facts, identify the interests of the parties, and explain the outcome. An example is provided below:

Case: *R* v *Savage* (1992)

Facts: Mrs Savage threw a glass of beer over another woman in a public house. Unfortunately the glass slipped out of her hand and cut her victim. Mrs Savage accepted that she intended a battery, but argued that she did not even see the risk of the glass slipping and cutting her victim, therefore lacked the *mens rea* for ABH.

Interests: The victim: an interest in her assailant being punished for the injury as well as for the soaking with beer;

The prosecution/society: an interest in deterring others from taking risks with dangerous weapons such as beer glasses;

The defendant: an interest being punished only for an offence for which she had *mens rea*.

Outcome: The defendant was guilty of ABH: the House of Lords decided that no additional *mens rea* is required for ABH than for battery.

You should now be able to:

■ understand what is required in an essay on the topic of balancing conflicting interests.

AQA Examination-style questions

Chapter 20: Law and morality

Discuss the nature of legal and moral rules. Consider the extent to which the law should reflect moral rules. *(30 marks)*

Chapter 21: Law and justice

Explain the meaning of justice. Consider whether it is reasonable to expect the law always to achieve justice. *(30 marks)*

Chapter 22: Judicial creativity

Discuss the extent to which a judge should develop the law through the operation of the doctrine of judicial precedent and by different approaches to statutory interpretation. *(30 marks)*

Chapter 23: Fault

Establishing liability based on fault is regarded as a fundamental principle of English law. Explore the arguments in support of this view, and critically comment on the exceptions to its application. *(30 marks)*

Chapter 24: Balancing conflicting interests

Consider how successful English law is in balancing conflicting interests. *(30 marks)*

Index

Key terms are in bold as are their page numbers.